UNDERSTANDING AND INTERPRETING CHINESE ECONOMIC REFORM

Jinglian Wu

THOMSON
™
SOUTH-WESTERN

Australia · Brazil · Canada · Mexico · Singapore · Spain · United Kingdom · United States

Understanding and Interpreting Chinese Economic Reform
Jinglian Wu

Composed by G&S Book Services

Printed in Singapore by Seng Lee Press PTE LTD

1 2 3 4 5 08 07 06 05

This book is printed on acid-free paper.

ISBN: 1-587-99197-7

This publication is designed to provide accurate and authoritative information in regard to the subject matter covered. It is sold with the understanding that the publisher is not engaged in rendering legal, accounting, or other professional services. If expert assistance is required, the services of a competent professional person should be sought.

For permission to use material from this text or product, submit a request online at http://www.thomsonrights.com.

Library of Congress Cataloging-in-Publication Data

Wu, Jinglian.

Understanding and interpreting Chinese economic reform / Jinglian Wu.—1st ed.
    p. cm.
    Includes bibliographical references and index.
    ISBN 1-58799-197-7
    1. China—Economic policy.   2. China—Economic conditions.   I. Title.

HC427.W798 2005
338.951'009'049—dc22   2005017747

For more information about our products, contact us at:

Thomson Learning Academic Resource Center 1-800-423-0563

Thomson Higher Education
5191 Natorp Boulevard
Mason, Ohio 45040
USA

CONTENTS

Part One Introduction to Reform   1

Chapter 1   The Raise of the Issue of Reform   3

1.1   The Establishment of a Soviet-Style Socialist System   3

    1.1.1   Lenin's Assumption before the Revolution and Soviet Russia's Early Practice   3

    1.1.2   The Establishment of Stalin's System   8

1.2   An Economic Analysis of the Centrally Planned Economic System   12

    1.2.1   Neoclassical Economists' Theoretical Demonstration of the Feasibility of a Planned Economic System   12

    1.2.2   The Debate on Socialism among Western Economists in the 1920s and 1930s   13

    1.2.3   The Reexamination of Planned Economy in the Late Twentieth Century   17

1.3   Reform in the Soviet Union and Eastern European Socialist Countries   20

    1.3.1   The Effort of the Soviet Union to Improve the Economy and Its Failure   21

    1.3.2   Self-Management Socialist Reform in Yugoslavia   24

    1.3.3   The Gradual Reform in Hungary   26

    1.3.4   The Four Rounds of Reform in Poland   27

    1.3.5   The Aborted Reform in Czechoslovakia   28

    1.3.6   The Transition of Russia and Eastern European Countries to Market Economies under New Political Systems   29

1.4   The Establishment of the Chinese Planned Economic System and the Raise of the Issue of Reform   31

    1.4.1   The Establishment of the Centrally Planned Economic System in China   31

    1.4.2   The Raise of the Issue of Reform in China   36

Chapter 2   The Evolution of China's Reform Strategy   43

2.1   Administrative Decentralization (1958 to 1978)   44

    2.1.1   The Establishment of the Policy of Delegating Power to and Sharing Profit with Local Governments   44

    2.1.2   The Implementation of the Policy of Transferring Administrative Functions to Lower Levels   46

2.1.3   Disorder Caused by Transferring Administrative Functions to Lower Levels and Its Remediation   49

2.1.4   An Economic Analysis of Administrative Decentralization   54

2.2   Incremental Reform (1979 to 1993)   57

2.2.1   The Emergence of the Strategy of Incremental Reform   58

2.2.2   The Shift of the Focus of Reform from "Inside the System" to "Outside the System"   62

2.2.3   The All-Round Implementation of Incremental Reform   64

2.2.4   The Emergence of the Dual-Track System   68

2.2.5   The Negative Outcomes of the Long-Time Practice of Incremental Reform   71

2.3   Strategy of "Overall Advance" (1994 to Present)   74

2.3.1   The Attempt at Changing Reform Strategy and Launching All-Round Reform in 1984–1986   75

2.3.2   The Third Plenary Session of the 14th CCCPC Started a New Era of Overall Advance of Reform   82

2.3.3   In-Depth Development of the Strategy of Overall Advance   85

Part Two   Reform in Different Sectors   91

Chapter 3   Rural Reform   93

3.1   The Agricultural Operation System before the Contracting System Reform   93

3.1.1   From Cooperatives to People's Communes   96

3.1.2   Basic Conditions in Rural China before Reform   102

3.2   Implementation and Economic Effects of "Contracting Output Quota to Each Household"   104

3.2.1   The Three Ups and Downs of "Contracting Output Quota to Each Household" before 1976   104

3.2.2   Quick Spread of the Household Contracting System   108

3.2.3   Economic Results of the Household Contracting System   114

3.2.4   Reform of Property Rights by the Contracting System   117

3.2.5   Impact on the Development of TVEs   118

3.3   Existing Problems and Prospects for Further Reforms   120

3.3.1   Reforming the Purchase and Marketing System of Agricultural Products   121

3.3.2   Improving the Land System   126

3.3.3   Alleviating the Burden on Farmers   128

3.3.4   Solving Contradictions between Small Farmers and
Big Markets   130

3.3.5   The Issue of the Transfer of Rural Surplus Laborers   133

Chapter 4   Reform of State-Owned Enterprises   139

4.1   The Enterprise System of Traditional SOEs and the Reform with the Main
Theme of Power-Delegating and Profit-Sharing   139

4.1.1   Major Features of the Enterprise System of Traditional SOEs   139

4.1.2   The Reform with the Main Theme of Power-Delegating and
Profit-Sharing   142

4.1.3   The Essence of the Reform of Power-Delegating and
Profit-Sharing   148

4.1.4   Achievements and Deficiencies of the Reform of
Power-Delegating and Profit-Sharing   151

4.2   Corporatization of Large SOEs   154

4.2.1   Progress in Corporatization of Large SOEs   155

4.2.2   Governance Problems of Transformed Companies   158

4.3   Further Reform Measures to Be Taken   163

4.3.1   Further Lowering the Proportion of State Equity Shares   163

4.3.2   Strengthening the Internal Control Systems of Large
Enterprises   166

4.3.3   Overcoming Defects of Insider Control and Instituting Checks
and Balances between the Owner and the Management   168

4.3.4   Bringing the SASAC into Play to Exercise Shareholder Rights in
Accordance with the Law   171

4.3.5   Learning from International Experience and Strengthening
Corporate Governance   173

Chapter 5   Development of Nonstate Sectors   177

5.1   Blind Worship of State Ownership and Its Breakdown   177

5.1.1   The Establishment of the Dominance of State Ownership
in China   178

5.1.2   Practice of the Reform and Opening up Continuously Breaking
the Restrictions of Traditional Ownership Theory   181

5.1.3   The Debate over Ownership and the Establishment of the
Guiding Principle of "Allowing Diverse Forms of Ownership
to Develop Side by Side"   186

5.2   The Layout Readjustment of the State Sector: Advancing in Some Areas
        while Retreating in Others   189

    5.2.1   The Guiding Principle for the Layout Readjustment of the
                State Sector   189

    5.2.2   Letting Go of and Invigorating Small and Medium SOEs   192

5.3   The Emergence of a Diverse Ownership Structure with Multiple Forms
        of Ownership Developing Side by Side   198

    5.3.1   The Rapid Development of Nonstate Sectors   198

    5.3.2   The Emergence of Diverse Ownership Structures with
                Multiple Forms of Ownership Developing Side by Side
                in Some Regions   199

5.4   Impediments to Further Development of Nonstate Sectors   204

    5.4.1   Improving the Business Environment of Nonstate Sectors   204

    5.4.2   Enhancing Support to Small and Medium Enterprises   206

    5.4.3   Relying on Nonstate Enterprises to Develop High-Tech
                Industries   208

    5.4.4   Nonstate Enterprises Should Make Even Greater Endeavors   211

**Chapter 6   Reform of the Banking System and Development
                of the Securities Market   217**

6.1   The Concepts of "Money" and "Finance" in a Planned Economy and
        Changes in China's Financial System in the 1980s   217

    6.1.1   Changes in Enterprise Financing   219

    6.1.2   The Introduction of New Financial Instruments and the Start
                of the Capital Market   219

    6.1.3   Changes in the Organizational Structure of Financial
                Institutions   220

    6.1.4   Changes in the Central Bank's Approaches to Macroeconomic
                Control   220

6.2   The Banking Reform in the 1990s and Its Future Direction   222

    6.2.1   Major Problems in China's Banking System before the
                1994 Reform   222

    6.2.2   The Progress of the Banking Reform since 1994   226

    6.2.3   New Challenges for the Banking Reform in the New
                Millennium   229

6.3   The Development of China's Money Market   234

    6.3.1   The Current Situation of China's Money Market and
                Its Problems   234

6.3.2   The Further Development of China's Money Market   236

6.4   The Development and Improvement of the Securities Market   237

6.4.1   The Development of China's Securities Market since the Reform and Opening Up   237

6.4.2   Problems in China's Securities Market and Proposed Solutions   239

Chapter 7   Reform of the Fiscal and Taxation System   255

7.1   Government Finance in a Planned Economy   255

7.2   Fiscal and Taxation Reform from 1980 to 1993   258

7.2.1   Changes in the Financial Relations between the Central Government and Local Governments   259

7.2.2   Changes in the Financial Relations between the Government and Enterprises   263

7.2.3   Institutional Defects of the Fiscal Responsibility System   265

7.3   All-Round Reform of the Fiscal and Taxation System in 1994   269

7.3.1   Main Requirements of the Third Plenary Session of the 14th CCCPC for Fiscal and Taxation System Reform   269

7.3.2   The Tax-Sharing System for Fiscal Budget   270

7.3.3   Basic Requirements of the Taxation System Reform   272

7.4   Reform of the Fiscal and Taxation System after 1994   274

7.4.1   Straightening Out "Extra-Budgetary Revenue"   275

7.4.2   Further Improving the Tax-Sharing System   279

7.4.3   Realizing the Transition toward a Public Finance System   281

7.4.4   Proposals for New Reform Measures   285

Chapter 8   Opening to the Outside World   291

8.1   The Evolution of China's Foreign Economic Relations and Development Strategy   291

8.1.1   1949–1971: Self-Seclusion   291

8.1.2   1972–1978: Import Substitution   293

8.1.3   1978–2001: Combination of Export Orientation and Import Substitution   293

8.1.4   After the Accession to the WTO in 2002: An Open Economy   294

8.2   The Spatial Evolution of Opening to the Outside World   295

8.2.1   Establishing Bases for Opening to the Outside World in the 1980s   295

8.2.2   Expanding the Regions Open to the Outside World
in the 1990s   297

8.2.3   Development Prospects of Special Economic Zones   299

8.3   Foreign Direct Investment   300

8.3.1   Growth and Characteristics of Foreign Direct Investment
in China   300

8.3.2   Promoting the Growth of Local Enterprises   305

8.4   The Development of Import and Export Trade   311

8.4.1   The Process of the Reform of the Foreign Trade System   311

8.4.2   The Development of Foreign Trade   315

8.4.3   Problems Demanding Immediate Solutions   317

8.5   Prospect of China's Opening to the Outside World   319

8.5.1   The Accession to the WTO Is a New Milestone in China's
Opening to the Outside World   319

8.5.2   China Will Enter a New Era of All-Round Opening to the
Outside World   319

8.5.3   Active Participation in Regional Economic Cooperation   320

Part Three   Macroeconomic and Social Issues   325

Chapter 9   Establishment of a New Social Security System   327

9.1   The Social Security System before Reform and the Reform Plan of the
Third Plenary Session of the 14th CCCPC   327

9.1.1   The Establishment of a Social Security System in China   327

9.1.2   Drawbacks of the Traditional Social Security System   329

9.1.3   Targets for Social Security System Reform Established by the
Third Plenary Session of the 14th CCCPC   332

9.1.4   Suggestions of the World Bank on Pension Reform   335

9.2   The Implementation of the Reform and Its Problems   336

9.2.1   Pension Insurance Reform   337

9.2.2   Medical Insurance System Reform   346

9.2.3   Unemployment Insurance   349

9.2.4   Minimum Living Guarantee System   351

9.2.5   Rural Social Security   352

Chapter 10   Macroeconomic Policies in the Transitional Period   355

10.1   Macroeconomic Issues and Macroeconomic Policies   355

10.2   Inflation between 1980 and 1994   356

    10.2.1   Inflation Is a Common Problem in the Transitional Period   356

    10.2.2   Four Rounds of Overheated Economy and Changes in Macroeconomic Policies between 1980 and 1994   359

10.3   Deflation and Remedial Policies between 1997 and 2002   374

    10.3.1   Causes of Insufficient Aggregate Demand   374

    10.3.2   Policies to Increase Domestic Demand and Their Effect   375

    10.3.3   Changes in Macroeconomic Situation   378

10.4   Short-Term Problems and Mid- and Long-Term Risks in China's Economy   378

    10.4.1   The Root Cause of the Problems in the Chinese Financial System Was the High Input and Low Efficiency of the Economy   379

    10.4.2   Essential Measures Needed to Avoid a Crisis   383

Chapter 11   Social Relations and Government Functions in the Transitional Period   385

11.1   Social Contradictions in the Transitional Period   385

    11.1.1   The Transitional Period Is a Period in Which Social Relations Are under Great Tension   386

    11.1.2   Evolution of the Social Structure and Social Contradictions during China's Transitional Period   389

    11.1.3   Increase in Corrupt Activities   391

    11.1.4   Enlarging Income Disparity among Social Strata   398

11.2   Constructing a Good Market Economy   403

    11.2.1   Different Attitudes toward Reform   403

    11.2.2   Maintaining Social Justice Was a Critical Issue in the Transitional Period   407

11.3   Government Functions in Economic Transition   413

    11.3.1   The Important Functions of the Government in the Transitional Process   413

    11.3.2   The Necessity of Change in Government Functions   416

11.4   Active Promotion of Political Reform   417

    11.4.1   The Necessity of Political Reform   417

    11.4.2   Major Contents of Political Reform   423

    11.4.3   Nurturing a Civil Society and Improving the Self-Organizing Ability of the Society   429

Part Four   Brief Conclusion   431

Chapter 12   Concluding Remarks   433

12.1   Economic and Political Goals Becoming Increasingly Clear in the Process of Reform   433

12.2   Promoting Reform and Comprehensively Improving the Socialist Market Economic System   437

Bibliography   441

Postscript by the Translator   447

Name Index   449

Subject Index   453

List of Supplements

Insights

Insight 1.1   Socialist Model in the Early Days of the Soviet Union   6

Insight 1.2   On the Basic Economic Characteristics of Socialism: The Soviet Textbook of *Political Economy*   10

Insight 1.3   Brus's Decentralized Model   15

Insight 1.4   *On the Ten Major Relationships* by Mao Zedong   39

Insight 2.1   The Beginning of China's Reform Economics   60

Insight 2.2   The Third Plenary Session of the 12th CCCPC and *Decision on Reform of the Economic Structure*   75

Insight 2.3   Debate on Reform Strategy of 1986   79

Insight 2.4   The Third Plenary Session of the 14th CCCPC and *Decision on Issues Regarding the Establishment of a Socialist Market Economic System*   83

Insight 2.5   The 15th National Congress of the CPC and Jiang Zemin's Report   87

Insight 3.1   The People's Communes Campaign   100

Insight 3.2   Contract by Farmers in Xiaogang Village, Fengyang County, Anhui Province   110

Insight 4.1   Managerial Rights Prescribed in *Regulations on Transforming the Management Mechanism of Industrial Enterprises Owned by the Whole People*   148

Insight 4.2   Enterprise Law of 1988 and Its Impacts on Company Law of 1993   153

Insight 5.1   The Reform of Small and Medium Enterprises in Zhucheng and Shunde   194

Insight 6.1   The Banking Reform Plan Approved by the Third Plenary Session of the 14th CCCPC   224

Insight 6.2   China's Commitment to Open the Banking Sector upon Entry into the WTO   229

Insight 6.3   "Big Debate on the Stock Market" in Early 2001   247

Insight 7.1   Public Goods and Public Finance   281

Insight 8.1   The Experience of Suzhou Industrial Park   309

Insight 9.1   Basic Principles of the Social Security System Established by the Third Plenary Session of the 14th CCCPC   333

Insight 11.1   Deng Xiaoping's View on the Reform of the System of Party and State Leadership   419

Figures

Figure 5.1   Nonstate Sectors Speeding Up Economic Growth (2000)   200

Figure 6.1   Financial Institutions in China in the Early 1990s   221

Figure 6.2   Monthly Chart of the Composite Index of Shanghai Stock Exchange (from January 1999 to January 2003)   250

Figure 8.1   Foreign Direct Investment in China (US$ billion)   301

Figure 8.2   Growth of China's Foreign Trade (1978–2001)   315

Figure 10.1   Growth of Total Investment of Society in Fixed Assets (in real terms)   380

Figure 10.2   Rapid Growth of Loans: Year-to-Year Growth %   381

Figure 10.3   Increase in ICOR in China   382

Figure 11.1   Ratio of Per Capita Disposable Income of Urban Households to Per Capita Net Income of Rural Households in China   402

Tables

Table 1.1   Annual Growth Rate of the Soviet Economy (%)   21

Table 1.2   Changes in Productivity in the Soviet Union (%)   22

Table 2.1   Gross Value of Industrial Output by Ownership (%)   66

Table 2.2   Total Retail Sales by Ownership (%)   66

Table 2.3   Degree of Openness of China's Economy (%)   67

Table 2.4   Economic Growth during 1978–1990   69

Table 2.5   GDP by Ownership (%)   89

Table 3.1   Gross Output Value of Farming, Forestry, Animal Husbandry, and Fishery (RMB Billion)   116

Table 3.2   Per Capita Annual Total Income and Annual Net Income of Rural Households (RMB)   117

Table 3.3   Number of TVEs and TVE Employment (thousand unit/thousand people)   120

Table 5.1   Investment and Employment by Ownership (%)   199

Table 5.2   Economic Growth in Zhejiang (year-on-year growth, %)   202

Table 5.3   Economic Growth in Jiangsu (year-on-year growth, %)   203

Table 5.4   Economic Growth in Guangdong (year-on-year growth, %)   203

Table 6.1   Real Interest Rate of Loans of State Banks (1985–1989)   222

Table 6.2   The Financing Structure of Chinese Enterprises (RMB billion, %)   239

Table 7.1   Fiscal Revenue, Expenditure, and Deficit as Percentages of GDP (%)   268

Table 7.2   Central Fiscal Revenue as Percentages of Total Fiscal Revenue and GDP (%)   269

Table 7.3   Fiscal Revenue and Deficit as Percentages of GDP   275

Table 8.1   China's Share in World Trade   292

Table 8.2   China's FDI by Origin (US$ billion)   303

Table 8.3   Sector Distribution of Foreign-Invested Enterprises at the End of 2001   304

Table 8.4   Reduction in the Average Statutory Tariff Rate in China   313

Table 8.5   Trade Dependence Ratio of the Chinese Economy (% of GDP)   316

Table 8.6   China's Export Merchandise Mix (Total National Exports = 100)   317

Table 10.1   Price Indices since 1978 (year-to-year growth, %)   360

Table 10.2   China's Macroeconomic Situation during 1978–1983 (year to year, %)   362

Table 10.3   China's Macroeconomic Situation during 1983–1986 (year to year, %)   364

Table 10.4   China's Macroeconomic Situation during 1986–1991 (year to year, %)   369

Table 10.5   China's Macroeconomic Situation during 1992–1996 (year to year, %)   373

Table 10.6   Growth of Investment in Fixed Assets by Sector (year to year, %)   378

Table 10.7   China's Macroeconomic Situation during 1997–2002 (year to year, %)   378

Table 11.1   Standard of Poverty Line and Rural Poverty Reduction in China (1990–1998)   400

PREFACE

For over two decades China's economy has sustained rapid and steady growth. This phenomenal development is attracting more and more attention worldwide. As China's development is having and will continue to have significant impact on the global economy, people, whatever their attitude toward China, are eager to know and understand how the change and growth were made possible. However, understanding China's economy, particularly its reform and development, is not easy. Even those who live here and have been involved in the tremendous transition of a quarter century cannot claim to have fully understood the hows and whys when the changes were taking place. Therefore, there is a demand for a book to systematically analyze and explain China's economic reform from the perspective of modern economics. As an economist who has witnessed and participated in the great transition of the country, I feel obliged to undertake the task.

In addition to my official job as a senior research fellow with a governmental advisory institution, I am an educator in the field of economics. In 1995 I began teaching the course "Chinese Economy" for doctoral candidates at the Graduate School of the Chinese Academy of Social Sciences (CASS) and later extended the same course to MBA and EMBA programs at China Europe International Business School (CEIBS). The courses I teach have developed in line with the economic reform in China. Interaction with my students over the years has helped me to improve and enrich the courses. Meanwhile it made the writing of a book on China's economic reform both imperative and possible. By 1998 a textbook entitled *Economic Reform in Contemporary China: Strategy and Implementation* with twelve chapters had taken shape. Published in early 1999, the textbook has also been used in my lectures to doctoral students at the School of Economics, Peking University. Since its publication, the book has also been popular with the general reading public interested in China's economic development and reform.

Since the textbook was first published, further changes have taken place in the economic and social life of China. Economists' understanding of the factors at work in China's economy also deepened. I found it necessary to update my original book. Now, with great pleasure, I present my new book to English-speaking readers.

In this brief introduction to my book, I would like to say a few words on the analytical framework and methodology. In studying the transition of former socialist states from a centrally planned economy to a market economy, economists used to classify the transitional strategies of different countries into two major types. One is the well-known "shock therapy" or "big bang" approach, which was exemplified by Russia and

other Eastern European countries in their pursuit of rapid privatization and price liberalization; the other is gradualism, which was exemplified by China in its transition toward a market economy at a much slower pace. This kind of comparison focuses on the
speed of the transition and takes it as the key criterion in studying the differences in the
strategies. To my mind, this method is too superficial to reach any significant conclusion. Although the method is still used by many economists in China, it has been all but
abandoned outside China since the turn of the century.

I prefer the theoretical framework proposed by Professor János Kornai, an economist
at both Harvard University and Collegium Budapest. According to Professor Kornai
there are two pure strategies in post-socialist economic transition. Strategy A, or the
strategy of organic development, perceives the creation of a favorable environment for
bottom-up development of the private sector as the most important task. Strategy B, or
the strategy of accelerated privatization, puts the emphasis on the elimination of state
ownership as quickly as possible through speedy privatization of state-owned enterprises
(SOEs). The experience of Central and Eastern European countries has proved Strategy A to be more effective because it facilitates capital accumulation and the development of an entrepreneurial class and accelerates the formation of the market system
based on the rule of law. In contrast, Strategy B is ineffective because it cannot achieve
the aforementioned effects and may even produce negative results, such as the emergence of an oligarchy that monopolizes an anarchic market and brings endless harm to
the economy.

I think that in studying the economic reform in China, Kornai's framework can be
used, with some modification to suit the country's specific situation. Comparison of the
transitional strategies is to be made by analyzing whether the emphasis is on the development of nonstate sectors or on the reform of SOEs. It is very interesting to note that
since the beginning of the economic reform the Chinese leadership has been emphasizing SOE reform, which more or less fits Kornai's description of Strategy B; however,
the transition itself has followed another path, similar to Kornai's Strategy A. For example, the contracted responsibility system implemented in the rural areas in the early
1980s generated millions of household farms and liberated Chinese peasants' natural entrepreneurial spirit. The mushrooming of township and village enterprises and private
firms that followed opened up the market and fostered large numbers of entrepreneurs;
and they, in turn, raised a strong demand for an orderly market system and lent support
to the deepening of SOE reform.

China's economic reform is a very complex process. Even though it has a clearly
defined objective—to change the system of a planned economy into a system of a market economy—the interest of different groups of people in the society is affected in
the process. Policies and measures taken to realize the goal of transition are invariably

influenced by the interplay of different interest groups. Therefore, the process has inevitably taken a zigzag route. To describe the intricacies of this process in a single book is a big challenge. In an attempt to explain them as clearly as possible, I divide my book into four parts.

There are two chapters in Part One, Introduction to Reform. In Chapter 1, The Raise of the Issue of Reform, I try to answer two questions: (1) how the socialist system, a social ideal that pursues social justice and common well-being, had evolved into the centrally planned economy; and (2) why, after having established such a supposedly ideal system, most of the socialist economies demanded fundamental change. Chapter 2, The Evolution of China's Reform Strategy, is an overview of the reform history by dividing it into three major periods: (1) 1958–1978, administrative decentralization; (2) 1979–1993, incremental reform; and (3) 1994 to present, an overall advance toward a market economy with breakthrough in key areas.

Part Two discusses the reform in different sectors of the economy in six chapters, each focusing on the transition in one key sector: Chapter 3, Rural Reform; Chapter 4, Reform of State-Owned Enterprises; Chapter 5, Development of Nonstate Sectors; Chapter 6, Reform of the Banking System and Development of the Securities Market; Chapter 7, Reform of the Fiscal and Taxation System; and Chapter 8, Opening to the Outside World.

In the three chapters in Part Three, Macroeconomic and Social Issues, I discuss respectively how to establish a new social security system, how to stabilize the macroeconomy by adopting appropriate policies to deal with problems arising under special circumstances of the transitional period, and the social relations and the government functions in the transitional period.

In the only chapter of Part Four, Concluding Remarks, I state my views on how to establish a sound socialist market economy, focusing on future tasks geared to achieving social justice and common well-being in the Chinese society.

I would like to conclude with a few words to my readers. As China's economic reform is an unfinished and ongoing revolution, my understanding and knowledge of it will be improved and deepened as the reform progresses. My objective in writing this book is to call for more studies and exchanges of ideas among professionals and other interested people. I hope to arouse more interest, concern, and thinking on the issues in China's economic reform. With our common effort, an orderly and sound market economy based on the rule of law will be established in China and the country will develop into a land of social justice and common well-being.

Wu Jinglian

Part I

Introduction to Reform

Chapter 1

The Raise of the Issue of Reform

The reform of the socialist economic system in China started nearly fifty years ago, when, in 1956, the Eighth National Congress of the Communist Party of China (CPC) decided to launch the "economic management system reform." In addition to China, other socialist countries in Europe and Asia also made various explorations in reform during the second half of the twentieth century. Reform, in this book, refers to socialist countries' transition from the traditional system of socialist economy—a centrally planned economy—to a market economy.

1.1 The Establishment of a Soviet-Style Socialist System

On its founding in 1949, the People's Republic of China adopted the concept of learning from the Soviet Union and set up a Soviet-style socialist system in the mid-1950s.[1] Shortly after this system was transplanted to China, its serious shortcomings became apparent, and the issue of reform was raised. Before studying China's economic reform, we need to understand how Soviet-style socialism evolved, what its basic characteristics were, and what reform actions were taken by the Soviet Union and Eastern European countries that adopted the Soviet-style socialist model.

1.1.1 Lenin's Assumption before the Revolution and Soviet Russia's Early Practice

Vladimir I. Lenin's (1870–1924) socialist model not only inherited Marx's theory but also had its own features. Karl Marx and Friedrich Engels envisioned that the process of public ownership replacing private ownership (i.e., the socialization of property rights) was a natural process already taking place when capital was accumulated. The "general law of capitalist accumulation" is that "the cheapness of commodities demands, ceteris paribus, on the productiveness of labor, and this again on the scale of production.

---

[1] Mao Zedong declared on the eve of the founding of the People's Republic of China in 1949, "Follow the path of the Russians—that was their [progressives in China] conclusion." (Mao Zedong, "On the People's Democratic Dictatorship (Lun renmin minzhu zhuanzheng) (June 30, 1949)," *Selected Works of Mao Zedong (Mao Zedong xuanji) (The Four-in-One Edition)*, Beijing: People's Publishing House, 1966, p. 1471.)

Therefore, the larger capitals beat the smaller." "In any given branch of industry centralization would reach its extreme limit if all the individual capitals invested in it were fused into a single capital. In a given society the limit would be reached only when the entire social capital was united in the hands of either a single capitalist or a single capitalist company."[2]

Marx also said, "The monopoly of capital becomes a fetter upon the mode of production, which has sprung up and flourished along with, and under it. Centralization of the means of production and socialization of labor at last reach a point where they become incompatible with their capitalist integument. This integument is burst asunder. The knell of capitalist private property sounds. The expropriators are expropriated."[3]

He further predicted that after completing the deprival of an extremely small number of capitalists who monopolized the means of production, the whole society, on the basis of public ownership of the means of production, would become one immense factory.[4]

The Lenin model is characterized by the idea of a state machine holding coercive power and functioning as the organizer of socialist economy, thus avoiding the idealism of an "immense social factory" and "association of free men." Lenin, in his book *The State and Revolution,* written just before the October Revolution in Russia, likened a socialist economy to a "State Syndicate," a super enterprise monopolized by the state. He said that in a socialist society (i.e., the first stage of a communist society), all citizens would be converted "into workers and other employees of one huge 'syndicate'—the whole state," and "the whole of society will have become a single office and a single factory, with equality of labor and pay."[5]

The introduction of the state machine distorted the public ownership theory of Marxism. Prior to Lenin, Marxists despised the "superstitious belief in the state." They believed that "the state is . . . at best an evil inherited by the proletariat after its victorious struggle for class supremacy." They proposed to create conditions so that "a new generation, reared in new and free social conditions, will be able to throw the entire

---

[2] Karl Marx, *The Capital (Ziben lun) (1867),* Chinese edition, Vol. 1, Beijing: People's Publishing House, 1975, p. 688.
[3] Karl Marx, "Historical Tendency of Capitalist Accumulation (Zibenzhuyi jilei de lishi qushi)," *The Capital (Ziben lun) (1867),* Chinese edition, Vol. 1, Beijing: People's Publishing House, 1975, pp. 831–832.
[4] In *The Poverty of Philosophy,* Marx said, "If one took as a model the division of labor in a modern workshop, in order to apply it to a whole society, the society best organized for the production of wealth would undoubtedly be that which had a single chief employer, distributing tasks to the different members of the community according to a previously fixed rule." See Karl Marx, "The Poverty of Philosophy (Zhexue de pinkun) (1847)," *Selected Works of Marx and Engels (Makesi Engesi xuanji),* Chinese edition, Vol. 1, Beijing: People's Publishing House, 1995, p. 163. In *The Capital,* Marx symbolized production under public ownership as the planned division of labor in a factory. "It is very characteristic that the enthusiastic apologists of the factory system have nothing more damning to urge against a general organization of the labor of society, than that it would turn all society into one immense factory." See Karl Marx, *The Capital (Ziben lun) (1867),* Chinese edition, Vol. 1, Beijing: People's Publishing House, 1975, p. 395.
[5] Vladimir I. Lenin, *Selected Works of Lenin (Liening xuanji),* Chinese edition, Vol. 3, Beijing: People's Publishing House, 1995, p. 202.

lumber of the state on the scrap-heap."[6] Engels said, "The first act in which the state really comes forward as the representative of the whole of society—the taking possession of the means of production in the name of society—is at the same time its last independent act as a state. The interference of the state power in social relations becomes superfluous in one sphere after another, and then dies away of itself. The government of persons is replaced by the administration of things and the direction of the processes of production."[7] In contrast, Lenin and his successors raised the function of the state to an extremely high position and viewed state ownership as the sole economic base for socialism.

Bolsheviks, after seizing state power in the October Revolution, should have founded socialist economy according to the Lenin model. However, divided opinions existed among leaders of the Russian Communist Party on whether state ownership could function as the only economic base in Russia at the time, where a small-peasant economy still dominated. Even Lenin himself hesitated. In his essay, "'Left-Wing' Childishness and the Petty-Bourgeois Mentality,"[8] written in May 1918, Lenin expressed the consideration of the gradual transition from a historical period of coexistence of multiple ownerships to complete socialism based on state ownership.

However, the foreign intervention and the outbreak of the civil war caused the immediate implementation of complete nationalization and shift to a command economy. It was necessary to implement all-round administrative control over the economy and rationing system in wartime. But leaders of the Russian Communist Party at that time regarded this as a significant step in realizing the ideal of socialism. Therefore, the first planned economy in the world was established in the form of "wartime communism" in Soviet Russia.

"Wartime communism" was only a caricature form of the "State Syndicate" model proposed by Lenin in 1917. But it was regarded as a standard economic system of socialism and was written into the Program of the Russian Communist Party approved by its Eighth National Congress in 1919. Thereafter, the economic system and policies of wartime communism were defined as the classical economic system of socialism in the booklet, *The ABC of Communism*,[9] written by two famous theorists of the Russian

---

[6] Friedrich Engels, "The 1891 Preface to Marx's 'The Civil War in France' (Makesi Falanxi neizhan 1891 nian danxingben daoyan) (1891)," *Selected Works of Marx and Engels (Makesi Engesi xuanji)*, Chinese edition, Vol. 2, Beijing: People's Publishing House, 1972, p. 336.

[7] Friedrich Engels, "Anti-Dühring: Herr Eugen Dühring's Revolution in Science (Fan Dulin lun) (1878)," *Selected Works of Marx and Engels (Makesi Engesi xuanji)*, Chinese edition, Vol. 3, Beijing: People's Publishing House, 1995, p. 631.

[8] Vladimir I. Lenin, *Selected Works of Lenin (Liening xuanji)*, Chinese edition, Vol. 3, Beijing: People's Publishing House, 1995, pp. 510–540.

[9] Nikolai Bukharin and Evgenii A. Preobrazhenskii, *The ABC of Communism (1919)*, English edition, London: The Communist Party of Great Britain, 1922. This booklet received Lenin's high praise and had a widespread and profound influence on the first generation of Chinese revolutionaries. Deng Xiaoping, in his South China speeches in 1992, commented that "In studying Marxism-Leninism we must grasp the essence and learn what we need to know. . . . It is formalistic and impracticable to require

Communist Party, Nikolai Bukharin (1888–1938) and Evgenii Preobrazhenskii (1886–1937), as their interpretation of the Program of the Russian Communist Party.

Insight 1.1

Socialist Model in the Early Days of the Soviet Union

In March 1919, the Eighth National Congress of the Russian Communist Party (Bolshevik) passed the first Party Program after seizing state power. The new Party Program presented a practical principle framework for this unprecedented advent of socialism, which was authoritatively interpreted by theorists of the Russian Communist Party in their books such as *The ABC of Communism* (Bukharin and Preobrazhenskii) and *The Economics of the Transition Period* (Bukharin).

The theorists held that the "mathematical limit" of the trends of accumulation and concentration of capital would turn the whole national economy into an "absolutely united trust." The proletariat, after seizing state power, should first of all strip big capital and achieve nationalization. Afterwards, all economic activities, according to an overall state plan, should be unified and managed by a National Economic Commission and subordinate industrial bureaus at various levels. Meanwhile, commodity markets should be eliminated, currency should be made a mere unit of calculation, and production should be organized nationwide.

The theorists argued that, in a backward country like Russia, a practical means of transforming a small-peasant economy to a great socialist economy is to develop state-run farms and urban agriculture. In rural Russia, practical ways to unite numerous small economies are through communes and labor organizations. For farmers, communes are unions not only in working, but also in distribution and living. In terms of product distribution, consumer cooperatives, joined by all the residents, are self-governed by their members. Furthermore, the new Soviet regime should build a unified distribution institution to allocate the necessities of subsistence, such as food and housing.

---

that everyone read such works. It was from *The Communist Manifesto* and *The ABC of Communism* that I learned the rudiments of Marxism." (Deng Xiaoping, "Excerpts from Talks Given in Wuchang, Shenzhen, Zhuhai and Shanghai (Zai Wuchang, Shenzhen, Zhuhai, Shanghai dengdi de tanhua yaodian) (January–February 1992)," *Selected Works of Deng Xiaoping (Deng Xiaoping wenxuan)*, Vol. 3, Beijing: People's Publishing House, 1993, p. 382.)

> According to these theorists, banks should also be nationalized and unified as a statistical organization for production and a financial allocation institution. All the banking businesses should be monopolized by the state. A socialist society will, eventually, eliminate the bank by turning it into the chief accounting department of the society. Monetary currency would also retreat gradually from circulation. Currency would be canceled first in the exchange of products among state-owned enterprises, then in settlements between the state and its workers; the next step would be to replace currency by commodity exchanges between the state and small producers, after which it would be eliminated inside small economies and eventually die out together with small economies.
>
> (Compiled from Nikolai Bukharin and Evgenii Preobrazhenskii, *The ABC of Communism (1919)*, English edition, London: The Communist Party of Great Britain, 1922; Nikolai Bukharin, *The Economics of the Transition Period (Guodu shiqi jingjixue) (1920)*, Chinese edition, Beijing: Joint Publishing, 1981.)

Strict military discipline and the rationing system assisted Russian communists in saving the newly born Soviet regime but this also resulted in severe economic and social problems, which the populace could no longer withstand after the civil war. When domestic dissatisfaction mounted, Lenin realized that it was wrong "to organize the state production and the state distribution of products on communist lines in a small–peasant country directly as ordered by the proletarian state,"[10] and it was necessary to explore other approaches for establishing the economic base for socialism. Therefore, Soviet Russia implemented its New Economic Policy, with its primary objectives of resuming "commodity exchange," developing "commerce suitable for the needs of the socialist construction," and implementing "principle of business" and "business accounting" in every industrial and commercial enterprise. As a result, the New Economic Policy was implemented and a market system was reinstated under the condition that the state kept control of the economic lifelines of the country.[11]

---

[10] Vladimir I. Lenin, *Selected Works of Lenin (Liening xuanji)*, Chinese edition, Vol. 4, Beijing: People's Publishing House, 1995, p. 571.
[11] In April 1922, *The Resolution on Industry* of the 12th National Congress of the Russian Communist Party (Bolshevik) pointed out, "As we had turned into a market economy, we should give the freedom to enterprises in their economic activities. . . . The administrative means of the management committee has been replaced by flexible economic means," *A Collection of Resolu-*

When deliberating on the New Economic Policy, Lenin insisted that turnover freedom was trade freedom and trade freedom was retrogression to capitalism; a real plan should be an integral and all-inclusive one. However, the implementation of the New Economic Policy changed Lenin's mind. In a speech delivered in 1921 in commemoration of the fourth anniversary of the October Revolution, Lenin pointed out that there was no contradiction between the realization of the unified state plan through market mechanism and a planned economy. He said, "The New Economic Policy does not aim to change the unified state plan or to go beyond this plan; it is only to adjust approaches to realize this plan." [12] In other words, Lenin agreed that the Soviet state, in the context of the time, might achieve development in a planned way (i.e., development in proportion) of the national economy on the basis of market practices plus government planning and coordination.

1.1.2 The Establishment of Stalin's System

By 1924, industrial and agricultural production in the Soviet Union had basically recovered. In the same year, Lenin passed away. After that, two opposing views on the future of the New Economic Policy emerged within the Communist Party of the Soviet Union (CPSU), resulting in a new debate about the continuation of the New Economic Policy among the leadership.

The fuse of the debate was the approach and speed of the Soviet Union's industrialization, but the essence of the debate was whether the Soviet Union should continue the New Economic Policy and a market economy or establish a planned economic system with administrative centralization. In the debate, the leaders of the CPSU divided into three political factions: the Left headed by Leon Trotsky (1879–1940), the Right headed by Nikolai Bukharin, and the Center headed by Joseph Stalin (1879–1953).

The debate focusing on industrialization in the Soviet Union was one between "embryology" and "teleology" in terms of methodology. Holding the viewpoint of embryology, Bukharin followed the logic that socialist industrialization should be planned on the basis of the existing economic situation. He argued that the larger the actual demand of farmers was, the quicker industry would develop; as the accumulation of the farmer economy accelerated, industrial accumulation would also accelerate. To ally with farmers, it was necessary to implement the New Economic Policy and retain the market system. Supporters of teleology advocated subjectively prescribing the direction and plan

tions of the Communist Party of the Soviet Union (Sugong jueyi caobian), Chinese edition, Vol. 2, Beijing: People's Publishing House, 1964, pp. 259–261.

[12] Vladimir I. Lenin, "To Comrade Krzhizhanovsky (Zhi Ge Ma Ke'errizhanuofusiji) (1921)," Collected Works of Lenin (Liening quanji), Chinese edition, Vol. 52, Beijing: People's Publishing House, 1988, p. 40.

of economic development because of the requirement of accelerated socialist industrialization. Grigorii Alexandrovich Feldman (1884–1958), one of the teleology advocates in the debate, claimed that the proletariat, as the principal of production, was able to allocate its force at will between the production of the means of production and the production of consumer goods. Teleology advocates, who eventually defeated Bukharin's embryology by virtue of Stalin's political power, actually regarded a state plan that reflected the government's will as an objective economic rule, and therefore laid a foundation for the implementation of forced collectivization and the establishment of the Stalinist economic model.

After defeating the Left faction and the Right faction one after the other in the inner-party fight, Stalin practiced a more Leftist policy than had the Left faction, criticized Right opportunism and its "blind faith in spontaneous forces of the market," and negated the New Economic Policy. Based on the victory of his Anti-Right Opportunist Campaign, Stalin launched forced collectivization and established a centrally planned economic system in 1929.

Stalin exerted administrative mandatory power of a proletarian dictatorship to the extreme and turned Lenin's theoretical model of State Syndicate into a reality. Stalin formulated the equation: Socialist Economy = Dominant State Ownership + Planned Economy, which ruled socialist countries for over half a century. In *Political Economy,* compiled by the Institute of Economics of the Academy of Sciences of the USSR under Stalin's personal supervision, state ownership and economic plans formulated and executed by state organs were regarded as the basic economic characteristics of socialism. Moreover, state ownership was even considered the foundation of the entire socialist system. Although Stalin's definition of socialism clearly reflected the "blind faith in the state" that was strongly criticized by classical Marxist authors, it was regarded as an unalterable principle of Marxism for a fairly long time by leaders in some socialist countries.

Many experts on the Soviet Union attributed forced collectivization and establishment of administrative socialism with state coercive power to Stalin's brutality. However, this analysis was oversimplified. There was no difference in principle between the centrally planned economic system of administrative socialism built by Stalin and Lenin's State Syndicate model, and the practice of pursuing a state development plan through state coercive power to attain national goals was a Russian tradition since Tsar Peter I, the Great (1672–1725). Because the Soviet Union selected the route of industrialization with priority given to heavy industry (military industry, in fact), a command economic system was inevitable. During the implementation of industrialization with priority given to heavy industry at an ultrahigh speed and with a weak economic base, it was impossible to use light-industry products to exchange for grain and agricultural raw materials and to create accumulation. Thus, coercive methods were applied to collect agricultural products and "tribute" from farmers.[13]

Stalin also made some alterations to Lenin's socialist economic system. He introduced the market force (the law of value) into his model in the form of "business accounting" when Russia's First Five-Year Plan (1928–1932) got into trouble.[14] After World War II, he further acknowledged that "so long as the two basic production sectors remain, commodity production and commodity circulation must remain in force, as a necessary and very useful element in our system of national economy."[15] Nevertheless, all these were piecemeal patches that never touched the basic framework of a planned economy based on state ownership.

For a long time, Stalin's viewpoints were regarded as the standard theory, and the Stalin model as the criterion of the Soviet Union, which was imitated by many other socialist countries.

Insight 1.2

On the Basic Economic Characteristics of Socialism:
The Soviet Textbook of *Political Economy*

This textbook, published in 1954, was compiled by the Institute of Economics of the Academy of Sciences of the USSR under Stalin's personal supervision.

The textbook presents the belief of its authors that the socialist relations of production are a system based on public ownership of the means of production in two forms: state property (property of the whole people) and cooperative and collective farm property. Under such a system,

---

[13] Stalin believed that Bukharin's principal mistake was "his opportunist distortion of the Party line on the question of the 'scissors' between town and country, on the question of the so-called 'tribute.'" Stalin emphasized that farmers should also pay supertax apart from normal taxes to the state through the "price scissors" between industrial products and agricultural produce. This supertax was "to stimulate the development of our industry and to do away with our backwardness." See Joseph Stalin, "The Right Deviation in the CPSU (B) (Lun Liangong (Bu) dangnei de youqing) (1929)," *Selected Works of Stalin (Sidalin xuanji)*, Chinese edition, Vol. 2, Beijing: People's Publishing House, 1979, pp. 148–149.

[14] In June 1931, Stalin, at a conference of economic executives, strongly criticized "equalitarianism" in the Soviet economy. He suggested doing away with wage equalization to give workers an incentive to rise to a higher position and introducing and reinforcing business accounting in state-run enterprises. See Joseph Stalin, "New Conditions: New Tasks in Economic Construction (Xinde huanjing he xinde jingji renwu) (1931)," *Selected Works of Stalin (Sidalin xuanji)*, Chinese edition, Vol. 2, Beijing: People's Publishing House, 1979, pp. 276–297.

[15] Joseph Stalin, "Economic Problems of Socialism in the USSR (Sulian shehuizhuyi jingji wenti) (1952)," *Collected Works of Stalin (Sidalin wenxuan)*, Chinese edition, Beijing: People's Publishing House, 1962, pp. 578–582.

exploitation is completely eliminated by implementing the principle of distribution according to work; the development of the national economy is planned and aims at the maximum satisfaction of laborers' ever-mounting requirements by continuously promoting production.

The textbook emphasizes the dominant status of state ownership. It states that state property is "the advanced form of socialist property;" it reflects "the most mature and consistent" socialist relations of production; state property plays "the leading and determining role in the entire national economy."

The prospect for the two forms of socialist public ownership is definitely to transition to complete ownership by the whole people (state ownership).

The basic economic law of socialism is the securing of the maximum satisfaction of the constantly rising material and cultural requirements of the whole society through the continuous expansion and perfection of socialist production on the basis of the highest technology. It determines the whole process of the development of socialist production, the purpose of socialist production, and the means of achieving it.

The planned (proportional) development of the national economy is another economic law of socialism. It requires the use of a plan to guide the economy, and this plan is the most important function of a socialist state as the organizer of the economy.

Commodity production and circulation under socialism are limited to consumer goods. Labor is not a commodity; therefore, wages are no longer the price of labor. Money in a socialist society is an economic instrument for planning the national economy and for calculating and supervising the production and distribution of commodities. The state-run and cooperative markets play a decisive role in commodity circulation, where prices are set by plan.

(Compiled from the Institute of Economics of the Academy of Sciences of the USSR, *Political Economy,* London: Lawrence & Wishart, 1957.)

1.2 An Economic Analysis of the Centrally Planned Economic System

1.2.1 Neoclassical Economists' Theoretical Demonstration of the Feasibility of a Planned Economic System

The first to provide an economic proof of the feasibility of socialist assumptions about a planned economy based on public ownership were not Marxist economists but neoclassical economists. Vilfredo Pareto (1848–1923), in *Socialist System* (1902–1903) and *Manual of Political Economy* (1906), initially pointed out that a plan formulated and carried out on the basis of economic calculations by a "socialist ministry of production" could optimize resource allocation. Pareto's follower, Enrico Barone (1859–1924) expounded Pareto's idea in details in his famous article, "The Ministry of Production in the Collectivist State" (1908).

As we know, the assumptions of neoclassical economics are perfect competition, complete information, and zero transaction costs. Therefore, institutional arrangements had nothing to do with efficiency, and the enterprise, no matter whether a family workshop or a big factory consisting of the whole society, would not affect the cost of a product. Under the assumptions of neoclassical economics, Pareto and Barone demonstrated that resource allocation under the condition of a centrally planned economy based on state ownership (called "collectivism" by Barone) shared the same nature as resource allocation under the condition of competition and market institutions: both were aimed at finding the solution to a set of simultaneous equations of resource allocation.[16] If the solution was found, it (a price vector) could provide the relative prices needed to balance supply and demand. Barone pointed out that the solution to this set of equations could be found either by hundreds of thousands of market transactions or by direct calculation conducted by the "ministry of production," that is, the planning organ of the central government. If the ministry of production could find the solution to economic equilibrium equations, work out the prices of scarce resources based on this solution, and order production units to arrange production according to the principle of marginal cost equal to price, an economic plan might have the same results as competitive market forces. So, he believed that a socialist planned economy was feasible.

The concepts of Pareto and Barone inspired sympathizers of socialism to form the idea of "market socialism" in the debate on socialism that occurred in the Western academic circles in the 1920s and 1930s.

---

[16] Joseph Alois Schumpeter gave a brief description of Barone's argument in his book, *Capitalism, Socialism and Democracy*. (Joseph Alois Schumpeter, *Capitalism, Socialism and Democracy*, New York: Harper, 1942.)

1.2.2 The Debate on Socialism among Western Economists in the 1920s and 1930s

The debate on whether a socialist economic system was feasible was raised by Austrian economists Ludwig von Mises (1881–1973) and Friedrich von Hayek (1899–1992). They thought that market price and competition mechanism were especially important to resource allocation. The price expressed in currency units offered a prerequisite to the possibility of rational economic calculation. They also believed the only means of setting prices was market competition. However, the absence of market mechanism in socialist countries made it impossible to set rational prices and establish a relevant incentive mechanism.

"Sympathizers of socialism" promptly made their responses. Maurice Dobb (1900–1976), the main representative of the so-called school of centralized solution, advocated revoking the consumer's right to free choice and carrying out centrally planned pricing to make the plan correspond to reality and be efficient. According to him, such measures prevented the fluctuation and distortion of the market and enabled efficient resource allocation. Unlike Dobb, Fred Manville Taylor (1855–1932), Abba P. Lerner (1903–1982), and Oskar Lange (1904–1965) proposed to solve the problem by the "competitive solution" of having the planning organ simulate the market. This viewpoint was the most influential among sympathizers of socialism.

Born in Poland and having completed his study in America before the debate on socialism started, Lange was among the most influential economists. He published his paper "On the Economic Theory of Socialism"[17] in two separate parts in October 1936 and February 1937, respectively. In this paper, based on Barone's analysis of 1908, Lange proposed that prices indicating consumer preferences could be used as guiding criteria for resource allocation in a socialist economy, and the planning organ could set prices by simulating the market in the manner of trial and error, a method equivalent to the competitive market mechanism. Lange's "competitive socialism model" divided the socialist economic system into three decision-making tiers. The top tier was the Central Planning Commission with two functions: (a) setting prices of the means of production according to supply and demand and (b) distributing social gains (rents and profits) from utilizing state-owned production resources. The middle tier was made up of industry administration departments that determined the development of various sectors of production. The bottom tier was comprised of state-owned enterprises and households. According to price signals, enterprises carried out production based on two principles:

---

[17] Oskar Lange, *On the Economic Theory of Socialism*, Minneapolis: University of Minnesota Press, 1938.

(a) to set outputs at such levels that the prices of products equal their marginal costs and (b) to minimize production costs at such output levels. Households could freely allocate personal income and decide the amount of labor to supply. The essence of the Lange model was to simulate the market by the central planning organ. The planning organ adjusted prices according to supply and demand, while enterprises decided what and how many products to produce according to price signals. This assumption of improving economic efficiency by competitive forces in the context of state ownership was later called "market socialism."

Responding to the viewpoints of the sympathizers of socialism, Hayek published a series of works in the 1930s and 1940s detailing how the Dobb model and the Lange model were impractical in real life. His three most representative articles are "Socialist Calculation I: The Nature and History of the Problem" (1935), "Socialist Calculation II: The State of the Debate" (1935), and "Socialist Calculation III: The Competitive 'Solution'" (1940).[18] In "Socialist Calculation I," following Mises' viewpoint, Hayek pointed out that because the socialist central planning authorities could not rationally calculate values and prices, it could not rationally allocate resources. In "Socialist Calculation II," he demonstrated that prices could not be rationally calculated based on Dobb's assumption of a "centralized solution" because of the central planning authorities' incomplete information and knowledge and inaccuracy in consumer choices. Meanwhile, simulated competition under the control of central planning authorities could not achieve the same performance in resource allocation as did competitive systems based on private property. In "Socialist Calculation III," Hayek further expounded in detail about the infeasibility of the Lange model.

This debate took place in the Western academic circles and had no impact on the development of domestic affairs in the Soviet Union. At that time, Hayek's economic theory was not yet fully formed and the viewpoints defending the socialist economic system, such as Lange's, were obviously constrained within the framework of neoclassical economics. Another reason the debate did not have an impact was because Western economies were then stranded in the global crisis that started in 1929, plus the dark side of the Soviet economy had not been fully exposed. Yet the viewpoints and arguments of both sides of the debate had an influence on theoretical discussions and reform practices later.

---

[18] Friedrich August von Hayek, *Individualism and Economic Order,* Chicago: University of Chicago Press, 1948.

Insight 1.3

Brus's Decentralized Model

Wlodzimierz Brus (1921–) is an exponent of the Polish school of market socialism and a representative figure of the Eastern European school of reform, which rose in the 1960s and 1970s and advocated combining plan with market mechanism. Brus's decentralized model had a great influence on reforms in all socialist countries.

Brus divided economic decision making into three tiers. The first tier was macroeconomic decision making; the second tier was enterprise decision making involving local issues; and the third tier was decision making on economic activities of households and individuals. According to whether these three tiers of decision making were centralized (the administrative approach) or decentralized (the economic approach), Brus divided economic operation models into four categories:

1. a model in which decision making is centralized at all three tiers, like the economic system of wartime communism;

2. a model in which decision making is centralized in the first tier (macro decision making) and the second tier (enterprise decision making), but decentralized at the third tier (individual decision making), which was called the centralized model (i.e., the Soviet model);

3. a model in which decision making is centralized at the first tier (macro decision making), but decentralized at the second and third tiers (enterprise and individual decision making), which was called the decentralized model and was, in general, the destination model of the reforms in Eastern European countries; and

4. a model in which decision making is decentralized at all three tiers, as exemplified by Adam Smith's laissez-faire economy.

Brus thought that the first and fourth models were absolutely inadvisable, and a choice could be made only between the second and third ones. He advocated the decentralized model.

Brus pointed out that the centralized model had the advantages of forced mobilization of resources, prompt action, and wide scope for selection, but it was also plagued by defects, such as the "ratchet effect,"* neglect of economic results, and lack of a system to hold people accountable. When there were large quantities of idle resources available, this model's merits and demerits balanced; but its demerits grossly outweighed its merits when resources were in short supply so that it was imperative to switch to intensive growth.

Brus suggested to combine plan with market mechanism and to practice the decentralized model, or the "model of central planning with regulated markets." In this model, the decision-making powers of the three tiers were divided as follows. The top tier was the central government with its two functions: (1) setting prices for the means of production and (2) distributing social gains (rents and profits) from utilizing state-owned production resources and making investment decisions. The middle tier was comprised of enterprises, which produced according to economic parameters like prices, wages, loans, and taxes set by the Central Planning Commission to pursue maximized profits while maintaining among themselves free contract relationships between buyers and sellers via the market. The bottom tier was comprised of households, which could freely choose their jobs and dispose of their incomes.

In Brus's view, his decentralized model not only fully utilized market mechanism under state regulation but also kept the development of the national economy under plan. Regulated markets would not weaken the planned economy but, rather, improve the plan. However, his model did not alter the ownership structure dominated by state ownership and maintained the control of central planning over investment decisions; it allowed the market to affect enterprises' decision making, but the influence of the market forces was limited to short-term decisions of enterprises. Thus, it would hardly be an integrated system of efficient resource allocation.

Brus changed his ideas after immigrating to Britain in the early 1970s. He criticized his own concepts of strengthening the planned economy by market mechanism and completely turned to supporting market-oriented reform.**

---

* A ratchet is a gear that can run only forward but not backward. When an economic mechanism has the same nature as a ratchet, it motivates economic agents to take specific measures to seek advantages and avoid disadvantages. For example, if an enterprise's profit target is set by "base plus growth," the enterprise, in gen-

eral, will be unwilling to exceed the planned profit target to avoid possible difficulties in fulfilling plans for the next year.

**See Wlodzimierz Brus, "From Revisionism to Pragmatism: Sketches to a Self-Portrait of a 'Reform Economist' (1988)," János Mátyás Kovács and Márton Tardos (eds.), *Reform and Transformation in Eastern Europe*, London: Routledge, 1992; Wlodzimierz Brus and Kazimierz Laski, *From Marx to the Market: Socialism in Search of an Economic System*, Oxford: Clarendon Press, 1989.

After World War II, Lange returned to Poland and occupied an important position in the government. The Polish school of economics headed by Lange advocated market socialism and had a widespread influence on reform in Eastern Europe. However, from the failure of reforms in Eastern European socialist countries, people learned that the low efficiency of centrally planned economies had its root causes in the system itself and could not be solved by improvements in technology.[19]

1.2.3 The Reexamination of Planned Economy in the Late Twentieth Century

A thorough theoretical analysis of planned economy did not occur until the 1980s, when scholars reexamined it based on modern economics and arrived at the conclusion that it is impossible for such an institutional arrangement to be efficient.

As Joseph Stiglitz (1943–) said in 1993 in the preface to the first edition of his *Economics,* the basic competitive model of neoclassical economics was perfected in the 1950s. "Since then, economists have gone beyond that model in several directions as they have come to better understand its limitations. Earlier researchers had paid lip service to the importance of incentives and to problems posed by limited information. However, it was only in the last two decades that real progress was made in understanding these issues, and the advances found immediate application."[20]

When we reexamine the socialist planned economy with tools of modern economics, we clearly understand its inherent defects.

The essence of a planned economy is to organize the whole society into a huge single factory and to allocate resources by the administrative means of the central planning organ. The key to this mode of allocation is to use a plan made in advance to allocate resources. The success of this mode of allocation depends on whether a plan that is made

[19] For criticism on market socialism, see János Kornai, *The Road to a Free Economy. Shifting from a Socialist System: The Example of Hungary,* New York: W.W. Norton & Company, 1990.
[20] Joseph Stiglitz, *Economics,* New York: W.W. Norton & Company, 1993, pp. xxxvi–xxxvii.

subjectively can reflect the objective actuality and optimize resource allocation, and whether the plan can be strictly implemented. In this case, there are two implicit premises for the efficient operation of a planned economy: (a) the central planning organ should have complete information on the economic activities of the whole society, including the conditions of material and human resources, the feasibility of technology, and the structure of demand (the complete information hypothesis) and (b) the interests of the whole society should be integrated and there should be no separate interests or different judgments of value (the single interest hypothesis). If these two requirements are not satisfied, a centrally planned economic system will not operate efficiently because of high information costs and incentive costs. The point is that these two premises are very hard to satisfy in real economic life. Therefore, insurmountable difficulties arise when making and carrying out decisions according to a centrally planned mode of resource allocation.

First, the operation of a planned economy incurs huge information costs. Modern production has the following features: (a) with rapid technological advance, there are many choices for product mixes, technological processes, and production plans; (b) consumption patterns are complicated and fast changing; and (c) as the division of labor deepens, members of society and economic units are sure to establish increasingly wider and more complex connections among them. In this situation, an explosion of information about demand and production occurs. To accurately and promptly collect trillions of bits of data scattered in every corner of the society for timely processing, to find solutions to tens of millions of equilibrium equations, and to work out all-inclusive plans to be assigned to implementing units tier upon tier, an extremely flexible and efficient information system is needed. Otherwise, these tasks can never be accomplished.

In a planned economic system, there are no horizontal links and feedback mechanisms between producers and consumers. Economic information is transmitted vertically via top-down commands and bottom-up reports between higher levels and lower levels in an administrative system. Information is likely to be delayed and congested as a result of long distances and narrow channels. Even worse, information is likely to be distorted because of the many links in the transmission. Production units are unable to acquire information about demand and technology directly and thus cannot respond flexibly to complex and changing demands and technical possibilities.

Hayek pointed out early that no manager, however omniscient and omnipotent, could have knowledge of the relative scarcity of millions of resources dispersed throughout a country. Only through the medium of the price system can this knowledge be transmitted effectively to the whole society so relevant people have the necessary information for decision making.[21] Through an analysis of transaction costs, we can arrive at the conclusion that if the central planning organ controlled and handled all micro affairs, the cost of obtaining all the necessary information to ensure smooth operation of the economic system would be infinitely high and thus absolutely impossible.

In essence, incentive mechanism is also an issue of transaction costs. In resource allocation by plan, decisions are made by the central planning organ, which represents the interests of the whole society, and are implemented by all members of the society, organized according to the principle of hierarchy. This situation requires that all members and organizations of the society act like the limbs of a "social Robinson Crusoe," as described by Marx; their objective function is to be loyal to the tasks assigned by the higher level without attention to their own special interests; they neither distort information when providing data and reporting work outputs to the planning organ nor deviate when implementing the unified plan of the society.

In reality, such a case is simply impossible. Under socialism, every economic agent, including the planner himself, has his own interests that do not conform to common interests. Therefore, distortions and deviations are unavoidable at every link in the process of making and implementing the plan as a result of the contradiction between individual interests and common interests. Conflicts also occur among economic agents because of conflicting interests. To overcome such distortions and deviations, the costs—including the costs of formulating the plan, supervising the implementation of the plan, and avoiding opportunism—would be immense. Therefore, it can be concluded that the lack of efficiency in a planned economy is closely related to the nature of this mode of resource allocation and is an innate defect that cannot be overcome.

A market economy is quite different. The relative prices of various resources set by market competition are parameters of full information. Prices carry information about the scarcity of various resources relative to others. Individual members of the society can make decisions based on the relative prices of commodities so information costs are significantly lower than those in a planned economy. Meanwhile, every participant in market activities is subject to the constraints of both competition and property rights, so supervision costs are also significantly lower. Therefore, a market economy is an efficient mode of resource allocation because it can save transaction costs. Efficiency cannot be greatly improved in an economy unless a market system is adopted and whether or not a social economic system is efficient fundamentally determines whether

---

[21] Hayek has published much on this topic. See Friedrich August von Hayek, "Use of Knowledge in Society," *The American Economic Review,* 1945, Vol. 35, No. 4, pp. 519–530; "The Pretence of Knowledge: Nobel Memorial Lecture (December 11, 1974)," *The American Economic Review,* 1989, Vol. 79, No. 6, pp. 3–7.

or not it can survive and develop. In other words, without high economic efficiency, the high ideal of socialism becomes a "castle in the air" or the so-called "socialism of common poverty" because of its lack of a material base. Therefore, between a planned economy and a market economy, we actually have no choice.[22]

1.3 Reform in the Soviet Union and Eastern European Socialist Countries

The advantage of a planned economy lies in the fact that resources can be mobilized and concentrated by administrative means for designated purposes; its fatal weaknesses are excessively high information costs and low economic efficiency resulting from a lack of incentives. At the initial stage of economic development when resources are abundant and there is enough room for extensive growth, under the threat of war, in a state of emergency, or in a recovery stage when rules exist for the allocation of resources, a planned economy can maintain strong growth momentum by taking advantage of its strong capability of mobilizing resources and the fact that the material well-being of economic agents are easy to satisfy. Once conditions change, however, the weaknesses of a planned economy become apparent very quickly.

The Soviet Union maintained a higher growth rate than many capitalist countries before World War II and during the postwar recovery period. Abram Bergson (1914–2003), an American economist, estimated that the average GNP growth of the Soviet Union between 1928 and 1955 ranged from 4.4 to 6.3 percent. The annual growth rate of Soviet industry was 19.2 percent during the First Five-Year Plan period (1928–1932), 17.8 percent during the Second Five-Year Plan period (1933–1937), and 13.2 percent during the Third Five-Year Plan period (1938–1940, cut short by World War II). From 1913 to 1950, the Soviet Union's total product of society increased by 17.2 times, its gross value of industrial output increased by 12 times, its output value of the means of production increased by 26 times, and its total value of national income increased by 7.8 times.[23] The planned economic system made contributions to the Soviet Union's industrialization and preparation for the Anti-Fascist War. However, for this the Soviet Union paid a high price of huge losses in material wealth and human lives.

As early as the 1950s, the disadvantages of the centrally planned economic system began to surface. Starting in the early 1960s, the growth rate of the Soviet Union decreased every year (see Table 1.1); efficiency also decreased and technological innovation slowed

---

[22] Wu Jinglian, "Market Economy and Socialism (Shichang jingji yu shehuizhuyi)," *Chinese Social Sciences Quarterly (Zhongguo shehui kexue jikan)*, 1992, Vol. 1, No. 1; see also *A Planned Economy or a Market Economy (Jihua jingji haishi shichang jingji)*, Beijing: China Economic Publishing House, 1992, pp. 206–225.

[23] Abram Bergson, *The Real National Income of Soviet Russia since 1928*, Cambridge, Mass.: Harvard University Press, 1961.

Table 1.1   Annual Growth Rate of the Soviet Economy (%)

	1951–1960	1961–1965	1966–1970	1971–1975	1976–1980	1981–1985
Statistics of Soviet government	10.1	6.5	7.8	5.7	4.3	3.6
Estimates by CIA, U.S.	5.6	4.9	5.1	3.0	2.3	0.6
Estimates by Soviet scholars	7.2	4.4	4.1	3.2	1.0	0.6

Source: Edward A. Hewett, *Reforming the Soviet Economy: Equality versus Efficiency,* Washington, D.C.: The Brookings Institution, 1988, pp. 37–59.

down, resulting in a widening gap between the Soviet Union and capitalist countries. Furthermore, this deterioration accelerated, which raised the issue of the reform of the existing economic system.

1.3.1 The Effort of the Soviet Union to Improve the Economy and Its Failure

After the death of Stalin, leaders of the CPSU were eager to make progress in improving the Soviet economy. In 1957, Nikita Sergeevich Khrushchev (1894–1971) launched the "regional economic council (*sovnarkhoz*) reform" characterized by delegating power to local governments. The goal of this reform was to shift the administration of the national economy from the central government and central departments to regional governments. The major measures adopted included dismantling 25 ministries at the union level and 113 ministries at the republic level and transferring their functions to 105 regional economic councils; transferring enterprises that used to be under the central government and republic governments to regional governments so the share of industrial output value controlled by the central government decreased from 45 percent to 6 percent; and changing the way of balancing planned material resources from central government–based to regional government–based. This reform did not change the nature of the economic system or overcome the inherent defects in allocating resources by administrative decrees. On the contrary, it created chaos in the economy as it intensified regional fragmentation and disrupted existing patterns of economic links. The failure of the Khrushchev reform caused the "palace coup" in the Soviet leadership that removed Khrushchev from office in 1964.

Aleksey Nikolayevich Kosygin (1904–1980) succeeded Khrushchev as premier and restored the centralized management system characterized by departmental control. In 1965, the Soviets, led by Kosygin, initiated new reform featuring the easing of planning control, the expansion of enterprise autonomy, and the systematic introduction of "economic accounting (*khozrachet*)." The reform achieved short-term growth in production and revenue, but economic decline set in soon because of the weakening of incentive effects and the deterioration of government finance. As a result, the Kosygin reform was terminated at the end of the 1960s.

After Kosygin's failure, Soviet leaders stopped trying to reform the economic system. Instead, they attempted to patch this system within the framework of the planned economy as follows:

• To switch the mode of economic growth. Since the First Five-Year Plan started in 1928, the Soviet Union had maintained a much higher economic growth rate than those of Western countries. So why did the Soviet economy lag behind Western economies later? Economists concluded that the reason lay in the mode of growth. The earlier rapid growth of the Soviet Union was based on extensive growth, that is, growth obtained by huge inputs of production factors in general and capital in particular, regardless of cost. As a result, the high growth rate did not generate much real benefit; as resources became increasingly scarce, it became increasingly difficult to maintain that high growth rate without much real benefit. To overcome this defect, Soviet economists proposed switching from extensive growth to intensive growth. Soviet leaders adopted this proposal and gave priority to developing science; strengthening research and development; and accelerating innovation, importation of technology, and the technological renovation of enterprises during the Ninth Five-Year Plan (1971–1975). They requested that the "switch from extensive growth to intensive growth" be accomplished during this five-year period. However, Soviet leaders did not recognize the most important fact that extensive growth originated from the planned economic system. They proceeded to focus their attention on technology and tried to speed up technological progress by administrative decrees and huge investments with only a few patches to the system. As a result, labor productivity improved, but capital productivity declined a lot (see Table 1.2). The Soviet economy was never able to achieve high growth through improving efficiency (i.e., intensive growth) before

Table 1.2 Changes in Productivity in the Soviet Union (%)

	1961–1965	1966–1970	1971–1975	1976–1980	1981–1984
Total factor productivity	0.5	1.2	−0.5	−0.9	−0.3
Labor productivity	3.4	3.2	2.0	1.5	1.9
Capital productivity	−3.5	−2.0	−4.0	−4.0	−3.4
Land productivity	4.4	5.6	2.9	2.7	2.8
Extensive/intensive growth	0.10	0.23	−0.14	−0.35	−0.11

Source: Hewett, *Ibid.*, p. 74.

it collapsed. On the contrary, total factor productivity continued to decline with each passing year.

- To achieve scientific planning. The other measure to improve the planned economy was to try to achieve scientific planning by using modern calculation technology, and to strengthen and improve the management of planning. Before Mikhail S. Gorbachev (1931–) assumed the position of Secretary General of the CPSU in 1985, Soviet leaders insisted that "planning was and now still is a main lever for managing socialist economy."[24] Meanwhile, they promised to improve planning methods. It was fair to say that Soviet planning organs applied modern technology at a substantial level. No longer limited to input-output tables, they applied various mathematical models when formulating the plan. Starting in 1969, the State Planning Commission of the Soviet Union adopted a complete quota system, including raw material consumption quotas, material storage quotas, designed capacity utilization quotas, and equipment storage quotas, to strengthen the quota management of enterprises' economic activities. During the Tenth Five-Year Plan started in 1976, quota management was extended to labor consumption, wages, capital and its utilization, etc., and a system of planning targets for the economic efficiency of social production was set up jointly by the State Planning Commission and various research institutions. In particular, the CPSU, at its 24th National Congress in 1971, decided to build an "automatic planning calculation system" based on the existing national calculating network and unified automatic communication network. They believed that this system, combined with economic and mathematical methods, programs, organizational techniques, and communication tools, would perfect the planning. The first phase of this system, initiated by the State Planning Commission of the Soviet Union with support from more than 140 research institutions and designing institutions, was completed in 1976, and its second phase in 1980.[25] Until then, the Soviet plan-formulating software was perfect in technical terms. However, the Soviet economy slid into fifteen years of stagnancy in the early 1970s due to the intrinsic defects of the planned economic system.

The poor performance of the Soviet economy was reflected not only by the continuous decline in the growth rate but also by the continuous decline in efficiency. According to the calculation of a Soviet scholar, Abel Aganbegyan, total factor productivity (TFP) growth of the Soviet Union between 1961 and 1984 vacillated between

---

[24] Aleksandr Vasilévich Bachurin, *Managerial Approach of Planned Economy (Jihua jingji guanli fangfa),* Chinese edition, Beijing: Joint Publishing, 1980.

[25] Jin Hui, Lu Nanquan, and Zhang Kangqin (eds.), *On the Soviet Economy: Management System and Major Policies (Lun Sulian jingji: guanli tizhi yu zhuyao zhengce),* Shenyang: Liaoning People's Publishing House, 1982.

−0.9 percent and 0.5 percent, except when it rose for a short time to its best performance of 1.2 percent during the Kosygin reform.[26]

After Gorbachev assumed office in 1985, the first measure he adopted was the so-called "acceleration strategy" to re-energize the economy and inspire the public. However, the strategy to pursue "acceleration" and avoid reform did not speed up economic growth, but, rather, resulted in zero growth. This forced Gorbachev to put forward reform in 1987, but the goal and approaches of that reform were not clear. It was not until mid-1989 that the aim of transitioning to a market economic system was defined. Unfortunately, Soviet leaders at that time had lost control over the overall situation and were stuck in political conflicts. All the plans, schemes, and programs for reform that were formulated one after another did not touch the economic system. The national economy and people's living standards plummeted, which led to violent upheavals and the eventual collapse of the Soviet regime.

1.3.2 Self-Management Socialist Reform in Yugoslavia

In 1948, the Yugoslavian Communist Party was expelled from the Soviet bloc by the Communist Information Bureau (Cominform), an international organization of the Soviet bloc. To seek public support amid complete isolation, Yugoslavian leaders broke away from the Stalin model in the early 1950s and started the independent development of self-management socialism. Yugoslavia's reform included three phases:

1. From the early 1950s to the early 1960s: emphasizing and expanding "enterprise autonomy." Although Yugoslavia did not establish real enterprise autonomy because the basic framework of the planned economy remained, the expansion of enterprise autonomy motivated the initiative of the leaders and staff in enterprises and accelerated economic growth. This, in return, prompted Yugoslavian leaders to further reform.

2. From the early 1960s to the early 1970s: practicing "market socialism." From 1961, the Yugoslavian government successively lifted planning control over wages, investment, foreign trade, and prices. Enterprises were completely free to decide their product mix, supply and marketing, income distribution, and investment. Government's control over prices was reduced to an insignificant level. Yugoslavia's economy started becoming active. However, two significant defects remained in the economic system. First, the property rights system lacked efficiency. According to Edvard Kardelj (1910–1979), leader of the Yugoslavian Communist

---

[26] Quoted from Edward A. Hewett, *Reforming the Soviet Economy: Equality versus Efficiency,* Washington D.C.: The Brookings Institution, 1988, pp. 69–70.

Party and chief designer of Yugoslavia's self-management socialism, Yugoslavia's social ownership is a kind of nonownership. In other words, "property belongs to all and none as well." In fact, it was collective ownership by in-service employees of enterprises. Enterprises' pursuit of the maximization of employees' income resulted in the "Illyrian short-term behavior syndrome,"[27] which got its name from the famous "Illyrian model" of Professor Benjamin Ward of the University of California at Berkeley. It includes such symptoms as the pursuit of "retaining less and distributing more," "investing by borrowing money," and high technical content in investment. Second, underdeveloped and chaotic markets and a lack of effective macroeconomic control and market regulation led to intensified inflation, rocketing unemployment, widening income disparity, and, consequently, social unrest. This gave an excuse to antireform forces to blame the market for all these social problems. As a result, Yugoslavian leaders in the early 1970s pushed aside managerial and technical professionals (i.e., the so-called "technocrats"), who supported a free economy, and reinforced government control.

3.   From the early 1970s to 1988: practicing "contractual socialism." Responding to the problems in market socialism, the 1974 Constitution of Yugoslavia defined concepts of "associated labor," "self-management agreement," and "social contract." In the new constitution, "enterprise" was no longer a legal organization but an "organization of associated labor." Several "organizations of associated labor" might constitute an enterprise group called a "composite organization of associated labor." The activities of commercial organizations such as "organizations of associated labor" were coordinated by "self-management agreements" and "social contracts." A self-management agreement was an agreement between commercial organizations on prices, terms for supply, credit, and investment. It was used to replace the relation between market supply and demand and price mechanism. In reality, however, self-management agreements could not have much binding force on parties that fixed the prices. As a result, Yugoslavia's economy fell into chaos with "neither a planned nor a market economy." "Social contracts" were made between enterprises and the government on issues like social economic development and enterprises' financial obligations. Administrative means were widely used by governments at various levels to deal with economic problems. Governments, almost daily, would formulate a number of administrative laws and orders to regulate the economic behavior of commercial organizations. These

---

[27] Benjamin Ward, "The Firm in Illyria: Market Syndicalism," *The American Economic Review,* 1958, Vol. 48, No. 3, pp. 566–589. Illyria is an ancient name for Yugoslavia.

"contracts" combined market forces and administrative powers in a strange manner. Yugoslavian economist Aleksander Bajt (1921–) considered "the contract, to some extent, a kind of feudal economic management."[28] Apart from low economic efficiency and social instability, the expanded local (republics and autonomous provinces) powers strengthened administrative decentralization, fragmented the domestic market, and led to the so-called "multi-center nationalism."[29] In the 1980s, Yugoslavia finally fell into serious economic and political crises.

1.3.3 The Gradual Reform in Hungary

Under the leadership of Janos Kadar (1912–1989), a senior communist leader, Hungary launched "New Economic System" reform on January 1, 1968.

The Hungarian New Economic System had the following features: short-term economic decisions were made to meet the demand of maximizing profits by enterprises themselves according to market situation; decisions on plans for development and structural adjustment of great impact, policies for price subsidies of consumer goods, and principles for public services were made by the central planning organ in the perspective of macro-balance. Details of the reform included: (a) the most important construction projects were decided by central planning and financed with state investment, while other investment projects were decided and financed jointly by the central authorities and enterprises; (b) market prices and fixed prices co-existed, with market prices playing the leading role in the pricing system after 1987; (c) the growth rate of salary and bonus of each enterprise was tied to its profit; (d) financial commodities, like bonds, emerged and commercial banks with comprehensive functions were established starting in 1987; (e) the government, step by step, removed restrictions on small, non-state-owned enterprises, and allowed small private enterprises to be established within a strictly limited scope but large private enterprises were still prohibited; and (f) restriction of imports by licenses continued.

Influenced by some schools of the Eastern European reform ideology of combining the merits of planning and market, Hungary did not abolish the planning system even

---

[28] Aleksander Bajt, "Experience of Economic Reform in Yugoslavia (Nansilafu jingji tizhi gaige jingyan) (1985)," The Development Economics Department of the Economic Research Institute of the Chinese Academy of Social Sciences (ed.), *Economic System Reform in China: A Collection of Papers at the Bashanlun Conference—International Conference on Macroeconomic Management (Zhongguo jingji tizhi gaige—Bashanlun Hongguan Jingji Guanli Guoji Taolunhui wenji),* Beijing: Chinese Economic Publishing House, 1987, pp. 72–82.

[29] "President of the Presidium of the League of Communists of Yugoslavia, Vidoje Žarković, indicated in September that 'multi-center nationalism came into being in Yugoslavia when federal centralism was eliminated' and 'multi-center nationalism was the main cause for the economic crisis' in Yugoslavia." See Lou Jiwei, "Learn from Experience of Yugoslavia and Avoid Enhancing Decentralization at Local Government Level (Xiqu Nansilafu jingyan, bimian qianghua difang fenquan) (1985)," *Comparison of Economic and Social Systems (Jingji shehui tizhi bijiao),* 1986, No. 1.

after twenty years of reform. Instead, it used a government indirect control system to replace direct intervention in enterprises. Financial repression still existed, and markets were strictly segmented. Meanwhile, however, the strict planning system was gradually toppling. Therefore, the Hungarian gradual reform did not overcome the defects inherent in the planned economic system, nor could it prevent the collapse of the political system built on this economic system. However, the reform helped avoid severe social unrest and prepared the country for a smooth transition to a market economy.

1.3.4 The Four Rounds of Reform in Poland

When Poland completed industrialization and agricultural collectivization in the mid-1950s, new problems occurred in its social and economic life. In 1956, when Khrushchev's liberalization policies of destalinization spread to Poland, agricultural cooperatives were dissolved. Since then, Poland attempted four rounds of reform, none of which succeeded.

1. In 1957 and 1958, reform was focused on power delegating and profit sharing. But it came to a standstill in 1958 because the program had failed to prepare people mentally and organizationally.

2. In the mid-1960s, reforms in the Soviet Union and Eastern European countries reached a climax. With rising economic tensions, Wladyslaw Gomulka (1905–1982), leader of the Polish Communist Party, launched the second round of reform, which, still lacking sufficient mental and organizational preparations, did not make any substantial progress. It did not ease the economic and social tensions, and finally led to the bloody conflict between the Polish people and government in December 1970.

3. The third round of reform in Poland was launched in 1973, with a "high-speed development strategy" as its guideline. This reform not only failed to change the traditional system fundamentally, it also caused the tensions in economic life to grow with each passing day. The wrong development strategy resulted in Poland's economy slipping into a widespread, unmanageable depression after a short period of prosperity. In the end, the conflicts between the workers (headed by the Solidarity Trade Union) and the government in 1980 pushed the precarious Polish economy to the edge of collapse.

4. The Polish Communist Party and government organized an economic reform committee in the autumn of 1980 to prepare for the fourth round of reform, but this reform again failed to overcome existing difficulties and save the situation.

1.3.5 The Aborted Reform in Czechoslovakia

Before World War II, Czechoslovakia was among the group of European developed countries ranked after Britain and France. Under the Soviet-style, centrally planned economic system, however, high growth was achieved only for a few years during the recovery period immediately after the war. In 1962, Czechoslovakia's economy was in crisis, and intense dissatisfaction arose among workers. At this point, the Czechoslovakian Communist Party appointed Ota Sik (1919–2004), a reform economist, to be responsible for reform program design. On January 1, 1967, Czechoslovakia, led by Vice Premier Sik, formally launched a marketization reform, which was more thorough than that of Hungary. However, after the economic reform was carried out, leaders of the Czechoslovakian Communist Party sensed the danger of losing power and then turned against reform policies. This, afterwards, led to an inner-party crisis and the step-down of conservatives. At the same time, the Czechoslovakian people staged a democratic movement later known as the Prague Spring in 1968 in support of the reform. This upsurge of democratic movement and acceleration of economic reform in Czechoslovakia alarmed leaders of the Soviet Union. They resorted to force in the end, invaded Czechoslovakia on August 20, 1968, arrested leaders of the Czechoslovakian Communist Party and government, and forced them to sign the Moscow Treaty, which completely negated the reform of the Prague Spring. A centrally planned economic system was restored and reform was aborted. Afterwards, despite some minor reform attempts, the deteriorating economic and political situation in Czechoslovakia could not be reversed, and the political system collapsed in 1989.

Important lessons can be drawn from the reform experiences of the Soviet Union and Eastern European countries.

- The low efficiency of planned economic systems has roots in the intrinsic defects of such systems. Efficiency cannot be improved without thorough reform of the old system.

- A true reform must be market-oriented and the key to success lies in the establishment of a competitive market system and enterprise system.

- Reform needs an overall design with the aim of establishing a market economic system and the implementation of various reform measures should be coordinated.

- Economic reform must be supported by the people and be carried out in a stable political environment.

1.3.6 The Transition of Russia and Eastern European Countries to Market Economies under New Political Systems

According to the so-called "Washington Consensus" (i.e., a set of policies such as price liberalization and privatization of state-owned enterprises), Russia practiced the "Shock Therapy" after the collapse of the Soviet Union in 1991 with undesirable results such as economic recession, rampant organized crime, social instability, and embezzlement of state assets. At the same time, some former Eastern European socialist countries, which also experienced social and political upheavals, chose other approaches to transition to a market economy and entered an era of coordinated development of their economies and societies. Hence, a few economists tended to categorize various kinds of transition to a market economy into "Shock Therapy" and "Gradualism" and made comparison between the two.

Hungarian economist János Kornai (1929–) made a different conclusion about the strategies of transition to a market economy. He argued that the implied standard for labeling "Shock Therapy" or "Gradualism" was speed, which was by no means a main criterion to measure success of reform. In his view, there are two pure strategies in compact form for the transition to a market economy: Strategy A is called the strategy of organic development and Strategy B is called the strategy of accelerated privatization.[30]

The main characteristics of Kornai's Strategy A are:

- the most important task is to create favorable conditions for bottom-up development of the private sector;

- most of the companies in state ownership will have to be privatized, and the basic technique for doing so is sale;

- any give-away distribution of state property must be avoided;

- preference must be given to sales schemes that produce an ownership structure with a core owner;

- the budget constraint on companies has to be hardened to ensure the financial discipline essential to operating a market economy.

The main characteristics of Kornai's Strategy B are:

- the most important task is to eliminate state ownership as fast as possible;

---

[30] János Kornai, "Ten Years after 'The Road to a Free Economy': The Author's Self-Evaluation," Boris Pleskovic and Nicholas Stern (eds.), *Annual World Bank Conference on Development Economics 2000*, Washington, D.C.: World Bank, 2001, pp. 49–66.

- the main technique for privatization is some form of give-away, for instance, a voucher scheme;

- dispersed ownership may actually be preferred;

- emphasis is not given to bottom-up development of private enterprises;

- a hard budget constraint is not required because of the expectation that privatization will automatically harden the budget constraint.

Kornai believed that the transition experiences of former socialist countries showed that Strategy A, which promoted organic development of the private sector, was the correct choice. What happened in Hungary and Poland showed the merits of Strategy A: healthy development of the private sector and tightening budget constraint made enterprises experience a process of natural selection of survival of the fittest; the chains of mutual debt among companies were broken, financial discipline was strengthened, and the standing of private contracts improved; and a start was made to consolidate the banking sector. All these developments promoted productivity and alleviated unemployment.

In contrast, by focusing on the speed of privatization of state-owned enterprises, Strategy B was, at most, a second-best choice that, if handled improperly, might create the combination of oligopoly and privileged government and end up with endless troubles. The saddest example of the failure of Strategy B was provided by Russia, where every feature of Strategy B appeared in an extreme form: people were forced to accept a privatization scheme that favored oligopoly; large amounts of state property were transferred into the hands of management and privileged bureaucrats; the ownership of natural resources, particularly oil and gas, was expropriated by the "oligarchs"; and market order and financial discipline were destroyed completely. Economic statistics underscored the differences: between 1989 and 1998, labor productivity rose by 36 percent in Hungary, 29 percent in Poland, and 6 percent in Czechoslovakia, but declined by 33 percent in Russia.[31]

The rise and fall of socialism in the twentieth century and half a century's reform in the Soviet Union and Eastern European countries provided valuable reference for the study of economic reform in China.

---

[31] János Kornai, "Ten Years after 'The Road to a Free Economy': The Author's Self-Evaluation," Boris Pleskovic and Nicholas Stern (eds.), *Annual World Bank Conference on Development Economics 2000,* Washington, D.C.: World Bank, 2001, pp. 49–66. See also Xiao Meng, "The Road of Hungary: An Interview with Professor János Kornai (Xiongyali daolu: zhuanfang Yanuoshi Ke'ernai Jiaoshou)," *Speculation on the Post-Socialist Transition (Hou shehuizhuyi zhuangui de sisuo),* Changchun: Jilin People's Publishing House, 2003, pp. 299–312.

1.4 The Establishment of the Chinese Planned Economic System and the Raise of the Issue of Reform

1.4.1 The Establishment of the Centrally Planned Economic System in China

Before the victory of the Chinese revolution, the program of the Communist Party of China (CPC) was to establish "a new-democratic society under the joint dictatorship of all the revolutionary classes of China" after achieving the victory of the democratic revolution, guided by Mao Zedong's (1893–1976) idea, put forward in his 1940 essay "On New Democracy," of achieving the success of the Chinese revolution in two stages. The economic base for the new-democratic society would be the new-democratic economy, which was defined as a mixed economy allowing the existence of a private capitalist sector that "cannot dominate the livelihood of the people" in accordance with the principle of "the regulation of capital" [32] and having the big banks and the big industrial and commercial enterprises owned by the state. [33]

In 1945, the political report "On Coalition Government" delivered by Mao Zedong at the Seventh National Congress of the CPC further developed the viewpoints put forward in "On New Democracy." "On Coalition Government" stated that in the new-democratic society, capitalism should have adequate room for development. Mao said, "Some people fail to understand why, so far from fearing capitalism, Communists should advocate its development in certain given conditions. Our answer is simple. The substitution of a certain degree of capitalist development for the oppression of foreign imperialism and domestic feudalism is not only an advance but an unavoidable process. It benefits the proletariat as well as the bourgeoisie, and the former perhaps more. It is not domestic capitalism but foreign imperialism and domestic feudalism which are superfluous in China today; indeed, we have too little of capitalism." [34] Mao, in his explanation of this report, indicated that "The report, different from the paper 'On New Democracy,' is to establish the necessity of the development of capitalism in a vast scale and the priority of anti-despotism. . . . The development of capitalism in a vast scale under the New Democratic regime has no harm but only benefit." [35]

---

[32] The principle of "the regulation of capital" originated from the *Manifesto of the Kuomintang's First National Congress* during the period of Kuomintang-Communist cooperation, which declared that "Enterprises, such as banks, railways and airlines, whether Chinese-owned or foreign-owned, which are either monopolistic in character or too big for private management, shall be operated and administered by the state, so that private capital cannot dominate the livelihood of the people: this is the main principle of the regulation of capital."

[33] Mao Zedong, "On New Democracy (Xin minzhuzhuyi lun) (January 1940)," *Selected Works of Mao Zedong (Mao Zedong xuanji) (The Four-in-One Edition)*, Beijing: People's Publishing House, 1966, pp. 662–771.

[34] Mao Zedong, "On Coalition Government (Lun lianhe zhengfu) (April 24, 1945)," *Selected Works of Mao Zedong (Mao Zedong xuanji) (The Four-in-One Edition)*, Beijing: People's Publishing House, 1966, p. 1061.

[35] Mao Zedong, "The Explanation to 'On Coalition Government' (Dui "Lun Lianhe Zhengfu" de shuoming) (March 1945)," *Collected Works of Mao Zedong (Mao Zedong wenji)*, Vol. 3, Beijing: People's Publishing House, 1996, pp. 272–279.

Before the founding of the People's Republic of China (PRC), the enlarged meeting of the Political Bureau of the Central Committee of the Communist Party of China (CCCPC) in September 1948 and the Second Plenary Session of the Seventh CCCPC in March 1949 reiterated the program of constructing the new-democratic political system and economic system in China.[36] With the approach of victory, Mao, based on his new assessment of the relationship with the bourgeoisie after the founding of the PRC, reminded party leaders that "Now I would like to lay bare the truth with one remark that after the completion of the bourgeois-democratic revolution, the main domestic contradiction will be the contradiction between the proletariat and the bourgeoisie."[37] Nevertheless at that time, he estimated that it would take a long time to launch an all-out attack on capitalism. When Liu Shaoqi[38] (1898–1969) mentioned that socialist policies should not be adopted immediately after the victory of the democratic revolution and that the CPC could "partner for at least 10 to 15 years" with the bourgeoisie to build the new-democratic economy, Mao added, "When, on earth, should we launch an all-out attack? We may need to wait 15 years after the victory."[39]

In the first few years after the founding of the PRC, when the Agrarian Reform was in progress and the Korean War was being waged, Liu Shaoqi and other leaders, according to "On New Democracy" and the decision of the Second Plenary Session of the Seventh CCCPC, decided that "measures of limiting the private capitalist sector not be launched too early."[40] Mao Zedong himself also warned his colleagues against "hitting out in all directions" and "making too many enemies."[41]

---

[36] Mao Zedong, "Report to the Second Plenary Session of the Seventh Central Committee of the Communist Party of China (Zai Zhongguo Gongchandang Di Qi Jie Zhongyang Weiyuanhui Di Er Ci Quanti Huiyi shang de baogao) (March 5, 1949)," *Selected Works of Mao Zedong (Mao Zedong xuanji) (The Four-in-One Edition)*, Beijing: People's Publishing House, 1966, pp. 1425–1440.

[37] Mao Zedong, "Report and Conclusion at the Meeting of the Political Bureau of the CCCPC (Zai Zhongyang Zhengzhiju Huiyi shang de baogao he jielun) (March 1948)," *Collected Works of Mao Zedong (Mao Zedong wenji)*, Vol. 5, Beijing: People's Publishing House, 1996, pp. 131–150.

[38] One of the top leaders of the CPC and the PRC, who was elected Vice Chairman of the CCCPC in 1956, President of the PRC twice in 1959 and 1965, and was persecuted to death during the Great Cultural Revolution.

[39] Bo Yibo, *Review of Some Important Decisions and Events (Ruogan zhongda juece yu shijian de huigu)*, Vol. 1, Beijing: The Central Party School Publishing House, 1991, pp. 46–66.

[40] Liu Shaoqi made this proposition at the Second Plenary Session of the Seventh CCCPC. After entering Beijing, he reiterated this viewpoint and criticized "Left" mistakes to go beyond New Democracy in his *Tianjin Speeches* in April and May of 1949 and in his *Telegram to the Northeast Bureau on the Policy towards National Capitalists* on May 31, 1949, drafted for the CCCPC. See Bo Yibo, *Ibid.*, pp. 46–66.

[41] Mao Zedong, "Don't Hit Out in All Directions (Buyao simianchuji) (June 6, 1950)," *Selected Works of Mao Zedong (Mao Zedong xuanji)*, Vol. 5, Beijing: People's Publishing House, 1977, pp. 21–24. Unlike those of other leaders, this instruction of Mao was only a tactical one. When tracing back to the situation at that time in a later occasion, Mao said, "At the Third Plenary Session in 1950, I spoke against hitting out in all directions. The agrarian reform had not yet been carried out in vast areas of the country, nor had peasants come over entirely to our side. If we had opened fire on the bourgeoisie then, it would have been out of order." The Agrarian Reform, especially the organization of farmers into agricultural producers' cooperatives, "will isolate the bourgeoisie once and for all and facilitate the final elimination of capitalism. On this matter we are quite heartless! On this matter Marxism is indeed cruel and has little mercy, for it is determined to exterminate imperialism, feudalism, capitalism, and small production to boot." See Mao Zedong, "The Debate on the Cooperative Transformation of Agriculture and the Current Class Struggle (Nongye hezuohua de yi chang bianlun he dangqian de jieji douzheng) (October 11, 1955)," *Selected Works of Mao Zedong (Mao Zedong xuanji)*, Vol. 5, Beijing: People's Publishing House, 1977, p. 196.

From 1949 to 1952, Chinese leaders did plan their work in accordance with the idea of "preparation for three years and construction for ten years" before taking steps toward socialism.[42] Even in September 1949, when the Chinese People's Political Consultative Conference (CPPCC) discussed the constitutional Common Program, a proposal by some democrats to mention socialism in the Common Program was turned down by the CPC leaders.

In 1952, when both the Agrarian Reform and the Korean War were drawing to an end, the action principle changed significantly. When writing comments on a document by the United Front Work Department of the CCCPC on June 6, 1952, Mao claimed that "the contradiction between the working class and the national bourgeoisie has become the principal contradiction in China; therefore the national bourgeoisie should no longer be defined as an intermediate class."[43] On September 24, 1952, at a meeting of the Secretariat of the CCCPC, he proposed that China should start the transition to socialism immediately and complete it in the main in ten to fifteen years, rather than wait ten years or more. In November 1952, at another meeting of the Secretariat of the CCCPC, he said that the bourgeoisie as well as capitalist industry and commerce should be eliminated.[44] On June 15, 1953, he formally put forward the General Line for the Transition Period at a meeting of the Political Bureau of the CCCPC. He criticized the policy of "firmly establishing the new-democratic social order" proposed by Liu Shaoqi, claiming that it was a viewpoint of "Right deviationism."[45]

In August 1953, the General Line for the Transition Period was formally made the guiding principle for the party, and it stated that "The time between the founding of the People's Republic of China and the basic completion of socialist transformation is a period of transition. The Party's general line or general task for the transition period is basically to accomplish the country's industrialization and the socialist transformation of

---

[42] During May to July 1951, Liu Shaoqi, according to Mao Zedong's opinion, expounded to the party's senior leaders the guiding principle of "preparation for three years and construction for ten years." See Liu Shaoqi, "Preparation for Three Years and Construction for Ten Years (San nian zhunbei, shi nian jianshe);" "Speech at Chun'ouzhai (Chun'ouzhai tanhua)," the Party Literature Research Center of the CCCPC (ed.), *Liu Shaoqi on Economic Construction in New China (Liu Shaoqi lun xin Zhongguo jingji jianshe)*, Beijing: Central Party Literature Publishing House, 1993, pp. 178–210.

[43] Mao Zedong, "The Contradiction between the Working Class and the Bourgeoisie Is the Principal Contradiction in China (Xian jieduan guonei de zhuyao maodun) (June 1952)," *Collected Works of Mao Zedong (Mao Zedong wenji)*, Vol. 6, Beijing: People's Publishing House, 1999, p. 231.

[44] For the process in which Mao changed his original position and put forward the "General Line for the Transition Period," see Bo Yibo, *Review of Some Important Decisions and Events (Ruogan zhongda juece yu shijian de huigu)*, Vol. 1, Beijing: The Central Party School Publishing House, 1991, pp. 64–65, 213–230.

[45] Mao Zedong, "Refute Right Deviationist Views that Depart from the General Line (Pipan likai zongluxian de youqing guandian) (June 15, 1953)," *Selected Works of Mao Zedong (Mao Zedong xuanji)*, Vol. 5, Beijing: People's Publishing House, 1977, pp. 81–82. See also Mao Zedong, "The Outline for a Speech at the Political Bureau Meeting (Zai Zhengzhiju Huiyi shang de jianghua tigang) (June 1953)," *Mao Zedong's Manuscripts since the Founding of the PRC (Jianguo yilai Mao Zedong wengao)*, Vol. 4, Beijing: Central Party Literature Publishing House, 1990, p. 251.

agriculture, handicrafts and capitalist industry and commerce over a fairly long period of time. This general line should be the beacon illuminating all our work, and wherever we deviate from it, we shall make Right or 'Left' mistakes."[46] The CCCPC-approved *Outline for Studying and Publicizing the Party's General Line for the Transition Period* of the CCCPC Propaganda Department noted that "The essence of this general line is to make socialist ownership of the means of production the only economic base for our country."[47]

On October 15, 1953, in his talk with Chen Boda[48] (1904–1989) and Liao Luyan[49] (1913–1972), Mao Zedong indicated that the essence of the General Line was "the solution of the problem of ownership," expanding state ownership and changing private ownership into either collective or state ownership. "Only thus can productive force be expanded and the country's industrialization accomplished."[50]

In 1955, Mao orchestrated a "socialist upsurge" in rural China. This campaign started with criticism of the "Right deviationism" represented by Deng Zihui (1896–1972), the chief official responsible for rural affairs and head of the Rural Work Department of the CCCPC, followed by the mobilization of farmers to join agricultural producers' cooperatives. It took only about one year to abolish the family farm system and to switch over to cooperatives. Then, cooperatives were merged into bigger ones and eventually switched over to people's communes in 1958.

As individual farmers disappeared, private industry and commerce also lost their reasons for existence.[51] In October 1955, Mao urged owners of private industry and commerce to "be ready for communism" (i.e., nationalization), at an informal meeting of

---

[46] Mao Zedong, "The Party's General Line for the Transition Period (Dang zai guodu shiqi de zongluxian) (August 1953)," *Selected Works of Mao Zedong (Mao Zedong xuanji)*, Vol. 5, Beijing: People's Publishing House, 1977, p. 89.

[47] Propaganda Department of the CCCPC, "Strive for Establishing a Great Socialist Country by Motivating All Forces—The Outline for Studying and Publicizing the Party's General Line for the Transition Period (Wei dongyuan yiqie liliang ba wo guo jianshe chengwei yi ge weida de shehuizhuyi guojia er douzheng—guanyu dang zai guodu shiqi de zongluxian de xuexi he xuanchuan tigang) (December 1953)," *A Collection of the Reading Materials for the Socialist Education Program (Shehuizhuyi jiaoyu kecheng de yuedu wenjian huibian)*, Vol. 1, Beijing: People's Publishing House, 1957, pp. 341–374.

[48] An ultra-Leftist, Mao's former political secretary, then Vice Head of the Rural Work Department of the CCCPC, later Editor in Chief of the monthly theoretical journal *Hongqi* ("Red Flag") of the CPC and Head of the notorious CCCPC Cultural Revolution Group.

[49] Then Vice Head of the Rural Work Department of the CCCPC, later Minister of Agriculture, who was persecuted to death during the Great Cultural Revolution.

[50] Mao Zedong, "Two Talks on Mutual Aid and Cooperation in Agriculture (Guanyu nongye huzhu hezuo de liang ci tanhua) (October and November 1953)," *Collected Works of Mao Zedong (Mao Zedong wenji)*, Vol. 6, Beijing: People's Publishing House, 1999, pp. 298–301.

[51] "Unified purchase and marketing of grain cut off the connection between farmers and markets. . . . By the end of 1954, there were 1,700 joint state-private enterprises nationwide. . . . At that time, those switched to joint state-private ownership were mainly large- and medium-sized enterprises, and small-sized enterprises and backward medium-sized enterprises were in trouble. . . . It was hard for them to survive in the competition with state-owned and joint state-private enterprises, and thus they were willing to switch to joint state-private ownership of a whole trade. With the arrival of the upsurge of the cooperative transformation of agriculture, capitalist industry and commerce also had an upsurge of joint state-private ownership of a whole trade." (*Xue Muqiao Memoir (Xue Muqiao huiyilu)*, Tianjin: Tianjin People's Publishing House, 1996, pp. 218–222.)

the Executive Committee of the All-China Federation of Industry and Commerce on transformation of private commerce and industry.[52] Under these circumstances, owners of private industrial and commercial businesses in large numbers applied to the state for "socialist transformation" in the form of "joint state-private ownership of individual enterprises of a whole trade."

Thus, although the General Line for the Transition Period was put forward in 1953 with an original plan to complete the socialist transformation of individual agriculture and private capitalist industry and commerce in fifteen or more years, it took only three years to establish public ownership, with state ownership and quasi-state, collective ownership as its major forms, as the only base for the national economy. On the basis of public ownership, a Soviet-style, centrally planned economic system was established nationwide.

This sudden shift from New Democracy to socialism was in Mao's plan before the founding of the PRC, but was a surprise to most people, including some senior party officials. The major reasons for its accomplishment in such a short period were as follows.

- For quite a long time, it had been regarded as an unalterable principle of socialism to abolish the market system and establish a planned economy characterized by highly centralized administrative coordination, following the example of the Soviet Union. After the founding of the PRC, "Soviet experts" completely transformed the Chinese economics education by instilling Stalin's political economy and making it the only prevailing theory of economics. According to this theory, it was natural to establish a centrally planned economic system.

- After the outbreak of the Korean War, China had to give top priority to national defense. Therefore, Chinese leaders chose the institutional arrangement that would mobilize and allocate resources through central planning so that limited resources could be used to build up heavy industry, especially its core of military industry.

- Having borne the humiliation of being a semi-colony for one hundred years, both the Chinese leaders and the Chinese public had a strong desire to catch up with and surpass Western developed countries. They believed that by following the example of the Soviet Union, wielding state power, and mobilizing and

---

[52] Mao Zedong had two talks with representatives from the commercial and industrial circles on October 27 and 29, 1955. See *Collected Works of Mao Zedong (Mao Zedong wenji)*, Vol. 6, Beijing: People's Publishing House, 1999, pp. 488–503.

concentrating human, financial, and material resources, China would be able to achieve modernization in a very short time.

• China had been a country full of small peasants for quite a long time and government control over society was a deeply rooted tradition. After the founding of the PRC, Mao Zedong, by virtue of his high prestige gained in the long revolutionary struggles, established a totalist government under his leadership.[53] This laid the political foundation for accomplishing the socialist transformation and implementing the planned economic system within only a few years.

1.4.2 The Raise of the Issue of Reform in China

Upon its establishment in the mid-1950s, the planned economic system in China met with numerous criticisms. Enterprises, which had enjoyed much autonomy in the economy of New Democracy, became subordinates to higher-level administrative organs. They lost their vigor as they were forced to give up decision-making power regarding human, financial, and material resources as well as supply, production, and marketing. Meanwhile, the decline in managerial initiative and service quality of industrial and commercial enterprises brought about many complaints from consumers.

Some Chinese economists sharply criticized the planned economic model during the autumn of 1956 to the spring of 1957 when Mao was promoting the policy of "letting a hundred flowers blossom and a hundred schools of thought contend (*baihua qifang, baijia zhengming*)"[54] and when the political atmosphere was quite free and academic discussion was quite active. A well-known representative of them was Sun Yefang (1908–1983), then Vice Director of the National Bureau of Statistics.

Sun felt keenly the inherent defects of a centrally planned economy in his job. Beginning with two papers in 1956, "Base Plan and Statistics on the Law of Value" and "Start with Total Output Value,"[55] he criticized the planned economy and the theoretical system behind it and proposed his own theoretical system of socialist economy.

As an economist, Sun was especially noteworthy for his keen insight and great courage. Influenced by his family background and the experiences of his youth, Sun

---

[53] Totalism is a concept introduced by Professor Tang Tsou (1918–1999) of the University of Chicago. Different from the concept of "totalitarianism" in Western political science, it refers to a particular state that controls every part of social life with powerful political organizations so as to transform or rebuild the society. See Tang Tsou, *Twentieth Century Chinese Politics: From the Perspectives of Macro-history and Micromechanism Analysis (Ershi shiji Zhongguo zhengzhi: Cong hongguan lishi yu weiguan xingdong jiaodu kan)*, Hong Kong: Oxford University Press, 1994.

[54] A policy put forward by the CPC in 1956. It was designed to promote the development of arts and sciences by tolerance in exchange of views but soon went into mothballs after the Anti-Rightist Campaign in 1957.

[55] Sun Yefang, *Selected Works of Sun Yefang (Sun Yefang xuanji)*, Taiyuan: Shanxi People's Publishing House, 1984, pp. 117–146.

thoroughly believed in the power of markets. As would be expected, many of his policy propositions in dealing with real-world problems were clearly market-oriented.

Based on his theory of socialist economy, Sun proposed to "promote the status of profit target in the planned economic management system."[56] With this idea as the main theme, Sun designed his model of socialist economy. The key proposition of the model was, in his words, "centralizing power on major issues while decentralizing power on minor issues," where the criterion of "major" and "minor" was the scale of fund. "Power on major issues," to be retained by the government, referred to decision-making power with regard to extended reproduction with new fund; while "power on minor issues," to be granted to enterprises in line with the law of value, referred to decision-making power with regard to simple reproduction with existing fund. In other words, the feature of Sun's model was to offer more autonomy to enterprises in their daily decisions (i.e., decisions on "simple reproduction") on condition that state ownership and the control of the state plan over enterprises' supply and marketing were maintained. It can be seen that Sun's model of "centralizing power on major issues while decentralizing power on minor issues" and Brus's decentralized model were essentially the same.

However, as he was educated by Soviet political economy in his early years, Sun had limitations in his criticism of the traditional model of socialist economy. There was a profound internal contradiction in his theoretical economic system. He opposed the "theory of natural economy" and presented incisive arguments such as "the law of value dominates all other laws." However, he denied the "theory of commodity economy" that allowed market functions under socialism. He asserted that his "law of value" was not the law of market, but the law that the average amount of socially necessary labor determines the value of commodity.

Although Sun emphasized only the importance of the law of value and used profit target merely as an accounting tool, his proposals still made him the first victim of the anti-revisionist purge in China that started in the mid-1960s. He was labeled as a "revisionist" worse than Liberman[57] by Kang Sheng (1898–1975), an ultra-Leftist Party leader in charge of ideological affairs at the time.

At that time, Gu Zhun (1915–1974), an economist at the Economics Institute of the Chinese Academy of Sciences, expressed the most penetrating viewpoints on the issue.

---

[56] Sun Yefang, "On Issues of the Financial and Economic System within the Sector under Ownership by the Whole People (Guanyu quanmin suoyouzhi jingji neibu de caijing tizhi wenti) (1961)," *Selected Works of Sun Yefang (Sun Yefang xuanji)*, Taiyuan: Shanxi People's Publishing House, 1984, p. 367.

[57] Evsei Grigorevich Liberman (1897–1983), Soviet economist. The suggestion he made in 1961 on Soviet economic reform was considered the theoretical basis for the Kosygin reform of 1965.

He pointed out in 1956 that the problem of socialist economy was that it abolished the market system. To promote efficiency, socialism might choose an economic system in which enterprises could make decisions according to spontaneous rises and falls in market prices.[58] In other words, market forces should play a decisive role in resource allocation. Unfortunately, this did not draw the attention of most economists, who were still constrained by the narrow-mindedness of traditional theory of socialist economy. Shortly, Gu Zhun was labeled a "bourgeois Rightist" and his academic viewpoint was judged as heresy and fell into oblivion. Nevertheless, Gu Zhun was the first to propose market-oriented reform in the development history of Chinese reform theory.

Party and government leaders made responses to the aforementioned economic situation. Chen Yun (1905–1995), a party leader in charge of economic affairs, proposed that a few adjustments in economic policies should be made so as to establish a socialist economic structure with "three mains and three supplements." They were (a) in terms of industrial and commercial business, state-run and collective-run enterprises should be its main part while a certain amount of individual businesses can be supplement to state-run and collective-run enterprises; (b) in terms of production plan, planned production should be its main part while free production according to market situation within the scope allowed by the plan can be supplement to planned production; and (c) in terms of the unified socialist market, the state market should be its main part while the free market within a certain scope and guided by the state can be supplement to the state market.[59]

The most important among these responses was Mao Zedong's instructional opinion on the reform of the Soviet-style, centrally planned economic system. In early 1956, Chinese leaders summarized the work of the first few years in the First Five-Year Plan in preparation for the Eighth National Congress of the CPC, scheduled for August 1956. The summarization showed that the economic system established in the mid-1950s had many defects though it had the advantages of a command economy in intensively mobilizing resources and concentrating them on key construction projects to accelerate industrialization with a focus on the growth of heavy and military industries. Awareness of the defects of the traditional system was reflected in Mao's speech, "On the Ten Major Relationships," made at the meeting of the Political Bureau of the CCCPC in April 1956. Mao believed that the major defect of this system was the over-

---

[58] Gu Zhun, "On Commodity Production and the Law of Value under Socialism (Shi lun shehuizhuyi zhidu xia de shangpin shengchan he jiazhi guilü) (1956)," *Collected Works of Gu Zhun (Gu Zhun wenji),* Guiyang: Guizhou People's Publishing House, 1994, p. 32.

[59] Chen Yun, "New Issues after the Completion of Socialist Transformation in the Main (Shehuizhuyi gaizao jiben wancheng yihou de xin wenti) (1956)," *Selected Works of Chen Yun (Chen Yun wenxuan) (1956–1985),* Beijing: People's Publishing House, 1986, pp. 1–13.

centralization of power in the central authorities, with too much control and too little flexibility.[60]

Therefore, the fundamental measure to reform the existing system was to delegate power to governments at lower levels and enterprises. Following this guiding principle of Mao, in 1958 China started its first economic reform after the establishment of a socialist economy. In the actual implementation of this reform, some amendments were made to Mao's 1956 principle. These amendments emphasized the division of powers and benefits among administrative organs at various levels. This was the idea of "administrative decentralization," according to which China started its economic reform in 1958.

Insight 1.4

On the Ten Major Relationships by Mao Zedong

To prepare for the Eighth National Congress of the CPC in the fall of 1956, Mao Zedong, after Liu Shaoqi, heard reports on the work of thirty-four ministries and commissions and a few provinces and municipalities from February to May 1956. From these reports, a number of issues of overall importance were identified, including the proportional relationship among agriculture, light industry, and heavy industry; the relationship between industry in the coastal regions and industry in the interior; the scale and speed of the national defense industry; the distribution of rights, responsibilities, and interests among the state, collectives, and individuals; the relationship between the central government and local governments; and the question of whether and how to learn from the Soviet Union in the future, among others.

The Political Bureau of the CCCPC boiled these issues down to ten major relationships after repeated discussions. The Political Bureau believed that, with the increasing influence of peaceful and cooperative forces in the world, it seemed unlikely that there would be a new war of aggression against China or another world war in the near future, and there would probably be a period of peace for at least a decade. Based on this

---

[60] Mao Zedong, "On the Ten Major Relationships (Lun shi da guanxi) (April 25, 1956)," *Selected Works of Mao Zedong (Mao Zedong xuanji),* Vol. 5, Beijing: People's Publishing House, 1977, pp. 272–276.

assessment, Mao Zedong suggested decreasing the speed of the conventional weapon industry and increasing that of the metallurgical, machinery, and chemical industries. Before this, Liu Shaoqi also pointed out when hearing the reports that China should attach importance to light industry and agriculture and give full play to the potential of coastal industry, the enthusiasm of local governments, and the role of technical personnel. Besides, it was essential to know what to accept and what to reject when learning from the Soviet Union. These ideas had significant impact on Mao Zedong's later presentation of the "ten major relationships."

From late April to early May 1956, Mao illustrated the ten major relationships at the enlarged meeting of the Political Bureau and the Supreme State Conference respectively. After Mao's death, the draft of the speech was revised by Hu Qiaomu* (1912–1992) and published in *Selected Works of Mao Zedong (Volume 5)*.

The ten major relationships are:

1. The relationship between heavy industry on the one hand and light industry and agriculture on the other. The proportion of investment in agriculture and light industry must be appropriately increased.

2. The relationship between industry in the coastal regions and industry in the interior. During peaceful times, China should promote industry in the coastal regions.

3. The relationship between economic construction and defense construction. The proportion of military and administrative expenditures should be properly reduced.

4. The relationship between the state, the units of production, and the individual workers. Attention should be paid to the interests of all three parties.

5. The relationship between the central and the local authorities. China should enlarge the powers of the local authorities to some extent and give them greater independence to bring their initiative into play.

6. The relationship between the Han nationality and the minority nationalities. China should put the emphasis on opposing Han chauvinism. Local nationality chauvinism must be opposed, too.

7. The relationship between party and non-party. There should be a long-term coexistence and mutual supervision between the CPC and democratic parties. Bureaucracy should be opposed and party and government organs streamlined.

8. The relationship between revolution and counter-revolution. Counter-revolutionaries should be transformed so as to turn negative factors into positive ones.

9. The relationship between right and wrong. The policy of "learning from past mistakes to avoid future ones and curing the sickness to save the patient" should be applied to those comrades who have committed mistakes.

10. The relationship between China and other countries. China should learn from the strong points of all nations and all countries but must learn with an analytical and critical eye, not blindly, and mustn't copy everything indiscriminately and transplant mechanically.

(Compiled from Mao Zedong, "On the Ten Major Relationships (Lun shi da guanxi) (April 25, 1956)," *Selected Works of Mao Zedong (Mao Zedong xuanji),* Vol. 5, Beijing: People's Publishing House, 1977; Bo Yibo, *Review of Some Important Decisions and Events (Ruogan zhongda juece yu shijian de huigu),* Vol. 1, Beijing: The Central Party School Publishing House, 1991.)

*One of the senior leaders of the CPC, secretary to Mao Zedong in the 1940s, alternate secretary of the Secretariat of the CCCPC in the late 1950s and early 1960s, and president of the Chinese Academy of Social Sciences in the late 1970s.

CHAPTER 2

THE EVOLUTION OF CHINA'S REFORM STRATEGY

The fundamental theme of China's reform is the transition from a centrally planned economy to a market economy. Economic reform in China was initiated in September 1956, when the Eighth National Congress of the Communist Party of China (CPC) decided to launch the "economic management system reform." This chapter analyzes the various reforms instituted in China to transform the economy over the last five decades.

At the very beginning, the so-called "economic management system reform" was no more than a set of policy adjustments aimed at improving the performance of the economy and "injecting vigor into the economy," without any definite institutional goal. It was not until a quarter of a century later, in the mid-1980s, that a market orientation was gradually established. However, many different opinions and viewpoints had been expressed about how to achieve the goal of a market economy. As a result, a variety of measures were taken to reform the original economic system between 1956 and the present. Backed by different theories, these measures took the Chinese economy in different, sometimes opposite, directions. Therefore, a simple, chronological review of all these measures would not result in a thorough analysis because of their interweaving nature and context.

Because of these reasons, this chapter divides the course of China's reform into three stages by major reform measures, analyzes the advantages and disadvantages of these measures, and comments on the theories and ideas behind them, as follows:

1. 1958 to 1978: Administrative decentralization reform with emphasis on the central government transferring power to and sharing profit with governments at lower levels.

2. 1979 to 1993: Incremental reform, or reform of "outside the system" preceding "inside the system" (i.e., focusing on nonstate sectors and off-plan parts of the economy and promoting their development).

3. 1994 to present: Reform highlighted by a strategy of "overall advance with key breakthroughs" to establish a socialist market economy.

During China's economic reform, various reform measures in various stages were often interwoven; in other words, reform measures in the previous stage often nurtured something forthcoming in the subsequent stage, and reform measures in the coming stage often contained legacies of measures instituted in the preceding stage. The analysis in this chapter focuses on the typical reform measures of each of the three chronological stages described.

2.1 Administrative Decentralization (1958 to 1978)

September 1956, the First Session of the Eighth National Congress of the CPC decided to reform the economic management system under the guidance of Mao Zedong's "On the Ten Major Relationships" and to implement the reform at the beginning of 1958.

At the end of 1957, the Central Committee of the Communist Party of China (CCCPC) decided to launch the Great Leap Forward campaign,[1] initiated by Mao Zedong. The proposed economic management system reform had to be conducted in ways conducive to the launch of the Great Leap Forward.

2.1.1 The Establishment of the Policy of Delegating Power to and Sharing Profit with Local Governments

The central theme of the economic management system reform of 1958 was delegating power to and sharing profit with local governments. This policy was not completely in line with Mao Zedong's original idea, proposed in "On the Ten Major Relationships," of delegating power to and sharing profit with economic units and individual workers as well as local governments. The major reason for such a change was closely related to the political situation during 1957 and 1958, which made the idea of delegating power to and sharing profit with economic units and individual workers no longer satisfy the requirement for maintaining political correctness.

First, concerning delegating power to and sharing profit with state-owned enterprises (SOEs), even before the Eighth National Congress of the CPC, many people from economic departments began with great enthusiasm to study Yugoslavia's experiment in "enterprise autonomy." At the Congress, the issue of giving autonomy to state-owned enterprises was a hot topic. In the "Political Report" delivered by Liu Shaoqi on behalf of the CCCPC at the Congress, a proposition to "guarantee that enterprises have adequate autonomy on issues of plan management, financial management, cadre management, worker assignment, and welfare facility establishment under the unified leader-

---

[1] A rash attempt to industrialize China during 1958–1960 under the guidance of the CPC's "general line for socialist construction (namely, go all out, aim high and achieve greater, faster, better, and more economical results in building socialism)" and Mao Zedong's plan to "catch up with Britain in three years and surpass America in ten years." It was characterized by overambitious targets, arbitrary orders, exaggerated statistics, and practices of extreme egalitarianism in the name of communism, and brought about disastrous consequences: grain yield reduced by 28 percent from 1958 to 1960, population reduced by 2 percent from 1959 to 1961, and industrial output reduced by 48 percent from 1960 to 1962.

ship and unified planning of the State" was put forward.[2] In the national survey of the economic management system conducted in late 1956 and early 1957 by the State Economic Commission, the demand for delegating decision-making power to enterprises was great. Later in 1957, however, the CPC's attack on the theory of self-management socialism of the Yugoslavian Communist Party escalated, and enterprise autonomy was condemned as the core of "Yugoslavian revisionism." Consequently, the issue of expanding enterprise autonomy was eliminated from the CPC's reform agenda.

Second, concerning delegating power to and sharing profit with individual workers, Mao Zedong's original idea was in line with trends in other socialist countries around 1956. In addition to the aforementioned self-management socialism of Yugoslavia that implied in-service employee ownership of enterprises, in early 1956, Khrushchev, First Secretary of the Communist Party of the Soviet Union (CPSU), also proposed to enhance "material incentive" to SOE employees when he fiercely attacked Stalin's economic policies.

However, the idea of delegating power to and sharing profit with individual workers became politically problematic in 1957. At that time, not only was the CPC attacking Yugoslavian revisionism, but also a difference in opinions about Stalinism emerged between the CPC and the CPSU. In addition, Mao Zedong had been personally in favor of spiritual incentive instead of material incentive and during the Anti-Rightist Campaign[3] of 1957, he blamed individualism as the spiritual root cause of the anti-party and anti-socialism ideology of Rightists and demanded people to "shake off the shackles of fame and wealth." At such a moment, arousing people's enthusiasm by material incentive was obviously at odds with the mainstream ideology.

In such a political environment, only local governments and officials at various levels could be the objects of power delegating and profit sharing. In other words, the central theme of the reform became the division of power and profit among administrative bodies at different levels. Thus, transferring power and, consequently, profit to local governments at various levels became the basic theme of the reform of 1958. From then on, the economic management system reform was defined as transferring administrative functions to lower levels (*tizhi xiafang*). Such thinking about reform had a far-reaching impact on China's economic reform and development in later days.

---

[2]Liu Shaoqi, *Political Report of the CCCPC to the Eighth National Congress of the Communist Party of China (Zhongguo Gongchandang Zhongyang Weiyuanhui xiang Di Ba Ci Quanguo Daibiao Dahui de zhengzhi baogao)* (September 15, 1956), Beijing: People's Publishing House, 1956.

[3]In April 1957, the CCCPC decided to launch a rectification campaign against bureaucratism, factionalism, and subjectivism within the party by inviting free airing of views from the public. Two months later, when some radical views against the CPC and socialism surfaced, the Chinese leaders overreacted and launched an all-out crackdown. By late summer of 1958, 550,000 outspoken people, mostly intellectuals and officials, were singled out as "bourgeois Rightists" and persecuted. This act of intolerance sowed seeds of disaster for the ensuing Great Leap Forward because almost nobody dared to speak out any more. By the end of 1981, almost all cases of "Rightists" were reversed.

2.1.2 The Implementation of the Policy of Transferring Administrative Functions to Lower Levels

The Third Plenary Session of the Eighth CCCPC in September 1957 launched the Great Leap Forward campaign and started the economic management system reform to prepare an institutional foundation for the Great Leap Forward. At the meeting, Chen Yun, head of the five-member CCCPC Economic Affairs Group,[4] delivered the *Report on Issues of Improving the State Administrative System and Increasing Agricultural Output.* Three related documents, drafted under the leadership of Chen Yun, namely, *Provisions on Improving the Industrial Management System (draft), Provisions on Improving the Commercial Management System (draft),* and *Provisions on Dividing the Power of Fiscal Administration Between Central and Local Governments (draft),* were passed in principle at the meeting and were submitted to the Standing Committee of the National People's Congress. Approved by the Standing Committee on November 14, these three documents were to be implemented in 1958. The essence of these three documents was to transfer some industrial, commercial, and financial administrative functions to local administrative bodies so that the initiative and enthusiasm of both local governments and enterprises can be brought into full play and the unified planning of the state can be accomplished according to local conditions.

Specifically, the transfer of economic administrative functions to lower levels of 1958 included several key actions, as follows.

2.1.2.1 Transferring the Power of Planning

In September 1958, the CCCPC promulgated the *Provisions on Improving the Planning Administration System.* In the *Provisions,* the original planning administration system, in which unified plans were formulated and balanced by the State Planning Commission and issued successively to lower levels, was changed into a system that was based on the overall balance by regions with coordination between specialized departments and regions. In other words, the new system was centered on local authorities, and plans were formulated and balanced from lower levels successively to higher ones so that local economies could become systems of their own. The CCCPC stipulated in this document that local governments were permitted to adjust their own targets of industrial and agri-

---

[4] The top decision-making body on economic affairs under the Political Bureau of the CCCPC; established in January 1957 and consisted of Chen Yun (Head), Li Fuchun, Bo Yibo, Li Xiannian, and Huang Kecheng. In June 1958, it was replaced by the CCCPC Financial and Economic Leading Group consisted of Chen Yun (Head), Li Fuchun (Vice Head), Li Xiannian (Vice Head), Zhou Enlai, Tan Zhenlin, Bo Yibo, Luo Ruiqing, Cheng Zihua, Gu Mu, Yao Yilin, and Xue Muqiao. This group was made a figurehead after Mao Zedong launched the Great Leap Forward and was dissolved in 1959. The CCCPC Financial and Economic Leading Group was restored in February 1962 to clean up the mess of the Great Leap Forward and dissolved again during the Great Cultural Revolution. Again, it was restored in March 1980 with Chen Yun as Head to clean up the mess of the "Imported Leap Forward."

cultural production; to make overall plans for the construction scale, projects, and distribution of investment within their regions; to regulate the use of materials and equipment within their regions; and to have at their disposal certain proportions of the overfulfilled outputs of some important products.

2.1.2.2 Transferring the Control over Enterprises

On April 11, 1958, the CCCPC and the State Council issued *Provisions on Transferring the Control of Industrial Enterprises,* which stipulated that, except for a small number of important, special, or experimental ones, all enterprises belonging to ministries of the State Council were to be transferred to local governments. On June 2, 1958, the CCCPC notified ministries of the State Council to complete the transfer of control over enterprises to lower levels by June 15. Thus, 88 percent of the enterprises and public institutions that used to belong to ministries were transferred to local governments at various levels, some even to subdistricts and communes.[5] The proportion of industrial output of enterprises directly under the central government fell from 39.7 percent in 1957 to 13.8 percent in 1958.[6]

2.1.2.3 Transferring the Power of Materials and Equipment Allocation

First, both the categories and quantities of materials and equipment allocated by the State Planning Commission and administered by ministries were reduced drastically. Categories of materials and equipment allocated by the commission and administered by ministries were reduced from 530 in 1957 to 132 in 1959, a three-fourths reduction. The administration of these reduced categories was transferred to provinces, municipalities, and autonomous regions. Second, instead of being planned and distributed by the central government, the remaining one-fourth of materials and equipment was managed by matching demands and supplies locally and distributing balances, with the central government control limited to the distribution of balances. Third, in terms of supply, except for railroads, military industries, foreign exchanges, and national reserves, all enterprises, either central or local, should apply for materials and equipment to and get supplies from the provinces, municipalities, and autonomous regions where they were located.

---

[5] As a country with a vast territory and a huge population, China has a five-tier system of local governments: (a) province, municipality directly under the central government (municipality in short), autonomous region, and special administrative region; (b) prefecture and prefecture-level city (city in short); (c) district, county, and county-level city; (d) subdistrict, administrative town (town in short, formerly people's commune), township (formerly people's commune); and (e) neighborhood, administrative village (village in short, formerly production brigade). In municipalities, the second tier is missing and districts are directly under municipalities.

[6] Zhou Taihe et al., *Economic System Reform in Contemporary China (Dangdai Zhongguo de jingji tizhi gaige),* Beijing: China Social Sciences Press, 1984.

2.1.2.4 Transferring the Power of Reviewing and Approving Capital Construction Projects and Credit Administration

Concerning the review and approval of capital construction projects, it was stipulated that for locally built, large-scale construction projects above the norm, only summaries of planning assignments needed to be submitted to the State Planning Commission for approval; the design and budget were to be approved by local governments. For projects below the norm, local governments could make decisions on all issues. In July 1958, the central government decided to carry out an investment responsibility system— within their scope of investment responsibility, local governments could make decisions and accumulate funds by themselves. Local governments could therefore start any business, including large-scale projects above the norm, within the limits of funds allocated from the central government and funds raised by themselves. At the same time, credit administration was transferred to local bank branches. The original, highly centralized credit system was abolished and a new system of "transferring deposits and credits to local bank branches and managing balance nationwide" was implemented. Local bank branches were allowed to "lend no matter how much is needed and no matter when it is needed" in accordance with local needs out of "production going all out."

2.1.2.5 Transferring the Power of Finance Administration and Tax Collection

To increase the financial capacity and expand the financial authority of local governments, the old system of "expenditure deciding revenue, adjusted every year" was changed into a system of "revenue deciding expenditure, management by different levels, sharing according to different categories, and fixed for five years." Seven types of taxes, such as urban real estate tax, recreation tax, and stamp tax, were reclassified as fixed revenues of local governments. Bulk taxes, such as commodity circulation tax, goods tax, business tax, and income tax, were to be shared between the central government and local governments. The old practice of no local sharing in the profits of enterprises directly under the central departments was abolished to allow local governments at the province/municipality level to have a 20-percent share in the profits of central enterprises. In addition, local governments were also given authority to reduce, exempt, and add taxes.

2.1.2.6 Transferring the Labor Administration

Recruitment plans could be executed with the confirmation of provincial-level authorities, and approval of the state ministries and commissions was no longer necessary.

Although delegating power to and sharing profit with enterprises was eliminated from the publicly announced program for the reform of 1958, in reality, a few measures of delegating power to and sharing profit with enterprises were taken in addition to those delegating power to and sharing profit with local governments. First, the targets of the mandatory plan of the State Planning Commission for industrial enterprises were reduced from 12 to 4 (outputs of major products, total number of employees, total wage bill, and profits). Second, the original system of enterprise incentive fund, or factory director's fund,[7] (retaining an industry-specific proportion of profits) was replaced by a system of "full profit retention"[8] (retaining an enterprise-specific proportion of profits). Third, the power of enterprises concerning personnel assignment was enlarged. Enterprises were responsible for managing their staff except for key managerial and technical positions. Enterprises were also granted the right to adjust their organizational structures and staffing, as long as the total number of staff was unchanged. Fourth, enterprises were granted the right to adjust the use of part of their capital and to increase, reduce, or scrap fixed assets.

2.1.3 Disorder Caused by Transferring Administrative Functions to Lower Levels and Its Remediation

Together with people's communes in the countryside, the decentralized planned economic system, created by delegating power to every lower level of local governments within the overall framework of a planned economy and resource allocation by administrative orders, laid the institutional foundation for the Great Leap Forward. Supported by this foundation, local governments at all levels responded to the call of Mao Zedong "to surpass Britain in three years and to surpass America in ten years"[9] by maximally

---

[7] Under this system, after achieving its quotas of total output value, profit, and remittance of profit, each enterprise could draw an enterprise incentive fund not less than 4 percent of the total wage bill from the planned profit and above-quota profit in accordance with a department-specific proportion set by the state. However, the enterprise incentive fund should not exceed 10 percent of the total wage bill.

[8] The profit retention proportion was first calculated for each department in charge. The future profit retention proportion is the total of the four items of expenditure during the First Five-Year Plan period (including enterprise incentive fund as well as technological upgrading and sporadic capital construction appropriated by the finance, etc.) and 40 percent of retained above-quota profit divided by total achieved profit of the same period. Once determined, the retention proportion remains unchanged for five years. Within the scope of the total retention, each department in charge could decide the retention proportion for each enterprise according to its specific conditions.

[9] On November 18, 1957, Mao Zedong pointed out in his speech at the Moscow Meeting of Representatives of the Communist and Workers' Parties that "Comrade Khrushchev told us that the Soviet Union can surpass America within 15 years. So I suppose we can catch up with or surpass Britain within 15 years." (Mao Zedong, "Speech at the Moscow Meeting of Representatives of the Communist and Workers' Parties (Zai Mosike Gongchandang he Gongrendang Daibiao Huiyi shang de jianghua)," *Mao Zedong's Manuscripts since the Founding of the PRC (Jianguo yilai Mao Zedong wengao),* Vol. 6, Beijing: Central Party Literature Publishing House, 1992, p. 635.) Afterwards, the supposed time period was shortened with the launch of the Great Leap Forward. In April 1958, Mao Zedong claimed that "It will not take as long as supposed before to catch up with capitalist countries in the industrial and agricultural production." "It will take ten years to catch up with Britain and ten more years to catch up with America." (Mao Zedong, "Introduction to a Cooperative (Jieshao yi ge hezuoshe)," *Mao Zedong's Manuscripts since the Founding of the PRC (Jianguo yilai Mao Zedong wengao),* Vol. 7, Beijing: Central Party Literature Publishing House, 1992, p. 177–179.) He declared at the enlarged meeting of the Military Commission of the CCCPC on June 21, 1958 that "We will surpass Britain in the main within 3 years and surpass America within 10 years. It is quite sure." (Bo Yibo, *Review of Some Important Decisions and Events (Ruogan zhongda juece yu shijian de huigu),* Vol. 2, Beijing: The Central Party School Publishing House, 1993, p. 702.)

exercising their power of resource allocation to launch capital construction projects, recruit workers, and commandeer resources from peasants in attempts to accomplish impossible plan targets, such as to double steel output every year.[10] As a result, all geographic regions, departments, and units scrambled for resources, and industrial and agricultural productions were thrown into disarray. There were 1,589 large- and medium-sized projects under construction in 1958, 1,361 in 1959, and 1,815 in 1960, with the number of projects in any single year exceeding the total number of projects during the entire First Five-Year Plan period (1953–1957). Investment in fixed assets increased from RMB 14.33 billion in 1957 to RMB 38.87 billion in 1960, with a three-year (1958–1960) total of RMB 100.74 billion, 71 percent more than the total of RMB 58.85 billion during the First Five-Year Plan period. Because of transferring the power of labor administration to lower levels, the number of SOE employees increased from 24.51 million at the end of 1957 to 45.32 million at the end of 1958, a net increase of 20.81 million, or 84.9 percent. By the end of 1960, the number of SOE employees had reached 59.69 million; the urban population exceeded 130 million, an addition of more than 30 million to the 99.49 million at the end of 1957.[11]

Widespread economic disorder led to deteriorating economic efficiency, and the consumption of huge amounts of resources only generated all sorts of exaggerated statistics with which local officials could please their superiors and win rewards. Facts revealed later indicate that all the "record-breaking" statistics of steel and grain productions were untrue.

However, many leaders in those days still indulged in spinning fantasies. On the eve of the outbreak of a nationwide famine, Mao Zedong was contemplating how to deal with "surplus" grain stock.[12] He proposed solutions such as adopting the fallow system and the practice of "eating all you want."[13] In people's communes, practices of "each

---

[10] According to Mao Zedong, two fundamental principles of the Great Leap Forward were "taking grain as the key link and ensuring an all-round development" and "taking steel as the key link to drive everything else forward." Impractical quotas were set for grain and steel production as a result. In 1958, the *Fifteen-Year Program Compendium for Socialist Construction (Draft) (Shiwu nian shehuizhuyi jianshe gangyao (chugao)),* formulated by the CCCPC, required that by 1972, the yield of grain per *mu* (a Chinese unit of area equal to 1/15 of a hectare or 1/6 of an acre) nationwide should be 2,500 to 5,000 kg; the yield of cotton per *mu* be 250 to 500 kg; and arable land nationwide be divided into three parts of one-third each: one-third for crops; one-third fallow or for green manure crops; and one-third for trees and grasses. In June 1958, Mao Zedong himself worked out a plan for steel production: to reach 11 million tons in 1958, more than twice the 5.35 million tons produced in 1957; to reach 25 million tons in 1959, surpassing Britain; and to reach 60 million tons in 1962. (Bo Yibo, *Review of Some Important Decisions and Events (Ruogan zhongda juece yu shijian de huigu),* Vol. 2, Beijing: The Central Party School Publishing House, 1993, pp. 679–702.)

[11] Zhou Taihe et al., *Economic System Reform in Contemporary China (Dangdai Zhongguo de jingji tizhi gaige),* Beijing: China Social Sciences Press, 1984, pp. 73–75.

[12] On August 4 and 5, 1958, Mao Zedong inspected Xushui County and Anguo County. In Xushui, he asked what to do with surplus grain stock and proposed the solution of assigning peasants to work half-days and to partake half-days in cultural activities, learning science, recreational activities, and studying middle-school and university courses. In Anguo, he proposed that since the grain harvest was large enough, each person could consume 300 kg to 350 kg of grain per year and land could be cultivated in alternate years. (See Bo Yibo, *Review of Some Important Decisions and Events (Ruogan zhongda juece yu shijian de huigu),* Vol. 2, Beijing: The Central Party School Publishing House, 1993, p. 739.)

[13] At that time, it was said that "food is free of charge" was an invention by Ke Qingshi (Party Secretary of Shanghai). (Bo Yibo, *Review of Some Important Decisions and Events (Ruogan zhongda juece yu shijian de huigu),* Vol. 2, Beijing: The Central Party School Publishing House, 1993, p. 745.) Public canteens spread quickly among people's communes and their rule is "to eat all you

taking what he needs," such as the public canteen, the "five guaranteed," and the "ten guaranteed,"[14] were widely adopted.

By the end of 1958, the negative consequences of all these absurd actions in defiance of objective laws began to surface, including plummeting production, mounting losses in enterprises, widening shortages in supplies of daily necessities, and the economy slid into abyssal difficulties.

Faced with this grave situation, leaders, including Mao Zedong, demanded actions to "compress the air" and to correct "Left deviation" at the Zhengzhou Meeting in November 1958, at the enlarged meeting of the Political Bureau in Wuchang in the same month, and at the Seventh Plenary Session of the Eighth CCCPC in April 1959. The State Council also took back control over many major enterprises. In July to August 1959, the enlarged meeting of the Political Bureau and the Eighth Plenary Session of the Eighth CCCPC were convened in Lushan (the Lushan Meeting). At the beginning of the meeting, Mao Zedong proposed to summarize the experience since the Great Leap Forward and to solve some specific problems. He claimed that failure to keep balance was the major shortcoming of the Great Leap Forward, which disrupted the proportional relationships of the entire national economy. He believed that there had been overdelegation of powers in the administration of human resources, financial resources, commerce, and industry, and thus proper proportions of those powers had to be taken back by central and provincial governments.[15] However, because Peng Dehuai[16] (1898–1974), a member of the Political Bureau, wrote a letter to Mao to demand a soul-searching to draw lessons from the experiences of the Great Leap Forward and the People's Communes Campaign, Mao decided to prolong the meeting and to switch its theme from "correcting Left deviation" to "opposing Right deviation." The Anti-Right Deviation Campaign led to the continuation of the Great Leap Forward and the second go-communism craze,[17] further worsening the economic crisis. The grain yield in China was 170 million tons in 1959, 30 million tons less than the grain yield of 200 million tons in 1958. The grain yield was further reduced to 143.5 million tons in 1960, lower than that of 143.7 million tons in 1951. Since the information of this

---

want." For related news reports, see "What Happens after Food Is Free of Charge (Chifan bu yao qian yihou)," *People's Daily (Renmin ribao)*, October 8, 1958; "The First Banner of Communism (Gongchanzhuyi de di yi mian qizhi)," *Xinhua Daily (Xinhua ribao)*, October 23, 1958.

[14] The "five guaranteed" were guaranteed output, job, cost, income in cash, and food supply. The "ten guaranteed" were guaranteed food, clothing, medical care, burial, marriage, education, housing, heating, haircut, and entertainment expenses.

[15] Mao Zedong, "Eighteen Issues Discussed at the Lushan Meeting (Lushan Huiyi taolun de shiba ge wenti) (June–July 1959)," *Collected Works of Mao Zedong (Mao Zedong wenji)*, Vol. 8, Beijing: People's Publishing House, 1999, pp. 75–82.

[16] One of the top leaders and top military commanders of the CPC and Commander of the Chinese People's Volunteers in the Korean War, who was conferred the rank of Marshal in 1955, was removed from his position as Minister of Defense in 1959, and was persecuted to death during the Great Cultural Revolution.

[17] Practice of extreme egalitarianism in the name of communism, characterized by indiscriminate, unpaid-for transfer of resources among collectives at the same level or different levels.

nationwide famine was suppressed and relief measures were inadequate, cases of edema caused by malnutrition prevailed in urban areas and deaths due to famine numbered in tens of millions in rural areas.[18]

Not until the fall of 1960 did the leadership of the CCCPC finally decide to implement the policy of "readjustment, consolidation, reinforcement, and upgrading." They appointed Chen Yun as the person in command and took drastic measures to overcome the grave economic difficulties caused by the Great Leap Forward and the Anti–Right Deviation Campaign. These measures included the following:

- In January 1962, the CCCPC convened an enlarged working conference (the so-called Conference of Seven Thousand Cadres), which was attended by cadres at the central level, central bureau level, provincial level, prefecture level, and county level. At this meeting, Mao Zedong made a gesture of taking responsibility for mistakes to cool the grievances of cadres and called on everybody to strengthen unity, discipline, and centralization to get work done and to overcome difficulties.[19] Meanwhile, the CCCPC Financial and Economic Leading Group headed by Chen Yun was restored to exercise unified leadership in the readjustment of the national economy.

- As requested by the CCCPC Financial and Economic Leading Group, a series of measures were taken to recentralize the administration of government finance, credit, and enterprises and to establish a system even more centralized and stricter than that of 1950 when the financial and economic work were unified. For example, the so-called *Ten Provisions* on tightening up planning discipline and a series of other decisions were made to take back the delegated power. A vertical system of leadership under the central government was exercised in banking, government finance, and statistics. Most of the enterprises transferred to local governments were brought back under the control of central departments.

- Scarce resources were reallocated by this highly centralized administrative system. Small iron and steel mills run by the masses with either indigenous or modern methods were all dismantled; thirty million workers recruited from rural areas

---

[18] Estimates by various scholars put the number of "abnormal deaths" nationwide caused by the Great Leap Forward and the People's Communes Campaign between fifteen and thirty million. See Sun Yefang, "Strengthen Statistics Work and Reform the Statistics System (Jiaqiang tongji gongzuo, gaige tongji tizhi)," *Journal of Economic Management*, 1981, No. 2. See also Basil Ashton et al., "Famine in China, 1958–1961," *Population and Development Review*, 1984, Vol. 10, No. 4; Denis Twitchett and John K. Fairbank, *The Cambridge History of China: Volume 14, The People's Republic, Part 1, The Emergence of Revolutionary China, 1949–1965*, Cambridge: Cambridge University Press, 1987.

[19] Liu Shaoqi, "Report at the Enlarged Working Conference of the CCCPC (Zai Kuoda de Zhongyang Gongzuo Huiyi shang de baogao) (January 1962)," *Selected Works of Liu Shaoqi (Liu Shaoqi xuanji)*, Vol. 2, Beijing: The Central Party School Publishing House, 1985, p. 349.

during the Great Leap Forward were all sent back home; and urban industrial enterprises were reorganized by closing down, suspending operations, merging, or switching production lines. The economy was stabilized after only several months of readjustment and had basically recovered by 1963.

However, as people rejoiced over the restoration of economic order, they also experienced again all the disadvantages of a centrally planned economy and started to deliberate on reform once again.

Until the downfall of the Gang of Four[20] in 1976, market-oriented reform was politically unacceptable because of the obstacle of the ideological creed that administrative order is the only way to allocate resources under socialism. As a result, transferring planning power to governments at lower levels was left as the only choice for economic reform, resulting in several attempts similar to the administrative decentralization reform of 1958. In 1970, a large-scale economic management system reform, famous for its slogan that "decentralization is a revolution and the more decentralization, the greater the revolution," was a restage of transferring administrative functions to lower levels of 1958 in a new historical setting. In 1970, Mao Zedong, based on his assessment of the international situation, assumed that another world war was imminent and the top priority then was to be prepared against a foreign enemy's full-scale invasion. As a result, the decentralization of 1970 had a clear political and military goal of making preparation for the war. The country was divided into ten cooperation regions and every cooperation region, every province, and every city was to establish an independent and integrated industrial setup, with which it could equip itself for war and meet the need of "each fighting in its own way." The consequences of this large-scale decentralization were no different at all from the decentralization of 1958. Enthusiasm to "go in for industry in a big way" and to pursue overambitious growth targets was stirred up from the cooperation region level down to the people's commune level. Concurrently, competition for resources motivated by local interests sank the national economy into disorder, just as it did in 1958.[21] After the death of Lin Biao[22] (1907–1971), the economic management

---

[20] A clique of ultra-Leftists ascending to power during the Great Cultural Revolution, including Jiang Qing (Mao's wife), Zhang Chunqiao, Yao Wenyuan, and Wang Hongwen, the first three of whom were members of the notorious CCCPC Cultural Revolution Group.

[21] Zhou Taihe and others summarized the actions and outcomes of this "big change in the economic system focusing on blind transfer to lower levels" as three parts: "First, blindly transferring enterprises to lower levels and intensifying the chaos in operation and management. Second, practicing the 'all-round responsibility system' in fiscal revenue and expenditure, materials and equipment allocation, and capital investment and achieving no expected results. Third, simplifying the taxation, credit, and labor-wage systems and weakening the role of economic levers." (See Zhou Taihe et al., *Economic System Reform in Contemporary China (Dangdai Zhongguo de jingji tizhi gaige)*, Beijing: China Social Sciences Press, 1984, pp. 134–146.)

[22] One of the top leaders and top military commanders of the CPC, who was conferred the rank of Marshal in 1955, was elected Vice Chairman of the CCCPC in 1958, was designated as the successor to Mao Zedong in 1969, and died in a plane crash in Mongolia in his attempt to flee to the Soviet Union in 1971.

system was recentralized in the "criticizing Lin and rectification campaign" directed by Zhou Enlai[23] (1898–1976) and the "all-round straightening out campaign" directed by Deng Xiaoping (1904–1997).

In a word, reforms of transferring administrative functions to lower levels (i.e., administrative decentralization) during 1958 to 1976 always ended up in disorder and recentralization later. Decentralization and ensuing disorder was followed by recentralization and ensuing stagnancy, resulting in cycles of decentralization–disorder–recentralization–stagnancy.

2.1.4 An Economic Analysis of Administrative Decentralization

Sun Yefang, a distinguished economist, was the first in China's academic circles to criticize the idea of transferring administrative functions to lower levels. In an internal research report submitted in 1961, Sun pointed out that the core issue of the economic management system was not the relationship between the central government and local governments, or between departments and regions, or, in other words, the division of power among administrative authorities at different levels. Rather, the core issue was "the power and responsibility of enterprises as independent accounting units as well as their relationship with the State, or, in other words, the independent power of operation and management of enterprises." According to Sun, only if an enterprise has power can the state arouse its enthusiasm to shoulder the responsibility given to it by the state. He believed that unless this issue was resolved, it would be impossible to resolve the issues of the relationship between the central government and local governments, or between departments and regions.[24] However, Sun's criticism was still presented in the theoretical framework of power delegating and profit sharing and arousing enthusiasm instead of from the perspective of efficient allocation of scarce resources. Therefore, he failed to explain theoretically why delegating power to and sharing profit with local governments could not solve the problem while delegating power to and sharing profit with enterprises (i.e., expanding enterprise managerial power) would raise the efficiency of the national economy.

Under the rule of "Left" guideline, even expanding enterprise autonomy in the framework of a planned economy, as proposed by Sun, was not allowed by the authorities then. Sun, after proposing this viewpoint, was criticized as a revisionist and persecuted. His criticism of administrative decentralization was not accepted until 1976.

---

[23] One of the top leaders of the CPC and the PRC, who served as Vice Chairman of the CCCPC and Premier of the State Council of the PRC for decades until his death.

[24] Sun Yefang, "On Issues of the Financial and Economic System within the Sector under Ownership by the Whole People (Guanyu quanmin suoyouzhi jingji neibu de caijing tizhi wenti) (1961)," *Selected Works of Sun Yefang (Sun Yefang xuanji)*, Taiyuan: Shanxi People's Publishing House, 1984, pp. 242–246, 286–287.

Because of the lack of a theoretical understanding of the erroneous nature of administrative decentralization reform, a few more measures of delegating power to and sharing profit with local governments were introduced after 1978 even though they were no longer regarded as the main theme of reform. These measures included the revenue sharing system (*fenzaochifan*) introduced nationwide in 1980 in the fiscal and taxation system; the long-time practice of the multi-tier macroeconomic control in the implementation of the macroeconomic management and monetary policy; and starting in the mid-1980s, the practice of granting some cities the status of "cities specifically designated in the state plan" so that they held the same planning power as provincial governments in the planning system.[25] These measures greatly influenced the reform process afterwards and they are to be discussed in Chapters 7 and 10.

Not until the mid-1980s did people come to a clear understanding of administrative decentralization. In a discussion of the advantages and disadvantages as well as the continuation or discontinuation of the revenue sharing system in the academic circles, some economists, using tools of modern economics, criticized the idea and practice of making transferring administrative functions to lower levels the main theme of reform.[26]

The basic idea of these economists was that the aim of reform should not be defined as decentralization in general terms because there were actually two types of decentralization, namely economic decentralization (i.e., market-oriented decentralization), which was aimed at a market economy, and administrative decentralization, which maintained the framework of a planned economy. Because the direction of China's reform was to build a market economy,[27] decentralization in China could only be economic decentralization, not administrative decentralization.[28] The economists opposing

---

[25] The cities that used to have the privilege of being "cities specifically designated in the state plan" were Shenyang, Dalian, Changchun, Harbin, Nanjing, Ningbo, Xiamen, Qingdao, Wuhan, Guangzhou, Shenzhen, Chengdu, Chongqing, and Xi'an.

[26] Wu Jinglian, "On Urban Economic Reform—Speech at the Cadres Conference in Shenyang on August 2, 1984 (Lun chengshi jingji gaige—1984 nian 8 yue 2 ri zai Shenyang Shi Ganbu Huiyi shang suozuo baogao)," *Research on Issues of Economic Reform (Jingji gaige wenti tansuo),* Beijing: China Outlook Press, 1987, pp. 218–227. See also Wu Jinglian, "The Key Issue in Urban Reform Is Invigorating Enterprises—Speech at the Weekly Forum of *World Economic Herald* in Shanghai on September 15, 1984 (Chengshi gaige de guanjian shi zengqiang qiye de huoli—1984 nian 9 yue 15 ri zai Shanghai Shijie Jingji Daobao Xingqi Jiangyanhui shang de baogao)," *World Economy Herald,* September 24, 1984 or *Selected Works of Wu Jinglian (Wu Jinglian xuanji),* Taiyuan: Shanxi People's Publishing House, 1989, pp. 389–413. See also Lou Jiwei, "Decentralization at Local Government Level Should Not Be Practiced Any More (Ying bimian jixu zou difang fenquan de daolu) (1985)," Wu Jinglian, Zhou Xiaochuan et al., *Overall Design of the Reform of China's Economic System (Zhongguo jingji gaige de zhengti sheji),* Beijing: China Outlook Press, 1988, pp. 204–216.

[27] Wu Jinglian pointed out, "All genuine reforms in socialist countries are market-oriented." See Wu Jinglian, "The Postscript to 'Research on Issues of Economic Reform' (Jingji Gaige Wenti Tansuo houji) (June 17, 1986)," *Research on Issues of Economic Reform (Jingji gaige wenti tansuo),* Beijing: China Outlook Press, 1987, pp. 434–437.

[28] As early as the 1960s and 1970s, the distinction between economic decentralization and administrative decentralization had been made by some Western scholars. For example, American scholar Herbert Franz Schurmann pointed out in 1966 that there were two types of decentralization in socialist economies. Decentralization I delegated decision-making power down to production units, whereas Decentralization II delegated power only to subordinate administrative units. He believed that when China started to think about system reform in 1956, the idea of Decentralization I dominated; the reform decided in 1957 was a mix of Decentralization I and Decentralization II; however, the reform actually carried out in 1958 was Decentralization II. This mode of decentralization led to chaos, and recentralization became necessary. See Herbert Franz Schurmann, *Ideology and Organization in Communist China,* Berkeley: University of California Press, 1966. In 1977, American comparative economist

administrative decentralization demonstrated their viewpoints from the perspective of the efficient mechanism of allocating scarce resources.

First, a planned economy allocates resources by administrative orders. This mode of resource allocation demands centralization. For a planned economy to be feasible, one of the prerequisites is for the central organ to compute a centralized calculation, determine planned quotas in a unified way, and ensure the strict enforcement of orders and prohibitions. Otherwise, the whole economy will suffer disorder as a result of divided leaderships with different agendas. Therefore, a decentralized planned economy is worse than a centralized planned economy.

Second, the only way to avoid both stagnancy in a centralized planned economy and disorder in a decentralized planned economy is to conduct market-oriented reform and to build an economic system in which market plays a fundamental role in resource allocation. Independent market players in a market economy decide what to produce, how many to produce, and for whom to produce, according to price signals and their self-interest. Economic decentralization is the only right direction of reform.

Third, it is true that administrative decentralization can motivate governments at lower levels in the short term. Measures of administrative decentralization adopted after 1978, such as the fiscal responsibility system, achieved the goal of encouraging local governments to increase revenue and reduce expenditure at the beginning. However, these measures soon revealed their shortcomings of not only weakening the unified leadership crucial for a planned economy but also encouraging local protectionism. By the mid-1980s, barriers between regions, market fragmentation, and administrative protection for local enterprises had become major obstacles to the development of a unified national market so that the Chinese economy at this point was called a "vassal economy" by some scholars. At that time, local governments' protection for vested interests hindered the process of breaking down barriers between regions and establishing a unified market.[29] Institutional change is characterized by path dependence.[30] The farther one is

---

Morris Bornstein pointed out in his testimony to the U.S. Congress on economic reforms in Eastern Europe that there were two different concepts of decentralization: administrative decentralization and economic decentralization. The former aimed to improve the existing administrative measures to make them more effective, and the latter aimed to switch to a regulated market economy. See Morris Bornstein, "Economic Reform in Eastern Europe," *Eastern-European Economies Post-Helsinki*, Washington, D.C.: U.S. Government Publishing Office, 1977, pp. 102–134.

[29] The negative consequences of administrative decentralization are thoroughly discussed in Wu Jinglian and Liu Jirui's book, *On Competitive Market System (Lun jingzhengxing shichang tizhi)*, Beijing: China Financial and Economic Publishing House, 1991, pp. 154–168. Barriers between regions and market segmentation remained major obstacles to the formation of a unified national market until China's entry into the WTO in 2001. Supachai Panitchpakdi, Director-General of the WTO, showed the severity of the situation by the example of Shanghai and Wuhan municipal governments imposing extra license fee and sales tax on cars produced by each other to protect local producers. (Supachai Panitchpakdi and Mark L. Clifford, *China and the WTO: Changing China, Changing World Trade*, Singapore: John Wiley & Sons Ltd. (Asia), 2002.)

[30] Path dependence is originally a feature of system evolution discovered in the study of nonlinear systems. Douglass C. North generalized this concept to institutional change. He pointed out that "the present choice set is narrowed by choices made in the past." Once institutional change is on a certain path, its existing direction will reinforce itself in later development. Hence, economic and political institutions may improve along the right path, or go away from their goals by following a wrong path. Or even worse, they may be locked in an inefficient state. Once locked in, it will be extremely difficult to exit. North claimed that

down a path deviating from the main path, the higher the exit cost is. The exit cost may even be so high that one is locked in this deviating path. Once locked in, it is impossible to exit without great social upheaval, according to economist Douglass C. North.

Economists noticed that administrative decentralization brought about another consequence. Market relations can hardly develop in a highly centralized planned economy. While strengthening local protectionism, administrative decentralization left some room for market relations to grow in gaps of competition among regions. As a result, China did not end up in a situation similar to that of the Soviet Union in which a highly centralized planned economy left no room for the growth of nonstate sectors. Township and village enterprises (TVEs) in China are good examples of this situation. The main reason for the rapid growth of TVEs in some localities is that, in pursuit of local interests, local officials used their administrative power to offer protection and convenience to TVEs in terms of financing, production, and marketing.[31] History witnessed similar situations in the birth of market relations. In autocratic oriental countries, absolute monarchical power and inadequate legal protection of private property prevented market relations from developing. In feudal Western Europe, market relations grew in gaps between different feudal manors; as market forces gradually expanded, free cities and the bourgeoisie emerged.

2.2 Incremental Reform (1979 to 1993)

China's economic development took a favorable turn after the Third Plenary Session of the 11th CCCPC in December 1978. After years of exploration, China found a new approach to reform. After the failed experiment of expanding enterprise autonomy and the stagnancy of SOE reform, China adopted some patching-up measures to keep the state sector running and switched its main effort to nonstate sectors for new growth. This strategy was called incremental reform. Achievements by China's economy during the following one or two decades could be largely attributed to this strategy. However, the continuation of this strategy led to a series of problems. This section analyzes the

---

turning of existing direction usually needs external force, such as an exogenous variable, or a regime change. See Wu Jinglian, "Path Dependence and China's Reform—Comments on the Speech of Professor North (Lujing yilai yu Zhongguo gaige—dui Nuosi Jiaoshou jiangyan de pinglun)," *Where to Find Macro Wisdom (Hechu xunqiu dazhihui)*, Beijing: Joint Publishing, 1997, p. 351−358.

[31] Xu Chenggang and Qian Yingyi clarified their viewpoints in their paper "Why Is China's Economic Reform Different from Others: M-Form Hierarchy and the Entry and Expansion of Nonstate Sectors (Zhongguo jingji gaige weishenme yuzhongbutong—M xing de cengjizhi he feiguoyou bumen de jinru yu kuozhang) (1993)," Qian Yingyi, *Modern Economics and China's Reform (Xiandai jingjixue yu Zhongguo jingji gaige)*, Beijing: China Renmin University Press, 2003. They claimed that, different from Eastern Europe and the Soviet Union that adopted a "U-form economic structure" organized on the basis of functional and specialized departments, China, since 1958, adopted an "M-form economic structure" based on geographical regions in a multi-tier and multi-region fashion. This was the main reason for the continuous entry and vigorous expansion of nonstate sectors during China's reform.

emergence of this strategy, its achievements, its problems, and the necessity to switch to a new reform strategy.

2.2.1 The Emergence of the Strategy of Incremental Reform

Reform after the downfall of the "Gang of Four" in 1976 started with expanding enterprise autonomy. Ten years of the Great Cultural Revolution (1966–1976) had driven the Chinese economy to the verge of collapse. During the process of "bringing order out of chaos" in political ideology and economic policy after the Great Cultural Revolution, most economists and leaders on economic affairs agreed with Sun Yefang's viewpoint that expanding enterprise autonomy and boosting enterprise vitality should be the core of reform. They were also influenced by Yugoslavia's "enterprise autonomy" to a large extent. Ma Hong (1920–), Jiang Yiwei (1920–1993), and Dong Fureng (1927–2004) were among the most famous advocates of micro-reform focusing on SOEs.

Some other economists thought beyond enterprise reform. Xue Muqiao (1904–), a leading economist and a veteran leader on economic affairs in the central government, pointed out in *China's Socialist Economy,* published in 1979, that there were two pressing issues for China's economic reform to address: "first, to reform the management system of enterprises (including collective economic units) to change them into vigorous grass-roots business units; second, to reform the management system of the national economy to meet the requirements of large-scale social production."[32]

At that time, however, most practitioners' attention was paid to the first group of economists—those most influenced by Sun Yefang. For example, Ma Hong pointed out in September 1979 that "the economic management system reform should begin with expanding enterprise autonomy," to expand the enterprises' decision-making power concerning human, financial, and material resources, as well as planning.[33] His proposition reflected the viewpoints of most economists and leaders on economic affairs, and was echoed enthusiastically by leaders of SOEs, as well.

Jiang Yiwei argued that neither the centralization mode nor the administrative decentralization mode was advisable because the former was an argument for a state-based economy and the latter was an argument for a region-based economy. He believed that a sound reform "should have enterprises (including industrial enterprises, commercial enterprises, agricultural enterprises, etc.) as basic economic units. Enterprises should practice independent operation and independent accounting under the unified leader-

---

[32] Xue Muqiao, *China's Socialist Economy (Zhongguo shehuizhuyi jingji wenti yanjiu),* Beijing: People's Publishing House, 1979, p. 185.
[33] Ma Hong, "Reform Economic Management System and Expand Enterprise Autonomy (Gaige jingji guanli tizhi yu kuoda qiye zizhuquan)," *Selected Works of Ma Hong (Ma Hong ji),* Beijing: China Social Sciences Press, 2000, pp. 228–245. This paper was submitted to the Academic Seminar of Beijing's Social Sciences Circles in Commemoration of the 30th Anniversary of the People's Republic of China.

ship and supervision of the State. They should enjoy deserved rights on the one hand and fulfill their obligations to the State on the other." He argued that "an enterprise should be an association of all its employees . . . it should be controlled by its employees," practicing independent operation and accounting.[34] Dong Fureng interpreted expanding enterprise autonomy as changing "the state ownership form of whole-people ownership," believing that economic units of whole-people ownership "should have independence under the unified leadership of the State and practice all-round, independent and strict economic accounting. . . . With the common interests of all workers safeguarded and promoted and under the guidance of the unified plan, workers in each economic unit are entitled to direct involvement in the operation with due consideration of the interests of the unit and their own."[35]

Top leaders responded to such a prevailing mood among economists and leaders on economic affairs. At the principle discussion meeting and the planning meeting on economic affairs held by the State Council from July to September 1978, materials about enterprise reform and foreign investment spurring economic growth in Yugoslavia and Romania were handed out. Li Xiannian (1909–1992), Vice Premier of the State Council, pointed out in his final report that "a major flaw in the economic system reform of the past twenty years was putting too much emphasis on the division and transfer of administrative powers, leading to a cycle of 'decentralization–recentralization–decentralization.' Necessary independence must be granted to all enterprises in future reform, making them actively instead of passively carry out economic accounting to increase overall economic efficiency."[36]

Li's idea was echoed by the decision of the Third Plenary Session of the 11th CCCPC in December 1978. The communiqué of the session reiterated the policies proposed by Mao Zedong in his article, "On the Ten Major Relationships," and pointed out that a major shortcoming of the old economic system lay in its overcentralization of power. "Power should be audaciously delegated to lower levels under unified leadership. Local governments as well as industrial and agricultural enterprises should have more autonomy of management under the guidance of a unified state plan," so as to "bring into play the initiative, enthusiasm, and creativity of central departments, local governments, enterprises, and individuals, thus bringing vigorous growth to all sectors of socialist economy."[37]

---

[34] Jiang Yiwei, "Argument for an Enterprise-Based Economy (Qiye benwei lun) (1979)," *Social Sciences in China (Zhongguo shehui kexue),* 1980, No. 1.

[35] Dong Fureng, "On the Form of Our Country's Socialist Ownership (Guanyu wo guo shehuizhuyi suoyouzhi xingshi wenti) (1979)," *Economic Research Journal (Jingji yanjiu),* 1979, No. 1.

[36] Li Xiannian, *Selected Works of Li Xiannian (Li Xiannian wenxuan),* Beijing: People's Publishing House, 1989, p. 330.

[37] "Communiqué of the Third Plenary Session of the 11th CCCPC (Zhongguo Gongchandang Di Shiyi Jie Zhongyang Weiyuanhui Di San Ci Quanti Huiyi gongbao) (December 22, 1978)," the Party Literature Research Center of the CCCPC (ed.), *A Selection of Important Documents since the Third Plenary Session (Sanzhongquanhui yilai zhongyao wenxian xuanbian),* Beijing: People's Publishing House, 1982.

Inspired by this idea, Sichuan Province initiated the reform of expanding enterprise autonomy to delegate power to and share profit with enterprises. In October 1978, Sichuan Province selected six enterprises to conduct an experiment in expanding enterprise autonomy and achieved good results. Later, the experiment in Sichuan Province was extended to one hundred SOEs. In July 1979, the State Council released a series of official documents, including *Provisions on Enlarging the Decision-Making Power for Operation and Management of State-Run Industrial Enterprises, Provisions on Implementing Profit Retention in State-Run Enterprises, Interim Provisions on Levying Fixed Assets Tax on State-Run Industrial Enterprises,* and *Interim Provisions on Implementing Full Loan Financing for Working Capital in State-Run Industrial Enterprises,* requesting all local governments and central departments to select some enterprises to conduct the experiment in expanding enterprise autonomy in line with these regulations. By the end of 1979, the number of experimental enterprises had reached 4,200 nationwide. In 1980, the experiment expanded to 6,600 large- and medium-sized SOEs, which accounted for 60 percent of the national budgeted industrial output and 70 percent of national industrial profits. During the first few months of the experiment, employees in experimental enterprises were strongly motivated to increase output and profit. However, similarly to Russia's Kosygin reform of 1965, the limitations of the reform soon became apparent.

The enterprises that were entitled to certain autonomy under the new system had neither the constraint of fair market competition nor the guidance of a price system reflecting the degree of commodity scarcity. Therefore, allowing enterprise enthusiasm to fully manifest itself was not always conducive to the efficient allocation of resources of the society. Besides, in those days, the growth target of industry was set too high, generating great pressure to increase investment and resulting in exploding aggregate demand, soaring fiscal deficits, and economic disorder. Meanwhile, reform in nonstate sectors and off-plan parts of the economy was under constant exploration and emerged gradually as the mainstream of reform.

Insight 2.1

The Beginning of China's Reform Economics

In the early 1980s, with the deepening of research and expansion of international exchange, China's reform theory gradually developed beyond the practice of expanding enterprise autonomy of the late 1970s. A complete set of ideas and policies centering on the "theory of socialist commodity economy" were established.

The leading exponents of this school of reform were Xue Muqiao, Du Runsheng (1913–), Yu Guangyuan (1915–), and Liao Jili (1915–1993), all of whom were senior economists and leaders on economic affairs.

Xue Muqiao is among the first economists to advocate the idea that Chinese socialist economy in the current stage is a commodity economy.* In 1979 and 1980, he repeated his two basic viewpoints in his articles: (a) socialist economy is commodity economy on the whole (i.e., does not just have commodity production and commodity exchange partially) and (b) the functions of the market should be brought into full play under the guidance of the plan. In his *Preliminary Opinions on Economic System Reform,* which he drafted for the System Reform Office of the State Council in the early summer of 1980, Xue Muqiao specifically pointed out that "the current socialist economy in China is a commodity economy in which public ownership of the means of production dominates and diverse economic sectors coexist. The principle and direction of China's economic reform should be to uphold the dominant position of public ownership of the means of production, to consciously apply the law of value in accordance with the requirement of developing commodity economy, and to turn the unitary system of plan regulation into one where market regulation is given full play under the guidance of the plan." When explaining his *Opinions* to first party secretaries of all provinces, municipalities, and autonomous regions in September 1980, Xue said that "the so-called economic system reform is to resolve the issue of establishing what kind of socialist economy in China. It is an issue about the fundamental direction of socialist construction. The plan of the economic management system reform to be drafted in the future will be an 'economic constitution.'"** This speech enlightened China's reformers and had a great impact on leaders of the state at the time. Although endorsed by many people, Xue's idea was not adopted in government decisions because it was not presented as a systematic theory and because market was strongly opposed by the traditional ideology at that time.

Another veteran economist of great influence on Chinese economic reform theories and policies was Du Runsheng. He devoted himself to research on rural economy for a long time and once assisted Deng

Zihui,*** a leader on rural affairs who was criticized by Mao Zedong as an "unrepentant Right deviationist for ten years." In the early 1980s, by promoting the household contracting system, Du Runsheng regained his influence on China's rural economic policy making. He extensively drew on the theoretical achievements of modern economics and advocated establishing a market economic system in an all-round way.

Yu Guangyuan, who worked in ideological departments for a long time, criticized Stalin and Mao's economic theories and economic systems from the perspective of restoring the Marxist original definition. He and his followers were in favor of the economic system of enterprise autonomy and social ownership developed by the Yugoslavian Communist Party. (See Chapter 1, Section 1.3 for this system.)

Many economists who had received their education in economics after the founding of the PRC contributed their efforts to market-oriented reform, including Liu Guoguang (1923–) and Dong Fureng who had studied in the Soviet Union and received the degree of doctorand in economics there. They learned from both the successes and failures since the founding of the PRC, and also benefited from the fruits of reform economics in former socialist countries of Eastern Europe. All these experiences enabled them to contribute to the criticism of the Soviet-style centrally planned economic system and the promotion of China's reform.

*"Commodity economy" is in fact another name for market economy.

**Xue Muqiao, "Notes on 'Preliminary Opinions on Economic System Reform' (Dui Guanyu Jingji Tizhi Gaige de Chubu Yijian de shuoming)," *On China's Economic System Reform (Lun Zhongguo jingji tizhi gaige)*, Tianjin: Tianjin People's Publishing House, 1990, pp. 219–255. See also Xue Muqiao, *Xue Muqiao Memoir (Xue Muqiao huiyilu)*, Tianjin: Tianjin People's Publishing House, 1996, p. 357.

***One of veteran leaders of the CPC and the chief official on rural affairs after the founding of the PRC. He was criticized time and again by Mao Zedong for advocating "four freedoms" in labor hiring, loan making, land leasing, and land trading after the Agrarian Reform, opposing the rash advance in collectivization in the mid-1950s, and advocating the household contracting system after the failure of the Great Leap Forward.

2.2.2 The Shift of the Focus of Reform from "Inside the System" to "Outside the System"

In the early 1980s, amid macroeconomic disorder and stagnant SOE reform, a debate over planned economy and market regulation arose among leaders on economic affairs and economists, mainly between two views.

One view advocated plan-oriented reform to improve the planning and keep its dominant position. The unsuccessful reform of expanding enterprise autonomy in SOEs strengthened the position of statesmen and theorists advocating planned economy as the mainstay. They believed that the difficulties occurring at the time were caused by overemphasis on the roles of market and money and advocated reversing the market orientation of reform, improving planning, and tightening up planning discipline.

Economists advocating reform held an opposing view. They believed that the difficulties were not caused by market-oriented reform itself, but by the inappropriate way it was carried out. In fact, people advocating market-oriented reform had been aware of the shortcomings of reform measures with power-delegating and profit-sharing being the main way and with market mechanism applied only partially. In 1980, Xue Muqiao, who was then in charge of the System Reform Office of the State Council, pointed out explicitly the limitations of the reform of power delegating and profit sharing. He proposed to focus the reform effort on the reform of the price control system and the reform of circulation channels, to gradually abolish the administrative pricing system and establish a commodity market and a financial market. The essence of his proposal was to establish an economic system based on the market.[38]

At that time, the statesmen and theorists advocating planned economy as the mainstay won the upper hand, resulting in the political negation of the proposition that socialist economy is commodity economy and the establishment of the guideline of planned economy as the mainstay with market regulation as the supplement.[39] Under such circumstances, the SOE reform lost its direction. Although the contracting experiments were still carried out in several industrial and commercial enterprises like Capital Steel,[40] the issues of giving enterprises full management authority, letting them assume full responsibility for profits and losses, and establishing a system of commodity economy were seldom mentioned.

---

[38] Xue Muqiao, "Some Opinions on Economic System Reform (Guanyu jingji tizhi gaige de yixie yijian) (June 1980);" "Price Readjustment and Reform of the Price Control System (Tiaozheng wujia he wujia guanli tizhi de gaige) (July 1980)," *On China's Economic System Reform (Lun Zhongguo jingji tizhi gaige),* Tianjin: Tianjin People's Publishing House, 1990, pp. 211–218, 325–340.

[39] See the interview between *Hundred Year Tide* magazine and Wu Jinglian: "About the Debate between Planned Economy and Market Economy (Guanyu jihua jingji yu shichang jingji de lunzheng)," *Hundred Year Tide (Bai nian chao),* 1998, No. 2, pp. 1–10. Under the circumstances, then, at the 12th National Congress of the CPC in September 1982, Hu Yaobang had to affirm in his report on behalf of the CCCPC that "a fundamental issue in economic system reform is to adhere to the principle of 'planned economy as the mainstay with market regulation as a supplement.'" When *Selected Works of Deng Xiaoping (1975–1982)* was published in 1983, the wording of "combining plan regulation and market regulation" in Deng Xiaoping's 1980 article of *The Present Situation and the Tasks before Us* had to be changed to "letting market regulation play a supplementary role under the guidance of planned economy." The wording was not changed back until Deng Xiaoping himself reviewed the new edition of *Selected Works of Deng Xiaoping* in 1994.

[40] In May 1979, six departments including the State Economic Commission and the Ministry of Finance selected eight SOEs including Capital Steel for the experiment of enterprise reform featured by profit retention in Beijing, Tianjin, Shanghai, etc. In 1981, Capital Steel started to experiment in the practice of "responsibility for progressive quota of turned-in profits," under which the enterprise would guarantee a turned-in profit with an annual growth rate of 7 percent and retain above-quota profit

When the reform of expanding enterprise autonomy in the state sector fell into plight, the Chinese leaders headed by Deng Xiaoping shifted the focus of reform from the urban state sector to the rural nonstate sectors. A major measure was lifting the ban on contracting output quota to each household.[41] In September 1980, the CCCPC decided to allow peasants to carry out the household contracting system (*jiating chengbao jingyingzhi*) at their will.[42] Within only two years, the household contracting system,[43] or the family farm system, replaced the people's commune system of three-tier ownership with production team as the basic unit among the overwhelming majority of the rural population. The rural economy took on an entirely new look. Township and village enterprises, mainly collective-owned, were springing up vigorously under such favorable circumstances. From then on, China adopted a new strategy different from the strategy of the Soviet Union and Eastern European countries that emphasized the reform of existing SOEs. Instead of taking major reform measures in the state sector, China focused its reform effort on nonstate sectors, aiming at establishing market-oriented enterprises so as to let them drive the growth of the economy. The new strategy was called the strategy of "outside the system" preceding "inside the system," or the strategy of incremental reform.

2.2.3 The All-Round Implementation of Incremental Reform

After the initial success of incremental reform in agriculture, the Chinese government applied it to other industries to promote the growth of nonstate sectors. In addition, the already implemented policy of opening to the outside world generated a number of joint ventures of mixed ownership with foreign investment in coastal regions. Gradually, these nonstate enterprises became the main force in China's economic development.

---

and the state would not provide investment to the enterprise by fiscal allocation any more. This practice was carried out until the mid-1990s.

[41] According to the *Decision of the CCCPC on Issues Regarding Accelerating the Development of Agriculture,* which was discussed at the Third Plenary Session of the 11th CCCPC in December 1978 and adopted at the Fourth Plenary Session of the 11th CCCPC in September 1979, "distributing land for individual farming" and "contracting output quota to each household" in ordinary areas were explicitly prohibited. The *Decision* wrote: "Distributing land for individual farming shall not be allowed. Contracting output quota to each household shall not be practiced except for some special cases in sideline production and for some isolated households in remote mountainous areas."

[42] In September 1980, the CCCPC transmitted with endorsement *Some Issues Regarding Further Strengthening and Improving the Responsibility System for Agricultural Production (Summary of the Symposium of First Secretaries of Party Committees of Provinces, Municipalities, and Autonomous Regions on September 14 to 22, 1980),* which pointed out that "In those remote mountainous areas and poverty-stricken backward regions and in those production teams that have been relying on state-resold grain for food, loans for production, and social relief for living for a long period of time, if the masses have lost their confidence in the collective and request contracting output quota to each household, such requests should be granted and either contracting output quota to each household or contracting responsibility to each household may be practiced and such arrangements are to be kept unchanged for a fairly long period of time." (See the Party Literature Research Center of the CCCPC (ed.), *A Selection of Important Documents since the Third Plenary Session (Sanzhongquanhui yilai zhongyao wenxian xuanbian),* Beijing: People's Publishing House, 1982, p. 507.)

[43] In addition to its popular name of *baochan daohu* (contracting output quota to each household), *jiating chengbao jingyingzhi* (the household contracting system) has several other names in the Chinese language, a clear indication of the spontaneous, multi-origin and bottom-up nature of Chinese rural reform. See Chapter 3, Section 3.2 for more information.

The strategy of developing nonstate sectors was carried out in the ways discussed in the following three sections.

2.2.3.1 Encouraging the Growth of Nonstate Enterprises

Allowing the growth of nonpublic sectors has always been a politically sensitive issue in China. Even in the process of bringing order out of chaos after 1976, such dogmas as "the larger in size and the more public in ownership, the better" and "the task of the communist party is to extinguish capitalism" remained dominant in people's minds. Therefore, at the beginning of reform, nonpublic sectors had to develop in roundabout ways.[44] Not until the legalization of "contracting output quota to each household" based on household operation were such ideological shackles broken. Together with the effort by the government to eliminate ideological and policy impediments to the development of nonstate sectors, collective-owned and individual-owned township and village enterprises (TVEs) sprang up like mushrooms. Within the ten years between 1979 and 1988, the number of peasants working in industrial and commercial TVEs reached 100 million. Private enterprises also started to develop after 1983.

Nonstate sectors immediately displayed their advantages on their emergence and grew with each passing day. In the 1980s, the growth rate of industrial output of nonstate sectors was about twice that of the state sector. In the mid-1980s, nonstate sectors, including the collective sector, the individual business sector, and the private sector (see Chapter 5, Section 5.1 for definitions of these sectors), came to occupy a decisive position in both industrial production and the whole national economy. Their share in industrial output amounted to more than one-third (see Table 2.1). Their share grew even more rapidly in retail sales (see Table 2.2).

Since the economic activities of nonstate sectors were mainly market-oriented, as nonstate sectors developed, markets of a limited scope gradually came into being, and market forces began to play an increasingly important role in resource allocation.

2.2.3.2 Integrating Parts of China into the International Market by Opening to the Outside World

The development of a domestic market is always a long process in the economic development of any country. Because Old China had a very weak commercial culture and

---

[44] For instance, in the late 1970s, argument for allowing private merchants to engage in long-distance transport of goods for sale was that it could serve as an expedient measure to solve the problem of unemployment. Argument for allowing private businesses to hire labor was a numerical example found in Chapter 9, Volume 1 of Karl Marx's *The Capital,* which demonstrates how to calculate the exploitation rate with assumed figures and shows that an employer with fewer than eight employees is not an exploiter but still an individual laborer. Using that numerical example, economists advocating reform succeeded in convincing the political leaders to loosen the restriction on hiring labor. Since 1980, the Chinese government drew a distinction between individual businesses with fewer than eight employees and larger private enterprises, and called the former "individual business sector," as opposed to the then prohibited "private sector."

Table 2.1   Gross Value of Industrial Output by Ownership (%)

Year	1978	1980	1985	1990
State sector	77.6	76.0	64.9	54.6
Collective sector	22.4	23.5	32.1	35.6
Nonpublic sectors*	0.0	0.5	3.0	9.8

*Nonpublic sectors refer to the collection of all nonstate and noncollective economic entities, such as individual businesses, private enterprises, and foreign-invested enterprises.
Source: The National Bureau of Statistics, *China Statistical Yearbook (Zhongguo tongji nianjian),* Beijing: China Statistics Press, various years.

Table 2.2   Total Retail Sales by Ownership (%)

Year	1978	1980	1985	1990
State sector	54.6	51.4	40.4	39.6
Collective sector	43.3	44.6	37.2	31.7
Nonpublic sectors*	2.1	4.0	22.4	28.7

*Nonpublic sectors refer to the collection of all nonstate and noncollective economic entities, such as individual businesses, private enterprises, and foreign-invested enterprises.
Source: The National Bureau of Statistics, *China Statistical Yearbook (Zhongguo tongji nianjian),* Beijing: China Statistics Press, various years.

tradition, and thirty years of practicing planned economy in the People's Republic of China almost completely wiped out market forces, it was even harder to develop a domestic market in China. Under such circumstances, the Chinese government adopted an ingenious policy—getting parts of China with proper conditions integrated into the international market by opening them to the outside world. By doing so, the so-called advantages of backwardness could be exploited, competitive forces could be introduced, and the formation and expansion of the market could be accelerated.

In 1979, special policies and flexible measures were adopted for Guangdong Province and Fujian Province so that they could take advantage of their geographical closeness to Hong Kong and Macao. In 1980, four special economic zones—Shenzhen, Zhuhai, Shantou, and Xiamen—were set up. In 1985, fourteen coastal port cities were opened up. An open belt of considerable width along the coast, along the border, and along the Yangtze River gradually took shape after China started to open to the outside world.

Coastal open areas made great contributions to the growth of exports and the introduction of foreign technology and capital. China's foreign trade dependence ratio increased continuously (see Table 2.3). Foreign loans and foreign direct investment (FDI) started to flood into China.

Table 2.3   Degree of Openness of China's Economy (%)

Year	1978	1985	1990
Ratio of total exports and imports to GNP	9.9	24.2	31.9
Ratio of total imports to GNP	5.2	14.7	14.8
Ratio of total exports to GNP	4.7	9.5	17.1

Source: The National Bureau of Statistics, *China Statistical Yearbook (Zhongguo tongji nianjian)*, Beijing: China Statistics Press, various years.

In the initial stage of the reform and opening up, loans from foreign countries accounted for a greater part of foreign capital than FDI. Since the 1990s, FDI has increased rapidly and become the major form of incoming foreign capital. In the first seven years of reform (1979–1985), total FDI was only US$7.4 billion, but it rose to US$18.6 billion between 1986 and 1991.

Opening to the outside world facilitated domestic economic reform. Participating in the fierce competition of the international market gave business managerial personnel in China both a good understanding of the international market and a great sense of urgency to improve product quality and reduce production costs. To survive competition, it was necessary for Chinese enterprises to operate with more autonomy and to improve operation and management. Participation in competitive import and export markets also brought the domestic price structure closer to the international norm, and thus accelerated the price reform.

2.2.3.3 Implementing Regional Advance of the Reform and Opening Up by Establishing Experimental Areas

Because market-oriented reform could not be carried out throughout the country simultaneously, and the reform had to be systematically conducted, setting up experimental areas in some coastal regions, where both developed markets and suitable conditions were available, was a good choice. When such areas applied the two approaches of the reform and opening up (encouraging the growth of nonstate enterprises and integrating into the international market) in combination, a regional "microclimate" was created in which the new economic system could run effectively to a certain degree. Such successful experiences would also provide examples for inland areas and drive reform there. Facts proved that this was another effective approach to reform—regional advance.

Regional advance helped raise living standards of people in those areas considerably. In his speech, *Make a Success of Special Economic Zones and Open More Cities to the Outside*

World, in 1984, Deng Xiaoping predicted that coastal regions would be the first to become wealthy. He said, "We are not in a position to adopt the suggestion to encourage high wages and high consumption as our policy nationwide. However, as we develop the coastal areas successfully, we shall be able to increase people's incomes, which accordingly will lead to higher consumption. This is in conformity with the laws of development."[45] After more than ten years of development, by the early 1990s, a vast area with a rudimentary market and a vigorous economy had emerged along the Chinese coastline from the Liaodong Peninsula to Guangxi Province. Even inland, some preliminarily invigorated areas emerged. These areas became powerful bases for promoting market-oriented reform, where market force was projecting its impact in all directions.

Incremental reform over more than a decade brought fast growth to the Chinese economy. During the twelve-year period from 1978 to 1990, on average, GDP grew by 14.6 percent annually, and the per-capita disposable income of urban residents grew by 13.1 percent annually (see Table 2.4).

2.2.4 The Emergence of the Dual-Track System

To ensure the survival and development of nonstate enterprises in an environment where the system of allocating resources by plan had not yet been changed, the Chinese government made a special institutional arrangement, namely, the dual-track system in price and other aspects that enabled nonstate enterprises to obtain a supply of raw materials and sell their products via a market.

In a planned economy, the means of production were transferred among units in the state sector by the state and price was just a tool for accounting among these units. Furthermore, consumer goods were uniformly distributed by state commercial departments with their prices uniformly set by price control departments at various levels. Therefore, there was almost no real market except country fair trade (free market), which accounted for only a very tiny proportion of the goods sold. Moreover, compared with the Soviet Union and Eastern European socialist countries, China's planned economy had even stronger administrative control. During a long period before 1979, the rationing system for daily necessities was so pervasive as to give China a strong flavor of an economy in kind. Such conditions had to change after TVEs, individual businesses, and other nonstate enterprises emerged in the early 1980s. Otherwise, they would not be able to survive because of the absence of regular channels of supply and marketing.

---

[45] Deng Xiaoping, "Make a Success of Special Economic Zones and Open More Cities to the Outside World (Banhao jingji tequ, zengjia duiwai kaifang chengshi) (February 1984)," *Selected Works of Deng Xiaoping (Deng Xiaoping wenxuan),* Vol. 3, Beijing: People's Publishing House, p. 52.

Table 2.4   Economic Growth during 1978–1990

Year	1978	1980	1985	1990
GDP (RMB billion)	362.41	451.78	896.44	1,854.79
Total industrial output (RMB billion)	423.70	515.40	971.60	2,392.40
Total exports and imports (RMB billion)	35.50	57.00	206.67	556.01
Total exports (RMB billion)	16.76	27.12	80.89	298.58
Total retail sales of consumer goods (RMB billion)	155.86	214.00	430.50	830.01
Per-capita disposable income of urban residents (RMB)	343.4	477.6	739.1	1510.2

Source: The National Bureau of Statistics, *China Statistical Yearbook (Zhongguo tongji nianjian)*, Beijing: China Statistics Press, various years.

In the initial phase of the reform and opening up, to solve the problems of the channels of supply and marketing and the pricing of products for nonstate enterprises, various nonstandard practices were adopted, such as bartering between enterprises[46] in the name of cooperation. *Provisions on Enlarging the Decision-Making Power for Operation and Management of State-Run Industrial Enterprises* adopted by the State Council in 1979 allowed enterprises to sell products exceeding the planned quotas and thus opened the second track (the market track) of commodity circulation.[47]

In the early 1980s, nonstate sectors expanded rapidly. By 1984, nonstate enterprises accounted for 31 percent of the gross value of industrial output of the nation. They would not be able to survive without free trading in the market. Meanwhile, the scope of off-plan production and trading of SOEs was also expanding. The *Circular on Lifting Control over the Prices of Overfulfilled and Producer-Marketed Industrial Means of Production* issued by the State Administration of Commodity Prices and the State Bureau of Materials and Equipment in January 1985, allowed enterprises to sell and buy off-plan products at market prices, thus officially introducing the dual-track system for the supply and pricing of the means of production. Those state-owned enterprises enjoying the right to get planned allocation of materials and equipment before 1983 could still get the same quantities of materials and equipment as they did in 1983 (namely the "83 base quotas") at allocation prices. The parts exceeding the "83 base quotas" could be purchased in the market at market prices.

---

[46]Bartering between enterprises means that one enterprise exchanges its products for necessary equipment and raw materials with another enterprise.

[47]In July 1979, *Provisions on Enlarging the Decision-Making Power for Operation and Management of State-Run Industrial Enterprises (Guanyu kuoda guoying gongye qiye jingying guanli zizhuquan de ruogan guiding)* granted enterprises limited power to sell and price their off-plan products. Specifically, "Products made according to the supplementary plan are first to fill the orders from commercial, foreign trade, and materials and equipment departments. Enterprises can sell their products not purchased by commercial, foreign trade, and materials and equipment departments at the price set by the State, or let commercial, foreign trade, and material departments sell their products on a commission basis. If an enterprise has excess productive capacity, it may process supplied materials for other enterprises."

The formal establishment of the dual-track system provided nonstate sectors with the basic operation environment for their survival and development. Such an institutional arrangement was compatible with the strategy of developing nonstate sectors and played a positive role in the rapid development of nonstate sectors and the whole national economy in the early stage of the reform and opening up.

With the increasing share of nonstate sectors in the national economy, the quantities of commodities circulating outside the plan was also increasing. Therefore, the scope of market pricing was gradually enlarged. Meanwhile, as foreign trade expanded, the international market prices exerted great influence on the domestic market prices, gradually closing the gaps between relative prices in the domestic market and those in the international market. Commodities priced by plan no longer held a dominant position in total domestic commodity turnovers by the early 1990s.

Economists expressed different opinions regarding the merits and demerits of the dual-track system created by partial liberalization. American economists Kevin Murphy, Andrei Shleifer, and Robert Vishny believed that resources would be misallocated unless controls over prices were lifted all at once.[48] But Lawrence Lau, Qian Yingyi, and Gérard Roland proved the Pareto-improving nature of dual-track liberalization of prices based on a general equilibrium analysis.[49] Moreover, the introduction of the dual-track system might make reform more acceptable for those officials who benefited from it. A majority of economists believed that the dual-track system broke the monopoly of plan in resource allocation and granted newly born nonstate sectors with room and conditions for growth, and thus definitely had more merits than demerits in the early stage of transition. However, it would also enable some people with powerful connections to gain from rent-seeking activities and to form social groups to block further marketization reform. Moreover, these corrupt activities would arouse public resentment and thus cause social instability.[50] In particular, the dual-track system created inequity in op-

---

[48] Kevin M. Murphy, Andrei Shleifer, and Robert W. Vishny, "The Transition to a Market Economy: Pitfalls of Partial Reform," *The Quarterly Journal of Economics,* August 1992, Vol. 107, No. 3, pp. 889–906.

[49] Lawrence J. Lau, Qian Yingyi, and Gérard Roland, "Pareto-Improving Economic Reforms through Dual-Track Liberalization," *Economics Letter,* 1997, Vol. 55, No. 2, pp. 285–292; "Reform without Losers: An Interpretation of China's Dual-Track Approach to Transition," *Journal of Political Economy,* February 2000, Vol. 108, No. 1, pp. 120–143. Using a model based on industrial organization theory, Zhang Jun explained the role of the dual-track system in the continuous growth of China's industrial output. He believed that the plan track ensured the full exploitation of the existing productive capacity of the state sector and the achievement of planned output while the market track increased output and gradually establish a competitive market structure by introducing nonstate sectors to compete with the state sector. Therefore, "pitfalls of partial liberalization of prices" and recession caused by the "Shock Therapy" were avoided. See Zhang Jun, *Introduction to China's Transitional Economy (Zhongguo guodu jingji daolun),* Shanghai: Lixin Accounting Press, 1996, pp. 59–78; *Economics of Dual-Track System: China's Economic Reform (1978–1992) (Shuangguizhi jingjixue: Zhongguo de jingji gaige (1978–1992)),* Shanghai: Shanghai Joint Publishing and Shanghai People's Publishing House, 1997, pp. 219–288.

[50] There was a viewpoint claiming that the "monetization of power" brought about by the dual-track system was a correct approach to promote reform. A researcher of the Research Institute of the State Commission for Restructuring Economic Systems stated, "In a dual-track economy, there is a mechanism for administrative power to allocate resources (i.e., voucher). Under certain conditions, the monetization of voucher will lead to the monetization of power, i.e., the power to allocate voucher is in fact the power to allocate money. In other words, power itself can be measured by money. . . . When the central and local in-

eration conditions between SOEs that could obtain subsidies in disguised forms and nonstate enterprises that could only obtain raw materials, equipment, and loans at market prices. As a result, the dual-track system became an obstacle to the further growth of nonstate sectors as these sectors developed.[51]

Chapter 1, Section 1.3 of this book introduced Kornai's theoretical framework about the merits and demerits of transition Strategy A and Strategy B of post-socialist countries. Kornai pointed out that after the sudden changes in the Soviet Union and Eastern Europe, many former socialist countries adopted Strategy B and conducted privatization of SOEs hastily with the aim of giving away those enterprises as soon as possible but ended up with no good results. Countries that adopted Strategy A, like Hungary, promoted bottom-up growth of the private sector and generated positive effects on the successful transition to a market economy. After a minor adjustment in Kornai's criteria for categorizing different strategies (i.e., analyzing the issue from the perspective of whether to focus on developing new private enterprises or to focus on transforming preexisting SOEs), his theoretical framework can be used in the analysis of the transition of socialist countries from a planned economy to a market economy.

The reform in the Soviet Union and Eastern European socialist countries and the reform in China in the late 1970s all had SOE reform as the core. Practice has shown that it is extremely difficult to transform SOEs into real enterprises. China's strategy of incremental reform created conditions for the birth of new nonstate enterprises, accelerated the accumulation of private capital, trained a large contingent of entrepreneurs, and greatly strengthened market forces. In addition, incremental reform played a positive role in preparing and promoting the readjustment of the layout of the state sector and SOE reform.

2.2.5 The Negative Outcomes of the Long-Time Practice of Incremental Reform

The strategy of incremental reform played a positive role in promoting China's reform in the 1980s. In contrast, the Soviet Union and Eastern European socialist countries fixated on the reform of the state sector. Because noticeable success in the reform of the state sector would be hard to achieve in a short term, it would be difficult for the state sector to simultaneously undergo reform and support the economic life of the whole

---

terests no longer coincide, independent interests emerge, which are fully capable of turning power into money. Such an act of corruption is very reasonable from an economic point of view. As long as the mechanism of the monetization of voucher is functioning and administrative power derived from plan is at least partially retained, it is very natural that the power to allocate various resources can be used as a sort of capital." ("A Reform Idea Drawn from the Practice of 'Granting Policy': Diao Xinshen Talks About 'Monetization of Power' in Dual-Track Economy ('Gei zhengce' yinchu de gaige silu—Diao Xinshen tan shuanggui jingji zhong de 'quanli huobihua')," *Economics Weekly (Jingjixue zhoubao),* March 5, 1989.)

[51] Gérard Roland, *Transition and Economics: Politics, Markets and Firms,* Cambridge, Mass.: MIT Press, 2000.

2

society as the dominant sector of the economy. That was why, after ten to twenty years of reform, all these countries were trapped in a predicament. By comparison, China's reform of "outside the system" preceding "inside the system" had the following three advantages: (1) the rapid development of a group of enterprises and regions with economic vigor could make people and cadres feel the effects of reform in terms of their immediate self-interest and realize that only reform would lead to vigorous development; (2) the increasingly vibrant nonstate sectors could absorb the unavoidable reform-related economic turbulence and maintain economic prosperity and political stability; and (3) the demonstration effect of and the competition pressure from nonstate sectors could promote the reform of the original state sector. In a word, the development of nonstate sectors and the development of the state sector promoted each other and created such a situation that the only way out was to maintain economic prosperity by sticking to marketization reform.

The purpose of the incremental reform strategy in China was to reduce obstacles to reform, to accumulate forces of reform, and to shorten the duration of reform so as to eventually establish a unified system of a market economy. Therefore, the state sector was sure to be reformed, after all. When the outside-the-system reform had paved the way for the all-round establishment of the institutions of a market economy, an overall and coordinated reform had to be launched in the state sector, which controlled most of the important resources of the national economy. This process ensured the all-round transition from a planned economy to a market economy. However, in the mid-1980s, when most reformers did not have a clear theoretical understanding of market-oriented reform and were still accustomed to experiments by "crossing the river by groping for the stones," it was very difficult for most people to accept the necessity of switching the reform strategy.

Because the reform strategy failed to be switched in time, intense conflicts occurred between the invigorated outside-the-system sectors and the inside-the-system sectors that were still fettered by the traditional economic system, many loopholes existed in the economic system, and stable economic development was constantly threatened. As Masahiko Aoki (1938–) pointed out in *Comparative Institutional Analysis: A New Approach to Economic System,*[52] because various institutions in a system are strategically complementary, when one or more institutions change, other institutions either change accordingly or obstruct the functioning of the new institutions due to their incompatibility with the new institutions. Therefore, system change should be of overall advance

---

[52]Masahiko Aoki and Masahiro Okuno (eds.), *Comparative Institutional Analysis: A New Approach to Economic System (Jingji tizhi de bijiao zhidu fenxi),* Chinese edition, Beijing: China Development Press, 1999, pp. 30–31, 306–310.

in nature although the change can be implemented in steps. Otherwise, the system will run only at enormous cost.

The negative effects of the sluggish reform of the state sector and the coexistence of the two tracks were mainly manifested in the following ways:

1. Financial conditions of SOEs deteriorated. Although nonstate sectors had achieved considerable progress since 1979, the development of SOEs lagged far behind, mainly for two reasons. First, the state sector retained much of the enterprise system of the traditional planned economy, its improvement in efficiency was very limited, and its output growth was mainly supported by vast inputs of resources, especially investment. Second, the state sector carried out the reform of power-delegating and profit-sharing to expand enterprise autonomy, but did not establish effective constraints of ownership and market competition, which led to insider control[53] and further softened budget constraint over SOEs.[54] Thus, the state sector as the mainstay of the national economy became increasingly feeble.

2. The pressure of inflation always existed and hyperinflation broke out from time to time. Since 1979, the rapid growth of China's economy was always accompanied by wild economic fluctuations. The persistence of a huge fiscal deficit made hyperinflation a constant threat. The fiscal deficit was the result of deteriorating financial conditions of the state sector as the main source of fiscal revenue and the lack of a complete transformation of the state fiscal system and the heavy burden of fiscal expenditure. Meanwhile, because of the coexistence of a planned economy and a market economy, the effectiveness of planning control greatly decreased while macroeconomic control compatible with the market system was yet to be established. This situation meant that the monetary authorities were unable to achieve the monetary policy goals and to maintain macroeconomic stability. These factors caused lasting pressure of hyperinflation in China's dual-track economy. Once the economic growth rate reached double digits, hyperinflation would break out soon.

3. Rampant rent-seeking activities (accumulating personal wealth by abusing public power) and administrative corruption were widespread. The coexistence of a

---

[53] A concept employed by Professor Masahiko Aoki of Stanford University in his analysis of modern corporate governance. See Masahiko Aoki, "Controlling Insider Control: Issues of Corporate Governance in Transition Economies (Dui neiburen kongzhi de kongzhi: zhuangui jingji zhong gongsi zhili jiegou de ruogan wenti) (1994)," Masahiko Aoki and Qian Yingyi (eds.), *Corporate Governance in Transitional Economies: Insider Control and the Role of Banks (Zhuangui jingji zhong de gongsi zhili jiegou: neiburen kongzhi he yinhang de zuoyong)*, Beijing: China Economic Press, 1995, pp. 15–36.

[54] The concept of soft budget constraint of SOEs was put forward by János Kornai, a Hungarian economist, in his analysis of the Hungarian economy in transition. See János Kornai, *Economics of Shortage*, Amsterdam: North-Holland Publishing Company, 1980.

command economy and a market economy provided abundant opportunities for rent-seeking activities[55] and other forms of corruption. The crucial causes of the problem were that (a) as a result of the strategy of "outside the system" preceding "inside the system," the economy had been monetized to a large extent, but administrative power that had a dominant position in the planned economy were still interfering with market transactions; (b) reform had created independent enterprises, but most resources, such as means of production, land, investment, and credit, were still under the control of the government and were still distributed by administrative means. Thus, the whole economy became a gigantic hotbed of rent-seeking activities.

4. The gap between the rich and the poor continued to widen. Since the beginning of the reform and opening up, the average income level of Chinese residents increased considerably, but the income gap among them widened rapidly as well. The main reasons were (a) the incremental reform strategy applied different policies to different regions, departments, and economic sectors, resulting in rapid widening of the income gap among different social groups; (b) the negative factors mentioned earlier, such as deteriorating financial conditions of SOEs, hyperinflation, and rampant corruption, widened the gap between the rich and the poor; and (c) huge waste and low efficiency resulting from the sluggish reform of urban industrial and commercial sectors made it impossible to create enough employment opportunities to absorb rural surplus laborers, which led to more and more agricultural laborers crowded on less and less arable land, unable to shake off poverty and attain prosperity.

In sum, sustainable and stable economic growth was threatened by the aforementioned contradictions, which, once intensified, might result in social and political upheavals.

2.3 Strategy of "Overall Advance" (1994 to Present)

Maintaining the dual-track system received praises from some people both at home and abroad[56] and was particularly supported by many local officials and SOE leaders who benefited from it. However, its limitation and negative effects became increasingly ob-

---

[55] See Wu Jinglian, "Rent-Seeking Theory and Some Negative Phenomena in China's Economy (Xunzu lilun yu wo guo jingji zhong de mou xie xiaoji xianxiang) (1988)" and "The Preface to the Second Edition of 'Corruption: Exchange between Power and Money' (Fubai: Quanli yu Jinqian de Jiaohuan zaiban qianyan)," *Corruption: Exchange between Power and Money (Fubai: quanli yu jinqian de jiaohuan),* 2nd edition, Beijing: China Economic Publishing House, 1993, pp. 1–9.

[56] John McMillan and Barry Naughton, "How to Reform a Planned Economy: Lessons from China," *Oxford Review of Economic Policy,* 1992, Vol. 8, No. 1, pp. 130–143.

vious. Initiated by Deng Xiaoping, an attempt at launching all-round reform was made in the mid-1980s.

2.3.1 The Attempt at Changing Reform Strategy and Launching All-Round Reform in 1984–1986

As an advocate of incremental reform, Deng Xiaoping did not rest on the early achievements in nonstate sectors. When nonstate sectors became strong enough to provide support to all-round reform, Deng Xiaoping proposed to shift the strategic focus of reform to the state sector.

When meeting guests from Japan in June 1984, Deng Xiaoping, as Chairman of the Military Commission of the CCCPC and Chairman of the Advisory Commission of the CCCPC, pointed out that after the success of reform in rural China, "the urban reform will include not only industry and commerce but science and technology, education, and all other fields of endeavor as well."[57] The Third Plenary Session of the 12th CCCPC, held in October 1984, discussed the implementation of this shift and adopted the *Decision of the CCCPC on Reform of the Economic Structure*. With this, the strategic focus of China's reform shifted from rural to urban areas.

Insight 2.2

The Third Plenary Session of the 12th CCCPC and *Decision on Reform of the Economic Structure*

On October 20, 1984, the 12th Central Committee of the CPC convened its Third Plenary Session in Beijing. At the session, the *Decision of the CCCPC on Reform of the Economic Structure* (hereinafter the *Decision*) was adopted "to speed up the reform of the whole economic system focusing on urban areas" and "to develop socialist commodity economy."

The *Decision* asserted that "the fundamental task of socialism is to develop social productivity. . . . Whether it promotes the growth of the productive forces . . . is the most important criterion for the success of any reform. . . . The full development of a commodity economy is an insurmountable phase in the development of the society and the economy

---

[57] Deng Xiaoping, "Building a Socialism with a Specifically Chinese Character (Jianshe you Zhongguo tese de shehuizhuyi) (June 1984)," *Selected Works of Deng Xiaoping (Deng Xiaoping wenxuan)*, Vol. 3, Beijing: People's Publishing House, 1993, p. 65.

and a necessary requirement for the realization of the economic modernization of China. Only with a fully developed commodity economy, can the whole economy be fully invigorated so that enterprises can have higher efficiency and more flexible operation to cope with the complex and changing social needs."

The *Decision* also asserted that three measures should be taken to develop a socialist commodity economy. First, a "reasonable price system that sensitively reflects changes in social labor productivity and relations between supply and demand should be established. . . . Price system reform is the key to the success of the reform of the whole economic system." Second, the separation of government administration from enterprise management and the separation of ownership and control should be realized. "Improving the vitality of enterprises, especially large- and medium-sized SOEs, is the central theme of the reform of the whole economic system focusing on urban areas." Third, diverse economic forms and business modes should be developed actively, and the guiding principle of the state, the collective, and the individual going all out should be adopted. "Diverse economic forms and business modes developing side by side is our long-term guideline and the need of the advance of socialism."

Deng Xiaoping spoke highly of the session and the *Decision*. He said that "the forthcoming Third Plenary Session of the Twelfth Central Committee will go down in Chinese history as a very important event."* "When the resolution to be adopted by the Third Plenary Session of the Twelfth Central Committee is promulgated, people will see we aim at nothing less than a comprehensive reform."** "The document on reform of the economic structure is a good one, because it explains what socialism is in terms never used by the founders of Marxism-Leninism. There are some new theories. I think it has clarified things." "I thought it read like the draft of a textbook on political economy that integrated the fundamental tenets of Marxism with the practice of socialism in China."***

(Compiled from the Party Literature Research Center of the CCCPC (ed.), *A Selection of Important Documents since the 12th National Congress of the CPC (Shierda yilai zhongyao wenxian xuanbian)*, Beijing: People's Publishing House, 1986.)

*Deng Xiaoping, "Our Magnificent Goal and Basic Policies (Women de hongwei mubiao he genben zhengce) (October 1984)," *Selected Works of Deng Xiaoping (Deng Xiaoping wenxuan)*, Vol. 3, Beijing: People's Publishing House, 1993, p. 78.

** Deng Xiaoping, "We Regard Reform as a Revolution (Women ba gaige dangzuo yizhong geming) (October 1984)," ibid, p. 82.

*** Deng Xiaoping, "Speech at the Third Plenary Session of the Central Advisory Commission of the Communist Party of China (Zai Zhongyang Guwen Weiyuanhui Di San Ci Quanti Huiyi shang de jianghua) (October 1984)," ibid., pp. 91, 83.

The *Decision of the CCCPC on Reform of the Economic Structure,* made at the Third Plenary Session of the 12th CCCPC, declared the start of all-round reform focusing on urban areas and defined establishing and developing a socialist commodity economy as the goal of reform and thus was a landmark in the history of China's reform.

To carry out the *Decision,* the *Proposal for the Seventh Five-Year Plan (1986–1990)* (hereinafter the *Proposal*) was put forward at the National Conference of the CPC in 1985. The *Proposal* demanded reform in three interrelated aspects: (a) changing enterprises into business operators with full management authority and full responsibility for profits and losses; (b) improving the market system; and (c) establishing a macroeconomic control system functioning mainly by indirect means. The *Proposal* demanded that "effort should be made to lay the foundation for a vigorous socialist economic system in the following five or more years." The Seventh Five-Year Plan formulated according to the *Proposal* defined details of the aforementioned requirements.

At the beginning of 1986, Zhao Ziyang (1919–2005), then Premier of the State Council, put forward a tentative plan of coordinated reform that focused on price, taxation, and fiscal systems. He declared that the guideline for the State Council in 1986 was to improve macroeconomic management on the premise of continuously reinforcing and improving macro-control, to improve supply conditions on the premise of restraining demands, and to make preparation for achieving a decisive progress of reform in 1987.[58] Afterwards, Zhao delivered several important speeches on the reform situation and requirements during the earlier stage of the Seventh Five-Year Plan. He pointed out that it might be harmful to let the old and new systems coexist and conflict with each other for too long a time. Therefore, significant measures should be taken to establish the dominance of the new system in 1987 and 1988. With this aim, he argued that a big stride forward was needed to establish the market system and to practice indirect control to enable enterprises to really assume full responsibility for profits and losses and to compete on a more or less equal footing. "To be more specific, next year's

---

[58] Zhao Ziyang, "Speech at the National Conference on Economic Affairs (Zai Quanguo Jingji Gongzuo Huiyi shang de jianghua)," *People's Daily (Renmin ribao),* January 13, 1986.

reform may be designed and studied in the following three aspects: price, taxation, and government finance. They are interrelated. . . . Reform of the price system is the key and other reforms should center on it."[59]

To implement the proposed coordinated reform, the State Council set up the Economic System Reform Program Design Office in April 1986. Under the direct leadership of the State Council and the CCCPC Financial and Economic Leading Group, the office drew up programs for coordinated reform during the earlier stage of the Seventh Five-Year Plan with a focus on price, taxation, government finance, banking, and foreign trade. The program for the price reform was to start with prices of the means of production in 1987. The specific measures of the price reform were similar to what Czechoslovakia adopted in the mid-1960s, which Ota Sik had introduced to his Chinese colleagues in 1981: "adjustment first and liberalization second."[60] In other words, first, adjust prices in an all-round way based on calculation; then, spend one or two years to liberalize prices in an all-round way so as to merge the two tracks. The main measures taken in the fiscal system were to change the current revenue-sharing system into a tax-sharing system, and to introduce value-added tax.[61]

In August 1986, these programs were approved at the executive meeting of the State Council and endorsed by Deng Xiaoping, who, on September 13, 1986, spoke highly of them when hearing the report of the CCCPC Financial and Economic Leading Group and instructed officials to carry them out accordingly. However, Zhao Ziyang, the leader of the State Council, changed his mind in October that year. Instead of implementing coordinated reform in price, taxation, government finance, banking, and foreign trade, he changed direction to focus on the reform of SOEs and implemented the so-called "five contracting/responsibility systems"[62] in 1987 and 1988 and thus returned to the old practice of maintaining the coexistence of a market economy and a planned economy in the hope of improving the performance of the state sector with some trivial repairs. The loss of this golden opportunity to push reform forward resulted

[59] Zhao Ziyang, "Speech at the Meeting of the CCCPC Financial and Economic Leading Group on March 13, 1986 (1986 nian 3 yue 13 ri zai Zhonggong Zhongyang Caijing Lingdao Xiaozu Huiyi shang de jianghua)" and "Speech at the Executive Meeting of the State Council on March 15, 1986 (1986 nian 3 yue 15 ri zai Guowuyuan Changwu Huiyi shang de jianghua)," *mimeograph.*

[60] Ota Sik, "On the Mode of Socialist Economy (Lun shehuizhuyi jingji moshi) (1981)," the Academic Reference Room of the Economic Research Institute of the Chinese Academy of Social Sciences (ed.), *Socialist Economic System Reform (Lun shehuizhuyi jingji tizhi gaige),* Beijing: China Law Press, 1982, pp. 105–114.

[61] Lou Jiwei, Xiao Jie, and Liu Liqun, "Some Thoughts on the Mode of Economic Operation and the Fiscal and Taxation Reform (Guanyu jingji yunxing moshi yu caizheng shuishou gaige de ruogan sikao) (1986);" Lou Jiwei and Liu Liqun, "Tentative Ideas on Reforming the Fiscal System and Solving the Deficit Problem (Gaige caizheng tizhi jiejue caizheng chizi wenti de shexiang) (1986);" Wu Jinglian, Zhou Xiaochuan et al., *Overall Design of the Reform of China's Economic System (Zhongguo jingji gaige de zhengti sheji),* Beijing: China Outlook Press, 1988, pp. 111–151.

[62] Namely, the enterprise contracting system, the department contracting system, the all-round fiscal responsibility system, the all-round foreign trade responsibility system, and the responsibility system of credit quota by region.

in the economic crisis of 1988, the political disturbances of 1989, and the ensuing resurgence of conservative thinking.[63]

Insight 2.3

Debate on Reform Strategy of 1986

In the mid-1980s, different viewpoints among economists about the direction of reform centered on whether to implement the coordinated reform programs of 1986, especially on whether to implement the price reform.

1. The Argument for Enterprise Reform as the Main Theme

Professor Li Yining (1930–) of Peking University is the chief proponent of "enterprise reform as the main theme." In early 1983, under the leadership of the Secretariat of the CCCPC, he participated in drafting the documents for the Third Plenary Session of the 12th CCCPC. In April 1986, he put forward a famous proposition that "If China's reform fails, the failure may be due to the failure in the price reform; if it succeeds, the success must be owing to the success in the ownership reform."[a]

Professor Li Yining demonstrated this proposition by saying, "The aim of the price reform is to create for economic reform an environment conducive to the development of a commodity economy, while the ownership reform, or the enterprise system reform, involves such basic issues as interests, responsibilities, and incentives."[b] At present, China's economy is in disequilibrium. "In disequilibrium, the effect of price regulation is limited, and it is unrealistic to rationalize economic relations through the price reform. The only option for our country is to carry out the ownership reform first, and then based on its initial success, to gradually improve the market system. Meanwhile, relative prices of commodities should be adjusted in several stages before the eventual launch of an

---

[63] For an explanation on this issue, see Wu Jinglian, "From 'Incremental Reform' to 'Overall Advance'—Speech at the Third Seminar of the Central Party School for Chief Leaders at the Province/Ministry Level on April 13, 1994 (Cong zengliang gaige dao zhengti tuijin de gaige zhanlüe—1994 nian 4 yue 13 ri zai Zhongyang Dangxiao Di San Qi Shengbuji Zhuyao Ganbu Yantaoban shang de fayan)," *On Building the Infrastructure of a Market Economy (Gouzhu shichang jingji de jichu jiegou)*, Beijing: China Economic Publishing House, 1997, pp. 44–56.

overall reform of the price-wage system."[c] Therefore, the sequence of reform proposed by Professor Li was to "skip the price reform and carry out the ownership reform first,"[d] to accomplish the ownership reform in about fifteen years and then to start the price reform.[e] His "ownership reform" referred to combining the standard "shareholding system" and the nonstandard "contracting system" to transform state-owned enterprises into "enterprises of public ownership that would really assume full responsibility for profits and losses"[f] by means of "contracting first and shareholding second," "shareholding first and contracting second," "both shareholding and contracting," or "shareholding without contracting."

To skip the price reform and carry out the ownership reform, "disequilibrium strategies" should be adopted to achieve "equilibrium by quota." For example, in enterprise contracting, a nonstandard approach to determine the base quota of contracting should be applied; in banking, credit quota regulation instead of interest rate regulation should be the main approach; in government finance, a combination of fiscal expenditure regulation and differential tax rate regulation should be adopted instead of pure tax rate regulation; in the commodity market, "equilibrium by quota" should be achieved through quota regulation of both supply and demand.[g] This viewpoint had been unpopular at the beginning of the debate of 1986; but after October, it was adopted by the leader of the State Council and was put into practice in 1987 and 1988.

Another arch-opponent of coordinated reform in price, taxation, and government finance was the person in charge of Capital Steel, a large SOE. He argued, in the name of the Economic Research Institute of Capital Steel, that reform should be based on contracting and reform would go astray if enterprise contracting was absent.

2. The Argument for Overall and Coordinated Reform

This viewpoint was developed in the process of designing the programs for coordinated reform in price, taxation, and government finance of 1986. As early as 1985, in their report to the leader of the State Council, a group of graduate students from the Chinese Academy of Social Sciences, Guo Shuqing, Liu Jirui, Qiu Shufang, and others, pointed out that because the dual-track system was an internally conflicting system, its long-time existence would inevitably lead to disorder in economic activities, or even abortion of reform.[h] Later, Guo Shuqing, Lou Jiwei, Liu Jirui, Xu Meizheng, and others, drafted programs for comprehensive and coordinated reform under the support of the leader of the State Council.[i] Wu Jinglian, Zhou Xiaochuan, Lou Jiwei, Li Jiange, and others, who were working for the Economic System Reform Program Design Office of the State Council, published many works on reform during the earlier stage of the Seventh Five-Year Plan. Centered on the idea of a "commodity economy" (i.e., market economy), a reform theory in the name of the "argument for coordinated reform," or the "argument for market economy," was developed.[j] The key points of this theory were as follows:

1. The fundamental characteristic of the old system is that scarce resources are allocated by administrative orders and mandatory plans. This mode of resource allocation cannot overcome the grave defects in its information mechanism and incentive mechanism and thus cannot attain high efficiency. It is superficial to diagnose the ills of the traditional system as overcentralization of power. If this mode of resource allocation by plan is not changed, any attempt to fundamentally improve the performance of the economy by power delegating and profit sharing will be doomed to failure.

2. The only substitute for the mode of resource allocation by administrative orders is the mode of resource allocation based on market mechanisms, which can overcome the defects in the information mechanism and incentive mechanism of a command economy and most efficiently allocate and utilize economic resources.

3. A market economy is an integral system consisting of three parts: (a) enterprises with full management authority and full responsibility for profits and losses; (b) a competitive market system; and (c) a macroeconomic control system that regulates mainly through the market. These three parts are interconnected and interwoven. Hence, economic reform should be carried out simultaneously and with coordination among these three related parts.[k]

[a] Li Yining, "Basic Ideas on Economic Reform—Speech at the Symposium in Commemoration of the May 4th Movement at Peking University on April 25, 1986 (Jingji gaige de jiben silu—1986 nian 4 yue 25 ri zai Beijing Daxue Wusi Kexue Taolunhui shang de baogao)," *Ideas on China's Economic Reform (Zhongguo jingji gaige de silu)*, Beijing: China Outlook Press, 1989, p. 3.

[b] Ibid.

[c] Li Yining, "Further Explanation on Basic Ideas on Economic Reform—Answers to the Questions Raised at the End of 'Management of National Economy' Course by Participants of the Professional Training Program

for Cadres at the School of Economics of Peking University on June 2, 1987 (Guanyu jingji gaige jiben silu de jin yi bu shuoming—1987 nian 6 yue 2 ri zai Guomin Jingji Guanlixue Kecheng jieshu qian dui Beijing Daxue Jingji Xueyuan Ge Ban Ganbu Zhuanxiuban xueyuan suoti wenti de huida)," *Ideas on China's Economic Reform (Zhongguo jingji gaige de silu),* 1989, p. 315.

[d] *Financial News (Jinrong shibao),* January 18, 1988.

[e] *Theoretical Information Daily (Lilun xinxi bao),* November 3, 1986. See also *Financial News (Jinrong shibao),* December 3, 1987.

[f] "The Focus of Deepening Reform Is the Reform of Forms of Public Ownership—A Talk with Li Yining, a Famous Economist (Shenhua gaige de zhongdian shi gongyouzhi xingshi de gaige—zhuming jingjixuejia Li Yining de yi ci tanhua)," *Financial News (Jinrong shibao),* December 3, 1987.

[g] Li Yining, *Chinese Economy in Disequilibrium (Feijunheng de Zhongguo jingji),* Beijing: Economic Daily Press, 1990.

[h] Guo Shuqing, Liu Jirui, and Qiu Shufang, "All-Round Reform Urgently Needs an Overall Plan—an Important Issue Concerning the Success or Failure of Reform (Quanmian gaige jixu zongti guihua—shiguan wo guo gaige chengbai de yige zhongda wenti)," *Comparison of Economic and Social Systems (Jingji shehui tizhi bijiao),* 1985, No.1.

[i] Guo Shuqing, Lou Jiwei, Liu Jirui, et al., "Study on the Overall Plan of System Reform (Guanyu tizhi gaige zongti guihua de yanjiu) (August 1985)," *Review of Economic Research (Jingji yanjiu cankao ziliao),* 1986, No. 35.

[j] Wu Jinglian, Zhou Xiaochuan, et al., *Overall Design of the Reform of China's Economic System (Zhongguo jingji gaige de zhengti sheji),* Beijing: China Outlook Press, 1988.

[k] Wu Jinglian, "Economic Mechanisms and Coordinated Reform (Jingji jizhi he peitao gaige) (1985)," *Selected Works of Wu Jinglian (Wu Jinglian xuanji),* Taiyuan: Shanxi People's Publishing House, 1989.

2.3.2 The Third Plenary Session of the 14th CCCPC Started a New Era of Overall Advance of Reform

After the economic crisis of 1988 and the political disturbances of 1989, some conservative statesmen and theorists blamed these upheavals on market-oriented reform. They branded "abolishing the planned economy and realizing marketization" as "changing the socialist system and implementing a capitalist system."[64] Accordingly, another resurgence of conservative thinking occurred. A new upsurge of the reform and opening up did not take place until the beginning of 1992, when Deng Xiaoping made his famous South China speeches[65] to promote the reform and opening up.

In October 1992, the 14th National Congress of the CPC set the reform target of establishing a socialist market economy. In November 1993, the *Decision on Issues Regarding the Establishment of a Socialist Market Economic System* was adopted at the Third Ple-

[64] Wang Renzhi, "About Anti-Bourgeois Liberalization—Speech at the Symposium on Party Construction Theory on December 15, 1989 (Guanyu fandui zichanjieji ziyouhua—1989 nian 12 yue 15 ri zai Dangjian Lilun Yanjiuban de jianghua)," *Seeking Truth (Qiushi),* 1990, No. 4.

[65] Deng Xiaoping, "Excerpts from Talks Given in Wuchang, Shenzhen, Zhuhai and Shanghai (Zai Wuchang, Shenzhen, Zhuhai, Shanghai dengdi de tanhua yaodian) (January–February 1992)," *Selected Works of Deng Xiaoping (Deng Xiaoping wenxuan),* Vol. 3, Beijing: People's Publishing House, 1993, pp. 370–383.

nary Session of the 14th CCCPC, and important breakthroughs were made on the following issues.

First, a new reform strategy of "overall advance with key breakthroughs" was explicitly put forward, demanding that the reform should not be confined to peripheral issues, but firmly carried out in the state sector and that a socialist market economic system should begin to take shape by the end of the twentieth century.

Second, a blueprint was made for reforms in five key areas of the fiscal and taxation system, the banking system, the foreign exchange control system, the enterprise system, and the social security system.

From the beginning of 1994, the Chinese government took important measures to implement reforms in these five key areas. Meanwhile, the State Council ordered that experiments be conducted in establishing a modern enterprise system according to the *Company Law* to gain experience before implementation nationwide. Since then, China's reform entered a new stage of overall advance.

Insight 2.4

The Third Plenary Session of the 14th CCCPC and *Decision on Issues Regarding the Establishment of a Socialist Market Economic System*

From November 11 to 14, 1993, the Third Plenary Session of the 14th CCCPC was held. The session discussed and adopted the *Decision on Issues Regarding the Establishment of a Socialist Market Economic System* (hereinafter the *Decision*), which provided a comprehensive and systematic presentation of reform targets. The *Decision* was divided into ten parts: (1) new situation and tasks facing China's economic system reform; (2) transform the operation mechanism of SOEs and establish a modern enterprise system; (3) cultivate and develop a market system; (4) change government functions and establish and improve a macroeconomic control system; (5) establish a reasonable income distribution and social security system; (6) deepen the reform of the rural economic system; (7) deepen the reform of the system of foreign economic relations and extend the scope of opening to the outside world; (8) further reform the system of science and technology and the education system; (9) intensify the construction of the legal system; and (10) strengthen and improve the leadership of the party and strive for the target of preliminarily establishing a socialist market economic system by the end of the twentieth century.

The *Decision* proposed a reform strategy of "combining overall advance with key breakthroughs" and demanded that "care must be taken to make gradual and orderly advance of reform and opportunity must be seized to make breakthroughs in key areas to drive the overall reform situation."

The *Decision* defined the goals and implementation programs of reform for subsystems of a socialist market economy in fiscal and taxation, banking, foreign exchange control, enterprises, and social security. They were:

1. Establishment of a New Fiscal and Taxation System

To transform the existing fiscal responsibility system (also called the central-local fiscal responsibility system) into a "tax-sharing system" based on a rationalized division of power and responsibility between the central and local governments.

To standardize the taxation system in accordance with the principle of unified tax law, equitable tax burden, simplified tax structure, and fair division of power so as to establish a taxation system that meets the requirement of a market economy in order to promote fair competition.

2. Reform of the Financial/Banking System

To establish a banking system in which state-owned commercial banks are kept as the mainstay, diverse forms of financial institutions are allowed to develop side by side, and policy-related banking is separated from commercial banking; also to establish a unified and open system of financial markets with orderly competition and strict regulation.

Specific tasks include: (a) to establish a central bank system that can carry out monetary policy independently under the leadership of the central government; (b) to commercialize the operation of the existing state-owned specialized banks and diversify commercial banks; and (c) to set up policy banks such as the China Development Bank, the Export-Import Bank of China, and the Agricultural Development Bank of China so as to take over the policy-related business previously done by the specialized banks of raising funds at low interest rates for those projects of long construction cycle, low profitability, but significant externalities within a state-designated scope.

3. Reform of the Foreign Exchange Control System

China's central government decided to take two steps in reforming the foreign exchange control system. First, to abolish the dual exchange rate system in domestic and foreign enterprises in sequence for merging the two exchange rates and achieving the managed convertibility of RMB under the current account. Second, to abolish control over capital flow and make RMB a fully convertible currency when the time is right.

4. Reform of SOEs

The *Decision* pointed out that "the operation mechanism of SOEs must be further transformed and a modern enterprise system, which is characterized by clearly established property rights, well defined power and responsibility, separation of enterprise from government, and scientific management, must be established." Later, the *Company Law of the People's Republic of China* was passed by the National People's Congress according to the *Decision*.

5. Establishment of a New Social Security System

It was decided to set up a multi-layer social security system to include social insurance, social relief, social welfare, special care and placement, social mutual aid, and private saving security, in which a system combining social pooling funds with individual accounts was to be instituted for old-age pension and medical insurance for urban workers.

(Compiled from the Party Literature Research Center of the CCCPC (ed.), *A Selection of Important Documents since the 14th National Congress of the CPC (Shisida yilai zhongyao wenxian xuanbian)*, Beijing: People's Publishing House, 1996.)

2.3.3 In-Depth Development of the Strategy of Overall Advance

By the mid-1990s, China's reform had made significant progress in establishing a macroeconomic control system and adjusting the ownership structure. The fundamental indicator of the progress was that the state sector no longer monopolized the whole economy, and its share in the national economy was significantly reduced. However, the bottleneck to reform—the establishment of the ownership foundation of a market economy—had not been broken. As late as 1993, most scarce economic resources were still in the hands of the government and SOEs, despite the fact that the state sector accounted for less than half of GDP. One example was that the state sector consumed more than 70 percent of bank loans. In addition, the dominance of the government and SOEs in the national economy made it impossible to establish a sound banking system, a sound fiscal and taxation system, etc., which were compatible with a market economy.

The root cause of this situation was that the old state sector, or the State Syndicate as proposed in Lenin's *State and Revolution,* or the Party-State Inc. in modern language, is the core of the old system, and vested interests attached to it are deep-rooted. Some people, especially elites of the society, have high stakes in maintaining this system. If people with vested interests in the old system do not care about the interests of the entire society as much as they care about their own, they will use all kinds of excuses (including political excuses) to block the process of reform and restructuring of the state sector. Therefore, reform and restructuring will encounter a great deal of resistance.

Another historic breakthrough in reform of the state sector was made at the 15th National Congress of the CPC in 1997. At the congress, the Soviet viewpoint that "the higher the proportion of the state sector in the national economy, the better" was discarded; keeping public ownership as the mainstay of the economy and allowing diverse forms of ownership to develop side by side was stipulated as the basic economic system in the primary stage of socialism for at least one hundred years.

Accordingly, the third-generation leader Jiang Zemin called for adjustment and improvement of the ownership structure of the national economy and the establishment of a long-term basic economic system based on the criterion of the three favorables (i.e., whether it promotes the growth of productive forces in a socialist society, increases the overall strength of the socialist state, and raises the people's living standards). The three items of adjustment were (a) to reduce the scope of the state sector and to withdraw state capital from industries nonessential to the national economy; (b) to seek various forms for materializing public ownership that can greatly promote the growth of the productive forces and to develop diverse forms of public ownership; and (c) to encourage the development of nonpublic sectors of the economy such as the individual business sector and the private sector and to make them important components of a socialist market economy.

In 1998, the aforementioned decision of the 15th National Congress of the CPC was incorporated into the *Amendments to the Constitution of the People's Republic of China,* specifically, "In the primary stage of socialism, the State upholds the basic economic system of keeping public ownership as the mainstay of the economy and allowing diverse forms of ownership to develop side by side. . . . Nonpublic sectors of the economy, such as the individual business sector and the private sector, within the limits prescribed by law, are important components of a socialist market economy. . . . The State protects the lawful rights and interests of the individual business sector and the private sector."

Insight 2.5

The 15th National Congress of the CPC and Jiang Zemin's Report

From September 12 to 18, 1997, the 15th National Congress of the CPC was held in Beijing. Jiang Zemin delivered a report entitled *Hold High the Great Banner of Deng Xiaoping Theory for an All-Round Advance of the Cause of Building Socialism with Chinese Characteristics into the Twenty-First Century* (hereinafter the *Report*). The most important breakthrough in the *Report* was the announcement that "keeping public ownership as the mainstay of the economy and allowing diverse forms of ownership to develop side by side" is the basic economic system in the primary stage of socialism for at least one hundred years. The *Report* also called for adjustment and improvement of the ownership structure according to the principle that "any form of ownership that meets the criterion of the "three favorables"* can and should be utilized to serve socialism."

Although the *Report* repeated existing propositions, such as "public ownership playing a dominant role" and "the state sector playing a leading role," it redefined their meanings and outlined the execution of adjusting the ownership structure in details, specifically:

1. Adjust the layout of the state sector by "advancing in some areas while retreating from others." The state needs to control only "major industries and key areas that concern the lifelines of the national economy. . . . Even if the state-owned sector accounts for a smaller proportion of the economy, this will not affect the socialist nature of our country." **

2. Strive to seek various forms for materializing public ownership that can greatly promote the growth of the productive forces. "All man-

agement methods and organizational forms that mirror the laws governing socialized production may be utilized boldly."

3. "Nonpublic sectors are important components of a socialist market economy. Nonpublic sectors of the economy, such as the individual business sector and the private sector, should be continuously encouraged and guided so as to ensure their sound development."

(Compiled from Jiang Zemin, *Hold High the Great Banner of Deng Xiaoping Theory for an All-Round Advance of the Cause of Building Socialism with Chinese Characteristics into the Twenty-First Century—the Report to the Fifteenth National Congress of the CPC (Gaoju Deng Xiaoping lilun weida qizhi, ba jianshe you Zhongguo tese shehuizhuyi shiye quanmian tuixiang 21 shiji—zai Zhongguo Gongchandang Di Shiwu Ci Quanguo Daibiao Dahui shang de baogao)* (September 1997), Beijing: People's Publishing House, 1997; and other materials.)

*In his South China speeches in 1992, Deng Xiaoping proposed that "The chief criterion for making that judgment should be whether it promotes the growth of the productive forces in a socialist society, increases the overall strength of the socialist state and raises living standards." See Deng Xiaoping, "Excerpts from Talks Given in Wuchang, Shenzhen, Zhuhai and Shanghai (Zai Wuchang, Shenzhen, Zhuhai, Shanghai dengdi de tanhua yaodian) (January–February 1992)," *Selected Works of Deng Xiaoping (Deng Xiaoping wenxuan)*, Vol. 3, Beijing: People's Publishing House, 1993, p. 372.

**Decision on Several Important Issues Regarding Reform and Development of State-Owned Enterprises* (*Guanyu guoyou qiye gaige he fazhan ruogan zhongda wenti de jueding)*, by the Fourth Plenary Session of the 15th CCCPC in 1999, defined four fields in which the state sector should have control. They are (a) industries related to national security, (b) industries of natural monopolies, (c) industries providing important public goods and services, and (d) key enterprises in backbone industries and high-tech industries.

At the turn of the twenty-first century, an outline for a market economy based on mixed ownership emerged (see Table 2.5).

At this moment, the issue about how to ensure that the market economy established in China was a good market economy instead of a bad market economy was raised. In other words, social and political reforms in line with marketization reform were placed on the agenda.

Such demand has been echoed by the decisions of leading organs of the party and the government. In 1997, the 15th National Congress of the CPC called for "building a socialist country under the rule of law." In 2002, the 16th National Congress of the CPC put forward requirements to push political reform forward, to promote political civilization, to develop democratic politics, and to build a country under the rule of law.

Table 2.5   GDP by Ownership (%)*

Year	State Sector	Collective Sector	Nonpublic Sectors**
1990	47.7	18.5	33.8
1995	42.1	20.2	37.7
1996	40.4	21.3	38.3
1997	38.4	22.1	39.5
1998	38.9	19.3	41.9
1999	37.4	18.4	44.2
2000	37.3	16.5	46.2
2001	37.9	14.6	47.5

*Quoted from Xu Xiaonian and Xiao Qian, "Another New Economy (Ling yi zhong xinjingji)," *Report of the Research Department of China International Capital Corporation Limited (Zhongguo Guoji Jinrong Youxian Gongsi Yanjiubu baogao),* 2003.
**Nonpublic sectors refer to the collection of all nonstate and noncollective economic entities.
Source: The National Bureau of Statistics, *China Statistical Yearbook (Zhongguo tongji nianjian),* Beijing: China Statistics Press, various years.

The *Decision on Issues Regarding the Improvement of the Socialist Market Economic System* by the Third Plenary Session of the 16th CCCPC in September 2003 was a programmatic document for social and political reforms. It indicated that China's economic, social, and political reforms will continue to advance in an all-round way in the future.

PART 2

REFORM IN DIFFERENT SECTORS

CHAPTER 3

RURAL REFORM

From the mid-1950s to the end of the 1970s, the focus of China's reform was placed on state-owned industry and commerce with no breakthrough being made. The new situation of "an enchanting sight in spring time" for China's economy appeared only in the autumn of 1980 when the household contracting system (*jiating chengbao jingyingzhi*)[1] was implemented on a large scale in rural China. Therefore, rural reform was the genuine starting point and the driving force of China's economic reform. The purpose of this chapter is to analyze the causes and achievements of rural reform as well as the prospects for future reform and development in rural China.

3.1 The Agricultural Operation System before the Contracting System Reform

Experiences in the agricultural development of various countries show that the family farm system is the operation system best suited for agricultural production. This mode of operation works best for agriculture because of some specific features of agricultural production. As pointed out by economist Chen Xiwen, agricultural production is characterized by two salient features. First, agricultural production processes are integrated with the life processes of animals and plants; the production processes of agriculture in its narrow sense (crop cultivation) are integrated with the life processes of plants whereas the production processes of agriculture beyond its narrow sense (animal husbandry and fishery) are integrated with the life processes of animals. This requires that the producer constantly and carefully look after the life and growth of animals and plants as the object of his labor and make appropriate intervention in accordance with their growth conditions. Second, agricultural production is greatly affected by climate and other natural processes, such as sunshine, temperature, precipitation, and air currents, all of which are beyond human control and ever changing. These features pose special requirements for agricultural producers in contrast to their industrial counterparts. The conditions of

---

[1] Also called the household responsibility system (*jiating zerenzhi*), the responsibility system in agricultural production (*nongye shengchan zerenzhi*), etc.

animals and plants and information about natural changes in sunshine, temperature, precipitation, and air currents must be closely monitored in real time, and decisions must be correspondingly made in a timely fashion. As such, for agricultural producers (laborers) to possess total control, including specific control and residual control, is the most effective institutional arrangement.[2]

Of course, it may be feasible and efficient to have an institutional arrangement in which the owner mainly engages in management while direct production activities are conducted mainly by employed laborers. However, the issue of effective incentive is difficult to resolve when agricultural production activities are conducted mainly by employed laborers. In agricultural production, since the life processes of animals and plants are continuous, only the total effort made by the laborer can manifest itself as the final output of those animals and plants. This situation differs from manufacturing where the quantity and quality of the effort by each laborer in each phase of the production process can be measured. If the measurement of agricultural laborers' efforts is made without reference to the final output, that is, without each laborer working on the entire lifecycle of those living things, it is impossible to accurately measure each laborer's effort. The issue is further complicated because agricultural production jobs vary a great deal according to line of business, location, and season. However, if agricultural production activities are conducted on a household basis, the incentive issue is very easy to solve. As a family is a close-knit entity with common economic interests, the differences in objectives and conflicts of interest among family members are minimal, and they rarely give thought to the effort and income of individual family members, transaction costs are significantly reduced.

Specifically, household operation has several advantages.

- It results in the optimal labor combination. Household coordination hardly has any transaction costs because family members share common objectives and have harmony of interests.

- It has a very low decision-making cost. Most family decisions are collectively made by key members with sufficient information. Family decision making has the advantages of being quick, flexible, convenient, and authoritative, and is easily adaptable to changes in circumstances.

---

[2] Chen Xiwen, *Rural Reform in China: Retrospect and Prospect (Zhongguo nongcun gaige: huigu yu zhanwang),* Tianjin: Tianjin People's Publishing House, 1993, pp. 57–60. Specific control and residual control can be separately owned, as in the case of a modern corporation where ownership (residual claim and residual control) and control (specific control) are held by shareholders and executives respectively.

- It has a strong capacity to bear risks. The blood ties among family members result in very strong cohesion, and the calculation of return on investment in the family farm is usually adequate.

- It simplifies distribution of income within the family, which not only saves distribution cost but also avoids the costs of measurement, calculation, division, and supervision.

- It has low management cost, low labor organizing cost, and low opportunity-taking cost.

All in all, since the family is the basic economic cell of society, which integrates production, consumption, education, and fostering of children and has enduring stability, the natural division of labor within the family reduces decision-making costs and minimizes measurement, supervision, and other transaction costs. All these have given household operation unparalleled superiority over other modes of operation in agricultural production. Thus, as stated by economist Justin Y. Lin and his colleagues, "Because agriculture does not display many characteristics of a scale economy, and because supervising and measuring agricultural work is difficult, agriculture is suitable for household operations."[3]

In socialist countries, the argument that collective agriculture is superior to household agriculture used to be prevalent. Even those who maintained a relatively open attitude toward the farmer issue and opposed the practice of "cooperative transformation first and mechanization second" were motivated by the belief that because productive forces determine relations of production, collectivization is the inevitable result of mechanization, and what they opposed was not collectivization per se, but the change in relations of production running ahead of the development of productive forces. After the household contracting system was implemented in rural China, many people still believed that this system was a measure of expediency adopted only when agricultural productivity was low. Agriculture would certainly "go collective" again when agricultural productivity improved and agricultural production mechanized. All these views shared a common theoretical basis in an assertion made by Karl Marx based on conditions in the United Kingdom that large-scale production was superior to small-scale production in agriculture, and therefore nationwide agricultural operation would generate greater momentum to production. In fact, as early as the end of the nineteenth century, a debate over whether large-scale production was superior to small-scale production in

[3]Justin Y. Lin, Cai Fang, and Li Zhou, *The China Miracle: Development Strategy and Economic Reform,* Revised edition, Hong Kong: The Chinese University Press, 2003, p. 143.

agriculture occurred in the socialist movement. At that time, such leading figures in the Social Democratic Party as Edward David (1863–1930) and Edward Bernstein (1850–1932) raised doubts about Karl Marx's assertion and said that peasant economy with the family as the unit had the potential for further development. Karl Kautsky (1854–1938) pointed out in his book, *The Agrarian Question,*[4] that large-scale production can be necessarily superior to small-scale production in agriculture only when other conditions are the same. Lenin expressed his assent to Kautsky's view in his book, *Development of Capitalism in Russia.*[5] The development of agriculture in developed countries in the twentieth century indicates that even when agriculture is mechanized and highly socialized, the family farm system still has superiority and vitality. The UK, where the corporate farm system with wage labor was once implemented, has now returned to the family farm system, which is a powerful testimony that household operation is superior in agricultural production.

3.1.1 From Cooperatives to People's Communes

On completion of the Agrarian Reform of 1948 to 1952 in all regions of China, through which each rural resident obtained a share of land, Chinese agriculture was confronted with a choice between two paths of development. At that time, two groups held opposing views within the leadership of the Communist Party of China (CPC). Supported by Liu Shaoqi, one group included Deng Zihui, leader in charge of rural affairs in the Central Committee of the Communist Party of China (CCCPC), among others. This group was faithful to the guiding principle confirmed at the Seventh National Congress of the CPC in 1945, which dictated that realization of socialism should take two steps: first, to develop the new democracy, to be followed by the second step, a march toward socialism. They believed that farmers should be given the freedom to buy and sell land, lease land, hire labor, and borrow money and that the idea to immediately shake, weaken, or deny the foundation of private ownership and collectivize agriculture would be a mistaken, dangerous, and unrealistic thought of agrarian socialism. Represented by Mao Zedong, the other group believed that the Agrarian Reform had already completed the democratic revolution; therefore, "composing the article of socialist revolution" should be put on the agenda. Their approach was to energetically promote mutual aid teams and cooperatives to achieve the "socialist transformation of agriculture."[6]

---

[4] Karl Kautsky, *The Agrarian Question (Tudi wenti)* (1899), Chinese edition, Shanghai: The Commercial Press, 1936.
[5] Vladimir Lenin, "Preface to 'Development of Capitalism in Russia' ('Eguo zibenzhuyi de fazhan' xuyan) (1908)," *Complete Works of Lenin (Liening quanji)*, Chinese edition, Vol. 3, Beijing: People's Publishing House, 1959.
[6] Conversation between Mao Zedong, Deng Zihui, and Du Runsheng in November 1952. See Du Runsheng, "My Recollection of Several Meetings between Mao Zedong and Me in the 1950s (Yi wushi niandai wo yu Mao Zedong de jici huimian)," *Collected Works of Du Runsheng (Du Runsheng wenji)*, Taiyuan: Shanxi People's Publishing House, 1998, p. 784.

The result of this contention was a campaign launched by Mao Zedong in mid-1955 against the "Right opportunism" of Deng Zihui, leader in charge of rural affairs and head of the Rural Work Department of the CCCPC, and others and then an "upsurge of socialism in rural areas" promoted by party and government organs at various levels. The reason for Mao Zedong to choose the second path was related to two more important choices he made in 1952 that involved the entire national economy:

1. the decision to immediately start the transition to socialism and a planned economy at the end of 1952 and the beginning of 1953 and

2. the decision to implement industrialization with priority given to the development of heavy industry during the First Five-Year Plan, starting in 1953.

In this context, it became necessary to organize farmers into collective economic organizations under state control so that the state could obtain, by nonmarket means, capital, grain, and raw materials indispensable to industrialization with priority given to heavy industry.

Mao Zedong repeatedly mentioned that "large amounts of funds are needed to accomplish both national industrialization and the technical transformation of agriculture, and a considerable part of these funds has to be accumulated through agriculture."[7] "Without enough food and other daily necessities, it would be impossible to provide for the workers in the first place, and then what sense would it make to talk about developing heavy industry?"[8] As early as January 1952, Chen Yun, Secretary of the Secretariat of the CCCPC in charge of economic affairs, pointed out that grain harvests would not be enough for many years to come, and "therefore, compulsory purchase of grain is necessary. . . . At present, we need to do the preparatory work. During the summer harvest of 1952, a combination of cooperative-mobilized purchase and local government compulsory purchase should be adopted in key regions for experiment to see how it works. If the experiment is successful, compulsory purchase shall be expanded after the autumn of 1952 and be gradually implemented nationwide."[9] In October 1952, it was declared that starting in December 1952, planned purchase and marketing (i.e., unified purchase and marketing (tonggou tongxiao)) of grain was to be implemented nationwide, in which all surplus grain would be gathered by the state at a state-stipulated

---

[7]Mao Zedong, "On the Cooperative Transformation of Agriculture (Guanyu nongye hezuohua wenti) (July 31, 1955)," *Selected Works of Mao Zedong (Mao Zedong xuanji)*, Vol. 5, Beijing: People's Publishing House, 1977, p. 182.

[8]Mao Zedong, "On the Ten Major Relationships (Lun shida guanxi)," *Selected Works of Mao Zedong (Mao Zedong xuanji)*, Vol. 5, Beijing: People's Publishing House, 1977, p. 268.

[9]Chen Yun, "Guidelines and Tasks for the Financial and Economic Work in 1952 (1952 nian caijing gongzuo de fangzhen he renwu)," *Selected Works of Chen Yun (Chen Yun wenxuan) (1949–1956)*, Vol. 2, Beijing: People's Publishing House, 1984, p. 160.

price. Later, Chen Yun stated that "if we continue with free-market purchase, I am afraid that the Central People's Government would have to be a 'beggar' everyday and have as a hard time as 'the last day of the lunar year'[10] everyday." He said that before implementing unified purchase and marketing, he had pondered deeply over the idea to determine whether it would have caused any trouble. "However, in retrospect, if it had not been so, what then should have been done? The only way out would have been to use all foreign exchange to import grain. But then there would have been no money to buy machinery equipment, and there would have been no national construction, nor establishment of industries."[11] Therefore, in October 1952, before carrying out the First Five-Year Plan, the Chinese government decided to implement unified purchase and marketing of agricultural products such as grain and cotton.

When there were tens of millions of independent rural households, it was very hard to implement unified purchase and marketing. As the unified purchase price was usually lower than the market price, compulsory purchase by the government met with strong resistance from individual farmers who the government could hardly control. In 1954, social unrest related to grain occurred in both urban and rural areas, with "every family talking about grain and everybody commenting on unified purchase." This resulted in the necessity to "organize" farmers to further bring them under control. Accordingly, Mao Zedong launched a socialist upsurge of the cooperative transformation of agriculture (i.e., the Cooperative Transformation Campaign) in 1955. This campaign started with criticism of the "Right opportunism" represented by Deng Zihui. Under the strong pressure of this political campaign, it took only about one year to abrogate the family farm system in agriculture and achieve the "advanced cooperative transformation." Under the condition that cooperative members could freely join and withdraw, agricultural cooperatives, as a mutual aid and cooperative organization of laborers, were able to solve the problems of labor supervision and measurement by the so-called "self-enforcing contract."[12] During the initial period of the mutual aid and cooperation campaign in China before 1955, when "mutual aid teams (*huzhuzu*)" and "elementary cooperatives (*chujishe*)" were basically organized voluntarily by farmers and when they were few in number, these elementary cooperatives showed some institutional efficiency and agricultural production increased. However, the Cooperative Transformation Campaign, launched in 1955, changed the nature of cooperatives from

---

[10] In old China, the last day of the lunar year was the usual deadline for repayment of debts and thus a terrible time for the poor.
[11] Chen Yun, "Implementing Unified Purchase and Marketing of Grain (Shixing liangshi tonggou tongxiao) (October 10, 1953)," *Selected Works of Chen Yun (Chen Yun wenxuan) (1949–1956)*, Vol. 2, Beijing: People's Press, 1984, pp. 208–211.
[12] Justin Y. Lin, "Collectivization and China's Agricultural Crisis in 1959–1961 (Jitihua yu Zhongguo 1959–1961 nian de nongye weiji) (1990)," *Institution, Technology and Agricultural Development in China (Zhidu, jishu yu Zhongguo nongye fazhan)*, Shanghai: Shanghai People's Publishing House and Shanghai Joint Publishing, 1994, pp. 16–43.

elementary ones with voluntary participation to quasi-state-owned "advanced cooperatives (*gaojishe*)" organized under social coercion. At the end of 1955, there were only five hundred advanced cooperatives nationwide with member households accounting for 3.45 percent of the total number of rural households. By the end of 1956, one year after launching the Cooperative Transformation Campaign, 540,000 advanced cooperatives existed with member households accounting for 88 percent of the total number of rural households. Advanced cooperative transformation was fully achieved by the winter of 1957, and 120 million rural households nationwide were organized into 753,000 advanced cooperatives.[13]

In "advanced agricultural producers' cooperatives" (i.e., advanced cooperatives), the property of the individual farmers were merged into indivisible collective property. Under conditions where members were not allowed to freely withdraw and cooperatives were managed by cadres, cooperatives were no longer different from state-owned enterprises, except that the state was not responsible for paying out wages. Nevertheless, the scale of these advanced cooperatives was relatively small, with each cooperative comprised of only one hundred to two hundred households, and they were established separately from the grassroots governments. For the "convenience for exercising leadership," the CCCPC issued a directive on March 30, 1958, requesting that small cooperatives be consolidated into larger ones. Liu Shaoqi named these larger cooperatives "communes." In July 1958, Mao Zedong formally called for merging advanced cooperatives into "people's communes" that were "large in size and public in ownership" and "integrating government administration with commune management." Hence, a campaign of "organizing people's communes on a big scale" (i.e., the People's Communes Campaign) was launched nationwide. By the autumn of 1958, the entire rural China had been switched over to people's communes.

At the beginning, the people's commune implemented "one-level accounting," that is, pure commune ownership, and land and other means of production previously owned by advanced cooperatives were transferred to the commune and allocated by the commune in a unified way; the labor force of the entire commune was organized according to military establishment and allocated by the commune in a unified way. Based on this property rights system, unified management, unified distribution, and unified responsibility for profits and losses of the commune were thus implemented. Farmers were organized in the commune as a military organization with such stringent discipline that even meals were taken in public canteens.

---

[13]Justin Y. Lin, *Institution, Technology and Agricultural Development in China (Zhidu, jishu yu Zhongguo nongye fazhan)*, Shanghai: Shanghai People's Publishing House and Shanghai Joint Publishing, 1994, pp. 19–21.

Insight 3.1

The People's Communes Campaign

On July 1, 1958, speaking at a mass rally to celebrate "July 1st" at Peking University, Chen Boda conveyed the latest directive from Mao Zedong, "Comrade Mao Zedong said that our direction should be to organize gradually and orderly the 'industry, agriculture, commerce, education, and defense' into a big commune, thereby forming the basic unit of the Chinese society." On August 9, 1958, during his countryside inspection in Shandong Province, Mao Zedong said that "You had better set up a people's commune; its advantage is that it can integrate industry, agriculture, commerce, education, and defense, which is of convenience for exercising leadership." From August 17 to 30, the Political Bureau of the CCCPC convened an enlarged meeting in Beidaihe, a coastal summer resort. In addition to calling on the party and the people to make the greatest efforts to achieve the objectives of the Great Leap Forward, the resolution of the meeting also pointed out that "The people's commune will be the best form of organization for construction of socialism and gradual transition to communism. . . . The realization of communism in China is no longer something distant in future, and we should actively make use of the form of the people's commune to try to find out a specific approach to communism."

Afterwards, a large-scale campaign of switching over to people's communes (the "People's Communes Campaign" in short) rapidly sprang up in rural China. By the end of October 1958, more than 740,000 advanced cooperatives had been reorganized into 26,000 people's communes, with, on average, 28.5 advanced cooperatives merged into one people's commune and more than 4,500 rural households in each commune. After advanced cooperatives merged into people's communes, all public properties of the original advanced cooperatives were handed over to the communes. Commune members handed in all their private plots together with all other means of production, such as private house sites, draught animals, and forests; they were allowed to retain only a small quantity of livestock and poultry. The commune set up production brigades (later called administrative districts) as units of production management and economic accounting, but the commune took the sole responsibility for profits and losses of all the production brigades. It was also stipulated that the workpoint system (*gongfenzhi*) should be uniformly implemented as the basis for compensation; at the same time, the free supply system (*gongjizhi*) of grain was to be practiced, i.e., grain was to be supplied to households for free according to the number of persons instead of the number of laborers in each household; and a public canteen was to be established for each production team.

However, many serious problems soon emerged in the People's Communes Campaign and this compulsory institutional change of switching over to people's communes brought disastrous consequences. Grain output declined by 15 percent in 1959 and it further decreased by 10 percent in 1960. Combined urban and rural grain consumption per capita dropped from 203 kilograms in 1957 to 163.5 kilograms in 1960—a drop by 19.5 percent; grain consumption per capita in rural areas dropped even more, by 23.4 percent. As a result, edema caused by malnutrition was prevalent among urban residents and millions of people died of starvation in rural areas.* Therefore, agriculture became the sector that suffered most under the planned economic system. The superiority of the people's commune was questioned by most farmers. This situation forced the state to retreat from its original policy.

In February 1959, the Political Bureau of the CCCPC decided to reduce the size of people's communes and the total number of them was consequently increased from 26,000 to 75,000. From 1960 to 1962, the CCCPC decided that the people's commune should implement a system of "three-level ownership with the production team as the basic accounting unit." After 1961, commune members were allowed to operate small private plots and small-scale household sideline production. After February 1962, production teams (average size ranging from twenty to thirty households, equivalent to an elementary agricultural producers' cooperative) became the primary owner of collective properties.

In 1979, after the "Decade of Turmoil,"** starting with the Xiangyang Commune in Guanghan County, Sichuan Province, the reform of separating government administration from commune management was launched. After 1980, the household contracting system was widely adopted in rural China; at the same time, separation of government administration from commune management was also implemented. As of 1984, more than 99 percent of people's communes nationwide had completed the process of separating government administration from commune management, and 91,000 township/town governments and 926,000 villagers' committees were established. As a result, people's communes no longer existed.

(Compiled from the State Commission for Restructuring Economic Systems, *A Decade of Economic System Reform in China (Zhongguo jingji tizhi gaige shi nian),* Beijing: Economic Management Press and Reform Press, 1988; and other materials.)

*For more information on estimates of the number of abnormal deaths after the Great Leap Forward and the People's Communes Campaign, refer to Chapter 2, Section 2.1.3.

**"Decade of Turmoil" is the decade of the Great Cultural Revolution from 1966 to 1976.

3.1.2 Basic Conditions in Rural China before Reform

During the "three-year period of hardships" (1960–1962) following the Great Leap Forward and the People's Communes Campaign, the Chinese government adjusted its agricultural operation system and rural policies several times. In February 1962, the CCCPC issued the *Directive on the Issue of Altering the Basic Accounting Unit of People's Communes in Rural Areas,* designating the production team as the basic accounting unit. This system of "three-level ownership with the production team as the basic accounting unit" continued as the basic economic system in rural China until the end of the Decade of Turmoil (i.e., the Great Cultural Revolution of 1966–1976).

In the autumn of 1959, rural fairs were reopened, and in the summer of 1960, private plots were restored and public canteens dissolved. In 1961, the system of production-team-based ownership was established, for farmers to retain a small fraction of household-operated production was recognized as legal within a limited scope, and temporary employment of surplus rural laborers in cities was conditionally allowed.

Even with these adjustments, however, the agricultural operation system and rural policies of the government still remained unfavorable to the development of productivity and were opposed by farmers. The crux of the problem was that after the Cooperative Transformation Campaign and the People's Communes Campaign, farmers lost control over the agricultural economy and claim to the surplus of their labor, and the system of integrating government administration with commune management (including the residence registration system, the grain coupon system, and the grain rationing system) restricted farmers' freedom of mobility so that their human capital had no way of being fully utilized. All in all, farmers lost the right to dispose of their own property. What to produce, how much to produce, and where to get the means of production were all to be decided by government departments at various levels; the production plan was made known to each of the levels below, and each level pressed for its implementation in seasons of planting and harvesting; once the plan was made by higher-level government departments according to leaders' preference, farmers were supposed to passively accept it. The state implemented unified purchase and marketing of major agricultural products, such as grain, cotton, and rapeseed, which were monopolized by state-owned commercial enterprises and quasi-state-owned "supply and marketing cooperatives (*gongxiao hezuoshe*)," allowed only limited rural fair trading, and forbade long-distance transport of goods for sale.

In terms of incentive, the workpoint system was implemented for cooperative members during the era of advanced cooperatives.[14] Because of the long cycles, the strong seasonality, and the wide spatial distribution of agricultural production, the measurement of effort was extremely difficult and supervision cost very high.[15] During the era of people's communes, most localities adopted a practice of low-accuracy measurement of effort by implementing "rigid allotment of base workpoints." In other words, the production team formulated the same workpoint standard for laborers of similar age and the same sex, and then recorded their workpoints according to their working days. In the collective production of people's communes, with commune members "showing up for work in big groups and making as much sound and fury but as little effort as possible," the consequence of such supervision and incentive was that "it is all the same whether you do more or less and whether you do better or worse." Therefore, "free-riding" became a common phenomenon, which struck a heavy blow to farmers' enthusiasm for work.

Farmers toiled all year round, and yet the income was extremely low. Quite often, they could not even ensure that there would be enough food and clothing for their fam-

---

[14] Evaluation of work and allotment of workpoints was done in various ways: (a) "Rigid allotment of base workpoints" was to determine the standard workpoints for each day of work (the base workpoints) in a range of 6 to 10 for each commune member based on his/her physical capacity, skills, and usual performance and to allot him/her base workpoints for each day of work regardless of the actual performance. (b) "Flexible allotment of base workpoints" was to determine base workpoints in the same way as (a) but to allot workpoints according to adjustment on the base workpoints based on regular appraisals of the actual performance of each member by other commune members collectively. (c) "Quota-based workpoints allotment" was to determine quotas of workpoints for various kinds of farm jobs according to their degree of difficulty and to allot workpoints according to farm jobs performed.

[15] See also the analysis by Justin Y. Lin on the ineffectiveness of labor supervision and measurement in the collective sector in "The Household Responsibility System in China's Agricultural Reform: A Theoretical and Empirical Study (Zhongguo nongye jiating zerenzhi gaige de lilun yu jingyan yanjiu) (1988)," Justin Y. Lin, *Institution, Technology and Agricultural Development in China (Zhidu, jishu yu Zhongguo nongye fazhan)*, Shanghai: Shanghai People's Publishing House and Shanghai Joint Publishing, 1994, pp. 44–75.

ilies, and basically they had no savings to speak of. In 1957, the average annual net income of each farmer was RMB 73.37. The figure was RMB 133.57 in 1978,[16] an increase of only RMB 60.20 in twenty-one years.[17] Moreover, about 250 million farmers did not have enough food and clothing.[18]

Farmers were the main victims of this system and related policies, and they had been showing their discontent mainly by being slack in work and making repeated requests for "backtracking as far as possible" to return to individual farming. Therefore, after every compulsory institutional change, waves of "contracting output quota to each household"[19] would always appear in various localities.

3.2 Implementation and Economic Effects of "Contracting Output Quota to Each Household"

3.2.1 The Three Ups and Downs of "Contracting Output Quota to Each Household" before 1976[20]

"Contracting output quota to each household (baochan daohu)" was an innovation of Chinese farmers during reform, although it was not historically unprecedented. In the long history of Chinese agricultural development, such an institutional arrangement had existed where small-scale household operation was combined with relatively large-scale land ownership.

China has a continental monsoon climate, where precipitation concentrates in the summer and agriculture relies on irrigation. Large-scale irrigation projects had to be built, and their construction had to be organized by the state. As a result, since the time immemorial, Chinese agriculture has maintained a three-in-one setup of irrigation, land, and farming. In the Qin and Han dynasties, a land allotment system was adopted. The basic pattern of this system was that the land, owned by the state (i.e., the imperial court) and overlords, was rented to farmers for farming. The state imposed taxes, and overlords collected land rents. Therefore, land ownership was separated from land-use right, and the interest relationship between the owner of the land and the user of the land was adjusted through the contract.

[16] The Agricultural Statistics Department of the National Bureau of Statistics, *Tremendous Changes in the Living Conditions of Chinese Farmers (Wo guo nongmin shenghuo de juda bianhua)*, Beijing: China Statistics Press, 1985, p. 9.
[17] Ibid., pp. 5–7.
[18] The Agriculture Research Team of the National Bureau of Statistics, *Monitoring Report on Poverty in Rural China—2000* (Zhongguo nongcun pinkun jiance baogao—2000), Beijing: China Statistics Press, 2000, Table 2 of the Preface.
[19] See Section 3.2.2 for a narrow definition and a broad definition of "contracting output quota to each household." The latter is equivalent to "the household contracting system" and thus includes "contracting responsibility to each household."
[20] For a detailed description of this process, see Chen Xiwen, *Rural Reform in China: Retrospect and Prospect (Zhongguo nongcun gaige: huigu yu zhanwang)*, Tianjin: Tianjin People's Publishing House, 1993, pp. 39–49. This section is to a great extent based on his description.

In the Tang Dynasty, a land tenancy system was established. All land, no matter whether it was government land or private land, were rented out to farmers for tillage. Fixed-rent contracts were the norm while crop-sharing contracts were less common. In the Ming Dynasty, the land system became more sophisticated and a permanent tenancy system came into being. This so-called permanent tenancy system refers to the system of "farmland with three possessors:" the proprietor, the major leaseholder, and the tenant. The proprietor was the original landlord who possessed the "field base right (*tiandiquan*)." The major leaseholder, having made capital investment to enhance land productivity by building irrigation systems on the leased land, realigning the field, and enhancing soil fertility, possessed the "field surface right (*tianmianquan*)," that is, they were tenants with permanent tenancy. These major leaseholders usually subleased the land to ordinary tenants, enabling them to build their own family farms on rented plots. Thus, the three layers of farmland operation were formed.

After the cooperative transformation, land ownership was transferred to the collective. However, farmers generally had a spontaneous tendency of hoping to lease the collective land to build their own family farms. In 1956 (following the establishment of advanced cooperatives), in 1959 (following the founding of the people's commune system), and in 1962 (following the havoc of the second go-communism craze in 1960–1961), the tendency to resort to output-quota contracting had three upsurges, but all were ruthlessly suppressed. During the Eighth Plenary Session of the 10th CCCPC in September 1962, Mao Zedong even "brought up again the issue of class struggle" and personally renounced "three freedoms and one contracting" (free markets, private plots, self-responsibility for profits and losses, and household contracting) as manifestations of efforts to restore capitalism.

As early as the autumn of 1956, just one year after advanced cooperatives were established across the nation, some localities spontaneously started the practice of paying farmers according to their agricultural output. This practice of "contracting output quota to each household" originated in Wenzhou Prefecture in Zhejiang Province, Wuhu Prefecture in Anhui Province, and Chengdu Prefecture in Sichuan Province. Wenzhou Prefecture alone had more than one thousand advanced cooperatives practicing "contracting output quota to each household." Li Yunhe, then Deputy Party Secretary of Yongjia County in Wenzhou Prefecture, summarized his experience with "contracting output quota to each household," as practiced by the Liaoyuan Cooperative in the county, in his article "'Assigned Operation System' and 'Contracting Output Quota to Each Household' Are Good Ways to Resolve the Principal Contradiction within the Cooperative," published in *Zhejiang Daily*.[21] Although, after this, *People's*

---

[21] *Zhejiang Daily (Zhejiang ribao),* January 27, 1957.

Daily consecutively published signed articles criticizing this practice, "contracting output quota to each household" continually spread. In the summer of 1957, after the launch of the Anti-Rightist Campaign, the situation radically changed. The CCCPC issued *Instructions for a Large-Scale Socialist Education for All Rural Population* on August 8, 1957, and launched a campaign of "mass debates between socialist and capitalist roads." In this campaign of mass debates (i.e., campaign of criticism), "contracting output quota to each household" was labeled "marching along the capitalist road." On October 9, *People's Daily* published a story entitled *Wenzhou Prefecture Redresses the Wrong Practice of 'Contracting Output Quota to Each Household,'* from which the following is quoted:

> At an enlarged meeting held in mid-August, the Wenzhou Prefecture Committee of the CPC conducted debate and criticism against 'contracting output quota to each household,' arrived at a common understanding, and decided to resolutely and drastically redress this wrong practice. All counties in Wenzhou Prefecture also conducted criticism and debate among cadres, many of whom criticized themselves for their Right-deviationist thinking.

On October 19, *People's Daily* published a signed article entitled *Mobilizing What Kind of Enthusiasm of Farmers,* pointing out that the main reason for the wrong practice of "contracting output quota to each household" to be popular in many cooperatives was that it fit perfectly the capitalist thinking of some well-to-do middle peasants and gained their active backing and support." Subsequently, party newspapers in various localities published articles in succession, sternly criticizing "contracting output quota to each household."

The second upsurge of "contracting output quota to each household" took place in 1959. During and after the People's Communes Campaign, rural China was dominated by the go-communism craze, the tendency to exaggerate, the tendency to be authoritarian, the tendency to give arbitrary orders, and the tendency for cadres to behave as the privileged. All these did great harm to farmers. Seeing that agricultural production and the minimum living standard of farmers could scarcely be maintained and trying to save themselves, some localities started to practice "contracting output quota to each household" when they made the production team the basic accounting unit. Unfortunately, their attempt coincided with the Anti-Right-Opportunist Campaign, and "contracting output quota to each household" was regarded as a major manifestation of "Right opportunism" and criticized. On November 2, 1959, *People's Daily* published a commentator's article, saying that "during the three months of May, June, and July in 1959, the ghost of capitalism appeared in rural China, attempting to draw the people back to the old road of mutual aid teams or households of individual farming that are 'small in scale and private in ownership.'" This article also said that "'contracting output quota to each household' is the proposition and activity of 'Right opportunism.' . . .

'Contracting output quota to each household' is a practice of extreme backwardness, retrogression, and reaction." Therefore, "this poisonous weed of 'contracting output quota to each household' must be uprooted and burned up completely, not even a mite of it is to be retained!" *Guangming Daily* also published an article on December 4 entitled "'Contracting Output Quota to Each Household' Is the Program of Right Opportunists for Capitalist Restoration in the Countryside."

Not very long after these renunciations however, the disastrous consequences of the Great Leap Forward and the People's Communes Campaign became apparent, especially in rural areas. Again, for the third time, "contracting output quota to each household" was demanded by farmers. At that time, farmers in many localities were suffering from hunger and cold and were dying "abnormal death" (euphemism for death from malnutrition-related causes) in large numbers, and collective economic organizations could no longer maintain the minimum living standard of commune members. Under these circumstances, Anhui Province was the first to adopt the practice of "fixing output quota for each plot and designating responsibility for each person,"[22] hoping to preserve lives and restore agricultural production by doing so. As of March 1961, production teams under people's communes implementing the practice of "responsibility plots" already comprised 39.3 percent of the total number of production teams in Anhui Province. Some other localities also adopted similar practices.

In Mao Zedong's view, however, the system of "three-level ownership with the production team as the basic accounting unit" within the framework of collective economic organizations should have been enough to solve the problem of stifled initiatives of farmers. He regarded "contracting output quota to each household" as private in nature and could by no means accept it. Therefore, it was expressly pointed out in *Directives on Conducting Socialist Education in the Countryside* issued on November 13, 1961 by the CCCPC, that "all practices of 'contracting output quota to each household' and individual farming in disguised forms in very few localities are not in conformity with the principle of socialist collective economic organizations, and therefore wrong; . . . Effort should be made to gradually guide farmers to change these practices."

At the enlarged working conference of the CCCPC held in January 1962 (i.e., the Conference of Seven Thousand Cadres), Mao Zedong criticized the mistake of the leader of the Anhui Provincial Committee of the CPC in supporting farmers to adopt the practice of "responsibility plots." On March 20, 1962, the Anhui Provincial Committee of the CPC worked out the *Resolution on Rectifying the Practice of "Responsibility Plots."* Nevertheless, some other leaders still believed that "contracting output quota to each household" might be, after all, an option to address the situation of that time. For

---

[22] "Responsibility plots" in short, one of the many forms of "contracting output quota to each household."

instance, after listening to the work report on East China at a meeting in late June 1962, the Secretariat of the CCCPC was divided in their opinion concerning the practice of "contracting output quota to each household," with half for it and half against it. At the meeting, Deng Xiaoping quoted a saying of farmers in Anhui Province, "black or yellow, all are good cats so long as they catch mice." Chen Yun and Deng Zihui both proposed to Mao Zedong and other members of the Standing Committee of the Political Bureau of the CCCPC that in some localities, "contracting output quota to each household" might still be practiced to stimulate farmers' enthusiasm and quickly restore agricultural production.[23]

The volatile issue of "contracting output quota to each household" thus became the focus of Mao Zedong's return to the subject of class struggle. In a working conference of the CCCPC held in Beidaihe from July 25 to August 24, 1962, Mao again criticized "contracting output quota to each household." He believed that within a year after implementing "contracting output quota to each household," class polarization would be very serious. In the Tenth Plenary Session of the Eighth CCCPC during September 24 to 27, 1962, Mao Zedong delivered a speech on the themes of class, the situation, and contradictions and solidarity within the party, and once again criticized the "tendency to return to individual farming," the "tendency to reverse verdicts," and the "tendency to paint everything black." He further propounded his viewpoint that class struggle must be "talked about every year, every month, and every day." On May 20, 1963, the CCCPC issued the *Decision on Several Issues in Current Rural Work (draft),* with the claim that serious class struggle had occurred in rural China, the slogans that "class struggle and proletarian dictatorship should never be forgotten" and "grasp class struggle and all problems can be solved," and the decision that a large-scale socialist education campaign should be launched in the countryside across the nation. The Socialist Education Campaign (1963–1966) turned out to be the prelude to the decade of the Great Cultural Revolution.

3.2.2 Quick Spread of the Household Contracting System

After the decade of the Great Cultural Revolution, confronted with the devastation of the rural economy everywhere, the party and government leaders in some localities anxiously searched for a way out of their plight. When farmers in these localities once again demanded "contracting output quota to each household," they received support from these open-minded cadres.

At that time, the responsibility system for agricultural production (*nongye shengchan*

---

[23] Ma Qibin et al., *The Communist Party of China: 40 Years in Power (Zhongguo Gongchandang zhizheng sishi nian),* Revised edition, Beijing: The Communist Party of China History Publishing House, 1991, p. 217.

zerenzhi) [24] adopted in various localities could be categorized in three major ways—job contracting, output-quota contracting, and responsibility contracting—and in three major forms—contracting job to each work group, contracting output quota to each household, and contracting responsibility to each household (also called the all-round responsibility system). [25] Nowadays, people often refer to "contracting responsibility to each household" as "contracting output quota to each household" although the two concepts were different originally.

"Contracting job to each work group (*baogong daozu*)" was in fact a form of labor organization within the framework of collective economic organizations. Its basic practice involved the production team giving out a contract for a quantity of work to the work group; specifying the time, quality requirements, and due remuneration; and rending rewards and punishments according to how well the task was completed by the work group awarded the contract. As there are clear specifications on quantity, quality, time limits, and due remuneration for the work, and the work group usually organized themselves as they saw fit, "contracting job to each work group" should reduce labor supervision cost and "free-riding" behavior, and therefore, better mobilize production enthusiasm of laborers in the collective—at least when compared with the operation form of "much fanfare but few practical results."

The essence of "contracting output quota to each household (*baochan daohu*)" is that it alters the way of labor assessment from directly measuring the quantity of work to measuring both the quantity and quality of labor by output. Its basic practice is to give plots to farmers under contracts stipulating output quotas; the quota part of output is handed in to the production team, and the above-quota part of output is retained by the household awarded the contract or shared with the production team according to predetermined proportions. "Contracting output quota to each household" is different from "contracting job to each work group" in that (a) it avoids difficulties in assessing the fruits of labor in each phase of agricultural production by expanding contracting from a certain phase to the entire process of production and (b) it avoids difficulties in supervising labor and curbing "free-riding" behavior in agricultural production by changing the party awarded the contract from work groups to households.

"Contracting responsibility to each household (*baogan daohu*)" implies fundamental changes in agricultural production from collective operation to household operation on contracted land. Its basic method is that the collective (generally represented by the villagers' committee), as the land owner, contracts plots to farmers to operate according to

---

[24] An official and inclusive name for virtually all kinds of "contracting systems" and "responsibility systems" practiced in rural China since the late 1970s.

[25] Zhou Taihe et al., *Economic System Reform in Contemporary China (Dangdai Zhongguo de jingji tizhi gaige)*, Beijing: China Social Sciences Press 1984, pp. 269–270.

the number of persons in the family or both the number of persons in the family and the number of laborers in the family; farmers fulfill their responsibilities to the state in terms of taxation and compulsory or contracted purchase as well as their responsibilities to the collective with contributions to a public accumulation fund and a public welfare fund; and all the remaining produce belongs to the farmers and is at their disposal. The biggest difference between "contracting responsibility to each household" and "contracting output quota to each household" is that the unified operation and distribution by the production team has been abrogated in the former. Essentially, "after handing in a sufficient amount to the state and contributing a sufficient amount to the collective, each household keeps all remaining harvest" is the farmers' description of "contracting responsibility to each household."

Insight 3.2

Contract by Farmers in Xiaogang Village, Fengyang County, Anhui Province

For nine months of 1978, there had not been a soaking rain in Anhui, and so severe a drought had not occurred in a century. There was no way crops could be sowed that autumn. In view of these circumstances, the Anhui Provincial Committee of the CPC decided to "lend land to tide over a lean year," that is, the collective would lease 0.3 *mu* of land to each farmer to plant vegetables; land that could be planted with wheat would not be subject to compulsory purchase as long as it was planted; and whoever planted grain and oil crops in uncultivated hills and lake shoals could take the harvest. Through this land lending, "contracting output quota to each household" was revived in Anhui. In early September, at a meeting of four levels of cadres called by the Chuxian Prefecture Committee of the CPC, a few commune party secretaries revealed that some villages were secretly practicing the contracted responsibility system with remuneration linked to output in the form of "contracting output quota to each work group." They called this practice a "secret weapon" to fight the drought. Among villages practicing "contracting output quota to each household," the most famous was Xiaogang Village in Fengyang County, Anhui Province.

In the beginning, the Xiaogang Production Team of twenty households was divided into four work groups, but this did not work well. Then, this production team was divided further into eight work groups, but they still failed to do well. Yan Hongchang, the newly elected vice team leader, went to an experienced veteran farmer, Guan Tingzhu, for advice. Guan mentioned that the "life-saving plots" (another name for responsibility plots) in 1961 were very effective; once implemented, output increased. "Great! We will just do that, contracting land directly to households!" Yan Hongchang replied. At a meeting of team members, team leader Yan Junchang said, "We will just implement contracting directly to households. In autumn, after handing in a sufficient amount to the State and contributing a sufficient amount to the collective, each household keeps all remaining harvest, and we will not need workpoint recording any more." This was unanimously agreed by the participants. Among the twenty-one farmers participating in the meeting, three affixed their personal seals while eighteen put their thumbprints on a written pledge as follows:

December 1978

Location: Home of Yan Lihua

We distribute land to households, to which head of each household has agreed by signing his signature or affixing his seal. If this works, each household pledges to pay its share of the required agricultural tax in grain to the State and not to ask for money or grain from the State any more. If this does not work, we cadres are willing to be condemned to prison or even death, and commune members collectively pledge to raise our children to the age of 18.

In the following year, grain output of Xiaogang Production Team totaled more than 65,000 kilograms. This event subsequently became the symbol of a major breakthrough in China's economic system reform. In 1979, the Anhui Provincial Committee of the CPC designated the spontaneous practice of "contracting output quota to each household" in Shannan Commune of Feixi County as an official experiment.

(Compiled from Yang Jisheng, *The Deng Xiaoping Era—Record of Actual Events in Two Decades of Reform and Opening up in China (Deng Xiaoping shidai—Zhongguo gaige kaifang ershi nian jishi)*, Vol. 1, Beijing: Central Compilation & Translation Press, 1998.)

The wave of "contracting output quota to each household," with the "all-round responsibility system" as its main form, first sprang up in Anhui Province, as detailed in Insight 3.2. By the end of 1978, the number of production teams practicing "contracting output quota to each household" in Anhui Province reached 1,200. In 1979, this number increased to 38,000, accounting for about 10 percent of the production teams in the province. In other localities in Sichuan, Guizhou, Gansu, Inner Mongolia, and Henan, "contracting output quota to each household" also expanded in a considerable scale. However, the CCCPC at that time still embraced the tenet of the "Two Whatevers."[26] Therefore, only a few provincial committees of the CPC, such as those of Anhui and Sichuan, expressly committed to supporting "contracting output quota to each household." Even though the *Decision of the CCCPC on Issues Regarding Accelerating the Development of Agriculture (draft),* reviewed by the Third Plenary Session of the 11th CCCPC in December 1978, criticized the "Left" mistakes long existing in agriculture since the founding of the People's Republic of China (PRC) and stressed that the guiding ideology should be rectified and the enthusiasm of eight hundred million farmers should be fully brought into play, it failed to thoroughly break away from "Left" thinking. The *Decision* still stipulated that "distributing land for individual farming shall not be allowed" and "contracting output quota to each household shall not be allowed." At the Fourth Plenary Session of the 11th CCCPC in September 1979, the *Decision of the CCCPC on Issues Regarding Accelerating the Development of Agriculture* was formally adopted, and the policy of two "shall not be allowed" was changed into the policy of one "shall not be allowed" and one "shall not be practiced." Specifically, "distributing land for individual farming shall not be allowed" and "contracting output quota to each household shall not be practiced" was the exact wording. The change from "contracting output quota to each household shall not be allowed" to "contracting output quota to each household shall not be practiced" somewhat relaxed the tone of the message. Besides, certain exceptions were permitted.

At the enlarged meeting of the Political Bureau of the CCCPC, held in August 1980, the mistakes of Hua Guofeng[27] (1921–), who maintained a "Left" stance even after the Great Cultural Revolution, was criticized and Deng Xiaoping took over control of the leadership. In September of the same year, the CCCPC transmitted with endorsement *Summary of the Symposium of First Secretaries of Party Committees of Provinces, Municipalities, and Autonomous Regions* under the title of *Some Issues Regarding Further Strengthening*

---

[26] The "Two Whatevers" refers to the slogan that "whatever decision Chairman Mao made should be safeguarded firmly; whatever instructions he gave should be followed unswervingly."

[27] Interim top leader between Mao Zedong and Deng Xiaoping, who ordered to arrest Gang of Four and ended the Great Cultural Revolution after Mao's death in 1976 but insisted on continuing Mao's policies. Resigned from the positions of Premier of the State Council in 1980 and of Chairman of the CCCPC in 1981.

and Improving the Responsibility System for Agricultural Production. This document pointed out emphatically that the responsibility system should be promoted according to local conditions and with categorized guidance, "The existence of multiple modes of operation, multiple forms of labor organization, and multiple methods of remuneration should be permitted. . . . Do not stick to one model or impose uniformity in all cases. . . . In those remote mountainous areas and poverty-stricken backward regions and in those production teams that have been relying on state-resold grain for food, loans for production, and social relief for living for a long period of time, if the masses have lost their confidence in the collective and request contracting output quota to each household, such requests should be granted and either contracting output quota to each household or contracting responsibility to each household may be practiced and such arrangements are to be kept unchanged for a fairly long period of time."

After this document was issued, the contracting system of various forms all experienced rapid growth. Among them, the fastest growing were "two contractings," i.e., "contracting output quota to each household" and "contracting responsibility to each household." During 1980, the proportion of production teams implementing "two contractings" increased from 1.1 to 14.9 percent. In January 1982, the first "No. 1 Document"[28] on rural economic policies by the CCCPC and the State Council expressly pointed out that "generally speaking, linking remuneration to output requires contracting. . . . Contracting to work groups, to households, or to laborers only represents different scale and size of the labor organization, not necessarily indicating advancedness and backwardness of production. . . . 'Job contracting,' 'output-quota contracting,' and 'responsibility contracting' only represent different methods of distributing fruits of labor. 'Responsibility contracting' is mostly 'output-quota contracting with fixed deduction,' which eliminates distribution by workpoints and is not only convenient but also welcome by the masses." This document therefore gave "responsibility contracting" an official policy basis. In June 1982, production teams implementing "two contractings" nationwide accounted for 86.7 percent of the total, and this number further increased to 93 percent by the beginning of 1983. The majority of these were "contracting responsibility to each household."[29] By this time, the two concepts of "contracting output quota to each household" and "contracting responsibility to each household" had already been integrated into one. "Contracting responsibility to each household"

---

[28] In January 1982, the CCCPC transmitted with endorsement the *Summary of the National Conference on Rural Work* as the No. 1 Document of the CCCPC of the year. That conference was held in December 1981.

[29] The Rural Development Research Institute of the Chinese Academy of Social Sciences, "Reform of Rural Economic System in China (Zhongguo nongcun jingji tizhi de gaige)," the State Commission for Restructuring Economic Systems, *A Decade of Economic System Reform in China (Zhongguo jingji tizhi gaige shi nian),* Beijing: Economic Management Press and Reform Press, 1988.

became the mainstream of the household contracted responsibility system with remuneration linked to output (*jiating lianchan chengbao zerenzhi*),[30] signifying the completion of the transition of China's agricultural operation system from the collective economic system of people's communes to the system of family farms built by farmers on the "contracted" land.

The two main reasons why the operation system in rural China could be changed in an extremely short period of time were as follows.

1. The "contracting system" was a relatively familiar institutional arrangement to farmers and the most acceptable system to them, as well. Under the condition that the system of collective land ownership is maintained, it is the most convenient option for farmers to "contract (lease)" land owned by the collective for long periods of time and build their family farms on this contracted or leased land. "Contracting output quota to each household" was exactly this kind of agricultural operation.

2. There was no serious social obstacle for the transition to the contracting system. During transition, as farmers had gains without losses and no harm was done to the interests of the other social groups, this reform was easily accepted by the public. Under the planned economic system, farmers were different from workers in that they could not receive welfare and security as urban workers did. Farmers would always have to assume risks by themselves and be responsible for their own livelihoods. There was no "big-pot meal" for them to eat. Therefore, with the transition, they had something to gain but nothing to lose. Furthermore, the fact that the catastrophe of the Great Cultural Revolution brought the Chinese economy to the verge of collapse made some practical-minded rural cadres also believe that they should support farmers in their institutional innovation of "contracting output quota to each household." In the meantime, "contracting output quota to each household" would not cost these cadres much in terms of power and interests; on the contrary, it would benefit their families and themselves. Therefore, in the transition to the household contracting system, many cadres played positive roles.

3.2.3 Economic Results of the Household Contracting System

The household contracting system, implemented during the late 1970s and the early 1980s, brought about tremendous changes to Chinese agriculture. Implementation of

---

[30] Another, and more formal, name for "the household contracting system."

the contracting system in rural China greatly promoted agricultural development. According to calculations by Justin Y. Lin, the total contribution of various measures of rural reform to rural output growth from 1978 to 1984 was 48.64 percent, of which the contribution of the contracting system was 46.89 percent.[31] One of the most direct economic effects was that agricultural output increased by a great margin. Between 1978 and 1984, agricultural production in China had experienced unprecedented changes since the founding of the PRC. In 1984, total national grain output reached a record high of 407.31 million tons, up by 33.6 percent as compared with 1978, with an average annual growth rate of 4.95 percent; total output of cotton measured 6.258 million tons, 1.89 times higher than that of 1978; output of oilseeds totaled 11.91 million tons, 1.28 times higher than that of 1978; total output of sugar crops was 47.8 million tons, 1.01 times higher than that of 1978.[32]

Also, both animal husbandry and fishery experienced tremendous growth. In 1988, the national output of pork, beef, and mutton combined was 21.936 million tons, increased by 1.56 times as compared with 1978, with an average annual growth rate of 9.9 percent—equivalent to 2.75 times the average annual growth rate during the twenty-six years prior to 1978; the national output of dairy products was 4.189 million tons, 3.3 times higher than that of 1978, with an average annual growth rate of 15.7 percent. In 1988, the national output of aquatic products was 10.61 million tons, 1.28 times higher than that of 1978, with an average annual growth rate of 8.6 percent.[33] The increase in agricultural, animal husbandry, and fishery products greatly improved people's standard of living. In 1988, grain per capita nationwide was 363 kilograms; cotton 3.8 kilograms; oilseeds 12.1 kilograms; pork, beef, and mutton combined 20.2 kilograms; and aquatic products 9.7 kilograms. They respectively increased by 13.5, 65.2, 120, 124, and 98 percent as compared with 1978.[34]

During and after the 1980s, agricultural production in China continued to grow (see Table 3.1). With such increases in agricultural production, the rural industrial structure in China was rationalized each passing day; the proportions of forestry, animal husbandry, side-line production, and fishery increased considerably. First, in crop cultivation, the share of cash crops in 1988 reached 18.4 percent, an increase of 6.5 percentage points over 1978; the output value of grain crops fell to 58.2 percent.[35] Second,

[31] Justin Y. Lin, *Institution, Technology and Agricultural Development in China (Zhidu, jishu yu Zhongguo nongye fazhan)*, Shanghai: Shanghai People's Publishing House and Shanghai Joint Publishing, 1994, p. 95.
[32] Zhu Rong et al. (eds.), *Agriculture in Contemporary China (Dangdai Zhongguo de nongye)*, Beijing: Contemporary China Press, 1992, p. 375.
[33] Ibid., p. 369.
[34] Ibid., p. 369.
[35] The National Bureau of Statistics, *Four Decades of Advance in Great Strides (Fenjin de sishi nian)*, Beijing: China Statistics Press, 1989, p. 23.

Table 3.1   Gross Output Value of Farming, Forestry, Animal Husbandry, and Fishery (RMB Billion)

Year	Total of Farming, Forestry, Animal Husbandry, and Fishery	Farming	Forestry	Animal Husbandry	Fishery
1978	139.7	111.8	4.8	20.9	2.2
1980	192.3	145.4	8.1	35.4	3.3
1985	361.9	250.6	18.9	79.8	12.6
1990	766.2	495.4	33.0	196.7	41.1
1995	2,034.1	1,188.5	71.0	604.5	170.1
2000	2,491.6	1,387.4	93.7	739.3	271.3

Source: The National Bureau of Statistics, *China Statistical Yearbook (Zhongguo tongji nianjian)*, Beijing: China Statistics Press, various years.

the share of the gross output value of agriculture in the gross rural output value dropped from 68.6 percent in 1978 to 46.8 percent in 1988; the share of rural industry increased from 19.4 percent to 38.1 percent; the share of rural construction increased from 6.6 percent to 7.1 percent; the share of rural transport service increased from 1.7 to 3.5 percent; and the share of rural commerce increased from 3.7 to 4.5 percent.[36]

In addition, specialized households engaging in rural industry, rural construction, rural transport service, and rural commerce had rapidly developed. In 1981, specialized households were still rare in rural China. But they numbered 15.61 million in 1982, 24.84 million in 1983, and 25.6 million in 1984. Driven by the contracting system, industrial enterprises in rural China adopted multiple forms of organization and operation, with four types predominating: township enterprises, village enterprises, joint household enterprises, and individual enterprises. By 1988, there were 386,900 joint entities in rural China engaging in industry, construction, transport, commerce, catering, service, and other sectors with 3.85 million employees, original value of fixed assets of RMB 7.154 billion, and net income of RMB 780 million.[37]

Along with the growth of agriculture, the income of Chinese farmers increased substantially. In 1980, rural per capita net income obtained from the basic accounting units of the collective economic organizations (i.e., production teams) was only RMB 85.9; rural per capita net income was RMB 191 when side-line production income was added.

---

[36] Ibid., p. 366.
[37] The National Bureau of Statistics, *China Statistical Yearbook (Zhongguo tongji nianjian) (1989)*, Beijing: China Statistics Press, 1989.

Table 3.2   Per Capita Annual Total Income and Annual Net Income of Rural Households (RMB)

Year	1978	1980	1985	1990	1995	2001
Total Income	152	216	547	990	2,338	3,307
Net Income	134	191	398	686	1,578	2,366

Source: The National Bureau of Statistics, *China Statistical Yearbook (Zhongguo tongji nianjian)*, Beijing: China Statistics Press, various years.

By 1985, the per capita net income of farmers increased to RMB 398,[38] doubling in five years. The strength of the overall rural economy in China also had grown substantially. In 1985, total rural output value was RMB 634 billion, about four times the RMB 162.7 billion in 1978.[39]

3.2.4 Reform of Property Rights by the Contracting System

The effect on productivity of the contracting system was only one aspect of the issue. The contracting system also had great impacts on the economic system and even the political system. Among all these impacts, however, the foremost was that Chinese farmers acquired property rights.

Before rural reform, farmers hardly had any property of their own except their houses. In 1978, about a quarter of the production teams in the country had an annual per capita income of less than RMB 50. The estimated worth of each household property was no more than RMB 500. Even collective property was skimpy. In 1978, the total value of fixed assets of the collective sector in rural China was RMB 72 billion, less than RMB 240 per laborer, which was equivalent to only 2.56 percent of RMB 9,400—the average value of fixed assets per laborer of state-owned industry.[40] Because the government had control over the production, distribution, and pricing of agricultural products, the state had been obtaining a great deal of revenue from agriculture through the price scissors and other means since the 1950s. According to the calculation of some relevant departments, from 1951 to 1978, agriculture, through accumulation, provided RMB 434 billion for industrialization, which equals RMB 98 billion of tax revenue plus RMB 512 billion of the price scissors between industrial and agricultural products minus RMB 176 billion of state investment in agriculture. During the seventeen years from

---

[38] The National Bureau of Statistics, *China Statistical Yearbook (Zhongguo tongji nianjian) (1981) and (1985)*, Beijing: China Statistics Press, 1981 and 1985.

[39] The National Bureau of Statistics, *China Statistical Yearbook (Zhongguo tongji nianjian) (1989)*, Beijing: China Statistics Press, 1989, p. 228

[40] *Investigation and Study (Diaocha yu yanjiu)*, 1978, No. 12.

1962 to 1978, only in five years was grain production profitable, with average profits per *mu* ranging from RMB 2 to 5; all the other years saw losses. Therefore, even the simple reproduction of agriculture could hardly sustain. During the twenty-one years from 1957 to 1978, the annual net income per capita of farmers increased only from RMB 73.37 to RMB 133.57, an average increase of less than RMB 3 per year. Taking the increases in commodity prices into account, the actual annual increase in rural per capita net income was RMB 1.[41] However, about half the central government's revenues were from agriculture either directly or indirectly. From 1952 to 1978, exports of agricultural and side-line products and their processed goods accounted for 62.6 to 90.6 percent of China's exports.[42] Therefore, most of the income created by farmers was contributed to the state.[43]

After the reform of the household contracting system, assets owned by Chinese farmers grew tremendously. As of 1992, total assets in rural China amounted to RMB 9,519.6 billion, of which, 22.71 percent were private household property and 77.29 percent were collective land properties and enterprise assets. Over 95 percent of the total collective assets had been contracted to rural households and individuals for operation on a long-term basis; less than 4 percent were operated collectively.[44] After the reform, Chinese farmers acquired three forms of property ownership. The first was personal property, mainly consisting of bank savings,[45] private houses, private means of production, and means of livelihood. The second was land-use right. Land was owned by the collective, but farmers had the right to use. Moreover, land had been contracted to farmers on a long-term basis, so they now enjoyed an unprecedented usufruct. The third was the growth of farmers' human capital. Farmers, now able to manage their activities themselves, greatly changed their mindset and attitudes and improved their abilities in the process of traveling and seeking employment.

3.2.5 Impact on the Development of TVEs

The predecessors of township and village enterprises (TVEs) were "commune and brigade enterprises" under the system of people's communes. There was a major differ-

---

[41] Chen Jiyuan (ed.), *Social and Economic Changes in Rural China (Zhongguo nongcun shehui jingji bianqian)*, Taiyuan: Shanxi Economy Press, 1993, pp. 585–586.

[42] Zhou Rili, "Evaluation of Achievements in a Decade of Reform and Ideas for Development in Rural Areas (Nongcun shi nian gaige de chengguo pingjia yu fazhan silu)," *Anhui Daily (Anhui ribao)*, December 30, 1989.

[43] According to research, gross accumulation by agriculture in 1980 was RMB 36.074 billion; deducting the portion used for the countryside by the state, the net capital outflow of agriculture was RMB 27.862 billion. See Feng Haifa and Li Wei, "Quantitative Study on Chinese Industrial Capital Accumulation Provided by Agriculture (Wo guo nongye wei gongye tigong zijin jilei de shuliang yanjiu)," *Economic Research Journal (Jingji yanjiu)*, 1993, No. 9.

[44] The National Bureau of Statistics, *China Statistical Yearbook (Zhongguo tongji nianjian) (1993)*, Beijing: China Statistics Press, 1993.

[45] Savings in rural credit cooperatives by farmers in 1992 amounted to RMB 210.78 billion. See the National Bureau of Statistics, *China Statistical Yearbook (Zhongguo tongji nianjian) (1993)*, Beijing: China Statistics Press, 1993, p. 664.

ence between the two systems. "Commune and brigade enterprises" must adhere to the "three-locally principle," namely, obtaining raw materials locally, processing locally, and marketing products locally. In other words, they were not supposed to develop market-oriented processing, but rather to confine their operation within the scope of a self-contained economy. Therefore, at least by the original intention of the leadership, "commune and brigade enterprises" should belong to the so-called "traditional natural economy" in development economics.[46] By contrast, TVEs originated and developed when the household contracting system was already implemented in agriculture. So, TVEs were in sync with the development of a market economy.

During the Great Leap Forward of 1958 and the decentralization of 1970, the people's communes in various localities had all set up some machining and repair enterprises mainly related to agricultural machinery. To prevent rural industry from generating pressure on urban industry, the authorities had adopted various political and economic measures to limit the development of commune and brigade enterprises strictly within the scope of a self-contained rural economy.[47]

All this changed with the introduction of the household contracting system. First, the new system caused rural surplus laborers to emerge from their original concealment under the people's commune system and lawfully gain the freedom to seek employment in nonagricultural industries. This provided adequate labor supply for the development of TVEs and it also enabled all sorts of "able persons" in rural China to bring into play their spirit of innovation, or "entrepreneurship" as described by Joseph Alois Schumpeter (1883–1950). Second, the introduction of the household contracting system also released the rural productive force that had long been fettered under the people's commune system, enabling agricultural production to yield a considerable surplus that could be turned into investment in the development of rural industry. Third, after the implementation of the household contracting system, farmers' increasing demand for consumable goods because of their rising living standard and the intensifying exchange of goods between urban and rural areas opened up markets for TVE products. After the 1980s, TVEs in China in general, and TVEs in such coastal regions as Middle Zhejiang, the Yangtze River Delta, the Pearl River Delta, and the Jiaodong Peninsula in particular, made considerable progress. Since the mid-1990s, rural industry has accounted for about one-third of industrial production in China. A number of TVEs have grown rapidly, despite market competition, to become leaders in their respective industries.

---

[46] Jahn Fei and Gustav Ranis, *Development of the Labor Surplus Economy: Theory and Policy*, Homewood, Ill.: R. D. Irwin, 1964.

[47] Chen Xiwen, *Rural Reform in China: Retrospect and Prospect (Zhongguo nongcun gaige: huigu yu zhanwang)*, Tianjin: Tianjin People's Publishing House, 1993, pp. 76–77.

Table 3.3   Number of TVEs and TVE Employment (thousand unit/thousand people)

Year	1978	1980	1985	1990	1995	2000
Number of TVEs	1,524	1,425	12,225	18,504	22,027	20,847
Number of TVE employees	28,266	29,997	69,790	92,648	128,621	128,196

Source: The National Bureau of Statistics, *China Statistical Yearbook (Zhongguo tongji nianjian)*, Beijing: China Statistics Press, various years; the TVE Bureau of the Ministry of Agriculture, *Annual Statistical Bulletin and Financial Statements of TVEs Nationwide (Quanguo xiangzhen qiye tongji nianbao ji caiwu juesuan ziliao)*, 2000.

3.3 Existing Problems and Prospects for Further Reforms

Owing to bumper harvests in several consecutive years, farmers faced depressed prices and difficulties in selling their crops around 1984. That, plus the policy adjustment of increasing prices of agricultural means of production, resulted in agricultural production falling into stagnation between 1985 and 1988. Since then, these two situations occurred alternately. Whenever there was a bumper harvest, the government attempted to purchase agricultural products at protective prices to prevent cheap grain from hurting farmers; however, the government resorted to increasing the purchase price to provide incentives for farmers to increase production whenever agricultural production decreased. With continuous upward adjustment of purchase prices of agricultural products since 1993, the relationship between supply of and demand for domestic agricultural products took a new turn around the mid-1990s when agricultural products started to produce structural and regional surpluses as opposed to the overall shortages in the past. With these kinds of surpluses, prices of agricultural products such as grain, cotton, oil, and sugar in the domestic market have fallen for several consecutive years since 1998. Falling agricultural prices led to decelerating growth of farmers' incomes and a widening income disparity between urban and rural residents. As a result, the "three rural problems"—stagnant rural economy, poor rural residents, and backward rural society—have become an issue of wide concern. There have been different diagnoses proposed as causes of the problems, and different prescriptions for solutions. Some people hold the viewpoint that the agricultural production operation system based on family farms can no longer be compatible with the requirements of developed productivity, and the way out is collectivization. However, the majority holds the view described in Section 3.1 of this chapter that the problem did not lie in the family farm system, but rather in imperfections in the supporting economic systems and government policies.

Specifically, the five issues that will be discussed in the following sections need to be solved urgently.

3.3.1 Reforming the Purchase and Marketing System of Agricultural Products

It was pointed out in Section 3.1 that the establishment of a planned economic system in China was spearheaded by unified purchase and marketing of grain and cotton, introduced in 1952. After the implementation of the household contracting system in the early 1980s, the framework of this unified purchase and marketing system was still maintained, which caused a great deal of tension between the production system and the circulation system. After shortages of grain and cotton were reversed, the CCCPC and the State Council announced in their No. 1 Document of 1985 the decision to reform the unified and quota purchase system of agricultural products. It proposed to expand the role of market regulation under the guidance of state planning and to implement the dual-track system of planned price for quota purchase and market price for nonquota purchase. At the beginning of 1992, the government leadership proposed to reform the purchase, marketing, and pricing system of grain in the form of "different decisions for different regions and different implementations for different provinces." As a result, various localities lifted control over grain retail markets. By the end of 1993, control over grain selling prices had been lifted in more than 98 percent of all counties and cities across the nation.

However, owing to a sudden rise in grain prices and panic purchasing in some localities at the end of 1993, the situation changed dramatically. To ensure grain supply, the central government implemented in May 1994 a provincial governor (municipality mayor) responsibility system for regional balancing of grain and successively adopted the following measures:

1. raising the government purchasing price of quota grain by 46.6 percent in 1994, 29.0 percent in 1995, and 5.8 percent in 1996;[48]

2. requiring that state grain departments amass a bigger pool of grain;

3. allowing local governments to grant allowances on top of the purchasing price of quota grain when necessary;

4. stipulating that state-owned grain stores sell certain kinds of grain at government-prescribed prices.

These measures were effective in stabilizing the quantity of purchase and ensuring the grain ration supply to low-income urban residents. Notwithstanding, state grain de-

---

[48] The National Bureau of Statistics, *China Statistical Yearbook (Zhongguo tongji nianjian) (2001),* Beijing: China Statistics Press, 2001, p. 294.

partments in some localities breached the State Council's regulation of fixing the purchasing price according to market change. They lowered the purchasing price and purchased grain from farmers by imposing arbitrary quotas and then resold grain at higher prices to make profits. After two years of bumper harvests in 1995 and 1996, grain prices fell again[49] and farmers had difficulty selling grain. To ensure that farmers would continue to produce grain, in August 1997, the State Council issued the *Circular Concerning Unrestricted Purchase of Non-Quota Grain at Protective Price,* requiring that all localities promptly set up grain protective price: the price for quota grain could be no lower than that of the previous year, while the price for nonquota grain should be the base price for quota grain. On completion of the quota grain purchase assignment, all localities should resolutely purchase without restriction surplus grain from farmers at protective price.

After promulgation of this policy, all local grain departments quickly changed their purchasing practices from purchasing nonquota grain at price fixed according to market change to purchasing nonquota grain without restriction at protective price. Accordingly, the quantity of grain purchased increased considerably, and grain depots in various localities were all filled to their capacities. Along with the continuous increase in grain stock, grain operation losses and unpaid bank credit also increased. By 1997, accumulated losses in the form of unpaid bank credit by state-owned grain trading enterprises for the past years reached RMB 100 billion, or over RMB 30,000 per employee for the state grain system of three million employees. As of March 1998, the balance of grain loans nationwide was as high as RMB 543 billion, indicating grain operation losses of RMB 214 billion by deducting the gross value of grain stock, or RMB 70,000 per employee of the state grain system.[50] Although various localities carried out the regulations of the State Council on unrestricted purchase of nonquota grain at protective price, as the overall grain supply exceeded demand, market price still fell for three consecutive years—1996, 1997, and 1998—and so did farmers' income from agriculture.

In response to problems of mismanagement by state-owned grain purchasing and marketing enterprises, the State Council issued the *Decision on Further Deepening Reform of the Grain Circulation System* in May 1998. In the *Decision,* it was pointed out that the basic principle of the reform of the grain circulation system was "four separations and one improvement:" separation of government administration from enterprise management, separation of reserve from distribution, separation of central government responsibilities from local government responsibilities, separation of new financial accounts

---

[49] On a year-to-year basis, grain purchasing price dropped by 9.8 percent in 1997, 3.3 percent in 1998, and 12.9 percent in 1999. Ibid.

[50] Zhang Chi, Wang Shuo, and Li Yong, "RMB 214 Billion, What a Huge Grain Fund Deficit (2140 yi, hao da ge liangkuan kulong)," *End-of-Month Issue of Securities Market Weekly: Finance and Economy (Zhengquan shichang zhoukan yuemo ban: caijing)* October 1998.

from old financial accounts, and improvement of the grain pricing mechanism (i.e., gradual achievement of marketization).

According to earlier discussions of one hundred domestic and overseas experts, the marketization of the grain purchase and marketing system could proceed in three steps: (a) during the early part of the Ninth Five-Year Plan from 1996 to 2000, "assuring quantity while liberalizing price" should be implemented; (b) during the middle part of the Ninth Five-Year Plan, "reducing purchase while liberalizing price" should be implemented and purchase by quota should only guarantee the grain ration of low-income residents and other necessarily guaranteed grain use; and (c) toward the end of the Ninth Five-Year Plan, with improvement of the special reserve system, full price liberalization should be implemented.[51]

On June 3, 1998, the national video working conference on grain purchase and marketing, convened by the State Council, further proposed that grain purchase and marketing reform should focus on the implementation of three policies. The so-called "three policies" were that (a) grain enterprises should purchase without restriction surplus grain from farmers at government-prescribed protective price; (b) grain purchasing and storage enterprises should implement "selling at mark-up price," i.e., selling at purchasing price plus minimum mark-up; and (c) purchasing funds lent by the Agricultural Development Bank of China to grain trading enterprises should "flow within a closed loop" according to the rules of "loan being linked to stock and money following grain."

To ensure the implementation of the three policies, in November 1998, the State Council issued the *Opinion on Current Promotion of Reform of the Grain Circulation System*, requiring strengthening of the control over the grain purchasing market so that grain dealers, distributors, and grain processing enterprises were not allowed to purchase grain from farmers directly in grain-producing regions or from the fair trade market, except from the state-owned grain purchasing and storage enterprises.

As can be predicted by an analysis based on principles of economics, this set of policies could hardly be implemented. In some regions, the policy for grain purchasing and storage enterprises to purchase without restriction surplus grain from farmers at protective price could hardly be fully implemented; under a market economy, the order prohibiting private grain dealers from purchasing and marketing grain could hardly be enforced; and with a continuously declining grain market price, it would be very difficult for state-owned grain enterprises to realize selling at mark-up price. What actually happened was a sharply rising subsidy burden on the state finance system, an excessively high level of grain stock, and heavy losses incurred by grain purchasing and

---

[51] The Department of Policy, System Reform, and Regulations and the Soft Science Committee of the Ministry of Agriculture, "Views and Suggestions from One Hundred Chinese and Foreign Experts on Issues of Grain and Agricultural Development in China (Zhongwai bai ming zhuanjia tantao Zhongguo liangshi ji nongye fazhan de guandian he jianyi)," *Chinese Rural Economy (Zhongguo nongcun jingji)*, 1996, No. 12.

storage enterprises. To many experts, the reform of the grain purchase and marketing system that was needed was to let market forces play their fundamental role by gradual marketization. The *Opinion on Further Deepening Reform of the Grain Circulation System* issued by the State Council in July 2001 pushed the grain circulation system closer to marketization and liberalized the grain retail markets of eight provinces and municipalities of major consuming regions, including Zhejiang, Shanghai, Fujian, Guangdong, Hainan, Jiangsu, Beijing, and Tianjin.

After liberalizing grain retail markets in major consuming regions nationwide, the focus of decision makers and most experts was on how to liberalize grain retail markets in major producing regions and how to protect the interests of grain farmers in the process. In terms of general orientation, the marketization of the grain purchase and marketing system will be realized sooner or later in China. Feasible reform involves a complete liberalization of grain purchase and marketing in major producing regions to let the market play its full role, together with direct subsidies to grain farmers in major producing regions. In September 2002, the State Council arranged for Anhui Province to conduct reform experiments with direct subsidies to grain farmers in Laian County and Tianchang County. Similar reform experiments were also carried out in 2002 in selected localities in Hunan, Hubei, Jilin, Henan, and Zhejiang provinces.

The direct subsidy reform primarily consisted of "two liberalizations and one adjustment," that is, liberalization of grain purchasing price, liberalization of grain retail markets, and adjustment to replace the indirect subsidy of state purchase without restriction at protective price with a direct subsidy in the form of state payments to farmers covering the price difference between the protective price and the market price. After the grain retail markets in experimental localities are liberalized, all enterprises, regardless of the nature of their ownership, are eligible to engage in the grain purchasing business as long as records are filed with the state grain departments and the industrial and commercial administration departments, with verification and registration from the latter, as well. Based on conditions in the aforementioned provinces, it is clear that direct subsidies have achieved positive results. The subsidies have not only increased farmers' income and alleviated the burden on government finance, but also invigorated the grain market and greatly facilitated the structural adjustment of agriculture and grain mix.

The *Decision of the CCCPC on Issues Regarding the Improvement of the Socialist Market Economic System* (hereafter the *Decision*) approved by the Third Plenary Session of the 16th CCCPC in October 2003 clarified the requirements of "improving the market system for agricultural products, liberalizing the grain purchasing market, and practically protecting the interests of grain farmers by carrying out direct subsidies to farmers instead of indirect subsidy through circulation."

In a similar manner, the reform of the cotton purchase and marketing system also experienced twists and turns over its implementation. In 1992 and 1993, cotton production dropped considerably,[52] which once again revealed the tension between cotton supply and demand, resulting in stagnation of the reform of the cotton purchase and marketing system. In August 1994, the State Council convened a national working conference on cotton in Beijing, and proposed a policy for cotton purchase and marketing known as "three non-liberalizations," that is, price, purchase, and marketing were not to be liberalized. Subsequently, in September 1994, the State Council issued the *Circular on Getting the Job of Cotton Purchase and Marketing in 1994 Done,* deciding to continue the unified purchase, processing, and distribution by supply and marketing cooperatives. No other units or individuals were allowed to purchase, process, and distribute cotton.

After the mid–1990s, cotton production increased for several consecutive years. In addition, a number of domestic chemical fiber plants successively began operation and greatly increased the supply of cotton substitutes. As a result, conditions were ripe for re-starting the reform of the cotton circulation system. In November 1998, the State Council promulgated the *Decision on Deepening Reform of the Cotton Circulation System.* The primary actions of the reform were:

- starting on September 1, 1999, control over cotton price would be lifted, and the price would mainly be determined by the market;

- the distribution channel of cotton would be broadened so that supply and marketing cooperatives and their cotton enterprises, cotton processing plants of agricultural departments, state farms, and spinning enterprises with certified qualification, could directly purchase, process, and distribute cotton, but private cotton dealers and other units without certified qualification were not allowed to purchase and process cotton;

- a public inspection system of cotton was to be introduced gradually and supervision and control over cotton quality be strengthened;

- a cotton trading market would be cultivated and a national cotton trading network supported by major cotton producing and consuming regions and centered on the cotton trading market be established.

---

[52] Cotton output nationwide dropped from 5.675 million tons in 1991 to 4.508 million tons in 1992; the figure further dropped to 3.739 million tons in 1993. See the National Bureau of Statistics, *China Statistical Yearbook (Zhongguo tongji nianjian) (2002),* Beijing: China Statistics Press, 2002, p. 107.

Afterwards, the State Council instituted adjustments and reforms several times. For example, the State Council removed monopolies on the basis of liberalizing cotton purchase; it implemented "double-separation" for supply and marketing cooperatives, that is, separation of cooperatives from enterprises and separation of storage from distribution; it straightened out and maintained cotton market order, tightened qualification certification and control over cotton purchasing and processing enterprises to ensure cotton quality; it actively promoted industrialized cotton operation by encouraging cotton spinning enterprises to engage in various cooperations with cotton farmers.

These reforms played a very important role in establishing a cotton purchase and marketing system compatible with a market economy. Notwithstanding, the problem of establishing cotton circulation enterprises with international market competitiveness, as well as an orderly market system, remains to be solved by further reforms.

3.3.2 Improving the Land System

The essence of the household contracting system is to separate land ownership from land-use right to a certain extent, and grant farmers land-use right during the contract period without changing land ownership. This land system innovation enabled farmers to build up their family farms on the "contracted" land, and this played a decisive role in promoting rapid growth in agricultural production. Nevertheless, the contracting system still had its limitations, as reflected in the following several aspects.

First, the land-use right obtained by farmers through contract was still imperfect. As the household awarded the contract did not possess a legal and permanent land-use right (that is, the "field surface right" mentioned in Section 3.2 of this chapter), the household felt great uncertainty, and therefore lacked incentive to make investment in the land. For this reason, most farmers' income was used on nonagricultural production investment. From 1978 to 1988, the net income of farmers increased about three times, but during the same period, the amount of investment in residential construction increased by about twenty times. In 1984, agricultural investment of collectives and individuals in rural areas accounted for 15.5 percent of the total rural investment, but this figure dropped to 11.9 percent in 1987. In contrast, nonagricultural investment rose from 84.5 to 88.1 percent.[53] Dwindling investment in land by farmers year after year led to a decline in land productivity. To overcome these defects, the central government twice extended the period of farmland contracts. In 1985, various localities throughout the nation signed a fifteen-year contract. In 1993, the CCCPC proposed to further ex-

---

[53]Chen Jiyuan (ed.), *Social and Economic Changes in Rural China (Zhongguo nongcun shehui jingji bianqian)*, Taiyuan: Shanxi Economy Press, 1993, p. 534.

tend the land contract period for another thirty years. Although the decision was warmly welcomed by farmers, contract period extension by no means fully resolved the issue of property rights. So, farmers still had misgivings about land investment and this also caused some difficulties for promoting new agricultural technologies.

Second, without clearly defined property rights, free transfer of the land-use right could not occur, and therefore larger scale agricultural operations could not proceed on the basis of land property optimization and reorganization, but only through administrative orders.

Third, land was transferred to nonagricultural uses in the process of accelerated industrialization and urbanization, but farmers had no legal claim to adequate compensation for the loss of their land-use right. Huge earnings from large amounts of land transferred from agriculture to nonagriculture were held back and swallowed up by various levels of government as well as industrial and commercial enterprises. According to estimates by economist Chen Xiwen, low-priced farmland requisition caused at least RMB 2,000 billion worth of losses to farmers since the commencement of the reform and opening up.[54] Moreover, farmers whose land had been occupied with no or inadequate compensation and who could not transfer themselves to nonagricultural industries, lost their means of making a living, which usually resulted in major social problems.

In view of these problems in the land system, the central government, in addition to stressing that the land contract period would remain stable for thirty years, also formulated laws to guarantee that farmers can fully exercise their rights of contractual operations within the contract period. In August 2002, the National People's Congress passed the *Law of the PRC on Land Contracts in Rural Areas* (hereafter the *Land Contract Law*). It expressly stipulated that:

1. the state protects the long-term stability of rural land contract relations according to law;

2. the state protects the rights of the party awarded the contract to transfer contractual operations with compensation, of their own will, and according to law;

3. the party awarded the contract has the right to use the land, to keep the income from the land, and to transfer the land-use contract, and that party is entitled to compensation for lawful requisition and appropriation of the contracted land according to law;

---

[54]Chen Xiwen, "Speech at the Chang-An Forum in February 2003 (2003 nian 2 yue zai Chang'an Luntan shang de jianghua)," *21st Century Business Herald (21 shiji jingji baodao)*, February 13, 2003.

4. land circulation proceeds are owned by the party awarded the contract according to law.

Nevertheless, even after the promulgation of the *Land Contract Law,* there were still problems to be solved. First, rural collectives owned rural land, and yet the law failed to clearly define how the rural collective is formed and how farmers, as members of the collective, exercise their rights and functions. As land is the last line of defense for farmers' survival, if there were institutional defects in this line of defense, troubles would be bred in rural areas, and even the entire society. Second, as the use right of contracted land was limited by the contract period, the property rights of farmers were limited as well. For instance, farmers had no adequate legal means to resist acts of administrative authorities to requisition land for commercial purposes without adequate compensation. In short, the land property rights system required further improvement and reform in the future; procedures for farmers to exercise their rights as the owner of the village collective needed to be clarified; a permanent use right of contracted land (i.e., "field surface right") should be granted; and "field surface right" transfer, lease, and succession should be explicitly defined so as to better represent and protect farmers' rights and interests.

3.3.3 Alleviating the Burden on Farmers

The Chinese government had issued orders and instructions many times to rigidly stipulate that the burden of "three retention fees and five contribution fees" on farmers should not exceed 5 percent of the per capita net income of the rural family in the previous year.[55] However, these policy measures hardly had any effect. In 2000, the government resolved to reform the rural tax and fee system. In March 2000, an experiment in rural tax and fee reform was first launched in Anhui Province. In February 2001, the experimental reform scheme was introduced in 107 counties of more than 20 provinces. In March 2002, the State Council decided to further expand the experiment in 16 provinces and autonomous regions. By the end of 2002, more than 20 provinces and municipalities conducted rural tax and fee reform on a large scale, involving a rural population of 700 million. The fundamental ideas for this reform were to abolish administrative fees such as township contribution fees and government funds such as rural education pooling fund, collected solely from farmers; to abolish uniformly prescribed

---

[55] "Three retention fees and five contribution fees" were three fees for the public accumulation fund, the public welfare fund, and administrative expenses as well as five fees for school establishment at the township and village levels, family planning, special care to disabled servicemen and families of martyrs and servicemen, militia training, and repair and construction of rural roadways that farmers turned in to township governments. See the State Council, "Regulations on the Control of Expenses and Labor Service Shouldered by Farmers (Nongmin chengdan feiyong he laowu guanli tiaoli)," *People's Daily (Renmin ribao),* December 13, 1991.

accumulation labor service and compulsory labor service; to abolish slaughter tax and reduce agricultural tax and agricultural specialties tax; to collect village retention fees as agricultural surtax in a unified way, with a maximum of 20 percent of agricultural tax. The village retention fees would be controlled at the township level and used at the village level.[56] Results achieved throughout the country indicated that rural tax and fee reform could alleviate the burden on farmers by about 30 percent.[57] In 2003, the State Council extended this reform to all rural China.

At the same time, the Ministry of Finance and the State Administration of Taxation decided to gradually eliminate agricultural specialties tax, except for some special products such as tobacco leaves. In October 2003, the *Decision* of the Third Plenary Session of the 16th CCCPC said that agricultural tax would be further reduced in the future to alleviate the burden on farmers.

Although rural tax and fee reform has indeed alleviated the burden on farmers, it has by no means fundamentally solved the problem. The root causes of the problem are the bloated organizations and redundant personnel of governments at the grassroots level. After reform, revenues of townships and villages were reduced while their expenditures remained rigid, and transfer payments from central government finance were not enough to fill the gaps. Under the pressures of fund shortages, new taxes and fees began to be imposed on farmers in a few rural areas where tax and fee reform had been implemented; in some rural areas, the standard tuition fees and miscellaneous fees for primary and junior high schools have been raised without authorization, which has once again aggravated the burden on farmers. If fundamental measures are not taken, the specter of the so-called "Huang Zongxi Law" may haunt China again.[58]

It follows that to completely solve the problem of the overburden on farmers, the rural social and political organization in China must be changed. Taking the bloated organization and redundant personnel of local governments in rural China as an example,

---

[56] Ma Xiaohe et al., *A Study on Rural Tax and Fee Reform in China (Nongcun shuifei gaige yanjiu),* Beijing: China Planning Press, 2002, p. 156.

[57] Ibid., p. 49.

[58] The so-called "Huang Zongxi Law" was the recapitulation by Professor Qin Hui of Tsinghua University of the analysis made by the thinker Huang Zongxi (1610–1695) in the Ming and Qing dynasties, that in Chinese history every tax system reform led to an aggravation of tax. (Qin Hui, "The Reform of Integrating Fees into Taxes and the Huang Zongxi Law (Bingshuizhi gaige yu Huang Zongxi dinglü)," *Farmers in China: Historical Retrospection and Practical Choices (Nongmin Zhongguo: lishi fansi yu xianshi xuanze),* Zhengzhou: Henan People's Publishing House, 2003, pp. 17–23.) Huang Zongxi pointed out that, in Chinese history, reform of integrating fees into taxes had occurred several times, including the "double tax law" in the Tang Dynasty, the "one lash law" in the Ming Dynasty, and "integrating poll tax into land tax" in the Qing Dynasty. After each tax reform, as a portion of nontax miscellaneous impositions had been abrogated, the burden on farmers had been alleviated to some degree. However, as there was no way to stop local authorities from establishing new miscellaneous impositions on top of the already augmented regular taxes, after a time, the burden on farmers would rise to a higher level than that before the reform. Huang Zongxi called this phenomenon the "evil of aggravation without alleviation." Vice Premier Wen Jiabao solemnly declared, when participating in discussions of Hubei delegation of the National People's Congress on March 6, 2003, "Communists are entirely to work for the people's benefits. We can certainly downsize township/town governments, lay off excessive staff, and get out of the vicious cycle of 'Huang Zongxi Law.'"

the root cause of this situation is that the administrative organization at the grassroots level is the extension of the "big government," and its cadres have been in charge of too many things. Therefore, the policy of better staff and simpler administration should be implemented. Meanwhile, rural democratic reform at the grassroots level should also be accelerated. Villagers' self-government should be improved according to the *Organic Law of Villagers' Committees of the PRC* of 1998. At the same time, direct election of grassroots governments should be expanded and mass supervision over township/town and county cadres should be strengthened. Only by doing so can the arbitrary imposition of miscellaneous fees by cadres be stopped, along with corruption and extravagance in various forms.

3.3.4 Solving Contradictions between Small Farmers and Big Markets

At the present, one of the most serious problems to be solved in rural China is to overcome the contradictions between farmers engaged in small-scale operations and big markets. Agricultural production is scattered in space and seasonal in time. In contrast, the consumption of agricultural products is concentrated in space and continuous in time. In particular, the current scale of agricultural operations in China is small; the quantity of any agricultural product supplied to the market by any individual farmer is very limited. Therefore, there is a major contradiction between small farmers' supply and big markets' demand. The solution to this contradiction between small farmers and big markets has become an important issue in promoting the rural economy and improving the farmers' position in market transactions.

A common practice for connecting scattered individual farmers with markets is the so-called "company + farmer" model. Under this model, "flagship companies" engaging in industrial and commercial businesses and possessing strong advantages in capital, technology, and market information, establish relatively stable economic contact and benefit-sharing mechanism with numerous farmers. Farmers provide the companies with agricultural products as raw materials or primary products for processing and marketing according to conditions stipulated in contracts for purchase in advance. These companies usually provide assistance to farmers in the form of seeds/seedlings, technology, and funds.

At present, there are already some successful "company + farmer" economic groups in China. They have played a positive role in invigorating the rural economy and raising farmers' incomes. However, two problems often occur in the practice, harming the interests of either the farmers or the companies. One problem is that the companies take advantage of their powerful connections or private information about the market, while farmers may find themselves in a weak position, dominated by the flagship companies. As a result, the farmers share little in the value-added downstream processing of primary products. The problem manifests itself in several ways. The first is the low rate of contract performance. According to statistics, in 1998, among the 16,948 flagship companies that had contracts with farmers, 38 percent of them failed to keep their promises of protective prices when purchasing farmers' products; in 2000, the contract performance rate of "order-form agriculture" was less than 20 percent. Second, contract formulation can be incomplete, without adequate technical supervision and quality testing measures specified. Third, administrative interference was unavoidable. Fourth, farmers have a weak position in negotiation.[59] Some flagship companies, relying on their own advantageous position, exploited farmers by lowering the product grade and forcing prices down, or acquired resources such as land and credit at favorable terms under the pretense of supporting farmers. The other problem is that, compared to scattered farmers who have the power to make decisions, companies often found themselves in a weak position when collecting and mastering information about production. In particular, damages to companies' interests, such as low rates of contract performance on the part of farmers, always occur when companies have no powerful connections.

According to experiences in market economy countries, one of the most effective approaches to link individual farmers with markets is for farmers to set up their own cooperative economic organizations to provide various preproduction and postproduction services. These cooperative economic organizations are communities of interest for their members. They are not profit-oriented, and their purpose is to serve the members. In developed market economy countries, cooperatives in the realm of circulation play very important roles in providing an interface between small farmers and big markets. For instance, in many countries in Western Europe and North America, more than 80 percent of their farmers have joined different types of cooperatives. In the agricultural product market in Western Europe, products distributed through cooperatives account for 60 percent of the total. Ninety percent of the dairy products in Denmark are marketed by cooperatives. Flowers, fruits, and vegetables marketed by cooperatives in the Netherlands account for 95, 78, and 70 percent of the national market, respectively. Agricultural cooperatives in the United States are also highly developed. There are cereal marketing cooperatives, vegetable trading cooperatives, and fruit trading cooperatives. There are two thousand or so cereal marketing cooperatives in the United States and one-third of all U.S. farmers market their cereal products through cooperatives. Those cooperatives control a 60-percent share of the domestic cereal market and provide 40 percent of American cereal exports. At present, 60 percent of agricultural

---

[59] Zhang Xiaoshan et al., *Connecting the Farmer and the Market—An Exploratory Study on Farmers' Intermediaries in China (Lianjie nonghu yu shichang—Zhongguo nongmin zhongjie zuzhi tanjiu)*, Beijing: China Social Sciences Press, 2002.

cooperatives in the United States are trading cooperatives. The most well-known, large-scale trading cooperatives include Farmland Industries, Inc., of Kansas City; Cenex Harvest States Cooperatives of St. Paul; Sunkist Growers, Inc., in California; and Blue Diamond Growers (almond processing and marketing) in several states. Those cooperatives market many agricultural products, including cereal grains, vegetables, and fruits for many farmers and provide them with market demand and technical information. They are not only bridges and links between farmers and markets, but also an important way for farmers to avoid market risks and protect their own interests.

During the Cooperative Transformation Campaign of the mid-1950s, a great number of agricultural producers' cooperatives known as "collective economic organizations" were set up in China. However, these cooperatives were in fact controlled by the state in much the same way as state-owned enterprises. Later, with agricultural producers' cooperatives as the model, even the original supply and marketing cooperatives and credit cooperatives organized on a voluntary basis were transformed into quasi-state-owned organizations, characterized by vertical integration and a strong flavor of government-run units. After the beginning of the reform and opening up, the Chinese government restored supply and marketing cooperatives and credit cooperatives that had been officially absorbed into the state sector during the Great Cultural Revolution. However, these cooperatives failed to recover their original nature as cooperative organizations formed by members on a voluntary basis and managed by members.[60] In contrast, some new cooperative economic organizations were spontaneously set up by farmers and other operators, such as various types of professional cooperatives, professional and technical associations, and agricultural service centers. As they are market-oriented and organized entirely according to the principle of voluntary participation, joint operation, democratic management, and return of benefits, they were therefore warmly welcomed by farmers. The *Decision* of the Third Plenary Session of the 16th CCCPC demanded that "support should be given to farmers, according to the principle of voluntary participation and democratic management, to develop various rural professional cooperative organizations."

To continue developing rural cooperative economic organizations in the future, the

---

[60] In China, as of the end of 2000, there were more than 28,000 grassroots supply and marketing cooperatives, with employees of the entire system numbering 3.62 million. Rural grassroots credit cooperatives numbered approximately 40,000, with principal capital of RMB 72 billion. In addition, there were also 2.234 million community cooperative economic organizations transferred from the people's communes, of which, 37,000 were at the township/town level and 2.197 million at the village level and below. Although community cooperative economic organizations were called cooperatives, most of them nevertheless affiliated to township/town governments and villagers' committees. In addition, they usually performed the economic administration functions of grassroots governments. Therefore, some people called township/town agriculture-industry-commerce corporations "representatives of the government, playing the role of the secondary township/town governments." See Zhang Xiaoshan et al., *Connecting the Farmer and the Market—An Exploratory Study on Farmers' Intermediaries in China (Lianjie nonghu yu shichang—Zhongguo nongmin zhongjie zuzhi tanjiu)*, Beijing: China Social Sciences Press, 2002, pp. 14, 91–92.

following problems must be solved. First, improvement of the cooperative legislation should be done as quickly as possible. To support the development of cooperatives, many countries confirmed their legal status by legislation. For instance, the United Kingdom passed the first Cooperative Act in the world in 1852, Germany promulgated a unified Cooperative Law in May 1889, the United States adopted the Capper-Volstead Act in 1922, and other countries also formulated laws pertaining to cooperative organizations.[61] Currently, China has not enacted any cooperative-related legislation. Many cooperatives or professional associations have been registered at the administrative bureau for industry and commerce, the civil administrative bureau, the agricultural bureau, or the association of science and technology. But some are not allowed to register anywhere.

Second, the original supply and marketing cooperatives, credit cooperatives, and other cooperative organizations should undergo thorough marketization reform to overcome their inclination to avoid practicing democratic management or serving members but rather maintaining cadres as masters of everything. These old cooperatives need to be transformed into genuine cooperative economic organizations, run according to the principle of the cooperative system.

Third, cooperative economic organizations should gradually expand their scale of operation across regions by implementing operation and management standardization, specialization, and professionalism. What needs to be stressed more, however, is that administrative measures to "go collective" should never be used in these organizations' development. Cooperative economic organizations should rely on market forces to develop and expand on their own according to the principles of voluntary participation, democratic management, and mutual benefit.

3.3.5 The Issue of the Transfer of Rural Surplus Laborers

The most deep-rooted cause of the "three rural problems" in China lies in the strong contradiction between an excessive rural population and scarce agricultural resources. China currently has a population of approximately 1.3 billion, of which more than half are farmers. The quantity of resources per farmer, especially land resources, is extremely small, and the trend of diminishing returns on land is obvious. Because each farming household has only about 8 *mu* (i.e., 1.33 acre) of farmland on average, if the huge quantity of surplus laborers cannot be transferred, the income level of farmers cannot increase significantly, nor can their production and living conditions improve no matter what measures the government adopts, such as increasing prices of agricultural products.

---

[61] Zhang Xiaoshan and Yuan Peng, *Theories and Practice of Cooperative Economy—A Comparative Study between China and Foreign Countries (Hezuo jingji lilun yu shijian—zhongwai bijiao yanjiu)*, Beijing: China City Press, 1991, pp. 57–73.

Therefore, to solve the "three rural problems," the fundamental approach is to transfer rural surplus laborers to nonagricultural industries.

The historical experiences in the economic development of various countries in the world have shown that the transfer of rural surplus laborers to nonagricultural industries is not only a basic component of industrialization, but also a fundamental approach to improve the living standard of farmers. All industrialized countries encountered this problem in their industrialization, although some were able to solve it faster than others, and this, to a great extent, led to differences in the course of industrialization in various countries. For instance, the agricultural population in the United States in 1870 accounted for 50 percent of the total. The figure went down to 30 percent in 1920 when industrialization was generally completed. It was further reduced to 11.6 percent in 1955 and 2.2 percent in 1985. In Japan, the agricultural population was as high as 70 percent of the total in 1870, but it dropped to 48.3 percent in 1950 and 5.9 percent in 1993. In South Korea, the agricultural population was 63.2 percent of the total in 1963, but it was only 12.5 percent in 1995.[62] Compared with industrialized countries, China has a larger population base with a higher proportion of farmers, and therefore faces a more pressing problem of transferring rural surplus laborers to nonagricultural industries. According to estimates, at present, there are about 150 million rural surplus laborers to be transferred to nonagricultural industries in China. If 8 million of them are transferred each year, it will take about twenty years to complete the process. This has become one of the most severe problems confronting China in its process of industrialization.

To facilitate the transfer of rural surplus laborers to nonagricultural industries, vigorous development must be achieved in small and medium enterprises to provide more working opportunities for rural surplus laborers. A comprehensive review of the history of more than two decades of the reform and opening up in China indicates that the transfer of rural surplus laborers to nonagricultural industries was gradually accelerating during the first decade, but the process obviously slowed down in the second decade.

The fundamental reason for the acceleration in the first decade was because China adopted a strategy to vigorously develop nonstate sectors, particularly, township and village enterprises (TVEs). This brought about the following consequences:

1. Rapid growth of agricultural production and universal prosperity triggered an increase in rural accumulation, an essential condition for the transfer of rural surplus laborers;

[62]Justin Y. Lin and Chen Jianbo, "Growth during System Transition: Let More People Participate in the Process and Share the Benefits of Growth (Tizhi zhuanxing zhong de zengzhang: rang geng duo ren canyu zengzhang de guocheng he fenxiang zengzhang de haochu)," *Economic Information Daily,* September 30, 2003.

2. On that basis, TVEs sprang up like mushrooms after rain, creating a great number of new jobs for rural surplus laborers;

3. The urban sector and the export sector of the economy made great progress and also took in a portion of rural surplus laborers to work in cities.

By the mid-1980s, the transfer of rural surplus laborers had reached a historical high. But, in the late 1980s, the transfer slowed down considerably not only because of TVEs' poor accumulation ability, decelerating quantitative expansion, and reduced capacity of unit capital to absorb laborers as a result of their increasing organic composition of capital, but also because of the state sector's stagnant reform, declining efficiency, and increased number of laid-off workers. The symptoms of "SOE disease" displayed by some TVEs owned by township/town governments also reduced their vitality and growth rate and slowed down the transfer. From 1984 to 1988, TVEs alone had absorbed on average about twelve million farmers annually to work in nonagricultural industries. After 1989, however, this figure dropped to five to six million.

After the 15th National Congress of the CPC in 1997, nonstate small and medium enterprises rapidly developed. Correspondingly, the transfer of rural surplus laborers to nonagricultural sectors also sped up. In addition to developing nonstate small and medium enterprises, however, the urbanization issue is also related to the transfer of rural surplus laborers.

Over the past two and half decades, TVEs have developed in two different ways. One was to adopt the "three-locally principle," in which TVEs were scattered in rural areas with their employees "leaving the farmland but not the village home, entering the factory but not the city." This approach was generally adopted by TVEs in the inland regions. The other type of TVEs adopted the market-oriented guideline, in which TVEs were built near cities, in administrative towns, or small nonadministrative towns. In those cases, these small towns where TVEs concentrate usually develop into new cities. TVEs in the coastal regions usually adopt this approach to development.

With these two different development models for TVEs as a backdrop, two different views appeared among economists in China.

One opinion supports the first approach, believing that under conditions in China, the capacity of cities and towns to absorb rural laborers is limited, whereas nonagricultural industries in rural areas play a decisive role in absorbing these surplus laborers. Therefore, relying on cities and towns to expand nonagricultural industries is neither advisable nor practical. The only way out is to shift the focus to rural areas and to ensure the on-site transfer of surplus laborers by developing rural industry. Since the commencement of the reform and opening up, rapid development of rural industry has turned the Chinese economy into a "triple economy structure," which is unique in the world, that is, an economic system formed by the agriculture sector, the rural industry sector, and the urban sector. This opinion argues that people must fully appreciate the uniqueness of China, take a critical view in adopting theories and policies pertaining to the "dual economy," and base rural development and rural labor transfer on the development of rural industry, which will also promote the development of the whole national economy.[63]

Some other economists hold the opposite view, however, believing that these kinds of enterprises scattered in rural areas have serious weaknesses. In addition to resulting in widespread sources of pollution and, therefore, difficulties in control and prevention, these kinds of scattered enterprises are usually low in efficiency as they can neither generate the agglomeration effects necessary for industrial development nor make use of what urban enterprises can, such as urban public service facilities, public support systems, cooperation based on division of labor among enterprises, and the convenience of a hub of communication.[64]

The development of the two types of TVEs over the past dozen years seems to have supported the second view. One important reason why some TVEs have failed to successfully develop in the inland regions is because they are scattered in rural areas, incurring high costs with low efficiency. Based on these experiences, it appears that the transfer of rural surplus laborers should be combined with the urbanization process.

Small towns,[65] because they are close to the countryside, with relatively low thresholds for entry, are comparatively more suitable for rural surplus laborers with relatively little accumulation of material capital and human capital. Since the inception of the reform and opening up, small towns have developed very fast and absorbed a great number of rural surplus laborers. At the end of 1978, there were only 2,173 administrative towns across the nation. However, by the end of 1998, administrative towns had increased to 19,216, with a total town population of 170 million. By the end of 2002, administrative towns numbered 19,811, nine times the number in 1978, accounting for more than 50 percent of the total number of townships and towns (39,240). The total

---

[63]Li Keqiang, "The Triple Economy Structure in China (Lun wo guo jingji de san yuan jiegou)," *Social Sciences in China,* 1991, No. 3. See also Chen Jiyuan and Hu Biliang, "The Triple Economy Structure and the Transfer of Rural Labor in China (Zhongguo de san yuan jingji jiegou yu nongye laodongli zhuanyi)," *Economic Research Journal,* 1994, No. 4.

[64]Gu Shengzu, "Where Is Chinese Rural Surplus Labor Heading? (Zhongguo nongcun shengyu laodongli xiang hechu qu)," *Reform,* 1994, No. 4, pp. 79–87.

[65]Small towns are the link between the city and the countryside, the "tail of the city, head of the countryside," with both features of the city and the countryside. They are the political, economic, and cultural centers of a certain area of the countryside, with relatively strong radiating capacities. In their extension, small towns have both a narrow and a broad sense. Small towns in the narrow sense usually refer to administrative towns (including towns in areas just outside city limits, according to the definition of random sample surveys by relevant departments and commissions of the State Council, such as the National Bureau of Statistics and the State Commission for Restructuring Economic Systems). Small towns in the broad sense refer to small market towns above a certain scale in addition to administrative towns; small market towns include the locations of township governments and the headquarters of more than two thousand state-owned farms as well as small market towns developed from administrative villages and the locations of clusters of TVEs. "Small towns" in this book refer to administrative towns.

town population had grown to 220 million, while the total population of the areas under their jurisdictions had reached over 640 million.

Small towns are only a fraction of the urban system. Comprehensive advance of urbanization requires coordinated development of large, medium, and small cities and small towns. Before the reform and opening up, the urbanization process in China was very slow. In 1951, the urbanization level was 11.8 percent; in 1978, it was only 17.9 percent. Since the commencement of the reform and opening up, the urbanization process in China has accelerated. Administrative cities increased from 223 in 1980 to 660 in 2002. The urbanization level increased from 17.9 percent in 1978 to 39.1 percent in 2002.

Statistics from the *World Development Report 1997* of the World Bank reveals that GNP per capita in China in 1995 was US$620, and the urbanization level was 30 percent. The average urbanization level in the same year of the eleven countries with GNP per capita between US$500 and 730 was 42.5 percent. This gap in urbanization level means that China urbanized about 150 million less rural population than it should have. Calculated according to purchasing power parity (PPP) by the World Bank, China's GNP per capita in 1996 was US$2,920. The average urbanization level of the nineteen countries with GNP per capita between US$2,000–3,800 (PPP) was 50.8 percent. So, according to this measurement, China urbanized about 250 million less rural population than it should have. In 1996, the average urbanization level of the world reached 45.5 percent, that of developed countries was generally more than 70 percent, and that of developing countries was on average over 40 percent. The urbanization levels of some developing countries with similar levels of economic development to China and of some newly industrialized countries were also considerably higher than that of China. For instance, the urbanization level of Brazil was 78 percent; Argentina, 88.4 percent; Australia, 84.7 percent; New Zealand, 86.1 percent; South Korea, 82.3 percent; North Korea, 61.5 percent; and the Philippines, 54.9 percent. The urbanization level of China was only 29.4 percent during the same period of time, grossly lagging behind.

Therefore, to vigorously develop small and medium enterprises, to increase urbanization in an orderly fashion, to abolish restrictions on farmers seeking employment in urban areas, to create more employment opportunities for farmers, to improve the environment for the transfer of rural surplus laborers, and to accelerate the employment of rural surplus laborers in nonagricultural industries are all arduous tasks for China to undertake for many years to come.

In October 2003, the 16th National Congress of the CPC put forward the requirement to "improve the environment for the transfer of rural surplus laborers," which included establishing and improving the training mechanism for rural laborers, promoting the reform and adjustment of TVEs, developing regional economies at the county level, enlarging the scope of rural employment, and abolishing restrictions on farmers seeking employment in urban areas to create more employment opportunities for farmers. Additional requirements were implemented to unify urban and rural labor markets step by step by providing better guidance and management, formulate the system of equal employment in both urban and rural areas, deepen the reform of the residence registration system, and improve the management of the transient population to direct the rural surplus laborers to transfer in a steady and orderly way. To accelerate urbanization, the rural population with stable jobs and residences in urban areas may be allowed, according to local rules, to have residence registration in their places of employment or residence and thus enjoy the same rights and undertake the same obligations as the local people. The implementation of these measures can significantly accelerate China's transfer of rural surplus laborers to urban nonagricultural industries.

CHAPTER 4

REFORM OF STATE-OWNED ENTERPRISES

An important part of the transitional process from a traditional centrally planned economy to a modern market economy is the transformation of the corporate sector, the basic economic unit, from a dependent unit in the State Syndicate to real enterprise. The significance of the transformation of the corporate sector is that it creates the microeconomic foundation for a modern market economy. There are three basic approaches for this transformation: the first is to develop private enterprises; the second is to withdraw state-owned capital from ordinary competitive industries; and the third is to transform traditional state-owned units, turning them into modern enterprises compatible with a market economy. Coordinated action in these three approaches will gradually result in diverse forms of ownership developing side by side. From the discussion on transition strategy in Chapter 1, of these three approaches, the development of the private sector is the most fundamental. However, in terms of chronological order, the issue of state-owned enterprise (SOE) reform was the first one raised. Hence, this chapter focuses on the subject of SOE reform.

4.1 The Enterprise System of Traditional SOEs and the Reform with the Main Theme of Power-Delegating and Profit-Sharing

China entered socialism "with drums beating and gongs clanging" in 1956. The Soviet-style state-owned and state-run enterprise system was soon established throughout the nation. To understand why it must be reformed, we must first know the characteristics of this type of system.

4.1.1 Major Features of the Enterprise System of Traditional SOEs

4.1.1.1 Basic Production Units of the "Immense Social Factory" Run Directly by the Government

The traditional state sector was established according to the Lenin model of State Syndicate (see Chapter 1). After the residence registration system separated urban China from rural China, all nonagricultural industries in cities were organized into a gigantic enterprise and all urban laborers became employees of the government. In this Party-

State Inc.,[1] the so-called "state-owned enterprise" (which had been known as a "state-run enterprise" for a long time in the past) was essentially a grassroots production unit for cost accounting, but did not have various attributes that an enterprise should have. Attached to the party and government organs, an SOE had the basic task of carrying out all the instructions and directives from its superiors. In terms of economic activities, the primary task of an SOE was to accomplish the plan mandated by the government, rather than bringing into play its "vigor" and engaging in innovative activities. Government departments determined everything for an enterprise through planned directives: what to produce, how many to produce, how to produce, where to get raw and processed materials, and to whom the products would be sold. The role of the management of an enterprise was simply to carry out the instructions. Therefore, some economists have argued that there was no real enterprise under the traditional system.[2] SOEs had neither the motivation nor the capacity to make decisions for optimal allocation of resources based on their own interests and changes in market. Vertically, they were subordinate to the administrative organs that both held the ownership of enterprises and served as the regulator of society and economy.

4.1.1.2 Multiple Roles and Multiple Objectives

Under the highly integrated system of the party, the state, and the economy, SOEs were not only production units but also grassroots organizations of the party-state political system with extensive social functions.[3] Correspondingly, as the owner of SOEs, the state integrated its function as enterprise owner with its other political and social functions. As a result, the multiple objectives of SOEs conflicted with each other. The state regarded SOEs as instruments to achieve its political and economic objectives, such as to establish a strong military industry and to catch up with and surpass Western countries. Therefore, managers of SOEs were regarded as cadres of the party and were governed in the same way under the same system as staff of the party and government organs. Moreover, SOEs integrated the functions of employment, social security, and social relief, providing a full spectrum of social services from cradle to grave.

---

[1] Due to the absolute dominance of the ruling party in the state organization of the Stalin model, Hungarian economist Maria Csanadi called this kind of state sector "Party-State Economy," or "Party-State Inc." (Maria Csanadi, *Party-States and Their Legacies in Post-Communist Transformation (Studies of Communism in Transition)*, Cheltenham, U.K.: Edward Elgar Publishing, 1997.)

[2] Japanese economist Ryutaro Komiya pointed out in his paper for the China-Japan Economics Symposium held in Okinawa on May 11–14, 1985 that "My impression is that there is no, or almost no, enterprise in China." See Wu Jiajun and Wang Haibo (eds.), *Economic Theories and Economic Policies (Jingji lilun yu jingji zhengce)*, Beijing: Economic Management Press, 1986, pp. 328–329.

[3] These functions of SOEs were pushed to the utmost in the era of the Great Cultural Revolution. The slogan at that time was, "Enterprises are fortresses of proletarian dictatorship."

4.1.1.3 Dissevered Ownership

State ownership was exercised through an organizational system dissevered horizontally and vertically, without symmetry between power and responsibility. First, the tasks of running SOEs were shared by the central government and local governments at various levels. Based on administrative affiliation, SOEs were managed by governments at various levels. Second, at each level of government, the power to run SOEs was segmented into several government departments as well. Generally, the decision-making power regarding investment and production was held by administrative organs like the planning commission and the economic commission; the power to appoint, remove, assess, and supervise chief executives of enterprises belonged primarily to the organization department of the party and the personnel bureau of the government; under the financial system of unified control over revenues and expenditures, the government finance department acted as the financial department of SOEs, administering their cash flows, revenues, and expenditures and collecting taxes, fees, and profits; replacing the labor market with administrative measures, the labor department allocated labor forces for SOEs, and they set human resource policies involving employment, salaries, bonuses, etc. for SOEs. This was an ineffective institutional arrangement because it dissevered unified ownership and allowed departments of the party and the government to exercise their part of the ownership according to their own requirements and even their own interests. The performance of an enterprise depended on how each department exercised its power, but the departments each exercised their power without taking corresponding responsibility.

4.1.1.4 Highly Softened Budget Constraint

Due to the nonexistence of a product market and a production factors market, SOEs did not need to consider supply and demand of the market. Nor did they need to face market competition. The major work of the factory director was to deal with government organs. First, the system of management and mode of operation was to ensure the achievement of government objectives instead of meeting market demand. Second, they frequently had to negotiate with superior administrative organs to get more resource supplies and to get tasks that were more favorable and easier to accomplish. The most important characteristic of the relation between SOEs and the government is "soft budget constraint" as defined by János Kornai. Because key economic parameters such as prices of inputs and outputs and capital input and taxation—which would decide survival and development of enterprises—were all controlled by the state, enterprises could always change the constraints they faced through negotiation with the government. "If the firm is struck by financial difficulties, the state will bail it out with tax allowances, credits at preferential terms, financial grants, taking over the losses, or permitting price increases. . . . If such interventions are quite frequent, the firm's behavioral norms are established in expectation of it."[4]

4.1.2 The Reform with the Main Theme of Power-Delegating and Profit-Sharing

Efforts at SOE reform can be traced back to the beginning of the establishment of the SOE system in China. From 1956 until 1993, when the Third Plenary Session of the 14th Central Committee of the Communist Party of China (CCCPC) proposed that the direction of SOE reform was to be the institutional innovation of enterprises and the establishment of the modern enterprise system, the primary goal of SOE reform had been to have SOEs "run well and invigorated" on the premise that no change was to be made in the basic institutional framework of SOEs. The specific criterion for being run well and invigorated was either a decrease in losses or an increase in profits on the books. In spite of various reform measures in practice, the essence was to change the distribution of power, responsibility, and benefit between the government and the "insiders" of enterprises (i.e., the managers and workers), that is, to delegate power to and share profit with the insiders of enterprises.

All reform measures with the main theme of "power-delegating and profit-sharing (*fangquan rangli*)" were based on a series of basic diagnoses of the problems of SOEs. According to these diagnoses, the poor performance, low profitability, and inferior competitiveness of SOEs were not due to their basic institutional framework, but rather to the following factors: (a) decision-making power was excessively concentrated in the central government; (b) the government implemented administrative intervention in businesses; (c) the managers and workers of enterprises lacked initiative; (d) the party and government organs chose inappropriate persons to be factory directors (managers) or did not adequately supervise them; (e) the debt burdens of enterprises were too heavy, as were their social burdens; (f) enterprises lacked funds for technological upgrading; (g) enterprises had too many redundant workers; and so on. It was believed that all these problems could be solved through power-delegating and profit-sharing without changing the basic institutional framework of SOEs. There were three major forms of power-delegating and profit-sharing: "transferring enterprises to governments at lower levels (*qiye xiafang*)," "expanding enterprise autonomy (*kuoda qiye zizhuquan*)," and the "enterprise contracting system (*qiye chengbao*)."

---

[4]János Kornai, *Economics of Shortage,* Amsterdam: North-Holland Publishing Company, 1980.

4.1.2.1 Transferring Enterprises to Governments at Lower Levels

This was the primary measure for reforming SOEs in China from 1956 until 1978. The so-called "transferring enterprises to governments at lower levels" referred to transferring enterprises that had been directly under the central departments to local governments at the province, prefecture, or county level for administration. The logic was that the low efficiency of SOEs was caused by the excessive concentration of the control over SOEs in the hands of the central government so that administrative organs were far away from enterprises in location and unable to make correct and timely decisions. If enterprises were transferred to local governments closer in location and interests, the government control over enterprises and the performance of enterprises would improve.

The idea of "transferring enterprises to governments at lower levels" made its first appearance at the Eighth National Congress of the Communist Party of China (CPC) in September 1956. Following the guidelines put forth in "On the Ten Major Relationships" by Mao Zedong, the Congress urged that "based on the principle of unified leadership, management at different levels, acting in accordance with local conditions, and adapting measures to changing situation, efforts should be made to improve the administrative system of the state; to divide the control over enterprises, public institutions, planning and finance; and to appropriately enlarge the control of provinces, autonomous regions, and municipalities directly under the central government."[5] In November 1957, the State Council issued specific regulations for implementation. Out of a total of 9,300 enterprises and public institutions directly under the central departments, 8,100 were transferred to local governments in 1958. The share of enterprises directly under the central departments in national total of gross value of industrial output (GVIO) decreased from 39.7 percent in 1957 to 13.8 percent in 1958.[6] As discussed in Chapter 2, economic disorder resulting from the comprehensive delegation of administrative power together with the Great Leap Forward campaign forced the government to recentralize the control over SOEs. Between 1961 and 1963, many SOEs were gradually taken back by the central departments, and along with newly established ones, enterprises directly under the central departments in national total of GVIO rose to 42.2 percent in 1965.[7]

The failure of transferring enterprises to governments at lower levels in 1958 did not change most people's diagnoses of the causes of the disease of SOEs. Therefore, as the preexisting problems of SOEs emerged again after the recentralization of the control

---

[5] Bo Yibo, *Review of Some Important Decisions and Events (Ruogan zhongda juece yu shijian de huigu)*, Vol. 1, Beijing: The Central Party School Publishing House, 1991, p. 551.
[6] Zhou Taihe et al., *Economic System Reform in Contemporary China (Dangdai Zhongguo de jingji tizhi gaige)*, Beijing: China Social Sciences Press, 1984, p. 70.
[7] Ibid., p. 100

over SOEs, delegating power to local governments once again became the solution chosen by policy makers. In 1966, Mao Zedong once again proposed, "It is not good to concentrate everything in the hands of the central authorities and impose rigid controls."[8] In the chaos of the Great Cultural Revolution, under the slogan that "decentralization is a revolution and the more decentralization, the greater the revolution," the State Council organized and implemented another round of transferring enterprises to governments at lower levels in 1970. After this round of decentralization, the number of enterprises in civilian industry directly under the central departments dropped to 142; the share of enterprises directly under the central departments in national total of GVIO declined once again to 8 percent.[9] The result of this round of decentralization was similar to that of 1958: it exacerbated the chaotic situation of the economy and ended up with recentralization.

The only change accomplished by administrative decentralization by transferring the control over SOEs from the central government to local governments was a change in the relationship between various levels of governments regarding the control over SOEs. It did not change the basic relationship between the government and the enterprise, let alone other aspects of the SOE system. Hence, it failed to improve the performance of SOEs. On the contrary, since resource allocation through administrative orders inherently required a high degree of consistency in command and control by the government, administrative decentralization inevitably led to malfunction of the centrally planned system and to economic disorder.

4.1.2.2 The Guiding Principle of Delegating Power to and Sharing Profit with Enterprises and the Reform of Expanding Enterprise Autonomy

After 1977, most enterprise leaders and economists were against reform of SOEs by "transferring enterprises to governments at lower levels." Generally agreeing with the viewpoint of Sun Yefang,[10] they believed that the lack of growth and efficiency of SOEs was caused by too much control and excessively tight control over them, and that the direction of reform should be delegating power to and sharing profit with enterprises. In the late 1970s, loosening control and delegating power as well as expanding autonomy and sharing profit became the mainstream belief of leading economic departments.[11]

---

[8] Mao Zedong, "Letter on Farm Mechanization (Guanyu nongye jixiehua wenti de yi feng xin) (March 12, 1966)," *People's Daily (Renmin ribao)*, December 26, 1977.

[9] Zhou Taihe et al., *Economic System Reform in Contemporary China (Dangdai Zhongguo de jingji tizhi gaige)*, Beijing: China Social Sciences Press, 1984, p. 137.

[10] See Chapter 1 for Sun Yefang's criticism on transferring enterprises to governments at lower levels.

[11] Yuan Baohua, an important leader of China's SOE reform, expounded in an interview on the process of decision making on the guiding principle of expanding autonomy and sharing profit. See He Yaomin, "Expanding Autonomy and Sharing Profit: the Breakthrough Point in SOE Reform—An Interview with Yuan Baohua (Kuoquan rangli: guoyou qiye gaige de tupokou—fang Yuan Baohua tongzhi)," *Hundred Year Tide (Bainian chao)*, 2003, No. 8.

Based on this new belief, the government of Sichuan Province chose six enterprises, including Chongqing Steel Factory, to experiment with expanding enterprise autonomy in October 1978. The so-called expanding enterprise autonomy is to relax the control by plan over enterprises by government departments and to permit the enterprise management to make the business decisions that had been made by the government in the past; that is, to transfer part of the control from the government to the enterprise management. In the experiments with the six enterprises in Sichuan Province in 1978, the first decision-making rights transferred to the enterprises included the following. First, the enterprises were allowed to retain a certain amount of profits and individual workers could receive a certain amount of bonus payments based on output increase and cost reduction. Second, they were granted autonomy to increase the supply of their products with a strong market demand and to accept customers' materials for processing, on the premise of accomplishing the state plan. Third, they were given the freedom to sell superfluous materials, as well as products that state-owned trading enterprises would not want to purchase, and they could also sell their new products on a trial basis. Fourth, on accomplishing the state plan, they were authorized to set up an enterprise fund and retain a portion of profits. Fifth, they were given the autonomy to appoint middle-level managerial staff.[12]

In July 1979, the State Council issued five related documents, including the *Several Provisions Pertaining to Expanding Decision-Making Power in Operation and Management of State-Run Industrial Enterprises* and the *Provisions Pertaining to Institution of Profit Retention in State-Run Enterprises,* which extended reform measures of expanding enterprise autonomy and profit retention to enterprises nationwide. As of 1980, the measures had been extended to 6,600 large and medium-sized SOEs that accounted for 60 percent of budgeted industrial output value and 70 percent of profits. Between the end of June 1979 and the end of June 1980, the profits of experimental enterprises in Shanghai and Tianjin accounted for over 80 percent of total profits, and those of Beijing 94 percent of total profits. Early in the reform of expanding enterprise autonomy, enterprises showed strong enthusiasm for increasing production and income. However, efficiency was not visibly improved, and before long, problems of chaotic economic order, skyrocketing fiscal deficit, and inflation emerged, bringing this reform into question by many. At the end of 1980, the Chinese government decided to readjust the national economy and SOEs shifted from the reform of expanding enterprise autonomy to the responsibility system for accomplishing the state plan.

Profit retention was the original form of profit-sharing. The definition of profit

---

[12]Zhou Taihe et al., *Economic System Reform in Contemporary China (Dangdai Zhongguo de jingji tizhi gaige),* Beijing: China Social Sciences Press, 1984, p. 166.

retention is that SOEs are permitted to retain a certain portion of profits and to use it for themselves instead of submitting profits in full to the state finance department as in the past. The State Council documents of 1979 divided retained profits into three parts (collectively known as the three funds): the production development fund, the employees' welfare fund, and the employees' bonus fund. The proportion of retained profits was the main parameter to adjust the relationship between the state and the insiders of enterprises in terms of economic benefit, and varied with time and location. The reform of substituting tax payment for profit delivery from 1983 to 1984 converted most profits, previously remitted to the state finance department by SOEs, to tax payments to the state finance department in the forms of enterprise income tax and "regulation tax." After the taxation system reform of 1994, SOEs basically did not need to remit profits to the state finance department, but rather, they paid enterprise income tax at a uniform rate.

4.1.2.3 The Enterprise Contracting System

There were various opinions why the reform of expanding enterprise autonomy had failed to achieve the expected success. The mainstream belief of the leading government department in charge of SOE reform attributed the failure to insufficient power-delegating and profit-sharing. Therefore, they proposed to introduce into industrial and commercial enterprises the contracting system that had been successful in rural reform.[13]

The contracted managerial responsibility system (*chengbao jingying zerenzhi*)[14] in enterprises is a special form of power-delegating and profit-sharing. Its unique feature is that a contract is established between relevant government organs and the management of the enterprise to specify the terms of power-delegating and profit-sharing, as well as the obligations of the insiders (managers and workers) of the enterprise.

In the early 1980s, the household contracted responsibility system with remuneration linked to output (the household contracting system in short) proved successful in the rural areas. Since a suitable way to reform SOEs was still not found then, the contracting system was introduced into SOE reform.

Under the contracting system, the party awarding the contract hands over its property to the party awarded the contract for management. The two parties reach an agreement that ensures the owner a fixed amount of profit; any profit exceeding this amount is then retained by the party awarded the contract or is shared by the two parties according to predetermined proportions. It is, in essence, a kind of hierarchical arrange-

---

[13] For example, the leader of the State Economic Commission commented on expanding enterprise autonomy of 1978 to 1980 by saying that "the five documents were called documents of autonomy-expanding and profit-sharing, but both autonomy-expanding and profit-sharing were really limited in practice." See He Yaomin, ibid.

[14] The official name for the enterprise contracting system.

ment of property rights in which the owner in the lower hierarchy, under the condition of paying fixed rent or proportional rent, can get residual control from the owner in the upper hierarchy during the contract period and can enjoy residual claim to operation surplus after deduction of rent.

In early 1983, the leader of the Secretariat of the CCCPC put forth the slogan that "bring the contracting system to cities and all problems can be solved" and urged the introduction of the enterprise contracting system in all urban industrial and commercial enterprises. During a period of just two to three months, the system was implemented in all SOEs nationwide. But it led to chaotic economic order and rising prices, which forced the leader of the State Council (i.e., Zhao Ziyang) to urge the CCCPC to make a decision to stop implementing the contracting system and to hasten the reform of "substituting tax payment for profit delivery." In June 1983 and October 1984, there were two successive steps for the reform of substituting tax payment for profit delivery. Without necessary reforms in other aspects of the system, substituting tax payment for profit delivery alone still could not enable enterprises to have full managerial autonomy and full responsibility for profits and losses and to participate in fair competition.

At the end of 1986, the leader of the State Council stopped implementing the strategy of coordinated reform and shifted to a strategy with enterprise reform as the main theme. At that time, there was already some intention of using the corporate system (then called the shareholding system) as the main form for the new enterprise system. However, as people were quite unfamiliar with the corporate system, and both basic economic conditions and the legal environment required by the modern corporate system were not ready, people once again chose the contracting system, which was easy to accept. In December 1986, the State Council urged "implementation of diverse forms of the contracted managerial responsibility system and granting of sufficient managerial autonomy to managers." The second surge of enterprise contracting was in mid-1987. By the end of that year, 78 percent of all SOEs covered by the national budget (80 percent of them being large- and medium-sized enterprises) had implemented the contracting system.

The basic principle of the contracting system of SOEs was "fixing the base quota, guaranteeing the remittance, retaining what exceeds the quota, and making up what falls short of the quota." Its main forms included (a) responsibility for fixed quota of profit remittance; (b) proportional sharing of profits; (c) responsibility for a progressive quota of profit remittance; (d) responsibility for loss reduction in loss-incurring enterprises; and (e) Two Guaranteed and One Linked (guaranteed profit and tax remittance, guaranteed technological upgrading projects, and total payroll linked to achieved taxes and profits).

The contracting system neither gave enterprises full managerial autonomy nor promoted the separation of government administration from enterprise management or fair competition among enterprises. At the same time, it solidified the existing system, obstructed the adjustment and optimization of the economic structure, impaired the improvement of economic efficiency, and further increased the difficulties for reform. Although people afterward proposed various correcting measures such as risk-deposit contracting, determining contract terms scientifically, and contracting through public bidding in an attempt to improve the contracting system, it was still impossible to achieve the goal of enabling enterprises to have full responsibility for profits and losses. The root cause of the problem was the innate defects in the institutional arrangement of the contracting system. After granting part of the residual control and residual claim to the party awarded the contract, the definition of the enterprise's property rights became more obscure, the conflict of interest between the two parties was intensified, and mutual infringements by both parties became more likely to occur. By the end of the 1980s and the beginning of the 1990s, except for a very few exceptions, people in all walks of life, including enterprise leaders, no longer thought that the contracting system was a good way to reform SOEs in China.

4.1.3 The Essence of the Reform of Power-Delegating and Profit-Sharing

For many years, the Chinese government's major approach to enterprise reform had been power-delegating and profit-sharing.[15] The State Council issued *Regulations on Transforming the Management Mechanism of Industrial Enterprises Owned by the Whole People* on July 24, 1992. It reaffirmed fourteen managerial rights that enterprises should enjoy.

Insight 4.1

Managerial Rights Prescribed in *Regulations* on *Transforming the Management Mechanism* of *Industrial Enterprises Owned by the Whole People*

Managerial rights of enterprises refer to the rights of possessing, using, and disposing the property that the state has granted to them to manage and operate in accordance with law.

1. Enterprises shall enjoy the right to make decisions on production and operation.

---

[15] According to Yuan Baohua's recollection, on the recommendation of Li Xiannian, a delegation from the State Economic Commission investigated some Japanese enterprises from October to December, 1978. The delegation strongly felt that enterprise reform was necessary in China and that more autonomy should be given to enterprises. After hearing the debriefing of this delegation, Li Xiannian said, "To run the economy well, the first thing is to run enterprises well and to expand enterprise autonomy." See He Yaomin, ibid.

2. Enterprises shall enjoy the right to price products and services.

3. Enterprises shall enjoy the right to sell products. After enterprises fulfill their production quotas of the mandatory plan, they may sell above-quota products by themselves.

4. Enterprises shall enjoy the right to purchase materials and equipment.

5. Enterprises shall enjoy the right to import and export. Enterprises may freely select foreign-trade agents nationwide to handle the business of import and export, and shall enjoy the right to participate in negotiations with foreign traders.

6. Enterprises shall enjoy the right to make decisions on investment.

7. Enterprises shall enjoy the right to allocate retention funds.

8. Enterprises shall enjoy the right to dispose of assets.

9. Enterprises shall enjoy the right to set up joint ownership enterprises and to merge.

10. Enterprises shall enjoy the right to employ labor.

11. Enterprises shall enjoy the right to make decisions on personnel matters.

12. Enterprises shall enjoy the right to distribute salaries and bonuses.

13. Enterprises shall enjoy the right to set up internal organizational structure.

14. Enterprises shall enjoy the right to refuse arbitrary imposition of quotas.

Managerial rights of enterprises are under the protection of law. No department, unit, or individual should intervene or infringe on these rights.

(Compiled from the State Council, "Regulations on Transforming the Management Mechanism of Industrial Enterprises Owned by the Whole People (Quanmin suoyouzhi gongye qiye zhuanhuan jingying jizhi tiaoli), (July 24, 1992)," *A Collection of Important Laws and Regulations on SOE Reform (Guoyou qiye gaige zhongyao fagui huibian)*, Beijing: Central Party Literature Publishing House, 1999, pp. 261–271.)

Many of these managerial rights that an enterprise should enjoy are normally exercised by the board of directors entrusted by owners under the modern corporate system. These include the right to decide independently to modify the scope of production and operation in its own industry or across industries; the right to set prices independently; the right to decide on the apportionment and usage of various funds from retained profits after paying taxes; the right to determine the establishment, adjustment, and dissolution of internal organizations and to decide manning quotas of the enterprise; and so on.[16] According to the *Regulations,* the rights to make decisions on investments, mergers, and splits belong partly to the enterprise and partly to the state. These rights usually belong to the board of directors of a corporation, or sometimes even to the general meeting of shareholders. Therefore, the so-called separation of ownership of the state and managerial rights of the enterprise refers essentially to sharing residual control between the state and the insiders of enterprises.

Profit-sharing has two implications. First, profit-sharing guarantees power-delegating. The management of an enterprise can decide independently to buy assets, upgrade technology, develop new products, create a new enterprise, and independently determine an incentive system for employees only if they have the right of disposal of retained profits. Second, in terms of incentives, profit-sharing links the personal benefits of the insiders to the enterprise's performance. Only if the enterprise makes profits can they retain a portion; the usual situation is that the more profits an enterprise makes, the more profits are at the disposal of the insiders, either formally or informally. Therefore, profit-sharing essentially refers to sharing residual claim between the state and the insiders of enterprises.

Sharing of residual control and residual claim between the state and the insiders of enterprises through power-delegating and profit-sharing has some important features. From the perspective of residual claim, although the insiders can actually share residual income with the state, they basically do not share risks with the state because they do not have equity investment in the enterprise. The aim of letting the enterprise assume full responsibility for profits and losses was doomed to fail from the beginning because

---

[16] Such provisions can be related to the misconception among some leaders on economic affairs and economists in China regarding the division of rights between the enterprise owner and the manager. For example, some scholars once investigated Japanese enterprises and came to the conclusion that the success of Japanese enterprises lay in the institutional arrangement of making the owner a figurehead. (See Wu Jiajun, *Japan's Joint-Stock Companies and China's Enterprise Reform (Riben de gufen gongsi yu Zhongguo de qiye gaige),* Beijing: Economic Management Press, 1994.) This misconception has continued all along. An economist who investigated many Japanese enterprises proposed that in the reform of SOEs, diversification and dispersion of share ownership should be achieved by cross-shareholding among corporations to stabilize the structure of share ownership and to allow the manager to dominate the enterprise, to make the owner a figurehead, and to have full management authority. Furthermore, a reasonable interest structure should be established and an "interest defense" be built so that the manager's interests are linked to managerial performance by salary and bonus rather than to share ownership. On this basis, the enterprise would have full responsibility for profits and losses. (See "Are Independent Directors 'Cakes Drawn to Allay Hunger'? (Duli dongshi shifou huabingchongji)," *China Business Post (Caijing shibao),* August 21, 2001.)

the so-called enterprise in real life is nothing more than its insiders. Since the insiders do not have equity investment, they will always assume responsibility for profits, but never for losses. In effect, those who assume responsibility for losses can only be the owners and creditors of the enterprise. From the perspective of residual control, although the state has granted the insiders of enterprises extensive rights, including some of the rights belonging to the owner, the state has insisted on its sole power in appointment and dismissal of the management of SOEs. The state also retains certain control over issues such as important investment projects, mergers and acquisitions, splits, and asset restructuring.

4.1.4 Achievements and Deficiencies of the Reform of Power-Delegating and Profit-Sharing

SOE reform with the main theme of power-delegating and profit-sharing did achieve certain positive results. As part of the economic reform program in China, these reform measures, while maintaining social and political stability, gradually disengaged SOEs from a traditional planned economy and let them begin to participate in and adapt to market competition with nonstate enterprises. In each key industry, a few high-performance SOEs emerged.

The reason for the reform of power-delegating and profit-sharing to achieve these positive results was that the division of ownership between the state and the insiders of enterprises improved the traditional SOE system in several important aspects. First, in terms of the incentive mechanism, as the management and workers of SOEs could actually share in the profits with the state, SOEs, which had been passive accessories of administrative organs and content with nothing more than the accomplishment of the state plan, were infused with the profit motive to varying degrees. For those enterprises with prospects of significantly improving profitability as long as the management and workers worked hard enough, this incentive was especially strong. The profit motive enabled enterprises to have the initiative and impulse of self-development. Second, in terms of the information mechanism and decision-making efficiency, in contrast to when government organs dominated everything, decision making was decentralized enormously because of the greatly expanded managerial autonomy of the management of enterprises and the greatly reduced administrative intervention of the government. The burden of information collecting and processing was shifted from the government to enterprises, enabling the decision making by enterprises to be more timely and effective than that by the government in the past.

However, the achievements of the reform of power-delegating and profit-sharing were quite limited. The main reason was that it did not change the basic institutional framework of SOEs and thus could not solve many of the aforementioned problems of

SOEs, such as multiple objectives, function of the owner being dissevered horizontally and vertically without symmetry between power and responsibility, and soft budget constraint. Meanwhile, attempts to improve the management performance of enterprises by dissevering the owner's rights between the state and the insiders also generated significant negative effects.

First, the reform of power-delegating and profit-sharing did not change the basic institutional framework and ways for the state to exercise its ownership. It made reforms unavoidably fall into a dilemma. In order to overcome maladies of the traditional system of SOEs and to reduce administrative intervention of the government in the operation of enterprises, the government had to delegate more managerial power to the insiders of enterprises, for it had to be either the government organs or the insiders of enterprises under this basic institutional framework. However, since the insiders of enterprises were not the real owner investing capital in the enterprises, power delegating to a certain extent would unavoidably lead to unchecked insider control. To keep insider control in check, the only system that could be relied upon was still government intervention, namely, strengthening the supervision and intervention by the party and government organs, which in turn would incur the perennial maladies of managing enterprises through administrative means by the government.

Second, the reform of power-delegating and profit-sharing did not change the basic institutional framework of SOEs. As business entities under the factory system, SOEs had a closed structure of ownership that would not admit multiple investment entities. Due to the lack of a modern corporate governance structure centered on a board of directors, enterprises under the factory system could rely only on the factory director responsibility system under the leadership of the party committee and had to rely on the party committee and workers and the superior party and government organs to supervise the factory directors. On one hand, this kind of governance structure often fell into a paralytic state due to the poorly defined division of power and responsibility between the factory director and the party committee; on the other hand, it often led to unchecked insider control and corruption.

Third, the reform of power-delegating and profit-sharing caused chaotic relationships of property rights and a serious problem of unchecked insider control due to the disseverance of ownership of SOEs between the state and the insiders. In the context of the reform of power-delegating and profit-sharing and following the philosophy of separation of ownership and control, the 1988 *Law of the PRC on Industrial Enterprises Owned by the Whole People* made a series of provisions that caused distortion of the enterprise property system. This distortion included defining factory directors as legal representatives of enterprises. Without a corporate governance mechanism like a board of directors, granting legal representatives a series of decision-making powers to run enterprises was essentially to grant them de facto partial ownership. This de facto partial ownership gave many legal representatives of enterprises a strong incentive to try to turn this ownership into de jure complete ownership. Maladies of this incentive mechanism were demonstrated in a series of corruption cases of legal representatives of SOEs.

Insight 4.2

Enterprise Law of 1988 and Its Impacts on Company Law of 1993

Based on the contracting system of SOEs and written in 1988, the *Law of the PRC on Industrial Enterprises Owned by the Whole People* (the *Enterprise Law* hereafter) was often viewed as the norm for the new type of SOEs. Its definition of the principle of separation of ownership and control has had widespread influence on enterprise reform.

1. The property of state-owned enterprises belongs to the whole people. The state grants managerial rights to enterprises according to the principle of separation of ownership and control. Enterprises hold rights of possessing, using, and disposing of the property that has been granted by the state for management and operation.

2. Enterprises acquire the status of a legal person according to law, and undertake civil liability with the property granted by the state for management and operation. The law protects the property granted by the state for management and operation against any infringement.

3. The factory director (manager) responsibility system should be implemented in enterprises. Factory directors are legal representatives of enterprises.

The aforementioned provisions mean that in state-owned industrial enterprises subject to the *Enterprise Law,* the state, as the property rights owner of enterprises, grants basic property rights to factory directors (managers), as "legal representatives"* of enterprises as legal persons, and holds only abstract ownership. Such provisions confound the specific control held by salaried executives within the limits of rights granted by the owner with the residual control held by the owner and become the legal basis for insider control so widespread in transformed SOEs.

This obliteration by the *Enterprise Law* of the difference between the function and power of professional managers and the property rights of the owner also manifested to some extent in the *Company Law* of 1993. Articles 45, 68, and 113 of the *Company Law* all prescribe that the board chairman is the legal representative of the company, no matter whether the company is a limited-liability company, a joint stock limited company, or a wholly state-owned company. Using law to designate the board chairman as a natural representative of a company violates a basic principle of civil law, the principle of private autonomy. Hence, it has bred various malpractices.**

*"Legal representative" of an enterprise is a special concept that was introduced at the beginning of SOE reform in China. Article 44, Section 2 of *Civil Procedure Law of the PRC (for Trial Implementation)* of 1982 prescribed that "Any enterprise or institution, State organ, or public organization may be a party to a civil proceeding, and the principal person in charge of such a unit will act as the legal representative." The Supreme People's Court provided a further definition of legal representative in *Opinions on Implementing the Civil Procedure Law (for Trial Implementation)* of 1984 that "The legal representative of any enterprise or institution, State organ, or public organization should be its chief executive." Article 38 of *General Principles of the Civil Law of the PRC* of 1986 prescribed that "According to law or the corporate memorandum of association, the person in charge performing functions on behalf of the corporation is the legal representative of the corporation." Thus, the concept of legal representative was established in China's laws.

**See Wu Jinglian, "Should a Company Have a Fixed 'Legal Representative'? (Gongsi yingfou sheli guding de 'fading daibiaoren') (1996)," in Wu Jinglian, *On Building the Infrastructure of a Market Economy (Gouzhu shichang jingji de jichu jiegou)*, Beijing: China Economic Publishing House, 1997, pp. 117–124. See also Fang Liufang, "Legal Status, Rights, and Conflict of Interest of Legal Representatives in SOEs (Guoqi fading daibiaoren de falü diwei, quanli he liyi chongtu)," *Studies of Comparative Law (Bijiaofa yanjiu)*, 1999, Vol. 13, No. 1.

4.2 Corporatization of Large SOEs

The Decision on Issues Regarding the Establishment of a Socialist Market Economic System, adopted at the Third Plenary Session of the 14th CCCPC in November 1993, stated that deepening SOE reforms should "emphasize the institutional innovation of enterprises." This marked a shift in SOE reform strategy from power-delegating and profit-sharing to the institutional innovation of enterprises. How then to achieve this innovation? The answer of the *Decision* was to establish a modern enterprise system, which referred to modern corporations. However, the *Decision* did not give a specific definition for modern corporate governance, but rather, described it as an enterprise system characterized by "clearly established property rights, well-defined power and responsibility, separation of enterprise from government, and scientific management."

The significance of the *Decision* of the Third Plenary Session of the 14th CCCPC was that it set corporatization as the direction of SOE reform in the form of the ruling party's document.

4.2.1 Progress in Corporatization of Large SOEs

On December 29, 1993, the National People's Congress passed the *Company Law of the People's Republic of China,* which went into effect on July 1, 1994. In November 1994, the State Council decided to convene the "National Working Conference for Experiments in Establishing a Modern Enterprise System" and to select one hundred SOEs as pilot studies for corporatization. Due to the lack of emphasis on using diversification of share ownership to restructure existing SOEs into real enterprises, most enterprises involved in the experiment simply converted themselves to wholly state-owned companies that were similar to modern corporations only in form. Therefore, the prescheduled evaluation at the end of 1996 showed that almost no experimental enterprise had achieved the minimum standards of a modern corporation. It was not until the 15th National Congress of the CPC in 1997 and particularly until the Fourth Plenary Session of the 15th CCCPC in 1999, which reiterated the requirements for corporatization, that corporatization reform of large and medium-sized SOEs entered the period of establishing modern corporations according to internationally prevalent norms.

The *Decision on Several Important Issues Regarding Reform and Development of State-Owned Enterprises,* adopted at the Fourth Plenary Session of the 15th CCCPC in 1999, brought forth some new requirements for the corporatization of large and medium-sized SOEs. First, it emphasized corporate governance after corporatization by pointing out that "corporate governance structure, which can establish checks and balances between the owner and the manager, is the core of the corporate system" and required that all the corporatized SOEs establish effective corporate governance. Second, it required that, except for a minority of enterprises that could be monopolized by the state, the rest should "actively develop corporations with multiple equity-holding entities" and should introduce nonstate equity investment. It mandated that large and medium-sized SOEs, especially well-performing ones suitable for the shareholding system, should be converted to shareholding enterprises by initial public offering (IPO), establishment of Chinese-foreign joint ventures, and use of cross-shareholding among enterprises. These steps would develop a sector of mixed ownership, with the state holding a controlling interest in important enterprises.

Corporatization of large and medium-sized SOEs after 1998 basically included three successive steps: (1) separation of administrative function and enterprise function; (2) reorganization of monopoly enterprises into competitive enterprises; and (3) IPO on domestic and overseas securities markets after asset restructuring.

4.2.1.1 Separating Administrative Function and Enterprise Function

During the era of a planned economy, the government integrated its function as the administrator of society and economy with its function as the owner of state assets. Such being the case, economic units were both administrative organs and so-called "enterprises." To separate administrative function and enterprise function so they could be performed by different organizations, the new government that took office in 1998 took an important step. It transferred administrative function of ministry-level institutions ("national industry corporations" and "group corporations" that belonged to the central government and had both administrative and enterprise functions), to "state bureaus" under the State Economic and Trade Commission,[17] thus turning these national industry corporations and group corporations into enterprises without administrative function.

4.2.1.2 Breaking Up Monopolies

Under a planned economy, to maximize the scale of operation, usually only one enterprise was set up in one industry or one sub-industry. This enterprise held a monopoly status in its industry. After 1998, the state broke up monopolies to promote competition by splitting and restructuring those enterprises. Taking the petroleum industry as an example, before the reform and opening up, the state established the Ministry of the Petroleum Industry and the Ministry of the Petrochemical Industry to manage upstream businesses and downstream businesses, respectively. The Ministry of Petrochemical Industry, which managed the downstream businesses, was restructured into the China Petrochemical Corporation (SINOPEC) in 1983. Later, in 1988, the Ministry of the Petroleum Industry, which managed the upstream businesses, was restructured into the China National Petroleum Corporation (CNPC). SINOPEC and CNPC became two administrative corporations, holding both administrative and enterprise functions. In June 1998, after transferring the administrative function of both corporations to the State Bureau of Petroleum Industry under the State Economic and Trade Commission, the government decided to restructure them into comprehensive petroleum companies. The specific approach was to transfer downstream businesses such as oil refining and retailing of SINOPEC in northern China to CNPC, to transfer the oil fields of CNPC in southern China to SINOPEC, and to permit them to invest and operate in each other's territory. These two corporations, in addition to the China National Offshore Oil Corporation (CNOOC), which was originally engaged in offshore

---

[17] Administrative functions in foreign trade and telecommunication were not performed by state bureaus under the State Economic and Trade Commission; instead, they were performed by the Ministry of Foreign Trade and Economic Cooperation (MOFTEC) and the Ministry of Information Industry (MII), respectively.

petroleum extraction, became the three comprehensive petroleum companies competing with each other in China. Similar approaches were employed to create a competitive situation in other industries. For some industries of natural monopoly, the government also adopted successful practices of other countries in reforming monopoly industries in the recent twenty years to limit monopoly operations within the most necessary scope and to subject these enterprises to strict supervision.

4.2.1.3 Restructuring for IPO

After the aforementioned reforms, SOEs generally still had bloated organizations, redundant personnel, heavy burdens of debt, and low-quality assets. One of two approaches could be used to convert them into real enterprises. The first approach was to spin off noncore assets by splitting and redundant personnel by early retirement and recommendation for reemployment, and to restructure core assets for IPO. The second approach was to carve out core assets from the original enterprise and restructure them for IPO, but to leave historical burdens such as noncore assets, nonperforming financial claims, and redundant personnel to the original enterprise to improve the financial performance of the newly established enterprise to ensure the success of IPO. The first approach proved more effective but would take a longer time. The second approach took effect more quickly but it left more unsolved problems. China mainly employed the second approach. For example, in October 1999, CNPC carved out its core assets of extraction–refining–chemical–retailing and restructured them into PetroChina Company Limited (PetroChina) for IPO in Hong Kong and New York. Among the original 1.54 million employees of CNPC, 1.06 million were retained by the remaining enterprise, while the other 0.48 million were employed by PetroChina. PetroChina changed its wholly state-owned nature by introducing some public investors and strategic investors via IPO in March 2000 on stock markets in Hong Kong and New York in the form of H-share[18] and American Depositary Receipt (ADR), respectively.

Former large SOEs that listed in domestic and overseas stock markets, in order, included Qingdao Beer (1993 H-share of Hong Kong, A-share of Shanghai in the same year), China Mobile (1997 Red Chip Share of Hong Kong), PetroChina (2000 H-share of Hong Kong), China Unicom (2000 Red Chip Share of Hong Kong, 2002 A-share of Shanghai), SINOPEC (2000 H-share of Hong Kong), and Baoshan Iron & Steel Co., Ltd. (2000 A-share of Shanghai).

---

[18] H-shares are shares issued by companies incorporated in Chinese mainland but listed on the Stock Exchange of Hong Kong. A-shares are issued by companies incorporated in Chinese mainland and traded in RMB in domestic stock exchanges. "Red Chips" are shares issued by companies incorporated in Hong Kong and listed on the Stock Exchange of Hong Kong but owned (directly or indirectly) in significant proportions by the Chinese government or a Chinese SOE.

On the basis of diversification of share ownership, most transformed SOEs have built a basic framework of corporate governance according to the *Decision on Several Important Issues Regarding Reform and Development of State-Owned Enterprises,* adopted by the Fourth Plenary Session of the 15th CCCPC.

4.2.2 Governance Problems of Transformed Companies

The idea accepted by many people for reforming the state assets management system after the Third Plenary Session of the 14th CCCPC was a three-layer model. The first layer is the government, which set up a state assets management commission to perform the function of the state as the owner, to separate the function of the administrator of society and economy and the function of the owner of state assets, as described in the *Decision* of the Third Plenary Session of the 14th CCCPC. However, because there were too many SOEs under the jurisdiction of governments at various levels and the span of control of the state assets management commission was too wide, state assets management institutions (i.e., investment institutions authorized by the state,[19] as described in Article 64 of the *Company Law*) were designated as the second layer. The specific forms intended then included state investment companies, state holding companies, state assets management companies, group corporations of enterprise groups meeting certain requirements, and so on.[20] These institutions were to exercise shareholder rights in transformed companies at the third layer.

In later practice, the original intention to separate the government's function as the administrator of society and economy and its function as the owner of state assets by establishing the state assets management commissions at the first layer was not really implemented. The central government and most local governments did not set up this kind of institution. Although the state assets management commissions were set up quite early in localities such as Shanghai and Shenzhen, the separation of the two functions did not really materialize. These state assets management commissions were not entities, but "virtual" institutions composed of incumbent government leaders and leading officials of related functional departments. In practice, the planning commissions, the economic and trade commissions, the organization departments of party committees,

---

[19] Tian Yanmiao (the Economic Law Section of the Commission of Legislative Affairs of the NPC Standing Committee) et al. (eds.), *Provision Interpretation and Legal Application of Company Law of the People's Republic of China (Zhonghua Renmin Gongheguo Gongsifa tiaowen jieshi ji falü shiyong),* Beijing: China Democracy and Legal System Press, 2000, p. 122.

[20] Hong Hu, "Explanation to 'Program of Selecting a Group of Large- and Medium-Sized SOEs for Experiments in Modern Enterprise System (draft)' (Guanyu Xuanze Yi Pi Guoyou Dazhongxing Qiye Jinxing Xiandai Qiye Zhidu Shidian de Fang'an (Caoan) de shuoming)," in the Enterprise Department of the State Economic and Trade Commission of the PRC (ed.), *A Collection of Documents of the National Working Conference for Experiments in Establishing Modern Enterprise System (Quanguo Jianli Xiandai Qiye Zhidu Shidian Gongzuo Huiyi wenjian huibian),* Beijing: Reform Press, 1995, p. 85.

and the finance departments still exercised the right to invest, the right to appoint senior executives, and the right to profits, respectively, and thus it was impossible for the state assets management commissions to be independent of the administrative function of the government.

Establishing authorized investment institutions as the second layer included the following situations. First, line ministries and bureaus of some industries were restructured into holding companies or assets management companies to perform the function of the state shareholder in enterprises that were originally affiliated with them. Second, existing administrative corporations, such as national industry corporations, were authorized to perform the function of the state shareholder in enterprises that were already under their control. Third, group corporations of some large enterprise groups were authorized to perform the function of the state shareholder in their affiliated enterprises. For example, one part of the experiment extended to 120 large enterprise groups in 1997 was to approve the group corporations of those enterprise groups that met certain requirements as investment institutions authorized by the state.

Some of these authorized investment institutions were created in the process called "first have a son, then have a father," that is, to first transform an SOE into a company and then create a "shell company" to act as the state shareholder of that company.

This institutional framework left transformed SOEs with some grave institutional defects.

4.2.2.1 Listed Companies Failed to Become Corporate Entities with Full Independence

To maintain control by the government, corporatization usually left listed companies dominated by state-owned shares. Furthermore, shareholder's rights of these controlling shares were usually exercised by wholly state-owned authorized investment institutions (i.e., holding companies, group corporations, assets management companies, and so on). This led to two consequences. First, directors with the support of authorized investment institutions (usually their senior executives) dominated the boards of directors of listed companies. Meanwhile, although the China Securities Regulatory Commission required that there be "three separations (separation in personnel, assets, and accounts)" between listed companies and their parent companies, board chairmen of listed companies (usually CEOs of their parent companies) were exempted from this requirement. Furthermore, according to the provisions of the *Company Law* of 1993, the board chairman of a joint stock limited company is the legal representative of the company. As a result, even those listed companies that achieved diversification of share ownership were under the complete control of wholly state-owned authorized investment institutions and could not have independent operation as was required by a market economy. Second, using "remaining enterprises" that were built on the old system as authorized investment institutions on behalf of the state to control the listed companies built on the new market economic system was obviously detrimental to the goal of transforming the listed companies into businesses with market competitiveness.

4.2.2.2 "Remaining Enterprises" Controlled Listed Companies

The restructuring of SOEs in China was usually done by "carving out for IPO," in other words, state holding companies, state assets management companies, national industry corporations, and enterprise groups carved out their better-performing assets to set up joint stock limited companies for IPO financing. The assets and staff not carved out remained in the original enterprises, or authorized investment institutions, otherwise known as "remaining enterprises." Since remaining enterprises undertook the burden of assets, debts, staff, products, and other things not suitable to be carved out for IPO, many of them had the need to constantly obtain resources from their listed subsidiaries in order to survive. Since remaining enterprises were usually the controlling shareholders of their listed subsidiaries, they also had enough power to do so. Therefore, cases of parent companies grabbing money from the stock market through listed companies and cases of parent companies "hollowing out" listed companies mushroomed. Some group corporations, as authorized investment institutions, even adopted the practice of transferring high-quality assets to other enterprises or even to some individuals while leaving debts with the group corporations, which then filed for bankruptcy to default the debts. This practice posed a huge risk to the government and banks.

4.2.2.3 Ownership Was Exercised by the Insiders

Since the state shareholder was usually determined by authorization, shareholder rights of state-owned equity in most transformed companies were exercised by other wholly state-owned enterprises authorized by the state, such as state holding companies, state assets management companies, group corporations of enterprise groups, and "shell companies." In most cases, these authorized enterprises did not achieve the separation of ownership and control. They had just one unified "leading team" and leading team members were both representatives vested with full authority of the state-owned equity as well as executives employed by them. As a result, it was these leading team members that represented the interests of the state shareholder to supervise and motivate themselves as executives of transformed enterprises.

The core of corporatization is the establishment of an effective corporate structure. However, in the process of corporatization in China, the most prominent problem was unchecked insider control,[21] a problem that is likely to emerge in the transitional process from planned economy to market economy. After studying enterprises in the process of economic system transition in Eastern Europe and the Commonwealth of Independent States, Aoki Masahiko of Stanford University, USA, pointed out that insider control is "a potential phenomenon inherent in the transitional process,"[22] and efforts should be made to overcome it. In China, this phenomenon exists widely in enterprises that have gained managerial autonomy in the reform, enterprises under the contracting system, and most of the pilot enterprises of the shareholding system. The Third Plenary Session of the 14th CCCPC decided that the reform direction of large SOEs was to establish a modern enterprise system. Since modern corporations have the inherent nature of separation of ownership and control, the bad practice of insider control has adulterated the corporate system and even become some kind of legal norm or administrative norm. First, the belief that the essence of the corporate system is the separation of shareholders' ownership and the enterprise's corporate property rights is prevalent. As discussed before, in the reform of past decades, the idea of excluding the owner from the enterprise came into being and thus the aforementioned separation actually meant disseverance of ownership. Second, the *Company Law* continued to use provisions of the *Enterprise Law,* adopting the practice of designating a fixed legal representative or "legal-person (corporate) representative" for a corporation. China had never had the concept of legal person as a group until its most recent history. Many people often thought a legal person to be one man. In daily economic life, people would often say, "John Doe is the legal person of our company." As a result, a salaried executive designated as the legal representative of a company became the incarnation of the legal person, and corporate property also became property that the legal representative, corporate legal-person representative, or legal person could dispose at his or her will. Authorized management further aggravated this tendency.

4.2.2.4 Multi-Tier Legal Person System Was Prevalent

Backed by such policies as authorization and setting up enterprise groups, the long-existing phenomenon of the "multi-tier legal person system" in Chinese SOEs has

---

[21] "Unchecked insider control" is a defect that is likely to exist in the governance structure of modern corporations. When shareholders of a modern corporation lose residual control of the corporation due to overdiversification of share ownership or other reasons, the problem of a mismatch between residual control and claim to residual income emerges. Companies controlled by insiders often make decisions against shareholders' interests and embark on a road to decline and demise. In recent years, there was an extensive literature in Management in Western countries on how to prevent this problem from happening, illustrating its harmfulness to the management of enterprises.

[22] Masahiko Aoki, "Controlling Insider Control: Issues of Corporate Governance in Transition Economies (Dui neiburen kongzhi de kongzhi: zhuangui jingji zhong gongsi zhili jiegou de ruogan wenti) (1994)," in Masahiko Aoki and Qian Yingyi

further developed. There are subsidiaries ("daughter companies") under authorized enterprises, and there are "granddaughter companies" or even "great-granddaughter companies" under "daughter companies." All of these companies have independent legal
person status, and the number of tiers can reach five, six, or even more. In many large
groups, the management of the enterprises authorized by the government to exercise
state ownership have no idea how many offspring their enterprises have in total. At
most, they know only the number of second-tier enterprises directly under them and
the total number of enterprises in the third tier. Furthermore, the influence of the state
as the owner gradually weakens as the number of tiers increases.

This organizational form has many problems. First, the multi-tier legal person system
is a concept conflicting with "legal person" in civil law. As we know, the so-called legal
person refers to an organization that has the capacity for civil rights and conduct and
that enjoys civil rights and undertakes civil obligations independently according to law.
Meanwhile, a natural person refers to an independent individual who has inherent "natural power." In this respect, a legal person cannot be multi-tier. Under the multi-tier
legal person system, second-tier and third-tier legal persons do not have completely independent rights. This is how it was in the days of a patriarchal society: even though a
man was already an adult, as long as his father was still alive, the man was still subject to
the patriarch and did not have complete independence.

The supposed advantage of the multi-tier legal person system is that it can mobilize
enthusiasm of member enterprises by this kind of property arrangement. However, in
fact, just as in the case of an extended family living under the same roof in old-time
China, this practice that permitted each branch to set up its own private coffer and private savings often causes conflicts of interest among member enterprises (the so-called
"incentive incompatibility" problem in economics). As we know, an effective incentive
system must have incentive compatibility—it must mobilize the enthusiasm of lower-
level organizations or individuals and at the same time ensure that the mobilized enthusiasm serves the objectives of the higher-level organization; otherwise, it would mobilize the enthusiasm of lower-level organizations to act against its objectives. From the
perspective of enterprise organization, the institutional structure of the multi-tier legal
person system violates the basic principle of incentive compatibility and causes conflict

---

(eds.), *Corporate Governance in Transitional Economies: Insider Control and the Role of Banks (Zhuangui jingji zhong de gongsi zhili jiegou: neibuiren kongzhi he yinhang de zuoyong)*, Beijing: China Economic Press, 1995, pp 15–36. Some Chinese economists held opinions on this issue different from those of Aoki and others. They argue that "Some form of insider control in SOEs can generate direct incentive effects and harden budget constraint, thereby significantly improving the operational effectiveness of SOEs." (See Zhang Shuguang, "Innovation in Enterprise Theories and Transformation of Analytical Methodology: Concur-
rent Comments on Zhang Weiying's 'Entrepreneur of the Enterprise: A Contract Theory' (Qiye lilun chuangxin ji fenxi fangfa gaizao—jianping Zhang Weiying de Qiye de Qiyejia— Qiyue Lilun)," *China Book Review (Zhongguo shuping)*, 1996, Vol. 10, pp. 44–45.

of interest among various parts of the enterprise. According to modern enterprise theory (incomplete contract theory), if the responsibilities of contracting parties can be clearly specified in a contract, all economic activities can be accomplished by fair trade among contracting enterprises. This way, the enthusiasm of contracting parties can be mobilized to the highest degree to accomplish complementary activities. As for matters that cannot be clearly specified in the contract, they are only suitable for transactions within an institution under the management of an administrative authority. Otherwise, problems may emerge, such as mutual infringement, mutual threats, endless disputes over minor issues, and friction among independent entities with conflicting interests, leading to a sharp rise in transaction costs. In some enterprise groups in China, there is this kind of friction among the core enterprise and member enterprises. For example, because many independent enterprises share one brand, member enterprises often seek private gain (of the member enterprise) at public expense (of the group company) by turning out low-quality products with shoddy work and inferior material, and they will refuse to mend their ways despite repeated admonition and education. This is very natural, as the root cause of the problem does not lie in the greed of a few individuals, but rather in an institutional arrangement with conflict of interest.

In the early stages of industrial development in various countries, after larger enterprises amalgamated smaller ones through mergers and acquisitions, they organized these smaller enterprises into a group in the form of a holding company. This was a common practice and represented progress. Nevertheless, to apply the multi-tier legal person system universally and to popularize it universally will make its negative aspect become more and more conspicuous.

4.3 Further Reform Measures to Be Taken

4.3.1 Further Lowering the Proportion of State Equity Shares

To corporatize SOEs, diversification of share ownership must be achieved first. There are a number of ways to bring in new types of equity holders.

4.3.1.1 Debt-Equity Conversion

In the mid-1980s, the state finance department discontinued free fiscal appropriations to SOEs. Instead, funds were channeled to SOEs as bank loans with interest. After this reform, known as "substituting fiscal appropriations with bank loans," SOEs chronically relied on bank loans for financing. By the mid-1990s, the debt-to-asset ratio of all SOEs combined was as high as 85 percent or so, and 37 percent of nonfinancial SOEs were already in insolvency, even as calculated by book value.[23] The high volume of liability of SOEs included a huge amount of overdue loans, which were nonperforming loans on the banks' balance sheets.

In view of this situation, many domestic and overseas economists suggested that the creditors (mainly state banks) apply debt-equity conversion to some of these liabilities. Doing this can create new types of owners for SOEs and hasten the processes of corporatization and diversification of share ownership in SOEs, while at the same time it can reduce nonperforming loans in banks, thus mitigating financial risk. At the end of 1998, the State Council decided to establish four asset management corporations (AMCs) to take over nonperforming loans from four big state-owned commercial banks (the Big Four), respectively. In 1999, the four AMCs—Cinda, Huarong, Great Wall, and Orient—were established successively and took over nonperforming loans of about RMB 1,400 billion at book value from the Big Four and the China Development Bank and immediately started debt-equity conversion for about 600 SOEs chosen by the State Economic and Trade Commission. The total amount of nonperforming loans converted to equities was about RMB 460 billion.

In a modern market economy, debt-equity conversion is a kind of business operation. The reason creditors choose to convert debt into equity is that they believe that instead of applying immediate bankruptcy liquidation to debtor enterprises, if they can restructure these enterprises in the capacity of owners, they may recover more of their debt claims. However, the debt-equity conversion by the four AMCs in 1999 was more of an administrative arrangement than a business operation. The debt-equity conversion was one of the "three super-weapons" for a scheme to get large and medium SOEs "out of the difficult position in three years."[24] Its main purpose was to convert interest payments of the debtor enterprises into profits on the books, therefore putting the loss-making enterprises in the black—in essence, government subsidies to these enterprises. The enterprises for debt-equity conversion were also decided by the State Economic and Trade Commission; AMCs were not allowed to choose these on their own. After the debt-equity conversion, although AMCs became shareholders or even controlling shareholders, they did not in fact perform the function of shareholders due to various limitations. By the end of 2002, most equities held by AMCs in the debt-equity con-

---

[23] Wu Jinglian et al., *The Strategic Restructuring of the State Sector (Guoyou jingji de zhanlüexing gaizu)*, Beijing: China Development Press, 1998, p. 26.

[24] On July 18 to July 24, 1997, Premier Zhu Rongji inspected ten large-sized SOEs—including Anshan Iron and Steel Group Corporation, Liaoyang Petrochemical Company, and Fushun Aluminum Factory—and held informal discussions with more than thirty leaders from enterprises in trouble and enterprises performing well, respectively, to assess the situation of reform and development of SOEs and to discuss how to eliminate losses and how to do a good job of running SOEs. During this inspection, Zhu Rongji pledged to get large- and medium-sized SOEs that were in the red out of trouble in about three years. (See *People's Daily (Renmin ribao)*, July 31, 1997.)

version were still not cashed out. As a result, the AMCs' efforts to dispose of nonperforming loans still have not made a significant impact on the structure of share ownership of SOEs. However, as AMCs continue to cash out the debts and equities they hold to overseas and domestic nonstate investors, the structure of share ownership of relevant SOEs will be further changed.

4.3.1.2 Inviting Private Investors to Become Shareholders

The debt-equity conversion deals with only the existing capital stock of SOEs. SOEs also need to increase capital by equity financing for further development and the capital increment created this way also brings new types of owners. In the reforms after 1992, there were two channels for domestic private investors to become shareholders of SOEs.

First, employees of SOEs invested to become shareholders. As early as the mid-1980s, the government launched some pilot projects of establishing shareholding companies by issuing new shares to employees. Most newly established enterprises of the shareholding system then issued shares mainly to their own employees because there was basically no other way to get nonstate equity investment. This situation did not change much until the early 1990s. At the end of 1991, there were 3,200 pilot enterprises of the shareholding system of various kinds all over the nation and 2,751 of them had their own employees as shareholders.[25] After 1994, during the experiments to establish the modern enterprise system, issuing new shares to employees was also the most convenient and commonly used way to achieve diversification of share ownership and to establish limited liability companies instead of wholly state-owned companies.

Second, stocks were issued to public investors on the stock market. One characteristic of the modern corporate system is the transferability of rights and interests of investors, which allows the corporate system to raise funds from public investors at a fast pace and on a large scale. Therefore, after SOEs were transformed into companies, new types of owners could be created when raising funds by issuing shares, thus achieving diversification of share ownership. In the reform of SOEs in China, however, the potential of equity financing on the stock market to change the ownership structure of SOEs was not fully realized. At the end of December 2002, the number of all classes of listed companies was 1,224 in China and the shares traded in the stock market accounted for only 34.7 percent of the total.[26]

There were two major reasons for the failure of the equity financing on the stock market to effectively drive diversification of share ownership of SOEs. First, in order to

---

[25] Wu Jinglian, *Modern Corporation and Enterprise Reform (Xiandai gongsi yu qiye gaige),* Tianjin: Tianjin People's Publishing House, 1994, pp. 222–223.
[26] <http://www.csrc.gov.cn/CSRCSite/tongjiku/199911/default.html>.

retain the state control over these companies, the government set a ceiling for the portion of shares that could be issued to the public by dividing the shares of these companies into tradable and nontradable shares, thus making equity financing on the stock market less likely to affect the ownership structure of these enterprises in a fundamental way, and even less likely to change the control of these companies. Second, because of the inadequate protection of public shareholder rights, for the insiders and sponsor shareholders (usually shell companies as the state shareholder) of these companies, equity financing on the stock market did not impose a burden of repayment of principal and interest, as was the case for bank loan financing. Nor did it mean a cost in terms of loss of control over these companies. Therefore, it became a financing channel with the softest constraint. The drive for gain at such a huge magnitude made the corporatization transformation degenerate into a procedure of IPO for "grabbing money" rather than a reform of the management mechanism of enterprises.

4.3.1.3 Developing Institutional Investors

In developed market economies, especially Anglo-American economies, institutional investors hold prominent status in the shareholding structure of companies. In the United States in 1994, 46.2 percent of total equities of all companies were held by various institutional investors, of which two major types of institutional investors—pension funds and mutual funds—accounted for 25.9 percent and 11.9 percent, respectively.[27] In the corporatization transformation of SOEs in China, institutional investors are also a potentially important type of owner. Among them, pension funds have the greatest potential because a large part of the existing state equity is in fact financed by past contributions of workers for the purpose of social security. It has come hand in hand with the state's social security commitment to older workers, which is an implicit debt of the state. Many economists have been advocating "cutting a chunk" from the existing state assets and transferring it to social security funds as compensation for liability to older workers of SOEs in the pension system reform. If these measures are carried out, they could effectively kill two birds with one stone, namely improving the social security function by resolving the historical legacy in the pension system reform while also creating new institutional investors outside the government.

4.3.2 Strengthening the Internal Control Systems of Large Enterprises

For large enterprises, one important aspect of establishing good corporate governance is the establishment of an effective internal control system as per the requirements of mar-

---

[27] Margaret Blair, *Ownership and Control,* Washington, D.C.: The Brookings Institution, 1995, p. 46.

ket competition. At present, most large Chinese enterprises have adopted the multi-tier legal person system. Even private enterprises have imitated SOEs by restructuring themselves into enterprise groups of the multi-tier legal person system once they have developed to a certain size.

In the historical development process of industrial and commercial enterprises, there was once an organizational form of enterprises similar to China's multi-tier legal person system. This was the holding company structure (abbreviated as "H-form").[28] H-form mostly appeared in enterprises formed by horizontal mergers and acquisitions. After amalgamation, each subsidiary in this structure retained its status as a legal person so that it had significant independence from the headquarters. This structure was once widely used in Europe. In the UK, for example, the holding company structure was the most popular structure to control subsidiaries. In the United States, H-form gradually lost its popularity and was replaced by the multidivisional structure (M-form). On the eve of World War I, virtually no one in big industrial companies in the United States managed business in H-form.

Small enterprises born in the industrial revolution in the eighteenth and nineteenth centuries generally adopted the unitary structure (U-form) of organization. As industrial and commercial enterprises were expanding at the beginning of the twentieth century, the organizational form of holding companies emerged. The best-known example of H-form enterprise was General Motors Corporation under the leadership of William Durant from 1908 until 1920. Durant made General Motors Corporation quickly expand to be the biggest motor company in the world by acquiring small motor companies such as Chevrolet. Inside the corporation, small companies that had been acquired still retained their status as independent legal entities, and the parent holding company simply gave them guidance in business principles. Because of its loose organizational structure, General Motors Corporation fell into disorder and its performance deteriorated. In 1924, after the DuPont and Morgan families took over General Motors, the corporation was restructured under the leadership of Alfred Sloan, Jr. and revived with a multidivisional structure.[29] The so-called multidivisional structure is an enterprise organizational form in which several divisions are set up under the headquarters. These divisions have considerable decision-making power for daily management and operation and are just "profit centers" without independent balance sheets. The divisions

---

[28] In the developmental process of industrial and commercial enterprises over nearly a century, enterprises adopted three hierarchical organizational forms successively. The first one was centralized unitary structure (U-form); the second was holding company (H-form); and the third was a multidivisional structure (M-form). For an analysis of the three hierarchical organizational forms, see Alfred Dupont Chandler, Jr., *Strategy and Structure: Chapters in the History of the American Industrial Enterprise,* Cambridge, Mass.: MIT Press, 1962. See also Oliver E. Williamson, *The Economic Institutions of Capitalism.* New York: The Free Press, 1985.

[29] Alfred P. Sloan, *My Years with General Motors,* New York: Currency & Doubleday, 1963, pp. 42–57.

adopt the strategy of separation of revenue and expenditure and simply monitor the business profitability, with no right to dispose of profits. Oliver Williamson, an American authoritative economist in business management, stated that only under conditions of limited material resources used mutually and interdependently did enterprises adopt H-form instead of M-form.

M-form is both a decentralized structure and a centralized structure. That is to say, it decentralizes as much as possible the general decision-making power of production and even of investment, but highly centralizes strategic decisions and financial accounting. The basic units in this structure are semi-independent profit centers established by trademarks of products or regions; each profit center is organized in accordance with U-form. Above the profit centers is the headquarters, composed of senior executives and in charge of resource allocation for the entire company and the supervision and coordination of subsidiary units. Thus, the separation of policy making and operational management is achieved and the division of decision-making work is improved. Senior executives are able to free themselves of the work of daily management and operation and concentrate on strategic decisions. Because of centralized and unified accounting, the decentralization of decision-making power for production and investment will not result in loss of control, corruption, or waste. Thus, centralization and decentralization mutually promote each other and bring out the best in each other. Therefore, the multidivisional structure has become the basic organizational form of large nonfinancial corporations in various countries.[30]

4.3.3 Overcoming Defects of Insider Control and Instituting Checks and Balances between the Owner and the Management

In order to achieve this goal, we must solve the problems discussed in the following sections.

4.3.3.1 Making Sure That the Owner Is Present

The general meeting of shareholders is the supreme organ of power of a company, holding the final control (residual control). This guarantees fundamentally the effective functioning of corporate governance structure. To achieve this in Chinese enterprises, the erroneous ideas and legal provisions of excluding the owner from the enterprise formed in the reform of power-delegating and profit-sharing must be changed and the problem of "absence" of the owner must be solved to ensure that the owner holds final control over the enterprise.

---

[30] Alfred Dupont Chandler, Jr., *Strategy and Structure: Chapters in the History of the American Industrial Enterprise,* Cambridge, Mass.: MIT Press, 1962.

Of course, to solve the problem of absence of the owner, we should carry out diversification of share ownership and diversification of the forms of public ownership. However, at present, most companies transformed from SOEs still have a high proportion of state ownership. As a result, many people have suggested establishing holding companies (or state assets management companies) to settle the problem of absence of the owner and nominal property rights in the state sector. Establishing a holding company solves the problem of absence of the owner for the subsidiaries under the holding company, but the holding company, as a corporate body itself, also has the problem of whether the owner is absent or not. The key to establishing the correct relation between the state ownership and enterprise operation is to settle the problem with the interface, or the linking part, between the government and the enterprises. Establishing holding companies cannot ultimately solve this problem. The principal manager is authorized by the government to represent the state in operation of the enterprise, but this approach cannot make the owner present and set up a normal mechanism of checks and balances in the corporate governance structure.

4.3.3.2 Making Sure That the Board of Directors Fulfills Its Fiduciary Duties in the Interest of Shareholders

In modern companies, the shareholders entrust the company's property to the board of directors. The board of directors appoints and removes senior executives and supervises them regularly. The board of directors has fiduciary duties, and any shareholder can sue the directors if he or she believes that they have breached their fiduciary duties. Anglo-American company laws permit directors to take positions of executive officers concurrently (as opposed to German companies, where a member of the board of supervisors cannot take a position on the management board). Therefore, how to make outside directors (including independent directors), who do not get paid by the company, have some clout and perform fiduciary duties faithfully becomes the key to ensuring the effective functioning of the corporate governance structure.

In China, the insiders dominate the boards of directors in a great number of newly established companies and there is a tradition of paternalism and personal despotism. Therefore, the practice currently adopted in many localities of management by the so-called legal representatives authorized by the state has several problems: (a) the scope of authorization is not clear; (b) the party being awarded the authorization is not a collective but an individual; (c) there are some conflicts of interest between the party being awarded the authorization (the insiders) and the party awarding the authorization (the owner); and (d) the party being awarded the authorization does not have completely clear legal responsibility. These problems must be solved.

4.3.3.3 Making Sure that the Board of Directors Carries Out Supervision over Senior Executives

Theoretically speaking, the board of directors is the supreme organ of decision making in a corporation; however, in practice in a modern economy, the board of directors retains only certain powers, such as the right to decide on significant changes in property relations. To a large extent, the board delegates the practical control on the company's daily management to senior executives. The main function of the board of directors is to appoint and remove senior executives and to supervise them regularly. To ensure the realization of investors' interests and the company's goal, the board of directors must select, assess, award, or punish chief executive officers and carry out daily supervision of them. The board of directors, especially independent directors, should keep a firm hand on the power to appoint senior executives and to decide on their compensation and should do frequent audits of all of the company's financial activities.

In the modern corporation, the international practice of setting up a corporate governance structure is that the general meeting of shareholders elects the directors to constitute the board of directors, and then the board of directors appoints the company's senior executives who are responsible for the company's daily management. However, this common practice of the corporate system is incompatible with China's current system of the party's organization department and the government's personnel department appointing the officers of enterprises. Although many large- and medium-sized enterprises have corporatized themselves, their high-level managers and even middle-level managers are still appointed by the organization departments of higher-level authorities. The board chairman and the board of directors do not always perform their fiduciary duties conscientiously for the shareholders, and it is also very hard for the general meeting of shareholders to demand that they act in accordance with the investors' goal of making a profit. If the general manager and the executive team are not appointed by the board of directors, the board of directors will not have independent fiduciary duties, and their incentive to carry out supervision over senior executives on behalf of the shareholders will be weakened. This practice simply must be changed. In order to prevent criminals and other unqualified people from occupying important positions of publicly held companies, the party organization department and the government personnel department can carry out qualification checks on candidates for the board of directors and the general manager according to the actual situation in China and the international practice of criminal record checks on candidates for the board of directors of public companies. However, this qualification check should not become a direct appointment.

4.3.3.4 Letting the Securities Market Play a Role in Strengthening Corporate Governance

In the Anglo-American model of corporate governance, the securities market, especially the secondary market, makes a great contribution to the effective functioning of the corporate governance structure. It provides very strong incentives and constraints on senior executives through the operations in the securities market such as "voting with feet" (disgruntled investors pulling out their money), hostile takeover, and stock options for CEOs. At present, the securities market in China is greatly distorted and it really cannot play any role in that aspect.

4.3.3.5 Providing Adequate Incentive to Executives

To ensure that they make great effort to achieve shareholders' goal, executives should not only be strictly supervised but also strongly motivated; otherwise, incidents damaging the interests of enterprises, such as the "phenomenon of age 58"[31] will occur. Incentives for executives can be in the form of promotion, on-the-job consumption, bonus, subsidized share ownership, stock options, etc. Each form has its own pros and cons and the incentives can be used in combination. When choosing the forms of incentives, attention should be paid to the compatibility of the executives' incentives with the achievement of the owners' goal. In developed market economies, stock options are the most frequently used form of incentive for executives. In an efficient securities market, since the stock price reflects the expected profitability of the company, to give executives stock options not only achieves good compatibility with shareholders' goals but also provides strong incentive. If the employed manager does not run the company well, he cannot get a penny from stock options; if he runs it well, he can earn a large reward. However, this method needs highly effective corporate governance and highly effective supervision of the securities market, and great effort is required to create these two conditions.

4.3.4 Bringing the SASAC into Play to Exercise Shareholder Rights in Accordance with the Law

According to the decision of the 16th National Congress of the CPC in 2002, the National People's Congress passed a resolution to create the State-Owned Assets Supervision and Administration Commission (SASAC). The creation of the SASAC ensures that

---

[31] "Phenomenon of age 58" refers to the phenomenon that frequently occurred in SOEs in recent years, in which some senior executives started to accumulate wealth by embezzling public funds and exchanging their enterprises' intellectual property for personal gains when they approached age 60 because they would lose all their power when they retired at age 60.

the SOE reform in China will be led by an authoritative institution committed to upholding shareholder rights with full authority. The essential function of the SASAC is to further advance the readjustment of the layout of the state sector; to carry out the corporatization transformation of SOEs that have not been corporatized; to exercise owners' rights on behalf of the state in the companies that have already been transformed (including wholly state-owned companies, state-controlled companies, and companies with noncontrolling state participation); and to set up a mechanism of checks and balances between the owners and the managers to make these companies' corporate governance become more effective.

4.3.4.1 Further Advancing the Strategic Readjustment of the Layout of the State Sector

The SASAC should continue to carry out the guiding policy of the 15th National Congress of the CPC, planning as a whole and implementing step by step, to make the state sector withdraw in an orderly fashion from industries where it does not have an advantage. Resources thus freed can be used to improve the public service of the government and to strengthen pivotal industries and key fields as well as fields that nonstate sectors are unwilling to enter. This will enable the state sector and nonstate sectors to put their own advantages to full use.

At the same time, during the period when state capital is being withdrawn from some industries, effective measures should be taken to refrain and correct phenomena caused by a few people that damage social justice and erode public property. The SASAC should set criteria to regulate the change in state property rights and mobilize every part of the society to carry out the supervision in order to guarantee justice of procedures in aspects such as pricing and applying for purchase.

4.3.4.2 Expediting the Corporatization Transformation of SOEs

After the creation of the SASAC, the "authorized investment" mode of state assets management should step down from the historical stage as quickly as possible. Under the jurisdiction of the SASAC, the first-tier enterprises can either maintain their status as authorized investment institutions or be transformed into corporations so that they become bigger and stronger on the basis of the modern corporate system. Units maintaining their status as authorized investment institutions will no longer be enterprises, but agencies of the SASAC for the reform of the state sector, and they should be led by civil servants appointed by the SASAC. These authorized investment institutions can take charge of the restructuring and corporatization transformation of their SOE subsidiaries by themselves or let domestic or overseas assets management companies do the same. After accomplishing the corporatization transformation, the original authorized investment institutions and their subsidiaries can become operational companies specializing in production operation, or they can become holding companies specializing in capital operation. In either case, once the corporatization transformation is accomplished, the enterprise should be set free and be managed directly by the SASAC as an equity owner in accordance with the *Company Law*. Even a wholly state-owned company should appoint a board of directors according to the *Company Law,* and the state shareholder should exercise its rights within the framework of the *Company Law*.

4.3.4.3 The SASAC Exercising Shareholder Rights in Accordance with Law in Transformed Enterprises

The *Company Law* is a basic law that regulates the behavior of corporations. The SASAC exercises the rights to supervise people, operate businesses, and manage assets of corporations transformed from SOEs on behalf of the state shareholder, but these should be done within the framework of the *Company Law*. The current phenomena that state assets management institutions overstep their authority or do not fully exercise their power should be rectified firmly.

For government administration departments to continue to carry out their administrative approval of the corporatization transformation of SOEs, especially approval of investment projects, is a special measure adopted to prevent investment risk and strengthen financial budget constraint when the owner is absent. The practice indicates that this is not a scientific or effective method. Once the SASAC had been founded and the investor (i.e., the owner) was present, the SASAC started performing the function of the owner, such as setting up effective corporate governance, transforming the financial constraint mechanism to impose an endogenous hard financial budget constraint, and undertaking business risk. Correspondingly, the duty of the government should be shifted from playing the role of the investor to providing administrative scrutiny on such issues as environmental protection to safeguard public interests. The SASAC also should not bypass the general meeting of shareholders and the board of directors, intervening directly in the investment and management of the enterprise. If it does so, the SASAC plus the preexisting government agencies will certainly restrict the enterprise to death.

4.3.5 Learning from International Experience and Strengthening Corporate Governance

Improving corporate governance and dealing appropriately with the conflict between the "insiders" and the "outsiders" is an ongoing task to ensure the smooth functioning of the modern corporate system. In the 1970s, the conflict was revealed in different forms in companies of the Anglo-American model and the German model, respectively. The problem with the Anglo-American model was that, due to the highly dispersed ownership, most small shareholders would rather be free-riders, leading to inadequate owners' control and supervision over managers. The problem with the German model was that the corporate governance was excessively biased toward workers' interests.[32] Both tendencies damaged the shareholders' interests and hurt the competitiveness of companies.

In the early 1990s, in order to solve this problem, countries using the Anglo-American model started the "corporate governance movement" to enhance the shareholders' value and strengthen the control of the company. One important feature distinguishing the corporate governance movement from other reforms of corporate and securities laws was that various nongovernment organizations issued self-disciplining and guiding codes of conduct to urge enterprises to improve their corporate governance procedure, and then the state institutions acknowledged these codes as administrative regulations. Enhancing corporate governance has become a global trend; China can draw on the experiences of other countries regarding this. In China, the Shanghai Stock Exchange issued the first guidance of this kind in 2000. In January 2002, on the government side, the China Securities Regulatory Commission and the State Economic and Trade Commission issued a compulsory *Code of Corporate Governance for Listed Companies in China*.

The corporate governance movement contains the essential components discussed in the following sections.

4.3.5.1 Instituting the Independent Director System

In the 1970s, some developed countries started to introduce the independent director system into listed companies. The key for independent directors to play a role within the board of directors lies in their independence. Although different countries and regions have different definitions for an independent director, "independent" in the definitions accepted by most people has the following meanings: (a) the independent director is independent of the management and has never taken an executive position or other position in the company; (b) the independent director is independent of business associates of the company, does not represent the interests of any law firm or accounting firm that has a business relationship with the company, and is not a major client or supplier of the company; and (c) the independent director is independent of the controlling shareholder, does not hold a lot of shares of the company, and does not represent any important shareholder. At present, independent directors occupy more and more seats and play an increasingly important role in the boards of directors of big com-

---

[32] Henry Hansmann from Yale Law School and Reinier Kraakman from Harvard Law School called the Anglo-American model the "manager-oriented model" and the German model the "labor-oriented model." According to them, the most effective corporate governance model is the "shareholder-oriented model." See Henry Hansmann and Reinier Kraakman, "Essay: The End of History for Corporate Law," *Georgetown Law Journal*, Vol. 89, January, 2001, pp. 439–467.

panies of various countries. According to an investigation by the Organization for Economic Cooperation and Development (OECD) in 1999, in large listed companies the proportion of independent directors in the board of directors was 62 percent in the United States, 34 percent in the United Kingdom, and 29 percent in France. In 2001, the China Securities Regulatory Commission issued a provision calling for instituting the independent director system universally in listed companies.

4.3.5.2 Enhancing the Board of Directors' Supervision over Executives

The early boards of directors held plenary meetings only occasionally. After the 1970s, some companies started to set up special committees, such as the audit committee, the compensation committee, and the nominating committee. In 1977, the New York Stock Exchange mandated the establishment of an audit committee made up of independent directors in listed companies. The rules for listing on the market stipulate that (a) the views of independent directors should be specified in the board resolutions; (b) a related-party transaction may not take effect until approved by independent directors; (c) two or more independent directors may propose that a special meeting of shareholders be called; and (d) independent directors may directly report to the meeting of shareholders, the U.S. Securities and Exchange Commission, and other relevant agencies. The *Sarbanes-Oxley Act* (SOX Act), passed by the U.S. Congress in 2002, required that each listed company have an audit committee entirely composed of independent directors. Furthermore, in some large U.S.-listed companies, the nominating committee and the compensation committee of the board are also entirely composed of independent directors.

4.3.5.3 Enhancing the Transparency of Corporate Operation

Globally, efforts to enhance the transparency of corporate operation have two main aspects. One is to encourage every country to adopt internationally accepted accounting standards such as the International Accounting Standards (IAS). The other is to strengthen information disclosure to the board of directors. The board of directors is the core corporate body managing the company on behalf of shareholders' interests, and is also the main protector of the interests of minority shareholders. Generally speaking, directors have a higher ability to understand and evaluate the financial and operational situation of the company, so it is especially important to disclose information to the board of directors. The scope of the disclosure includes the annual business plan, budget, and long-term planning; the operational situation of the company and each department; the audit report, deviations from the agreed policies and guidelines; trading of the company's shares by directors; important investment deals; and the risks faced by the company.

Corporate governance reform is often driven by crises and scandals. In the 1990s, the corporate governance reform in the United Kingdom, the United States, and other countries was triggered by waves of scandals of insider control in the context of highly dispersed ownership. In 2002, a series of corporate governance scandals—most notably the Enron case and the WorldCom Company case—inspired new deliberations and new reform efforts for corporate governance.

However, the Anglo-American corporate governance movement mainly strengthens residual control of the capital owners (shareholders), but little attention is paid to the risks and rights of other stakeholders such as executives. The experiences of continental European countries on this issue are also worth studying.

CHAPTER 5

DEVELOPMENT OF NONSTATE SECTORS

In 1956, as private enterprises were eradicated in China, the Chinese economy became dominated by state ownership. However, it was impossible to set up a market economy based on a monopoly of state ownership. Therefore, since its beginning in 1978, market-oriented reform in China demanded the abolition of the state monopoly on ownership and the creation of private enterprises. Since then, the growth of the private sector has driven the complete remodeling of state-owned enterprises and laid a new foundation of diverse forms of ownership developing side by side for a market economy.

In an environment dominated by the state sector, the growth of nonstate sectors[1] was a process full of twists and turns. Nonstate sectors managed to gain a foothold in the economy as a result of incremental reform after 1978. By the mid- to late 1980s, nonstate sectors were well developed and their contribution to economic growth exceeded that of the state sector. However, it was not until the 15th National Congress of the Communist Party of China (CPC) of 1997 that the blind worship of state ownership spread by the Soviet textbook, *Political Economy,* was finally broken down. As a result, nonstate sectors finally broke free of ideological constraints to become important components of China's market economy, and China's economic reform finally embarked on the correct path to enter a new era of socialist market economy. This chapter begins with this breakdown of blind worship of state ownership of Soviet socialism.

5.1 Blind Worship of State Ownership and Its Breakdown

According to the notion of socialist political economy of the Soviet Union, the dominance of the state sector and a planned economy based on state ownership are essential economic features of socialism. In the process of the reform and opening up, this traditional notion was gradually broken and nonstate sectors gradually developed. The development of the situation led to objections from people self-labeled as "insisting on socialism" and a hot debate ensued regarding ownership structure during 1996 and 1997. The result of this debate was that it was widely accepted that nonstate sectors are

---

[1] The term "nonstate sectors (*minying jingji*)" loosely refers to the collection of sectors of the economy not owned by the state.

important components of a market economy and that diverse forms of ownership should be allowed to develop side by side. In 1997, the 15th National Congress of the CPC defined China's basic economic system as keeping public ownership as the mainstay of the economy and allowing diverse forms of ownership to develop side by side.

5.1.1 The Establishment of the Dominance of State Ownership in China

In Chapter 1, it was mentioned that the socialist society conceived by Marx and Engels is an association of free men. This association of free men, through the possession of entire productivity, makes it possible for people to work with public-owned means of production, thus forming a society based on collective possession of the means of production. But Marx and Engels never claimed that a socialist society is a huge factory organized and managed by the state or that state ownership is the economic base of socialism. They did say that after seizing political power, "the proletariat will use its political supremacy to wrest by degrees, all capital from the bourgeoisie, to centralize all instruments of production in the hands of the state, i.e., of the proletariat organized as the ruling class, and to increase the total of productive forces as rapidly as possible"[2] and that "the proletariat seizes state power and to begin with transforms the means of production into state property."[3]

However, this does not necessarily mean that the founders of Marxism viewed state ownership as the goal of socialism. Engels wrote that, "the state is . . . at best an evil inherited by the proletariat after its victorious struggle for class supremacy, whose worst sides the proletariat, just like the Commune, cannot avoid having to lop off at the earliest possible moment, until such time as a new generation, reared in new and free social conditions, will be able to throw the entire lumber of the state on the scrap-heap."[4] Marx and Engels, as thinkers loyal to their own ideals, held the idea that transforming the means of production into state property, "it thus puts an end to itself as proletariat, it thus puts an end to all class differences and class antagonisms, and thus also to the state as state." Therefore, "The first act in which the state really comes forward as the representative of the whole of society—the taking possession of the means of production in the name of society—is at the same time its last independent act as a state." After that, the state "withers away."[5]

The concept that state ownership is the economic base of socialism originated with

---

[2] Karl Marx and Friedrich Engels, "The Communist Manifesto (Gongchandang xuanyan) (1848)," *Collected Works of Marx and Engels (Makesi Engesi quanji)*, Chinese edition, Vol. 1, Beijing: People's Publishing House, 1995, p. 272.
[3] Friedrich Engels, "Anti-Dühring: Herr Eugen Dühring's Revolution in Science (Fan Dulin lun) (1878)," *Selected Works of Marx and Engels (Makesi Engesi xuanji)*, Chinese edition, Vol. 3, Beijing: People's Publishing House, 1995, p. 320.
[4] Friedrich Engels, "The 1891 Preface to Marx's 'The Civil War in France' (Makesi Falanxi Neizhan 1891 Nian Danxingben daoyan) (1891)," *Selected Works of Marx and Engels (Makesi Engesi xuanji)*, Chinese edition, Vol. 3, Beijing: People's Publishing House, 1995, p. 13.
[5] Friedrich Engels, "Anti-Dühring: Herr Eugen Dühring's Revolution in Science (Fan Dulin lun) (1878)," ibid., p. 320.

Lenin and Stalin, not Marx or Engels. According to Lenin, the whole society would become a State Syndicate under socialism. Stalin turned this concept into reality. Between 1928 and 1930, Stalin utilized the coercive power of the state to carry out agricultural collectivization, to abolish nonstate sectors, and to establish the Soviet economy based on state ownership and collective ownership controlled by the state.

To provide justification for the Soviet Union's practice, Stalin fabricated an official theory that the basic economic system of socialism can only be state ownership. The textbook, *Political Economy,* written by the Institute of Economics of the Academy of Sciences of the USSR under Stalin's personal supervision, includes authoritative statements concerning this theory. It states that "socialist property exists in two forms: (1) state property (property of the whole people) and (2) cooperative and collective farm property." Of the two, "state property is the predominant and guiding form of socialist property," and it embodies "the most mature and consistent" socialist relations of production. "The leading and determining role in the entire national economy belongs to state property, as the advanced form of socialist property." Collective property exists as a temporary expedient in the phase where the level of agricultural productivity is not high enough. The socialist nature of collective property is also determined by "the condition that state property predominates in the national economy." When agricultural productivity improves to a certain extent, collective property should gradually transform to whole-people property (state property).[6] This blind faith in the state, or "a superstitious reverence for the state and everything connected with it,"[7] which had been strongly opposed by Engels yet promulgated by the Soviet textbook of *Political Economy,* had a strong influence on the economic systems and policies of socialist countries. For many years, it was deemed to be a perfectly justified socialist principle and any debate about it was strictly prohibited.

China's economic system before reform was established under the guidance of this theory. The Chinese economy before 1949 was dominated by the private sector. Private businesses accounted for two-thirds of total industrial output and more than 85 percent of total retail sales; moreover, the influence of private banks and old-style banking houses was significant.[8] The establishment of the dominance of the state sector by eliminating other economic sectors in 1955 and 1956 was the result of taking Russia as the model and accelerating the socialist transformation.[9]

---

[6] Institute of Economics of the Academy of Sciences of the USSR, *Political Economy,* London: Lawrence & Wishart, 1957.
[7] Friedrich Engels, "The 1891 Preface to Marx's 'The Civil War in France' (Makesi Falanxi Neizhan 1891 Nian Danxingben daoyan) (1891)," *Selected Works of Marx and Engels (Makesi Engesi xuanji),* Chinese edition, Vol. 3, Beijing: People's Publishing House, 1995, p. 13.
[8] Xue Muqiao, *Memoir of Xue Muqiao (Xue Muqiao huiyilu),* Tianjin: Tianjin People's Publishing House, 1996, p. 201.
[9] "Taking Russia as the model" was originally proposed by Sun Zhongshan (Sun Yat-sen, 1866–1925). Mao Zedong came to the same conclusion in *On the People's Democratic Dictatorship:* "The October Revolution helped progressives in China, as throughout

As mentioned in Chapter 1, during the early days of the People's Republic of China, the majority of the CPC leaders intended to carry out the plan stipulated by the Seventh National Congress of the CPC in 1945, which would have meant three years of preparation in the recovery period and ten to fifteen years of construction of a society of New Democracy before the beginning of the transition to a socialist society. In 1953, however, Mao Zedong proposed the Party's General Line for the Transition Period, requiring that the transition to a socialist society be basically completed in ten to fifteen years. After this timeframe was formally accepted as the party's guideline in 1954, the socialist transformation campaign soon swept across the nation. The task of exterminating "capitalism and small production to boot," [10] which had been scheduled to take more than a decade to complete, was actually accomplished in less than two years. The Chinese economy was then dominated by the state sector and the quasi-state, collective sector, while nonpublic sectors died out almost completely.

According to the dominant viewpoint of the time, the goal of socialism is complete state ownership. During the Great Leap Forward of 1958, Mao Zedong advocated people's communes, which meant not only turning cooperatives of collective ownership in name into units of state ownership, which were large in size and public in ownership, as well as integrating government administration and commune management, but also attempting to achieve communism in one single step. Only because of the huge losses of life and property resulting from the Great Leap Forward and People's Communes Campaign did Mao Zedong withdraw from his position of immediate transition to complete whole-people ownership of communism. Reversing himself, Mao declared at the Sixth Plenary Session of the Eighth Central Committee of the Communist Party of China (CCCPC) at the end of 1958 that people's communes were still economic organizations of collective ownership. However, one of the resolutions of the Sixth Plenary Session of the Eighth CCCPC still demanded that "the transition from socialist collective ownership to socialist whole-people ownership be gradually achieved in order to completely accomplish whole-people ownership," and the goal of making the state sector the only economic sector be achieved in "15 years, 20 years, or a longer period of time." [11]

---

the world, to adopt the proletarian world outlook as the instrument for studying a nation's destiny and considering anew their own problems. Follow the path of the Russians—that was their conclusion." See Mao Zedong, "On the People's Democratic Dictatorship (Lun renmin minzhu zhuanzheng) (June 30, 1949)," *Selected Works of Mao Zedong (Mao Zedong xuanji) (The Four-in-One Edition),* Beijing: People's Publishing House, 1966, p. 1471.

[10] Mao Zedong, "The Debate on the Cooperative Transformation of Agriculture and the Current Class Struggle (Nongye hezuo-hua de yichang bianlun he dangqian de jieji douzheng) (October 1955)," *Selected Works of Mao Zedong (Mao Zedong xuanji),* Vol. 5, Beijing: People's Publishing House, 1977, p. 196.

[11] *Resolution of the CCCPC on Issues Regarding People's Communes (Zhonggong Zhongyang guanyu renmin gongshe ruogan wenti de jueyi)* (December 10, 1958).

5.1.2 Practice of the Reform and Opening Up Continuously Breaking the Restrictions of Traditional Ownership Theory

The introduction of market mechanism became the core task after China stepped into the era of the reform and opening up. Is it possible to introduce market mechanism and establish a market economy on the basis of state ownership? The answer is absolutely negative. However, in the early stages of reform, any attempt to weaken the dominant position of state ownership met with vehement opposition from traditional ideologists. Therefore, leaders of China's reform, such as Deng Xiaoping, adopted the tactic of "don't argue."

The gradual loosening of the traditional mentality and policies regarding ownership resulted from the interactions of two factors. First, the Chinese government adopted a series of pragmatic and flexible policies to offer more business opportunities to people. Second, as long as there were business opportunities, people would make the best use of them to engage in market transactions and start businesses. These activities were often carried out cautiously and in forms suitable to local policies and conditions. To obtain legal status for their enterprises, some entrepreneurs even made them artificially affiliated to collective enterprises or state-owned enterprises so that they wore a "red cap."

Roughly, the process of gradual introduction of nonstate sectors occurred as follows.

5.1.2.1 The Lifting of the Ban on the Individual Business Sector

After the Great Cultural Revolution, it became urgent to find employment for a large number of educated urban youths who had been dispatched to work in rural areas and then returned to cities. Under the circumstances, some economists suggested that the unemployed should be allowed to engage in self-employed businesses and long-distance transport of goods for sale.[12] In February 1979, this suggestion was accepted in a report drafted by the State Administration for Industry and Commerce and transmitted with endorsement by the State Council. It pointed out that the industrial and commercial administration at various levels "may, according to the needs of local markets and with the approval of relevant departments, give permission to idle labor with permanent residence registration to undertake individual businesses in repair, service and handicraft industries, but hiring labor shall not be allowed." In August 1980, *Circular of the CCCPC on Transmitting the Documents of the National Conference on Labor and Employment* confirmed "the guideline of combining employment through labor administrations, employment

---

[12] For instance, in March 1979, at the National Forum on Reforming Wage System, and in July 1979, in his report at the CPC Central School, Xue Muqiao suggested that urban unemployed youth be encouraged and assisted to look for employment by allowing them to engage in individual businesses and long-distance transport of goods for sale. (Xue Muqiao, "Comments on the Issues of Labor and Wage (Tantan laodong gongzi wenti) (March 1979)" and "Comments on the Issue of Urban Employment (Guanyu chengzhen laodong jiuye wenti de jidian yijian) (July 1979)," *Selected Economics Papers of Xue Muqiao (Xue Muqiao jingji lunwen xuan)*, Beijing: People's Publishing House, 1984, pp. 216–235.)

through organizing cooperatives on a voluntary basis, and employment through establishing individual businesses." It required that "the development of the urban individual business sector be encouraged and fostered."

As might be expected, it soon became necessary to hire labor to expand operations when individual business owners could no longer make full use of market opportunities by themselves alone. At that time, however, hiring labor was considered exploitation and was strictly forbidden. Nonstate sectors could not develop further if this rule remained in force. While drafting government documents, an economist[13] cited a numerical example in Marx's *The Capital* to assert that an individual business owner hiring fewer than eight laborers could still be considered an individual worker because the main source of his income was still his own labor. After this opinion was endorsed by political leaders, the State Council clearly stated in *Several Policies Regarding Urban Nonagricultural Individual Business Sector* of July 1981 that when necessary, an individual business owner "may hire one or two helpers; an individual business owner with high or special skills may have two, three, or no more than five apprentices."[14] From then on, fewer than eight hired workers became the borderline to distinguish individual businesses (*geti qiye*) from private enterprises (*siying qiye*).[15]

5.1.2.2 The Rapid Development of Contracted Family Farms

From the autumn of 1980 to the end of 1982, the household contracting system had been universally adopted in rural China. The people's commune system characterized by a structure of three-level ownership with the production team as the basic accounting unit disintegrated, and peasants set up their own family farms on land collectively owned by villages and contracted (leased) to them. As to the nature of this sector, although the official documents still called it a cooperative sector of collective ownership,[16] it was in fact a sector of sole proprietorships. At the beginning of each of the five consecutive years from 1981 to 1985, the CCCPC publicized its "No. 1 Document" regarding the consolidation of the household contracting system. Later on, in the deci-

---

[13] This economist is Lin Zili, who was working in the Research Department of the Secretariat of the CCCPC at that time.

[14] In *Provisions of the CCCPC and the State Council Pertaining to Exploring All Possibilities, Invigorating the Economy and Solving the Urban Employment Problem (Zhonggong Zhongyang Guowuyuan guanyu guangkaimenlu, gaohuo jingji, jiejue chengzhen jiuye wenti de ruogan guiding)* (October 17, 1981), this stipulation was formally stated as "As to individual businesses, the owners shall be permitted to hire no more than two assistants each; those having special skills may have no more than five apprentices each."

[15] Narrowly defined, "private enterprises (*siying qiye*)" and the "private sector (*siying jingji*)" in this book often refer to the group of enterprises owned by individuals and having eight or more employees and the sector of the economy composed of such enterprises, respectively.

[16] On September 1, 1982, at the 12th National Congress of the CPC, Hu Yaobang pointed out in his report entitled *Create a New Situation of Socialist Modernization Drive in an All-Round Way (Quanmian kaichuang shehuizhuyi xiandaihua jianshe de xin jumian)* that because of the rather low and very uneven standard of productivity development in China, it would be necessary for multiple economic sectors to coexist for a very long period of time. In the countryside, the main economic sector would be the cooperative sector of collective ownership by working people. . . . No matter whether in the countryside or in cities, the individual business sector should be encouraged to adequately develop within the scope prescribed by the state and under the control of industrial and commercial administration, so as to serve as a necessary and beneficial supplement to public sectors.

sion of the Eighth Plenary Session of the 13th CCCPC in 1991 and decision of the Third Plenary Session of the 14th CCCPC in 1993, it was clearly stipulated that the household contracting system must remain stable over a long period of time to further consolidate the family farm system.

5.1.2.3 The Rapid Development of Township and Village Enterprises (Xiangzhen Qiye)

As stated by Deng Xiaoping, "In the rural reform our greatest success—and it is one we had by no means anticipated—has been the emergence of a large number of enterprises run by villages and townships."[17] During the 1980s, township and village enterprises (TVEs) suddenly emerged as prominent players.[18] By the early 1990s, TVEs had become an important component of the Chinese economy and a vigorous driving force for its rapid growth. In 1992, the gross output value of TVEs was more than RMB 1,600 billion, almost equal to the national output value of 1985, of which the gross value of industrial output (GVIO) was more than RMB 1,200 billion, approximately 35 percent of the national total of GVIO of 1992 and almost equal to the national total of GVIO of 1986. Total employment in TVEs was more than 100 million, about the same as total employment in the state sector at that time; profits and taxes achieved was more than RMB 150 billion, of which taxes was approximately RMB 60 billion, with more than 30 percent of growth in taxes coming from TVEs.

TVEs of different regions had different characteristics and ownership structures. For quite a long time, the TVEs of the South Jiangsu area were highly praised as models. Their origins could be traced back to commune and brigade enterprises in the era of the Great Cultural Revolution. After the beginning of the reform and opening up, by virtue of their close relationships with Shanghai, these enterprises rapidly developed in technology and sales channels. TVEs in Wenzhou and Taizhou of Zhejiang Province were also highly developed, most of which were private enterprises grown from individual businesses. These various types of TVEs were generally categorized into the collective sector and thus received recognition and support from the government.

5.1.2.4 The Development of Foreign-Invested Enterprises in the Opening Up Process

The Third Plenary Session of the 11th CCCPC in 1978 adopted the guiding principle of reform and opening up and adjusted foreign economic policies, requiring that

---

[17] Deng Xiaoping, "We Shall Speed up Reform (Gaige de buzi yao jiakuai) (June 12, 1987)," *Selected Works of Deng Xiaoping (Deng Xiaoping wenxuan)*, Vol. 3, Beijing: People's Publishing House, 1993, p. 238.

[18] Chen Naixing et al., *Study on the Policy Guidance for the Development of Industry in Chinese Villages and Towns (Zhongguo xiangzhen gongye fazhan de zhengce daoxiang yanjiu)*, Beijing: Economic Management Press, 1994, p. 262.

state-owned enterprises in every region and every department "actively carry out equal and mutually beneficial economic cooperation with other countries in the world on the basis of self-reliance." The *Law of the PRC on Chinese-Foreign Equity Joint Ventures* of 1979 marked China's transition from prohibiting to actively encouraging foreign direct investment. The main aim of this transition was to acquire the latest technology and advanced management skills from foreign countries. Foreign-invested enterprises were of three different forms: (a) equity joint ventures, (b) contractual joint ventures, and (c) wholly foreign-owned enterprises. From 1979 to 1988, because of the controversy surrounding foreign investment, the Chinese government set up five special economic zones and fourteen coastal open cities for opening to the outside world in the first instance. As people's opinions about foreign investment changed, other regions began to adopt competitive policies to attract foreign investment.

After the aforementioned reforms, the Chinese economy embraced foreign-invested enterprises and sole proprietorships with some limitations. Until the early 1980s, however, private capitalist industry and commerce were still strictly prohibited. The *Constitution of the People's Republic of China* adopted in December 1982 stipulated that "The basis of the social and economic systems of the People's Republic of China is socialist public ownership of the means of production, namely, ownership by the whole people and collective ownership by working people. . . . The state sector is the sector of socialist whole-people ownership and the leading force in the national economy. The state ensures the consolidation and growth of the state sector. . . . The individual business sector of urban and rural working people, operated within the limits prescribed by law, is a supplement to the socialist public sectors." The private sector was not mentioned at all.

5.1.2.5 The Legalization of the Private Sector

After the green light was given to hiring workers and long-distance transport of goods for sale, the private sector developed rapidly with many enterprises hiring eight or more employees. In early 1983, some statesmen and theorists, still holding on to the planned economic system, claimed that capitalism was occurring everywhere and should be cracked down. The answer they received was "No discussion for three years." As a result, the private sector continued to develop under the protection of the policy of "Don't argue; try bold experiments and blaze new trails."[19] The 13th National Congress of the CPC in 1987 explicitly advocated a policy of encouraging the development

---

[19] Deng Xiaoping mentioned later in his "South China Speeches" that "It was my idea to discourage contention, so as to have more time for action. Once disputes begin, they complicate matters and waste a lot of time. As a result, nothing is accomplished. Don't argue; try bold experiments and blaze new trails." See Deng Xiaoping, "Excerpts from Talks Given in Wuchang, Shenzhen, Zhuhai and Shanghai (Zai Wuchang, Shenzhen, Zhuhai, Shanghai dengdi de tanhua yaodian) (January–February 1992)," *Selected Works of Deng Xiaoping (Deng Xiaoping wenxuan)* Vol. 3, Beijing: People's Publishing House, 1993, p. 374.

of the individual business sector and the private sector. In April 1988, the First Session of the Seventh National People's Congress passed an amendment to the *Constitution of the PRC,* which stated in Article 11 that "The State permits the private sector to exist and develop within the limits prescribed by law. The private sector is a supplement to the socialist public sectors. The State protects the lawful rights and interests of the private sector, and exercises guidance, supervision, and control over the private sector."

As pointed out in Chapter 2, the second stage of China's reform was characterized by incremental reform. The so-called increment largely refers to the new, nonstate sectors that gradually developed in the original national economy. The development of those new sectors was the basis for the steady and speedy growth of the Chinese economy in the 1980s.

At that time, there were huge market needs that could not be met by traditional state-owned enterprises and quasi-state-owned, collective enterprises. Therefore, private entrepreneurs strove to satisfy those needs by establishing their own businesses, which simultaneously helped alleviate local unemployment. As a result, local governments' attitudes toward the development of nonstate sectors were normally of tacit consent, protecting, supporting, and even encouraging. When such phenomena drew more and more attention, the central leadership began to adjust its ownership policies to accommodate the development of larger-scale and higher-level nonstate enterprises.

As shown in Tables 2.1, 2.2, and 2.4 in Chapter 2, in the late 1980s, the share of nonstate sectors in the national economy increased steadily while the share of the state sector shrank gradually.

During their economic reform processes, the Soviet Union and Eastern European countries also tried to introduce the private sector without changing the leading position of the state sector, but they failed. As a result, after fundamental changes in their political systems, these countries had to simultaneously carry out marketization reform and large-scale privatization. How did China manage to successfully introduce new ownership components without changing the leading position of the state sector?

Economists proposed different answers. Jeffery Sachs and Wing T. Woo held the view that the main reason for China's success in introducing the private sector into an economy of public ownership was that China was still in an elementary stage of social development, with plenty of surplus labor available to private enterprises. The Soviet Union and Eastern European countries, which were more developed than China, did not have this labor surplus, and thus marketization reform forced them to adopt a strategy of shock therapy.[20] Xu Chenggang and Qian Yingyi offered an

---

[20] Jeffrey Sachs and Wing Thye Woo, "Understanding the Reform Experiences of China, Eastern Europe and Russia," in Chung Lee and Helmut Reisen (eds.), *From Reform to Growth: China and Other Countries in Transition,* Paris: OECD, 1994; "Structural

alternative explanation that the rapid development of Chinese TVEs resulted from the fact that the Chinese planning system was significantly different from the unified planning system of the former Soviet Union. After the decentralization reform advocated by Mao Zedong, the social structure of China was similar to an M-form enterprise organized under the principle of multiple divisions. Therefore, it became possible for markets to develop within and between different jurisdictions.[21]

5.1.3 The Debate on Ownership and the Establishment of the Guiding Principle of "Allowing Diverse Forms of Ownership to Develop Side by Side"

The guiding principle of "keeping public ownership as the mainstay of the economy and allowing diverse forms of ownership to develop side by side" was put forward in the mid-1980s. However, the implementation of this principle altered from time to time. For instance, as has been mentioned earlier, the evaluation attached to the status and role of private enterprises was constantly on the rise. For example, the Third Plenary Session of the 14th CCCPC in 1993 gave a new interpretation of keeping public ownership as the mainstay of the economy by pointing out that "along with the flowing and restructuring of property, there will be more and more economic units with mixed ownership of property, resulting in new structures of property ownership. Although public ownership should be the mainstay in the whole national economy, some deviations should be permitted in some regions or in some industries. The mainstay status of public ownership is mainly shown by the fact that state-owned and collective-owned assets dominate in assets of the whole society, the state sector controls the most vital part of the national economy and plays a leading role in the development of the economy."[22]

Those decisions and the rapid development of nonstate sectors aroused much dissatisfaction in some statesmen and theorists, who still insisted on a planned economy. From 1995 to 1997, four lengthy articles with different contents and focuses yet similar thoughts were published to challenge the guidelines and policies adopted since the inception of the reform and opening up.[23] In early 1997, on the eve of the 15th Na-

---

Factors in the Economic Reforms of China, Eastern Europe and the Former Soviet Union," *Economic Policy,* April 1994, Issue 18, pp. 101–145.

[21] Xu Chenggang and Qian Yingyi, "Why China's Economic Reform Is Different from Others (Zhongguo de jingji gaige weishenme yuzhongbutong) (1993)" in Qian Yingyi, *Modern Economics and China's Reform (Xiandai jingjixue yu Zhongguo jingji gaige),* Beijing, China Renmin University Press, 2003, pp. 177–196.

[22] See *Decision of the CCCPC on Issues Regarding the Establishment of a Socialist Market Economic System (Zhonggong Zhongyang guanyu jianli shehuizhuyi shichang jingji tizhi ruogan wenti de jueding)* (approved by the Third Plenary Session of the 14th CCCPC on November 14, 1993). In 1997, the 15th National Congress of the CPC further explained the concepts of public ownership, public ownership as the mainstay, the leading role of the state sector in economic development, etc.

[23] Ma Licheng and Ling Zhijun, *Confrontation of Ideas: A Faithful Record of the Third Emancipation of Mind in Contemporary China (Jiaofeng: dangdai Zhongguo di san ci sixiang jiefang shilu),* China Today Publishing House, 1997. Details of the debate can be

tional Congress of the CPC, these statesmen and theorists published their third "ten-thousand-word article," "Some Theoretical and Policy Issues Concerning Upholding the Mainstay Status of Public Ownership,"[24] to intensify their attack on the policy of reform and opening up. In this article, it was suggested that the widespread acceptance of the new explanation of keeping public ownership as the mainstay of the economy by the Third Plenary Session of the 14th CCCPC was a "miserable fact." Meanwhile, the article asserted its own viewpoint of ownership in socialism, that is, "scientific socialism deems whole-people ownership (i.e., state ownership) as the advanced form of public ownership and the essential goal to pursue." In the authors' view, the mainstay status of public ownership should be the mainstay status of the state sector. To uphold this mainstay status, first, "the state sector, especially hundreds of thousands of small, medium, and large industrial enterprises of independent accounting as well as the most vital parts of the state sector, should be maintained as a unified and integrated system;" second, "the state sector should be leading the collective sector;" and third, "public sectors should place nonpublic sectors in a supplementary position." Furthermore, this ten-thousand-word article harshly criticized the unregulated increase of nonstate industrial enterprises in the reform and opening up process and the ensuing sharp decline in the share of state-owned industrial enterprises. The article claimed that if the socialist state vested with both political power and ownership could not effectively defend state-owned enterprises with political power, it would be no different from carrying out the erroneous line and gradualist strategy of Mikhail Gorbachev.

Economists supporting market-oriented reform responded openly to this ten-thousand-word article. The research carried out by the research group on "Strategic Restructuring of the State Sector" of the Development Research Center of the State Council was the most representative of them.[25] Their main arguments were:

1. As for the statement that "scientific socialism deems state ownership as the advanced form of public ownership and the essential goal to pursue," this is the

---

found in this book. Chapter 11 (Public or Private: Old Issue Turned into New Constraint), Chapter 12 (Anti-Peaceful Evolution: One More Central Task?), Chapter 13 (Ownership: Can Reform Overcome This Difficulty?), and Chapter 14 (Controversies and Debates at the Back of a Great Man) presented the contents of the four "ten-thousand-word articles" respectively. Chapter 15 (From Emancipation of Mind to Emancipation of Theory) recorded the responses and counter-criticisms by other Chinese thinkers.

[24] Special Commentator of *Contemporary Trend of Thought, Some Theoretical and Policy Issues Concerning Upholding the Mainstay Status of Public Ownership (Guanyu jianchi gongyouzhi zhuti diwei de ruogan lilun he zhengce wenti)*, mimeograph, revised between December 21, 1996 and January 20, 1997. For its main ideas, see Special Commentator of *Contemporary Trend of Thought*, "Hallmark of Keeping Public Ownership as the Mainstay and How to Uphold the Mainstay Status of Public Ownership (Yi gongyouzhi wei zhuti de jiben biaozhi ji zenyang caineng jianchi gongyouzhi de zhuti diwei)," *Contemporary Trend of Thought*, 1996, No. 4.

[25] Research Group on Strategic Restructuring of the State Sector of the Development Research Center of the State Council of the PRC, *Achieving the Strategic Restructuring of the State Sector (Shixian guoyou jingji de zhanlüexing gaizu) (May 8, 1997)*. For its main contents, see Wu Jinglian et al., *The Strategic Restructuring of the State Sector (Guoyou jingji de zhanlüexing gaizu)*, Beijing: China Development Press, 1998.

platitude about the basic economic feature of socialism put forward in the Soviet textbook of *Political Economy.* As these ideologies have become the main impediment to the reform and opening up process, it is quite necessary "to totally break away from the constraints of the Soviet model and the textbook of *Political Economy,* to give a clearer definition of socialism, and to adhere to the idea that the essence of socialism is the realization of common prosperity."

2. "Whether a country has the character of socialism is not determined by the share of the state sector in its economy. . . . As long as the party has correct policies to prevent the polarization between the rich and the poor, China's socialist character is securely guaranteed."

3. "There are various forms for materializing public ownership. We should encourage and support the exploration of various forms for materializing public ownership, such as various funds and foundations, various cooperative organizations, and community ownership. It is wrong to confine public ownership to state ownership and Soviet-style 'collective ownership,' or consider state ownership as 'the supreme form of public ownership and the essential goal for socialists to pursue.'"

4. Based on China's realities, "it is impossible for the limited state capital to support the enormous state sector," and therefore, "it is necessary for the state sector to reduce its scope, to make strategic restructuring . . . to withdraw from ordinary competitive industries so as to concentrate on strategic industries that the State must control."

5. The trend of modern scientific and technological revolution indicates that as the role of human capital and the contribution of individual creativity are increasingly important, the guiding principle of allowing diverse forms of ownership to develop side by side will still be adopted even in the early twenty-first century when China will have achieved preliminary modernization.[26]

The final conclusion of this debate was made by the 15th National Congress of the CPC in September 1997.[27] "Keeping public ownership as the mainstay of the economy and allowing diverse forms of ownership to develop side by side" was confirmed as

---

[26] Wu Jinglian, "Promote the Theoretical Innovation of Socialism to a New Level (Ba shehuizhuyi lilun chuangxin tigao dao yige xinde shuiping) (May 1997)," *China in Transition (Zhuangui Zhongguo),* Chengdu: Sichuan People's Publishing House, 2002, pp. 2–10.

[27] Jiang Zemin, *Hold High the Great Banner of Deng Xiaoping Theory for an All-Round Advance of the Cause of Building Socialism with Chinese Characteristics into the Twenty-First Century—the Report to the Fifteenth National Congress of the CPC (Gaoju Deng Xiaoping lilun weida qizhi, ba jianshe you Zhongguo tese shehuizhuyi shiye quanmian tuixiang 21 shiji—zai Zhongguo Gongchandang Di Shiwu Ci Quanguo Daibiao Dahui shang de baogao)* (September 1997), Beijing: People's Publishing House, 1997.

China's basic economic system for the primary stage of socialism. Nonpublic sectors were acknowledged as "important components of a socialist market economy." It was required to "strive to seek various forms for materializing public ownership that can greatly promote the growth of the productive forces. . . . All management methods and organizational forms that mirror the laws governing socialized production may be utilized boldly." Meanwhile, it was determined that the ownership structure should be readjusted according to the principle that "any form of ownership that meets the criterion of the 'three favorables'[28] can and should be utilized to serve socialism."

Obviously, the share of the state sector in the national economy would drop during this readjustment. Acknowledging this situation, the report of the 15th National Congress of the CPC and the decision of the Fourth Plenary Session of the 15th CCCPC asserted that the decline in the share of the state sector in the national economy would not alter the socialist character of China.[29]

The readjustment of ownership structure would be implemented in two ways: the strategic layout readjustment of the state sector and the promotion of the healthy development of nonstate sectors. These are to be discussed in detail in the following two sections.

5.2 The Layout Readjustment of the State Sector: Advancing in Some Areas while Retreating in Others

5.2.1 The Guiding Principle for the Layout Readjustment of the State Sector

In contrast to the rapid development of nonstate sectors, the situation of the state sector had been unsatisfactory since the commencement of the reform and opening up. This was the result of fundamental deficiencies in the enterprise system as well as the excessive scale and unreasonable layout of the state sector.

According to statistics from the former State Administration of State-Owned Assets, by the end of 1995, the total amount of operating state assets was approximately RMB 4,500 billion; the total amount of state assets in industry and commerce was approximately RMB 3,600 billion, excluding some specific sectors such as armies, post offices, and railways. Since 20 percent of all these assets in industry and commerce were

---

[28] The criterion of the "three favorables" refers to favorable to promoting the growth of the productive forces in a socialist society, increasing the overall strength of the socialist state, and raising the people's living standards.

[29] See Jiang Zemin, ibid. and *Decision of the CCCPC on Several Important Issues Regarding Reform and Development of State-Owned Enterprises (Zhonggong Zhongyang guanyu guoyou qiye gaige he fazhan ruogan zhongda wenti de jueding)* (approved by the Fourth Plenary Session of the 15th CCCPC on September 22, 1999).

nonproductive assets (such as housing, schools, hospitals, and so forth), the total amount of state assets used in production and business was less than RMB 3,000 billion. Yet these state assets were distributed among 291,000 enterprises in virtually all industrial and commercial fields, ranging from retail trade to long-range missiles. The average amount of state assets in each enterprise was only about RMB 10 million.

According to modern economics, the main role of public enterprises is to provide products or services that nonstate enterprises are unable or unwilling to provide. In ordinary competitive fields, state-owned enterprises are less flexible and competitive than nonstate enterprises. However, in China, the state sector was involved in almost all fields, including some fields inappropriate for government operation, and thus low efficiency and large-scale losses prevailed. Furthermore, the state sector was so dispersed and the assets for each individual enterprise were so small that even in some fields that would be best operated by state-owned enterprises, economies of scale and essential technological innovations were hard to achieve. Because too many state assets were put into ordinary profit-making undertakings, funds for governments to carry out their basic public services could not be guaranteed. For instance, although it was stipulated in the *Compulsory Education Law of the PRC* that the government should provide nine years of compulsory education, some localities required parents to pay tuition fees due to insufficient funding for education. Because some law enforcement agencies had insufficient funding, victims in some criminal cases were asked to pay fees.

In view of the insufficient capital funds for SOEs, some people suggested that the state muster financial resources and inject a great quantity of capital through the state treasury into state-owned enterprises to expand their scale and enhance their competitiveness. However, according to estimates by the Development Research Center of the State Council in 1997, if the existing distribution of state assets across industries and enterprises remained unchanged, the state would have to invest at least RMB 2,000 to 2,500 billion to make state-owned enterprises competitive enough on the market. Of this investment, RMB 600 billion would be needed to relieve enterprises of their bad debts, and RMB 1,800 billion would be used to replenish insufficient capital funds and to upgrade outdated production facilities. In addition, funds in the order of RMB trillions would be needed to replenish the pension funds of older employees and finance some urgent projects that the state should have launched but did not for lack of resources. Such huge amounts of funds were completely unavailable under the existing economic conditions.

Since the commencement of the reform and opening up, China's national savings structure had changed a great deal, and households had replaced governments and state-owned enterprises to become the main sources of savings. According to estimates by the World Bank, of China's total national savings in 1978, household savings accounted for

3.4 percent, government savings 43.4 percent, and enterprise savings 53.2 percent. In other words, 96.6 percent of national savings was owned by the state in 1978. In the 1990s, the ownership structure of China's savings had changed to one in which 83 percent of total national savings was from households, while governments and enterprises contributed only 3 percent and 14 percent, respectively. Since savings from state-owned enterprises was estimated at less than 7 percent of the total, only about 10 percent of national savings was owned by the state. Under a market economy, it would be impossible to simply rely on the accumulation of state-owned enterprises and the financial resources of the state to significantly increase the total amount of state assets.[30]

Reality made people realize that to change this situation, the state sector must be strategically restructured. The state sector needed to withdraw from ordinary competitive industries and concentrate on some strategic industries that need to be controlled by the state sector. Currently, "strategic industries" mainly refer to industries related to national security, such as important military industries and the coinage industry; large infrastructure project and other projects of significant externalities, such as projects to control major rivers and projects of major forest belts as well as social welfare undertakings, which generate large social benefit for numerous beneficiaries but that nonstate enterprises are unable or unwilling to carry out; large projects for nonrenewable resources (such as oil fields and coal mines) requiring huge investments with long payoff periods that are beyond the capacity of private capital but cannot be controlled by foreign capital and, thus, must be dominated by state capital; and the development of public domain high technologies that are of strategic significance to the long-term development of the nation.

There are two different approaches to restructuring the state sector. The first is by state planning. That is, the government proposes a plan, deciding which enterprises in which industries should be strengthened, which should be merged, and which should be closed down, and then carries out this plan by state investment or administrative allocation. In the past few decades, there have been many unsuccessful examples of piecing together giant enterprises such as trusts by the government in a vain attempt to avoid the institutional innovation of enterprises. It had been shown that restructuring state-owned enterprises by this approach of "arranged marriage" would not achieve the goal of optimizing the structure. On the contrary, because of strengthened administrative control and the process of economic reform, the conditions of the state sector might deteriorate. In the mid- and late 1990s, some departments and regions attempted to re-

---

[30] Quoted from Wu Jinglian et al., *The Strategic Restructuring of the State Sector (Guoyou jingji de zhanlüexing gaizu),* Beijing: China Development Press, 1998.

adjust industrial and enterprise structures under the leadership of the governments, with either the result that large-scale yet low-efficiency enterprises were created or the result that bad enterprises were not turned around while good enterprises were dragged down after mergers. Lessons should be learned from these failures.

The other approach is to improve the structures of industries and enterprises by optimizing and restructuring state assets on the basis of existing or emerging strong enterprises through financial operations on the capital market. These financial operations include financing by share-issuance, selling shares to cash out, mergers and acquisitions, debt restructuring, and bankruptcy liquidation. Many cases have shown that such restructuring not only gives full play to the superiority of the state sector in specific industries but also makes full use of the strength of other economic sectors.

The restructuring of the state sector through the capital market depends on the autonomous actions of independent enterprises. Therefore, turning state-owned enterprises into real enterprises is a prerequisite for restructuring the state sector. The first step is to change the functions of government to separate government administration from enterprise management, that is, to separate the government's economic administrative function from its function as the owner of state assets. Specific institutions that exercise owner's rights on behalf of the state should replace administrative institutions that combine government administration with enterprise management.

According to recent practice, the major difficulty in restructuring the state sector is caused by barriers between departments and regions that are mainly caused by combining government administration with enterprise management. Although administrative departments in charge are not the real owner, they have real control over enterprises. Their interests do not lie in increasing the value of assets, but rather in achieving other economic and noneconomic goals by virtue of such control. Therefore, to make state assets flow freely, the state assets management has to be reformed. In addition, the existing fiscal, taxation, and financial regulations that impede the free flow of capital across industries and enterprises, such as collecting enterprise income tax by administrative affiliation and allotting credit quotas by region, need to be changed as well.

5.2.2 Letting Go of and Invigorating Small and Medium SOEs

Small and medium enterprises (SMEs) have always been on the periphery of state economic policies in China. That position made small and medium SOEs the first target of ownership reform. These enterprises also provide a practical proving ground for the policy of categorized guidance for the reform and restructuring of the state sector.

In the early stage of the reform and opening up in China, the most frequently used policy toward small and medium SOEs was to delegate power to their management or to handle them as contracting operations. Compared with the direct supervision of administrative institutions, this method was more likely to maximize the enterprise management's enthusiasm for increasing production and income. However, contracting often led to "insider control" and widespread short-term thinking on management's part. This behavior was popularly described as "distributing bonuses whenever money is available, borrowing a loan whenever money is not available, and leaving repayment of the money to the next management." Some enterprise managers even used the enterprise capital to speculate in high-risk markets, such as the stock market, the futures market, and the real estate market. Other managers fabricated account books, reported false profits to hide true losses, and embezzled public property, turning the contracted responsibility system into ownership by factory director or ownership by factory director's family and relatives.[31]

TVEs were established under the direct leadership of township-level governments and above. Most of them were wholly owned by grassroots governments. Because of protection from grassroots governments and good financing conditions, TVEs used to be full of vigor in the early stages of reform. However, as reform deepened and TVEs grew larger, their weaknesses, which are similar to those of their SOE counterparts, became increasingly clear. By the 1990s, TVEs in many regions were experiencing slowdown in growth and deterioration in financial conditions. The number of financially distressed firms grew rapidly, highlighting the urgent need for transformation.

In 1995, the total number of industrial SOEs with independent accounting was 87,900. According to the standard of the National Statistics Bureau, about 15,000 of them were large and medium-sized enterprises, while the remaining 72,200 were all small. In addition, there were more than 500,000 TVEs under the jurisdiction of township-level governments and above. Obviously, the only way out for these 600,000 SMEs was to clarify property rights and transform them into real enterprises.

As early as November 1993, *Decision on Issues Regarding the Establishment of a Socialist Market Economic System* by the Third Plenary Session of the 14th CCCPC pointed out that "for small SOEs in general, some may switch to contracting operations or leasing operations; others may be restructured into shareholding cooperative enterprise or sold to collectives or individuals." However, because ideological impediments were still strong in many regions, this policy of "letting go of small enterprises" was not widely implemented before the 15th National Congress of the CPC in 1997, except in a few places, such as Zhucheng of Shandong Province and Shunde of Guangdong Province.

---

[31] Yu Chengzhi, "A Great Pioneering Undertaking in the History of Socialist Reform: The Universal Significance of the Mixed Ownership System of Shunde Industry (Shehuizhuyi gaigeshi shang de yida chuangju: Shunde gongye hunhexing chanquan zhidu de pubian yiyi)," *SEZ and Hong Kong & Macau Economy* (Tequ yu Gang Ao jingji), 1995, No. 4.

Insight 5.1

The Reform of Small and Medium Enterprises in Zhucheng and Shunde

State-owned enterprises in Zhucheng City of Shandong Province were few in number, small in scale, and poor in performance. Their losses were heavy burdens on the local government finance. In September 1992, the city government decided to experiment with shareholding system reform in those enterprises. Zhucheng Electric Machinery Factory was chosen as the first to try out this experiment. The city government proposed two schemes for the employees to choose from: (a) the state would hold controlling shares, and shares held by employees would not exceed 20 percent of the total; (b) employees would purchase the enterprise's assets, and the state would become a shareholder by contributing land as investment.

Employees dismissed both schemes. Instead, they asked for permission to purchase all of the enterprise's assets and to pay rent for land use. Finally, the government approved the employees' proposal, and Zhucheng Kaiyuan Electric Machinery Co., Ltd. was established. After the evaluation of assets, employees voluntarily purchased the net assets of the enterprise in the form of shares; a board of directors and a supervisory board were elected on a one-share-one-vote basis via secret ballot and based on nominations from the floor so that a system of democratic management by employees was set up.

Zhucheng Kaiyuan Electric Machinery Co., Ltd. performed well after the reform. As a result, the city's party committee and government decided in April 1993 to "implement the shareholding system reform in an all-round way" in enterprises under the control of the city government and township governments. The main approach of the reform was "a sale followed by a transformation with employees as shareholders." By July 1994, 274 enterprises (including 37 state-owned enterprises) at the township level and above had successfully transformed. The number of enterprises adopting the shareholding cooperative system was 210 (including 32 state-owned enterprises). Other approaches to transformation included limited liability companies, joint ventures with overseas investors, transfer property for free, bankruptcy, leasing, and merger.

In 1993 and 1994, Shunde City of Guangdong Province reformed several state-owned enterprises and collective-owned TVEs established in the early 1980s, focusing on transforming their ownership structure. The reform was carried out in three major steps: (a) evaluating assets and defining property rights; (b) deciding on the transformation plan of the enterprise; and (c) signing the transformation contract and setting up the new enterprise system. The basic methods of the transformation included turning into a listed or unlisted joint stock company, selling the ownership to managers and employees to form a mixed-ownership limited liability company, transferring part of the ownership to foreign investors to establish a new Sino-foreign joint venture, leasing, risk-deposit contracting, liquidation auction, etc. Simultaneously, Shunde adopted some complementary measures, including compensation for retired employees and the establishment of a social security system, improvement of the investment system, establishment of a chamber of commerce, etc.

By the end of 1994, 896 enterprises in Shunde were transformed, accounting for 82.7 percent of public-owned enterprises under the jurisdiction of township and city governments. Among those transformed enterprises, there were 2 listed joint stock companies, 7 unlisted joint stock companies, 32 joint ventures, 124 joint state-private enterprises, 431 public-owned private-run enterprises, 78 shareholding enterprises with shares held by employees, and 22 enterprises sold through auction. Of the total assets, governments at the city and township levels accounted for 61.2 percent, private capital for 22.6 percent, foreign capital for 15 percent, and public capital from outside Shunde for 1.2 percent. Just a few years after the reform, many vigorous enterprises flourished in Shunde, some of which have become the flagship enterprise in their industries.

(Compiled from Huang Shaoan and Huang Lijun, "Re-Analysis of the Zhucheng Phenomenon," *Journal of Reform,* No. 2, 1998; Liu Shiding, "Reform of the Structure of Asset Ownership of Enterprises in Shunde," *Journal of Reform,* No. 6, 1995.)

The guiding principle of the reform of state-owned enterprises fundamentally changed around 1995. In essence, the primary objective of the reform was switched from invigorating every state-owned enterprise to making strategic readjustments in the layout of the state sector. The main concept was "grasping large enterprises and letting go of small enterprises." To be specific, "grasping large enterprises" meant concentrating effort on one thousand large and medium-sized SOEs that were essential to the national economy. "Letting go of small enterprises" meant releasing and invigorating small and medium SOEs by means of merger, leasing, contracting, offering for sale, or bankruptcy.

This new guiding principle generated a great deal of intense discussion among economists and political leaders, and the resulting recommendation was that in implementing this principle, the focus should be on letting go of small enterprises; that is, transforming small and medium SOEs and enterprises affiliated to governments at the township level.

Letting go of small enterprises did not gain momentum until the second half of 1995. Based on information from various regions, methods of transforming small and medium SOEs were as follows:

- Transferring part or all of the property rights to employees to create a cooperative enterprise or a joint stock cooperative enterprise.

- Selling the enterprise in its entirety to nonpublic legal entities or individuals. The enterprise after the sale became a nonstate enterprise, a joint venture, or a foreign-invested enterprise, either as an independent firm or subsidiary of other firms.

- Transforming the enterprise into a limited liability company or a joint stock company in accordance with the procedures prescribed in the *Company Law of the PRC*. Some of the transformed companies retained state-owned shares; some companies' shares were mainly held by their employees; some belonged to Sino-foreign joint ventures; and in some others, shares were held by various owners.

- By acquisition and merger, transforming the enterprise into part or a subsidiary of another large, state-owned enterprise.

- Leasing all or part of the enterprise's assets to the management or employees of the enterprise or those of another enterprise. In most cases, only state-owned real estate such as land and buildings were leased to the new owner who then paid rental fees to the state and took full responsibility for the management of the enterprise.

However, some unhealthy practices occurred in the process of transforming SMEs that impaired the rights and interests of relevant stakeholders. Therefore, some economists claimed that it was necessary to correctly deal with the rights and interests of various parties in the process of letting go of small enterprises, especially in the evaluation of the enterprise's property and in handling the social security issues of employees to ensure social justice.

The first issue was the determination of the transfer price of the enterprise. The value of an enterprise depends on its future profits and is best determined through market competition. Therefore, it was difficult to accurately determine the value of the enterprise when the capital market was not yet fully developed. The mispricing most frequently at issue was the excessive low pricing for the enterprise. Sometimes the price could be considered as a giving-away of the enterprise. Local government had to adopt measures to avoid such mispricing, such as:

- Specific institutions were set up to act as representatives vested with the full authority of the sellers, handling legal issues related to prices and other issues regarding transferring property rights. No individual official was allowed to decide such legal issues on his or her own.

- Before the parties to the transaction negotiated the transfer price of the enterprise's property, an evaluation of the assets by a third party, that is, a qualified evaluation institution (such as a certified public accountant) should be arranged.

- Introducing market competition mechanism as the most effective way to prevent mispricing. Currently, China's centralized securities exchange markets are still quite immature. This impedes competitive trading via exchanges and the open sale of shares on markets.

Economists suggested that in the process of transformation, it should not be compulsory to turn all enterprises into joint stock cooperative enterprises held by existing managers and employees. Even when a shareholding cooperative system is adopted, the proportion of shares available for open sale should be as large as possible.

The second issue concerned compensation for social security funds of employees.[32] Because the assets of an enterprise are composed of owners' equity and liabilities, how to compensate employees for their social security claims accumulated against the state under the low-salary system became an issue in the transformation process. In practice, there are three main approaches to this issue. The first is to deduct the anticipated social security compensation from the selling price. After the sale, the new owner is then

---

[32] The issue of compensation for social security funds of employees is not limited to the process of "letting go of and invigorating small and medium enterprises;" all state-owned enterprises encounter this problem in their reform process.

obligated to pay pensions to retired employees and take care of other social security expenses. The second is to pay the employees a lump sum with part of the proceeds from transferring state-owned net assets. The third is to transfer part of the state-owned property rights to relevant social security institutions and use dividends and other returns to pay pensions and other social security expenses. Of the three approaches, the first is for new enterprises to take over the responsibility of social security payments from old enterprises. This approach is easy, but is not a long-term solution. The second approach amounts to paying employees social security benefits in a lump sum. It is simple, but may have many problems later. The third approach, although seemingly more complicated, may have more advantages in the long run. We return to this approach in detail in Chapter 9.

5.3 The Emergence of a Diverse Ownership Structure with Multiple Forms of Ownership Developing Side by Side

During the incremental reform, the nonstate sectors, emerging from scratch, grew up to break down the monopoly of the state sector and laid the foundation for their further development. In the mid-1990s, nonstate sectors received a further boost by the SOE reform policy of letting go of and invigorating small and medium enterprises. In 1997, the 15th National Congress of the CPC affirmed that "keeping public ownership as the mainstay of the economy and allowing diverse forms of ownership to develop side by side" was China's basic economic system, and nonstate sectors were important components of China's socialist market economy. This removed ideological impediments and laid down the political foundation for the development of nonstate sectors. The development of nonstate sectors has accelerated since then.

5.3.1 The Rapid Development of Nonstate Sectors

Since 1998, with the implementation of the guideline of the 15th National Congress of the CPC for readjusting the layout of the state sector and improving ownership structures, the share of nonstate sectors in the national economy has grown rapidly.

In early 1998, speeding up the development of nonstate enterprises became an urgent item on the government's agenda. At that time, more than ten million SOE employees were laid off every year. The reemployment of those laid-off SOE employees was a concern of the entire society. However, it was impossible for the state to devote resources to reemploy laid-off workers within the state sector. China was then transitioning out of a dual economy via the growth of the modern sector, and the reemployment of the urban unemployed was made even more difficult because hundreds of millions of rural surplus laborers were seeking employment in nonagricultural industries as well. If new jobs could not be created in large numbers, and the employment environment of the entire society could not be improved, the reemployment problem of laid-off SOE employees would be impossible to solve. Because small and medium nonstate enterprises were apparently the main sources of new jobs, the leaders of the State Council made prompt decisions to adopt a series of new measures to support the development of nonstate enterprises.

By the end of the twentieth century, nonstate sectors had taken over the largest share of China's national economy and become the fundamental driving force in China's economic growth (see Table 5.1).

Nonstate sectors were not only huge in size but also superior in performance. This can be seen in Figure 5.1 from the relation between the share of nonstate sectors in each region's economy and the GDP growth rate of each region: the larger the share of nonstate sectors, the faster the growth of GDP.

5.3.2 The Emergence of Diverse Ownership Structures with Multiple Forms of Ownership Developing Side by Side in Some Regions

The greatest success from China's economic reform is that nonstate sectors developed from supplementary components to major contributors of the whole national economy. It has been shown that nonstate sectors are the most active components of the market economy, a fundamental force in maintaining economic and social stability, and an important source of technological innovations. Nonstate sectors played an extremely important role in resisting economic recession and accelerating economic recovery after

Table 5.1   Investment and Employment by Ownership (%)

Year		1997	1998	1999	2000	2001	2002
Investment in Fixed Assets	State Sector	52.5	54.1	53.4	50.1	47.3	43.4
	Collective Sector	15.4	14.8	14.5	14.6	14.2	13.8
	Nonpublic Sectors*	32.1	31.1	32.1	35.3	38.5	42.8
Urban Employment	State Sector	53.1	41.9	38.2	35.0	31.9	28.9
	Collective Sector	13.9	9.1	7.6	6.5	5.4	4.5
	Nonpublic Sectors	33.0	49.0	54.2	58.5	62.7	66.6

*Nonpublic sectors refer to the collection of all non-state and non-collective economic entities.
Source: The National Bureau of Statistics, *China Statistical Yearbook (Zhongguo tongji nianjian)*, Beijing: China Statistics Press, 2003.

Figure 5.1   Nonstate Sectors Speeding Up Economic Growth (2000)

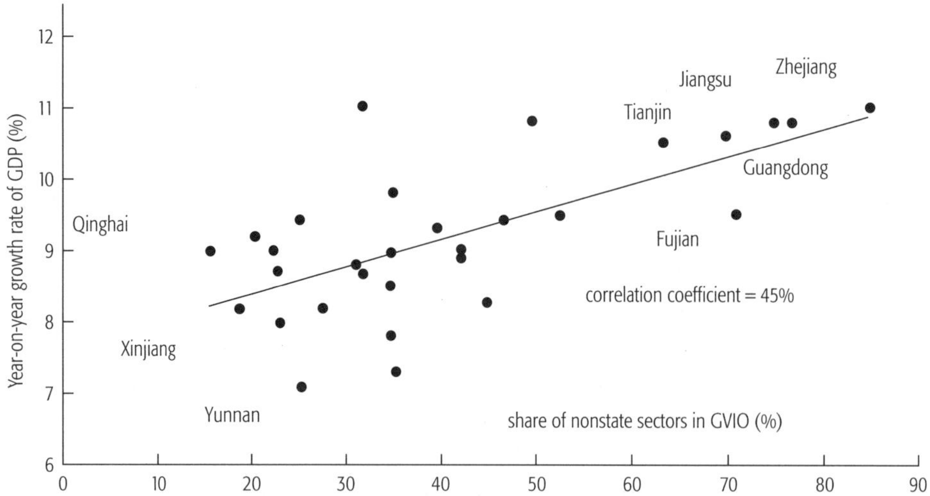

Note: GVIO here is the total GVIO of all state-owned industrial enterprises and nonstate industrial enterprises with annual sales revenue of RMB 5 million or more.
Source: The National Bureau of Statistics, *China Statistical Yearbook (Zhongguo tongji nianjian)*, Beijing: China Statistics Press, 2001; Data from China International Capital Corporation Limited (CICC).

the East Asian Financial Crisis in 1997; they acted as the main channel for the reemployment of urban laid-off workers, provided new opportunities for relieving rural poverty and boosting farmers' income, and drove the in-depth development of China's market economy.

These trends occurred mainly in China's southeast coastal regions, where the ownership structure had been improved and diverse forms of ownership developing side by side had become a reality. The enterprise system and business environment in these regions unleashed the entrepreneurial talent and enthusiasm in the Chinese people, resulting in rapid increase in social investment, unprecedented vigor of foreign trade, exceptional inflow of foreign direct investment, abundant employment opportunities, and stable social order. These regions have become the engines of the rapid development of the national economy.

Zhejiang Province was the first region to experience these trends. The main driving force of Zhejiang's economic development lay in the rapid growth of its small and medium nonstate enterprises and the resulting swift transfer of rural surplus laborers to jobs in urban industry and commerce. Starting from household workshops and small enterprises of "shop at the front and factory at the back," nonstate enterprises in Zhejiang evolved into enterprise clusters based on specialized markets, and their products were sold in markets throughout China and the world.

Before the reform and opening up, Zhejiang was only a moderately developed province. In 1980, its GVIO was only RMB 20.1 billion, and its nonstate industry and commerce were underdeveloped. Between 1981 and 1985, small and medium nonstate enterprises in Zhejiang expanded rapidly. In 1982, the number of rural and urban nonstate enterprises was 79,000, and the total number of employees in these businesses was 80,000, approximately eight times those figures in 1980. In 1985, there were 264,000 rural individual businesses and joint household enterprises, implying that hundreds of thousands of peasants were employed in nonagricultural industries. Correspondingly, the annual growth rate of the net income of rural residents was as high as 20.1 percent between 1980 and 1985. In 1986, the net income per capita of Zhejiang rural residents was the highest of all Chinese provinces and autonomous regions, excluding those municipalities directly under the central government. Since then, small and medium nonstate enterprises in Zhejiang have continued to grow rapidly. In 2000, the total industrial value added by urban and rural nonstate enterprises accounted for 49 percent of that of the whole province.

In the twenty years from 1981 to 2000, rural surplus laborers in Zhejiang took jobs in urban nonagricultural industries in huge numbers. The share of the agricultural labor force in the total work force declined from 67.7 percent in 1980 to 37.2 percent in 2000, a reduction of 30.5 percentage points. In other words, close to half the people who worked in agriculture in 1981 no longer worked on farms in 2000. The urbanization level rose from 14.9 percent in 1980 to 48.7 percent in 2000, an increase of 33.8 percentage points, 12.5 percentage points higher than the national average. Zhejiang's per capita GNP and per capita income ranked first in all provinces, second only to large cities, such as Shanghai and Beijing.[33]

Therefore, at the turn of the century, Zhejiang's economy could be characterized as having diverse forms of ownership developing side by side and rural and urban areas developing side by side (see Table 5.2).

In Jiangsu Province, some fluctuations in economic development occurred. In the 1980s, TVEs in the South Jiangsu model were quite competitive compared with those dominant state-owned enterprises. They were deemed the model for other rural areas in China. However, in the early 1990s, these quasi-state-owned enterprises, despite

---

[33] As to Zhejiang's economic development, see Shi Jinchuan, Jin Xiangrong et al., *Institutional Change and Economic Development: Investigation on the Wenzhou Model (Zhidu bianqian yu jingji fazhan: Wenzhou moshi yanjiu),* Hangzhou: Zhejiang University Press, 2002.

Table 5.2 Economic Growth in Zhejiang (year-on-year growth, %)

Year	GDP	Industrial Value Added	Investment in Fixed Assets	Total Exports
2000	11.0	12	18.5	51.1
2001	10.5	11	22.1	18.2
2002	12.3	13.5	24.9	28.0

Source: Zhejiang Provincial Bureau of Statistics, *Statistical Yearbook of Zhejiang (Zhejiang Tongji Nianjian)*, Beijing: China Statistics Press, various years.

their increased sizes, began to show weaknesses similar to those of state-owned enterprises, such as low efficiency and slow growth. In the past, Jiangsu had always been the first province to emerge from adversity and lead the national economy to recovery. However, in 1998 and 1999, economic performance in Jiangsu Province was worse than the national average.

When the 15th National Congress of the CPC put forward "grasping large enterprises and letting go of small enterprises" in 1997, it was commonly accepted that enterprise system reform needed to be furthered with TVEs in the South Jiangsu model. Great efforts were taken in the South Jiangsu area to let go of small enterprises. However, two problems appeared immediately. First, people in power sold enterprises to relatives and friends at extremely low prices. Second, when enterprises were transformed to the shareholding cooperative system, current employees not only could not get any compensation for the state's implicit liabilities of social security, but they were also forced to purchase shares of the enterprise or they would be fired. Such an unreasonable practice was strongly opposed by employees. The State Economic and Trade Commission promulgated notice to stop those wrong practices and, as a result, some localities stopped letting go of small enterprises.

TVEs in South Jiangsu started to learn from TVEs in Wenzhou and Taizhou of Zhejiang Province with great enthusiasm when they finally encountered serious crises. The former copied the latter's enterprise systems and undertook restructuring of property rights. Most of the South Jiangsu enterprises have been transformed into sole proprietorships or companies.[34] South Jiangsu's economic situation changed a great deal after that: GDP increased significantly, industrial production revived, and investment escalated. Foreign trade increases were especially satisfactory (see Table 5.3).

---

[34] As to the situation of Jiangsu TVEs in the late 1990s, see Xin Wang, "The Historical Ending of the South Jiangsu Model (Sunan moshi de lishi zhongjie)," *China Economic Times (Zhongguo jingji shibao)*, December 30, 2000. This article recorded various controversies arising from the reform and restructuring of collective enterprises in the South Jiangsu area.

Table 5.3   Economic Growth in Jiangsu (year-on-year growth, %)

Year	GDP	Industrial Value Added	Investment in Fixed Assets	Total Exports
2000	10.6	12.2	9.2	40.7
2001	10.2	11.5	10.3	12.1
2002	11.6	14.0	16.5	33.3

Source: Jiangsu Provincial Bureau of Statistics, *Statistical Yearbook of Jiangsu (Jiangsu Tongji Nianjian)*, Beijing: China Statistics Press, various years.

The export-oriented economy of South Jiangsu area was originally better than Zhejiang. In recent years, the Suzhou Industrial Park, jointly developed by China and Singapore, has utilized the administrative "software" (rules and regulations) of the Singaporean government. This software was later introduced to other Jiangsu development zones and contributed significantly to the improvement of the Jiangsu investment environment. Moreover, South Jiangsu area is close to Shanghai, the largest commercial and financial center of China. This helps further in attracting a large amount of foreign investment.

Guangdong is another region that experienced experimental reform early. Guangdong excels in export-oriented TVEs and has established an economy in which diverse forms of ownership have coexisted for a long time. However, around the turn of the century, as a result of its tardiness in reforming the state sector and improving the legal environment, Guangdong's economic performance was not as satisfactory as the Yangtze River Delta in general and Zhejiang in particular. Currently, some areas in Guangdong have begun to catch up by improving the investment climate and accelerating the reform of state-owned enterprises (see Table 5.4). If Guangdong can take full advantage of the process of complementary economic integration with Hong Kong, its future will be very promising.

Table 5.4   Economic Growth in Guangdong (year-on-year growth, %)

Year	GDP	Industrial Value Added	Investment in Fixed Assets	Total Exports
2000	10.5	12.8	7.9	18.3
2001	9.5	11.1	10.6	3.8
2002	10.8	13.3	12.5	24.2

Source: Guangdong Provincial Bureau of Statistics, *Statistical Yearbook of Guangdong (Guangdong Tongji Nianjian)*, Beijing: China Statistics Press, various years.

Nonstate enterprises are mostly SMEs, which have lots of advantages. First, those enterprises can be major sources of new jobs for the following reasons:

1. Most SMEs, especially those in the service industry, are labor intensive and thus require a large amount of labor.

2. They have low occupational requirements and have fewer constraints on labor with weak education backgrounds or low technical skills.

3. They do not require advanced technology or large investment and thus are relatively easy to start up.

4. They can create huge demand for investment and consumption, which, in turn, create opportunities for future development of other SMEs, especially in the service industry.

Second, SMEs are one of the major forces of innovation in the contemporary economy. Since the 1980s, alongside the development of high technology, the role of human capital (especially the intellectual part of human capital) becomes more and more prominent. Because small enterprises can establish a close link between innovation activities and material rewards for innovators, these types of business are superior in successfully developing high-tech products. In today's developed countries, small enterprises normally account for more than 95 percent of the total number of enterprises and more than 60 percent of the total employment. Moreover, small enterprises generate most of the breakthrough innovations and new employment positions.

5.4 Impediments to Further Development of Nonstate Sectors

In recent years, nonstate sectors in China have developed fast and contributed greatly to the national economy. However, there are still many problems in the business environment of nonstate sectors and in the organizational system, business strategy and incentive mechanism of nonstate enterprises. All these problems need to be solved to ensure further development of nonstate enterprises. SMEs in nonstate sectors have great competitive advantages and generate positive externalities of intensifying competition in the whole market, but they also have some innate disadvantages, and therefore need special support from the society.

5.4.1 Improving the Business Environment of Nonstate Sectors

In China, as a result of the legacy of ownership discrimination in a planned economy and ultra-left ideology, nonstate enterprises have both innate and acquired disadvantages. If the government had not removed impediments and provided the necessary support for nonstate enterprises, it would have been very difficult for them to develop. Since the late 1990s, the situation has been gradually improving.

First, discriminatory regulations have been abolished, and national treatment has been applied to nonstate enterprises. In the early stages of reform, many regions and departments divided enterprises into various grades and ranks in accordance with their ownership. The state sector received "upper-caste" treatment and the collective sector received "lower-caste" treatment but nonpublic sectors were often treated as outcaste. Some private entrepreneurs subconsciously viewed themselves as second-class citizens. This mindset affected every aspect of the economic system and economic policy and became a huge impediment to the development of nonstate sectors.

The decision of the 15th National Congress of the CPC established the political foundation for equal treatment for enterprises of various ownerships. China's accession to the WTO in 2001 further called for equal national treatment. Governments at various levels have promulgated rules and regulations to implement equal national treatment. For instance, according to *Opinions on Promoting and Guiding Domestic Private Investment* and *Opinions on Policies and Measures to Speed Up the Development of Service Industries during the Tenth Five-Year Plan Period,* promulgated by the State Planning Commission in December 2001, domestic private investment should be encouraged and permitted in all areas where foreign investment is encouraged and permitted. In investment areas with preferential policies, those policies shall apply equally to domestic private investment.

The Third Plenary Session of the 16th CCCPC clearly restated that "laws and regulations that hinder the development of nonpublic sectors must be abolished or revised in order to eliminate the institutional impediment. The market should be open to nonpublic sectors and nonpublic capital should be allowed to enter industries and fields that are not prohibited by any laws and regulations, such as infrastructure and public utilities. Nonpublic enterprises should be treated in the same way as other enterprises in investment, financing, taxation, land use, foreign trade, etc."[35]

Second, the financing environment of nonstate enterprises has been improved to some degree. A most pressing issue is the lack of smooth financing channels for nonstate enterprises. To solve the lack of credit guarantees for SMEs, every locality has set up credit guarantee institutions to share risks with banks. To further develop financing channels for nonstate enterprises, experimental efforts have been made to create various

---

[35] "Decision of the CCCPC on Issues Regarding the Improvement of the Socialist Market Economic System (Zhonggong Zhongyang guanyu wanshan shehuizhuyi shichang jingji tizhi ruogan wenti de jueding)" (approved by the Third Plenary Session of the 16th CCCPC on October 14, 2003), *People's Daily (Renmin ribao)*, October 21, 2003, p. 1.

kinds of financial institutions, including private banks and cooperative financial organizations, which are flexible in operation, allow for the easy establishment of relationships of mutual trust with nonstate enterprises, and help them carry out credit transactions.

Third, the credit culture of the society has been improving, and a market environment of the rule of law has been developing. A good market economy has to be based on fair and transparent game rules, in other words, on the rule of law. This is also important for the healthy development of nonstate enterprises. Currently, China's market order is still a mess, and bad business practices, such as bullying competitors and dominating the market, repudiating debts, and breach of promise, are prevalent. As a result, people perceive business as a dangerous undertaking.

The popular opinion in China that government should govern as little as possible is one-sided. The real problem is that government governs when it should not while it fails to govern when it should. It is the inescapable responsibility of the government to establish market rules, to develop market infrastructure, and to enforce the law fairly and strictly. In 2001, under the auspices of some government agencies, the first credit information institution was established in Shanghai on a trial basis. Afterwards, private credit information organizations began to develop as well. In 2002, the establishment of a society-wide credit system was put on the agenda, and lawful and open administration became a key item of government reform. The business environment for nonstate enterprises can be further improved only if China makes further progress in the establishment of the rule of law.

Fourth, chambers of commerce (trade associations) and other business/social organizations (such as community productivity promoting centers) have started to play an important role. In China, trade associations organized in a top-down fashion are often called "intermediary organizations" and were granted administrative power in trade management. This practice evolved from the "drive gears" and "transmission belts" under Lenin's proletarian dictatorship system and is not appropriate now. Chambers of commerce should be organizations of entrepreneurs with the mission of protecting entrepreneurs' interests and should be self-educated, self-supervised, and self-disciplined.

5.4.2 Enhancing Support to Small and Medium Enterprises

China's nonstate enterprises are mostly small and medium ones, which have some strengths, such as flexibility and competitiveness, but some weaknesses as well. For instance, a considerable number of SMEs have only limited capital and insufficient credit. It is hard for them to establish their own supporting functions such as market information and research and development. Moreover, their economic activities are characterized by positive externalities, and they enhance competition in the whole market by the so-called catfish effect.[36] Therefore, if they cannot receive the support they need from governments and social organizations, it will be hard for them to overcome their weaknesses, exploit their advantages, and generate positive externalities in the market. For that reason, major market economy countries consider supporting the development of SMEs as their basic national policy and provide systematic help to those enterprises.

Since 1998, the Chinese government has adopted the following measures to support the development of SMEs:

1. The Small and Medium Enterprise Department was established under the former State Economic and Trade Commission in 1998 to help SMEs solve problems encountered in their development. Many local governments have set up similar institutions to facilitate the development of SMEs.

2. Commercial banks have been required to set up small and medium enterprise credit departments to further improve credit service to SMEs. The range of lending interest rates for SMEs has been broadened to gradually liberalize the interest rate. Credit guarantee institutions for SMEs with a flavor of policy financing have been organized in each province and city. Reform of rural financing and building financial systems at the county and township levels have been listed as key items in ongoing financial reforms.

3. A series of preferential tax deductions and exemptions have been applied to SMEs by the Ministry of Finance and the State Administration of Taxation. For instance, the value-added tax rate for SMEs has been reduced from 6 to 4 percent.

4. The National People's Congress promulgated in June 2002 and began to implement on January 1, 2003, the *Law of the PRC on Small and Medium Enterprises.* Aiming to "improve the business environment of small and medium enterprises, facilitate the healthy development of small and medium enterprises, enlarge employment in both urban and rural areas, and maximize the significant effect of small and medium enterprises in the national economy and society development," this law established the legal status of SMEs, clarified the responsibilities of the government, and further confirmed the policy of facilitating the development of SMEs in legal forms. The implementation of this law and its supporting rules and regulations will create a good environment for the development of SMEs.

---

[36] Catfish are ferocious fish. It is said that fishermen put catfish into the water trough to stimulate other fish so that they take in oxygen by swimming at fast speed and thus do not die during transport.

5. The service of the government and the society to SMEs has been improved. SMEs are in urgent need of information about management, technology, industrial development, supply and demand in the world market, and so on. It would cost too much for each individual enterprise to acquire such information independently. It would be much more efficient for the government or a social organization to provide the information. When the government provides services, it needs to change its traditional leading methods under a planned economy or quasi-planned economy. The government needs to investigate what services it should provide and how to provide these services. It should not limit itself to some patchwork operation within the framework of the original mindset, but rather adapt to the new situation of a market economy by innovation. This is a new issue to be addressed by government institutions.

SMEs have been developing very fast since 1998. According to a joint survey by the Development Research Center of the State Council, China Entrepreneur Survey System (CESS), and other agencies,[37] by the end of 2001, there were 29.3 million SMEs in China with total employment of 174 million. In 2001, SMEs created 50.5 percent of China's GDP, created more than 75 percent of new jobs, and accounted for 43.2 percent of national tax revenue.

5.4.3 Relying on Nonstate Enterprises to Develop High-Tech Industries

Developing high technology (high-tech) is one of the basic guidelines emphasized by the Chinese government since the mid-1950s. At the CCCPC's Conference Concerning the Issues of Educated People, held January 14 to 20, 1956, the *Report Concerning the Issues of Educated People* by Zhou Enlai on behalf of the CCCPC put forward the slogan of "catching up with and surpassing advanced world levels of science and technology." Furthermore, the *Long-Term Plan of Development of Science and Technology from 1956 to 1967* was constituted, and resources were mustered for "marching toward science." In the early 1960s, when the new technological revolution was developing, the CCCPC made the *Decision Regarding the Industry Development,* demanding accelerated development of new industries, such as electronics. After the mid-1970s, the slogan of achieving "four modernizations" (i.e., modernizations of industry, agriculture, science and technology, and national defense) was reconfirmed. Modernization of science and technology was

---

[37] Ai Fang and Zhu Xingping, "Small and Medium Enterprises: Why Their Financing Is Difficult? (Zhongxiao qiye: rongzi jiu-jing nanzai na)," *Economic Daily (Jingji ribao),* July 2, 2002.

considered the most important of the four. Over the decades, to develop modern science and technology, the Chinese have made tremendous sacrifices and sustained efforts. However, the gap between the high-tech standard of China and that of advanced countries continued to widen. The root cause of the problem lay not in technology, but in institution.

A common mistaken belief about this issue is that as long as sufficient investment in research and development is made and enough large-scale enterprises are built, high-tech industries will grow rapidly. In China's campaigns for developing high-tech industries, the approaches adopted were largely the same: the government played a leading role in setting the priorities for research and development, mobilizing material and human resources to tackle key problems, and turning new technology into new products.

Another mistaken idea about the optimal approach for developing high-tech industries is that the government is the most capable entity to do it because the government has a far and broad vision, represents long-term interests of the nation, and has the ability to mobilize human, material, and financial resources. Therefore, the best results will be achieved if the government makes the plan, carries out the research, and organizes the manufacturing of high-tech products.

However, the experiences of various countries after World War II have shown that this is not true. In the 1980s and 1990s, in its competition with the United States to develop high-tech industries, Japan adopted the same approach it used when trying to catch up with advanced countries in America and Europe in the 1960s and 1970s (i.e., the government made the plan and organized the resources of the society to develop technology and manufacture products); however, this effort failed in Japan.

The first reason for Japan's failure in developing high-tech industries is that although it is not difficult for a government to acquire information for making plans and organizing resources for catching up, knowledge of technological innovation is not readily available to the government and has to be acquired by trial-and-error and the exploratory work of scientific and technical professionals.

The second reason is that high-tech development depends on the free creativity of professionals but government plans and administrative regulations can only stifle the enthusiasm and creativity of professionals.

The third reason is that if high-tech products are manufactured by government and state-owned enterprises, production processes will not be as efficient as those used by nonstate enterprises simply because there is no pressure of competition, no support of business income, no profit incentive.

Based on the experiences of other countries in the development of high-tech industries, China should take the following measures to develop its high-tech industries.

5.4.3.1 Let the Government Play the Right Role

Government should not do what it is not supposed to do, as described previously; however government should do what it is supposed to do. In the development of high-tech industries, activities that require the involvement of government include (a) establishing an organizational system and a legal system conducive to entrepreneurial activities in high-tech industries, (b) providing financial support for basic research and development of advanced technology without direct business income, and (c) organizing the development of public domain technology.

5.4.3.2 Establish an Effective Financing Mechanism

A long-standing mistaken idea about the financing mechanism for China's high-tech industries is to attribute the insufficient capital supply to the lack of venture capital companies and to believe that as long as venture capital companies exist, the financing issue of high-tech enterprises can be resolved. In fact, the predominance of venture capital in the financing of high-tech enterprises is a typically American phenomenon. In other countries, other financing channels satisfy the financial needs of high-tech enterprises. Most importantly, high-tech enterprises have different financing requirements in different stages of their development.

Various financing channels should be created in China to meet the different requirements of high-tech enterprises in different developmental stages. First, investors and professional funds should be encouraged to provide "angel capital," and nonstate enterprises and social organizations should be encouraged to establish "angel funds." Second, venture capital mainly in the form of limited partnership should be introduced. Third, an over-the-counter market (OTC market) and a second board market should be established to provide further financing for mature high-tech enterprises and a channel for the exit of venture capital. Fourth, regulations regarding mergers and acquisitions should be improved to provide another channel for the exit of venture capital. Fifth, order-based financing should be provided in addition to asset-based financing.

5.4.3.3 Separate High-Tech Enterprises from Universities and Research Institutes

A large proportion of technological professionals, who are experts in research and development, are currently working in research institutes and universities. Many of them are outstanding entrepreneurs and a vital new force of innovation in China's high-tech industries. If we can fully tap the potential of these professionals, their impact on China's high-tech industry would be enormous. Currently, the main organizational form to tap their potential is enterprises attached to universities and research institutes, which are an exclusively Chinese phenomenon. In modern society, because of the highly specialized division of labor, it is difficult for universities and research institutes to manage enterprises. Moreover, in this special type of state-owned enterprise, there is no direct incentive mechanism for inventors and entrepreneurs, which makes the enterprises inefficient. Normally, universities and research institutes can receive only limited income from the attached enterprises; however, those enterprises use the resources of the universities and research institutes so that their core businesses of teaching and research are compromised. This organizational form neither gives full scope to professionals' enthusiasm and creativity nor allows universities and research institutes to focus on their teaching and research. Therefore, these enterprises should be separated from the universities and research institutes as soon as possible and encouraged to develop independently.

5.4.3.4 Establish Excellent Innovation Bases

The government should, together with other institutions of the society (including commercial organizations and intermediaries), endeavor to establish "habitats" or "incubators" for start-up enterprises and to prepare conditions for professionals to tap their creativity. Because China's original conditions of social resources and related laws and regulations were not satisfactory, the initial incubators were usually set up and managed by the government. Entry into those incubators required approval by the government after the high-tech content of the entrant was verified. This practice was restrictive and was not effective in tapping the creativity of professionals. Therefore, it is necessary to gather resources from society and to allow various nonstate institutions to provide professional services to start-up enterprises such as consulting services, financial services, property management services, and secretarial services, and to make "incubators" available to the whole society.

5.4.4 Nonstate Enterprises Should Make Even Greater Endeavors

Nonstate enterprises have achieved enormous success in many areas. However, they will have to make sustained efforts as the main engines of China's economic growth in the context of globalization.

5.4.4.1 Improving the Enterprise System

A sound enterprise system is a basic condition for the healthy development of enterprises. However, whether developed from individual businesses or transformed from small and medium SOEs or quasi-state-owned TVEs, most of China's nonstate enterprises have similar weaknesses in this aspect. To make themselves bigger and stronger, nonstate enterprises must first lay a solid foundation for a sound enterprise system.

The theory of firm tells us that appropriate enterprise systems vary according to time, location, industry, and stage of development. There are many kinds of enterprise systems in a market economy. Roughly, they can be divided into sole proprietorships, partnerships, cooperative enterprises, and corporations. Corporations can be further divided into limited liability companies and joint stock limited companies. Each kind of enterprise system has its own peculiarities and suits the needs of enterprises of different industries, scales, and characteristics. Currently some localities in China provide categorized guidance for the transformation of small SOEs, and it is absolutely right to adopt different enterprise systems to satisfy different needs.

However, it remains to be investigated whether all the choices of enterprise system are appropriate in China. As enterprises operate, they need to take proper action to change inappropriate enterprise systems or inappropriate aspects of some enterprise systems. Some problems are just minor deviations from the correct course. However, if not corrected in time, they may finally result in the wrong course being followed. This has occurred often in the reform process and should be avoided in the future. Therefore, enterprises of different industries and sizes should, according to their own characteristics, adopt different governance structures and organizational forms. There is no best enterprise system suitable for all kinds of enterprises.

Although the specific structure of enterprise systems are not always the same, all effective enterprise systems have one common characteristic, that is, the boundary of property rights must be clearly defined. Enterprises with large scales also require an effective governance structure based on clearly defined property rights. As a result, this issue has two aspects. One is that the owner should be present. The other is that the enterprise's governance structure should be sufficiently effective. This is easy to achieve for a natural-person-owned enterprise, in which the owner manages the enterprise himself. In enterprise structures such as cooperatives or corporations, where managers are entrusted to run the enterprise and ownership and control are separate, the situation is not as simple and needs to be handled in accordance with the basic requirements of corporate governance as discussed in Chapter 4 of this book.

The mistake about the multi-tier legal-person system, as discussed in Chapter 4, should relate to nonstate enterprises as well. An effective way for nonstate enterprises to expand is to acquire other enterprises during their development process. It is also appropriate to maintain the independent status of the acquired enterprises for a period of time, as it helps retain the original owners and employees. Therefore, most large and medium-sized nonstate enterprises have adopted the organizational structure of enterprise groups that consist of closely affiliated enterprises (those not independent) and loosely affiliated enterprises (those maintaining the status of independent legal persons). However, those enterprise groups are not companies with centralized property rights. Moreover, they are different from the British-style group companies in which the parent company establishes a majority shareholding control over the subsidiary companies. Enterprise groups can be considered a special product of traditional Chinese culture. China is filled with small tenant peasants who are not accustomed to "legal person culture," that is, they are not accustomed to using hierarchical organizational forms with strict rules and regulations to organize large production operations. Instead, Chinese people are used to splitting property rights and distributing a share to every level to maintain relationships of economic cooperation. Such a system inevitably leads to "independent kingdoms" within the enterprise and conflict of interest and thus should be gradually transformed according to the principles of the corporate system.

In China, the issue of family enterprises needs specific attention in a discussion of enterprise systems. At the moment, two extremes of opinion predominate. The first holds that family enterprise is an enterprise system with great advantages and therefore should be supported and continued. The second holds that family enterprise is a primitive organizational form and needs to be transformed into a modern corporation as quickly as possible. As mentioned earlier, the appropriateness of a particular enterprise system depends on the particular situation of the enterprise in question. It is wrong to say that there is a kind of enterprise system appropriate for every situation. Generally, in Chinese society, where people treasure blood relationships, SMEs in the form of family enterprises have the advantages of enhancing internal cohesion and lowering transaction costs.

However, when enterprises become large, especially when the founders with strong management abilities have retired, and the enterprises need to be run by professional managers, it becomes an objective requirement to choose the modern corporate system with separation of property rights and managerial rights.

Even in such a situation, when the business environment lacks the well-functioning legal framework and credit system necessary to the operation of a modern corporate system, the family companies, in which the founders' families still play a decisive role on the board of directors, have advantages. However, it is an inevitable trend for family companies to go public. Therefore, those family companies, while making full use of the advantages of family relationships, need to introduce professional managers and grant them power to use their management skills to improve the company and transform it into a publicly owned corporation.

5.4.4.2 Formulating Appropriate Business Strategy

In their initial stages, nonstate enterprises normally take advantage of markets not covered by the state sector and adopt the low-price strategy. For instance, in Wenzhou and Taizhou in Zhejiang Province, thousands of small enterprises with "shops at the front and factories at the back" developed by selling in specialized markets. Those enterprises often changed their products according to market changes and did not have clear goals and strategies for development. This approach was suitable for newly established SMEs under conditions of seller's market dominated by the state sector. Since enterprises have become large and buyer's market has become the norm, there is not much space left for them to develop if they stick to their original approach.

First, when enterprises are small with small numbers of employees or employees made up of mainly family members, coordination can be accomplished through tacit understanding and agreement. However, when the enterprise has many employees from various sources, clear business and development strategies are needed to coordinate the efforts of employees, especially high- and middle-level managers, so that everyone strives for a common goal. As stated by Michael E. Porter, "Every firm competing in an industry has a competitive strategy, explicit or implicit." Otherwise, "left to its own devices, each functional department will inevitably pursue approaches dictated by its professional orientation and the incentives of those in charge."[38]

Currently, a habitual business strategy in nonstate enterprises is to use price wars as a main competitive weapon. In the past, demand exceeded supply in almost all product markets, and SOEs enjoyed dominant status and did not need to do their utmost to please customers. As the saying goes, "A princess need not worry about her marriage." In such a situation, products of small and medium nonstate enterprises were easily sold as long as their quality was not too bad and the price was low enough. As a result, many SMEs had a tradition of manufacturing in a rough way and selling low-quality products at low prices.

However, in China, the market situation has changed from seller's market, where demand exceeded supply, to buyer's market, where supply exceeds demand and competition is fierce. In such a situation, traditional price wars of cutthroat competition would lead to thinner and thinner profits until enterprises were forced to give up technological innovation or to use inferior materials and turn out substandard products to survive. As a result, the whole industry would be ruined.

As stated by Porter, there are three potentially successful generic strategic approaches to outperforming other firms in an industry: cost leadership, differentiation, and focus.[39]

---

[38] Michael E. Porter, *Competitive Strategy,* New York: Free Press, 1980, p. 1.

Price wars are implemented under the premise of overall cost leadership. However, as stated by Porter, this strategy requires continuous capital investment and improvement in process technology, strict supervision over workers, a low-cost distribution system, and other fundamental skills and resources.[40] Moreover, it requires well-designed organizational structures, clearly defined responsibilities, and strict control over costs. If these conditions cannot be satisfied, and a price war is launched by reducing profits and turning out low-quality products, then the enterprise is in fact committing suicide.

Just as management expert Shi Ziyi pointed out when criticizing the cut-throat competition among some Taiwanese enterprises, entrepreneurs should not always think of doing better than others in the market that has already been occupied; what is more important is to be more special than others.[41] Entrepreneurs should exploit their core competencies to create products different from others', to find positions in new market segments, and then to increase productivity, lower costs, and enhance competitiveness in those market segments. In other words, enterprises should apply the concept of "market segmentation," make every effort to avoid sharing the same market with other companies, adopt the customer-oriented strategy of differentiation, and explore new markets with specialized products designed for specific customers. Only this can turn the current situation of cut-throat competition among manufacturers of similar products to orderly competition.

Another problem frequently seen in the business strategy of China's nonstate enterprises is their excessive diversification. Many enterprises, after their initial success in one industry, enter other industries unrelated to their original industry, resulting in diverted financial, technological, and managerial resources and deviation from the strategy of differentiation. In brief, enterprises should do best in markets where they have competitive advantages. It is not wise for them to become involved in too many industries, and thus reduce their overall efficiency.

5.4.4.3 Associating with Government Officials Should Not Become the Basis for Establishing Businesses

Under the autocratic system of old China, the emperor and his officials held considerable power in resource allocation. Therefore, in the traditional Chinese business culture, associating with government officials and making deals between power and money were standard practice to ensure success. Since reform, because of the coexistence of the two

---

[39] Michael E. Porter, *ibid.,* p. 35.
[40] Michael E. Porter, *ibid.,* pp. 35–37, 45–46.
[41] Shi Ziyi, "Transformation of the Century (Shiji biange) (1996)," *Niche Strategy—Successful Tips for Small and Medium Enterprises (Liji celüe—zhongxiao qiye zhisheng zhidao),* Beijing: Joint Publishing, 2002, pp. 3–132.

economic systems, administrative power still plays an important role in resource alloca-tion. Therefore, rent-seeking activities, which were discussed in Chapter 2, still exist throughout the country. In recent years, the overall social and economic environment of China has improved to some extent, but this unhealthy business environment has not been eliminated. As a result, some entrepreneurs still hope to make their fortunes by making deals between power and money and employing tricks and skills often found in books telling stories of "merchants wearing high-ranking official hats," such as *Hu Xue-yan*.[42] These actions seriously impair the market order, degenerate commercial morals, and threaten the normal operation of markets. Moreover, it is the main source of the plague of crony capitalism. As anticorruption campaigns increase and orderly markets form, those upstart entrepreneurs who still rely on associating with corrupt officials to build their businesses will inevitably decline.

---

[42] A book about the life of a Chinese business magnet (Hu Xueyan, 1823–1885) in the Qing Dynasty, who not only amassed huge wealth but also won the favor of the imperial court.

CHAPTER 6

REFORM OF THE BANKING SYSTEM AND DEVELOPMENT OF THE SECURITIES MARKET

The financial system, which consists of various financial institutions (commercial banks, insurance companies, etc.) and financial markets (the money market, the bond market, the stock market, etc.), is one of the most important pillars of a modern economy. A key component of the transition from a planned economy to a market economy is to reconstruct the financial system to adapt to a market economy.

6.1 The Concepts of "Money" and "Finance" in a Planned Economy and Changes in China's Financial System in the 1980s

As has been discussed in Chapter 1, both Marx and Lenin believed that there should be no commodity- and money-based relationship under socialism. The certificates of credit in a certain form issued by central banks of various countries of planned economy (such as ruble in the Soviet Union or Renminbi (RMB) in China before the 1980s) are used only for measurement of the amount of labor provided by laborers and for the economic accounting of enterprises. According to Marxist political economy, such certificates are "no more 'money' than a ticket for the theater."[1] They are only tokens of the share of each member of the society in the total output and "do not circulate."[2]

---

[1] This refers to the "certificate of labor" or "labor-money" put forward by Robert Owen (1771–1858), in whose communes a certain number of certificates of labor are granted to each member according to their work in exchange for their deserved consumer goods. According to Marx, "Owen presupposes directly associated labor, a form of production that is entirely inconsistent with the production of commodities. The certificate of labor is merely evidence of the part taken by the individual in the common labor, and of his right to a certain portion of the common produce destined for consumption." "Owen's 'labor-money,' for instance, is no more 'money' than a ticket for the theater." (See Karl Marx, *The Capital (Ziben lun)*, Chinese edition, Vol. 1, Beijing: People's Publishing House, 1972, pp. 112–113.)

[2] According to Marx, "In the case of socialized production, the money-capital is eliminated. Society distributes labor-power and means of production to the different branches of production. The producers may, for all it matters, receive paper vouchers entitling them to withdraw from the social supplies of consumer goods a quantity corresponding to their labor-time. These vouchers are not money. They do not circulate." (See Karl Marx, *The Capital (Ziben lun)*, Chinese edition, Vol. 2, Beijing: People's Publishing House, 1972, p. 397.) Here Marx indicated that the voucher is different from currency because it does not circulate like currency, which "takes the form of a constant motion away from its starting-point" in the transaction and flows "from the hands of one commodity-owner into those of another." (See Karl Marx, *The Capital (Ziben lun)*, Chinese edition, Vol. 1, Beijing: People's Publishing House, Chinese edition, 1972, p. 134.) Instead, it serves as a voucher to exchange for goods and returns to its issuer, the state bank, after each transaction.

Due to this special nature of "money," the financial system in a planned economy is characterized by the following features:

1. Money is the only financial asset.

2. Money is "passive" in that it is used only as a tool for pricing and accounting. Accordingly, measures like "cash administration" are used to restrict and control the use of cash in order to prevent the "spontaneity" of resource allocation. Only industrial and commercial enterprises are allowed to obtain credit from the state bank, while credit among different enterprises ("commercial credit") is strictly prohibited.

3. The bank is only considered as the cashier for the state fiscal system, and one institution played the roles of both the central bank and commercial banks, resulting in the so-called "mono-bank system."

4. The bank plays an insignificant role in inter-temporal allocation of financial resources. Its financing to enterprises is limited to only credit financing for "non-budgeted working capital" (i.e., the part of working capital that is not employed perennially).

5. Households and individuals are not allowed to participate in any financial activities other than opening deposit accounts in the bank.

On the eve of the founding of the People's Republic of China in 1949, the Central Committee of the Communist Party of China (CCCPC) began to build its state bank on the basis of the preexisting banks in the Liberated Area of North China. From 1948 to 1978, the People's Bank of China (PBC) had been the only state bank in China, integrating the functions of the central bank such as financial supervision with those of policy banks and commercial banks such as savings and loans. In 1956, during the Socialist Transformation campaign, all private financial institutions were merged into the PBC, and a centralized and unified financial system thus came into being. The PBC was not only the financial supervisor and money issuer but also the state bank dealing with banking activities. As the state bank, the PBC established an organizational structure characterized by vertical command chain across the nation, unified the issuance of the Chinese currency RMB, and exercised unified supervision of various kinds of financial institutions. Moreover, it was in charge of adjusting money demand and supply to foster the fast development of the state sector of the economy through money issuance and monetary policy.

After the commencement of the reform and opening up in the late 1970s, China's economy experienced great changes in three aspects: (a) people's communes were replaced by households as units of agricultural production, which greatly expanded the scope of monetary activities; (b) nonstate industrial and commercial enterprises, which operated independently and were somewhat market-oriented, began to emerge; and (c) state-owned enterprises (SOEs) were given more decision-making power in financing. These factors enhanced the role of banks as financial intermediaries and called for restoring the various functions of the financial system. Beginning from the mid-1980s, China accelerated its financial reform. By the late 1980s, a rudimentary financial system came into being.

6.1.1 Changes in Enterprise Financing

As mentioned earlier, other than money, there were no financial assets in China for a long period after its transition to a socialist economy in 1956. The major source of enterprise financing was fiscal appropriations. Their perennially employed fixed asset investment and working capital ("budgeted working capital") came from the state budget. Only temporary funds used for daily operations ("non-budgeted working capital") depended on short-term loans from the PBC. After the commencement of the reform and opening up, things changed. First, the State Council stipulated in June 1983 that SOEs should gradually switch to bank loans to supplement their insufficient working capital. Second, in order to improve the supervision over investment in capital construction through "paid use," fiscal appropriations for investment in capital construction were replaced by bank loans in 1985 after years of trial. Those loans would be provided by the restored People's Construction Bank of China (the predecessor of the China Construction Bank) according to state planning of capital construction. The interest and principal of these loans were to be repaid as per contracted period and year respectively. As a result, fiscal appropriations as a source of financing were gradually replaced by bank loans. Before 1979, about two-thirds of the fixed asset investment of SOEs was financed by fiscal appropriations from the government. By the mid-1980s, however, the proportion had decreased to one-quarter.[3] In addition, some enterprises began to raise funds through the securities market.

Meanwhile, nonstate sectors have been developing gradually since the early 1980s. Nonstate enterprises had to support their operations through self-financing, as they could not get fiscal appropriations from the government.

6.1.2 The Introduction of New Financial Instruments and the Start of the Capital Market

Under the planned economic system, cash and bank deposits are the two major financial assets. After the commencement of the reform and opening up, the need for new

---

[3] *China Statistical Yearbook (Zhongguo tongji nianjian),* Beijing: China Statistics Press, various years.

financial instruments emerged with the increasing shares of household and corporate deposits in total national savings. The central bank took a series of actions to adapt to the changed situation. From 1980 to 1985, specialized banks began to discount commercial papers. In 1986, the PBC began to offer rediscount services to specialized banks and allowed commercial banks to trade financial assets. In 1981, the Ministry of Finance began to restore bond issues. In 1987 and 1988, the secondary markets of corporate bonds and treasury bonds were established respectively. In 1990 and 1991, the Shanghai Stock Exchange and the Shenzhen Stock Exchange were established successively for centralized trading of stocks. Moreover, investors began to trade treasury bond futures in these two exchanges in 1993 and 1994, respectively.

6.1.3 Changes in the Organizational Structure of Financial Institutions

The first step of the banking reform in China was to change the mono-bank system copied from the former Soviet Union. In 1979, the State Council decided that the Agricultural Bank of China (ABC) was to be restored to specialize in rural banking. The Bank of China (BOC) was spun off from the PBC to specialize in foreign exchange business. The restored People's Construction Bank of China became the bank specializing in financing investment in fixed assets. In 1983, the State Council decided that the PBC was to focus on its function as the central bank and transfer all saving and loan businesses to the newly established Industrial and Commercial Bank of China (ICBC).

Besides these nationwide specialized banks, smaller banks and non-bank financial institutions were also established in China. In the late 1970s, credit cooperatives were restored across rural China. In 1980, the People's Insurance Company of China (PICC) restored its domestic insurance operations, which had been stopped for nearly twenty years, and later Shenzhen Ping An Insurance Company (the predecessor of Ping An Insurance (Group) Company of China, Ltd.) was established in 1988. After 1984, many local banks and non-bank financial institutions such as trust and investment companies and financial leasing companies were established. In 1987, two nationwide joint-stock commercial banks, Bank of Communications headquartered in Shanghai and CITIC Industrial Bank affiliated with the China International Trust and Investment Corporation (CITIC), were established (see Figure 6.1).

6.1.4 Changes in the Central Bank's Approaches to Macroeconomic Control

As commercial financial institutions were gradually separated from the central bank, traditional approaches characterized by "unified control over deposits and loans" were discarded by the PBC. A new approach of "centralized planning, managing at different levels, linking deposits with loans, and controlling the balance" was adopted in 1979. In

Figure 6.1   Financial Institutions in China in the Early 1990s

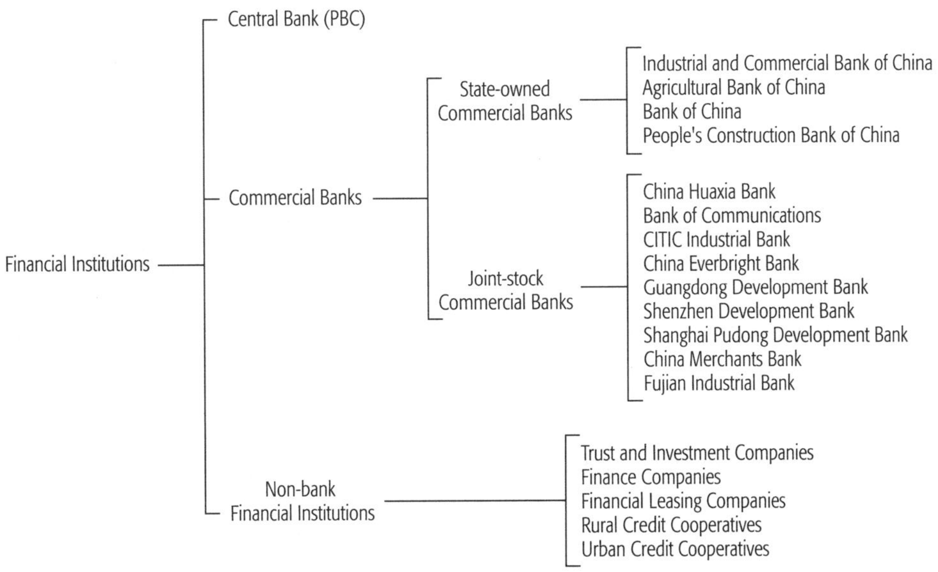

Financial Institutions
- Central Bank (PBC)
- Commercial Banks
  - State-owned Commercial Banks
    - Industrial and Commercial Bank of China
    - Agricultural Bank of China
    - Bank of China
    - People's Construction Bank of China
  - Joint-stock Commercial Banks
    - China Huaxia Bank
    - Bank of Communications
    - CITIC Industrial Bank
    - China Everbright Bank
    - Guangdong Development Bank
    - Shenzhen Development Bank
    - Shanghai Pudong Development Bank
    - China Merchants Bank
    - Fujian Industrial Bank
- Non-bank Financial Institutions
  - Trust and Investment Companies
  - Finance Companies
  - Financial Leasing Companies
  - Rural Credit Cooperatives
  - Urban Credit Cooperatives

Source: The PBC, *China Financial Outlook, 1994*, Beijing: China Financial Publishing House, 1994.

1981, "controlling the balance" was replaced by "balance responsibility." In 1985, the approach was further changed to "centralized planning, partition of funds, actual loans linked to actual deposits, and mutual financing." Under this system, provincial branches of each specialized bank borrowed funds from provincial branches of the PBC according to predetermined credit quotas, and then allocated funds to its sub-branches at different levels. These sub-branches deposited the allocated funds in local branches of the PBC and withdrew the money when they needed it. Borrowing happened among different banks at the same level, among different levels within the same bank, and among commercial banks and the central bank.

In the early 1990s, China's financial system was under strict administrative control by the central bank, with the typical characteristics of financial repression. The official interest rates were so low that the real interest rate at that time was often negative (see Table 6.1), and capital resources were not allocated efficiently by the market but allotted by administrative planning. As a result, economic growth with efficiency and macroeconomic stability could not be guaranteed. On the contrary, the national economy fluctuated greatly. Therefore, in-depth and substantial financial reform became imperative.

Table 6.1   Real Interest Rate of Loans of State Banks (1985–1989)

Year	Nominal Interest Rate[a]	Inflation Rate[b]	Real Interest Rate[c]
1985	4.68	11.0	−7.22
1986	4.68	7.0	−2.23
1987	6.69	8.8	−2.11
1988	7.56	20.7	−13.14
1989	10.26	16.3	−6.04

[a] Nominal interest rate = the (weighted average) annual interest rate based on which the PBC grants loans to financial institutions.
[b] Inflation rate = retail price index (year on year).
[c] Real interest rate = a − b.
Source: The Planning and Fund Department of the PBC, *Handbook of Current Interest Rates (Lilü shiyong shouce)*, Beijing: China Financial Publishing House, 1997.

6.2 The Banking Reform in the 1990s and Its Future Direction

From 1993 to 1994, China experienced another round of hyperinflation that revealed the serious problems in its banking system and forced the government to deepen its reform of the banking system.

6.2.1 Major Problems in China's Banking System before the 1994 Reform

The review of the banking system in the early 1990s showed that the role it played was far from the requirements of a market economy. The major problems were as follows:

1. The PBC was characterized by unclear functions, out-of-date means of adjustment, and unreasonable organizational structure and financial rules and therefore could not effectively perform its fundamental role in maintaining the stability of currency.

    First, the functions of the PBC were not clearly defined and it lacked independence. According to the *Interim Regulations of PRC on the Administration of Banks* of 1986, financial activities conducted by the central bank, specialized banks, and other financial institutions should be guided by the objective of economic growth, currency stability, and enhancement of social and economic benefits. Therefore, the monetary policy of the central bank had double objectives—to support economic growth and to maintain currency stability. In practice, the central bank was often pushed by the government to give priority to economic growth through expansionary monetary policy, which led to inflation and economic fluctuation. Second, the PBC established branches in line with the division of administrative regions and exercised macro adjustment at two levels (the central bank and its provincial branches). Consequently, local governments had strong influence on the decisions of the central bank branches, which not only crippled the authority of the central bank but also damaged the integrity of monetary policy and impeded the control over aggregate money supply. Third, the PBC relied on the control of administrative quota of credit as the major means of achieving objectives of monetary policy. Due to the reversed transmission of the pressure for easing monetary condition and the self-interest of the banking system, the effect of macro adjustment was very poor. Fourth, the profit retention system implemented at the PBC branches created incentives for oversupply of currency. Moreover, the branches also established many profit-oriented enterprises, which were against the nature of the central bank and naturally resulted in an endogenous mechanism of monetary expansion within the central bank.

2. Commercial businesses were not separated from policy-related businesses in specialized banks, which suffered from the combination of government administration and enterprise management. For businesses within the predetermined range, specialized banks had no independence as commercial banks due to strict control by the central bank. For businesses outside the predetermined range, specialized banks lacked effective constraints by the market mechanism.

    First, specialized banks not only needed to perform commercial functions but also had to grant policy-related loans. On the one hand, policy-related businesses could not get enough funds; on the other hand, commercial risks and losses were concealed by policy-related businesses. Second, specialized banks did have an interest-driven credit expansion mechanism, but had no corresponding risk control mechanism. Specialized banks lacked funds for planned loans, yet they granted non-planned loans in the forms of interbank lending and interbank transaction. The official interest rate was usually low and the real interest rate was negative in most of the years; in the meantime, the lawful market was hungry for funds and the price for funds (interest rate) was extremely high in the gray market and the black market. The huge interest rate gap among different markets resulted in rampant corruption and tremendous loss of interest income in the banking sector. As a result, the control of money supply ended in vain. Third, although the business circles and the economists called for the development of specialized banks in the direction of universal services and multiple functions, the government did not show any sign of giving up the segregated supervisory model. Meanwhile, the segregated supervisory system was imperfect and a large amount of loans flowed into the gray market and the black market through the so-called "off-balance-sheet businesses."

3. The market was in disorder and developed in a distorted way.

First, rules for market entry were neither clearly defined nor strictly enforced. It was not rare for unqualified investors to get access to the market. For example, many industrial and commercial enterprises were allowed to enter the interbank market, resulting in the loss of the originally envisaged meaning of the interbank lending market, and effectively creating another credit market with too long a maturity and too high an interest rate. Second, the treasury bond market lacked the support of the banking system and did not have an effective operation mechanism based on smooth coordination between the fiscal system and the banking system.

Insight 6.1

The Banking Reform Plan Approved by the Third Plenary Session of the 14th CCCPC

According to the *Decision of CCCPC on Issues Regarding the Establishment of a Socialist Market Economic System* of the Third Plenary Session of the 14th CCCPC in November 1993, the reform of the financial system included the reform of the banking system and the development of financial markets. The reform of the banking system was to be given priority, which mainly included the following initiatives:

1. Reform the central bank system. The PBC as the central bank should independently carry out monetary policy under the guidance of the State Council. Its major function should be to adjust the money supply and maintain currency stability by means of regular instruments in a market economy, such as reserve-deposit ratio, base interest rates, and open market operation, instead of control over credit quotas. Moreover, it should supervise financial institutions and ensure the financial order. Meanwhile, it should stop any business relationship with nonfinancial institutions. As per the currency's circulation all over the nation and demand for centralized adjustment, the PBC should establish branch offices as its representative organs. In addition, the PBC should make efforts to establish branch offices across administrative regions.

2. Develop commercial banks. The existing specialized banks should be gradually transformed into commercial banks, and rural and urban cooperative banks should be set up step by step if necessary. Commercial banks should introduce risk management and debt-asset ra-

tio management. The rates of interest for deposits and loans of commercial banks may float freely within specified bands.

3. Regulate and develop nonbank financial institutions.

4. Establish policy banks to separate policy-related business from commercial business. China Development Bank, the Export-Import Bank of China and the Agricultural Development Bank of China were to be established to undertake policy-related business defined by law.

According to the *Decision,* the development and improvement of financial markets should focus on the following aspects:

1. Develop the capital market by developing bond financing and equity financing actively but steadily, establishing a credit rating system for bonds and bond issuers to encourage a healthy development of the bond market, and effectively regulating initial public offerings (IPOs) to increase the size of the stock market.

2. Develop the money market by developing interbank lending and discount of commercial papers. The central bank should operate the treasury bond business and adjust money supply through open market operation of treasury bonds.

3. Give a full play to the functions of various supporting organizations (intermediaries) in service, communication, notarization, and supervision, with a focus on the development of accounting, auditing, and law firms, notarization and arbitration agencies, metrological and quality testing and certification agencies, credit consulting agencies, and asset and credit rating agencies.

4. Reform the foreign exchange control system by establishing a market-based, managed floating exchange rate system and a unified and normalized foreign exchange market, gradually realizing the convertibility of RMB.

(Compiled according to the *Decision of CCCPC on Issues Regarding the Establishment of a Socialist Market Economic System (Zhonggong zhongyang guanyu jianli shehuizhuyi shichang jingji tizhi ruogan wenti de jueding)* adopted by the Third Plenary Session of the 14th CCCPC on November 14, 1993.)

6.2.2 The Progress of the Banking Reform since 1994

According to the decision of the Third Plenary Session of the 14th CCCPC held in November 1993, the banking reform should be deepened with a market orientation from 1994, which mainly included the following aspects.

6.2.2.1 The Establishment of the Central Bank System

As mentioned earlier, the primary task of the banking reform is to turn the PBC into a real central bank. To this end, the following measures have been taken.

First, switching the monetary policy from multi-level adjustment to single-level (central) adjustment. The end of 1998 witnessed the establishment of large branches of the PBC in nine major cities, replacing the original thirty-one provincial branches based on the administrative regions, to further eliminate interference of local governments in the central bank's monetary policy and financial supervision. In 1997, the Monetary Policy Committee was established as a consultative agency on monetary policy.

Second, making indirect adjustment the core of the macro adjustment system. According to the *Law of the People's Bank of China* adopted by the National People's Congress in 1995, the objective of the PBC was to maintain the stability of currency and thereby promote economic growth. Accordingly, the intermediate objective of the PBC changed from regulating credit quotas to regulating money supply. Starting from the third quarter of 1994, the PBC established a monitoring statistical index of money supply and published the data on a regular basis. Meanwhile, the reform of monetary policy tools was also in steady progress. The first was the launch of rediscount business in 1995. The second was the launch of open market operation on a trial basis in April 1996. The third was the reform of the credit control system. In 1998, credit quotas for state-owned commercial banks were replaced by indirect control based on asset-liability ratio management and risk management. The fourth was the improvement on the interest rate mechanism. A unified nationwide interbank lending market came into being in January 1996; limit on interest rate in the interbank market was removed on June 1; a new interest rate administration system on foreign currency was adopted in September 2000; and urban commercial banks and rural credit cooperatives began to enjoy an enlarged range of deposit and lending interest rates during 2001 and 2002.

6.2.2.2 The Reform of Commercial Banks and Other Financial Institutions

Commercial banks, the principal part of China's banking sector, were the focus of the banking reform. The major measures taken were as follows.

First, the four preexisting specialized state banks (the "Big Four") were transformed to wholly state-owned commercial banks. According to the *Commercial Bank Law of the People's Republic of China* of 1995, the "Big Four" should stop doing any non-bank business, such as "trust and investment." These wholly state-owned commercial banks should adjust their disposition of branches and take back the power of their branches to grant loans without authorization from the headquarters.[4] All commercial banks should introduce modern management methods including asset-liability ratio management, internal risk control, conservative accounting, and the five-category loan classification.[5]

Second, non-wholly state-owned, joint-stock banks were established to foster competition within the banking sector. Besides those banks established before 1993, which are Bank of Communications, CITIC Industrial Bank, China Everbright Bank, Shenzhen Development Bank, Huaxia Bank, Pudong Development Bank, China Merchants Bank, Guangdong Development Bank, Fujian Industrial Bank, and China Investment Bank, two more joint-stock banks were established in 1995: China Minsheng Banking Corporation Limited and Hainan Development Bank, which targeted nonstate sectors and the Hainan Special Economic Zone respectively. Meanwhile, Huaxia Bank, originally affiliated with Capital Steel Co., Ltd., and China Investment Bank were transformed into independent banking corporations while China Everbright Bank became the first in China to introduce a foreign financial institution as a strategic investor. Urban credit cooperatives in cities also began to merge into urban commercial banks.

While reforming commercial banks, the PBC also reformed non-bank financial institutions. After consolidation, there were a total of 244 trust and investment companies by the end of 1997. The number of securities companies was 90 after their separation from the PBC. In 1998, the People's Insurance Company of China Group was split into three independent companies: the PICC Property, the Life Insurance Co. of China, and the China Reinsurance Co. In addition, there were eight branches of wholly foreign-owned insurance companies, one Chinese-foreign joint venture insurance company and two insurance intermediaries in China.

6.2.2.3 The Reform of the Foreign Exchange Control System

Before the reform and opening up, China adopted a foreign exchange control system under which all foreign exchanges from export were required to be surrendered at the

---

[4] Before this, branches of state-owned specialized banks were "legal persons" or "quasi-legal persons" and could provide credit services without authorization from the headquarters.

[5] The five-category loan classification means that commercial banks classify loans into five categories according to different degrees of risks. The five categories are respectively Pass, Special Mention, Substandard, Doubtful, and Loss. "Pass" borrowers are able to honor the terms of the contracts and there is no reason to doubt their ability to repay the principle and interest of loans in full and in a timely manner. "Special Mention" means that borrowers are able to serve their loans currently, although repayment may be adversely affected by specific factors. "Substandard" means that borrowers' abilities to service their loans are in question. Borrowers cannot depend on their normal business revenues to pay back the principle and interest so losses may ensue, even when guarantees are allowed. "Doubtful" means that borrowers cannot pay back the principle and interest in full and significant losses will be incurred, even when guarantees are invoked. "Loss" means that the principal and interest of loans cannot be recovered or only a small portion can be recovered after taking all possible measures and resorting to necessary legal procedures. The five-category loan classification system is prevalent in America, Canada, Southeast Asia, and most Eastern European countries as methods of classifying loans and controlling risks.

official exchange rate and the use of foreign exchange was allocated according to a centralized plan. As a result, the exchange rate of RMB was extremely overvalued. After 1979, foreign exchange control was gradually loosened and the practice of unified control over revenues and expenditures in foreign exchange was broken up. A dual-track system of official exchange rate and market exchange rate was adopted. A certain proportion of foreign exchange retention was allowed to encourage exports.

In 1994, the Chinese government made great changes to its foreign exchange control system. After January 1, 1994, all foreign exchange revenue and expenditure under current account of domestic institutions was to be surrendered to and bought from banks, respectively. Domestic enterprises were to take back and sell their foreign exchange revenue under current account to banks at the market rate except the legal retained part. The government terminated the plan and the approval system for foreign exchange expenditure under current account. Instead, domestic enterprises could buy foreign exchanges from banks at the interbank market rate with valid commercial documents or an import license. The interbank foreign exchange market was established and the original dual exchange rates were merged into a single rate to allow for the managed floating exchange rate system. From the second half of 1996, foreign-invested enterprises were included in this foreign exchange surrendering and buying system, and the convertibility of RMB under current account was realized ahead of schedule. On December 1 of the same year, China formally accepted Article 8 of the *International Monetary Fund Agreement,* thereby undertaking obligations of IMF members such as avoiding restrictions on current account and avoiding discriminating monetary policy.

The reform of the foreign exchange control system played an important role in the fast development of China's foreign trade and economic relations and in the further improvement of balance of payments after 1994.

6.2.2.4 The Establishment and Improvement of the Financial Supervision System

The modern financial system is a complex system consisting of three sectors of banking, securities, and insurance, which have their respective features and should be supervised in different ways. Taking into consideration the development stage of the financial sectors, the ability of financial supervision, and the segregated operation of the three sectors, the Chinese government decided to adopt a segregated supervisory structure. In the first half of 1993, the China Securities Regulatory Commission (CSRC) was spun off from the PBC as a specialized agency in charge of supervision over the securities market. Similarly, the China Insurance Regulatory Commission (CIRC) was spun off from the PBC in November 1998 as a specialized agency in charge of supervision over insurance services, insurance companies, and the insurance market. In March 2003, the

PBC transferred its role of supervision over commercial banks to the newly established China Banking Regulatory Commission (CBRC). Hence, a segregated supervisory structure for banking, securities, and insurance was formed.

6.2.3 New Challenges for the Banking Reform in the New Millennium

Although the last two decades of the twentieth century witnessed great achievements in China's banking reform, there are still many problems unsolved. Hence, the impact of China's accession to the WTO at the end of 2001 has been especially significant on its vulnerable banking system. How to reduce financial risks and enhance the competitive capacity of Chinese banks in both domestic and foreign markets is therefore a big challenge ahead.

Insight 6.2

China's Commitment to Open the Banking Sector upon Entry into the WTO

The financial sectors, including banking, insurance, and securities, were the most disputed fields in the negotiation of China's accession to the WTO. China's commitment to open the banking sector mainly included the following:

1. Regarding foreign exchange business, foreign financial institutions would be permitted to provide services in China without any geographic or client restrictions upon accession. In other words, foreign banks would be allowed to do business with all kinds of clients including Chinese residents and Chinese enterprises and to provide all kinds of foreign exchange business including company business and retail business without approval.

2. Regarding RMB business, foreign banks would be allowed to do RMB business in twenty cities stage by stage over four years after accession. Cities to be opened in the first stage would include Shanghai, Shenzhen, Tianjin, and Dalian; cities to be opened in the second stage would include Guangzhou, Qingdao, Nanjing, and Wuhan; cities to be opened in the third stage would include Yantai, Fuzhou, Chengdu, and Chongqing; cities to be opened in the fourth stage would include Kunming, Zhuhai, Beijing, and Xiamen; and cities to be opened in the fifth stage would include Shantou, Ningbo,

Shenyang, and Xi'an. Five years after accession, all geographic restrictions would be removed. In terms of clients, foreign banks would be permitted to do RMB business with Chinese enterprises in two years after accession and with all Chinese clients in five years. Foreign financial institutions licensed for RMB business in one region in China would be allowed to do inter-city RMB business with clients in any other region opened for such business.

3. Regarding business licenses, the financial regulatory authorities would grant business licenses solely on the basis of the prudential principle, which meant that there would be no economic needs test or quantitative limits on licenses. Any existing nonprudential measures restricting ownership, operation, and organizational form of foreign financial institutions, including restrictions on branches and grant of licenses, would be eliminated by no later than January 1, 2005.

Foreign financial institutions would be allowed to deal with the following businesses instantly upon accession: deposits and loans, financial leasing, payment and money transmission services, guarantees and acceptance, mergers and acquisitions, consultation on securities investment, intermediary agency, and other auxiliary financial services.

Foreign nonbank financial institutions would be allowed to provide car loans instantly upon accession.

(Compiled according to the PBC, *Contents and Timetable for the Opening of China's Financial Sectors after China's Entry into the WTO (Jiaru WTO hou Zhongguo jinrongye duiwai kaifang de neirong yu shijian)*, November 2001, http://www.21abroad.net/bank_card/2502047.html.)

6.2.3.1 Ensure the Stability of the Banking System

The banking system is the basis of finance. Research on financial crises in the twentieth century demonstrates that the scope and degree of financial crises largely depend on the degree of banking crises. Compared with the situation in developed countries, the banking sector plays a more important role in the financial system in China. Therefore, it is of more significance to China to maintain the stability of the banking sector.

After the East Asian financial crisis, the Chinese government took a series of measures to reduce the proportion of non-performing loans (NPLs) and increase the capital adequacy ratio of state-owned banks. China issued special treasury bonds of RMB 270 billion in 1998 to enhance the capital adequacy of state-owned banks. In 1999, four asset management corporations (AMCs), including Cinda, were established to take over NPLs of RMB 1,400 billion from the Big Four. By mid-2002, however, the NPLs of the Big Four rose to RMB 1,700 billion.[6] Moreover, none of them except the Bank of China met the capital adequacy requirement of the Basle Accord.[7]

It is therefore urgent for the Chinese government to reduce the NPLs ratio of state-owned banks and increase their capital adequacy to decrease financial risks. Possible measures are as follows: (a) the state makes additional capital investment; (b) the state disposes of the NPLs for a second time; (c) the banks solve the problem by themselves through improving management; (d) the state reduces business tax on these commercial banks to enhance their ability of reducing NPLs (the current tax rate is 8 percent; the central government has already removed its part of the tax of 3 percent and local governments should also remove the remaining 5 percent); (e) the banks establish a prudent financial system, implement the five-category loan classification system, and increase provisions for non-performing loans; and (f) the banks reduce their exposure of risks in the capital market.

6.2.3.2 Reform State-Owned Commercial Banks

The root cause of the Big Four's problems lies in their poorly defined relations of property rights and lack of proper governance structure. Although they are nominally state-owned banks, the owner is actually absent. As they have been regarded as administrative organs by the government for a long time, they not only lack a strict system of board of directors in a real sense but also have no normalized procedure for the appointment and dismissal of their presidents. As a result, without pressure from the government, no one really cares about the financial risk and economic efficiency of state-owned banks. Hence, the transformation of state-owned commercial banks into joint-stock banking corporations has become one of the most important reform tasks.

---

[6] See Xie Ping, "Next Round of Financial Reform: Six Alternatives (Xia yilun jinrong gaige: liuda fang'an)," *China Newsweek (Xinwen zhoukan),* 2002, No. 38. See also Wu Xiaoling, *The Proportion of Non-Performing Loans of the Big Four Will Drop to 15% and Below (Sida yinhang buliang daikuan jiang jiangdao 15% yixia),* October 16, 2002, www.cnstock.com: "The balance of non-performing loans at the end of June 2002 reached RMB 1,729.5 billion."

[7] The Statistic Bureau of PBC, *2002 Balance Sheets of Banks (Ge yinhang zichan fuzhai biao (2002 nian)).*

The reform of SOEs in the past twenty years was characterized by negligence of institutional transformation and overemphasis on IPO financing. In order to quicken the process of initial public offering (IPO), many enterprises "carve out" their core assets for IPO while leaving a large amount of non-core assets to the original enterprises as remaining enterprises (usually the so-called "authorized investment institutions"), and this practice hindered further reform. In view of this, institutional transformation should be given priority in the reform of state-owned commercial banks to change their ownership and governance structures in substance. Meanwhile, private enterprises, institutional investors and individuals both at home and abroad should be allowed to buy sufficient proportion of shares when establishing joint-stock limited banking corporations. Based on the shareholder diversification, healthy corporate governance of commercial banks should be established.

6.2.3.3 Develop Nonstate Banks Aggressively

Whether the financial sectors should be opened to private participation has been a long-time controversy on which no agreement has been reached in the financial circles in China. In fact, this should no longer be a problem after China's accession to the WTO. China promises to give foreign banks the same treatment as Chinese banks within five years after the accession. According to *Opinions on Promoting and Guiding Domestic Private Investment* and *Opinions on Policies and Measures to Speed Up the Development of Service Industries during the Tenth Five-Year Plan Period* promulgated by the State Planning Commission on December 11 and December 3 of 2001 respectively, "domestic private investment should be encouraged and permitted in all areas where foreign investment is encouraged and permitted;" in financial sectors that are heavily dominated by the state sector, restrictions on market entry of nonstate sectors should also be loosened gradually to offer them the same treatment as the state sector, thereby enabling them to participate in the development of the financial sectors on a large scope.

As far as the banking reform is concerned, there is a debate on whether the development of nonstate banks should be allowed in addition to the reform of state-owned commercial banks. In the discussion of the strengths and weaknesses of Strategy A and Strategy B for transition in Chapter 1, it has been pointed out that to establish a micro foundation for a market economy, effort should be devoted to the reform of SOEs but even more effort should be devoted to the development of new nonstate enterprises. The reason lies not only in the fact that nonstate enterprises develop faster than SOEs but also in the fact that nonstate enterprises impose competitive pressure on SOEs and provide conditions such as capital and market for the reform of SOEs. Therefore, the financial sectors must be opened to nonstate sectors and nonstate financial institutions should be strongly encouraged.

- Continue the reform of joint-stock commercial banks and urban commercial banks. There have been eleven joint-stock commercial banks since the establishment of Bank of Communications, the first one of this kind, in 1987. More than one hundred urban commercial banks were established during the reform of urban credit cooperatives in the late 1990s. These joint-stock banks still possess the characteristics of the old system, as they were initially set up and controlled by government or SOEs. More private capital both at home and abroad should be allowed to be invested in these banks to facilitate their transformation and help them establish effective corporate governance and lawful operations on the basis of a diversified ownership structure.

- Open the banking sector to nonstate capital and allow citizens to establish nonstate banks. In July 2003, Great Wall Financial Research Institute, a private institution of economists and financial professionals, put forward a plan for the trial operations of five nonstate banks, which were ready to apply for licenses from the China Banking Regulatory Commission.

- Reorganize rural credit cooperatives. Many credit cooperatives emerged in rural areas during the campaign of "cooperative transformation of agriculture." They were expected to perform better after the commencement of the reform and opening up. However, most of them have suffered huge losses due to poor operation in recent years. Since 1999, local governments in some regions have consolidated original rural credit cooperatives into rural credit cooperative unions at the county level or above. However, such measures may be far from enough to solve the fundamental problems of credit cooperatives, namely, poorly defined property rights and insider control. Therefore, existing rural credit cooperatives may adopt different forms of property rights to restructure and transform themselves into real financial enterprises. For those localities that really need rural credit cooperatives, it is imperative to clearly define their property rights and restore their nature of being cooperatives of their members.

- Normalize and develop informal financing. In the context of financial repression, informal financing tends to flourish to meet the huge demand of enterprises for financing in localities where nonstate sectors are developed. Possible forms of informal financing include loans among individuals, "underground banking houses," and "money-pooling organizations."[8] For most localities, the following actions

---

[8] Lu Mai, *The Development of Nonstate Sectors in West China (Xibu diqu de minying bumen de fazhan)*, mimeograph, 2001.

are needed: (a) legalization; (b) normalization; and (c) establishment of the credit system.

6.2.3.4 Switch from Specialized Banking to Universal Banking

The current *Commercial Bank Law of the People's Republic of China* bears resemblance to the one in effect between 1933 and 1999 in the United States. According to the *Law*, the system of specialized banking should be adopted in the financial sectors and commercial banks are not allowed to be involved in insurance and investment banking businesses. However, the experience of developed countries shows that universal banking is a trend of development. Even in China, financial institutions with universal banking in disguised form, such as financial holding companies, are emerging.

The fast development of financial holding companies both at home and abroad results from the competitive advantages of the model itself. The financial holding companies possess the following advantages: (a) economies of scale and scope; (b) diversified businesses; and (c) dispersed risks. Particularly in the context of China's accession to the WTO and the opening of domestic financial markets to foreign financial institutions, it may be an inevitable trend for local financial institutions to adopt the model of universal banking to compete with foreign universal banks.

As was criticized in the 1930s, universal banking may lead to extremely high financial leverage ratios due to the repeated cross-investment among different financial businesses. Such situations are conducive to illegal financial activities such as insider trading and market manipulation and thus cause great financial risks. Consequently, an effective China Wall should be established among the subsidiaries of a financial holding company under universal banking. Moreover, to minimize financial risks, it is essential to combine internal control and external supervision, rather than solely rely on the latter.

6.3 The Development of China's Money Market

6.3.1 The Current Situation of China's Money Market and Its Problems

According to the *Interim Regulations of the PRC on the Administration of Banks* issued in January 1986 by the State Council, specialized banks can call money from each other at negotiated interest rates. In December 1986, after hearing the report from the leaders of the central government, Deng Xiaoping said, "Great advances should be made in the reform of the banking system. Banks should perform all the functions of banks."[9] Ac-

---

[9]Deng Xiaoping, "On the Reform of Enterprises and of the Banking System (Qiye gaige he jinrong gaige) (December 19, 1986)," *Selected Works of Deng Xiaoping (Deng Xiaoping wenxuan)*, Vol. 3, Beijing: People's Publishing House, 1993, p. 193.

cording to this instruction from Deng Xiaoping, the principles and objectives for deepening the financial system reform were put forward at the Fifth Session of the Sixth National People's Congress in March 1987 and the 13th National Congress of the CPC in October 1987. One of the objectives of the reform was to develop and make effective use of various financial businesses and financial tools and to establish and develop capital markets of different sizes and at different levels in medium and large cities.

Since 1987, the interbank lending market, the interbank repo market, and the commercial paper market have come into being. By 1996, a unified national interbank lending market had emerged among the headquarters of sixteen commercial banks, with a total trading volume of RMB 587.2 billion in 1996. Starting from 2000, the same treatment was given to authorized branches of commercial banks, insurance companies, securities companies, securities investment funds, finance companies, and rural credit cooperative unions. By the end of 2000, there were 465 members in the interbank market, including most major financial institutions, and the trading volume in 2000 reached RMB 672.8 billion. In 1997, the interbank repo market started to operate at the China Foreign Exchange Trading Center. By the end of 2000, the cumulative trading volume in the interbank repo market had reached RMB 1,600 billion with 650 trading members. The commercial paper market started much earlier. In 1982, commercial paper acceptance and discount business within the same city first appeared in Shanghai on a trial basis. In 1985, the PBC issued *Provisional Regulations on Acceptance and Discount of Commercial Papers,* followed by *Trial Procedures of the PBC on Rediscount* in the next year, which gave the green light to rediscount business. By the end of 2000, the cumulative trading volume of commercial papers had reached RMB 674 billion and that of discount had amounted to RMB 631 billion.[10] Today, the interbank lending market, the interbank repo market, and the commercial paper market form the major part of China's money market.

However, many problems still exist in the current Chinese money market:

1. Inadequate market tools. The development of China's money market has been mainly in the interbank lending market and the interbank repo market while other markets are less developed. First, the treasury bond market, which should be the most important part of the money market, is not yet fully developed due to the lack of treasury bills with maturity less than one year. Second, transferable certificates of deposit, which were issued in large volume only in the late 1980s,

---

[10]Xie Ping, "Pension Insurance, Banking Sector and Money Market (Yanglao baoxian yu yinhangye ji huobi shichang) (2001),"
  Wei Jianing (ed.), *Pension Insurance and Financial Markets (Yanglao baoxian yu jinrong shichang),* Beijing: China Finance Press, 2002,
  p. 153.

have disappeared due to the stagnation of the market after 1990 caused by the low interest rate set by the PBC. Third, the commercial paper market is inactive despite issuances every year.

2. Low liquidity and inactive trading. China's money market had long been dominated by commercial banks until 1998 when the PBC allowed foreign banks and insurance companies to enter the interbank bond market. In 1999, 283 rural credit cooperative unions, 20 investment funds, and 7 finance and securities companies were also permitted to enter the interbank bond market. Since then the situation has improved. However, the commercial paper market is fragmented, and its trading is separated in thousands of dealers across the country, making commercial papers only a payment tool of enterprises or a substitute for loans. Not surprisingly, a large amount of commercial papers are actually sunk.

3. Fragmented market. China's money market has long been fragmented. Regional interbank lending markets based in large cities like Shanghai, Beijing, Wuhan, Shenyang, Chongqing, Xi'an, and Guangzhou are different in lending interest rates and trading rules. As a result, the liquidity of the money market is rather low.

4. Imperfect market infrastructure. A sound market infrastructure, including a trading network, a unified quotation system, a unified bond depository and clearing system for settlement of cash and securities, has been absent in China's money market.

All these problems have prevented China's money market from functioning properly as a mature market. The money market price cannot accurately reflect money demand and supply due to the fragmented market, inadequate market tools, and low liquidity. As a result, it is impossible to form an accurate benchmark interest rate and to enable it to function as a transmission mechanism of monetary policy.

6.3.2 Further Development of China's Money Market

Generally speaking, the development of the money market is to achieve two objectives: to establish a market system with sufficient liquidity of monetary assets and to provide the central bank with an effective transmission mechanism of monetary policy. Since 2000, China's money market has been moving toward these objectives. For example, in 2000, the PBC permitted twelve securities companies to enter the interbank lending market and the Industrial and Commercial Bank of China was allowed to open a commercial paper department in Shanghai, the first of its kind in mainland China. Moreover, the PBC Shanghai selected seven prefecture-level (city-level) branches in Zhejiang and Fujian provinces for repurchase of commercial papers on a trial basis. Meanwhile, four PBC branches, located respectively in Hangzhou, Fuzhou, Ningbo, and Xiamen, were authorized to examine and approve rediscount and repurchase of commercial papers of more than RMB 5 million per deal. The requirements for starting the rediscount and repurchase of commercial paper were also loosened. Moreover, the PBC Shanghai planned to further promote commercial paper acceptance business in large cities and to encourage financial institutions in these cities to engage in discount and cross-sector rediscount business for qualified enterprises. Commercial banks under the jurisdiction of the PBC Shanghai were encouraged to open specialized windows for commercial paper business.

Interest rate liberalization has been a hot issue in China's financial reform. In 2000, officials of the PBC once asserted that China would make steady progress in the reform of liberalizing interest rates in the next three years. Steps of the interest rate reform were to take the following order: (1) foreign currencies before Renminbi (i.e., liberalizing the interest rates for deposits and loans in foreign currencies before those in Renminbi); (2) loans before deposits (i.e., liberalizing the interest rates of loans before those of deposits); (3) rural before urban (i.e., liberalizing the interest rates in rural areas before those in urban areas); and (4) large deposits before small deposits (i.e., liberalizing the interest rates of large deposits before those of small deposits). However, the liberalization of interest rates (i.e., the determination of equilibrium prices of funds by market) also needs some other conditions such as a sound and unified money market and independent commercial banks. Thus, the gradual liberalization of interest rates will still be one of the most important tasks in China's future financial reform.

6.4 The Development and Improvement of the Securities Market

During the few decades before the reform, there was no securities market in China at all. Only after the launch of marketization reform at the end of the 1970s had the securities market in China begun to take shape and develop gradually.

6.4.1 The Development of China's Securities Market since the Reform and Opening Up

China's securities market started in 1980, when Fushun Office of Liaoning Branch of the PBC issued stocks for enterprises, and 1981, when the Ministry of Finance issued treasury notes. From 1991 to 2002, the accumulative total value of securities issued in China reached more than RMB 5 trillion and a securities market with a set of various securities came into being.

China's stock market has developed very rapidly. By the end of 2002, there were 1,220 listed companies in the Shanghai Stock Exchange and the Shenzhen Stock Exchange, the total number of shares of which amounted to 587.462 billion. By the end of 2002, the total capitalization of tradable shares had reached RMB 1.3 trillion and the total trading volume of 2002 amounted to RMB 3 trillion. There were 126 securities companies with more than 2,900 securities business units and more than 100,000 employees. The number of stock accounts was once recorded at 68 million. The fast development of the stock market has significantly changed the financing structure of enterprises. During the first one-and-a-half decades of the reform, the financing of enterprises was dominated by long-term credit financing, a natural result of the policies of full loan financing for working capital adopted in 1983 and substituting fiscal appropriations with bank loans for fixed asset investments in 1985. Since 1992, other types of financing, especially equity financing, have become an important part of corporate financing. From 1987 to 2001, the total amount of equity financing by listed companies amounted to RMB 623.3 billion.

China's bond market has experienced three phases in its development. The first phase is characterized by the immature over-the-counter (OTC) bond market represented by counter trading of bearer certificates. The second phase is characterized by the exchange bond market, such as the Shanghai Stock Exchange. The third phase is characterized by the mature OTC bond market represented by the interbank bond market. Currently, China's bond market consists of the interbank bond market as the OTC market and the Shanghai Stock Exchange and the Shenzhen Stock Exchange as the exchange market. After 1997, China's bond market, especially the treasury bond market, experienced fast growth. By the end of 2002, the total balance of China's bond assets had reached RMB 3.4 trillion, among which negotiable bonds were worth RMB 2.8 trillion. The total annual bond trading reached RMB 13.4 trillion, implying average daily trading of more than RMB 50 billion. The bond market attracted all kinds of institutional investors and individual investors, and was obviously outperforming the stock market in terms of every indicator. However, China's bond market is still dominated by treasury bonds and financial bonds issued by policy banks, while the market for corporate bonds is underdeveloped. In 2002, the bond financing by the government and enterprises was RMB 592.9 billion and RMB 32 billion respectively. Hence, the major functions of China's bond market are to provide investment tools for institutional and individual investors, to raise funds to support government financing, and to help the central bank switch to indirect adjustment by monetary policy, rather than to help with the efficient allocation of capital resources among enterprises.

China's securities market has made the following contributions to China's economic growth:

1. More channels for domestic investment and financing have been created and the original financial model of households depositing all savings in banks and enterprises relying solely on bank loans has been broken. As a result, the liquidity and allocation efficiency of capital are greatly improved.

2. The birth of the stock market has laid ground for the ownership diversification and improvement of governance structure of SOEs as well as for the possible strategic exit of the state sector from competitive fields in the future.

3. Capital stock in the national economy becomes more liquid, which greatly facilitates the adjustment of the industrial structure and the efficient use of capital stock through asset restructuring and mergers and acquisitions.

However, due to the problems to be addressed in the following paragraphs, the role of China's securities market is still very limited.

6.4.2 Problems in China's Securities Market and Proposed Solutions

In spite of its rapid development after the commencement of the reform and opening up, China's securities market still suffers from many problems. For example, the corporate bond market is underdeveloped and the stock market is hindered by inappropriate

Table 6.2   The Financing Structure of Chinese Enterprises (RMB billion, %)

Year	Total amount of financing	Loans in local and foreign currency[a] Increase	%	Equity financing[b] Increase	%	Commercial paper financing[a,c] Increase	%	Bond financing[a] Increase	%
1996	1,158.0	1,114.0	96.2	42.5	3.7	6.4	0.5	−4.9	−0.4
1997	1,258.3	1,140.0	90.6	128.5	10.2	−2.5	−0.2	−7.7	−0.6
1998	1,281.4	1,152.0	89.9	84.0	6.5	29.4	2.3	16.0	1.3
1999	1,207.6	1,072.1	88.8	94.1	7.8	29.4	2.4	10.2	1.0
2000	1,587.2	1,288.7	81.2	210.4	13.3	79.8	5.0	8.3	0.5
2001	1,401.6	1,252.4	89.4	116.9	8.3	17.6	1.3	14.7[d]	1.0

Note: Foreign currency is translated into local currency based on the current average exchange rate.
[a] Loans in local and foreign currency, commercial paper financing, and bond financing by financial institutions all refer to the increase in the current year.
[b] Equity financing in local and foreign currency includes rights offers and convertible bonds.
[c] Commercial paper financing = increase in ending balance of bank acceptance − increase in ending balance of bank discount, because the discounted part has been counted as indirect financing in loans of financial institutions.
[d] Bond financing in 2001 refers to bonds issued that year as the balance was not reported.
Source: The PBC and the CSRC.

positioning, overspeculation, and poor regulation. All these problems have hindered the proper functioning of China's securities market.

6.4.2.1 Extremely Underdeveloped Corporate Bond Market

In developed market economies, bond issuance is the major means of corporate financing, and funds raised through bond issuance are usually three to ten times those of stock issuance. In some countries, the number of repos and delisting shares is even greater than new issuances. In contrast, the issuance of corporate bonds is increasing rapidly, with a total value over the country's GNP. In the United States in 2002, for example, 1,592 listed companies issued corporate bonds, while only 199 companies issued shares. At the end of 2001, the balance of American corporate bonds reached US$3.8 trillion, accounting for 36.18 percent of its GDP. The difference in the positioning of bond financing and equity financing determines the structure of the securities market, in which the major role of the corporate bond market is to raise funds for enterprises, while that of the stock market is to optimize the allocation of social resources and to improve corporate governance structure.

After 1992, equity financing began to grow in China, while bond financing remained an insignificant channel for enterprise financing. In 2002, loans of financial institutions increased by RMB 1,920 billion. The total amount of funds raised from the securities market reached RMB 1,060 billion, of which RMB 627.8 billion was treasury bonds, RMB 307.5 billion was financial bonds issued by policy banks, RMB 96.2 billion was stocks, and RMB 32.5 billion was corporate bonds.[11] Corporate bonds accounted for only 3 percent of the total financing of the securities market and was even more insignificant compared with bank loans. The underdevelopment of China's corporate bond market is therefore evident.

Moreover, corporate bonds account for only a small share of China's bond market, demonstrating again the underdevelopment of China's corporate bond market. Government bonds are preferred by financial institutions and other investors as a tool of liquidity management because of their zero credit risk. In comparison, corporate bonds are regarded as a typical tool of capital investment. In the global context, the percentage of corporate bonds in the bond market has been increasing recently while that of government bonds has been decreasing. Corporate bonds accounted for 23.8 percent of the American bond market in 1990 and the figure increased to 30.3 percent by the end of 2001. In China, corporate bonds account for less than 3 percent of the bond market. The major tools of China's bond market are treasury bonds and financial bonds issued

---

[11] Team of the Monetary Policy Analysis of the PBC, *Report on the Implementation of China's Monetary Policy in 2002 (2002 Zhongguo huobi zhengce zhixing baogao),* Beijing: China Finance Press, 2003.

by policy banks with the state-owned commercial banks as the key investors, showing a strong flavor of government credit. The development of corporate bonds will facilitate the establishment of private credit in the bond market and promote the transition of the bond market from a government-credit-dominated to a private-credit-dominated market.

The extremely underdeveloped corporate bond market in China can be attributed to many factors. For example, the issuance of corporate bonds is subject to approval by the planning authorities, there are few objective and fair credit rating agencies in the market, and enterprises lack credibility. Moreover, the interest rate of bonds is restricted and is not determined by demand and supply. In summary, there are three major obstacles.

First, the functional positioning of corporate bonds is not appropriate. As mentioned earlier, corporate bonds are an important tool of corporate financing in a market economy. In China, however, corporate bonds are often regarded by the government as a tool for raising funds for fixed asset investment and are always bundled with fiscal appropriations and bank loans when planning departments consider projects. To facilitate the healthy development of China's corporate bond market, the first task is to get rid of this improper mindset.

Second, there are few sophisticated institutional investors in the corporate bond market. Compared with stocks, corporate bonds are more favored by institutional investors than by individual investors because of the asymmetry between the analysis cost and return. In developed economies, there are a variety of corporate bonds. For example, in the American bond market, there are millions of types of corporate bonds. Undoubtedly, it costs a lot to search for data and analyze the credit status and business situation of an enterprise. In contrast, the expected rate of return of corporate bonds is rather low due to their nature of fixed income. This is also the very reason for the remarkable economies of scale in corporate bond investment. Moreover, only professional institutional investors are potential customers of credit rating companies. In China, however, individual investors still account for the majority of corporate bondholders, which has resulted in two consequences. The first is that individual bondholders have little demand-side discipline over issuers. For such a complicated financial product with credit risk as corporate bonds, only institutional investors can exert effective demand-side discipline over issuers. It is often difficult for individual investors to accurately understand the credit risk and corresponding interest rate of corporate bonds because they lack the ability to conduct professional analysis. The second is that without institutional investors such as funds and insurance companies, it will be hard to expand the corporate bond market.

Third, the liquidity of corporate bonds is low due to the absence of an OTC market. Generally speaking, only bonds with low credit risk and simple clauses are suitable for trading in exchanges, while corporate bonds with high credit risk and complex clauses are suitable for trading in the OTC market. In developed countries like the United

States, only bonds issued by a few large companies are traded in securities exchanges in small volumes, mainly for the sake of publicity; the overwhelming majority of corporate bonds are traded in the OTC market with institutional investors, who are familiar with these corporate bonds, acting as market makers to maintain the liquidity of the secondary market. Currently, there are only a small number of corporate bonds with high credit rating listed and traded in the Shanghai Stock Exchange and the Shenzhen Stock Exchange with daily trading volumes less than RMB 50 million; most corporate bonds cannot meet the basic requirements to be listed in exchanges. As a result, the issuance cost of corporate bonds in the primary market is high due to the inactive secondary market, which hinders the further development of corporate bonds.

Measures that can be taken to solve these problems are as follows: (a) bring more institutional investors into the corporate bond market by launching corporate bond funds that invest primarily in corporate bonds, allowing banks to invest in corporate bonds, and lifting the restriction on insurance companies to invest in corporate bonds; (b) replace the approval system for bond issuance with the verification system and liberalize the interest rate of corporate bonds gradually to let the market set the price; (c) allow corporate bonds to be traded on the OTC bond market; and (d) set up China's own credit rating companies, and discipline them by new laws and regulations and institutional investors, allowing a virtuous cycle of the development of the credit rating system and the corporate bond market.

6.4.2.2 Inappropriate Positioning of the Stock Market and Problems Incurred

According to modern economics, the basic function of the stock market is to optimize the allocation of capital resources through stock trading and fluctuations of stock prices. Meanwhile, stock prices can be used to measure the performance of companies, thereby evaluating the business situation and monitoring the management. However, many problems may appear due to the characteristics of the stock market, such as imperfect market and asymmetric information.

During a fairly long period after China's stock market was established, the administrative authorities believed that the basic function of the stock market was to raise capital for enterprises, especially for SOEs, and adopted the policy that "the stock market should serve SOEs."[12] Accordingly, the administrative authorities in charge of securities took the following measures.

First, SOEs were given priority in IPO approval to raise funds and get out of finan-

---

[12] See "Former CSRC Chairman on the History of the Securities Market (Qianren Zhongguo zhengjianhui zhuxi huishou laishilu)," *China Business Post (Caijing shibao)*, December 11, 2000. See also "Public Opinions on Stock Market Should Not Be Biased, Both Jumps and Slumps Should Be Controlled (Gushi yulun buneng pianpo, baozhang baodie dou ying tiaokong)," *Securities Daily (Zhengquan ribao)*, March 16, 2002.

cial difficulty.[13] In developed market economies, the setup and IPO of companies follow the registration system. China, however, adopted the administrative approval system, or the substantive examination system. Before 2000, a company planning to be listed in exchanges had to first get recommendation from the provincial government and then get approval from the CSRC. After that, there were still many procedures of administrative approval regarding the IPO price and size. SOEs obtained the most chances, while few chances were given to nonstate enterprises. It was not until March 1998 that the first nonstate listed company, Sichuan New Hope Agribusiness Co., Ltd. (code: 000876) in Sichuan Province, appeared with controlling interest by the nonstate enterprise, New Hope Group. In addition, private capital acquired the controlling interests of several listed companies.

Second, stock prices were often manipulated to raise more funds for companies with listing qualifications. The administrative authorities helped listed companies to enjoy high premiums in IPO and rights issue by making encouraging speeches from time to time and "boosting the market with policies." Moreover, they also tried to boost stock prices by adjusting the supply and demand sides. Supply-side policies included (a) setting an IPO quota each year to limit the number of IPO; and (b) dividing stocks into "tradable shares" and "non-tradable shares" to allow only one-third of the shares to be traded on stock exchanges. Demand-side policy was to encourage various types of investors to buy stocks. As a result, the P/E[14] in the secondary market reached 40 to 60.[15] Under such circumstances, even though listed companies issued stocks at the high P/E of around 20 set by the administrative authorities, the huge gap between IPO price and secondary market price still attracted numerous retail investors, who were not aware of the danger of bubbles in the stock market.

This practice of "the government boosting the market and SOEs grabbing the money" caused a series of disastrous effects. Some companies with very poor performance were able to issue stocks with high premiums only because they gained approval from the administrative authorities. These companies not only enjoyed risk-free high returns from the primary and secondary markets but also raised funds through rights offering with high premiums. As a result, the stock market was turned into a paradise for rent seeking.[16] Most stocks were not worthy of investment because of their extremely

---

[13] For debates over the issue, see Liu Hong, *Academic Critical Biography of Contemporary Chinese Economists: Wu Jinglian (Dangdai Zhongguo jingjixuejia xueshu pingzhuan: Wu Jinglian)*, Xi'an: Shaanxi Normal University Press, 2002.

[14] Price-earnings ratio, P/E in short, refers to the ratio of the price of a stock to its earnings per share. P/E indicates how many years it will take for investors to get back their investment at the current level of earnings.

[15] Wu Jinglian, "Economic Reflection on Corruption and Anti-Corruption (Fubai yu fanfubai de jingjixue sikao), (May 20, 2002)," *China Supervision (Zhongguo jiancha)*, 2002, August Issue.

[16] The saying that China's stock market is a large paradise for "rent-seeking" was first put forward by Professor Zhang Weiying. See Zhang Weiying, "China's Stock Market Is Much Like a 'Rent-seeking' Paradise (Zhongguo gushi geng xiangge 'xunzuchang')," *China Business Post (Caijing shibao)*, March 9, 2001.

high P/E and low growth rate. Therefore, investors could not count on long-term return; instead, they could only try to earn money through speculative buying and selling. As a result, a speculative atmosphere permeated the entire stock market, making it "a casino without rules."

The realities of China's securities market in recent years have demonstrated that it is impossible for SOEs to get out of financial difficulty only by "grabbing money" from the securities market. On the contrary, this will only lead to the ultimate collapse of China's securities market. As far as the primary market is concerned, quota allotment plus the approval system should be replaced by the registration system. The issue of "all tradable" should be resolved in an appropriate way to realize the same benefits and rights for the same class of shares. Effective governance should be established in line with the *Company Law* in all listed companies, and internal monitoring by stockholders should be strengthened. Listed companies and the securities market should gradually upgrade themselves to international standards. As far as the secondary market is concerned, the government and supervisory institutions of securities exchanges should strengthen regulation over illegal activities, improve information disclosure, strictly implement trading rules of the stock market, and check and punish illegal activities.

6.4.2.3 Overspeculation and the Formation of Bubbles

Because of the poor quality of listed companies and high stock prices in the secondary market resulting from the wrong positioning of the stock market, the P/E is too high. The average P/E of negotiable shares even reached a ridiculously high level of 100 to 200 in the early 1990s, making stocks not worthy of investment. Although the average P/E has been up and down several times since 1993, it remained at about 40 for a long time. Moreover, the cash dividends of listed companies account for only about one-tenth of their profits, while in developed countries the ratio is about one-third. Therefore, compared with the P/E of the stock markets in developed countries,[17] the P/E of China's stock market is unattractive to long-term investors. Under such circumstances, it is impossible for investors to make profits from long-term investment. As a result, market participants can only try to profiteer from frequent buying and selling, which almost unavoidably leads to overspeculation.

Admittedly, speculation plays an important role in the effective functioning of the stock market,[18] because a precondition for trading any financial product is different pre-

---

[17] For data concerning the cash dividends of China's listed companies and a comparison with those of developed countries, see Sun Guofeng, "2000 Points in the year 2000: How Were the Bubbles Created (2000 nian 2000 dian, paomo shi zenyang xingcheng de)," *Caijing Magazine (Caijing)*, 2000, No. 9.

[18] For the role of speculation in the securities market and the futures market, see Wu Jinglian, "On 'Speculation' (Tantan 'touji')," *Where to Find Macro Wisdom (Hechu xunqiu da zhihui)*, Beijing: Joint Publishing, 1997, pp. 195–204.

dictions of the price changes by buyers and sellers. If there are only long-term investors, the market will lack liquidity and price discovery will not be realized. Only when some investors seek risky returns can trading continue. However, only when there is positive interaction between speculation and investment can optimal allocation of capital resources be achieved through the securities market. If there is only speculation, the securities market will become a zero-sum game,[19] where money is only transferred from one pocket to another without adding value or improving efficiency. This is exactly the reason that long-time speculation will unavoidably result in losses.

Overspeculation results in the formation of economic bubbles, which is directly related to the nature of markets for assets such as securities. According to modern microeconomics, an asset market, as an incomplete market, does not have equilibrium with Pareto efficiency. Instead, it can reach equilibrium between supply and demand at any point within a rather large range. In this kind of market, the price largely depends on the expectation of buyers and sellers on the future movement of the price. Moreover, the expectation is typically "self-sustaining" or "self-fulfilling." In other words, when the price of an asset (either physical asset or financial asset) changes, the higher it rises, the more people will buy the asset with the expectation that the price will keep rising. With more people buying the asset, its price will rise further, reinforcing the expectation that the price will keep rising. Therefore, a "big bull market" will appear if there are enough people rushing into the market and there is a continuous flow of money into the market. However, it is impossible for economic bubbles to expand forever. As soon as the price stops climbing, it will begin to decline, leading to the collapse of the market (crash). When the stock market crashes, the paper wealth accumulated through speculation in the bull market will evaporate and the so-called "wealth effect" will change into a "negative wealth effect." Some speculators with great financial might just take advantage of this characteristic of financial markets to snatch money from small investors by price manipulation.

Starting with the "Tulipomania" in Holland in the seventeenth century, various financial tragicomedies of "speculation mania—panic selling—crash of market"[20] were shown in succession on the global stage. Among them were the "South Sea Bubble" in the United Kingdom and the "Mississippi Bubble" in France in the eighteenth century,[21] the "Big Bull Market" and "Big Crashes" in the United States in the 1920s and

---

[19] "Zero-sum game" means that the total benefits of all parties involved in the game is fixed, and gains of one party are definitely equal to the losses of the other.

[20] Charles P. Kindleberger, *Manias, Panic and Crashes: A History of Financial Crises,* New York: John Wiley & Sons, Inc., 1989.

[21] See Charles Mackey, *Extraordinary Popular Delusions and the Madness of Crowds* (1841), which gives vivid descriptions of "Tulipomania," "South Sea Bubble," and "Mississippi Bubble."

1930s,[22] economic bubbles in Japan[23] and Taiwan[24] in the 1980s and 1990s, and the "Internet Bubble" in the United States at the turn of the century.[25]

In China, similar to what happened in the early stage of developed countries, over-speculation and bubbles also appeared in its infant securities market. With their privilege of conducting illegal activities without being punished, some individuals created speculation mania in the stock market, the futures market, and the real estate market, aggravating the problem of economic bubbles.

Economists held rather different opinions and attitudes about the problems in the securities market. Some economists were deeply worried about the situation then, believing that economic bubbles would jeopardize economic development and social stability because China was still at an early stage of economic development when down-to-earth hard work was a must. If many retail investors with limited financial resources were attracted into the bull market by a high expected return and the bubble burst, they might lose their hard-earned savings, incurring serious social consequences.[26]

Some other economists believed that "there is not enough speculation in China's securities market."[27] After the summer of 1993, while adopting a contractionary monetary policy and taking measures to suppress inflation, the macroeconomic authorities in China also restrained overspeculation and economic bubbles in the securities market and the real estate market. However, whenever the prices of financial assets dropped, some economists would raise a cry of warning that "the stock market is in bad shape" and "the stock market is the outcome of the reform and the stock market has to be saved to save the reform." Together with some government officials, these economists often urged the macroeconomic authorities to restore the stock market to its past "glory" of speculation mania by slowing down the pace of issuing stocks, increasing demand, and reducing taxes.[28] Even in 1996, when it was so evident that economic bubbles generated by speculation in the stock market, the real estate market, and the futures market caused significant damage, one economist still insisted that "the statement of 'economic bubbles' not only raises a false alarm but also gives a false account of the true situation," and that "there were no 'economic bubbles' at all during the period from 1993 to 1995."[29]

---

[22] John Kenneth Galbraith, *A Short History of Financial Euphoria,* Knoxville, Tenn.: Whittle Direct Books, 1990.

[23] Zhu Shaowen, "The Bursting of Japanese Economic Bubbles and Its Lessons (Riben paomo jingji de polie jiqi jiaoxun)," *Reform (Gaige),* 1993, No. 4.

[24] Xue Xiaohe, "How Taiwan Fell into the Trap of 'Money Game' (Taiwandao shi zenyang luoru 'jinqian youxi' de xianjing de)," *Reform (Gaige),* 1994, No. 1.

[25] Robert J. Shiller, *Irrational Exuberance,* Princeton, N.J.: Princeton University Press, 2000.

[26] Wu Jinglian, *Opinions on Stock Market during Its Ten Confused Years (Shinian fenyun hua gushi),* Shanghai: Shanghai Far East Publishers, 2001.

[27] *Asia-Pacific Economic Times (Yatai jingji shibao),* March 2, 1993.

[28] Mao Bihua, "China's Stock Market: The Predicament and the Way Out—Interview of Professor Xiao Zhuoji, a Famous Chinese Economist (Zhongguo gushi: kunjing he chulu—zhuming jingjixuejia Xiao Zhuoji fangtanlu)," *Capital Economy (Shoudu jingji),* No. 3, 1994.

[29] Li Yining, *Development Theory of Transformation (Zhuanxing fazhan lilun),* Beijing: One Mind Press, 1996, pp. 180–182.

Although the claim that "economic bubbles are helpful to economic development" could not maintain the everlasting flourish of the stock market, it was often endorsed by some interest groups and government officials as the basis for the principle that "the stock market should serve SOEs." In fact, the government gave a boost to the stock market several times during its development. For example, on May 19, 1999, the Shanghai Stock Exchange and the Shenzhen Stock Exchange began to "blowout" thanks to the intervention of the administrative authorities. The composite index of the Shanghai Stock Exchange rose from 1,059 points to 1,427 points (June 14) within only twenty trading days. On June 15, an editorial in *People's Daily* asserted that the rocketing stock prices reflected macroeconomic reality and market requirements. In other words, the rocketing prices were just a "normal restoring rise" because "current macroeconomic development remains healthy and sustainable, which provides a good foundation for long-term growth of the securities market." What China needed to do was to "align opinions, stay confident, and combine efforts to bring a normalized and vigorous securities market into the twenty-first century."[30] The statement made by the government enhanced investors' confidence and more investors rushed into the market. As a result, stock prices kept rising and the composite index of the Shanghai Stock Exchange reached a peak of 1,739.20 points on June 29, 1999.

Insight 6.3

"Big Debate on the Stock Market" in Early 2001

In October 2000, the fraudulent operations of fund management companies were disclosed in an article titled "The Inside Story of Funds" published in *Caijing Magazine*. Soon, ten fund management companies made a joint counter-statement. On October 29, in an interview by the reporter of a program of China Central Television (CCTV) titled "Half Hour for Economy," Professor Wu Jinglian condemned insider trading and market manipulation. On January 13, 2001, in another program of CCTV titled "Dialogue," Professor Wu again expressed his viewpoint about China's stock market and advocated normalizing the market. With tightening regulation of the market and investigations that started on January 9 and 10 on the manipulation of the stock prices by two listed companies, namely, Yi'an Technology and Zhongke Venturing, respectively,

---

[30] "Keeping Confidence and Achieving Normalized Development (Jianding xinxin, guifan fazhan)," *People's Daily*, June 15, 1999.

the stock prices slumped for four consecutive days starting on January 15. Then, a big debate on the stock market started in newspapers and on the Internet. On February 8, 2001, the publication of an article titled "Nine Questions for Professor Wu Jinglian" in *Securities Market Weekly* marked the escalation of the debate. On February 11, Li Yining, Dong Fureng, Xiao Zhuoji, Han Zhiguo, and Wu Xiaoqiu organized a talkfest with journalists and opposed the viewpoints of Professor Wu Jinglian. In March, Professor Wu Jinglian replied in a systematic and comprehensive way to his opponents in the preface to his book, *Opinions on the Stock Market during Its Ten Confused Years.*

The debate centered on the following questions: Is it good for everyone to speculate on stocks? Is there too much speculation in China's stock market? Is the P/E in China's stock market too high? How shall China treat market manipulators? Is it necessary to normalize the stock market, which is still in its infancy? What kind of market economy does China need to establish?

Opponents to Wu Jinglian argued the following points.

1. It was an integral part of a socialized investment system for everyone to speculate on stocks. There were still not enough people speculating on stocks in China. More and more people should be encouraged to speculate on stocks.

2. Without speculation, there would have been no stock market.

3. A high P/E ratio was not rare in emerging stock markets around the world. As China was short of capital and capital was insufficient in supply, it was natural for commodities with insufficient supply to have high prices. The average P/E of 50 to 60 was thus not too high, but rather reasonable.

4. If there had been no market manipulators and large institutional investors, the securities market would have become a pool of dead water. Without market manipulators, there would have been no securities market.

5. It would be abnormal for the stock market to be normalized in its infancy. The development of the stock market was actually a learning process for both regulators and investors, and errors should be al-

lowed. China's stock market was like an infant that needed care and protection, and it should not be treated with drastic medicine even if it was sick.

6. The essence of the debate was whether China should establish a market economy with a developed financial system and capital market or one with only small commodity wholesale markets.

Wu Jinglian and his supporters countered with the following arguments.

1. The expansion of the capital market did need more direct investment including investment in stocks. However, investment in stocks was totally different from speculation on stocks. It would be abnormal for everyone to speculate on stocks.

2. Speculation did indeed play an important role in a market economy. For example, it helped achieve market equilibrium and optimal allocation of resources. However, only when there was positive interaction between speculation and investment could it benefit the overall economy. Pure speculation could not increase social wealth.

3. Only when coupled with future growth potentials of companies could P/E ratio reflect and appraise the investment value of the stocks. If listed companies had great growth potential, their high P/E ratio would not be a problem. Considering the low growth rate and deteriorating ROI of China's listed companies, investors would suffer if the P/E ratio of these companies was too high.

4. The manipulation of stock prices by market manipulators to make huge profits was a crime per China's *Criminal Law* and should be punished by judicatory agencies.

5. Even a stock market in its infancy should be normalized.

6. The difference between the so-called traditional market economy and a modern market economy did not lie in the difference between real economy and virtual economy, or that between small commodity wholesale market and developed financial system. Rather, the issue was to establish a modern market economy based on the rule of law or a crony-capitalist economy characterized by intervention of power in market transactions and exploitation of people.

(Compiled according to "Five Economists Question Professor Wu Jinglian: Sudden Calls for Boosting the Stock Market (Wuwei jingjixuejia zhiyi Wu Jinglian, gushi "tuo" sheng zhouqi)" in *China Business Post (Caijing shibao)* on February 13, 2001 and *Preface to "Opinions on the Stock Market during Its Ten Confused Years" (Shinian fenyun hua gushi qianyan)* by Wu Jinglian, Shanghai: Far East Publishers, 2001.)

In spite of this criticism of the practice of China's stock market and the "big debate on the stock market" in early 2001, the strong support from some leaders and the positive feedback effect of the "big bull market" drove the composite index of Shanghai Stock Exchange up to the historical high of 2,247.69 points on June 7, 2001. The inevitable plunge of stock prices afterwards trapped not only most retail investors but also the entire society.

Figure 6.2   Monthly Chart of the Composite Index of Shanghai Stock Exchange* (from January 1999 to January 2003)

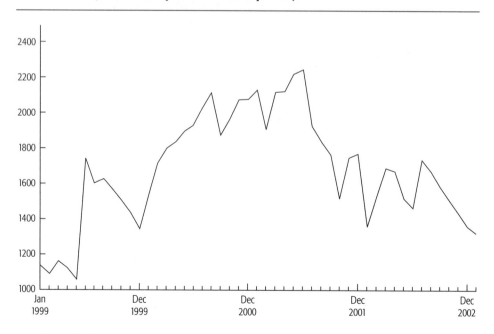

Source: Shanghai Stock Exchange.
*The values demonstrated at each point are the closing index of the last trading day of each month, except for the specially marked points.

According to international experience, the government can take the following possible measures to prevent overspeculation and economic bubbles: (a) abandon the wrong practice of "the government boosting the market and SOEs grabbing the money;" (b) speed up the reform of SOEs and improve the corporate governance of listed companies to lay a solid foundation for the development of the securities market; (c) adopt a prudent and stable monetary policy and other macroeconomic policies to maintain macroeconomic stability and to avoid violent fluctuation of the securities market; (d) come up with a solution acceptable to all relevant parties to the problem of tradable shares to realize "all tradable" as soon as possible; (e) speed up the legislation of securities trading, improve the regulation of various securities trading institutions and businesses, and strengthen the supervision of market to prevent new problems; and (f) remove restriction on the sphere of private investment to turn private capital into industrial investment and to turn bubble-generating "heat" into economy-driving "steam" for a new round of rapid economic growth.

A distinctive feature of the securities market is the severe information asymmetry between the supply side (investors) and the demand side (issuers). Issuers enjoy informational advantage because they know everything about the value of securities investment. In contrast, investors, especially retail investors, suffer from an informational disadvantage. If issuers are allowed to make full use of their informational advantage, investors will unavoidably suffer from all kinds of frauds. This is the very reason that market economies try their best to protect investors, especially retail investors, by enforcing the compulsory information disclosure system and punishing illegal activities. According to *Objectives and Principles of Securities Regulation* issued by the International Organization of Securities Commissions (IOSCO) in 1998, securities regulation should follow three objectives, namely, to protect investors; to ensure the fairness, efficiency, and transparency of the securities market; and to reduce systematic risk. Therefore, the key task of securities regulatory authorities is to enforce the compulsory information disclosure system.

In China's securities market, various illegal activities have been prevalent from its very beginning. Insider trading and market manipulation by some individuals with powerful connections or some enterprises affiliated to government institutions are neither promptly curbed nor duly punished.

In view of the intensified disorder in the securities market, the Chinese government started to strengthen regulation in 1993. However, for quite a long time, officials could not reach a clear conclusion on how to regulate the securities market. Many people preferred regulation by the substantive examination system (i.e., the administrative approval system). However, it had been proven both in theory and in practice that the administrative approval system was not only ineffective but also led to many problems such as the corruption of the regulatory authorities themselves and even more disorder in the securities market.[31]

According to the *Securities Law of the PRC,* which came into effect on July 1, 1999, the issuance of stocks in China should follow a verification system. Starting in April 2001, the approval system was officially replaced by the verification system. Compared with the original administrative approval system, the verification system improves in four aspects. First, the quota control is abandoned nominally. Second, the recommendation function of local governments and central authorities (i.e., the practice of two-level approval) is abandoned. Third, the issue price is to be determined through consultation between the issuer and the underwriter based on the market conditions and demand of institutional investors nominally. Fourth, the compulsory information disclosure is emphasized. However, the securities regulatory authorities still keep strong power of administrative control, and whether the rights and interests represented by certain securities can be traded in the primary market is often determined by the securities regulatory authorities first, which may easily hinder the securities transfer and appropriate allocation of risks. Hence, the verification system should gradually be replaced by the registration system, which is also called the declaration system.

Compulsory information disclosure should be enforced to improve the regulation of the securities market. The *Securities Law of the PRC* prescribes the disclosure obligation of listed companies, while the *Criminal Law of the PRC* defines insider trading and manipulation of stock prices as crimes. For quite a long period of time, however, criminal activities prohibited by Chinese laws, such as false statements, insider trading, and manipulation of market price, have been prevalent in China's securities market. Some people even openly took advantage of market disorder to grab tremendous profit without being punished. Obviously, the securities regulatory authorities should give priority to enforcing the compulsory information disclosure system and punishing illegal activities to meet the regulatory objectives of openness, fairness, justice, and credibility.

Moreover, it should be noted that the major reason for the problems in China's securities market is the poorly defined property rights of SOEs and "absence of the owner," which leads to wrongdoings of corporate executives and securities profession-

---

[31] For the two different approaches to regulation of the securities market and their respective advantages and disadvantages, see Gao Xiqing, "Theoretical Grounds for Compulsory Information Disclosure System in the Securities Market (Zhengquan shichang qiangzhixing xinxi pilu zhidu de lilun genju)," Shenzhen: *Securities Market Herald (Zhengquan shichang daobao),* October 1996, pp. 4–17. According to Professor Gao Xiqing, it was still difficult to tell whether the authorities had made a final choice between the compulsory information disclosure system and the substantive examination system. The substantive examination system was still a "sharp sword" cherished by the authorities of the securities markets. Since the setup of the CSRC four years ago, more than 360 companies had been approved by the CSRC for IPOs. Chiefs of thirty provinces, municipalities directly under the central government, autonomous regions, fourteen cities specifically designated in the state plan, as well as their subordinates at various levels, chief officials of ministries and commissions of the State Council, and enterprise executives made frequent visits to administrative authorities such as the CSRC for years to seek approval for IPOs for their regions, departments, and enterprises. Therefore, to give up such strong power would definitely require "a revolution at the very bottom of the soul" for any organization, especially an organization growing out of the traditional central planning system.

als. As phenomena of "absence of the owner" and "unchecked insider control" are prevalent in China's state-owned industrial, commercial, and financial enterprises, all or most gains will go to private individuals while losses will be borne by the state. This creates huge incentive for managers of enterprises to make risky speculation. For this reason, in the past few years, Chinese SOEs have repeatedly lost tens of millions of U.S. dollars in speculation in overseas futures markets. Financial experts analyzed several financial scandals in the late 1990s and concluded that external regulation (the China Securities Regulatory Commission and the central bank) plays only a limited role in controlling business risks. What matters more is internal control of enterprises. It is hard to identify the wrongdoings of executives and operators and correct them in time by means of external regulation. On the contrary, internal control is relatively more effective in detecting problems in time. Meanwhile, the owner of an enterprise, as the ultimate supervisor, also has enough motivation to exert strict control over first-line operators through corporate governance to protect his or her own interests. That is to say, internal control should be strengthened on the basis of effective corporate governance. Although they did not generate instant results, the measures taken by the CSRC in 2001 to improve the governance of listed companies laid a solid foundation for the healthy development of China's securities market.

Chapter 7

Reform of the Fiscal and Taxation System

After the founding of the People's Republic of China (PRC) in October 1949, the Chinese government established a highly centralized fiscal and taxation system based on the Soviet model, with no separation between government administration and enterprise management. This system made a considerable shift in 1958 toward administrative decentralization. However, after the failure of the Great Leap Forward and the restoration of the centralized system to remedy the chaos, the situation basically returned to where it had been. After the beginning of the reform and opening up in 1978, a major step to reform the fiscal and taxation system was to establish a multi-tier fiscal system of administrative decentralization, and, consequently, the revenue-sharing system (*fenzaochifan*)[1] and the all-round fiscal responsibility system (*caizheng dabaogan*) were kicked off in 1980 and 1988 respectively. However, this kind of administrative decentralization reform not only failed to establish a fiscal and taxation system compatible with a market economy but also intensified tensions within the existing fiscal and taxation system and reduced the budgetary revenue, especially the budgetary revenue of the central government, resulting in ever-enlarging government deficits. In 1993, the Third Plenary Session of the 14th Central Committee of the Communist Party of China (CCCPC) decided to carry out an overall reform of the fiscal and taxation system, which then successfully switched the fiscal and taxation system into a new track. Nevertheless, there are still many problems left over from the old fiscal system and to establish a sound public finance system compatible with a market economy is still a major task to be accomplished with great effort.

7.1 Government Finance in a Planned Economy

A characteristic of a planned economy is to organize the entire society into a giant enterprise ("immense social factory" or "State Syndicate"). By so doing, the differences between the public sector and the private sector are eliminated. As the head office of

---

[1] Literally, "eating from separate kitchens," *fenzaochifan* is a system of dividing revenue and expenditure between the central and local governments and holding each responsible for balancing its budget.

the State Syndicate, the government is responsible for supplying not only public goods but also private goods. Therefore, the leading characteristic of the fiscal and taxation system under a planned economy is the integration of public finance and business finance.

At the same time, under a planned economy, all powers for the supply of all goods are centralized in the hands of the government and are allocated only among different departments within the government. The public, as consumers of public goods and taxpayers, have neither the power to make decisions on the production of public goods nor the power to supervise the production of public goods. Since government finance under this model can neither effectively reveal the preference for public goods nor can it establish effective supervision and control over the government behavior in providing public goods, it is very unlikely to achieve effective supply of public goods.

After the founding of the PRC and the completion of the socialist transition, China established a fiscal and taxation system compatible with a planned economic system that underwent changes for many times afterwards. In February 1950, the national conference of government finance made the decision to "unify the financial and economic work of the nation" and established a fiscal system that strictly implemented unified control over revenues and expenditures. Except agricultural surtax in the amount of 5–15 percent of agricultural tax paid in grain and several small tax categories, all agricultural tax paid in grain and other tax revenues were controlled by the central government. Government expenditures were carried out according to the head count and the standard of provision stipulated by the central government. After the beginning of the First Five-Year Plan in 1953, a three-tier budgetary system of the central government, provincial governments, and county governments was established and the degree of centralization on budgetary management was slightly reduced. In 1954, a categorized sharing system of budgetary revenues was implemented, according to which the state budgetary revenues were categorized into fixed revenues, fixed-ratio shared revenues, and variable-ratio shared revenues. Fixed revenues of the central government included tariff, salt tax, revenue from monopolized sales of tobacco and alcohol, revenues of enterprises and public institutions under the central government and some other revenues; fixed revenues of local governments included seven kinds of local taxes (such as stamp tax), revenues of local state-owned enterprises and public institutions and some other revenues. Fixed-ratio shared revenues included agricultural/animal husbandry tax, industrial and commercial business tax, as well as industrial and commercial income tax. Variable-ratio shared revenues of the central government included commodity circulation tax and excise tax, which were used by the central government to cover the deficits of local governments and the ratios were decided by the Ministry of Finance on a yearly basis. Budgetary expenditures were divided according to administrative affiliation: expenditures of enterprises, public institutions, and administrative units under the central government were listed in the central government budget; expenditures of enterprises, public institutions, and administrative units under the local government were listed in the local government budget. During the period of the First Five-Year Plan, of the total national fiscal expenditure, the fiscal expenditure of the central government (including expenditures covered by revenues directly raised by the central government and revenues turned in by local governments) accounted for 74.1 percent of the national total, with only the remaining 25.9 percent for local governments. Key construction projects and main expenditures of the state were appropriated by the central government. The basic nature of the budgetary system of "three-tier management" was still centralization.

Henceforth, a highly centralized financial system was all the while maintained, apart from the period of "transferring administrative functions to lower levels" in 1958 when the systems of administrative decentralization such as "fixed shares for three years"[2] between the central and local governments, the all-round investment responsibility system, full profit retention in SOEs, and full loan financing for working capital, were tried.

For most of the period from 1953 to 1979, the fiscal and taxation system in China displayed the following three basic characteristics:

1. **Government finance and business finance were integrated into a unified national financial system.** Since a planned economy was a society-wide giant enterprise established on the basis of state ownership, the nature of its financial system was just as what was stated in *Dictionary of Economics and Management* in the mid-1980s: "Since the financial system of a socialist country is built on the basis of public ownership of the means of production and the national economy is under the unified leadership of the State, government finance includes relations of distribution not only outside the realm of production, but also inside the realm of production. Hence, a socialist public financial system consists of state budget, bank credit, and business finance."[3]

2. **The government used its power to raise the budgetary revenue, which mainly came from state-owned industry.** Under a planned economy, the government was able to use its power of pricing to set very low prices for primary products, such as grain and other raw materials, to transfer the surplus generated

---

[2] The policy of "fixed shares for three years" was conducted as follows: the local revenue was divided into three categories: fixed revenue, fixed-share revenue from enterprises, and variable-share revenue from commodity circulation tax, etc. Once the scopes of revenue and expenditure, revenue items and sharing ratios of the local finance were determined, they would not change for three years.

[3] Ma Hong and Sun Shangqing (eds.), *Dictionary of Economics and Management (Jingji yu guanli dacidian)*, Beijing: China Social Sciences Press, 1985, p. 422.

by nonstate sectors to state-owned industry and commerce and then to channel almost all the surplus of the national economy into the budget as profits and taxes of state-owned industry and commerce. Compared with other countries in the process of industrialization, the industrial sector in China had maintained very high profitability since the full establishment of the planned economic system in 1956. The situation gradually changed only after the commencement of the reform and opening up at the end of 1978. As such, from 1957 to 1980, profit remittance and tax payment from the industrial sector had always accounted for 50–66 percent of the government revenue.

3. **There were huge differences in financial burden across industries and enterprises in terms of profit remittance and tax payment.** As the whole country was a giant enterprise, the economic unit called "enterprise" was just a workshop or a working team of the State Syndicate and all surpluses, be they taxes or profits, belonged to the state from the very beginning. The reason why some surpluses had to be turned in to the taxation department in the form of taxes was that in the economic accounting of enterprises under the planned economic system, taxes slimmed down profits, and profits in turn slimmed down costs. Hence, in designing tax rates, the principle of "reasonable profit" was usually adopted. By using tax rates as a lever, the government left SOEs with a planned profit rate equal to a certain rate of social average profit rate.[4] Moreover, the government also made extensive use of the taxation policy to carry out its own agenda in industrial development by stipulating grossly different tax rates for different sectors and products. Therefore, under the planned economic system, the principle of equitable tax burden was not practiced; rather, a very complex tax rate structure with enormous difference was instituted. For instance, in 1980, the average rate of industrial and commercial tax was 18.9 percent for light industry (317 percent for the tobacco industry) but 4.6 percent for heavy industry. This resulted in the ratchet effect of "whipping the fast ox" and unfair competition among different industries and enterprises.

7.2 Fiscal and Taxation Reform from 1980 to 1993

From 1979 to 1993, the Chinese government adopted measures of "power-delegating and profit-sharing" in the state sector and instituted material incentives to "bring into

---

[4]Lev I. Maizenberg, *The Formation of Price in the USSR National Economy (Sulian guomin jingji zhong de jiage xingcheng)*, Chinese edition, Beijing: China Financial and Economic Publishing House, 1956.

play" the enthusiasm of local governments and enterprises. By doing so, both the relations between the central and local governments and the relations between the government and state-owned enterprises had changed.

7.2.1 Changes in the Financial Relations between the Central Government and Local Governments

After the end of the Great Culture Revolution in 1976, many issues neglected in the past demanded immediate attention. To fulfill promises made over the years to improve production and living conditions, many changes were introduced that increased expenditure and reduced revenue. The reform of "expanding enterprise autonomy," initiated at the end of 1970s, expanded enterprises' financial rights and increased salaries and bonuses, adding further difficulties to balancing state revenue and expenditure. As a result, there was a huge budget deficit in 1979, an enormous pressure on the central government finance. To bring into play the enthusiasm of local governments to increase revenue and reduce expenditure and to ensure the fiscal revenue of the central government, from 1980, the fiscal budgetary system of China was switched from the unitary system to the responsibility system, which not only offered incentives to local governments to increase revenue and reduce expenditure but also prevented the fiscal revenue of the central government from further declining.

7.2.1.1 The Revenue-Sharing System

In 1980, except in the three municipalities directly under the central government (namely, Beijing, Tianjin, and Shanghai) where "unified control over revenues and expenditures" was still practiced, a "revenue-sharing system" was introduced in all provinces and autonomous regions. Under this new fiscal administration system, revenue would be shared between the central and the local governments according to predefined formulae. In the twenty-six provinces and autonomous regions where the revenue-sharing system was practiced, four different formulae were adopted.

First, a formula of fixed-ratio fiscal responsibility was continually followed in Jiangsu Province. Jiangsu Province started with a fixed-ratio fiscal responsibility system in 1977. Under this system, the central government shared the revenue with the provincial government according to a ratio based on the historical ratios of provincial government fiscal expenditure to its revenue, and this ratio was supposed to be fixed for four years. In reality, this ratio was always adjusted each year through negotiations between the central and local governments. The ratio of revenue turned in to the central government to revenue retained by the provincial government was 58:42 in 1977, 57:43 from 1978 to 1980, and 61:39 in 1981.

Second, the system of "dividing revenue and expenditure, turning in a set quota or receiving a set subsidy," was implemented in Guangdong and Fujian provinces, which pioneered in the experiment of opening to the outside world. That was to set a fixed amount of turned-in or subsidy based on the final accounting of the revenue and expenditure of the two provinces in 1979, and once determined, this amount would remain fixed for five years. The fixed amount of turned-in for Guangdong Province was RMB 1 billion each year, while the fixed amount of subsidy for Fujian Province was RMB 1 billion. In the process of implementation, increased revenue and balance of expenditure were all retained for local use.

Third, in fifteen provinces, including Sichuan, Shaanxi, Gansu, Henan, Hubei, Hunan, Anhui, Jiangxi, Shandong, Shanxi, Hebei, Liaoning, Heilongjiang, Jilin, and Zhejiang, the system adopted was one of "dividing revenue and expenditure, taking different responsibilities according to different circumstances." The so-called "dividing revenue and expenditure" was to clearly divide the scope of revenue and expenditure between the central government and the local government according to administrative affiliation. In terms of revenues, revenue from enterprises under the central government and revenue from tariffs belonged to the central government finance as its fixed revenue; revenue from local enterprises, salt tax, agricultural/animal husbandry tax, industrial and commercial income tax, local taxes, and other local revenues belonged to the local government finance as its fixed revenues. Industrial and commercial tax was designated as variable-ratio shared revenues of the central and local governments. In terms of expenditure, the central government took responsibility for the following: working capital, capital for technological upgrading, and new product development expenses of enterprises under the central government; geological prospecting expenses; expenditures for national defense and preparation against war; aid to foreign countries; expenditure for material reserves; operating expenses for cultural, educational, medical, and scientific institutions; operating expenses for agricultural, forestry, water conservancy, and meteorological institutions; operating expenses for industry, transportation, and commerce departments; and administrative expenses at the central government level. The following were classified as local government expenditure: locally planned capital construction investment; working capital, capital for technological upgrading, and new product development expenses of enterprises under the local government; expenditure for supporting rural people's communes and operating expenses for agricultural, forestry, water conservancy, and meteorological institutions; operating expenses for industry, transportation, and commerce departments; urban maintenance expenses; outlay of urban population relocating to the countryside; operating expenses for cultural, educational, medical, and scientific institutions; pension and social relief expenses; and administrative expenses. Some special expenditures, such as relief expenses for serious natural calamities and development funds for supporting underdeveloped regions, would be allocated by the central government. The so-called "taking different responsibilities according to different circumstances" referred to the following: based on the predefined scope of revenue and expenditure and the budgeted revenue and expenditure of 1979, provinces with revenue exceeding expenditure would need to submit a fixed percentage of the surplus to the central government; provinces with revenue falling short of expenditure would receive a subsidy from the central government to be financed by a certain proportion of industrial and commercial tax; and provinces with revenue smaller than expenditure even though the central government gave up the entirety of industrial and commercial tax would receive additional central government subsidy in a fixed amount. The sharing ratios and the amounts of subsidy would remain unchanged for five years once determined. During the five years of practicing the fiscal responsibility system, the local governments that had more revenue could spend more and vice versa, and the local governments should independently arrange their own budget and seek balance between revenue and expenditure.

Fourth, in the five autonomous regions, including Inner Mongolia, Xinjiang, Tibet, Ningxia, and Guangxi, and the three provinces with more minority nationalities, namely, Yunnan, Qinghai, and Guizhou, the fiscal system pertaining to national autonomous areas remained unchanged. The existing special treatment to national autonomous areas was still maintained, with improvement in two aspects: first, the concept of fiscal responsibility was to be adopted in these areas as well, with reference to the third system specified in defining the scope of revenue and expenditure and determining the amount of central government subsidy, which should remain unchanged for five years rather than one year; second, the portion of local revenue growth would all be retained by the local government and the amount of subsidy by the central government to national autonomous areas would be progressively increased by 10 percent every year.

When the "revenue-sharing system" was introduced in 1980, decision makers regarded it as a transitional fiscal system for only five years, and planned to switch to the division of fiscal revenue between the central and local governments according to tax categories and redefine the scope of fiscal revenue and expenditure of government finance at various levels in 1985. However, after this system was instituted, other institutional changes had to take into consideration this established "revenue-sharing system" and end in minor adjustments within the framework of administrative decentralization. In 1986, when contemplating coordinated reform in price, taxation, government finance, banking, and foreign trade systems, the State Council intended to replace the "revenue-sharing system" with the "tax-sharing system." However, with the miscarriage of coordinated reform, not only was the revenue-sharing system not abolished, but it was solidified into a formal system—the all-round fiscal responsibility system in 1988.

7.2.1.2 The All-Round Fiscal Responsibility System

The "all-round fiscal responsibility system" introduced in 1988 was the continuation and development of the revenue-sharing system of 1980. It covered the country's thirty-seven provinces, municipalities, autonomous regions, as well as "cities specifically designated in the state plan" by six types of methods.

The first type was "responsibility for progressive increase in revenue" adopted by Beijing, Hebei, Liaoning, Zhejiang, Henan, and Chongqing. Specifically, the year-on-year increase of local revenue and the sharing ratio with the central government were determined on the basis of the actual revenue of 1987, the reasonable level of expenditure, and the growth rate in recent years. When the realized revenue fell within the range of the predetermined growth rate, it would be shared by the central government and the local government according to the predetermined sharing ratio. When the realized revenue exceeded the predetermined growth rate, the extra part of the revenue would be completely retained by the local government. When the realized revenue fell short of the predetermined growth rate, the local government would have to make up the gap with its own financial resources.

The second type was "total sharing" adopted by Shanxi, Anhui, and Tianjin. Specifically, this involved a verification of base amounts of revenue and expenditure according to actual records of revenue and expenditure of the previous two years and determination of a sharing ratio based on the ratio of actual local government expenditure to its total revenue.

The third type was "total sharing plus growth sharing," which was formulated by adding a component of growth sharing to the second type of method. Specifically, the revenue of any given year would be split into two parts. The first was the base amount, which would be shared according to total sharing ratio; the second was the incremental portion, which would be shared according to another sharing ratio, namely, the "growth sharing ratio." This method was implemented in three regions and their total sharing ratio and growth sharing ratio were respectively as follows: Dalian 27.74 percent and 27.26 percent; Qingdao 16 percent and 34 percent; and Wuhan 17 percent and 25 percent.

The fourth type was "responsibility for progressive increase in turned-in." This method was adopted by Guangdong and Hunan provinces. Specifically, taking the turned-in revenue of 1987 to the central government as the base, a progressively increasing amount would be turned in according to a certain growth rate.

The fifth type was "set quota for turned-in." This method was adopted by Shandong, Heilongjiang, and Shanghai. Specifically, based on the originally verified revenue and expenditure bases, a fixed amount for turning in would be collected from the difference between the base amounts of revenue and the expenditure. The amounts for turning in of the three regions were determined as follows: Shanghai RMB 10.5 billion; Shandong (excluding Qingdao City) RMB 289 million; and Heilongjiang (excluding Harbin City) RMB 299 million.

The sixth type was "set quota for subsidy." This method was practiced in Jilin, Jiangxi, Fujian, Shaanxi, Hainan, Inner Mongolia, Guangxi, Guizhou, Yunnan, Tibet, Qinghai, Ningxia, Xinjiang, Hubei and other provinces. Specifically, based on the originally verified revenue and expenditure bases, a fixed amount of subsidy would be granted to cover the difference between the expenditure base and the revenue base.

7.2.2 Changes in the Financial Relations between the Government and Enterprises

From 1979 to 1993, according to the requirements to "delegate power to and share profit with enterprises," the financial relations between the government and state-owned enterprises (SOEs) were adjusted, and the past practice of turning in all profits and taxes to the government finance and total fiscal allocation of all investments was replaced by the method of the "fiscal responsibility system" in various forms.

a. Since the end of 1978, the enterprise fund system, various forms of profit retention system, and system of responsibility for one's own profits and losses had subsequently been tried out in SOEs. With the exception of the three experimental units including the Capital Iron and Steel Corporation that had carried out the "system of responsibility for one's own profits and losses," the profit retention system was introduced in most of the other industrial and transportation SOEs, 6,600 of them by the early 1980s. Statistics showed that profits retained by industrial and transportation enterprises between 1978 and 1982 amounted to RMB 42 billion, certainly a considerable amount.[5]

b. From 1984 to 1986, a reform of "substituting tax payment for profit delivery" ("tax for profit" in short) was carried out in all enterprises in two steps, wherein most profits of SOEs were turned in to the state finance in the form of enterprise income tax.

The experiment of "tax for profit" was first conducted in fifteen industrial SOEs run by Guanghua County, Hubei Province in early 1979. Starting in January 1980, the

---

[5] Zhou Taihe et al., *Economic System Reform in Contemporary China (Dangdai Zhongguo de jingji tizhi gaige)*, Beijing: China Social Sciences Press, 1984, p. 457.

experiment was expanded to SOEs in Shanghai, Sichuan, Guangxi, Beijing, Guangdong, and Heilongjiang.

In April 1983, the State Council transmitted with endorsement the *Method on Trial Implementation of Substituting Tax Payment for Profit Delivery in SOEs* (the *Method* hereinafter) formulated by the Ministry of Finance, which was the first step of "tax for profit" reform. The key measure introduced by the *Method* was to increase the proportion of enterprise income tax in the pretax profit of SOEs while reducing the proportion of profit turned-in so as to achieve a coexistence of tax payment and profit remittance. The *Method* stipulated that large- and medium-sized SOEs would pay their income tax at a uniform rate of 55 percent and small SOEs at an eight-level progressive rate from 7 percent to 55 percent. In addition, due to considerable differences in the price environment of various enterprises, large- and medium-sized SOEs were also required to pay "regulation tax"—one rate for each enterprise according to their profits—to avoid unfair treatment in profit retention. Industrial and commercial income tax for collective and private enterprises was to apply an eight-level progressive rate from 10 percent to 55 percent. The statutory rate of income tax for foreign-invested enterprises was 33 percent; the rate was 15 percent for enterprises in special economic zones in addition to the privilege of "exemption from income tax in the first two years and reduction of income tax by half in the next three years." During the first step of the "tax for profit" reform, a total of 107,145 industrial, transportation, and commercial enterprises were involved, of which 28,110 were industrial enterprises, 2,236 transportation enterprises, and 76,799 commercial enterprises.[6]

In September 1984, the State Council transmitted with endorsement the *Report on Introduction of the Second Step Reform of Substituting Tax Payment for Profit Delivery in SOEs* and the *Measures of Trial Implementation of the Second Step Substituting Tax Payment for Profit Delivery in SOEs* formulated by the Ministry of Finance, and decided to implement the second step of "tax for profit" reform on October 1 of the same year. The key measures of the second step reform included a division of the income to be turned in to the state finance by SOEs into eleven tax categories and a gradual switch from the coexistence of tax payment and profit remittance to complete substitution of tax payment for profit delivery, with after-tax profits retained by enterprises. Specifically, the existing industrial and commercial tax was split into product tax, value-added tax, business tax, and salt tax; resource tax was imposed on certain mining enterprises; four categories of local taxes, namely real estate tax, land use tax, vehicle and vessel tax, and urban maintenance and construction tax, were restored or created; income tax was collected from profitable SOEs; and regulation tax was levied on large SOEs.

---

[6] Shen Jueren (ed.), *China's Economy: The Whole Stories of Important Decisions (Zhongguo jingji: Zhongda juece shimo)*, Nanjing: Jiangsu People's Publishing House, 1999, p. 537.

c. In 1987, the enterprise contracting system of "fixing the base quota, guaranteeing the remittance, retaining what exceeds the quota, and making up what falls short of the quota" was introduced into SOEs on a full scale. Although it was prohibited time and again by the central government by means of document dispatch, the common practice in various localities was that all taxes payable by the enterprise, including turnover tax and enterprise income tax, were all included in the fixed base quota; whenever the enterprise incurred a loss, government tax revenue would be affected. In this case, it was easy for enterprises to "retain what exceeds the quota" but difficult for them to "make up what falls short of the quota." Hence, "being responsible for profits but not losses" became a common practice. Statistics showed that during the period from 1987 to 1991, total unpaid taxes of contracted enterprises amounted to over RMB 5.1 billion, of which only 37 percent, or RMB 1.9 billion, was made up by enterprises themselves, while the remaining RMB 3.2 billion became the loss in government budget.[7]

7.2.3 Institutional Defects of the Fiscal Responsibility System

Although there were differences between the "revenue-sharing system" and the "all-round fiscal responsibility system," they were nevertheless both variants of the fiscal responsibility system. It was originally intended that implementation of the "revenue-sharing system" and the "all-round fiscal responsibility system" was to define the rights and responsibilities of the various levels of fiscal units and to give play to the "two enthusiasms" of the central and local governments while ensuring stability of the budgetary revenue of the central government. The implementation of this system had indeed prompted local governments at all levels to make great efforts in increasing production and revenue in the short term, but from the long-term point of view, its negative effects on effective resource allocation and market system establishment far outweighed its positive ones.

For one thing, it resulted in "unfair treatment" and "whipping the fast ox" among various regions. Under the fiscal responsibility system, the key parameters were the sharing ratios of various regions, which were determined through one-to-one bargaining between the central government and the local government in question on the basis of historical data. Because of this, all kinds of unfair circumstances would inevitably occur. Regions with historically low levels of economic development and designated as pilot units during the reform and opening up would benefit more from this system arrangement due to their low base and fast growth of revenue. In contrast, the traditional industrial bases had more financial difficulties, as they had had a higher original base of

---

[7] Naved Hamid and Pradumna B. Rana (eds.), *From Centrally Planned to Market Economies: The Asian Approach,* Vol. 2, Hong Kong: Oxford University Press, 1996, p. 123.

revenue, slower development and heavier burden of remittance since the reform and opening up. For instance, in the mid-1980s, the GDP of Guangdong Province was already close to that of Shanghai; Shanghai's annual revenue turned in to the central government was about RMB 12 billion while the quota to be turned in by Guangdong was about RMB 1 billion only. Consequently, the fiscal responsibility system became a "rent-seeking" system, encouraging people to seek benefits not from reform of government public service, but from making use of the public authorities to engage in "rent seeking."

What was more important, it intensified the drive to market segregation and hindered formation of a unified market. Based on administrative affiliation, the "revenue-sharing system" and the "all-round fiscal responsibility system" designated the profits and enterprise income tax of an SOE as fixed revenue of the government to which the enterprise was affiliated. To increase revenue, local governments at all levels employed all available means to expand the scale of capital construction and set up local SOEs by government investment on the one hand; while on the other, they widely exploited such measures as regional trade barriers, discrimination in taxes and fees, subsidy in disguised form so as to protect their "own" enterprises from external competition, resulting in widespread local protectionism across the country. Besides, different tax rates for enterprises of different localities and different ownerships breached the principle of equitable tax burden.

The fiscal responsibility system was criticized by many economists. Notwithstanding, there was another view, believing that although administrative decentralization was not the end of reform, it was nevertheless a step forward toward the direction of decentralization after all; moreover, as government officials at all levels gained benefits in the process of decentralization, it significantly reduced the resistance to reform. Indeed, in the short term, administrative decentralization has multiple benefits. However, when merits and demerits are weighted in a long-term framework, the "path dependence" nature of institutional transformation must be taken into consideration, and it should be noted that each step of reform should not become the obstacle for further reform. In fact, even though by bringing about benefits to local government officials, the fiscal responsibility system indeed reduced resistance and added momentum to reform, it nonetheless fostered the "vassal economy" of local protectionism, market segregation and tendencies of the market "dicing, stripping, slivering and mincing,"[8] moreover, on this basis, pressure groups backed by vested interests emerged, thereby obstructing advance of market-oriented reform such as the tax-sharing system.

---

[8]For the earliest criticism at market "dicing, stripping, slivering and mincing" in the process of reform in China, see Wu Jinglian and Liu Jirui, *On Competitive Market System (Lun jingzhengxing shichang tizhi),* Beijing: China Financial and Economic Publishing House, 1991, pp. 160–171.

It had also been pointed out by the British economist Max Boisot[9] and the British journal *Economist*[10] that the Chinese fiscal and taxation responsibility system was similar to the "tax farming" system of France in the eighteenth century. It could result in check posts everywhere along the road, obstructing business and travel and hindering establishment of a domestic market and development of a market economy. There were also economists who quoted the "likin disaster" suffered by regions south of the Yangtze River in China from the 1850s to 1920s, explaining the harm that a wrong fiscal and taxation system might have to the establishment of a domestic market.[11]

Parallel to the strategy of "administrative decentralization," the fiscal and taxation system stressed "bringing into play the local enthusiasm." On the one hand, it still retained the very rigid fundamental features of the old system, while on the other, it also incurred some new problems because of administrative decentralization. Obviously, this kind of fiscal system failed to meet the requirements of the more and more market-oriented economy and displayed several serious drawbacks.

7.2.3.1 Unstable Fiscal Revenue Base Made State Financial Resources Insufficient for the Government to Fulfill Its Social Duties

As mentioned, the main feature of the traditional fiscal and taxation system was that the state achieved its fiscal revenue in the form of taxes and profits turned in by state-owned industrial and commercial enterprises by taking advantage of the central government's pricing power and the monopolistic position of SOEs. After over a decade of reform, dramatic changes had taken place in China's economic structure. Many nonstate enterprises joined the competition, which drove down the profitability of SOEs. At the same time, the reform of power delegating and profit sharing enabled local governments and enterprises to try all means to turn in less tax and keep more revenue. What was worse, the management of tax collection was ineffective and local governments often reduced taxes on their enterprises or exempted their enterprises from paying taxes beyond their authority. Consequently, the share of fiscal revenue in the national economy was decreasing every year (see Table 7.1), while it still had to fund most of the existing activities. The resulting deficit increased so dramatically that the government could not even sustain its basic social services.

---

[9] Max Boisot, "Management and Organization of the State Sector in China," *World Bank paper in mimeograph*, August 1987.
[10] *Economist*, August 1, 1987, Vol. 304, Issue 7509.
[11] See Wu Jinglian and Liu Jirui, ibid., pp. 96–97. "Likin" was a miscellaneous tax on commodities independently collected by local governments starting in 1853 in order to raise funds for local militia as permitted by the Qing government. From South Jiangsu to the whole country, every region subsequently established likin offices and likin check posts and likin was repeatedly collected at the places of production, transit, and marketing. The "likin" system dealt a serious blow to the development of the newly emerging industry and commerce, and it was therefore termed the "likin disaster."

Table 7.1 Fiscal Revenue, Expenditure, and Deficit as Percentages of GDP (%)

Year	Fiscal Revenue	Fiscal Expenditure	Fiscal Deficit
1978	34.8	34.5	−0.3
1981	27.3	29.4	2.1
1986	25.2	27.4	2.2
1991	18.4	21.8	3.3
1992	14.2	17.7	3.4

Source: Christopher J. Heady, Wing Thye Woo, and Christine P. Wong, *Fiscal Management and Economic Reform in the People's Republic of China,* Hong Kong: Oxford University Press, 1995. See Chinese edition, Beijing: China Financial and Economic Publishing House, 1993, p. 12.

7.2.3.2 Rapid Decrease of the Budgetary Revenue of the Central Government

The fiscal responsibility system expanded the power of local governments to control their fiscal revenue without corresponding constraint mechanism, encouraging local fiscal institutions to act in local interests. At the same time, the budgetary revenue of the central government had only seen a short period of stability after the implementation of the revenue-sharing system in 1980, and began to decrease in 1986 (see Table 7.2). In the early 1990s, approximately half of the expenditure of the central government had to be financed by borrowing from banks.

7.2.3.3 Slackening Fiscal Discipline and Chaotic Fiscal System

The government shifted the burden of some expenditure items, including part of the expenses of administrative organs and the costs of primary education that should have been covered by the government finance, to the units concerned, forcing them to fund themselves by "raising funds" and "creating extra income." As a result, the scale of "extra-budgetary" revenue and expenditure continually expanded and "private coffers" proliferated through imposition of various kinds of charges and quotas in a multitude of names, which encouraged the unhealthy tendency to "marketize" public welfare under-takings, such as arbitrary charges in disguised forms for compulsory education, public health service, and other public services. Together with rampant corruptive practices like rent-setting and rent-seeking by government departments and making deals between power and money, all these aroused discontent of the society.

Under this context, the Third Plenary Session of the 14th CCCPC was held in November 1993, which decided to start an all-round reform of the fiscal and taxation system.

**Table 7.2   Central Fiscal Revenue as Percentages of
Total Fiscal Revenue and GDP (%)**

Year	As Percentage of Total Fiscal Revenue	As Percentage of GDP
1978	15.52	4.85
1979	20.18	5.73
1980	24.52	6.30
1981	26.46	6.40
1982	28.61	6.55
1983	35.85	8.26
1984	40.51	9.28
1985	38.39	8.59
1986	36.68	7.63
1987	33.48	6.15
1988	32.87	5.19
1989	30.86	4.86
1990	33.79	5.35
1991	29.79	4.34
1992	28.12	3.68

Source: The National Bureau of Statistics, *China Statistical Yearbook (Zhongguo tongji nianjian),* Beijing: China Statistics Press, various years.

7.3 All-Round Reform of the Fiscal and Taxation System in 1994

7.3.1 Main Requirements of the Third Plenary Session of the 14th CCCPC for Fiscal and Taxation System Reform

In November 1993, the *Decision on Issues Regarding the Establishment of a Socialist Market Economic System* laid down two key measures of the fiscal and taxation system reform of 1994.

The first measure was to replace the fiscal responsibility system with a tax-sharing system based on a reasonable division of authority between the central and local governments and establish mutually independent tax collection systems for the central and local governments. Taxes necessary for safeguarding the national rights and interests and implementing macro-control were categorized as central taxes while those directly related to economic development were shared between the central and local governments.

Categories of local taxes were augmented to increase local tax revenue. The proportion of fiscal revenue in GNP would be raised gradually through developing the economy, improving efficiency, and tapping new sources of revenue and the ratio of central fiscal revenue to local fiscal revenue would be set at a more reasonable level. The system of revenue return and transfer payment from the central to the local would be established to adjust income distribution across regions and, particularly, to aid the development of underdeveloped regions and the rejuvenation of old industrial bases.

The second measure was to reform and improve the taxation system according to the principle of unified tax law, equitable tax burden, simplified tax structure, and fair division of power. A system of turnover tax would be instituted with value-added tax (VAT) being the principal part. Consumption tax would be levied on a few commodities, and business tax would continue to be levied on most non-commodity operations. Income tax rate for SOEs would be lowered and state key energy and transportation projects fund and state budget regulation fund would be eliminated. Enterprises would pay taxes as required by law and the profit distribution between the state and SOEs would be straightened out. At the same time, enterprise income tax and personal income tax would be unified, the tax rates would be normalized and the tax base would be broadened. Some new taxes would be imposed, some old ones would be adjusted, cases of tax reduction and exemption would be reviewed, and tax collection management would be tightened up to close tax loopholes. The multiple budget system would be improved and normalized, and the government public budget and the state assets operation budget would be established. If necessary, social security budget and other budgets would be created. Fiscal deficit would be under strict control. The fiscal deficit of the central government would be solved through issuance of long-term and short-term government bonds instead of overdrawing at banks.

7.3.2 The Tax-Sharing System for Fiscal Budget

In the mid-1980s, the Chinese government once considered replacing the "fiscal responsibility system" with a "tax-sharing system" during the period of the Seventh Five-Year Plan (1986–1990), but the idea was aborted later on. In 1992, the experiment with the tax-sharing system reform was restored. According to the *Decision on Issues Regarding the Establishment of a Socialist Market Economic System* adopted at the Third Plenary Session of the 14th CCCPC, starting on January 1, 1994, the tax-sharing system would be implemented nationwide. The following are the four main contents of the system.

1. On the basis of separating the functions of the government from those of the enterprise, define functions of governments at provincial, county (county-level city),

and township (town) levels and divide authority among governments at different levels according to their functions.

2. According to the principle of matching authority with financial power, define the scopes of expenditure of governments at different levels according to their authority. The central government finance would mainly assume outlays necessary for state security, foreign affairs and operation of the central government organs and expenditure necessary for adjusting the structure of the national economy, coordinating regional development and implementing macro-control as well as expenditure for the development of undertakings under direct control of the central government. The rest would be in the scope of local government expenditure.

3. According to the nature of benefits and the principle of effective collection and management, divide tax revenue according to different tax categories. Taxes pertaining to safeguarding the national rights and interests and implementing macro-control would be categorized as central taxes; taxes linked closely to local economic and social development, scattered in sources, and suitable for local collection and management would be categorized as local taxes; principal taxes with stable revenue and large amount would be categorized as central-local shared taxes. The proportion of central fiscal revenue should be increased to about 60 percent in total fiscal revenue, while the proportion of central fiscal expenditure would be kept at about 40 percent in total fiscal expenditure.

4. Establish a system of formula-based transfers step by step and transfer part of central fiscal resources, which equals to about 20 percent of total fiscal revenue, to local governments with lower levels of revenue so as to gradually reduce the difference in the level of government services across regions.

Fixed revenue of the central budget includes: customs duties, consumption tax and VAT per the customs, consumption tax, income tax of enterprises under the central government, income tax of local banks, foreign-invested banks and nonbank financial institutions, revenue collectively turned in by the railway department, headquarters of various banks and head offices of various insurance companies (including business tax, income tax, profits, and urban maintenance and construction tax), as well as profits turned in by enterprises under the central government. With regard to export tax rebates for foreign-trade enterprises, except the 20 percent assumed by local governments in 1993 that was listed in the base to be turned in by local governments to the central government, all subsequent export tax rebates would all be assumed by the central finance.

Fixed revenue for local government budget includes: business tax (excluding business tax collectively turned in by the railway department, headquarters of various banks, and head offices of various insurance companies), income tax of local enterprises (excluding income tax of the aforementioned local banks, foreign-invested banks, and nonbank financial institutions), profits turned in by local enterprises, urban land use tax, personal income tax, fixed asset investment regulation tax, urban maintenance and construction tax (excluding the portion collectively paid by the railway department, headquarters of various banks, and head offices of various insurance companies), real estate tax, vehicle and vessel tax, stamp tax, slaughter tax, agricultural/animal husbandry tax, agricultural specialties tax, farmland use tax, deed tax, estate and gift tax, land appreciation tax, as well as revenue of paid state land leasing.

Central-local shared revenues are VAT and resource tax. For VAT, the central government would share 75 percent while local governments would take the remaining 25 percent. Resource tax would be classified according to different resource varieties: land resource tax would go to local government revenue while offshore petroleum resource tax would go to central government revenue. Securities exchange stamp tax would be shared equally between the central government and the local governments.[12]

7.3.3 Basic Requirements of the Taxation System Reform

Basic requirements of the taxation system reform were: normalizing the taxation system according to the principle of unified tax law, equitable tax burden, simplified tax structure and fair division of power; establishing a taxation system compatible with a market economy; straightening out distribution and promoting fair competition. The main points are as follows.

7.3.3.1 Implement a New System of Turnover Tax (Indirect Tax) with VAT Being the Principal Part

Turnover tax after the reform consisted of VAT, consumption tax, and business tax, uniformly applicable to domestic-invested and foreign-invested enterprises. After calculation, according to the principle of "neither too much nor too less," the normal VAT rate was set at 17 percent of the added value, with a preferential rate at 14 percent.

---

[12]In 2002, the ratio for sharing securities exchange stamp tax between the central and local governments changed to 97:3.

7.3.3.2 Unify Income Tax for Domestic-Invested Enterprises

Simplify and unify the income tax rate for enterprises of different ownership. A unified enterprise income tax would apply to all Chinese enterprises, including SOEs, collective enterprises, private enterprises, as well as corporations and other forms of joint ownership enterprises.

7.3.3.3 Unify Personal Income Tax

The focus of the 1994 reform was to consolidate the existing personal income tax, personal income regulation tax, as well as income tax of urban and rural individual business owners to establish a unified personal income tax. A progressive rate would be adopted for personal income tax.

7.3.3.4 Tighten Up Tax Collection and Management

Establish two tax collection systems, namely the State Administration of Taxation and local taxation bureaus. Central taxes and central-local shared taxes would be collected by the State Administration of Taxation, while the local taxes would be collected by the local taxation bureaus. Along with the work to tighten up tax collection and management, arbitrary imposition of charges and quotas and "extra-budgetary revenue" of governments at all levels would be straightened out and the retained items would be brought under the control of the approved budget revenue.

Although the 1994 reform involved enormous adjustment of interest relations, especially those between different regions, it proceeded fairly successfully on the whole. Through this reform, the fundamental framework of a fiscal and taxation system compatible with a market economy was established. In a sense, the 1994 reform was the institutional innovation with the most significant adjustment in the pattern of interests and the most far-reaching impact since the founding of the PRC. The reform of the tax-sharing fiscal system was proposed mainly in response to the shortcomings of the fiscal responsibility system. In addition to aiming at overcoming many of the defects of the fiscal responsibility system, its design also drew on the international successful experience with tax-sharing fiscal systems. Compared with all the previous reforms, the 1994 reform was not only committed to the adjustment of the structure of intergovernmental fiscal distribution, but also stressed on normalized, scientific, and impartial relations of intergovernmental fiscal distribution. It strove to establish a fiscal operation mechanism compatible with the inherent requirements of a market economy.

The fiscal operation after the reform proved that it was a successful one with very positive effects. First, the tax-sharing system changed the structure of the original fiscal responsibility system where multiple systems coexisted. It normalized the intergovernmental fiscal distribution relations and established a restraint mechanism wherein governments at all levels performed their own functions, carried out their own duties, and gained their own benefits as well as an attachment mechanism wherein benefits and expenses were shared between upper-level and lower-level governments. In addition, it rationalized the relations of authorities and responsibilities among governments at all levels. Second, fiscal transfer payment by the central government was strengthened considerably and formed a reasonable vertical distribution mechanism of financial resource. The promulgation of the *Method for Fiscal Transfer Payment during the Transition Period* initially established a normalized horizontal equalization mechanism of financial resource, which was favorable to the gradual narrowing of the gap in the level of government services across regions. Third, the tax-sharing fiscal system effectively facilitated the adjustment of industrial structure and the optimization of resource allocation, strengthened budget constraint to local government finance, and promoted reasonable economic behaviors of local governments. By earmarking for the central government most of VAT from industrial products and all consumption tax, the tax-sharing system, to a great extent, limited local protectionism and market fragmentation; whereas, by earmarking for the local government tax categories from the tertiary industry and agriculture-related tax categories, the tax-sharing system stimulated enthusiasm of the local government to develop the tertiary industry as well as farming, forestry, animal husbandry, and fishery. After the downward coasting in 1995, the proportion of fiscal revenue in GDP began to climb up in 1996, rising year after year, while the proportion of fiscal deficit in GDP began to decline in 1996.

After the East Asian financial crisis in 1998, China implemented a proactive fiscal policy dominated by bonds issuance to finance increased expenditure. Therefore, starting in 1998, deficit and the proportion of deficit in GDP increased rapidly (see Table 7.3).

7.4 Reform of the Fiscal and Taxation System after 1994

Even though the fiscal and taxation system in China switched to a new track in 1994, it nevertheless had a number of serious drawbacks and a few aspects unfit for the market economic system. The continuous improvement of the fiscal and taxation system in China on the basis of the 1994 reform was mainly in the following aspects: (a) straightening out and normalizing the "extra-budgetary revenue," (b) further improving the tax-sharing system, and (c) establishing the framework of public finance.

Table 7.3   Fiscal Revenue and Deficit as Percentages of GDP

Year	Fiscal Revenue (RMB Billion)	Fiscal Expenditure (RMB Billion)	Balance of Revenue and Expenditure (RMB Billion)	GDP (RMB Billion)	Fiscal Revenue as Percentage of GDP (%)	Balance of Revenue and Expenditure as Percentage of GDP (%)
1995	624.220	682.372	−58.152	5,847.81	10.7	0.99
1996	740.799	793.755	−52.956	6,788.46	10.9	0.78
1997	865.114	923.356	−58.242	7,446.26	11.6	0.78
1998	987.595	1,079.818	−92.223	7,834.52	12.6	1.18
1999	1,144.408	1,318.767	−174.359	8,206.75	13.9	2.12
2000	1,339.523	1,588.650	−249.127	8,940.36	15.0	2.79
2001	1,638.604	1,890.258	−251.654	9,593.33	17.1	2.62

Note: Starting in 2000, fiscal expenditure includes domestic and overseas debt payment of interest expense.
Source: The National Bureau of Statistics, *China Statistical Yearbook (Zhongguo tongji nianjian) 2002*, Beijing: China Statistics Press, 2002.

7.4.1 Straightening Out "Extra-Budgetary Revenue"

Governments at all levels in China had the so-called "extra-budgetary revenue." During the early period after the founding of the PRC when a highly centralized system of unified control over revenues and expenditures was implemented, extra-budgetary revenue was limited only to agricultural surtax and production revenue of institutional units. In 1957, extra-budgetary revenue was equivalent to 8.5 percent of budgetary revenue. During the Great Leap Forward, the scope of extra-budgetary funds began to expand as a result of the economic system reform and transfer of fiscal authority to lower levels. After the commencement of the reform and opening up, budgetary revenue was declining, but extra-budgetary revenue of governments at all levels saw a big increase each year for the following three reasons.

1. In the process of the reform, fiscal revenue was decreasing while government functions remained more or less the same and government institutions and staff were even expanding. To support government administration, new sources of revenue were created outside of the budget—collecting charges to make up insufficient tax revenue. For instance, the central government began to collect fees for "state key energy and transportation projects fund" in 1980; in 1989, fees were

also collected for "state budget regulation fund." There were more cases of local governments obtaining extra-budgetary revenues to finance expenditures.

2. After the implementation of the "revenue-sharing system" and transfer of fiscal authority to lower levels, local governments at all levels began to enjoy more and more power to control the local economy. Consequently, some administrative organs began to concoct various pretexts to extort excessive fees.

3. In the marketization process, for quasi-public goods where service cost and beneficiaries could easily be identified, such as highway facilities, the method of paid supply should be adopted as much as possible in the first place; and yet, with the unsound rule of law and the integration of government administration with enterprise management, this kind of charges were subject to neither market constraint nor administrative regulation. This provided administrative organs or quasi-administrative organs with a motive to expand their own revenue to concoct various pretexts for high charges.

As of the early 1990s, creating extra-budgetary revenue had become a common phenomenon from the central government to local governments. By the end of 1996, there were more than 130 items of charges expressively stipulated by the central government and 46 items of construction fees, surcharges, and funds approved by the central government; after aggravating at every lower level of local governments and competent departments, according to incomplete county and county-level city statistics, there were over 1,000 various items of charges and over 420 various kinds of funds. An investigation by the Office on Alleviation of Enterprise Burden of the State Council in 1997 revealed that all sorts of unreasonable burdens on industrial SOEs amounted to RMB 50–60 billion or so, accounting for 20 percent of their achieved profits and taxes and exceeding the total of their achieved profits of the same year.[13] According to the result of a straightening-out registration and level-upon-level tabulation of various kinds of funds nationwide, the national total of fund revenues in 1995 amounted to RMB 203.4 billion, equivalent to 32.6 percent of the fiscal revenue of the same year. An investigation on extra-budgetary funds by the Ministry of Finance in 1996 showed that at the end of 1995, the national total of extra-budgetary funds collected with approval from governments at the provincial level and above was RMB 384.3 billion, equivalent to 61.6 percent of the fiscal revenue of the same year. Even after several rounds of clean-

---

[13] Yang Zhigang, "Fund Analysis of the Chinese Government (Zhongguo zhengfu zijin fenxi)," *Comparison of Economic and Social Systems (Jingji shehui tizhi bijiao),* 1998, No. 5.

up by competent state departments, there were still 344 items of departmental charges/ administrative and institutional charges and 421 departmental funds in 1997 at the central level.[14] Items of charges at the provincial level and below were even more numerous. For instance, in a county-level city in Zhejiang Province, there were over 1,000 items of charges in 1995. A prefecture-level city had approximately 4,000 items of charges.[15] According to estimates by some financial experts, in 1997, the national total of extra-budgetary charges by governments at all levels was RMB 750–1,200 billion, equivalent to 1–1.5 times of the fiscal revenue of the same year.[16]

The expansion of extra-budgetary revenue of the government resulted in a series of evil consequences such as widespread corruption and waste by government institutions and officials, unbearable heavy burdens on enterprises and residents, which aroused strong public discontent. In 1998, Zhu Rongji, then the new premier, declared to implement the "transformation of administrative fees into taxes," in an attempt to straighten out items of extra-budgetary revenue. The straightening-out scheme included five items. First, to conduct a thorough clean up of all types of existing charges and to resolutely abolish obviously unreasonable items of charges with unfavorable public reactions. According to an analysis, items of charges already abolished or about to be abolished could well exceed ¼ of the items of charges at that time. Second, to conduct the "transformation of administrative fees into taxes" for most items of charges that were necessary to be retained. On the whole, the scope of transformation into taxes included items that payers could not directly benefit from as well as items of construction charges. Third, to distinguish charges for public welfare from administrative and institutional charges. Charges by public welfare undertakings such as schools and hospitals should be strictly straightened out; items that ought to be abolished must be abolished; items necessary to retain should be disconnected from administrative organs; responsibilities should be clarified among the government, public welfare units and the public; items of charge should be strictly defined. Moreover, market mechanism could be introduced

---

[14] *China Financial and Economic News (Zhongguo caijing bao)*, April 29, 1998.

[15] Jia Kang, "Basic Thinking on Tax and Fee Reform: Separation and Consolidation (Shuifei gaige de jiben silu: fenliu guiwei)," *Reform (Gaige)*, 1998, No. 4.

[16] According to the estimate by Jia Kang and Zhao Quanhou, fiscal revenue (total budgetary revenue) in 1996 was RMB 740.499 billion; after deducting extra-budgetary funds of the "state-owned enterprise and competent departments," government budgetary charges were RMB 83.587 billion; government extra-budgetary charges amounted to RMB 389.377 billion, estimated outside-system charges RMB 597.971 billion, government extra-budgetary charges plus estimated outside-system charges totaled up to RMB 987.305 billion, equivalent to 1.33 times of the total fiscal budgetary revenue. See Jia Kang and Zhao Quanhou, "Theoretical Analysis Framework and International Comparative Studies of the Tax and Fee System and Exploratory Discussion on Tax and Fee Reform in China (Shuifei tizhi de lilun fenxi kuangjia, guoji bijiao yanjiu yu Zhongguo de shuifei gaige tantao)," Liu Rongcang and Zhao Zhiyun (eds.), *Front Line of China's Financial Theories (Zhongguo caizheng lilun qianyan)*, Vol. 2, Beijing: Social Science Literature Publishing House, 2001, p. 449.

into these public welfare units to enhance their quality of service through competition. Fourth, to strictly normalize charges by intermediaries such as auditing, accounting, appraisal, and law firms. In the past, these intermediaries used to be affiliated with administrative organs, though their business was mainly enterprise behavior. Owing to their special relations with the government, there were often many practices of unreasonable charges. These intermediaries must be pushed onto the market and separated from government operations completely. Fifth, to retain a few items of charges. Items of charges that could neither be abolished nor transformed should be maintained as government-stipulated fees. These items to be maintained mainly include four categories: (1) charges on certificates and licenses for registration according to law; (2) charges by law courts on lawsuits; (3) franchised operation charges, such as taxi license plates; and (4) environmental protection fees, which mainly targeted polluting enterprises.[17]

One important aspect in straightening out and normalizing extra-budgetary revenue was rural tax and fee reform, which has been adequately discussed in Chapter 3.

By the turn of the century, efforts in straightening out and normalizing extra-budgetary revenue had paid off. According to the report by the Ministry of Finance, the record-high ratio of extra-budgetary revenue to budgetary revenue of the Chinese government was 1:1; but by 2000, the ratio had dropped to 0.28:1. In 2001, the Ministry of Finance carried out a reform in all budgetary units to separate revenue from expenditure. The focus of the reform was to disengage revenue from expenditure, separate collection from payment, and abolish extra-budgetary funds step by step by bringing them under budget control. In 2002, the Ministry of Finance stipulated that all departmental extra-budgetary revenue should be brought under budget control or special fiscal account control,[18] and thirty-four central government departments achieved this goal. Starting in 2003, all administrative and institutional charges and revenues from fines and confiscations should be turned in to the special fiscal account,[19] which signified the end of extra-budgetary revenue.

---

[17] *China Economic Times (Zhongguo jingji shibao)*, November 2, 1998.

[18] Xiang Huaicheng, "Report by Minister of Finance Xiang Huaicheng at the Fifth Session of the Ninth National People's Congress on Central and Local Government Budget Performance in 2001 and Budget Draft in 2002 (Caizhengbu Buzhang Xiang Huaicheng zai Di Jiu Jie Quanguo Renmin Daibiao Dahui Di Wu Ci Huiyi shang guanyu 2001 nian zhongyang he difang yusuan zhixing qingkuang ji 2002 nian zhongyang he difang yusuan caoan de baogao) (March 6, 2002)," *China Business Post (Caijing shibao)*, March 7, 2002.

[19] "All Charges and Fines Go to the Treasury from This Year: The Termination of 'Extra-Budgetary Revenue'" (*Shoufei fakuan jinnian qi tongjiao guoku, 'yusuan wai shouru' zhongjie),* China Business Post (Caijing shibao)*, January 3, 2003.

7.4.2 Further Improving the Tax-Sharing System

According to theories of intergovernmental fiscal relations and overseas experiences in the implementation of the tax-sharing system, a complete tax-sharing fiscal system should include the following aspects: (a) there should be a clear-cut and reasonable division of authority among governments at all levels, (b) governments at all levels should have a normalized and stable revenue system, and (c) a sound transfer payment system should be set up with public service equalization as the basic objective. In the last aspect, the tax-sharing system set up in 1994 had its obvious drawbacks.

First, when the "new taxation system" was implemented in 1994, the central government adopted the buffer measure of guaranteeing the "1993 base number" to protect the original interests of wealthier regions. According to the new system, the incremental central revenue from consumption tax (central tax) and VAT (central-local shared tax, with a central share of 75 percent) in excess of the central revenue from tax receipts in 1993 would be returned to the local government as compensation to guarantee that its revenue after implementing the new system would not be less than its actual revenue in 1993 (the 1993 base number). The portion left after compensation for the 1993 base number would be shared between the central and local government budgets by the ratio of 7:3. The reform met with little resistance as local governments were happy with the idea to set up the 1993 base number. However, due to the unscrupulous exaggeration of the base number in the last quarter of 1993 by some local governments, most of the incremental revenue from the two taxes was returned to local government budgets such that the central government budget was left with an insufficient amount for transfer payment to less-developed provinces and autonomous regions, thereby aggravating the imbalance of fiscal resources across regions.[20]

Second, according to the basic principles of public finance, the respective responsibilities of the central and local government finance should be divided in line with the range of benefits brought by the public goods: the central government should be responsible for providing nationwide public goods, such as income redistribution and macro-control, whereas the local governments should be responsible for providing regional public goods with limited range of beneficiaries, such as local administrative services and public security. Division of authority among governments at different levels by the current fiscal and taxation system was also unreasonable. Governments at the

---

[20] In 1997, the average financial resources per capita for population supported by the local finance nationwide was RMB 16,314; Shanghai, with RMB 53,566, being the highest, equivalent to 328 percent of the national average, Jiangxi Province, with RMB 10,850, being the lowest, or just about 66 percent of the national average, the absolute difference between the highest and the lowest was RMB 42,761, with relative difference of 3.96 times.

county and township levels were assuming many duties of nationwide public services, including popularizing the nine-year compulsory education and public medical service, taking on heavy duties of expenditure and yet without corresponding sources of revenue. The combination of heavy duties and inadequate transfer payments resulted in enormous differences in the level of public services. Across provincial-level units, the ratio of highest and lowest budget expenditure per capita rose from 6.1 in 1990 to 19.1 in 1999.[21]

Third, the 1994 reform of the tax-sharing system failed to address the issue of the unequal distribution of fiscal resources across regions by transfer payment. Local governments had neither adequate right of taxation to obtain additional revenue nor the right to raise public construction funds through borrowing.

Since 1995, the central government had taken out a certain amount of funds from its own incremental revenue for transfer payment. However, the fiscal resources of the central government available for transfer payment were limited and therefore it was very difficult to adjust the vested local interests. There were also technical problems such as incomplete statistical data and imperfect measurement method in the design of a transfer payment system. Because of this, the Ministry of Finance decided to temporarily implement a method for fiscal transfer payment during the transition period and promulgated the *Method for Fiscal Transfer Payment during the Transition Period*. It selected some objective and policy factors and adopted a relatively standard method to make limited transfer payment. The basic principles followed by the fiscal transfer payment during the transition period were: (a) not to adjust the vested local interests, (b) to be fair and just, and (c) to set priority and give special care to minority regions.

Specifically, the fiscal transfer payment amount during the transition period was composed of objective-factor transfer payment amount and policy-factor transfer payment amount. Objective-factor transfer payment amount was calculated and determined mainly by taking reference to the balance between the standard fiscal revenue and the standard fiscal expenditure of various regions as well as the objective-factor transfer payment coefficient. The standard fiscal revenue was calculated and determined by adopting the methods such as "standard tax base × standard tax rate" and "revenue base × (1 + relevant factor growth rate)," respectively, according to different tax categories; while the standard fiscal expenditure was calculated and determined by adopting different methods mainly according to classifications of staff outlay (excluding the health care and urban construction systems), public outlay (excluding the health care

---

[21] Huang Peihua, Deepak Bhattasali et al., *China: National Development and Local Finance (Zhongguo: guojia fazhan yu difang caizheng),* Beijing: CITIC Publishing House, 2003, p. 4.

and urban construction systems), health care undertakings expenses, urban maintenance and construction expenses, social security expenses, pension for the disabled and families of the deceased and social relief expenses, expenditure for supporting agricultural production, and expenditure for comprehensive development of agriculture. Policy-factor transfer payment was calculated and determined mainly based on the difference between the standard fiscal revenue and expenditure and policy-factor transfer payment coefficient of the minority regions. The formula for calculation of the fiscal transfer payment amount of various regions was as follows: fiscal transfer payment amount of certain region = objective-factor transfer payment amount of the region + policy-factor transfer payment amount of the region.[22]

In implementation, this transfer payment system displayed considerable randomness, which not only affected further deepening of the reform of the tax-sharing fiscal system, but also encouraged the phenomenon of visiting officials of central departments for money (*paobuqianjin*). A normalized fiscal transfer payment system was yet to be established and improved in the future reform.

7.4.3 Realizing the Transition toward a Public Finance System

Insight 7.1

Public Goods and Public Finance

Public finance refers to activities of raising and distributing funds by government for providing public goods. Public goods are a concept opposite to private goods. Public goods have two basic features:

---

[22] Objective-factor transfer payment of a region = (standard fiscal expenditure of the region − standard fiscal revenue of the region) × objective-factor transfer payment coefficient; objective-factor transfer payment coefficient = (sum total of transition period fiscal transfer payments of the current year arranged according to central government budget − sum total of policy-factor transfer payments of the current year) ÷ sum of the differences between standard revenues and expenditures of the regions where standard fiscal expenditure exceeds standard fiscal revenue; standard fiscal revenue of a region = local standard fiscal revenue at the same level of the region + central government revenue refund of the region + special central government subsidy to the region + rated original system subsidy to the region − original system quota of turned-in revenue of the region + settlement subsidy to the region + other subsidies to the region; standard fiscal expenditure of a region = standard staff outlay of the region + standard public outlay of the region + standard health care undertakings expenses of the region + standard urban maintenance and construction expenses of the region + standard social security expenses of the region + standard expenses of pension for the disabled and families of the deceased and social relief of the region + standard agricultural production support expenditure of the region + standard agricultural comprehensive development expenditure of the region; policy-factor transfer payment of a region = (standard fiscal expenditure of the region − standard fiscal revenue of the region) × policy-factor transfer payment coefficient.

1. Nonrivalrous—the use of public goods by one person will not reduce the use of the same goods by other persons, which means that the marginal cost for use of public goods by an additional person is zero.

2. Nonexcludable—the exclusion of any person from the use of public goods will incur a very high cost. A typical example is national defense.

Because of these features, public goods can therefore hardly be provided by the private sector. For instance, if national defense were provided only to those who pay, everybody would expect others to pay rather than themselves, and then enjoy the benefits for free as a "free rider." As such, input to national defense will be in serious shortage. Hence, in principle, public goods should be provided by government. But this is not tantamount to saying that government should directly produce all products and services constituting the public goods, since production of these products by the government may be of lower efficiency than private production. The government can certainly purchase them with fiscal funds.

There are also quasi-public goods between pure public goods and private goods. Quasi-public goods have a certain degree of rivalrousness or excludability. An example would be cable television, which has excludability but no rivalrousness. Since World War II, some countries have changed certain quasi-public goods, wherein their service cost and beneficiaries can be identified, into paid services provided by commercial organizations. This method of ensuring better use of resources is widely applied in many countries.

(Compiled based on Joseph Stiglitz, *Economics,* New York: W. W. Norton & Company, 1993, and other materials.)

Under the planned economy, the fiscal system in China was a system embracing financial activities of both public and private sectors carried out by a totalist government. After over two decades of reform, the fiscal system in China still retains many features of the fiscal system under the planned economy, resulting in a series of negative consequences. A great deal of financial resources is continually invested in SOEs in competitive fields. As discussed in Chapter 4, in competitive sectors, SOEs are less market-oriented and competitive than nonstate enterprises. Hence, this kind of allocation is in fact a waste of resources. Correspondingly, the government lacks adequate resources to support public services in the fields of public security, compulsory education, and public health care. According to recent statistics, due to shortage of necessary financial support, in most of rural China, the nine-year compulsory education stipulated in law has not yet been popularized. The sudden attack of Severe Acute Respiratory Syndrome (SARS) in 2003 exposed serious problems in the public health care system of China. All these indicate that China has not yet fully established its public finance system.

In 2000, the Chinese government proposed the goal of "establishing a framework of public finance compatible with the requirements of a socialist market economy." The primary task of establishing a preliminary framework of public finance was to "further adjust and optimize the structure of fiscal revenue and expenditure, gradually reduce investment in profitable and business fields, rigorously cut down administrative and institutional expenses, push business institutions onto the market and use the financial resources mainly for meeting the common needs of the society and for social security."[23] To this end, the state finance should adapt to the needs of transforming government functions, further adjust and optimize the structure of expenditure, and gradually normalize the scope of public finance expenditure. In the meanwhile, it should also gradually withdraw from ordinary competitive fields, reduce its financial aid to business development projects and applied research projects in enterprises, and increase its input in education, science and technology, health care, public security, social security, and infrastructure construction.[24]

In line with this effort, reform was also carried out in the following aspects of the budget system.

7.4.3.1 Deepen the Departmental Budget Reform

A reform of the departmental budget system was kicked off in the second half of 1999 to reflect both extra-budgetary and budgetary funds in departmental budgets according to a unified standard and to make the budgeting process more serious, scientific, and normalized. In 2000, budgets of four departments, namely the Ministry of Education, the Ministry of Agriculture, the Ministry of Science and Technology, as well as the Ministry of Labor and Social Security, were submitted to the National People's

---

[23] Li Lanqing, "Speech by Vice Premier Li Lanqing at the Opening Ceremony of the Seminar on Government Finance for Provincial/Ministerial-Level Officials (Li Lanqing Fuzongli zai Shengbuji Ganbu Caizheng Zhuanti Yanjiuban Kaibanshi shang de jianghua)," *Xinhua News (Xinhuashe Beijing dian),* November 20, 2000.

[24] Lou Jiwei, "Fiscal Reform and Development in China after Accession to WTO (Jiaru WTO hou de Zhongguo caizheng gaige yu fazhan) (2002)," Wang Mengkui (ed.), *China after Accession to WTO (Jiaru Shimaozuzhi hou de Zhongguo),* Beijing: People's Publishing House, 2003, pp. 27–31.

Congress for examination and approval. In 2001, the number was increased to twenty-six departments, with their budgets more specific in contents and more standardized in format. In 2002, all budgeting units of the central government prepared their budgets according to the unified standard and a new classification of government revenues and expenditures. By having unified control over budgetary and extra-budgetary funds, all departments increased the transparency of their revenues and expenditures. Meanwhile, the departmental budget reform of local governments also sped up toward unification and standardization. Departments at the provincial and prefecture/city levels in public security, law court, industrial and commercial administration, environmental protection, and family planning were all required to implement departmental budgets. Government finance at the provincial level should expand the scope of departmental budgets as much as possible, while government finance at the prefecture/city level should make preparations for the departmental budget reform.

7.4.3.2 Advance the Reform of the Fiscal and Treasury Administration System

To implement the reform of a centralized treasury receipt and payment system is to transform the decentralized budget receipt and payment system, which was established during the reform of administrative decentralization and featured by multiple accounts, to a modern treasury management system with a unitary treasury account wherein all deliveries and appropriations are to be received and paid by the treasury. Implementation of this reform is of great significance to ensure safe and effective operation of government funds, enhance the efficiency of government funds, and prevent corruption at the very source. In 2001, the State Council approved the *Reform Program of the Fiscal and Treasury Administration System* jointly proposed by the Ministry of Finance and the People's Bank of China. At the same time, an experiment was also conducted at the six central government departments including the Ministry of Water Resources, the Ministry of Science and Technology, the Office of Legislative Affairs, the Ministry of Finance, the Chinese Academy of Sciences, and the National Natural Science Foundation of China. In 2002, experiments in the reform were further extended to twenty-three central government departments, and carried out in Anhui, Sichuan, Fujian, Chongqing, Liaoning, Heilongjiang, Jiangsu, and Shandong. In addition, direct fiscal appropriations were also tried out for special funds for the central government to subsidize local governments.

7.4.3.3 Implement the Government Procurement System

According to the new requirement to prepare departmental budgets, government procurement budgets should be prepared, a centralized procurement catalogue should be compiled, and centralized government procurement should be implemented. Relevant methods for implementation should be worked out to institutionalize the government procurement under the rule of law. At the same time, the scope of direct appropriation should be extended, and a public bidding system should be introduced for government procurement to ensure the separation between administration and execution of government procurement. The auditing of government procurement should also be tightened up. In 2001, the government procurement amounted to RMB 65.3 billion nationwide, and in 2002, the figure reached RMB 100 billion, which is still expanding today.

It should be pointed out that the departmental budget reform and supporting reforms of the centralized treasury receipt and payment system and the government procurement system were only part of the effort to establish a framework of public finance. These measures centered on solving the problem of the supervision in the process of supplying public goods. To ensure the efficient supply of public goods, it is also necessary to solve the problem of revealing preference of the public for public goods. Hence, the fundamental measure to advance the budget system reform, establish a public finance system, and improve the efficiency of public goods supply is to reform and improve the system of the National People's Congress, strengthen its power in the preparation and execution of government budget as the legislative body, and institutionalize the government budget system under the rule of law.

7.4.4 Proposals for New Reform Measures

With the elapse of the five-year transition period after the accession to the World Trade Organization (WTO), it is necessary for China to accelerate its taxation system reform in line with the fundamental principles of the WTO and the international practice. In 2000, a research group on the topic of "Further Fiscal and Taxation System Reform in China," composed of both Chinese and foreign economists, proposed suggestions focusing on the following items.

7.4.4.1 Improve Value-Added Tax

Improving value-added tax (VAT) mainly includes two aspects: first, to convert production VAT to consumption VAT; second, to extend VAT coverage.

The current production VAT system allows the enterprise to deduct the input tax included in purchased raw materials, not the input tax included in fixed asset. Therefore, there is the problem of double taxation on capital goods, which can be avoided when production VAT is converted to consumption VAT.

After the VAT conversion, some existing preferential tax policies need corresponding adjustments: (a) switch from the current policy of import-stage VAT exemption for foreign-invested and domestic-invested projects on imported equipment to a policy of "collection first and deduction later" in principle, (b) abolish the current VAT rebate for foreign-invested enterprises on homemade equipment, and (c) abolish the current income tax deduction for technological upgrading on homemade equipment.

Moreover, the VAT coverage should be expanded according to the principle of multistage collection. As a first step, industries closely related to economic development, such as construction and installation, transportation, warehousing and leasing, and post and communications, should be included into the VAT coverage. When conditions are ready, the VAT coverage can further expand to real estate, some services, and the entertainment industry, leaving the banking and insurance industry and some other services to business tax. By expanding the coverage, the VAT chain is well connected and its neutrality and deduction functions can be brought into full play.

7.4.4.2 Normalize Taxation on Imports and Exports

Limited by the present fiscal and administrative capacities of China, the export tax rebate system in China has been changed many times since the taxation system reform but is still imperfect and incomplete, which distorts the VAT mechanism and lowers the competitiveness of Chinese products in the international market. Therefore, China should make active use of the export tax rebate mechanism permitted by the WTO, and further deepen the reform of taxation on imports and exports. Specific measures include the following.

1. Unify and normalize preferential taxation policies for imports, and establish an open, impartial, transparent, and effective system of tax collection and management for imports, which is supportive to the collection and management of import duty and domestic turnover tax and in line with the international practice. Adjust import taxation policies, restore taxation on imported fixed assets (including real estate) for production and operation use, and allow deduction in the subsequent stages.

2. Adapt to the new environment after the WTO accession, further improve the export tax rebate system, properly adjust export tax rebate policies, and gradually realize the objective of zero tax rate for exports. In line with the international practice, further expand export tax rebate coverage and include service trade and travel shopping export into export tax rebate coverage. Adopt effective preferential taxation measures to encourage imports and exports of high-tech products.

7.4.4.3 Adjust Consumption Tax and Business Tax Policies

In terms of consumption tax adjustment, aside from the realized adjustment of consumption tax rates for tobacco and liquor products and standardization of their tax base, consideration should be given to increasing the consumption tax rates on cars with large displacement engines and properly adjusting the tax rates and brackets of vehicles and motorcycles. In addition, some of the luxury goods and products closely related to environmental protection may also be brought into the coverage of consumption tax.

With regard to business tax adjustment, aside from the tax rate increase for the entertainment industry, the preferential policies to foreign-invested enterprises should be adjusted. The business tax exemption for intra-zone business receipts of foreign-invested financial institutions established in the special economic zones (SEZs) in the first five years should be abolished to ensure equitable tax burden on domestic-invested and foreign-invested enterprises.

7.4.4.4 Reform the Enterprise Income Tax System

The main problems with the existing enterprise income tax system include: separate income tax laws and regulations for domestic-invested and foreign-invested enterprises, inequitable tax burden across regions, unreasonable division of tax revenue between the central and local governments according to administrative affiliation, and irregular tax base. To solve all these problems, the enterprise income tax system reform needs to be carried out in the following lines.

Unify the enterprise income tax systems for domestic-invested and foreign-invested enterprises and consolidate the two laws, namely, the *Interim Regulations of Enterprise Income Tax of the People's Republic of China* and the *Enterprise Income Tax Law of Foreign-Invested Enterprises and Foreign Enterprises of the People's Republic of China;* normalize the tax base, define the scope and standard of pretax deduction in reference to the international practice, and unify the depreciation levels of domestic-invested and foreign-invested enterprises; straighten out and normalize the current preferential policies according to the principle of unified tax law, equitable tax burden, maintaining industry-specific preferential treatment, and phasing out region-specific preferential treatment; transform the existing practice of tax collection according to administrative affiliation; and reform the means of enterprise income tax collection.

The Ministry of Finance has pledged to gradually unify the enterprise income tax on domestic-invested and foreign-invested enterprises according to the principle of national treatment, and to create a more equitable tax environment for competition among all kinds of enterprises.[25]

---

[25] Lou Jiwei, "Fiscal Reform and Development of China after Its Entry into WTO (Jiaru WTO hou de Zhongguo caizheng gaige yu fazhan) (2002)," Wang Mengkui (ed.), *China after Its Entry into WTO (Jiaru Shimaozuzhi hou de Zhongguo),* Beijing: People's Publishing House, 2003, pp. 27–31.

7.4.4.5 Reform the Personal Income Tax System

Main contents of the personal income tax reform include: (a) transforming the pure schedular tax system into a mixed tax system combining comprehensive tax and schedular tax—including regular income such as wages and salaries, remuneration for personal services, and business income into the comprehensive tax category while retaining the schedular tax collection for other sources of income and (b) strengthening the tax collection method combining withholding at sources and filing tax returns by individuals, establishing an information processing system for individual earnings and large payments, and setting up an interdepartmental information exchange system and a third-party information reporting system of personal income to ensure effective collection.

Given the fact that interest income tax belongs to the central government, sharing personal income tax revenue between the central and local governments should be further clarified. The main consideration is that, as an important tax category with an income redistribution function, personal income tax is generally taken as a shared tax according to taxation theories and the international practice; moreover, after implementing the mixed tax system of comprehensive tax and schedular tax, the collection and refund of comprehensive income tax as well as information gathering also need cross-regional coordination and processing. As to the method of sharing, the preliminary view is that for the time being, it is proper that the central government exclusively enjoys taxes on investment income, including interest, dividends, and bonuses, while taxes on other income items are enjoyed by the local government.

Adjustment of the personal income tax rate is also under discussion. The purpose to implement the progressive tax on income is to redistribute income and narrow the gap between the rich and the poor. However, the American experience tells a different story. Extremely complicated and highly costly and distortionary, the American system of progressive income tax has created a situation where the ordinary citizens have a heavy burden while the rich always have ways to evade. Consequently, the progressive tax has in fact degenerated into a regressive tax.[26] Therefore, there are experts, both home and abroad, who advocate a uniform rate for personal income tax and at the same time, there are other scholars who favor a progressive tax rate.[27]

---

[26] Robert Hall and Alvin Rabushka, "Chapter 4: The Flat Tax and the Economy," *The Flat Tax,* 2nd edition, California: Hoover Institution Press, 1995. See also Wang Zeke, "Heavy Cost of the Federal Individual Income Tax of the USA (Meiguo Lianbang geren suodeshui de chenzhong daijia)," *Comparative Studies (Bijiao),* Vol. 3, Beijing: CITIC Publishing House, 2002, pp. 163–170.

[27] Lawrence J. Lau, "Some Thoughts on a Comprehensive Individual Income Tax for China (Youguan Zhongguo shixing zonghe geren suodeshui de yixie sikao)," *Comparative Studies (Bijiao),* Vol. 2, Beijing: CITIC Publishing House, 2002, pp. 129–141.

7.4.4.6 Reform and Improve Local Taxation System

As the economic situation changes, problems in the current local taxation system, such as two tax systems for the same tax object, excessively limited tax coverage, and unreasonable tax categories, have become more and more prominent. Accordingly, there is a need to speed up the reform and improvement of the local tax categories and establish local taxes with property tax and act tax as the mainstay. Detailed contents include: to consolidate the two different tax systems so that the tax burden will be the same for Chinese and foreign enterprises and citizens; abolish the outdated tax categories such as banquet tax; and impose new tax categories such as estate tax and securities transaction tax.

7.4.4.7 Speed Up the Transformation of Administrative Fees into Taxes

Discussions of the academic community and policy circles have focused on the following issues.

1. Rural taxation system reform. The on-going rural tax and fee reform is only the interim goal of the rural taxation system reform, and the final goal should be the gradual abolition of the existing agricultural tax and the establishment of a rural income tax system.

2. Social security financing. How to finance the public expenditure of social security, especially the implicit debts for repayment of pension funds of older employees of SOEs, has long been an issue of heated debates over the recent years. As to whether to transform social security contribution into social security tax or not, there has never been a consensus among different government institutions and the academic community. In this regard, there will be further discussions in Chapter 9 of this book.

3. Feasibility of transforming administrative fees into taxes in the aspects of urban maintenance and construction and resource protection. A suggestion is to transform administrative fees into taxes and to abolish all irregular charges.

4. Feasibility of replacing educational surcharge with tax.

5. Feasibility of transforming pollution fees into environmental protection taxes.

7.4.4.8 Adjust Taxation Rights

Based on the principle established in the *Law on Legislation of the People's Republic of China* and the overall arrangement of transforming administrative fees into taxes, the next important issue is to transfer the taxation rights to lower levels.

Among the eight aforementioned items of the fiscal and taxation reform, some items have been approved by the Third Plenary Session of the 16th CCCPC in October 2003 and are expected to be implemented in the subsequent years.[28]

---

[28] *Decisions of the CCCPC on Issues Regarding the Improvement of the Socialist Market Economy System* approved by the Third Plenary Session of the 16th CCCPC proposed the reform of the taxation system. It includes reforming export tax rebate system, unifying enterprise tax system, converting production VAT to consumption VAT, improving consumption tax, appropriately expanding tax base, revising personal income tax, implementing an integrated income tax system of consolidated and classified taxes, granting local government proper tax administration authority under the premise of unified tax administration, creating conditions for unifying urban and rural taxation system, etc.

CHAPTER 8

OPENING TO THE OUTSIDE WORLD

In the late 1970s, while taking the first steps in a new stage of economic system reform, the Chinese government also started to experiment with a new policy of opening up (*kaifang*), or opening to the outside world (*duiwai kaifang*). After more than two decades, China is now more open than its neighboring open economies of East Asia when they were at the same level of development as China is now. Reform of the domestic economy and opening to the outside world have been reinforcing each other and driving the fast growth of China's economy. With China's accession to the World Trade Organization (WTO) in November 2001, China's economy is entering a new era of all-round opening up.

8.1 The Evolution of China's Foreign Economic Relations and Development Strategy

As one of the earliest civilizations, China had extensive economic and cultural exchanges with various countries of the world in history. The "Silk Road" and the "Seven Expeditions to the Western Ocean by Zheng He (1371–1435)" were important evidences of China's historical openness to the outside world. In the sixteenth century, however, the declining Ming Dynasty implemented a self-seclusion policy, which evolved into a strict "closed-door" policy in the Qing Dynasty, when the imperial government imposed the "ban on maritime intercourse with foreign countries" (i.e., prohibiting the entry and exit of vessels, people, and goods, and isolating China from the outside world). Several centuries of self-seclusion rendered China impoverished and backward; during the same period, with the collapse of the feudal system in Western Europe, various capitalist countries greatly increased their productivity by developing the domestic market and tapping the international market, a striking contrast to the stagnation of China's economy.

Since 1949, China's foreign economic and trade relations have undergone four stages of different strategies.

8.1.1 1949–1971: Self-Seclusion

Neither before nor after the founding of the People's Republic of China (PRC) did the Chinese leadership consider establishing an entirely closed economy. However, the out-

Table 8.1   China's Share in World Trade

Year	World Trade Volume (US$ billion)	China's Share in World Trade (%)
1953	2.37	1.5
1957	3.11	1.4
1959	4.38	1.9
1962	2.66	0.9
1970	4.59	0.7
1975	14.75	0.8
1977	14.80	0.6

Source: The National Bureau of Statistics, *China Statistical Yearbook (Zhongguo tongji nianjian),* Beijing: China Statistics Press, various years; General Agreement on Tariffs and Trade (GATT), *International Trade,* Geneva: General Agreement on Tariffs and Trade, various years.

break of the Korean War in 1950 and the subsequent blockade of China by the United States and its allies forced China to cut itself off from the West. After 1956, in order to adapt to the centrally planned economic system, the Chinese government established a foreign trade system characterized by state monopoly. All the import and export businesses of an industry were monopolized by a state-run national import and export corporation[1] established by the industry. Import and export were carried out according to the mandatory plan assigned by the State Planning Commission: exports were purchased according to the state plan while imports were transferred and distributed according to the state plan, with the state finance system responsible for all profits and losses. Under this system, the function of import and export trade was defined as "supplying what each other needs," and it played only the role of "regulating supply and demand" with foreign countries.

After the Great Leap Forward was launched in 1958, and especially after the political and economic relations with the USSR ruptured in the early 1960s, the Chinese leadership emphasized self-reliance, encouraged every region to have "independent economic setup," and adopted the self-seclusion policy in foreign economic relations. From then until the 1970s, foreign trade in China was basically stagnant (see Table 8.1).

---

[1] National corporations under direct administration of the foreign trade department of the central government included China National Cereals, Oils and Foodstuffs Import and Export Corporation, China National Native Produce and Animal By-Products Import and Export Corporation, China National Textiles Import and Export Corporation, China National Silk Import and Export Corporation, China National Light Industrial Products Import and Export Corporation, China National Arts and Crafts Import and Export Corporation, China National Chemicals Import and Export Corporation, China National Machinery Import and Export Corporation, and China National Metals and Minerals Import and Export Corporation, among others.

8.1.2 1972–1978: Import Substitution

During the later half of the Great Cultural Revolution, the gaps in industry, technology, and management between China and industrialized countries grew even more apparent. Mao Zedong sensed the danger of a long period of self-seclusion: it would be impossible to achieve industrialization, let alone the ideal of "surpassing Britain and catching up with the United States," a goal set in earlier years. As a result, China improved its relations with the United States and normalized diplomatic relations with Japan in 1972, and adopted a policy of developing trade relations with Western countries. Especially during the Imported Leap Forward[2] of 1977–1978, China imported many sets of large-scale manufacturing and mining equipment. In 1978 alone, China signed contracts totaling US$7.8 billion for equipment related to chemical fertilizers and metallurgy, among other industries, which were for twenty-two large-scale projects. Import and export trade rapidly grew, with the total import and export volume 39 percent higher in 1978 than it was in 1977. However, at this time, China's purpose for developing foreign trade was not to build an open economy, but rather, to establish an economic system of independence and self-reliance by import substitution.

8.1.3 1978–2001: Combination of Export Orientation and Import Substitution

After the Great Cultural Revolution, the Chinese leadership learned their lesson from the past and came to an understanding that self-seclusion could only hinder China's economic development. Meanwhile, impressed by the experience of Japan and the "Four Little Tigers" of Hong Kong (China), Singapore, Taiwan (China), and South Korea in East Asia, where export-oriented sectors were developed to promote rapid growth of the overall economy, the Chinese government decided to adopt the guideline of opening to the outside world and implement the policy of export orientation.

In September 1978, Deng Xiaoping pointed out that "actively developing relations, including economic and cultural exchanges, with other countries on the basis of the Five Principles of Peaceful Coexistence"[3] would "enable us to make use of capital from

---

[2] At the First Session of the Fifth National People's Congress held in February 1978, Hua Guofeng delivered his Government Work Report entitled *Be United, Strive for Construction of a Socialist Modernized Power (Tuanjie qilai, wei jianshe shehuizhuyi de xiandaihua qiangguo er fendou)*, and the Congress approved the *Ten-Year Planning Compendium for the Development of the National Economy from 1976 to 1985 (draft) (1976 zhi 1985 nian fazhan guomin jingji shi nian guihua gangyao (caoan))*. Overambitious targets of economic development were set in both the *Report* and the *Compendium*, resulting in too much imported advanced equipment from abroad, which grossly exceeded the foreign exchange payment capacity and supporting capacity of China at that time and gave this episode the name of the "Imported Leap Forward."

[3] The Five Principles of Peaceful Coexistence are mutual respect for territorial integrity and sovereignty, mutual nonaggression, noninterference in each other's internal affairs, equality and mutual benefit, and peaceful coexistence.

foreign countries and of their advanced technology and experience in business management."[4] After several years of reform and opening up, he further pointed out, "The present world is open. One important reason for China's backwardness after the industrial revolution in Western countries was its closed-door policy. . . . The experience of the past thirty or so years has demonstrated that a closed-door policy would hinder construction and inhibit development."[5] "The lessons of the past tell us that if we don't open to the outside, we can't make much headway. . . . If we isolate ourselves and close our doors again, it will be absolutely impossible for us to approach the level of the developed countries in 50 years."[6]

Opening to the outside world under the leadership of Deng Xiaoping included the adoption of an export-orientation strategy, which was mainly to fully exploit China's comparative advantages in labor-intensive industries and to earn foreign exchange through "three supplied and one compensation (*sanlaiyibu*)," namely, processing supplied materials, processing according to supplied samples, assembling supplied parts, and compensation trade.

It has to be pointed out that although the authorities had decided on the foreign trade policy of export orientation, because of their lack of clear understanding of the differences between import substitution and export orientation, government officials in practice continued to execute the policy of import substitution. The export orientation strategy was not implemented immediately. For instance, from 1985 to 1992, China maintained an average statutory tariff rate above 43 percent. Until 1993, China still maintained a dual exchange rate system, and the official exchange rate of RMB was significantly overvalued.[7] Under such conditions, many processing enterprises actually served the domestic market.

8.1.4 After the Accession to the WTO in 2002: An Open Economy

China is one of the founding members of the General Agreement on Tariffs and Trade (GATT), the predecessor of the World Trade Organization (WTO). In 1986, China applied to restore its status as a founding member of the GATT. This very act signified China's determination to further open itself to the outside world and to integrate itself

---

[4] Deng Xiaoping, "Hold High the Banner of Mao Zedong Thought and Adhere to the Principle of Seeking Truth from Facts (Gaoju Mao Zedong sixiang qizhi, jianchi shishiqiushi de yuanze) (September 1978)," *Selected Works of Deng Xiaoping (Deng Xiaoping wenxuan)*, Vol. 2, Beijing: People's Publishing House, 1994, p.127.

[5] Deng Xiaoping, "Building a Socialism with a Specifically Chinese Character (Jianshe you Zhongguo tese de shehuizhuyi) (June 1984)," *Selected Works of Deng Xiaoping (Deng Xiaoping wenxuan)*, Vol. 3, Beijing: People's Publishing House, 1993, p. 64.

[6] Deng Xiaoping, "Speech at the Third Plenary Session of the Central Advisory Commission of the Communist Party of China (Zai Zhongyang Guwen Weiyuanhui Di San Ci Quanti Huiyi shang de jianghua) (October 1984)," *Selected Works of Deng Xiaoping (Deng Xiaoping wenxuan)*, Vol. 3, Beijing: People's Publishing House, 1993, p. 90.

[7] In 1993, the official exchange rate of RMB against the U.S. dollar was about 5.8, whereas the market exchange rate was between 11 and 12.

into the world economic system. During the fifteen years of negotiations before its official accession to the WTO in November 2001, the Chinese government instituted reform measures in many areas related to trade. For example, tariff barriers were significantly lowered, most import quotas were abolished, and the laws and the law enforcement system were improved, all enabling China's economy to be integrated into the world economic system.

The accession to the WTO means that China has accepted the rules of globalization to some extent. Significant reduction of tariffs and elimination of nontariff barriers have led to considerable weakening of trade protection in strategic industries. By changing government functions, accelerating the improvement of the market economic system, and reducing restrictions on foreign investment, China will create an attractive environment for capital, technology, and talent from overseas to build an open economy.

8.2 The Spatial Evolution of Opening to the Outside World

China's opening to the outside world has followed a path of gradual advance. After it was specified as a basic state policy and a key component of the economic development strategy in the late 1970s, opening to the outside world was implemented first on a regional basis. In other words, China's opening to the outside world has been advancing step by step in several stages and at several levels, with coastal regions as the strategic focus.

8.2.1 Establishing Bases for Opening to the Outside World in the 1980s

In the early 1980s, China began to establish bases for opening to the outside world in a few coastal cities. The reason for this decision was that, with a vast territory and many years of planned economic system it would be impossible to quickly establish the domestic market and to fully implement the policy of opening to the outside world to integrate with the international market. Therefore, with experience learned from other countries in establishing special economic zones (SEZs), the Chinese leadership exploited the advantages of some coastal cities such as Shenzhen of being close to Hong Kong, Macao, and Taiwan and being the hometown of a large number of overseas Chinese in order to create a "micro climate" for a market economy, to attract foreign capital, technology, and management, and to develop export-oriented industries. Specific steps taken included:

1. In May 1980, it was decided to implement special economic policies and flexible measures of opening to the outside world in both Guangdong and Fujian provinces.

2. In August 1980, SEZs were set up in Shenzhen, Zhuhai, Shantou, and Xiamen as experiments. SEZs are "regional export-oriented economies regulated mainly by market forces." Imported goods for self-use by enterprises in SEZs were exempted from tariffs and consolidated industrial and commercial tax. Tariffs and consolidated industrial and commercial tax on imported goods for sale were reduced by half; for the sale of self-produced goods within SEZs, consolidated industrial and commercial tax was also reduced by half.

3. In May 1984, it was decided to further open fourteen coastal port cities, namely, Dalian, Qinhuangdao, Tianjin, Yantai, Qingdao, Lianyungang, Nantong, Shanghai, Ningbo, Wenzhou, Fuzhou, Guangzhou, Zhanjiang, and Beihai (including Fangchenggang), and to offer foreign-invested enterprises there preferential treatment similar to that provided SEZs.

4. In February 1985, it was further determined to designate the Yangtze River Delta, the Pearl River Delta, the Xiamen-Zhangzhou-Quanzhou Triangle in South Fujian, the Jiaodong Peninsula, and the Liaodong Peninsula as open economic regions.

5. In April 1988, it was decided to establish the Hainan Special Economic Zone.

By then, the overall situation of all-round opening to the outside world in coastal regions was basically set up. Opening up in coastal regions not only directly promoted the rapid development of local economies, but also played a significant role in promoting regional economic development as well as the reform and opening up and the economic development of the whole nation.

First, these open regions made effective use of international resources, actively participated in international competition, and became pioneers of opening to the outside world in China. According to statistics, by the end of 1990, the accumulated investment in capital construction over the prior decade completed by the first four SEZs in Shenzhen, Zhuhai, Shantou, and Xiamen exceeded RMB 30 billion; a number of large-scale infrastructure and industrial projects had been completed. Foreign direct investment (FDI) in the fourteen coastal open cities during the Seventh Five-Year Plan (1986–1990) exceeded US$10 billion; more than two thousand of the "three categories of foreign-invested enterprises" (i.e., Chinese-foreign equity joint ventures, Chinese-foreign contractual joint ventures, and wholly foreign-owned enterprises) were put into operation. Opening to the outside world promoted the development of export-oriented sectors. The total export volume of the twelve coastal provinces, autonomous region, and municipalities in 1990 was approximately US$40 billion, accounting for about two-thirds of the total national export volume.

Second, opening to the outside world in these regions promoted rapid economic growth, making them the most vigorous regions. All-round opening up attracted a great deal of foreign investment and generated a great deal of foreign trade, which in turn led to rapid development. Gross value of industrial output in the first four SEZs jumped from only RMB 5.5 billion in 1985 to RMB 49.5 billion in 1990, an increase by eight times in only five years, with an average annual growth of 50 percent.

Third, these regions played a key role in connecting inland China with the international market. Enjoying their unique position as gateways to the outside world, these coastal open regions could fully play the role of connecting the inside of China to the outside world, and vice versa. By absorbing foreign capital, technology, and management, and developing export trade, these regions could gradually develop and strengthen themselves; then, they could gradually transfer foreign capital, technology, and management skills to inland regions so as to promote development there, as well. In addition, these SEZs and coastal open regions also daringly explored new economic systems and operating mechanisms, thus accumulating experience, setting up models, and providing references for economic system reform in the whole nation; they became the testing ground for reform. Opening to the outside world in the 1980s prepared China and provided experience for further opening to the outside world in the 1990s.

8.2.2 Expanding the Regions Open to the Outside World in the 1990s

In the 1990s, the Chinese government proposed the "four-along strategy" to further open China to the outside world.

1. "Along the coast" referred to development focused on coastal China from the Bohai Sea to the Beibu Gulf (Gulf of Tonkin).

2. "Along the border" referred to development focused on the border regions of Xinjiang, Inner Mongolia, and Heilongjiang to strengthen economic and trade exchange with countries of the Commonwealth of the Independent States (CIS) and development focused on the border regions of Yunnan and Guangxi to open trade routes to South Asia and Southeast Asia.

3. "Along the river" referred to the overall development and opening up of the Yangtze River Valley downstream from Chongqing, with the development of Pudong in Shanghai as the flagship; from there, the goal was to link the east and the west and to generate influence to the south and the north.

4. "Along the railway" referred to the regions along the railroad from ports in East China to the Altai Mountains in Xinjiang Autonomous Region, as part of the Eurasian "continental bridge" within Chinese territory.

Opening to the outside world in various regions across China in the 1990s was carried out in two directions. First, the territory along the banks of the Yangtze River was to be gradually built into another vast open belt after coastal regions of China, with the development and opening of Pudong in Shanghai as the "head of the dragon." This plan had the greatest strategic significance in expanding open regions in the 1990s. In April 1990, the Chinese government made a strategic decision to develop and open Pudong New Area in Shanghai. Deng Xiaoping, in his South China tour in 1992, made an important speech, pointing out that Shanghai had significant advantages in terms of human resources, technology, and management. Besides, Shanghai could generate influence in the Yangtze River Valley, which was the largest highly industrialized region in China. On both banks of the Yangtze River were comprehensive industrial bases with a high degree of specialization in Shanghai, Nanjing, Wuhan, and Chongqing, among others. As the Yangtze River economic belt possessed technological strength and covered a vast inland area, it could open itself to the outside world to a wider extent and at a higher level than other regions. No other region could substitute for the Yangtze River Valley because of its existing industrialization. Moreover, the Yangtze River economic belt boasted convenient transportation and a mature cultural environment. It could fully tap international resources by expanding its opening up process and attracting investment to stimulate the growth of local and inland economies. Therefore, in 1993, after implementing the development of Pudong in Shanghai, the Central Committee of the Communist Party of China (CCCPC) and the State Council decided to apply the opening-up policy to the five cities of Wuhu, Jiujiang, Wuhan, Yueyang, and Chongqing. As a result, Pudong in Shanghai, as the flagship in the development and opening up, would further strengthen its influence and leading role, and, at the same time, the largest highly industrialized region in the Yangtze River Valley would take off following the lead of the Pudong area.

Second, the process of opening up in inland provinces and autonomous regions was accelerated. Inland cites along the border were further opened to drive the economic development of inland provinces and autonomous regions forward. The inland provinces and autonomous regions of China have vast territories and abundant natural resources, and opening these areas to the outside world would facilitate the exploitation of these advantages. In 1993, the CCCPC and the State Council decided to open eleven provincial capital cities—Hefei, Nanchang, Changsha, Chengdu, Zhengzhou, Taiyuan, Xi'an, Lanzhou, Xining, Guiyang, and Yinchuan. In addition, the provincial capital cities of the four coastal and border provinces and autonomous regions of Harbin, Changchun, Hohhot, and Shijiazhuang were made open cities. They were allowed to enjoy the same preferential policies as those of coastal open cities, which infused vitality into the development of these provinces. Thus, by the mid-1990s, a new situation of all-round, multi-level, wide-scope opening to the outside world came into being.

8.2.3 Development Prospects of Special Economic Zones

The strategy of gradual opening to the outside world by starting with SEZs was developed to cater to the requirements of government management capacity and the system reform during the transition from a closed economy to an open economy. In the process of the reform and opening up, SEZs had been the showcase and testing ground, and had become the bases to utilize foreign investment, increase exports, and set up modern industries, especially modern manufacturing.

With the basic framework of a market economy in place and the accession to the WTO, the continuation of preferential treatment to enterprises in SEZs, such as reduced or exempted taxes, became nonconducive to the establishment of a large unified domestic market of fair competition, or to the reduction of disparity between coastal and inland regions. The Chinese government promised that after the accession, policies not in conformity with the WTO principles, such as national treatment and most-favored-nation (MFN) treatment, would no longer be adopted in SEZs. This meant that the policies extended exclusively to SEZs must be adjusted, and their primary functions must be changed, allowing them to win new competitive advantages through institutional innovations rather than through preferential policies such as tax incentives.

A new trend at the turn of the century was that many foreign enterprises shifted orders from their factories in other regions to those in China, or set up new plants in China to produce products for the international market. A consequent topic is whether China will become a world-class manufacturing base, or a "world factory."

Reasons for this trend are several. First, with a surging wave of new technological revolution and economic globalization, multinationals can now segment their production and business activities and search for the most suitable bases for different links in the production of the same product, resulting in unprecedented industrial relocation across countries. The continuous relocation of labor-intensive parts of production to developing countries means that these countries may become assembly and export bases for capital- and technology-intensive products. Second, China's political situation will remain stable. Third, China enjoys competitive advantages as a manufacturing base: it has a solid industrial foundation with adequate supporting capacities, an abundant supply of quality but cheap labor with labor cost remaining low in the foreseeable future, rules and regulations increasingly in conformity with international norms driven by the accession to the WTO, and a good infrastructure for participation in international division of labor. Therefore, China will be the most attractive base for global manufacturing. For example, since the second half of 2001, global demand for IT products has experienced a sharp decline; yet China's export of IT products has gone against the market trend and achieved two-digit growth. This fact demonstrates China's enormous potential to be a global manufacturing base.

The question now does not lie in whether China can become a global manufacturing base, but rather in how much benefit it can bring to indigenous enterprises and people in China. In discussing this issue, we have to take note of the fact that although China has cheap production costs because of its labor force of high quality, good discipline, and low wages, transaction costs are high because of defects in social organizations and institutions. If this problem cannot be solved, China can provide only a "cheap but good" labor force to foreign manufacturing enterprises, but cannot itself gain much benefit from development. To this end, efforts should be focused on all-round advance of reform to improve China's economic, social, and political institutions. Further discussion on this subject appears in Chapter 12 of this book.

8.3 Foreign Direct Investment

8.3.1 Growth and Characteristics of Foreign Direct Investment in China

Attracting foreign direct investment (FDI) is an important component of China's policy of opening to the outside world. It enables China to obtain valuable capital resources and, more importantly, it brings advanced technology, management skills, access to overseas market, and competitive pressure. All these are of critical importance to China's economic development.

Since the inception of reform and opening up in the late 1970s, the Chinese government has adopted a series of preferential policies to attract foreign investment. As a result, FDI has been growing year by year, a great achievement that has drawn worldwide attention (see Figure 8.1). By the end of 2002, the total number of foreign-invested enterprises approved nationwide was 424,196; the total contract value of FDI reached US$828 billion; and the total used value of FDI stood at US$448 billion. Since 1993, China has been the largest recipient of FDI among developing countries. In 2002, for the first time, China surpassed the United States to become the country using the largest amount of FDI in the world.

A new FDI trend that appeared in the mid-1990s was the fast growth of investment by international consortia and multinationals. According to the latest statistics, among the world's top five hundred nonfinancial corporations, more than four hundred have investment projects in China. Multinationals have set up approximately four hundred R&D centers of various types in China. As a result of the rising share of investment by and increasing capital- and technology-intensive projects of big multinationals, the technological content of foreign-invested projects has also increased considerably, which in turn has enhanced China's ability to participate in the international division of labor. Concentration of foreign investment in the Yangtze River Delta and the Pearl River Delta has made these regions important clusters of IT industry. With increasing impact

Figure 8.1   Foreign Direct Investment in China (US$ billion)

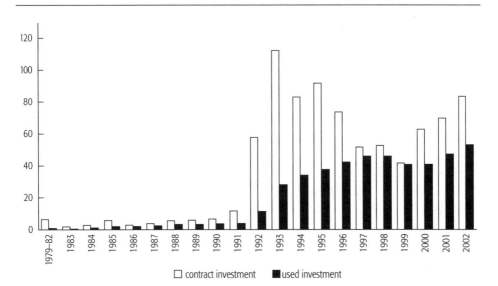

on the international market, China has now become the second-largest producer of IT products in the world, after the United States.

In the early stage of the reform and opening up, China had only a few open regions where land-use fee was low, labor was cheap, and the state granted preferential treatment in enterprise income tax, making them a paradise for low-level, small-scale investments. With the continuous expansion of open regions, domestic economic development, and the accession to the WTO, the first mover advantage of these first open regions is now diminishing. They will have to attract leading multinationals and conglomerates of large-scale operation and sophisticated technology in the future by exploiting their advantages in geographic location, investment environment, infrastructure, supply of parts and components, service system, talent quality, level of science and technology, and government efficiency. Simultaneously, inland regions with advantages in land and labor costs should focus on attracting small- and medium-sized investments.

Foreign investment in the early years was mainly in the form of Chinese-foreign equity joint ventures and Chinese-foreign contractual joint ventures (i.e., Chinese-foreign cooperative enterprises). Wholly foreign-owned enterprises gained popularity in subsequent years, and today, they have become the primary form of foreign investment in China. In 2002, they accounted for 65 percent of the total number of FDI projects, 69 percent of contract investment, and 60 percent of used investment.

In addition, other forms of investment, such as BOT financing and securities financing have also been introduced into China. Generally speaking, foreign investment may take the form of sole investment or joint venture according to the investors' free will. The *Catalogue for the Guidance of Foreign Investment Industries* formulated by the government only imposes restrictions on the share of foreign investment in certain service sectors and particular manufacturing industries as allowed by China's WTO accession protocol.

A new form of FDI is to participate in the reform of China's state-owned enterprises (SOEs). The first important measure in the reform of SOEs is to define property rights. The reform can either be "restructuring on the spot"—defining property rights, dividing shares, and establishing a corporation system while maintaining the existing ownership structure—or "restructuring with outside investment"—transforming SOEs into mixed-ownership companies or companies controlled or wholly owned by new investors by introducing new domestic and foreign capital. "Restructuring with outside investment" is of particular significance, as it[8] can help China's SOEs overcome the difficulties in breaking down the old institutional framework and the inadequacy of self-owned capital, thus accelerating the process of corporatization.

In terms of the sources of investment, East Asia has been most important for China, and among them, the Hong Kong Special Administrative Region has been the largest supplier of FDI in the form of individual as well as enterprise investment. Investment from other parts of the region also takes Hong Kong as its springboard. As of 2002, accumulated used investment from Hong Kong had reached US$204.9 billion.

Taiwan (China) is another important source of investment. Although statistics showed that accumulated used investment from Taiwan was only US$33.1 billion, fourth place among investment sources, the true amount is much higher, given the fact that many Taiwanese invest through a third place or party to avoid restrictions imposed by the Taiwan authorities on investing in mainland China. This accounts for why Hong Kong, the Virgin Islands, and the Cayman Islands are important gateways for outside investment. According to estimates, the actual investment from Taiwan was about two to three times more than the official statistics showed. Thus, Taiwan is in fact the second largest source of FDI in mainland China. In addition, developed countries such as the United States, Japan, and European countries are also important sources of investment (see Table 8.2). Also worth special mention is that among the FDI from the Triad of Japan, the European Union, and the United States, a large proportion is from leading

---

[8] Wu Jinglian, *Modern Corporation and Enterprise Reform (Xiandai gongsi yu qiye gaige)*, Tianjin: Tianjin People's Publishing House, 1994, pp. 261–268.

Table 8.2   China's FDI by Origin (US$ billion)

Country (Territory)	Used Investment in 2002	Accumulated Used Investment
Hong Kong (China)	17.861	204.875
Virgin Islands	6.117	24.388
U.S.A	5.424	39.889
Japan	4.190	36.340
Taiwan (China)	3.971	33.110
South Korea	2.721	15.199
Singapore	2.337	21.473
Cayman Islands	1.180	3.803
Germany	0.923	7.994
U.K.	0.896	10.696

Note: Accumulated used investment was accumulated from 1978.
Source: The National Bureau of Statistics, *China Statistical Yearbook (Zhongguo tongji nianjian),* Beijing: China Statistics Press, various years.

multinationals with large-scale and capital- and technology-intensive projects. These projects are conducive to improving the quality of China's foreign capital utilization.

Most FDI from the East Asian region comes to China to take advantage of the low cost of production factors such as labor, and is mainly engaged in labor-intensive production, with products primarily exported to their traditional markets. As a result, an interesting "triangular trade" phenomenon has formed. Large quantities of inputs are imported by mainland China from South Korea, Japan, and Taiwan (China), which are assembled or processed in China and then exported to developed markets, such as the United States and Europe. As a result, the original trade surplus of these East Asian economies with the United States has now become the large trade surplus of China with the United States. In 2001, China replaced Japan as the number one source of trade deficits with the United States. At the same time, these East Asian economies generated a great trade surplus with China.

In terms of the sector distribution of FDI in China, it is mainly found in manufacturing. By the end of 2001, manufacturing accounted for 70 percent of the total number of foreign-invested enterprises, 56 percent of total investment, and 60 percent of registered capital. FDI in the service industry was mainly concentrated in real estate. Shares of the primary industry in total investment and registered capital of foreign-invested enterprises were quite low, less than 2 percent (see Table 8.3). This is partly because China has comparative advantages in manufacturing, i.e., low costs of production

Table 8.3 Sector Distribution of Foreign-Invested Enterprises at the End of 2001

Sector	Number of Enterprises	%	Total Investment US$ million	%	Registered Capital US$ million	%	Foreign Registered Capital US$ million	%
	Number		US$ million		US$ million		US$ million	
Total	202,306	100.00	875,011	100.00	505,795	100.00	359,683	100.00
Farming, Forestry, Animal Husbandry, and Fishery	4,752	2.35	9,135	1.04	6,180	1.22	4,763	1.32
Mining and Quarrying	1,047	0.52	3,282	0.38	2,317	0.46	1,462	0.41
Manufacturing	141,668	70.03	491,322	56.15	305,250	60.35	214,931	59.76
Production and Supply of Electricity, Gas, and Water	1,268	0.63	49,505	5.66	20,039	3.96	11,606	3.23
Construction	5,139	2.54	21,547	2.46	11,862	2.35	7,743	2.15
Geological Prospecting and Water Conservancy	128	0.06	4,237	0.48	1,545	0.31	1,412	0.39
Transport, Storage, Post, and Telecommunications	3,499	1.73	41,442	4.74	20,432	4.04	15,163	4.22
Wholesale and Retail Trade and Catering Services	12,249	6.05	24,592	2.81	15,585	3.08	11,311	3.14
Banking and Insurance	74	0.04	2,089	0.24	1,965	0.39	1,415	0.39
Real Estate Management	11,925	5.89	149,094	17.04	72,244	14.28	55,536	15.44
Social Services	16,169	7.99	56,274	6.43	34,020	6.73	23,188	6.45
Health Care, Sports, and Social Welfare	469	0.23	2,774	0.32	1,543	0.31	1,128	0.31
Education, Culture and Arts, Radio, Film, and Television	530	0.26	1,390	0.16	982	0.19	675	0.19
Scientific Research and Polytechnic Services	1,851	0.92	4,334	0.49	2,752	0.54	2,171	0.60
Others	1,538	0.76	13,994	1.60	9,079	1.80	7,179	2.00

Source: The National Bureau of Statistics, *China Statistical Yearbook (Zhongguo tongji nianjian)*, Beijing: China Statistics Press, 2003. Percentages are calculated by the author.

and strong supporting capacity of domestic industries, and partly because China has long imposed rigorous restrictions on foreign investment in service industries.

In terms of the regional distribution of FDI in China, investment is mainly concentrated in coastal regions. In 2002, FDI in twelve coastal provinces, autonomous region, and municipalities accounted for 87.43 percent of the national total. The main reasons were that these areas were the first to be opened to the outside world and had a better investment environment, higher level of economic development, and a better industrial base. It should be noted that the disparity in investment environment between coastal and inland regions has become increasingly large as a result of the first mover advantage. Inland regions have lagged far behind in many aspects, such as infrastructure, institutional environment, cadres' mindset, and supporting capacities of local industries. Obviously, the concentration of FDI in coastal regions is not conducive to reducing the gap in regional development.

8.3.2 Promoting the Growth of Local Enterprises

The emerging global trend of opening up has intensified competition among countries in attracting foreign capital. China must make necessary adjustments in policies, focusing on improving the investment environment and government service, to attract more investment projects with more advanced technology.

In this regard, the most important development is to shift the focus from "preferential treatment" to "impartiality" in attracting foreign investment, creating a sound investment environment and gradually giving national treatment to foreign-invested enterprises. In the early stage of the reform and opening up, China's policy toward foreign capital was centered on preferential treatment, which was absolutely necessary at that time because foreign investors then were unfamiliar with the investment environment in China and were still doubtful about the opening-up policy. Furthermore, China's infrastructure and other conditions were also backward, and there were many restrictions on and discrimination in charges against foreign-invested enterprises. Therefore, in open sectors, preferential treatment, such as tax incentives, was used as major means to attract foreign investors.

With substantial changes in China's economic environment and increasing understanding of its market potential, the charm of preferential policies is diminishing, and foreign investors now attach more importance to an environment of fair competition and national treatment. Multinationals will be the mainstay of foreign investment in China in the future, who care more about long-term return on investment than about preferential policies. Since 1995, China has adjusted its policy on charges and taxes on foreign capital by, for instance, repealing consolidated industrial and commercial tax, imposing value-added tax (VAT), consumption tax, and business tax, abolishing the tax exemption for foreign-invested companies on imported cars, and merging the two exchange rates. Most foreign investors believe that a fair taxation environment for all enterprises is instrumental in attracting more foreign investment. At the same time, this policy adjustment can curb fake foreign investment and optimize the FDI structure.

Creating a sound competitive environment does not mean the immediate removal of all restrictions on investments by foreign citizens or of all protections for domestic infant industries. In recent years, the Chinese government has formulated a series of policies in accordance with the international practice to increase the attractiveness of China's industry to foreign capital, to regulate the behavior of various parties, and to encourage the entry of foreign investors and guide them into the normal track.

In 1995, the State Planning Commission, the State Economic and Trade Commission, and the Ministry of Foreign Trade and Economic Cooperation jointly issued the *Interim Regulations on the Guidance of Foreign Investment Directions* and the *Catalogue for the Guidance of Foreign Investment Industries*. The *Regulations* and the *Catalogue,* to be adjusted according to changes in circumstances, divided foreign investment projects into four categories: "encouraged," "restricted," "prohibited," and "permitted." Foreign investment projects of the "encouraged" and "permitted" categories enjoy preferential treatment according to laws and regulations. Foreign investment projects of the "restricted" category require approval by the ministries and commissions of the State Council or governments of provinces, autonomous regions, or municipalities directly under the central government, and cities specially designated in the state plan.

The new edition of the *Catalogue for the Guidance of Foreign Investment Industries* issued on March 31, 2002 listed three categories of industries: "encouraged," "prohibited," and "restricted." In the meantime, it further expanded the industries open to foreign investment.

Since 2001, in accordance with commitments made during negotiations for the accession to the WTO, China has successively amended the *Law of PRC on Wholly Foreign-Owned Enterprises,* the *Law of PPC on Chinese-Foreign Equity Joint Ventures,* and the *Law of PRC on Chinese-Foreign Contractual Joint Ventures* and abolished performance requirements for foreign-invested enterprises in export, local content, balance of foreign exchange, transfer of technology, and establishment of R&D units, thereby providing a legal guarantee to grant national treatment to foreign-invested enterprises in the aforementioned aspects.

In a word, the Chinese government adopted effective measures to improve the soft environment for foreign investment in the following aspects.

1. Improve the policy and legal environment for foreign investment; promote administration according to law; maintain stability, continuity, predictability, and

operability of policies and laws regarding foreign investment; and create a unified, stable, transparent, and predictable legal and policy environment.

2. Maintain and improve a fair and open market environment; resolutely suppress arbitrary inspections and imposition of charges, quotas, and fines on foreign-invested enterprises; break local protection and trade monopolies; protect intellectual property rights and crack down on infringement and piracy; improve the complaint system for foreign-invested enterprises.

3. Further open trade in services.

4. Encourage foreign investors to invest in high-tech industries, basic industries, and supporting industries.

5. Take active measures to attract more multinationals to invest in China.

6. Encourage foreign investment in the central and western regions of China.

From the experience of other developing countries, the major contribution of FDI to the host country lies in that it not only brings in the capital, technology, and management skills necessary for the economic development of the host country, but also improves its economic efficiency and competitiveness through market competition. Another important role of FDI is to promote the economic system reform in the host country. However, the greatest uncertainty for the host country is the relationship between FDI and domestic enterprises. Usually, FDI can produce a "crowding-out effect" in two aspects: in the product market, it has an adverse impact on the growth of domestic enterprises in competitive industries; in the factor market, it reduces capital and other factors available to domestic enterprises, or increases the latter's costs to obtain them, or both.[9]

During the initial stage of the opening up, there were strict restrictions on the sales by foreign-invested enterprises in China's domestic market. With the deepening of the reform, however, these restrictions on sales in the domestic market were gradually loosened, and were eventually eliminated after the accession. The rapid growth of foreign-invested companies in market shares and their acquisitions of Chinese enterprises raised great concern in the public on how to protect local companies and national industries while introducing foreign capital.

This problem demands a careful analysis. To open to the outside world and to let in foreign capital certainly means giving up some domestic market shares, but the overall

---

[9] Karl P. Sauvant et al., "World Investment Report 1999: Foreign Direct Investment and the Challenge of Development," *UNCTAD World Investment Report, No. WIR1999,* http://www.unctad.org/en/docs//wir99_en.pdf.

effects are more positive than negative and conducive to the healthy development of China's industry. When foreign businesses come in, they not only bring in capital, new technology, and management skills, but also intensify the competition in the domestic market. As long as the policies are right, competition functions as a screening mechanism to reward the superior and punish the inferior. Under fair competition, national enterprises, with their advantages of being local and being Chinese, will never decline; rather, they will survive and prosper in the domestic market and even in the international market. The so-called right policies refer to the following measures adopted while opening to the outside world.

1. Ensure fair competition in the domestic market and prevent unfair competition such as dumping.

2. Offer moderate protection to domestic infant industries where there are significant economies of scale.

3. In industries in urgent need of development in China, implement preferential policies, such as policy loans, that are in line with the international practice.

In some sectors, the problem of "snapping the Chinese market" by foreign investors by illegal means, such as dumping, certainly exists. However, what needs to be stressed is that, in addition to failure to implement the aforementioned necessary protection measures in line with the international practice, the main reasons for the problem are the following.

1. Reform lags behind opening up, resulting in low efficiency, poor management, and unfavorable business conditions of Chinese enterprises and their inability to compete with foreign-invested enterprises.

2. The traditional fund supply system is no longer operational and the capital market is still immature, leaving Chinese enterprises with no means of meeting their life-and-death financing needs. In contrast, foreign-invested enterprises can take advantage of their capital abundance and financing channels in the international financial market to elbow out or gobble up Chinese enterprises.

3. The reform to establish a modern enterprise system in SOEs has not achieved its objective, and a great number of skilled workers have resigned to join foreign-invested companies.

Given the situation, China has two choices: one is to slow down the process of opening up, or even to close the opened door to ensure the survival of Chinese enterprises; the other is to accelerate the reform of SOEs and improve their business environment to enable those with vigor to survive and win in fair competition. Both international and China's own experiences show that the first choice is not feasible and it is not a genuine way out for China. In an open world economy, to maintain self-seclusion is impossible. Even if self-seclusion could be maintained, China would end up unable to catch up with the trend of rapid technological revolution because there would be no way to exploit its comparative advantages through free trade, to develop itself by exploiting its strengths while avoiding its weaknesses, or to make use of the latest research findings from abroad. Excessive protection can only make national industries more and more backward and eventually collapse. What should be adopted is the second choice. On the one hand, all foreign-related laws should be improved to prevent foreign-invested enterprises from elbowing out Chinese enterprises by unfair competition and, at the same time, to provide appropriate protection to domestic infant industries; on the other hand, energy and effort should be focused on advancing the reform to fundamentally improve the enterprise mechanism and the business environment.

Insight 8.1

The Experience of Suzhou Industrial Park

Suzhou Industrial Park was founded in February 1994 according to an agreement between the Chinese and Singaporean governments. After nine years of development, the park had accommodated 103 foreign-invested enterprises, with an accumulated FDI of US$16.07 billion. In 2002, its GDP reached RMB 25.17 billion. Major features and experiences in the establishment of Suzhou Industrial Park are as follows.

1. An efficient, clean, and service-oriented government and team of civil servants. When it was established, the Suzhou Industrial Park Administrative Committee designed the organizational structure and workforce quotas based on the principles of simplicity, uniformity, and efficiency, as well as "small government, big community." The numbers of departments and staff members were only one-third as many as in similar administrative divisions. The committee established a set of strict rules and regulations regarding personnel, finance, and infrastructure as well as government procurement, and started to implement a system of universal social service provision in 1998. In addition, the committee strengthened the "pro-business" sense, i.e., the sense of serving investors, and established an investor service system and a highly efficient network for attracting investment.

2. A sound and rational social security system. In 1997, inspired by the Singaporean model and the trend of social security system reform in China, the park implemented a new accumulation fund system with individual accounts, which stipulated that enterprises and public institutions in the park were obliged to deposit 25 percent of the total amount of employees' salaries complemented with the same amount of contribution from employers to the individual accounts. Nine percent of the accumulated funds would be used for social pooling for pension and major illnesses, and the rest for individuals' housing purchase, medical care, pension, and unemployment relief. The new social security system proves to be an important benefit for employees working in the park and a big attraction for high-quality talents.

3. Market-orientated allocation of human resources. The park went to the market to recruit talents. By formulating an interim method for labor management and an employment permit system, the Administrative Committee has not only standardized the labor recruitment system, but also promoted an orderly flow of talents. In addition, the park also set up a human resources development company to provide investors with world-class human resource services.

4. Public housing and a complete set of supporting community services. Using the development of public housing in Singapore as a reference, the park launched public housing projects of high quality and reasonable price to meet the needs of the employees. The neighborhood center is a new form of community service based on the experience of Singapore in tertiary industry, public welfare, and management. Constructed with government investment, the center is a nonprofit organization, providing its nearby residents with integrated services in commerce, culture, education, and community services.

5. Continuous improvement of the legal system. The Administrative Committee of the park has been active in enforcing foreign-related economic laws and regulations, and established forty-four administrative rules and regulations, including *Administrative Rules on Urban Planning and Construction, Administrative Rules on Environmental Protection of Construction Projects, Administrative Rules on Foreign Investment,* and *Detailed Administrative Rules on the Management of Ordinary Special Accounts of Public Accumulation Fund,* etc., of which, forty have been approved for implementation.

In addition, the committee has acquired valuable experience and found an effective way in environmental protection, labor relations, vocational education, and customs management, among others.

(Compiled from Pan Yunguan et al. (eds.), *Reference and Practice—Continued Exploration on the Use of Singaporean Experience for Reference by Suzhou Industrial Park (Jiejian yu shijian—Suzhou Gongye Yuanqu jiejian Xinjiapo jingyan xutan)*, Shanghai: Shanghai Academy of Social Sciences Press, 2000; and relevant data from www.sipac.gov.cn.)

8.4 The Development of Import and Export Trade

The basic content of China's strategy of opening up was the development of foreign trade, which benefited not only from the reform of the foreign trade system but also from the enormous inflow of FDI. As a logical outcome of the spatial evolution of opening to the outside world, coastal regions in China were the main bases both for foreign capital utilization and foreign trade development.

8.4.1 The Process of the Reform of the Foreign Trade System

Since 1979, China has conducted a series of reforms in its foreign trade system and gone through a transition from a plan-oriented foreign trade system to a market-oriented foreign trade system.

8.4.1.1 Reform of Trading Rights

The government implemented several measures in reforming trading rights. These are as follows.

1. Transferred part of the trading rights to lower levels. Under the planned economic system, foreign trade was monopolized by twelve national import and export corporations. The monopoly in foreign trade hindered the realization of export potential. To encourage the initiatives of local governments and industrial departments, the central government gradually expanded their power to grant trading rights to foreign trade enterprises and export-oriented production enterprises; to approve the establishment of foreign-invested enterprises; and to approve "processing supplied materials, processing according to supplied samples, assembling

supplied parts, and compensation trade." At the same time, the government also expanded the trading rights of enterprises. Only exports that were huge in volume, significant to the national economy and the people's livelihood, particularly hot on the international market, or with special requirements were managed by specialized national import and export corporations affiliated to the Ministry of Foreign Trade and Economic Cooperation. The trading rights in all other merchandise were granted to local branches of national import and export corporations and foreign trade companies of industrial departments. All provinces, municipalities, autonomous regions, and cities specially designated in the state plan opened ports with direct trading rights to engage in foreign trade within an approved scope. Furthermore, the central government also approved the establishment of a new batch of specialized national import and export corporations affiliated to various ministries of industry and granted trading rights in products and supplies to a number of qualified large- and medium-sized enterprises. Except for a few categories of merchandise to be monopolized by national import and export corporations and another small portion subject to quota or license control, most merchandise can be freely exported and imported by enterprises with trading rights.

2. Granted production enterprises trading rights in their own products and supplies and explored approaches to the integration of industry and trade, of technology and trade, and of production and marketing. In view of the long-existing problems in quality, variety, and packaging as a result of the separation between industry and trade and between production and marketing, the central government approved some large-sized key industrial enterprises and enterprise groups to directly engage in foreign trade. It also helped to set up joint-ownership enterprises to integrate trade, industry, agriculture, and technology, and began to experiment with various forms to integrate industry and trade as well as production and marketing.

3. Granted foreign-invested enterprises with trading rights in their own products and supplies; that is, foreign-invested enterprises were entitled to manage the import of raw materials, parts, and components for self-use and the export of their own products.

4. Implemented policies conducive to the development of processing trade. China introduced bonded supervision over imports necessary for processing activities. At the same time, it abolished nontariff barriers, such as licenses and quotas for processing import, except for some sensitive merchandise. These policies helped to

Table 8.4   Reduction in the Average Statutory Tariff Rate in China

Year	Average Tariff Rate (%)
1992	43.2
1993	39.9
1994	35.9
1996	23.0
1997	17.0
2000	16.4
2001	15.3
2002	12.0
2003	11.0

Note: Tariff rates in the table are calculated without weighting.
Source: Yin Xiangshuo, *The Process and Achievements of China's Foreign Trade System Reform (Zhongguo duiwai maoyi gaige de jincheng he xiaoguo)*, Taiyuan: Shanxi Economy Press, 1998, p. 94–95; and other materials.

avoid distortion caused by high tariffs and nontariff barriers to trade, and effectively promoted the development of processing trade.

5. Granted private production enterprises with trading rights in their own products and supplies. In September 1998, the State Council approved the reform that granted private production enterprises and scientific research institutions with trading rights in their own products and supplies from 1999. Since then, the share of nonstate enterprises in total national import and export volume experienced a substantial increase.

8.4.1.2 Reduce Tariff Protection

In 1982, the average statutory tariff rate was 56 percent in China. In 1992, the figure was cut to 43.2 percent. The process of reducing tariff rates was accelerated in recent years. In 2003, the average tariff rate dropped to 11 percent (see Table 8.4). By the end of the post-WTO transitional period, the average tariff level in China will reach a level equivalent to that of other developing members of the WTO.

8.4.1.3 Gradually Abolish Nontariff Barriers

Nontariff barriers in China include trading rights restrictions, import quotas, import licenses, list of import substitutes, import invitation-for-bids (IFB) requirements on specific merchandise, as well as quality and safety standards. Quotas and licenses introduced in the early 1980s were the most important nontariff barriers. By the end of the

1980s, licensed merchandise had reached fifty-three categories, accounting for as much as 46 percent of all imported goods. In the 1990s, China gradually reduced the categories of licensed merchandise. By the end of the 1990s, less than 4 percent of taxable import merchandise was subject to the restriction of import license. In negotiations for the accession to the WTO, the Chinese government committed to remove all import quotas and licenses and to gradually abolish, within two to four years after the accession, the compulsory IFB requirement on the import of four major categories of goods, specifically, scientific apparatus, building equipment, agricultural equipment, and medical equipment.

8.4.1.4 Formulate and Establish Systems and Policies to Encourage Exports

These policies include export incentive funds to reward foreign trade enterprises and export production enterprises, several adjustments in foreign exchange rate based on the development of foreign trade and price variation of domestic merchandise, product tax/value-added tax rebates for export merchandise, preferential export credit for foreign trade enterprises and export production enterprises, and a system of foreign exchange retention from export proceeds.

1. Reform of the foreign exchange control system. Under the traditional domestic-oriented planned economy, foreign-related economic activities including import and export were regulated by the plan; foreign exchange was allocated by the government; and the role of exchange rate was insignificant. With the development of foreign economic relations, the impact of exchange rate on foreign-related economic activities became much more prominent. From 1981 to 1993, the government adjusted the official exchange rate many times. In 1994, the official exchange rate of RMB was merged with the market rate under a managed floating exchange rate system, and the convertibility of the Chinese currency (RMB) under the current account was achieved within three years. However, after the East Asian financial crisis of 1997, to relieve pressure on neighboring countries and to stabilize the overall situation of the world economy, China adopted the measure of intervention by the central bank to stabilize the exchange rate of the Chinese currency, which restricted considerably its floating band. At present, we need to restore the floating nature of the exchange rate of the Chinese currency when the right opportunity comes along.

2. Tax rebates for exports. It is a common international practice that exported products are not subject to domestic turnover tax, such as product tax and value-added tax (VAT). After the taxation system reform of 1994, China stepped up its effort to promote exports by tax rebates and began to offer VAT rebates on exports.

Nevertheless, as export tax rebates were huge in amount, lengthy in process, and complex in formality, the slow implementation of export tax rebates affected export growth as an important policy factor.

8.4.2 The Development of Foreign Trade

During the twenty-three years from 1978 to 2001, the volume of China's foreign trade increased by twenty-five times (see Figure 8.2). Correspondingly, China's rank in world trade jumped from No. 32 in the early stage of the opening up to No. 6. Import and export of some key categories of merchandise occupied important positions in the international market, making China an important player in the world trade system.

Processing trade was the key driver of trade expansion in China. In these twenty-three years, the average growth rate of foreign trade in China was far higher than the average growth rate of world trade. The expansion of China's economy and the resulting improvement of its international competitiveness were two basic reasons for the high growth of foreign trade in China, but the most important reason was the rapid development of processing trade. Starting in the late 1970s, China adopted a policy of developing businesses of "processing supplied materials, processing according to supplied samples, assembling supplied parts, and compensation trade." In the mid and late 1980s, China implemented the opening-up strategy of large-scale import and export. As this strategy was geared to the international trend of industrial relocation and exploited China's comparative advantages in the low costs of factors such as labor and land in the international division of labor, enormous success was achieved. From 1980 to 2001, the average annual growth rate of processing export reached 29.4 percent while the average

Figure 8.2   Growth of China's Foreign Trade (1978–2001)

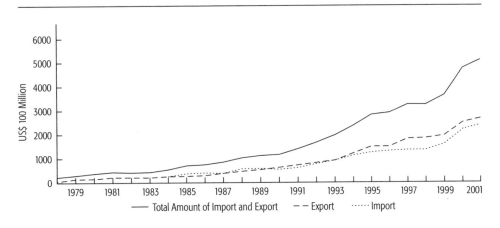

Table 8.5   Trade Dependence Ratio of the Chinese Economy (% of GDP)

Year	1978	1980	1985	1990	1995	1997	2002
Total Imports and Exports	9.8	12.6	23.0	30.0	40.3	36.1	49.6
Total Exports	4.6	6.0	9.0	16.1	21.3	20.3	26.0
Total Imports	5.2	6.6	14.0	13.9	19.0	15.8	23.6

Source: The National Bureau of Statistics, *China Statistical Yearbook (Zhongguo tongji nianjian)*, Beijing: China Statistics Press, various years.

annual growth rate of processing import reached 24.1 percent; the average annual growth rates of processing export and import were 19.8 percentage points and 13.8 percentage points higher than other forms of export and import respectively. The shares of processing export and import in total export and total import were 59.2 percent and 41.5 percent respectively.

With the continuous growth of foreign trade, China's trade dependence ratio also increased correspondingly.[10] In 2002, the trade dependence ratio of China reached 49.6 percent, and export dependence ratio 26.0 percent (see Table 8.5). Compared with the international standard, (a) the increase of the Chinese trade dependence ratio conformed to the international trend because the world average export dependence ratio increased from 14 percent in 1970 to about 25 percent in 1997; (b) the current trade dependence ratio of China is still below the world average; (c) if the difference in GDP structure of various countries is taken into consideration, the trade dependence ratio of manufacturing in China is lower than that of developed countries such as the United States and Germany, and far below the level of the so-called "small open economies;" (d) a high proportion of processing trade leads to exaggeration of the degree of dependence of China's economy on the international market when measured by the trade dependence ratio; and (e) if the influence of exchange rates is eliminated, according to the trade dependence ratio calculated by PPP (purchasing power parity), China's degree of openness (8.5 percent) is equivalent only to the average level of low-income countries (8.4 percent), and far below the average levels of middle-income countries (16.7 percent) and high-income countries (38.7 percent).[11]

---

[10] The trade dependence ratio is the index used to measure the degree of opening up and dependence of an economy on the international commodity market, usually indicated by the ratio of total volume of imports and exports to GDP. Because imports and exports of most countries are balanced in the long term, some economists also use the export dependence ratio (ratio of exports to GDP) or import dependence ratio (ratio of imports to GDP) to indicate the degree of dependence on trade.

[11] Long Guoqiang, "How to Look upon China's Trade Dependence Ratio (Ruhe kandai wo guo de waimao yicundu)," *Development Research Center of the State Council of PRC Research Paper*, No. 2000-089, http://www.drc.gov.cn/e/index.htm; *China Economic Times (Zhongguo jingji shibao)*, August 10, 2000.

8.4.3 Problems Demanding Immediate Solutions

China is already a trade giant in the world. Yet the following problems demand immediate solutions if China wants to become a trade power.

First, export suffers from poor merchandise mix and low grade. Before the reform and opening up, China mainly exported primary products, including intermediate products such as foodstuffs, mineral products, cotton yarn, etc. Over the past twenty years, the product mix of China's foreign trade has continuously been improving and the export mix has quickly been transformed from primary-product dominance in the early stage of the opening up to finished-product dominance (see Table 8.6). Today, China is the major exporter in the world of labor-intensive goods such as textiles, shoes, and toys. Thanks to the development of processing trade brought along by foreign investment, electromechanical products have become the largest category of China's exports, with a few items, such as IT products, occupying an important position in the international market. However, most of those apparently capital- and technology-intensive electromechanical products are only assembled in China, with their core components imported from abroad. Thus, the production activities that China engages in are still concentrated on the labor-intensive, low-value-added part of production. At

Table 8.6   China's Export Merchandise Mix (Total National Exports = 100)

Year	1980	1985	1990	1995	2000	2002
Primary Products	**50.2**	**50.6**	**25.5**	**14.4**	**10.2**	**8.8**
Foodstuffs	16.5	13.9	10.6	6.7	4.9	4.5
Other Agricultural Products	9.5	9.7	5.7	2.9	2.1	1.7
Fossil Fuel	23.5	26.1	8.4	3.4	3.2	2.6
Others	0.8	0.9	0.8	1.4	0.05	0.03
Finished Products of Processing Industry	**49.8**	**49.4**	**74.5**	**85.6**	**89.8**	**91.2**
Chemical Products	6.2	5.0	6.0	6.1	4.6	4.7
Textiles and Other Light Industrial Products	22.1	16.4	20.3	21.1	17.1	16.3
Electromechanical Products	4.7	2.8	9.0	21.1	33.1	39.0
Miscellaneous (including Ready-Made Clothes)	15.7	12.7	20.4	36.7	34.6	31.1
Others Non-Classified	1.2	12.5	18.7	–	0.09	0.02

Source: The National Bureau of Statistics, *China Statistical Yearbook (Zhongguo tongji nianjian)*, Beijing: China Statistics Press, various years.

present, few of the finished products exported by China contain technology with Chinese intellectual property rights; most Chinese exports are sold at low prices as a result of the lack of their own marketing network.

Given the global glut of production capacities, labor-intensive products with low production entry barriers are now experiencing cutthroat competition in the international market. Therefore, although China's export volume has grown rapidly, its trade terms [12] are deteriorating. What is worse, due to the low grade of export merchandise, China's export can adopt only the strategy of "winning by sheer numbers." With protectionism in international trade on the rise, this strategy is likely to meet with unfair treatment. At present, China is facing more antidumping investigations than any other country in the world. Because of the so-called "nonmarket economy provisions" [13] of fifteen years in China's WTO accession protocol, Chinese enterprises are at a disadvantage in responding to antidumping investigations. Moreover, China's export products are also faced with the risk that importing countries may quote special safeguard provisions against them. Faced with the proliferation of international technical and "green" trade barriers, Chinese export merchandise is in an unfavorable position in international competition as a result of its low grade. With the advent of the twenty-first century, the international economic circles began to spread a new "China threat theory," such as "China's export of deflation." Officials in charge of finance and economic affairs in Japan and the United States began to discuss publicly the issue of Chinese currency revaluation, adding new uncertainties to the external environment of China's exports.

Second, China's export market is overconcentrated in a few countries. In terms of market structure, China's exports are concentrated in the three big markets of the United States, Japan, and Europe. China, in particular, is highly dependent on the U.S. market, with 40 percent of China's exports of final products going there. An important reason for this is that a number of neighboring economies have relocated to China their production activities of final products that are intended to be exported to the United States, forming a unique "triangular trade" phenomenon. In this case, China imports large quantities of intermediate goods from Japan, South Korea, and Taiwan, and then exports them to the U.S. market after assembling and processing.

To address the overconcentration problem in the short run, China must accelerate the implementation of a market diversification strategy. It needs to further develop tra-

---

[12] Terms of trade refers to the ratio of average price of exported goods to that of imported goods. A decrease in this ratio means that the country must export more goods to exchange for the same amount of imported goods, indicating deteriorating terms of trade.

[13] Within fifteen years after its accession to the WTO, China will still be considered a country with a nonmarket economy; this is one of the most important concessions made by China in its negotiations for accession to the WTO. This clause enables foreign enterprises to easily win antidumping lawsuits as long as it can be proven that the selling price of Chinese products is lower than the cost of the products in market economies.

ditional markets such as the United States, Japan, Europe, and ASEAN for new export growth; to vigorously exploit the Russian market, regulate Chinese-Russian trade order, and expand Chinese-Russian bilateral trade; to promote the export of products to India by focusing on engineering projects and overseas processing and assembling; and to develop markets in the Commonwealth of the Independent States (CIS), Middle East, Latin America, Africa, and South Asia.

Third, the development of service exports is lagging behind. In recent years, the proportion of service exports in total exports of the various trade powers in the world continuously increased. In 1999, service exports of these countries equaled 24 percent of their merchandise exports. In contrast, the development of service exports in China was slow: its ratio to merchandise exports was 15 percent lower.

8.5 Prospect of China's Opening to the Outside World

8.5.1 The Accession to the WTO Is a New Milestone in China's Opening to the Outside World

The unswerving implementation of the policy of opening to the outside world by the Chinese government is evidenced by the fact that in 1986, China officially applied for restoration of its status as a founding member of the General Agreement on Tariffs and Trade (GATT). From 1948 when the GATT went into effect to 1995 when the GATT was transformed into the WTO, the number of members of the organization reached 105 and the trade volume among member economies accounted for 90 percent of the world's total. After fifteen years of tough negotiations, China finally entered the WTO. China's commitments upon the accession are mainly in two areas: one is to open markets, including merchandise markets and service markets; the other is to accept the WTO rules and to revise relevant Chinese laws and regulations according to these rules. China's accession to the WTO has further shown to the domestic and international communities that to establish an open market economic system is the committed policy of the Chinese government.

8.5.2 China Will Enter a New Era of All-Round Opening to the Outside World

Fulfillment of the commitments upon the accession will trigger extensive and profound changes in social and economic life in China. In terms of opening markets, over the past twenty and more years, under unilateral and bilateral frameworks, the degree of market opening significantly increased. But, as a whole, the absolute level of market protection was still high—higher than developed economies and developing economies as well.

After the accession, China's overall degree of market opening is parallel to the level of developing members, and in some sectors, it goes beyond the average level of developing members. Therefore, from a relatively closed economy to a relatively open economy, China will experience significant increase in the degree of market opening. In terms of revising laws and regulations, China has just set up a general framework of a market economy, and some reforms of critical importance to the market economic system, such as the establishment of a unified domestic market, SOE reform, and reform of the investment and financing system, have not yet achieved breakthroughs. The WTO rules are the basic requirements for an open market economic system. To deepen the economic system reform in line with the WTO rules is fundamentally consistent with the reform objective of establishing a socialist market economic system in China.

China needs to fulfill its commitments to open the domestic market and to revise laws and regulations in less than five years. Compared with opening to the outside world on its own initiative in the past two decades and more, China will have less discretion and flexibility in the future to control the opening pace. It is certainly an unprecedented task to realize such extensive market opening and system adjustment in such a short period.

The accession to the WTO is essential for China to meet the challenges of economic globalization, and will effectively promote China's reform and development. From the long-term point of view, it is a necessary journey for China to increase its participation in the international division of labor and seek development in the process of globalization. Nevertheless, all-round opening up imposes much higher demands on government management and adjustment ability. If the government fails to formulate a correct strategy and strengthen its adjustment ability, it is very likely that China will suffer instead of benefit from the process of opening up. To this end, we must be fully prepared.

8.5.3 Active Participation in Regional Economic Cooperation

Since the 1990s, regional economic integration has experienced rapid progress, becoming a prominent trend parallel with economic globalization. Among major trade countries, only Japan, South Korea, and China in Asia have not yet participated in institutionalized regional economic cooperation organizations. Nevertheless, in the past two years, both Japan and South Korea have adopted active policies on regional economic cooperation, and Japan has already signed a free-trade area agreement with Singapore.

Regional economic cooperation has the double effects of trade creation and trade diversion, although the second effect is more obvious. Countries from outside the region receive unfavorable trade treatment within the free trade area, and their market share for export erodes. For instance, China used to be the largest textile product supplier to the U.S. market, but was replaced by Mexico after the establishment of the North American Free Trade Area.

Participation in regional economic cooperation is also instrumental for countries with weak economic strength to speak with one voice in formulating international economic rules. The ability to influence international economic rule-making shows the overall national strength of a country and is instrumental for a country to make use of international rules to seek economic benefits. If developing countries can institute various forms of regional cooperation, their status and ability in formulating international economic and trade rules will be greatly improved.

Facing the trend of regional economic integration, economic experts suggest that China should, from the perspective of the global strategy of the nation, understand the importance and urgency of participating in regional economic cooperation and take a proactive attitude in strategy formulation and negotiations with neighboring countries to accelerate its participation in regional economic integration. China has several alternative schemes: "10 + 1 (ASEAN + China)," "10 + 3 (ASEAN + China, Japan, and South Korea)," "China, Japan, and South Korea," and the Shanghai Cooperation Organization, among others. In 2002, China reached a framework agreement with ASEAN concerning the establishment of a free-trade area before 2010. At the same time, China is also cooperating with policy research units in Japan and South Korea to study the issue of Northeast Asia regional cooperation. With the advance of regional cooperation, such as the "10 + 1" and "China, Japan, and South Korea," regional cooperation organizations in East Asia comparable to the European Union and the North American Free Trade Agreement may eventually emerge.

In the globalization of the world market, a system of orderly competition needs to be established to protect the equal rights of people of all countries. In the past two decades, developing countries have been advocating such a new order by consultation on an equal footing among all countries. However, over a considerably long period of time, developed countries reacted indifferently to this proposal. It was not until the end of 1997 when the financial crisis in East Asia dealt a serious blow to the economy of South Korea, which was newly accepted as a member of the so-called "rich countries' club," the Organization for Economic Cooperation and Development (OECD), that statesmen from developed countries began to realize that economies of all countries in the world are intimately related to each other and bound by a common cause. Since then, developed countries have adopted a more active attitude in salvaging countries ravaged by crisis and in preventing its spread. The financial crisis in countries like Russia and Brazil in 1998 further proved the necessity for international cooperation and the establishment of a healthy international economic system by joint efforts.

From October 3 to 5, 1998, the "Group of Seven" (G7)—the United States, Japan, Germany, France, the United Kingdom, Canada, and Italy—convened in Washington, D.C., where it discussed world economic issues of common concern (the G7 Economic Summit). At the same time, finance ministers from twenty-two countries attending the annual meetings of the International Monetary Fund (IMF) and the World Bank also discussed the issue of the world financial order. Participants also put forward many suggestions and declarations.

- It was pointed out by G7 in its communiqué that the most important thing at the moment was to restructure the financial systems of emerging markets and developed countries. Governments of all countries should limit their guarantees for loans to enterprises so as to prevent financial turmoil.

- It was suggested in the *Report of the Working Group on Transparency and Accountability* that a team composed of representatives of international organizations and regulatory authorities of various countries be set up as soon as possible to study how to compile and publish data on such institutional investors as investment banks, hedge funds, and pension funds.

- It was suggested in the *Report of the Working Group on Strengthening Financial Systems* that the host countries of banks, investment banks, or hedge funds, after applying adequate monitoring and control over these institutional investors, should set up a financial policy forum participated in by finance ministers, governors of central banks, and financial market regulatory authorities every year or every six months to discuss problems concerning the international financial system.

- It was suggested in the *Report of the Working Group on International Financial Crises* that government guarantees for loans to private enterprises should be limited and new financing mechanisms should be set up to provide emergency loans and enable markets under immediate impact to apply for loans from the IMF to prevent and avoid problems in a single market from spreading to other countries.

Relevant comments of the various countries during the G7 Economic Summit as well as the annual meetings of the IMF and the World Bank attended by finance ministers of twenty-two countries were positive signs. It indicated that more and more people realized the necessity of establishing a sound international economic order by consultation on an equal footing among all countries. China, as an influential developing country, should actively participate in the establishment of a new international economic order to seek steady development of the world economy.

During the first year after the accession, the Chinese government earnestly fulfilled its commitments, actively responded to challenges by accelerating reform, and regarded challenges as opportunities for reform and development. First, China revised its laws and regulations and issued a number of judicial interpretations according to its commitments and the WTO rules while abolishing a number of judicial interpretations not in conformity with the WTO rules. Thirty ministries and commissions under the State Council reviewed 2,300 department regulations regarding merchandise trade, service trade, intellectual property rights, and investment, of which 830 were abolished and 325 were revised. Local governments reviewed more than 190,000 local laws and regulations.

Second, administrative organs at various levels reviewed all their items of administrative approval; departments of the central government alone had more than 3,600 items reviewed, nearly half of which were abolished by May 2004.

Third, China reduced its trade protection level. According to China's WTO accession protocol, after January 1, 2002, China reduced import tariff on merchandise of over 5,300 tariff codes, with the average statutory tariff rate down from 15.3 to 12 percent: the average tariff on agricultural products was reduced from 18 to 15.8 percent, and the average tariff on industrial products was reduced from 14.7 to 11.3 percent.

Finally, China loosened its restrictions on market access for foreign investment in the service sector. In the retail sector, in 2002, China approved the establishment of eight joint ventures, which would open twenty-eight stores. In the banking sector, on November 7, 2002, the United Overseas Bank of Singapore officially opened its first branch in China. The Bank of East Asia, Credit Lyonnais, ABN AMRO Bank, and Deutsche Bank AG were either waiting for approval from the People's Bank of China or busy preparing for branch establishment. When China officially entered the WTO on December 11, 2001, it had already removed client restrictions against foreign banks on handling foreign exchange business and allowed these banks to operate RMB business in Shanghai, Shenzhen, Tianjin, and Dalian. Starting on December 1, 2002, the People's Bank of China further opened RMB business to foreign-invested financial institutions in Guangzhou, Zhuhai, Qingdao, Nanjing, and Wuhan. In the insurance sector, seven foreign-invested corporations have obtained their business licenses.

Earnest fulfillment of its commitments won high praise for China from the international community. The WTO carried out seventeen reviews of China's trade policies for the transition period. Results of the reviews indicated that China's fulfillment of its commitments upon the accession to the WTO was generally good. The American Chamber of Commerce made a general evaluation of the first nine months after the accession, with the result being "generally not bad."

The anticipated serious consequences did not occur in the first year after the accession, thanks to the active response of the government and enterprises. The expectation of adverse impact generated great momentum for further economic reform, adjustment of industry structure, and development of imports and exports. Sectors such as banking and automobile production that were once expected to meet major challenges have accelerated their reform and restructuring and achieved unprecedented development. Taking advantage of the global output reduction in bulk agricultural products resulting from natural calamities, agriculture has avoided adverse impact of import surge; at the same time, the product mix of agriculture has been adjusted, and international market expansion has been strengthened.

Meanwhile, foreign economic and trade relations have been exceptionally active. While the growth of global trade was only 1 percent, export growth in China reached 20 percent in 2002, making it the sixth largest trade power in the world. Moreover, in utilization of foreign capital, China surpassed the United States for the first time, becoming the largest recipient of FDI in the world.

One important lesson from the first year after the accession is that opportunities always exist along with challenges. The key to success is to turn the table by a proactive attitude and a correct strategy. If handled properly, pressure can be turned into motivation, challenges into opportunities, and disadvantages into advantages.

PART 3

MACROECONOMIC AND SOCIAL ISSUES

CHAPTER 9

ESTABLISHMENT OF A NEW SOCIAL SECURITY SYSTEM

After the founding of the People's Republic of China, a labor security system centered on urban state-owned work units was established. Workers covered by this security system received medical, pension, and other benefits from the state according to the stipulated benefit standards, protecting them against potential risks in life such as old age, illness, and death. Such protection was considered a fundamental right of workers. However, this kind of social security system was not only limited in coverage but also non-sustainable even within its limited coverage, as was evident after several decades of implementation. Meanwhile, the advance of economic reform, especially enterprise reform, posed an urgent need for the establishment of a social security system to cover the whole society as soon as possible to provide a social safety net and ensure stability amidst the great social transformation and economic restructuring.

9.1 The Social Security System before Reform and the Reform Plan of the Third Plenary Session of the 14th CCCPC [1]

After the founding of the People's Republic of China, the Chinese government established a defined-benefit, pay-as-you-go social security system modeled on the precedents of the USSR and other socialist countries.

9.1.1 The Establishment of a Social Security System in China

In February 1951, the central government issued the *Ordinance of the People's Republic of China on Labor Insurance,* stipulating that full-scale labor insurance to state employees and their dependents, such as old age insurance, medical insurance, and occupational injury insurance, be entirely planned by the state and implemented by enterprises. This *Ordinance* laid the foundation of social security for employees of state-owned work units. According to this *Ordinance,* the labor insurance system was first established in large industrial SOEs and was then gradually expanded to other industries such as state-owned

---

[1] CCCPC is the acronym for the Central Committee of the Communist Party of China.

commerce and trade. In rural areas, the practice of the traditional Chinese society was adopted with household provision as the major form of security.

Aside from the general feature of a pay-as-you-go system, the Chinese social security system was unique in that "work units" (factories, organs, and public institutions) were responsible for its implementation. Prior to the Great Cultural Revolution, the specific method for work units to implement social security was to deduct from income a fringe benefit fund in the amount of a fixed proportion of the payroll to cover the various items of labor insurance expenses. After the Great Cultural Revolution started, the fringe benefit fund was no longer enough to pay the social security expenses because of the increasing number of retired workers and the insufficient financial resources of enterprises amidst social turmoil. After 1969, therefore, enterprises switched from deducting the labor insurance fund in the amount of a fixed proportion of the payroll to having pension, public medical service, and other labor insurance benefits listed under nonbusiness expenditures. As a result, social security completely evolved into enterprise security.

In 1986, the State Council stipulated in the *Interim Regulations for the Implementation of the Labor Contract System in State-Owned Enterprises* that the pensions of new employees recruited under the labor contract system should be financed by pooling funds. While this somewhat changed the enterprise provision system of the Great Cultural Revolution era, the pension pooling remained small in scale and local in scope, and more importantly, the means of financing and management did not undergo corresponding adjustment to adapt to the economic reform. This situation continued until the early 1990s.

During the era of the planned economy, the social security system where "the state takes care of everything" was established and recognized as one of the major advantages of the socialist system. As work units were established as the grassroots organizations of the society under the planned economy, in which normal flow of labor force was no longer necessary, and workers and even their descendants could fully depend upon and adhere to their work units all their lives, the social security functions were quickly transmuted to "work-unit security." The contracting system reform of state-owned enterprises (SOEs) in the 1980s did not touch the labor and personnel system of enterprises, let alone lead to the emergence of the labor market or the market-oriented allocation of labor resources. Therefore, the issue of how to establish a social security system independent of the enterprise system was not raised. To a very limited extent, the labor contract system, introduced in 1986 for some new employees of SOEs, created an independent relationship between workers and enterprises and raised the issue of independent social security functions. This change, however, did not touch the fundamental issues of social security system reform, as "social pooling" for financing pensions for workers under the labor contract system was in fact still a pay-as-you-go system administered entirely by the government.

9.1.2 Drawbacks of the Traditional Social Security System

The traditional social security system established during the era of the planned economy has its basic drawbacks in two fundamental aspects of efficiency and fairness.

9.1.2.1 Loss in Efficiency

First, it elicited little enthusiasm from the contributor. The defined-benefit, pay-as-you-go system is, in essence, an intergenerational transfer from the current generation of workers to the previous generation of workers, which dampens the working enthusiasm of the former. Especially when the aging of a society has reached a relatively high level, the working generation may have to support too many aged people, and the contradictions will become more prominent. Due to the Chinese policy of opposing birth control in the mid-1950s and the 1960s, China's population explosion caused serious social problems. In the early 1970s, the Chinese government was forced to switch to a policy of strict birth control and the birth rate dropped sharply. In the mid-1980s, the phenomenon of an aging population began to appear in China and was further aggravated in the 1990s. In some old SOEs, the ratio of the number of retirees receiving pension to the number of active employees had generally become very high (ranging from $1:3$ to $1:1$). With time, the enterprises' burden of pension and medical expenses increased, seriously affecting incentives for the current working generation.

Second, its operation cost was very high. Under such a social security system, the funds came from two major sources: the fringe benefit fund and nonbusiness expenditures for enterprises and administrative expenditures for administrative organs. As enterprise finance and government finance were integrated under the planned economy, social security funds always came from government finance, directly or indirectly, whereas employees themselves did not make any contribution. There was no connection at all between the payment of the social security benefits and the contribution of the beneficiary. Under such a financing structure, the beneficiary was tempted to seek high benefits, with work units vying with each other to raise payment standards. No one was motivated to supervise the revenue and expenditure of the social security fund. In the meantime, this style of management was also very likely to breed bureaucracy and to increase operation cost.

Third, it caused unfair competition among enterprises and obstructed the flow of workers among enterprises. With the aging of the population, the burden on enterprises was increasingly heavy. This was especially the case for old enterprises with numerous retired employees. Their cost for pension and medical care was abnormally high, and some of them were even running into great financial difficulties. In contrast, some new enterprises had a relatively light burden as the average age of their employees was low and consequently fewer funds were needed to support the aged, sick, and retired, which put the old enterprises at a disadvantage in competition. Meanwhile, different standards of social security in different enterprises also obstructed the free flow of employees.

Finally, the old system could not adapt to the needs of reform. During the reform, economic structure underwent great changes and enterprise restructuring was frequent. If the social security system fails to perform its security functions and to build a social safety net, resistance to reform will increase, or even social unrest will occur. Hence, the old social security system is particularly unfavorable to enterprise reform.

9.1.2.2 Deviation from Fairness

Under the old social security system, deviation from fairness did not lie primarily in the imparity between different cohorts or different generations of beneficiaries, but rather in the unbalanced relationship between the state and the individual as well as among different social groups. As the state monopolized all social security resources and bore all social security obligations to the individual simultaneously, the hard constraint on resources reduced the individual's disposable income to a minimum level and limited the consumer's right to free choice to a minimum scope. On the other hand, because of the rejection of the role of market mechanism, most basic living resources were provided by the state as social welfare at a low price or even free in the form of consumer goods such as housing, medical care, children's schooling and employment, and articles for labor protection. Social welfare in the form of rationing in kind deprived individuals of their free choice of the most satisfactory basket of consumer goods, let alone the autonomous arrangement for their incomes over the entire life cycle.

It follows that the practice of the state—as the only producer and provider of consumer goods—to provide consumers with social welfare in kind can result in at least two direct consequences. One consequence is that the individual consumers are deprived of their right to free choice, and are fully subject to the decisions of the state as the producer, let alone the forming of social preferences regarding social security consumption through a public choice mechanism. Another consequence is that the state can carry out rationing in kind for different social groups at extremely low initial cost, resulting in hidden social inequality among different social groups.

First, under an urban-rural dual social structure, the state distributes most of the social security resources to urban residents. In China, the old social security system covered only some of urban residents (i.e., employees of SOEs and urban "big collectives"[2] as well as personnel of state organs), excluding unemployed urban residents and the vast number of rural residents. This constitutes a great unfairness to the latter.

Second, when social security resources were allocated in kind through work units, the level of benefits for each individual was dependent upon the availability of resources as well as the ability of work units to obtain resources under the planned allocation system. Because of this, there were great differences among different work units in terms of the welfare portfolio and levels of expenditure. Even among SOEs, there was a wide disparity: some could not enjoy the basic security because of inadequate plan quotas, while others enjoyed a high standard of welfare because of adequate resources or special political status.

The aforementioned unfairness became more prominent after the inception of the reform and opening up. First, with the disintegration of the people's commune system, the simple and crude rural social security system, such as rural cooperative medical service, had nothing left and hundreds of millions of rural households were left without even minimal social security protection. Second, in urban areas, nonstate sectors of the economy, including individual businesses, private enterprises, and Chinese-foreign joint ventures experienced rapid development, yet their employees were not covered by social security services. Third, the traditional model of in-kind allocation of social welfare became increasingly incompatible with enhancing enterprise independence, expanding market exchange relations, and increasing consumer choices. With the weakening of the planned allocation of in-kind social welfare, social security was more and more dependent on enterprise finance. Therefore, inequality caused by enterprise security was almost inevitable when different enterprises had different market performance and different financial positions. In the event that an enterprise could no longer bear the burden of increasing demand for social security payment, employee pension and medical expenses were hardly guaranteed. If an enterprise went bankrupt in the process of enterprise reform, which is normal under a market economy, there would be no guaranteed resources to nourish the living and bury the dead. This posed a great threat to social stability.

---

[2] Urban "big collectives" refer to enterprises established by local governments at the district level or above. This kind of enterprise is called a "collective" enterprise but is in fact owned and managed by the government.

9.1.3 Targets for Social Security System Reform Established by the Third Plenary Session of the 14th CCCPC

With the deepening of the economic system reform, the inherent defects of the old social security system were increasingly prominent, making its reform more necessary
than ever before. In 1984, in view of the great disparities in pension between new and
old enterprises, some cities and counties in provinces such as Sichuan, Guangdong,
Jiangsu, and Liaoning experimented with social pooling for pension expenses of SOEs,
taking the first step in transforming the pension system from enterprise insurance to social insurance. In 1986, the State Council issued the *Interim Regulations for the Implementation of the Labor Contract System in State-Owned Enterprises,* proposing to set up "pension fund accounts" for contract workers. In 1991, the State Council promulgated the
Decision on the Reform of the Pension Insurance System for Enterprise Employees and started
promoting social pooling of pension insurance funds in urban areas. At the same time,
in the mid-1980s, the Chinese government started experimenting with medical security system reform by implementing social pooling for medical expenses for major
illnesses in some cities. Nevertheless, all these reforms amounted to only minor improvements within the framework of the defined-benefit, pay-as-you-go system, and
therefore failed to overcome the fundamental defects of this system.

Under this context, some economists in China began to explore in the early 1990s
how to reform the traditional social security system. After investigating and studying the
successful reforms in countries such as Singapore and Chile, they formed a shared understanding on the goals for China's social security system reform. They argued that the
new system should be independent of the enterprise system to meet the needs of establishing and developing a market economy; it should not only embody social justice but
also provide incentives for hard work and high savings to promote long-term economic
development. Based on China's own experience and the experience of the transformation of the social security systems of various countries after World War II, the Chinese
government and economists reached the following consensuses on the goals of China's
social security system reform.[3]

First, the selection of a social security system should start from China's realities.
China is a developing country with a very low GDP per capita, and its primary goal is
to realize rapid and sustainable growth after the economic take-off. As far as distribution is concerned, it needs to observe the principle of "giving priority to efficiency with

---

[3] The State Commission for Restructuring Economic Systems, *The Social Security System Reform (Shehui baozhang tizhi gaige),* Beijing: Reform Press, 1995. This book collects some policies and schemes formulated by the State Council and its relevant departments during this period concerning social security reform and offers descriptions and explanations on the strategies behind
these policies and schemes.

due consideration to fairness." Starting from this fundamental principle, China should try to maintain the effectiveness of incentive mechanism in the selection of a social security system. While ensuring the basic social security, the new system should reinforce the incentive mechanism of "more pay for more work" and avoid the drawbacks of "big-pot meal" (i.e., indiscriminate egalitarianism).

Second, China should draw on the experiences of social security reforms in countries like Singapore and replace the defined-benefit, pay-as-you-go system with a defined-contribution, funded system (i.e., individual account system). This is because the pay-as-you-go system is characterized by intergenerational transfer that breaks the connection between welfare benefits and insurance premium payments and weakens the motive for contribution. It provides no incentive for public savings and is likely to create burdens on government finance.

Third, China should learn from the experience of countries like Chile and allow the beneficiary to entrust the administration and operation of the social security system to independent agencies, because direct administration by the government institutions is likely to create problems of low efficiency and corruption.

Last, attention should be given to its coordination with other social and economic reforms, particularly to its active role in promoting SOE reform and the formation of the capital market.

In November 1993, the *Decision of CCCPC on Issues Regarding the Establishment of a Socialist Market Economic System* was adopted at the Third Plenary Session of the 14th CCCPC, which decided that the individual account system should be introduced into the basic pension insurance and basic medical insurance, and that the administration of social security and the operation of social security funds should be separated. If these principles are implemented in practice, a diversified social security system will be established by attracting market forces to jointly bear social security responsibilities with the government.

Insight 9.1

Basic Principles of the Social Security System Established by the Third Plenary Session of the 14th CCCPC

In November 1993, the 14th CCCPC convened its Third Plenary Session and adopted the *Decision of CCCPC on Issues Regarding the Establishment of a Socialist Market Economic System.* One of the key elements of this *Decision* was to establish a new social security system in China, and its basic requirements were as follows.

1. Establish a multi-layer social security system. Social security policies should be uniform and management legalized. The level of social security should be compatible with the level of social development and the bearing capacities of all parties. Social security schemes for urban and rural residents should be different. Social mutual assistance should be encouraged, and commercial insurance should be developed as a supplement to social insurance.

2. Determine the source of funds and means of security according to different types of social security. Emphasis should be given to the improvement of enterprise pension and unemployment insurance systems, the strengthening of social service functions to alleviate burdens on enterprises, the promotion of the adjustment of their organizational structures, and the enhancement of their economic benefits and competitiveness. The pension and medical insurance funds of urban employees should be jointly contributed by the work unit and the individual through a combination of social pooling and individual account. The unemployment insurance system should be further improved, with insurance premiums contributed by the enterprise in the amount of a certain proportion of its payroll. The industrial injury insurance system should be universally established. Old-age provision for farmers should be mainly household provision supplemented by community support.

3. The administration of social security should be separated from the operation of social security funds. The social security administration agencies exist mainly to exercise administrative functions. Supervisory organs of social security funds should be established with the participation of representatives from government departments concerned and the public to supervise the receipts and expenses as well as the management of social insurance funds. While ensuring normal payment, safety, and liquidity of the funds, departments in charge of social security funds may use social insurance funds mainly to purchase treasury bonds according to law to preserve and increase the value of social insurance funds.

(Compiled from *Decision of CCCPC on Issues Regarding the Establishment of a Socialist Market Economic System (Zhonggong Zhongyang guanyu jianli shehuizhuyi shichang jingji tizhi ruogan wenti de jueding)*, Beijing: People's Publishing House, November 1993; and other materials.)

However, the concept for the government to monopolize all resources, rights, and responsibilities was so appealing that some institutions always doubted or even opposed the positive role played by nongovernment forces in the establishment of the social security system. By keeping away the nongovernment forces in the process, the reform deviated from the objectives established by the Third Plenary Session of the 14th CCCPC.

9.1.4 Suggestions of the World Bank on Pension Reform

Social security system reform was a worldwide issue in the late twentieth century. In 1994, the World Bank issued a report on pension policy research titled *Averting the Old Age Crisis: Policies to Protect the Old and Promote Growth,*[4] which systematically expounded its proposition on pension system reform.

According to this report, a complete pension system should not only be able to effectively protect the aged but also be able to promote economic growth. Specifically, the pension system should not only have the function of substituting individual savings or salary, redistributing income to those with low income, and preventing poverty as well as various kinds of risk associated with the aged, it should also be able to minimize the implicit costs that affect economic growth (such as reduction in employment, reduction in savings, misallocation of capital and labor, aggravation of financial burden, increase in administration cost, and evasion of contribution), allowing itself to be a sustainable and highly transparent long-term plan. To attain these two objectives, the existing pension systems of various countries must undergo reform according to the model of a multi-pillar system, consisting of the following three pillars.

1. *Public Pension Plan (Pillar I).* This plan is financed by government tax revenue on a pay-as-you-go basis; its purpose is limited only to redistributing income to the

---

[4] The World Bank, *Averting the Old Age Crisis: Policies to Protect the Old and Promote Growth,* New York: Oxford University Press, 1994.

poor and elderly and providing them with an institutional arrangement of co-insurance. Therefore, the tax rate should not be set too high, and the tax base may be expanded wider. For instance, income tax or consumption tax may be used instead of payroll tax to raise funds, maintaining the long-term efficiency of this form of financing.

2. *Mandatory Pension Plan (Pillar II).* This plan adopts two major forms, a compulsory occupational pension plan and a compulsory individual account. Its main purpose is to force people to set aside savings in advance to provide security in old age. This plan is non-redistributive, adopting a fully funded scheme, and all accumulated funds are managed in a decentralized manner.

3. *Pension Plan Voluntarily Created by Individuals or Enterprises (Pillar III).* This voluntary individual or enterprise savings plan is a supplement to the first two pillars mentioned and is a voluntary arrangement of preventive savings of individuals or enterprises for themselves or their employees. As far as the government is concerned, one of the effects of this kind of private action is that while relieving the pressure of the old age issue, it can also increase capital accumulation. Therefore, government often adopts various kinds of measures to encourage the growth of this type of plan.

The World Bank suggested that various countries establish their own pension insurance systems, based on their specific conditions, as different combinations of the aforementioned three pillars. In the transition from the old pension system to the new pension system, Kazakhstan adopted a series of transitory methods to achieve the three-pillar objective, from which we can draw some experiences.

It should be said that the proposal by the World Bank is basically consistent with the pension insurance framework decided on by the Third Plenary Session of the 14th CCCPC.

9.2 The Implementation of the Reform and Its Problems

According to the deployment of the Third Plenary Session of the 14th CCCPC, the establishment of the new social security system started in 1995, with a focus on the reform of the basic pension insurance system and basic medical insurance system for urban employees. While recognizing the impressive progress in the past decade in pension insurance, medical insurance, unemployment insurance, and occupational injury insurance, we are facing a number of pressing problems that demand immediate solution.

9.2.1 Pension Insurance Reform

Of the various items of the social security system, the pension system is the most important and has the most difficulties in meeting the requirement of the Third Plenary Session of the 14th CCCPC. In terms of the number, the urban basic pension insurance had already covered 111 million employees and 36 million retirees by the end of 2002,[5] but the problem is that the current pension insurance system is basically a pay-as-you-go system incompatible with the required combination of social pooling and individual account put forward by the Third Plenary Session of the 14th CCCPC.

The biggest difficulty in implementing the new pension insurance system with individual account is to provide pension funds for the retired and would-be retired employees (also called the "old ones" and the "middle ones," respectively). Under the old pay-as-you-go system, no individual account was opened, nor was any pension fund accumulated for the older employees. Thus, individual accounts opened for these older employees after pension insurance reform were basically empty. The balance of pension deposits in the hands of the government amounted to only a scanty RMB 30 billion, with a very unbalanced structure. In some old industrial bases where the proportion of older employees was relatively high, the pension system could no longer balance its revenue and expenditure. Under such conditions, the solution was for the state to repay the implicit debt by contributing to the pension fund that should have been accumulated for older employees (including both the "old ones" and the "middle ones"). During the long discussion of the social security system reform from 1993 to 1995, some economists and business leaders proposed two compensation schemes: (1) "cutting a chunk"[6] out of the existing state assets and (2) issuing "recognition bonds" by the Ministry of Finance.[7] However, because of the opposition from some government functional departments, neither compensation scheme was adopted.[8] Therefore, the only option

---

[5] The Ministry of Labor and Social Security and the National Bureau of Statistics, *2002 Bulletin of Labor and Social Security Undertakings Development Statistics*, May 7, 2003, http://www.stats.gov.cn/tjgb/qttjgb/qgqttjgb/t20030507_77008.htm.

[6] The so-called "cutting a chunk" refers to allotting a certain portion of state assets for repaying the government implicit debt to the pension fund for older employees of state-owned enterprises. When drafting the social security scheme in 1993, quite a few economists had proposed this suggestion. See Zhou Xiaochuan and Wang Lin, "Social Security: Economic Analysis and System Proposal (Shehui baozhang: jingji fenxi yu tizhi jianshe) (1993)," in Wu Jinglian et al., *Building Up a Market Economy: Comprehensive Framework and Working Proposals (Jianshe shichang jingji de zongti gouxiang yu fang'an sheji)*, Beijing: Central Compilation & Translation Press, 1996, pp. 211–258.

[7] "Recognition bonds" are government bonds issued by the Chilean government in 1981 during pension reform; its purpose was to repay the government's implicit debt to those employees who had quit from the government pension plan. Some Chinese economists believe that China may also adopt this kind of method to solve the problem of "empty accounts" of older employees (Zhou Xiaochuan and Wang Lin, ibid, pp. 244–245).

[8] The main argument against compensation for older employees is that the state has no liability to older employees. In fact, it is the consensus of the society that in the process of transition from the pay-as-you-go system to the funded system, the state owes a sum of implicit debt to older employees. And this is why during the corporatization transformation of state-owned enterprises, the state has to "buy out employment guarantee" of existing employees (that is, to "buy out" their status as employees of state-owned enterprises, and as the price of "buying out employment guarantee" is calculated by years of service, it is therefore also

was to borrow from the "young ones" to support the "old ones" by using a social pooling fund collected from enterprises.

It was against this background that, at the national conference on planning the reform of the pension insurance system in March 1995, the State Council proposed the
following two schemes to be adopted by each locality according to their local realities.

1. *Scheme I (also called the SCORES—the State Commission for Restructuring Economic
   Systems—Scheme): "big individual account, small social pooling."* All individual contributions made by an employee go to the individual account, and part of the enterprise contributions also go to the individual account in proportion to the society-
   wide average salary and the salary of the employee. At the retirement, the pension
   for the retired employee will be paid monthly from the individual account according to the savings amount (including principal and interest). The basic concept of this scheme is the combination of a defined-contribution system and a
   defined-benefit system, with the defined-contribution system being the mainstay
   of the scheme. Although it does not achieve the "fully funded"[9] individual account of the beneficiary, it is nevertheless very close to the principles stipulated by
   the Third Plenary Session of the 14th CCCPC, and instrumental in preventing
   the new social security system from slipping toward a defined-benefit, pay-as-
   you-go system. Unfortunately, this scheme is not very feasible because it does
   not provide a solution to the problem of how to source pension funds for older
   employees.

2. *Scheme II (also called the MOL (Ministry of Labor) Scheme): "big social pooling, small individual account."* Individual contributions made by an employee go to the individual account, and enterprise contributions go to the social pooling fund. At the
   retirement of an employee, if the deposits in his or her individual account are
   sufficient to pay the pension, then the payment is made in the same way as in
   Scheme I. If the deposits in the individual account are insufficient or the individual account is an "empty account," then the difference should be made up by
   the social pooling fund. Although Scheme II alters the "fully funded" individual

---

called "buying out years of service"). However, as the price of "buying out employment guarantee" depends on the current
financial condition of the state-owned enterprise with which the employee is affiliated, there is the phenomenon of "misery and
happiness being unequally distributed." Besides, when handed to the employees for their own disposal in the form of cash, this
portion of resources for security such as old-age pension is likely to be used for other purposes. Hence, "buying out employment guarantee" is not at all a good method of compensation.

[9] The so-called "fully funded" refers to the practice by countries like Singapore, where contributions by the employer and the
employee are all deposited in the individual account of the employee, and the benefit of basic pension insurance is paid entirely
from the fund thus accumulated.

account to a "partially funded" one and, to a greater extent, its "social pooling fund" has the feature of a pay-as-you-go system, it provides a relatively practical method to settle the issue of the source of pension funds for the "old ones" and the "middle ones" by social pooling; therefore, a majority of local authorities opted for this scheme.

However, in fact, Scheme II adopted the pay-as-you-go system and the individual account system for the "old ones" and the "young ones," respectively. In some old industrial cities where the proportion of the supported population was very high, the burden on enterprises to contribute to the social pooling fund was very heavy. According to a report by the United Nations Development Program (UNDP), the pension insurance premium rate in China on average was above 20 percent of the salary; when other insurance premiums were included, the gross rate of social security premiums was as high as 35 to 45 percent of the salary. In some old industrial cities like Shanghai, the pension insurance premium alone reached 28.5 percent of the salary of employees (of which 25.5 percent was collected from enterprises and 3 percent from individual employees[10]), whereas in some new emerging cities, the premium rate of the social pooling fund was very low, putting the former in a disadvantageous position in competition. From a long-term point of view, this kind of practice was also susceptible to the danger of returning the pension system to the defined-benefit, pay-as-you-go system.

These defects in the pension insurance system had the following negative consequences. First, enterprises participating in the pension insurance tended to delay or evade contribution. The collection rate of pension insurance fund contribution dropped year by year: from 95.7 percent in 1992 to 92.4 percent in 1993, 90.5 percent in 1994, 90 percent in 1995, and further down to 87 percent in 1996.[11] Second, nonstate enterprises, especially foreign-invested enterprises, believed that it was unfair for them to contribute to the social pooling fund to compensate older employees of SOEs and therefore were not willing to participate. Third, when there were fund shortages, there was no choice but to divert the funds in the individual accounts of existing employees such that theirs became "empty accounts" as well.

To overcome these problems, the State Commission for Restructuring Economic Systems and the Ministry of Labor proposed an improvement scheme[12] in June 1996,

---

[10] United Nations Development Programme, *China Human Development Report: Human Development and Poverty Alleviation*, 1997, Beijing: UNDP China, 1997, p. 62.

[11] Yang Yiyong, "Why the Collection Rate of Pension Insurance Fund Contribution Continually Declines? (Yanglao baoxian jijin shoujiaolü weihe buduan xiajiang?)," *Economic Highlights (Jingjixue xiaoxi bao)*, March 7, 1997.

[12] The Ministry of Labor, *Report Outline Concerning the Unification of Pension Insurance Systems for Enterprise Employees (Guanyu tongyi qiye zhigong yanglao baoxian zhidu de huibao tigang)*, June 9, 1996.

which came into effect in August 1997.[13] The core of this scheme was to unify the different schemes of various localities to establish the following framework: to set up individual accounts for employees at 11 percent of their salary, of which the individual would contribute 8 percent and the enterprise would contribute 3 percent; for the social pooling fund, the rate of enterprise contribution would be determined by the local government of the pooling area. Pension benefit payment would consist of two parts. The first part was the basic pension benefit, divided into several brackets according to the number of years of contribution, with payment in general not exceeding 25 percent of local average salary. The second part was the individual account pension benefit with monthly payment equal to the cumulative total of the individual account divided by 120. After the death of the employee or retiree, the individual account would not be inherited, but be used to comfort and compensate the bereaved family. Surrounding the framework, the reform scheme also proposed some other measures: to gradually increase the individual contribution rate, to gradually adjust the provision standard of basic insurance, and to improve fund operation, supervision, and management. In addition, the State Council also decided to hand over all the social pooling fund of pension insurance by industry to the local (provincial-level) insurance institutions for unified management.

The implementation of the unified system certainly played a role in improving pension financing and payment. It failed, however, in the transition from the old system to the new system to solve the most critical problem—the source of pension funds for the older employees whose payment still had to rely on social pooling and funds from the individual accounts of the existing employees.

Given its inherent defect, the basic pension insurance system began to fall into a payment dilemma in 1998: the current revenue was only RMB 145.9 billion while the expenditure amounted to RMB 151.16 billion. In 1999, twenty-five provinces/autonomous regions/municipalities across the country had deficits and funds diverted from individual accounts exceeded RMB 100 billion. Under such conditions, the central government had to use tens of billions in its budget to fill the gap between revenue and expenditure of the basic pension insurance every year.

Amidst the mounting financial pressure of the basic pension insurance, two opposing policy propositions emerged. The first proposition advocated "substitution of contributions with taxes" for social security by imposing social security tax. This viewpoint maintained that basic pension insurance premiums, basic medical insurance premiums, and unemployment insurance premiums could be consolidated into a unified social se-

---

[13] The State Council, "Decision of the State Council on the Establishment of a Unified Basic Pension Insurance System for Enterprise Employees (Guanyu jianli tongyi de qiye zhigong jiben yanglao baoxian zhidu de jueding)," *Xinhua News,* August 26, 1997.

curity tax on the basis of various schemes of the social security system reform already launched by the state. In practice, collection of social security contributions was quite difficult. In many localities, therefore, these contributions were already collected by the tax authorities on a commission basis. If a social security tax was imposed, the collection of social security tax could be guaranteed with the aid of the *Law on the Administration of Tax Collection* and the tax authorities. However, this proposition was vehemently opposed because it was equivalent to deviating from the direction of reform stipulated by the Third Plenary Session of the 14th CCCPC and returning to a pay-as-you-go system. Under such strong opposition, the suggestion of switching to social security tax was not adopted by the government.

In early 2000, some collective protests and group incidents broke out in some localities, participated in by employees of SOEs who disliked the low compensation for "buying out employment guarantee." This state of affairs made the leadership of the Chinese government realize that to carry out SOE restructuring was particularly dangerous when there was no social safety net. Hence, the Chinese government invited some economists to offer suggestions on how to set up a new social security system, the most representative of which was the reform scheme of an old-age social security system proposed by Professor Lawrence J. Lau of Stanford University. According to his suggestion, the government should set up an old-age social security system composed of two parts: the "public basic pension" (equivalent to the aforementioned Pillar I suggested by the World Bank) funded by the general tax revenue of the central government, and the "individual account in a central provident fund" (equivalent to the aforementioned Pillar II suggested by the World Bank) funded by the contributions of employees and employers. The individual account in a central provident fund would be under the unified management of the "Administration Board of the Central Provident Fund" under the "Trust Council for the Central Provident Fund" of the central government. Domestic or foreign fund managers, banks, or other financial institutions would be selected and entrusted with operation and management.[14] Professor Lau also suggested that the state use the existing state assets to repay the implicit debt that the government owed to the social security fund for retired, active, and laid-off employees of state-owned work units. The idea behind this scheme gained applause from many economists and recognition from the government leadership. At the same time, a number of research institutions began to estimate the implicit debt of the government to the older employees of state-owned work units. According to estimates by the World Bank, this

---

[14] Lawrence J. Lau, "A Proposed Pension System for the People's Republic of China (Guanyu Zhongguo shehui yanglao baozhang tixi de jiben gouxiang) (July 29, 2000)." For main contents of this article, see *Comparative Studies (Bijiao)*, Vol. 6, Beijing: CITIC Publishing House, 2003, p. 328.

figure accounted for 46 to 69 percent of China's GDP in 1997; according to some economists, the figure varied from 71 to 94 percent of GDP that year; estimates by a research group of SCORES were as high as 145 percent. Even if we assume that the implicit debt accounted for only 30 percent of China's GDP in 1997, the total amount could still have exceeded RMB 2 trillion.[15] Therefore, in late 2000, the State Council made a resolution to set up the Council for National Social Security Fund.[16]

As to how to replenish the individual accounts of the basic pension insurance, aside from the so-called "full replenishing" scheme of repaying all the implicit debt of the government to the older employees as mentioned earlier, there was also the so-called "partial replenishing" scheme proposed by the Ministry of Labor and Social Security. Partial replenishing referred to the scheme whereby only the individual contribution of the employee (5 percent of the salary at that time) was reckoned into the individual account, while the enterprise contribution (the average rate of contribution at that time was 20 percent) was used as the social pooling fund to make up the deficiency in the pension fund for the older employees. This scheme was similar to the Scheme II of 1995 (also called the "Ministry of Labor Scheme"), or "big social pooling, small individual account." Under this scheme, the role played by the individual account became insignificant, and there was no way to fully satisfy the pension requirement of the employee after retirement. Hence, it was certain that in the future the employee would still need another extensive plan of the pay-as-you-go system to make up for the deficiency in the pension fund. This idea, which was basically equivalent to the pay-as-you-go system and still had to rely on the government for financing, received wide criticism from both Chinese and foreign economists.[17]

American economist Martin S. Feldstein, once Chairman of the Council of Economic Advisers for President Reagan, believes that since the current real marginal product of capital in China is greater than the growth rate of aggregate wages, converting the

---

[15] Wu Jinglian, "Major Problems to Be Solved in the Reduction of State Shareholding (Shenme shi guoyougu jianchi yao jiejue de zhuyao wenti)," *Caijing Magazine (Caijing)*, 2002, No. 1.

[16] Officially established at the end of 2001, the National Council for Social Security Fund is a public institution under direct administration of the State Council; its responsibility is to manage the social security funds raised with the approval of the State Council or generated from investment proceeds that are under the control of the central government. As active financial transfer to the pension fund as repayment of the implicit debt with state assets has not yet started, under such conditions when the measures and tools of investment are still far from adequate, the focus of the National Council for Social Security Fund, since its establishment, has been on infrastructure construction, such as selecting fund management companies to act as investment trustees, striving to participate in new share rationing for sale in the capacity of a strategic investor, etc. At the present moment, tools of investment of the social security fund permissible within the scope of policy include bank deposits, government bonds, securities investment fund, stocks, and negotiable securities with a credit standing of above the investment ranking, such as enterprise bonds and financial bonds. Of these, the proportion of bank deposits and government bonds should not be lower than 50 percent, enterprise bonds and financial bonds not higher than 10 percent, securities investment funds and stock investment not higher than 40 percent. Investment with low risk was directly operated by the National Council for Social Security Fund, while investment with relatively high risk was entrusted to the investment trustee for investment operation.

[17] For instance, Zhou Xiaochuan and Wang Lin (1993, 1994), Wu Jinglian (1993, 1998–2003), James Estella (1995), Li Shaoguang (1998, 2000, 2001, 2003), Lawrence J. Lau (2000), Martin S. Feldstein (2000), Song Xiaowu et al. (2001), and Noriyuki Takayama (2002).

social pooling portion under the pay-as-you-go system to a funded system will considerably reduce the government's financial burdens.[18] Economist Guo Shuqing is also a leading exponent advocating a fully funded system. He advocates that (a) a full individual account system can wholly link the benefits of pension insurance with its contributions and completely obliterate the "welfare big-pot meal;" (b) a full individual account system will dismiss any illusions of the people, and therefore is conducive to the smooth collection of contributions; (c) the government can hardly misappropriate; (d) the system is highly transparent with low management cost; (e) it can obtain the optimal effects of accumulation and appreciation; (f) due to the accelerating process of urbanization, without individual accounts, government pension insurance liabilities will be increasingly heavy as time goes by.[19] Hence, from the long-term point of view, a fully funded system can better give consideration to both fairness and efficiency.

In July 2001, the State Council decided to carry out experiments in Liaoning Province on the improvement of the urban social security system according to the instruction of the Ministry of Labor and Social Security. The main contents are as follows.

- Managing the individual account and the social pooling fund separately, with the individual account operated as a funded account. The contribution to the individual account was reduced from 11 percent to 8 percent of the individual salary and was funded entirely by the individual, with the rate of the individual contribution increased by 3 percent. The rate of the enterprise contribution was maintained at 20 percent of the individual salary and all enterprise contribution would go to social pooling. The individual account accumulated as a funded account and was managed as a separate account from the social pooling fund. The social pooling fund was designated for payment of the basic pension of the retirees as well as that of those to be retired in the future. The individual contribution was accumulated as the individual account fund for payment of the individual account pension.

- Adjusting and improving the methods of pension calculation and payment. While maintaining the monthly standard of the basic pension to be equivalent to 20 percent of the average monthly salary of the province or the city of the previous year, it was stipulated that after fifteen years of contribution, for every year of additional contribution, the basic pension of the employee was increased by a certain rate, with the general standard of the basic pension to be controlled at around 30 percent. After the death of the pension receiver, the funeral allowance to be received

---

[18] Martin S. Feldstein, "Social Security Pension Reform in China (Zhongguo de yanglao baozhang zhidu gaige)," *Comparison of Economic and Social Systems (Jingji shehui tizhi bijiao)*, 1999, No. 2.

[19] Guo Shuqing, "To Establish a Fully-Funded Basic Pension Insurance System Is the Best Choice (Jianli wanquan jileixing de jiben yanglao baoxian zhidu shi zuijia xuanze)," *Comparison of Economic and Social Systems (Jingji shehui tizhi bijiao)*, 2002, No. 1.

by members of the bereaved family was paid by the social pooling fund. In addition, employees who had contributed for less than fifteen years would not be allowed to receive the basic pension.

- Encouraging enterprises to set up enterprise annuities by stipulating that the total enterprise contribution within 4 percent of the total wage bill may be listed as cost expenditure.

Although adoption of the aforementioned method has somewhat improved the financial conditions of the pension insurance system of Liaoning Province, this kind of improvement was achieved only with special transfer payments from the central government. To support the experiments in Liaoning Province, the central government specially provided several billion RMB in financial support over the past few years to make up the deficit in the province's basic pension insurance. Furthermore, even if the central government finance could afford the necessary expenses, what would be set up when the Liaoning model would be promoted nationwide would still be a pension insurance system dominated by the pay-as-you-go system, which could hardly be maintained in the long run. Out of this consideration, quite a few economists advocated returning to the basic thoughts on pension insurance of the Third Plenary Session of the 14th CCCPC as well as the compensation method drawn up in 2000.

Another layer of the urban pension insurance system in China is the annuities set up for employees by enterprises. This was called the "enterprise supplementary pension insurance system" before 2000 and was renamed "enterprise annuity" in 2000, with the intention to standardize the development of the enterprise supplementary pension insurance system based on established international practice. According to relevant provisions in the *Decision on the Reform of the Pension Insurance System for Enterprise Employees* issued in 1991 and the *Circular on Deepening the Reform of the Pension Insurance System for Enterprise Employees* issued in March 1995 by the State Council, the enterprise may freely decide to set up a supplementary pension insurance plan for its employees according to its own financial position, with the funds extracted from the enterprise's self-owned fund for employee bonus and welfare and put into the employees' individual accounts. The enterprise may also freely choose the plan administrator.[20]

However, the enterprise annuity plan has been developing very slowly. At the end of 2001, the number of employees participating in enterprise annuity plans nationwide was

---

[20] The State Council, "The Decision on the Reform of the Pension Insurance System for Enterprise Employees (Guanyu qiye zhigong yanglao baoxian zhidu gaige de jueding)," June 26, 1991, http://www.molss.gov.cn/correlate/gf199133.htm; "The Circular on Deepening the Reform of the Pension Insurance System for Enterprise Employees (Guanyu shenhua qiye zhigong yanglao baoxian zhidu gaige de tongzhi)," March 17, 1995, http://www.molss.gov.cn/correlate/gf19956.htm.

only 1.93 million, and the accumulated surplus amounted to RMB 4.9 billion.[21] There were three reasons for the relatively slow development. First, the burden of the contribution to the social pooling fund of the statutory compulsory social security plan was already quite heavy for many enterprises, so only a few enterprises with abundant financial resources were in a position to set up annuity plans. Second, there were no adequate incentives; for instance, it was still not clear whether preferential taxation policies should be provided for annuity contribution of enterprises. Third, there were some restrictions; for instance, it was stipulated by relevant departments that enterprises not participating in the basic pension insurance would not be eligible to set up enterprise annuity plans. And finally, the management and operation mechanism was not well established. In the most recent two years, financial institutions such as insurance companies have displayed rather high enthusiasm for the development of enterprise annuity plans. Participation of financial institutions will be instrumental to the development of enterprise annuity plans. Furthermore, one current viewpoint of the academic circles is to consolidate the individual accounts of the enterprise annuity and the basic pension insurance after its "replenishment," to enlarge the portion of Pillar II.

Although voluntary individual savings pension insurance has long been deemed as the third layer of the pension insurance system, a clearly established institutional framework and development plan have not yet been in place. The source of financing for this layer can be only the transfer of residents' bank savings. However, to make it a pension plan capable of providing for old age and distinct from the ordinary savings, it is still necessary for financial institutions to develop it as a new type of financial product adapted to provide for old age and then launch it in the market. Marketing this type of financial product needs special promotion, such as exemption or deferment of interest income tax.

Aside from enterprise employees, there is yet another important group of pension beneficiaries—employees working in such public institutions as government offices. For the pension insurance of this group, the funded system with contributions has never been implemented; rather, the traditional pay-as-you-go system has been used for financing. However, with the establishment of the civil service system and advance of the reform of the personnel management system, the tradition of lifetime employment will soon be obsolete, considerably raising the urgency to reform the pension insurance system of public institutions. The new system should adapt to the requirement of the personnel management system reform, and, likewise, should establish individual accounts

---

[21] The Ministry of Labor and Social Security and the National Bureau of Statistics, *2001 Bulletin of Labor and Social Security Undertakings Development Statistics (2001 niandu laodong he shehui baozhang shiye fazhan tongji gongbao),* February 10, 2003, http://news.xinhuanet.com/zhengfu/2003-02/10/content_722425.htm.

of pension insurance for employees of public institutions and set up specific fund plans with joint contributions of individuals and public institutions as employers to achieve the integration with enterprise pension insurance plans in both institutional arrangement and operation mechanism.

9.2.2 Medical Insurance System Reform

From the viewpoint of economic theories, the health care market is different from ordinary markets in many aspects, rendering it unable to fully achieve the optimal outcome that highly competitive markets can achieve. First, the health care market is plagued by asymmetric information. Second, competition in the health care market is not always based on a completely free price system. Third, special entry barriers exist in the health care market, as the government usually implements a special system of entry permissions for medical institutions. Fourth, with a medical security system, often a considerable portion of the medical expenses are paid by a third party, which may invalidate the normal budget constraint on the patient and enables the hospital to increase the price of medical care. And finally, serious problems of moral hazard and adverse selection exist in the medical insurance market. These particularities of the health care market have determined that comprehensive consideration should be given to the medical insurance system and the medical management system. Only when solutions to these problems inherent in the health care market are carefully considered will it be possible to establish a more effective medical security system.

The reform of the medical insurance system for employees in China started in the late 1980s. With the advance of economic system reform, both the government and enterprises became aware of the incompatibility of the traditional public health service system and the new economic system. The government and enterprises bore all expenses, offering no incentive for patients to reduce medical expenses, resulting in a rapid increase in medical expenses. At the same time, medical institutions took this opportunity to increase service costs, blindly importing medical equipment that caused inefficient resource allocation. Under the pressure of rapidly increasing medical costs, financing for medical expenses became all the more difficult. In view of these problems, in March 1989, the State Council transmitted with endorsement the "Main Points of the 1989 Economic System Reform" of SCORES, and decided to carry out reform experiments on the medical insurance system in four cities: Dandong, Siping, Huangshi, and Zhuzhou. Meanwhile, some other localities carried out experiments on their own initiative. This type of reform attempt lasted until 1993. The main objectives of the reform included shifting part of the medical expenses to individual employees, decentralizing the authority for management of medical outlays, and implementing social pooling for medical expenses for retirees as well as for employees with major illnesses. However, these reform measures did not succeed in stopping the rapid increase in medical expenses, and thus it became increasingly difficult for low- and medium-income classes to access medical care.

After the Third Plenary Session of the 14th CCCPC in 1993, relevant government departments began to experiment with a reform in Zhenjiang of Jiangsu Province and Jiujiang of Jiangxi Province, with a combination of social pooling and individual account as its core content. In April 1996, based on the experience in these two cities, the State Council approved *Opinions on the Expansion of Experiments on the Reform of the Medical Security System* jointly issued by four ministries and commissions including SCORES, and expanded the experiments to over fifty cities across the country. The key points of this scheme are as follows.

1. To establish a medical security system including four layers: (i) the basic medical insurance system as social endeavor; (ii) the supplementary medical insurance system as enterprise endeavor; (iii) the commercial medical insurance system as individual endeavor; and (iv) public medical assistance.

2. To feature the basic medical insurance system as "low standard, wide coverage." A low standard carries two meanings: (i) to moderately lower the standard of contribution of employing units and (ii) to guarantee only the basic medical care. Wide coverage also contains two meanings: (i) to widen the scope of medical insurance beneficiaries and (ii) to extend the service of medical insurance to include medical care, drugs, and services.

3. On the basis of basic medical insurance, to put into play the complementary roles of supplementary medical insurance and commercial medical insurance, and to finally have public medical assistance cover all that is left.

4. To implement unified management of basic medical insurance by the labor and social security department of the government.

Cities participating in these experiments studied possibilities based on the aforementioned *Opinions* and created many forms of the combination of social pooling and individual account, such as social pooling for major illnesses.[22] Based on the expanded experiments, the State Council issued in 1998 the *Decision on the Establishment of the Basic Medical Insurance System for Urban Employees,* and decided to establish the system by the end of 1999.

---

[22] Song Xiaowu et al., *China's Social Security System Reform and Development Report (Zhongguo shehui baozhang tizhi gaige yu fazhan baogao)*, Beijing: China Renmin University Press, 2001, pp. 95–99.

The *Decision* adhered to the principle of "low standard, wide coverage" and the combination of social pooling and individual account, mandating that all urban employers participate in a basic medical insurance system administered on a local basis. The contributions of the employer and the individual were 6 and 2 percent, respectively, of the payroll, among which 30 percent of the employer contribution was put into the individual account.

As of December 2002, a total of ninety-four million people nationwide participated in the basic medical insurance system; the balance of the basic medical insurance fund nationwide amounted to RMB 45 billion.[23] However, such chronic problems as high medical outlays, scarce medical resources, and their grossly imbalanced allocation still persist.

As the medical insurance reform involves the reform of financing and payment mechanisms on the demand side of the health care market, it must coordinate with the system reform on the supply side of the health care market and improve the information asymmetry between the consumer and the supplier in the medical service market so that correct market prices can be set to optimize the allocation of medical service resources. However, the slow progress in the reform of the medical service management system makes it difficult for the medical insurance reform as the demand side to achieve its anticipated results alone.

The most visible sign of the mismatch between the two reforms is that over the past years, the practice of allocating medical service resources by the administrative control system as was under the planned economic system has never changed; resources have been highly concentrated in big cities in the form of state-owned hospitals while small and medium cities and vast rural areas have been in severe shortage of resources. At the same time, the entry of domestic private capital and foreign capital has been stringently restricted. The government operates ordinary medical institutions (i.e., nonpublic medical facilities) that are supposed to be business operations, resulting in a great amount of public resources thrown into them without fully meeting their needs. Yet private capital is forbidden to enter the medical service market. Such institutional distortion and restriction on market entry result in a persistent shortage of medical service and therefore increases the cost considerably. In view of such a medical service system, the existing medical insurance plan can only be a high-cost plan with low accessibility for the low-income cohort. Taking the opportunity of medical insurance reform, some regions have attempted to separate the management of medical services and drug sales and to reduce

[23] The Ministry of Labor and Social Security and the National Bureau of Statistics, *2002 Bulletin of Labor and Social Security Undertakings Development Statistics (2002 niandu laodong he shehui baozhang shiye fazhan tongji gongbao)*, May 7, 2003, http://www.stats.gov.cn/tjgb/qttjgb/qgqttjgb/t20030507_77008.htm.

medical expenses by changing the situation of subsidizing medical services by drug sales; however, the results are not very obvious. Reform of the medical service management system will involve many other aspects. For example, medical professionals may have a personnel management system independent of hospitals, and they may be granted qualification for practicing medicine independently, enabling them to provide service on a contract basis independent of hospitals. This will not only increase the income of medical professionals but also improve the unbalanced distribution of medical service resources among different regions. Additionally, this will promote competition among hospitals.

As the financing, payment, and management mechanisms for the demand side of the health care market, the medical insurance plan cannot ignore the underlying features of the health care market as an imperfect market. An effective medical insurance plan should look after any possibility of market failure in the health care market. According to the analysis of Kornai and Eggleston,[24] a co-payment mechanism that requires patients to bear part of the expenses will be instrumental in hardening the budget constraint on demand. A medical insurance plan that requires individuals to bear a portion of their medical expenses will help to control the inordinate growth of medical expenses. However, given the fact that the health care market is plagued by information asymmetry, the pressure from medical service suppliers for increasing costs can only be resisted by strengthening the extent of organization of the medical insurance plans. As the extent of organization increases, the ability of patient organizations to access information and to bargain over prices with medical institutions will also improve. Hence, the reform of the medical insurance system in China is not simply a problem of financing and management, but of strengthening the ability of policyholders as consumers to influence the market prices by enhancing their extent of organization.

9.2.3 Unemployment Insurance

In 1986, China introduced the *Enterprise Bankruptcy Law* and the labor contract system in SOEs. To conform to the requirements of the SOE reform, the State Council issued the *Interim Regulations on Unemployment Insurance of State-Owned Enterprises,* thereby initiating an unemployment insurance system. On this basis, in April 1993, the State Council issued the *Regulations on Unemployment Insurance of State-Owned Enterprise Employees.* In November 1993, the unemployment insurance system was officially adopted in the *Decision on Issues Regarding the Establishment of a Socialist Market Economic System* of

---

[24]János Kornai and Karen Eggleston, *Welfare, Choice and Solidarity in Transition: Reforming the Health Sector in Eastern Europe,* Cambridge: Cambridge University Press, 2001.

the Third Plenary Session of the 14th CCCPC, and put onto a track of fast development since then. By the end of 2002, the unemployment insurance covered a total of 102 million people.[25]

The funds for the unemployment insurance system come from unemployment insurance premiums contributed by enterprises, interest proceeds from the unemployment insurance fund, and subsidies from the government. Normally, the rate of enterprise contribution is no more than 1 percent of its payroll, and no individual account is established. In the late 1990s, as the problem of lay-offs in SOEs aggravated, it was no longer possible for the unemployment insurance system alone to guarantee the basic living standard of laid-off workers. Therefore, the central government adopted a "triple-support" financing plan for laid-off workers. The central government, the local government, and the enterprise each contributed one-third to the payment of basic living expenses for laid-off workers. As unemployment insurance revenue was inadequate to meet expenditure, especially when a considerable portion of the living expenses of laid-off workers had to be covered by the unemployment insurance, in May 1998, it was determined at the Meeting on Reemployment of Laid-Off Workers of State-Owned Enterprises convened by the central government that the rate of unemployment insurance contribution would be increased from 1 percent to 3 percent of total wages, of which 1 percent would be borne by individuals.[26]

In recent years, the unemployment insurance has been declining. According to official statistics, in 2002, the number of people participating in the unemployment insurance plan decreased by 1.73 million compared to 2001.[27] Recently, some scholars suggested that the unemployment insurance be incorporated into the minimum living guarantee system for urban residents. In practice, however, the unemployment insurance fund is used in many regions to pay for reemployment training and employment services for the unemployed, but these are the functions not covered by the minimum living guarantee system for urban residents. Therefore, the future of the existing unemployment insurance system remains uncertain.

---

[25] The Ministry of Labor and Social Security and the National Bureau of Statistics, *2002 Bulletin of Labor and Social Security Undertakings Development Statistics (2002 niandu laodong he shehui baozhang shiye fazhan tongji gongbao)*, May 7, 2003, http://www.stats.gov.cn/tjgb/qttjgb/qgqttjgb/t20030507_77008.htm.

[26] CCCPC and the State Council, *Circular of CCCPC and the State Council Concerning Practically Better Carrying out the Work of the Basic Living Guarantee and Reemployment of Laid-Off Workers of State-Owned Enterprises (Zhonggong Zhongyang Guowuyuan guanyu qieshi zuohao guoyouqiye xiagang zhigong jiben shenghuo baozhang he zaijiuye gongzuo de tongzhi)*, June 9, 1998, http://www.molss.gov.cn/correlate/zf199810.htm. Also see the Ministry of Labor and Social Security, the State Economic and Trade Commission, the Ministry of Finance, the Ministry of Education, the National Bureau of Statistics and the All China Federation of Trade Unions, *Circular on Strengthening Management of Laid-Off Workers of State-Owned Enterprises and Establishment of Reemployment Service Centers (Guanyu jiaqiang guoyouqiye xiagang zhigong guanli he zaijiuye fuwu zhongxin jianshe youguan wenti de tongzhi)*, August 3, 1998, http://www.molss.gov.cn/correlate/LSBF19988.htm.

[27] The Ministry of Labor and Social Security and the National Bureau of Statistics, ibid.

9.2.4 Minimum Living Guarantee System

As the advance of China's economic reform demanded for a better social safety net, which was obviously impossible under the existing social security arrangement, the Chinese government decided to establish a minimum living guarantee (*dibao*) system for urban residents. In September 1997, the State Council issued the *Circular Regarding the Establishment of a Minimum Living Guarantee System for Urban Residents across the Country,* requiring that a minimum living guarantee system for urban residents in cities and towns be established during the period of the Ninth Five-Year Plan to guarantee the basic needs of urban residents. Its main points are as follows.

The beneficiaries of the minimum living guarantee system are urban residents of nonagricultural residence status with a per capita household income lower than the local minimum living standard, including the following three categories: (1) residents without a source of income, labor capacity, or supporters; (2) residents receiving unemployment benefits or unable to be reemployed upon their expiration, with a per capita household income lower than the minimum living standard; and (3) active employees, laid-off workers, or retirees with a per capita household income lower than the minimum living standard even after receiving wages, minimum wages/basic living expenses, or pensions, respectively.

The minimum living standard for urban residents is to be determined solely by the local governments on the basis of the local realities and the principle of securing basic needs while overcoming a dependency mentality. It should be parallel with the local cost of basic living and the bearing capacity of local government finance, and made known to the public after its approval by the local government. Adjustments should be made to reflect changes in prices of living necessities and improvement in the people's living standards.

Funds needed for the implementation of the minimum living guarantee system for urban residents should be listed by local governments at various levels in their fiscal budget and be incorporated into the special expenditure items for social welfare and managed as a separate account. Cities currently adopting the practice of sharing the financial responsibility for minimum living allowance between the government finance and the work units of the beneficiaries should gradually switch to the practice of government financing.

In recent years, various localities have achieved rapid development in the establishment of the minimum living guarantee system. Statistics show that by the end of September 2002, the number of poor residents enjoying the minimum living allowance nationwide had reached 19.63 million; the average minimum living standard nationwide was RMB 152 per capita per month; and the average minimum living allowance payment to beneficiaries nationwide was RMB 70 per capita per month.

In some well-off regions, attempts are being made to extend the minimum living guarantee system to rural residents. For instance, Zhejiang Province has implemented the minimum living guarantee system for all people in the province since October 2001.

9.2.5 Rural Social Security

China has a rural population of over nine hundred million. Under the People's Commune system, China's rural areas developed a social security system with the "Five Guarantees" (referring to care and material assistance such as food, clothing, housing, medical services, and burial for those without source of income, working capacity, or supporters) and a rural cooperative medical service (i.e., "barefoot doctors"). However, the degree of security was very low and the necessary expenses were borne mainly by collective economic entities. After the implementation of the household contracting system, the rural social security system lost its original source of financing (i.e., collective economic organizations) and fell apart. Under current conditions in the vast rural areas, there is virtually no effective supply of medical service resources. Restricted by low income, the farmers have no opportunity to enjoy the medical service resources allocated mainly to cities. Because of this, health of the rural population as well as the public health conditions in rural areas are compromised.

In October 1986, the Ministry of Civil Affairs decided to implement the rural pension insurance in regions with a fairly developed rural economy, with the community as the unit. However, the development of rural pension insurance was not successful. At the end of 2001, the number of people in rural areas participating in the pension insurance was about sixty million; by the end of 2002, the figure had dropped to around fifty-four million.

There are two basic problems facing the rural social security system: the first is the financing and management of funds to convert potential demand for social security in rural areas effective demand, and the second is the allocation of social security resources to ensure an effective supply. The settlement of these two basic problems requires the development of a rural social security system on both the demand and the supply sides at the same time. This has been subject to the constraint of a number of practical conditions.

The gap between urban and rural areas has had a long history in China, and it will not be eliminated in the foreseeable future. Under this constraint, the rural social security system must be developed separately from the urban social security system. It should not aspire to be grandiose, but rather, with a focus on the key issues, develop an overall plan for steady progress. Diversified views can be found among the academic circles and policymakers concerning the development strategy for rural social security. One view believes that the rural social security should combine social security with household provision, jointly funded by the state, the collective, and the individual. Another argument is that, in the rural society where the traditional mode of agricultural production has not yet completely changed, household provision is still the main way to resist various risks. Under such a traditional mode of production, the most appropriate model would be some kind of cooperative social security on the basis of voluntary participation by farmers, rather than the compulsory social security with social pooling. Hence, the development strategy for rural social security should be to guide rural communities to set up voluntary and informal cooperative security organizations.

One way to integrate the reasonable components of these different viewpoints is for the government to provide a suitable institutional framework to guide rural areas and farmers in raising and managing a rural cooperative social security fund and determining the specific social security benefits through the existing villagers' self-governing organizations. The social security financial aid provided by the government should be supplied to farmers in dire need through a mechanism with a positive incentive to increase its efficiency. The practice in some regions of providing farmers with a basic social security allowance by making use of an insurance mechanism is certainly a measure worthy of consideration.

As the income level of rural households remains quite low, it is impossible, without external assistance, for farmers to establish a rural social security system capable of providing protection against multiple risks. The development of a rural social security system will be a long-term process and should focus on the key issues. At present, however, the development of a medical service system including a public health system with social pooling may be more urgent than a pension insurance system.

Under the constraint of the present realities, rural medical resources should be allocated to institutional "growing points" with comparative advantage according to the theory of comparative advantage. For instance, the resources of traditional Chinese medicine can be developed and utilized in favor of rural areas. Medical professionals can collect, sort out, and authenticate the resources of traditional Chinese medicine. Protection can be provided in the form of qualifications for practicing traditional Chinese medicine and patents for traditional Chinese treatments with real therapeutic effects. Such endeavors can, to a great extent, alleviate the problem of sick farmers being unable to afford treatment because of the high-priced urban medical service resources.

CHAPTER 10

MACROECONOMIC POLICIES IN THE TRANSITIONAL PERIOD

In a planned economy, the whole society is organized into a giant company with the government as the administrative office. The administration of this "Party-State Inc." by the government results in government control of the entire national economy with no distinction between macroeconomic and microeconomic issues. With the transition from a planned economy to a market economy and the enlarged autonomy of microeconomic agents, macroeconomic issues have become the focus of the government. Moreover, because of the peculiarities of this transitional period, these issues need to be approached differently from how they are handled under a planned economy and how they are usually dealt with under a market economy. All these warrant special discussions of macroeconomic issues in this chapter.

10.1 Macroeconomic Issues and Macroeconomic Policies

Before World War II, mainstream economics did not divide microeconomics and macroeconomics in research on market economies. However, the reason for this lack of distinction was not the same as the reason for it in a planned economy. The logic of classical economics is that the totality of an economy is the sum of all economic entities (households and enterprises). Based on this logic, aggregate demand of the society is the sum of demands of all entities in the society, and aggregate supply of the society is the sum of supplies of all entities in the society. Because supply and demand are always in equilibrium in every business transaction in classical economics, the relation between aggregate supply and aggregate demand should also be in equilibrium. Obviously, this theory fails to explain any disequilibrium of aggregates in a market economy, as occurs in an economic crisis.

Although economic aggregates, such as economic growth and unemployment, were part of early economics studies, macroeconomics was not perceived as an independent branch of economics because classical economists thought that relative prices in market economies are indicators of the relative scarcity of various resources and can efficiently allocate resources. Furthermore, according to classical economics, changes in prices automatically work to bring supply and demand into equilibrium and achieve long-term stable growth.

The worldwide Great Depression in the 1930s severely challenged classical economic theory and led to the Keynesian revolution. John Maynard Keynes pointed out that the classical economic theory of market price fluctuations resulting in automatic equilibrium could not overcome short-term difficulties, but only explain long-term economic trends. According to Keynesian theory, the cause of economic recession is the insufficient aggregate demand for goods and services in the short run. Thus, Keynes proposed to use government fiscal and monetary policies to alleviate economic depression. By the end of World War II, major market economy countries, such as the United Kingdom and the United States, adopted Keynesian concepts by using expansionary macroeconomic policies to alleviate and prevent economic crisis, and these countries achieved notable success. At the same time, however, inflation arose with the alleviation of depression. In response to this situation, Keynesians advised contractionary macroeconomic policies to suppress inflation.

In 1958, based on unemployment rates and changes in wage rates in Britain between 1861 and 1957, A. W. Phillips, of the London School of Economics, suggested that there is a tradeoff between inflation and unemployment: when inflation rate is high, the unemployment rate is low, and when the inflation rate goes down, unemployment increases. Using U.S. data, economists Paul A. Samuelson (1915–) and Robert M. Solow (1924–) proved in 1960 that there is a negative correlation between inflation and unemployment and named it the Phillips curve. Keynesian economists believe that the Phillips curve offers guidance for macroeconomic policies in finding an optimum point along the Phillips curve where a moderate level of inflation is used to alleviate unemployment, or contractionary policies are used to alleviate the pressure of inflation.

Keynesian theory was challenged by economists Milton Friedman (1912–) and Edmund S. Phelps (1933–), who pointed out that there was no negative correlation between inflation and unemployment in the long run. Developments since have shown that both theories have merit, depending on whether they are applied to short-run analysis or long-run analysis. More discussion on this subject occurs in Section 10.3 of this chapter.

10.2 Inflation between 1980 and 1994

For a long time after China started reform and opening up at the end of 1978, inflation occurred again and again, and each was worse than the previous one.

10.2.1 Inflation Is a Common Problem in the Transitional Period

As mentioned in Chapter 1, in addition to China, most Eastern European socialist countries have been plagued by inflation as they sought to reform their economic systems during the transition to a market economy. Worsening macroeconomic situations were important factors in the economic collapses and social turbulence in Hungary, Poland, and Yugoslavia in the late 1980s.

Why does inflation frequently occur during the transition from a planned economy to a market economy? Many economists have studied this issue. They believe the reasons for this occurrence mainly are as follows.

First, hidden inflation is unveiled when economic change is implemented. Hungarian economist János Kornai said in 1980 that a planned economy was a kind of shortage economy.[1] In other words, the normal state of a planned economy is that aggregate supply is insufficient to satisfy aggregate demand. However, as prices of most goods under planned economic systems are fixed, aggregate supply shortage usually does not manifest itself as increases in prices; instead, supply shortages remain hidden by administrative suppression and find expression in rationing systems and additional search costs.

The core of the market system is its free-price mechanism. Therefore, after market-oriented reform began in China and European socialist countries, controls over prices of goods and services are lifted sooner or later, and resources start being allocated by the free fluctuation of prices. Once liberalized, prices of various goods rise and fall inevitably. If aggregate supply and aggregate demand match each other, there will be no prevalent shortage of supply, and relative prices will not constantly rise. However, when there is hidden inflation and administrative suppression of prices loosens, the hidden inflation becomes apparent. In this case, during marketization reform and price liberalization, continuing increases in prices are unavoidable.

Second, in the transition period, especially in its early phases, there exist many factors that increase expenditures and reduce revenues. The fundamental objective of economic reform is to establish a market economic system to lay an institutional foundation for sustainable and stable growth of the national economy. But the transition from a planned economy to a market economy takes years or decades to complete. During the transition, the fiscal system is affected by many factors that increase expenditures and reduce revenues. It takes time for reform to increase the overall efficiency of the whole national economy. During the transition, preexisting macroeconomic control measures of a planned economy gradually weaken and become ineffective, but at the same time, the regulating mechanisms of a market economy have not yet been established. This results in a "mechanism vacuum" or "mechanism deadlock," weakening the government control over aggregate fiscal revenue and expenditure and decreasing budgetary revenues and monetary income. Reform also means significant adjustments to the preexisting pattern of interests. To increase support of and neutralize opposition to reform, the

---

[1] János Kornai, *Economics of Shortage,* Amsterdam: North-Holland Publishing Company, 1980.

adjustments should not only help the disadvantaged in the old system, but also ensure that vested interests not suffer substantial losses. In addition, those who do suffer losses as a result of reform measures should be compensated, so, as a result, most people can benefit from reform. To ensure that as many benefit from reform as possible, the state needs to increase resources used to pay for the costs of reform. Overall, mechanism vacuum and the increased resources needed to support reform are likely to lead to increases in fiscal deficit, shortages of supplies, and instability of markets, and thus increased inflationary pressure in the early stages of reform.

Third, during the course of reform, deficiencies in macroeconomic control and policy mistakes make curbing inflation impossible at its early stages. As mentioned, fairly high inflation is unavoidable in the course of reform, but this does not mean that reform definitely leads to hyperinflation, let alone that an inflationary policy should be adopted to aggravate rising prices. As a matter of fact, the level of inflation differed greatly among the different countries transitioning their economies along with China. Some nations adopted effective measures in time to keep inflation within acceptable limits while others experienced out-of-control inflation that led to social unrest or even collapse of the political regime.

However, during the transition, achieving sound macroeconomic control often is a difficult task. First, a sound macroeconomic control infrastructure is a prerequisite to sound macroeconomic control. For example, it is necessary to have an independent and effective central bank system; a sound mechanism for transmitting monetary policy; and enterprises with hard budget constraint, among other factors. During transition, especially at its early stages, all these infrastructure components likely do not exist. Second, the application of fiscal, monetary, and income policies by the government to maintain macroeconomic stability is essentially an art of great delicacy. To let officials—who are used to operating with administrative orders in a planned economy but unfamiliar with modern economics—undertake macroeconomic control more often than not produces unsatisfactory results, to put it mildly. Finally, during transition, macroeconomic decisions are usually made by political leaders. When weighing long-term versus short-term interests, they, being politicians, tend to prefer the shorter view. As a result, when choosing between the need to maintain macroeconomic stability versus promoting faster long-term growth with efficiency and expansionary macroeconomic policies, the macroeconomic authorities often choose the second item as a priority over the first, a preference that definitely leads to hyperinflation.

10.2.2 Four Rounds of Overheated Economy and Changes in Macroeconomic Policies between 1980 and 1994

The fifteen years between 1980 and 1994 saw four rounds of severe economic fluctuation in China, which all began with expansionary macroeconomic policies, especially an expansionary monetary policy. The result was an overheated economy and surging prices for commodities (see Table 10.1). When the overheated economy and inflation caused severe negative effects both economically and politically, macroeconomic policies were switched to contractionary ones, and economic stability was restored after varying adjustment periods.

10.2.2.1 The First Round of Economic Fluctuation between 1978 and 1983

With the end of the Great Cultural Revolution in 1976, people were inspired, and there was enthusiasm for development and investment in a spurt of "go all out and go fast" throughout the nation, from the leadership to the masses. Without considering the actual grossly distorted economic structure and economic system, the leaders of China's central government failed to give priority to adjustments and reform, but rather organized the so-called Imported Leap Forward, following the tradition of high-target, high-input, low-efficiency, extensive growth. Formulated in February 1978, the *Ten-Year Planning Outline for the Development of National Economy during 1976 to 1985* set targets of, between 1978 and 1985, constructing or expanding 120 large projects and building 14 large bases of heavy industry all over the country. Within the eight-year period, China's gross value of industrial output was supposed to grow at an average annual rate of 10 percent or more, according to the *Outline*.

To make the new leap forward a reality, the principle discussion meetings of the State Council held July to September 1978, emphasized the need to obtain foreign advanced technology and equipment in large quantities. Within a few months after the meetings, China signed contracts to import nine large-scale chemical projects costing a total of RMB 16 billion and another twenty-two projects costing a total of RMB 60 billion, including Baosteel and one hundred sets of integrated coal-mining equipment. Such huge investment and so many large-scale projects simultaneously undergoing construction sent a tremendous shock throughout the national economy. In the wake of a decade of turmoil during the Great Cultural Revolution, China's national economy was at the brink of collapse. Adding new "sufferings" in the form of these massive investments to the "body on the sickbed" generated all kinds of symptoms of an overheated economy.[2]

---

[2] A system-related factor that caused this overheated economy was the reform of "expanding enterprise autonomy" undertaken by state-owned enterprises. The impact of this reform on macroeconomic conditions was discussed in Chapter 4.

Table 10.1   Price Indices since 1978 (year-to-year growth, %)

Year	Retail Price Index	Consumer Price Index (CPI)
1978	0.7	
1979	2.0	
1980	6.0	
1981	2.4	
1982	1.9	
1983	1.5	
1984	2.8	
1985	8.8	9.3
1986	6.0	6.5
1987	7.3	7.3
1988	18.5	18.8
1989	17.8	18.0
1990	2.1	3.1
1991	2.9	3.4
1992	5.4	6.4
1993	13.2	14.7
1994	21.7	24.1
1995	14.8	17.1
1996	6.1	8.3
1997	0.8	2.8
1998	−2.6	−0.8
1999	−3.0	−1.4
2000	−1.5	0.4
2001	−0.8	0.7
2002	−1.3	−0.8
2003	−0.1	1.2

Source: The National Bureau of Statistics, *China Statistical Yearbook (Zhongguo tongji nianjian)*, Beijing: China Statistics Press, various years.

For example, fiscal deficit increased quickly and extensively. While the fiscal surplus was RMB 1.01 billion in 1978, the astounding deficit was RMB 20.6 billion in 1979, or 5.2 percent of GDP, generating substantial pressure for monetary expansion. The annual growth rate of the cash supply (M_0) soared from 9.7 percent in 1978 to 24.4 percent in 1979 and 25.5 percent in 1980; the annual growth rate of bank credit balances rose from 10.2 percent in 1979 to 18.3 percent in 1980.

Under such macroeconomic conditions, prices of commodities began to rise although most were still under administrative control at that time. The retail price index increased by 0.7 percent in 1978, 2.0 percent in 1979, and 6.0 percent in 1980.

In view of this situation, the Financial and Economic Committee of the State Council, founded in March 1979 and headed by Chen Yun and Li Xiannian, put forward the Eight-Character Guideline of "readjusting, restructuring, straightening out and upgrading." However, this guideline could not be enforced for some time because of ongoing large-scale capital construction and the reform of enterprises by "power-delegating and profit-sharing" taking place at that time. The Central Committee of the Communist Party of China (CCCPC) decided in the winter of 1980 to "further readjust the national economy" more extensively in the next year.[3] This time, the readjustment of the national economy was carried out in the general milieu of "insisting on the dominance of the planned economy."[4] During the three years between 1979 and 1981, the following contractionary measures were taken: (a) investment in fixed assets and capital construction projects was scaled down, (b) outlays for national defense and administration expenditures was cut, (c) bank credit was put under tight control while savings accounts of enterprises were frozen, and (d) RMB 4.8 billion in government bonds were issued to enterprises by administrative order.

In response to these policies and measures, the inflation rate began to fall in 1981 and reached its trough at the beginning of 1983 (see Table 10.2). The balance of international trade turned from deficit to surplus as well.

Because this round of economic fluctuation involved certain characteristics related to changes in the pattern of interests resulting from economic reform, it was considered the first economic cycle after the inception of reform and opening up.

10.2.2.2 The Second Round of Economic Fluctuation between 1984 and 1986

In September 1982, the 12th National Congress of the CPC formally set the strategic goal of China's development, i.e., to quadruple the gross value of industrial and agricultural outputs by the end of the twentieth century. A corresponding strategic focus and implementation plan were also established. According to the original plan, during the twenty years between 1980 and 2000, the first ten years would involve laying the

---

[3]Chen Yun, "Economic Situation and Economic Lessons (Jingji xingshi yu jingji jiaoxun) (December 16, 1980)," *Selected Works of Chen Yun (Chen Yun wenxuan) (1956–1985)*, Beijing: People's Publishing House, 1986, pp. 248–254.
[4]Chen Yun, "On Planning and Market Issues (Jihua yu shichang wenti) (March 8, 1979);" "Several Important Guidelines on Economic Construction (Jingji jianshe de jige zhongyao fangzhen) (December 22, 1981);" "Enhance and Improve the Work of Economic Planning (Jiaqiang he gaijin jingji jihua gongzuo) (January 25, 1982)," all in *Selected Works of Chen Yun (Chen Yun wenxuan) (1956–1985)*, Beijing: People's Publishing House, 1986, pp. 220–223, 275–277, and 278–280.

Table 10.2   China's Macroeconomic Situation during 1978–1983 (year to year, %)

Year	1978	1979	1980	1981	1982	1983
GDP Growth	11.7	7.6	7.8	5.2	9.1	10.9
Increase in Retail Price Index	0.7	2.0	6.0	2.4	1.9	1.5

Source: The National Bureau of Statistics, *China Statistical Yearbook (Zhongguo tongji nianjian)*, Beijing: China Statistics Press, various years.

foundation, and the second ten years would see the economy take off. At that time, the plan aroused enthusiasm at all levels, and, encouraged by some central government leaders, starting in early 1984, many local governments started vying with each other, raising the target at every level, and demanding the enlargement of their investment to "quadruple ahead of schedule." Although leaders of the central government later repeatedly called for calm, some local governments adopted strategies of "starting your projects while those of everyone else are suspended" and "keep advancing amid criticism" based on their past experience. These local governments kept expanding, making it even more difficult to check the overheating of the economy. In September 1984, the Third Plenary Session of the 12th CCCPC turned its back on the resurgence of the planned economy ideology that had occurred between 1981 and 1983, and explicitly set the goal of reform as establishing a socialist commodity economy. In those days, the public readily embraced optimistic sentiments, believing that they would be able to carry out reform with a free hand, and the Chinese economy would soon take off. Meanwhile, October 1984 happened to be the grand celebration of the thirty-fifth anniversary of the founding of the People's Republic of China. Some leaders advocated the concept of "being able to earn and being willing to spend," so many government agencies and enterprises scrambled to raise salaries and to distribute bonuses and consumer goods such as clothing, adding more fuel to the flames of an overheated economy.

In addition, a technical error was made when measures to expand the autonomy of specialized banks to grant loans, which were supposed to be implemented in 1985, were formulated. The error was the stipulation that the central bank would use the total of actual loans granted by each specialized bank in 1984 as the base quota in setting the credit quota of that specialized bank in succeeding years. Therefore, every specialized bank, to raise its 1985 credit quota, competed with each other to expand the scale of bank credit by setting targets for every lower level and deliberately fabricating a larger base quota. Branches of specialized banks not only approved all loan applications from enterprises but also visited enterprises to solicit applications, requesting enterprises to borrow more.

The combined effect was that the money supply increased rapidly. Total amount of bank credit in 1984 increased by 28.8 percent on a year-on-year basis, and December of 1984 saw an increase of 84.4 percent compared with the same month the previous year. The supply of cash (M_0) increased by 49.5 percent on a year-on-year basis. At the end of the first quarter of 1985, M_0, M_1, and M_2 increased by 59 percent, 39 percent, and 44 percent, respectively, compared with the same period the previous year. As could be expected, starting with the second quarter of 1985, prices rose rapidly.

In late 1984 and 1985, economists and policymakers had different opinions about whether the economy was overheated and contractionary policies were necessary. As a result, the government was unable decide on policies in a timely manner. The then leader of the State Council agreed with the analysis that money circulation was abnormal[5] and believed that inflation was unfavorable to development and reform. He thus agreed to tighten macroeconomic control and to implement contractionary policies to stabilize the economy. With the approval of Deng Xiaoping at the end of January 1985, he called a meeting of provincial governors in early February, requesting them to take actions to halt the expansion of investment and consumption. Because of differing opinions within the central leadership, however, this effort failed to produce significant effect. Only with the intervention of Deng Xiaoping did different opinions on how to deal with inflation among the Chinese leaders converge. Under such conditions, the State Council demanded that all local governments formulate plans to stop further rises in prices. At the same time, the State Council decided to send out inspection teams to all provinces to supervise the reduction of capital construction projects.

Beginning with the third quarter of 1985, the growth rate of investment fell every month. Meanwhile, the People's Bank of China adopted a contractionary monetary policy, and in addition to enhancing control over credit quotas, it raised both deposit interest rates and lending interest rates twice in succession. Accordingly, the interest rates for working capital loans and capital construction loans both increased. As a result of these changes in both administrative and economic measures, the money supply in the second half of 1985 began to fall. In the first quarter of 1986, annual growth rates of M_0 and M_2 dropped to 14 percent and 13 percent, respectively, and the growth of the price index and GDP also fell quickly (see Table 10.3).

Accompanying the economic fluctuation of 1984 to 1986 were constant and vociferous debates on theories and policies. As early as the end of 1984, when signs of an

---

[5] Wu Jinglian, Li Jian'ge, and Ding Ningning, "The Current Situation of Money Circulation and the Measures to Deal with It (Danqian huobi liutong xingshi he duice) (December 31, 1984)," in Wu Jinglian and Hu Ji (eds.), *Dynamic Analysis and Policy Studies of Chinese Economy (Zhongguo jingji de dongtai fenxi he duice yanjiu)*, Beijing: China Renmin University Press, 1989, pp. 1–11.

Table 10.3 China's Macroeconomic Situation during 1983–1986 (year to year, %)

Year	1983	1984	1985	1986
GDP Growth	10.9	15.2	13.5	8.8
Growth of Investment in Fixed Assets	15.3	26.1	51.4	14.6
Increase in Retail Price Index	1.5	2.8	8.8	6.0

Source: The National Bureau of Statistics, *China Statistical Yearbook (Zhongguo tongji nianjian),* Beijing: China Statistics Press, various years.

overheated economy first appeared, economic policy advisory agencies and economists launched a fierce debate on the macroeconomic situation of the time. Economists advocating expansionary macroeconomic policies argued that increases in the money supply were required to implement the policy of "opening to the outside world and invigorating the domestic economy." The growth of the money supply exceeding the growth of economy was a requirement of economy itself, as reasonably higher money supply growth above that of the economy as a whole would promote production. Economists used their "theory of disequilibrium" to justify an inflationary policy. They argued that aggregate demand exceeding aggregate supply was the norm of a socialist economy. In a developing socialist country like China, in the foreseeable future, its national economy would always be in the "disequilibrium" state, with which aggregate demand exceeded aggregate supply. Any attempt to use macro control measures to suppress aggregate demand and to limit money supply would not only harm high-speed growth but also cause damage to the interests of all parties and, subsequently, weaken the support for reform. Therefore, contractionary macroeconomic policies were inadvisable.[6]

Contrary to this point of view, other economists argued that international experience repeatedly demonstrated that inflation was not only disadvantageous to development but also harmful to reform. In the meantime, considering societal acceptability, these economists believed that overall reform of the economic system, including the price system, should have the prerequisite that aggregate demand more or less matched aggregate supply; that the economic environment was rather easygoing; and that national financial resources were sufficient to avoid severe inflation when the government debuted the next round of major reform measures. Therefore, according to these econ-

[6] See Li Yining, "Several Theoretical Issues in Economic Reform Starved for Study (Guanyu jingji gaige zhong jidai yanjiu de jige lilun wenti)," *Economic Development and System Reform (Jingji fazhan yu tizhi gaige),* 1986, No. 5. See also Li Yining, *Political Economy of Socialism (Shehuizhuyi zhengzhi jingjixue),* Beijing: The Commercial Press, 1986, pp. 466–471.

omists, the party and the government should decisively move to reduce aggregate demand, increase aggregate supply, and rapidly implement the first batch of supporting reforms when the economic environment was improved to a certain extent, so the new economic system could start functioning and help the national economy enter a positive cycle as soon as possible.

Liu Guoguang was one of the advocates for the "argument for a good environment," or the "argument for an easy-going environment." In his *On the Relation between Economic Readjustment and Economic Reform in Brief* (1979),[7] *On Buyers' Market Again* (1983),[8] and *On Issues Regarding the Development of Socialist Commodity Economy*,[9] he repeated the necessity of keeping inflation in control and creating an "easy-going environment" for reform.

In this debate, the International Conference on Macroeconomic Management, also known as the Bashanlun Conference, sponsored by the State Commission for Restructuring Economic Systems, the Chinese Academy of Social Sciences, and the World Bank, September 2 to 7, 1985, played the leading role in correcting theoretical economic misconceptions. Through in-depth discussions among economists at this conference, a conclusion with sufficient scientific backing about what macroeconomic policies China should adopt was arrived at. In particular, James Tobin, dubbed a master in Keynesianism and monetary issues, silenced the argument in the name of Western mainstream economics that inflation is beneficial to economic development. Based on the World Bank's briefing on China's economic situation, Tobin pointed out that China was facing the risk of severe inflation. He proposed that China adopt "triple-contractionary policies," that is, a contractionary fiscal policy, a contractionary monetary policy, and a contractionary income policy, instead of the combination of a contractionary monetary policy and an expansionary fiscal policy that is usually adopted by Western countries to avoid a crisis when they face moderate inflation. The Bashanlun Conference also made the leader of the State Council fully resolved to implement stabilization policies.[10]

The policy derived from this debate was drawn by the National Congress of the CPC in September 1985. At the meeting, Deng Xiaoping pointed out that "if the growth rate were too high, it would bring many problems that would have a negative effect on the reform and on social conduct. It is better to be prudent. We must control the scale of

---

[7] Liu Guoguang, *Discussion about Economic Reform and Economic Adjustment (Lun jingji gaige yu jingji tiaozheng)*, Nanjing: Jiangsu People's Publishing House, 1983, p. 10.

[8] Liu Guoguang, *Selected Works of Liu Guoguang (Liu Guoguang xuanji)*, Taiyuan: Shanxi People's Publishing House, 1986, p. 434.

[9] *Social Sciences in China (Zhongguo shehui kexue)*, 1986, No. 6.

[10] China Society of Economic Reform, *Macroeconomic Management and Reform—Selected Speeches of the International Conference on Macroeconomic Management (Hongguan jingji de guanli he gaige—hongguan jingji guanli guoji taolunhui yanlun xuanbian)*, Beijing: Economic Daily Press, 1986.

investment in fixed assets and see that capital construction is not overextended."[11] The *Suggestions of the CCCPC Regarding the Seventh Five-Year Plan for National Economy and Social Development* made at this meeting said that according to the comprehensive analyses and scientific assessment of economic and social conditions in China, in the Seventh Five-Year Plan period (1986–1990), economic and social development should adhere to the four fundamental guiding principles, of which at least two directly pertained to macroeconomic policies.

1. "Reform should be given top priority and should be well-coordinated and mutually supportive of development. Fundamentally speaking, reform serves development. For the time being, arrangements for development should be favorable for the advance of reform. In order to pave the way for reform, the economic growth rate should be set at a reasonable level. Every care should be taken to prevent blindly vying with each other and going after the growth of output quantities and output values so as to avoid tension and dislocation in economic activities and to create a good economic environment for reform."

2. "Equilibrium of aggregate demand and aggregate supply should be maintained and accumulation and consumption should be kept at an appropriate ratio. The key issue here is that while the government should make appropriate arrangements for the livelihoods of the people, it also bears responsibility to keep tab on the country's financial strength to determine the reasonable scale of investment in fixed assets, realizing balances in the country's financial position, credit position, tangible resources, and foreign exchange, as well as an overall balance among them. They are basic conditions for ensuring appropriate proportions of the economy, a stable economic life, and smooth progress of the system reform."

To say the least, the argument made by the National Congress of the CPC was a profound summary, based on experiences and lessons since the commencement of reform, of how to correctly deal with the relations between reform and economic growth and between reform and economic environment, and it should have been used to guide China's macroeconomic policies. Unfortunately, before long these lessons learned at a high price seemed to be forgotten, and thus, much more severe inflation began in 1986 and broke out in full in 1988.

Apparently, whether or not an expansionary monetary policy should be adopted and an inflationary policy used to spur short-term economic growth was not just a theoret-

---

[11] Deng Xiaoping, "Speech at the National Conference of the Communist Party of China (Zai Zhongguo Gongchandang Quanguo Daibiao Huiyi shang de jianghua) (September 23, 1985)," *Selected Works of Deng Xiaoping (Deng Xiaoping wenxuan)*, Vol. 3, Beijing: People's Publishing House, 1993, p. 143.

ical argument, but was often goaded by real interests in economic and political terms. Consequently, there have always been people with reasons to advocate an inflationary policy. In early April 1988, based on his own in-depth analysis of China's economic situation, at the Third Sino-Japan Academic Exchange of Economics held in Beijing, the renowned Japanese economist Ryutaro Komiya pointed out that from the autumn of 1984 to mid-1987, China had suffered from rampant inflation and mammoth deficit in international trade. The very basic nature of this "overheated economy" was typical demand-pull inflation. "This phenomenon had not come to an end by mid-1987," said Ryutaro Komiya.[12]

For various reasons, Chinese economists and leaders attached less weight to this point of view than they ought to have. Support for the opinion that "inflation cannot be harmful, but only be helpful" reached its peak in the spring of 1988. Some economists even investigated economic situations of countries in Latin America to support their opinion that inflation rates of thousands of percent were not frightening at all. Chinese leaders were misled. It was not until the outbreaks of hyperinflation (monthly increases in the consumer price index equivalent to an annual increase of 80 percent) and panic buying in August 1988 that these economists were silenced, at least for the time being.

10.2.2.3 The Third Round of Economic Fluctuation between 1987 and 1990

As mentioned in Chapter 2 of this book, according to the Chinese government's original plan, its guideline for economic affairs for 1986 was to continue to stabilize the economy so as to prepare for "radical reform measures" in 1987. However, at the beginning of 1986, the Chinese economic growth rate was slowing down, and in February, GDP growth was reported as zero. At that time, the government decided to loosen control over bank credit. As a result, starting in the second quarter of 1986, the money supply increased sharply, which led to inflation resurfacing in the fourth quarter of 1987. But at this time, leaders were convinced of the misperception that "inflation cannot be harmful, but only be helpful." They believed that there was no macroeconomic problem in 1987, only a local problem of agricultural production. To dispel worries about inflation, the 1988 "No. 1 Document" of the CCCPC changed its usual theme from agricultural issues to macroeconomic issues. The document argued that the economy in 1987 achieved growth with efficiency and high speed without any risk of inflation. Thus, in mid-1988, the annual growth rates of M_1 and M_2 reached 33 percent and 29 percent, respectively.

---

[12]Ryutaro Komiya, "The 'Overheated Economy' from 1984 to 1987: Task of Improving Macroeconomic Management (1984–1987 nian de "jingji guore": gaishan hongguan jingji guanli de keti)," *Modern Chinese Economy (Xiandai Zhongguo jingji),* Chinese edition, Beijing: The Commercial Press, 1993, pp. 154–224.

In early May 1988, the Standing Committee of the Political Bureau of the CPC decided to complete the "crashing through the pass of price reform and wage reform" in the following five years. At the end of May, at a high-level meeting on implementation of this decision, economists Liu Guoguang and Wu Jinglian, based on the macroeconomic situation at that time, proposed "improving the situation first before crashing through the pass of price reform." Their reasons were that: (a) the upward movement of prices that started with agricultural products in the fourth quarter of 1987 was spreading to other sectors; (b) the "bottleneck constraints" of transportation and supply of capital goods were becoming more and more severe; (c) sporadic panic buying appeared everywhere and was continuously spreading; (d) a negative growth rate of bank savings appeared in April, indicating that the inflation expectation had begun to take shape. However, other economists' opinions were accepted by the then leaders of the government. According to their observations of economic situations in Latin America, these economists believed that even inflation rates of a thousand percent or more would not necessarily throw obstacles in the way of economic prosperity. As a result, government leaders concluded that crashing through the pass of price reform could be achieved despite hyperinflation and high growth rates.[13]

In the second half of 1988, things did not develop as government leaders had optimistically expected. The Political Bureau of the CPC in early June officially decided to start "crashing through the pass of price reform and wage reform," and inflation expectations immediately appeared among the population, followed by a swift rise in prices. The retail price index increased by 26 percent year-on-year in the second half of 1988, and panic buying was common in cities. Speculative buying and selling of allocated supplies and foreign exchange quotas and corruption became widespread, aggravating the public discontent, turning economic problems into political ones, and leading to political unrest.

To control explosive inflation, in the third quarter of 1988, the government began to precipitately scale down investment in fixed assets; suspend approval of off-plan construction projects; clean up and reorganize newly created business entities, especially trust and investment corporations; strictly control the group consumption of enterprises and institutions; tighten control over prices; and set price ceilings for critical capital goods. Following the "forced-landing" policy of macroeconomic adjustment formulated at the Central Working Conference in September 1988, the People's Bank of China adopted a set of contractionary monetary and credit policies, including stringent control over the scale of bank credit and, at one point, suspending granting bank loans

---

[13] Liu Hong, *Academic Critical Biography of Contemporary Chinese Economists: Wu Jinglian (Dangdai Zhongguo jingjixuejia xueshu pingzhuan: Wu Jinglian)*, Xi'an: Shaanxi Normal University Press, 2002, pp. 247–270.

to township and village enterprises. It also raised the reserve ratio on deposits of specialized banks and adjusted its interest rate policy. Because of the surge of inflation, increases in prices of goods far exceeded deposit interest rates, making real interest rates fairly large negative values. To slow down the decline of real interest rates, nominal rates of interest were raised twice in September 1988 and February 1989 by the central bank. To further stabilize the financial situation and to protect the interests of depositors, the central bank instituted an inflation-proof interest rate system for deposits with maturities of three years or longer.

Although these tough measures succeeded in lowering the inflation rate in a rather short time, it did not get there without a price. In the third quarter of 1989, the money supply index fell to its trough, the annual growth rates of M_1 and M_2 fell to -1 percent and 13 percent, respectively. Accordingly, retail prices fell as well, and the growth rate of the retail price index dropped to 0.6 percent on a year-on-year basis in the third quarter of 1990. At the same time, however, markets became sluggish, industrial production declined, enterprises operated below capacity, unemployment mounted, China's financial position deteriorated, and the economy slipped into recession, resulting in an unprecedented situation of an "over-cooled" economy (see Table 10.4).

10.2.2.4 The Fourth Round of Economic Fluctuation between 1991 and 1995

In the third quarter of 1989, while the government managed to check inflation and reduce the price index, sales turnover began to decline; inventories piled up; and enterprises' production was in disarray. In the fourth quarter of 1989, the People's Bank of China, at the behest of the State Council, started to inject a great deal of credit capital to "jump start" the economy that seemed at a standstill in its trough. The bank also substantially reduced deposit and lending interest rates in succession in March and August 1990, and April 1991. At the same time, the bank also reduced the interbank base rates for deposit and lending for financial institutions. However, because people had an expectation of low inflation and were under the influence of the psychological propensity "to buy when prices go up and not to buy when prices go down," the growth rate

Table 10.4   China's Macroeconomic Situation during 1986–1991 (year to year, %)

Year	1986	1987	1988	1989	1990	1991
GDP Growth	8.8	11.6	11.3	4.1	3.8	9.2
Increase in CPI	6.5	7.3	18.8	18.0	3.1	3.4

Source: The National Bureau of Statistics, *China Statistical Yearbook (Zhongguo tongji nianjian)*, Beijing: China Statistics Press, various years.

of GDP was merely 3.8 percent in 1990 although the growth rate of M_2 was as high as 28.0 percent.

In 1991, with a continuous injection of substantial amounts of money, the growth rates of M_1 and M_2 reached 23.2 percent and 26.5 percent, respectively, and industrial production, led by the nonstate sectors, started to bottom out. In the beginning of 1992, Deng Xiaoping made his famous "South China speeches," calling for accelerating reform and development. His speeches boosted the rising momentum of the economy and set off a surge of development all over the country.

In the positive national economic climate of 1992, various localities, departments, and enterprises all showed great enthusiasm. They initiated various measures to boost reform and opening up in their regions and units and played a very important role in enlarging the scope of market functions. However, the central government seemed to be passive toward promoting reform, and failed to take actions supporting reform in key sectors including government finance, banking, and state-owned enterprises. Reform in these sectors could not proceed without the facilitation of state agencies.[14] At the same time, as a result of the adoption of an expansionary monetary policy to spur economic growth, local governments at various levels devoted their attention to setting up development zones and launching infrastructure investment projects, setting off another round of economy bubbles in the form of crazes for development zones, real estate, bonds, stocks, and futures. The economy quickly overheated, and in 1992, M_1 and M_2 increased by 35.7 percent and 31.3 percent, respectively.

However, during the year between mid-1992 and mid-1993, many economists voiced different views regarding the macroeconomic situation. Some believed that the national economy had good momentum, and effort should be made to maintain this momentum. Others argued that signs of an overheated economy were already obvious, and appropriate measures should be adopted to rectify it. A popular analysis divided people into two groups according to the orientation of their macroeconomic policies. Those who believed that the economy was not yet overheated and nothing should be done belonged to the "reformists"; those who believed that the economy was already overheated and timely remedial measures should be taken belonged to the "conservatives." This analysis failed to conform to reality, however. In fact, the real situation at that time was much more complicated than this simplistic "dichotomization." Even people who apparently held the same views regarding the economic situation (whether it was overheated or not) might be widely different in their assumptions and policy propositions.

---

[14] Wu Jinglian, "Go All Out to Build Up the Basic Structure of a Market Economy (Quanliyifu, jianli shichang jingji de jichu jiegou)," *Reform (Gaige)*, 1992, No. 2, pp. 4–11.

Roughly speaking, there were actually four different viewpoints at that time. The first opinion attributed the overheated economy to the "over speed" at which the marketization reform had been pushed forward. The implication was that the reform should be slowed down, and control by plan should be tightened. The second opinion agreed with the first about the fact that the economy was overheated, but in contrast, proponents of this view insisted that the root cause of the overheated economy was that reform of key sectors had not been fast enough. They advocated for decisive measures to stabilize the economy and to accelerate reform. The third opinion was that the situation for economic development was excellent, and it maintained a fast speed and avoided the occurrence of an overheated situation and the risk of inflation. Proponents of this view were affirmative about economic affairs in the preceding period and believed that what had been done should be continued. The fourth opinion was one of dissatisfaction with the progress of the reform, but its proponents believed that the prospect of economic growth was still promising. They argued that inflation was inevitable for any country undergoing breakneck growth, so austerity measures should not be taken because they might reduce the momentum of fast growth. The debate among these four viewpoints dragged on for nearly a year. In the spring of 1993 the risk of inflation became too palpable to be veiled anymore. When the retail price index jumped up more than 10 percent compared with the same period of the previous year, and the six-month period between November 1992 and May 1993 saw the market exchange rate of RMB against US$ depreciated by 45 percent, inflation was obvious. After Deng Xiaoping personally intervened in April and May of 1993, the top leaders decided to adopt two sets of measures to restore macroeconomic stability.

The first set consisted of emergency measures. In June 1993, the Chinese government declared a sixteen-point plan to stabilize the economy, including areas of finance, fiscal administration, and investment: (1) increase deposit and lending interest rates and issue treasury notes to make up the fiscal deficit; (2) instruct specialized banks to call back loans that had exceeded the banks' credit quotas; (3) instruct the specialized banks to review and reexamine all interbank short-term loans to all kinds of financial institutions, and call back all illicit interbank short-term loans; (4) separate policy-orientated lending from commercial lending of specialized banks; (5) intensify the central bank function of the People's Bank of China; (6) demand that any corporation to be listed on the stock exchange obtain the approval of the central authorities; (7) cut down administrative expenses by 20 percent; (8) demand every region achieve sales quotas of treasury notes on or before July 15; (9) reexamine economic development zones approved by local governments; (10) reduce investment in capital construction; (11) increase capital investment in public transportation projects; (12) reform the system of foreign exchange retention; (13) ban the use of IOUs in lieu of cash when agricultural products were purchased from peasants; (14) prohibit local governments from illicitly "raising" funds from enterprises and farms; (15) send teams to twenty provinces, municipalities, and autonomous regions to investigate and examine the righteousness of financial activities; and (16) stop new price reform measures.

The second set of measures were more fundamental. Unlike all previous adjustments that had relied on tightening the control by plan, this round of economic adjustments relied on deepening reform to eradicate institutional root causes of the overheated economy. This change was epitomized in the *Decision on Issues Regarding the Establishment of a Socialist Market Economic System* passed by the Third Plenary Session of the 14th CCCPC in November 1993. The decision demanded great strides in all directions, including developing a new fiscal and taxation system, carrying out the reform of the banking system, and accelerating the reform of state-owned enterprises to ensure that a socialist market economic system would be initially formed by the end of the twentieth century.

The specific measures to stabilize the economy introduced in mid-1993 could be classified into three types: (1) administrative measures that included setting a definite time limit for banks to call back loans granted against rules and regulations, stepping up the control of credit quotas of specialized banks, reexamining investment projects, etc.; (2) economic measures that consisted of raising interest rates of bank deposits and lending twice, resuming inflation-proof bank savings, selling government bonds, etc.; and (3) execution of reform to get rid of microeconomic bases for inflation and to construct a macroeconomic adjustment system compatible with a market economy, including reform of state-owned enterprises, reform of the fiscal system, reform of the banking system, etc. Due to the grim macroeconomic situation at the time, priority was given to the emergency measures that could be effected quickly to stabilize the situation.

After the introduction of the sixteen-point plan in June 1993, it took only a short period to deter the momentum of the overheated economy. The growth rate of M_1 dropped from 34.0 percent in June to 15.6 percent in October; the growth rate of investment in the state sector fell from 74.0 percent to 58.0 percent; the growth rate of the capital goods price index declined from 53.0 percent to 31.4 percent; and the exchange rate of the U.S. dollar for RMB decreased from 11.5 to 8.7.

Keeping pace with the controversy on policy issues was the debate on how to understand and correctly deal with the relationship between checking inflation and alleviating unemployment. At that time, economists who advocated the theory that moderate inflation was beneficial submitted a new argument that, although inflation was an evil, it harmed everyone equally; so, everyone might be discontented with inflation, but no single group would be likely to stir social unrest. However, unlike inflation, unemployment is much more likely to lead to social unrest. Therefore, people should "choose the lesser of two evils" and live with some inflation to alleviate unemployment.

Table 10.5   China's Macroeconomic Situation during 1992–1996 (year to year, %)

Year	1992	1993	1994	1995	1996
GDP Growth	14.2	13.5	12.6	10.5	9.6
Increase in CPI	6.4	14.7	24.1	17.1	8.3

Source: The National Bureau of Statistics, *China Statistical Yearbook (Zhongguo tongji nianjian)*, Beijing: China Statistics Press, various years.

Economists who held a different point of view retorted that the foundation of the opinion that inflation and unemployment were negatively correlated was the outdated understanding of the Phillips Curve by old-fashioned Keynesians. However, modern economics had outgrown this outdated understanding long ago by realizing that the position of the Phillips Curve was not fixed, but depended on people's expectation about inflation. Therefore, the practice of picking an optimum trade-off point with inflation and unemployment levels that were both acceptable to a society along a fixed Phillips Curve had been rejected by most economists quite a while ago; nobody should repeat the mistakes of some countries after World War II that tried to alleviate recession with inflation but ended up with "stagflation."

To the argument that inflation harmed everyone equally and thus it would not lead to social instability, these economists' response was that this was a shortsighted view. In fact, inflation is a vicious tax with redistributive effects, which are favorable to the rich, not the "from hand to mouth" wage-earning class. Therefore, hyperinflation would cause tension in social relations and lead to social unrest.

Furthermore, the real meaning of easing monetary policy to reduce unemployment was nothing more than granting bank loans to enable state-owned enterprises on the brink of bankruptcy to pay salaries and benefits. Job creation by implicitly subsidizing SOEs with loans instead of enhancing their vigor and improving their efficiency by reform was a short-term solution to the unemployment problem, absolutely not a long-term solution. The most fundamental and intractable part of the unemployment problem in China was the hundreds of millions of unemployed and underemployed in rural areas. Although an expansionary monetary policy to subsidize state-owned enterprises and to maintain employment for their redundant employees could temporarily alleviate the pressure of laid-off state employees, it would not help transfer rural surplus laborers to nonagricultural industries. Thus, such a policy would not fundamentally alleviate the unemployment problem in China.[15]

---

[15] For main views of the controversy, see articles of Ding Hu, Wu Jinglian, Li Yining, Ma Bin, and Zhang Zhuoyuan, *Reform (Gaige)*, 1994, No. 2.

10.3 Deflation and Remedial Policies between 1997 and 2002

Since the beginning of the East Asia financial crisis in July 1997, the macroeconomic environment in both China and the world underwent dramatic changes. Recession replaced inflation to become the major problem faced by all countries of the world. Economists time and time again pointed out that "depression economics has returned."[16] China in 1997 started to suffer from insufficient aggregate demand, a sluggish market, and a declining growth rate. However, in China, these economic changes occurred for more complicated reasons than in other East Asian countries.

10.3.1 Causes of Insufficient Aggregate Demand

In the second half of 1997, China's national economy began to feel the pressure of insufficient aggregate demand. At year's end, a consensus was reached on the need to use macroeconomic policies to increase aggregate demand. Many factors contributed to insufficient aggregate demand. First were the lagging effects of austerity measures after 1993. For the past twenty years, in general, China's economy had followed the development pattern of upsurge-inflation-remedy-contraction-stagnation-recovery-expansion. The austerity measures that were implemented in the summer of 1993 had achieved significant success by the winter of 1996, and the inflation rate was nearly zero in 1997. Just as policy measures adopted by other countries to stabilize commodity prices usually had some lagging effects, China started moving toward deflation in 1998.

Second, in the strategic restructuring of the state sector, it was necessary to discard some redundant production capacity. For example, in three years the textile industry had to reduce its capacity by ten million spindles, or 25 percent of the existing capacity. As a result, state-owned enterprises had to lay off a great many workers. In 1997, the number of laid-off workers from state-owned enterprises totaled 12.75 million, and only a minority of these people managed to find new jobs. In 1998, another substantial number of SOE workers were laid off. Furthermore, during these years of reform, some township and village enterprises owned by local governments experienced slowdowns. All of these caused reductions in aggregate demand.

Third, in the process of reform, particularly the reform of the housing and social security systems, the removal of old systems under which the state took care of everything occurred much faster than the establishment of new systems. This discrepancy made the general public increase their saving and cut back on consumption, again, leading to a decrease in aggregate demand.

---

[16] Paul Krugman, *The Return of Depression Economics,* New York: W. W. Norton & Company, 1999.

The fourth reason was the impact of the East Asian financial crisis. Because of continuing economic and financial turbulence, neighboring countries suffered from severe depreciation of domestic currencies and diminishing purchasing power for imports. Consequently, demand for China's exports to these areas declined. Simultaneously, foreign direct investment in China from these areas substantially decreased. Overall, all these factors combined to result in economic contraction in China.

10.3.2 Policies to Increase Domestic Demand and Their Effect

In response to this situation, in early 1998, the Chinese government proposed guidelines to expand domestic demand to spur economic growth. These policy measures affecting both demand and supply sides of the economy were put in place after mid-1998.

10.3.2.1 Demand-side Policy

In early 1998, the Chinese macroeconomic authorities began to adopt policies to expand domestic demand. The first was a proactive fiscal policy, mainly in the form of investment financed by treasury bonds. Between 1998 and 2001, the authorities issued long-term treasury bonds for development totaling to RMB 510 billion, mainly invested in infrastructure construction, such as superhighways, transportation systems, power generation, and large water conservancy projects. In a relatively short time, this action succeeded in stopping the downward trend of investment. The second policy was for the total amount of supporting funds for projects financed by treasury bonds—in the form of commercial loans from the four state-owned commercial banks—to match the sum total of fiscal allocation funds. The third policy was a moderately expansionary monetary policy to supplement the fiscal policy. The central bank reduced deposit and lending interest rates seven times in succession and increased the money supply.

This economic policy of creating aggregate demand directly by the government had advantages in that it could quickly increase demand and stop downward investment trends. For example, after the East Asian financial crisis started in 1997, the CCCPC and the State Council in mid-1998 proposed to increase investment by RMB 160 billion. After the formalities of legislation, the fund was quickly allocated down through the government hierarchy by stages. However, to increase demand by this method, particularly on a perpetual basis, also resulted in some negative effects. First, government investment tended to "crowd out" private investment. Second, in competitive sectors, the efficiency of government investment would be lower than that of private investment. Third, and the most important, the treasury bonds issued for government investment would have to be redeemed eventually by increasing tax revenue. As a result, private investment would be hampered, worsening the investment environment. As a result, around the beginning of 2000, economists began to recommend that the proactive fiscal policy be gradually reduced.[17]

10.3.2.2 Supply-side Policy

As early as 1998, some economists suggested that under conditions of insufficient aggregate demand and slow economic growth, in addition to the expansionary fiscal policy on the demand side, supply-side policies should be adopted that would increase the involvement of enterprises. Although this proposition neither gained consensus among economists nor was formally declared, the Chinese government in practice did adopt supply-side policies because of the urgent needs for reform and the development of economic entities.

First, according to the requirement of the 15th National Congress of the CPC that the layout of the state sector should be adjusted by "advancing in some areas while retreating from others," hundreds of thousands of small and medium-sized SOEs were transformed into nonstate enterprises with a market orientation and clearly identified property rights.

Second, the macroeconomic authorities adopted a series of measures to improve the business environment for nonstate enterprises. These measures included setting up the Small and Medium Enterprise Department under the State Economic and Trade Commission to specifically facilitate the development of small and medium enterprises (SMEs), and emphasize the need for improving finance and credit services to SMEs. In response, credit guarantee companies or funds were established in all provinces and major cities to help improve financing options for SMEs. These measures improved the operating environment for nonstate enterprises, spurred private investment, and enabled nonstate SMEs to grow rapidly in some regions.

Third, the authorities accelerated adjustments to the layout of the state sector and the reform of state-owned enterprises. Industries dominated by large state-owned enterprises, such as petroleum, telecommunication, railroads, and electric power, were reorganized, and incorporation of these enterprises was carried out. The macroeconomic authorities also completed the following tasks: (a) separated government administration from enterprise management and set up a new framework of government regulation; (b) eliminated business monopolies and promoted competition between enterprises; (c) set up the basic framework of corporate governance based on shareholder diversification upon the completion of incorporation and listing in overseas or domestic securities markets.

---

[17] Wu Jinglian, "Economy Turns for the Better: Stronger Reform Measures Are Needed (Jingji zoushi chuxian zhuanji, haixu jiada gaige lidu) (2000)," *Reform: We Are Passing a Critical Moment (Gaige: women zhengzai guo daguan)*, Beijing: Joint Publishing, 2001, pp. 76–82.

All these measures increased the strength of enterprises by enabling different forms of ownership, improved financial positions, and better investment opportunities.

As time went on, however, the relative effectiveness of the demand versus the supply side policies changed. By 2001, supply-side policy effects had surpassed those of the demand-side policy. The supply side had become the major engine driving rapid economic growth of China. This is discussed in more detail in the following paragraphs.

First, nonstate enterprise growth enabled private investment to become the major part of total investment. A survey of the Development Research Center of the State Council[18] showed that between 1999 and 2001, growth rates of fixed asset investment in the collective sector, the individual business sector, and the "others" sector increased faster than that of the state sector. Contrasting vividly with slowdown in state investment growth, the average growth rate of domestic private investment in fixed assets reached 20.4 percent, 11.8 percent, 22.7 percent, and 20.3 percent, in the four years between 1998 and 2001, respectively. These rates were not only higher than those of the state sector during this period, but also higher than the growth rate of the total investment of society.

As domestic private investment gathered momentum, the dependence of the total investment of society on government investment was decreasing, and the capacity of autonomous investment was growing. According to a report by the National Bureau of Statistics, in 1999, 2000, and 2001, the share of treasury bond investment (including total investment funded by treasury bonds and investment funded by supporting funds) in the total investment of society in fixed assets declined to 8.1 percent, 8.8 percent, and 6.5 percent, respectively. The growth rate of budgetary investment funds also declined to 54.7 percent, 13.9 percent, and 13.2 percent, respectively. Concurrently, the growth rate of total investment of society rose to 5.1 percent, 10.3 percent, and 13.0 percent, respectively. In summary, strong autonomous private investment was driving the rebound of total investment of society (see Table 10.6).

Second, although the international economic situation was worsening, China maintained a high growth in exports. In 1999, the government granted permission for nonstate enterprises to export their own products. In 2001, although the three major world economies of the United States, Europe, and Japan showed no signs of recovery, and the absolute volume of global trade was dropping, China's exports grew substantially, and its share of global trade significantly increased.

---

[18]Lu Zhongyuan, "Analysis of the Situation of Private Investment (Minjian touzi taishi fenxi) (2002)," in Ma Hong and Wang Mengkui (eds.), *Research of Development in China—Selected Works of Development Research Center of the State Council (Zhongguo fazhan yanjiu—guowuyuan fazhan yanjiu zhongxin baogaoxuan)*, Beijing: China Development Press, 2003, pp. 109–121.

Table 10.6   Growth of Investment in Fixed Assets by Sector (year to year, %)

Year	Average of All Sectors	State Sector	Collective Sector	Individual Business Sector	Others	In Which			
						Share-holding	Foreign	Hong Kong and Taiwan	Joint Ownership
1998	13.9	17.4	8.9	9.2	11.6	40.4	−16.2	42.4	−50.9
1999	5.1	3.8	3.5	7.9	5.3	27.3	−12.6	−8.7	61.8
2000	10.3	3.5	10.7	12.2	28.5	63.9	−8.4	6.2	−3.2
2001	13.0	6.7	9.9	15.3	28.9	39.4	7.8	22.4	−0.2
2002	16.9	7.2	13.4	20.1	36.2	47.1	19.1	11.5	46.2

Source: The National Bureau of Statistics, *China Statistical Yearbook (Zhongguo tongji nianjian)*, Beijing: China Statistics Press, various years.

Table 10.7   China's Macroeconomic Situation during 1997–2002 (year to year, %)

Year	1997	1998	1999	2000	2001	2002
GDP Growth	8.8	7.8	7.1	8.0	7.5	8.0
Increase in CPI	2.8	−0.8	−1.4	0.4	0.7	−0.8

Source: The National Bureau of Statistics, *China Statistical Yearbook (Zhongguo tongji nianjian)*, Beijing: China Statistics Press, various years.

10.3.3 Changes in Macroeconomic Situation

As a result of efforts made by the Chinese government since 1998, the slowdown in economic growth was stopped by 2000, and the consumer price index also turned from negative to positive. By mid-2000, the economic situation was turned around (see Table 10.7).

Even in 2001 and 2002, when the external economic environment was unfavorable and government investment in total domestic investment was decreasing, China's GDP growth was still at eye-catching rates of 7.5 percent and 8.0 percent respectively, proving the effectiveness of the supply-side policy that invigorated the economy.

10.4 Short-Term Problems and Mid- and Long-Term Risks in China's Economy

In spite of the outbreak of Severe Acute Respiratory Syndrome (SARS) in 2003, China's national economy grew with a strong momentum. For several years in succession, China's GDP growth rates were high—between 7.5 and 8.0 percent. In 2003, GDP growth exceeded 9 percent. At the same time, the national economy did not show significant signs of inflation. This situation indicated that the Chinese economy had an inspiring outlook in the short term.

However, the story has another side. Despite more than twenty years of fast economic growth, many deep-rooted economic and social problems had not been solved. This backlog of problems made the microeconomic efficiency of enterprises low and the macroeconomic efficiency of the society low, which was epitomized by the relative inefficiency of the banking system. The negative consequences of high growth based on low efficiency were the mounting nonperforming loans (NPLs). At the same time, the unavoidable cost of economic transition was often expressed as "contingent losses" on the banks' balance sheets. For this reason, China's banking system during transition was very vulnerable.

In a modern market economy, the financial sector is the key sector that can generate a domino effect throughout the economy. Without a powerful and active financial system, the economy of any country cannot experience fast and steady growth. Because the financial sector is a merging point for all kinds of economic and social connections and conflicts, it tends to be the blasting fuse of economic and social crises. Especially since the collapse of the Bretton Woods system in the early 1970s,[19] the international financial market had experienced continuous fluctuations. A country's financial turbulence could easily affect another country through the globalizing international financial system. Since 1973, the frequency of financial crises in the world had almost doubled.[20] In the twenty years between 1979 and 1999, 69 incidents of financial crises occurred in both developing and developed countries.[21]

A comprehensive assessment of foreign and domestic conditions indicates that it is possible for China to have a financial crisis in the future. Some scholars even predict that, during the next twenty years, it is almost certain that China will have a financial crisis.[22]

10.4.1 The Root Cause of the Problems in the Chinese Financial System Was the High Input and Low Efficiency of the Economy

In recent years, China's economic growth has been sustained by investment (see Figure 10.1). The new round of growth acceleration since the second half of 2002 was

---

[19] The Bretton Woods system refers to agreements to set up a U.S. dollar–based international currency system, finalized in July 1944, in Bretton Woods, New Hampshire at a meeting of forty-four members of the United Nations and allies.

[20] Caprio, Gerard and Daniela Klingebiel, "Episodes of Systemic and Borderline Financial Crises," *World Bank Working Paper*, 1999.

[21] Eichengreen, Barry and Michael Bordo, "Crises Now and Then: What Lessons from the Last Era of Financial Globalization," *NBER (National Bureau of Economic Research, Inc.) Working Paper*, January 2002, No. w8716.

[22] Qian Yingyi and Huang Haizhou, "Financial Stability and Development in China after WTO Accession (Jiaru Shimao Zuzhi hou jinrong de wending yu fazhan) (2001)," in Qian Yingyi, *Modern Economics and China's Reform (Xiandai jingjixue yu Zhongguo jingji gaige)*, Beijing: China Renmin University Press, 2003, pp. 160–176.

Figure 10.1 Growth of Total Investment of Society in Fixed Assets (in real terms)

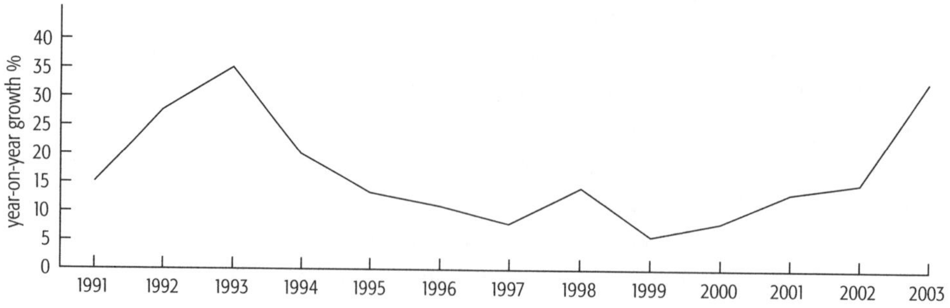

Source: Made by author with data from the National Bureau of Statistics.

mainly induced by investment. Between January and August of 2003, the completed total investment of society in fixed assets rose by 30 percent, up by 10 percentage points,
compared with the same period in the previous year.

The increases in investment were sustained by increases in loans (see Figure 10.2), as
pointed out by a 2003 investigation by some economists.[23] Between January and August of 2003, loans in local currency granted by all financial institutions recorded an
eight-month increase of RMB 2.1681 trillion, exceeding the previous year's 12-month
increase of RMB 1.848 trillion.

At present, because the age structure of the Chinese workforce is still on the young
side and the Chinese people have a tradition of saving, the savings rate in China is very
high, with savings comprising roughly 40 percent of GDP. Most Chinese resident savings are in the form of bank deposits. Banks use these deposits to make loans to enterprises (around 65 percent of total bank loans was made to state-owned enterprises), enabling them to make huge investments to support fast growth. A report of Standard &
Poor's Ratings Services pointed out that since 1995, the growth rate of total lending by
the Chinese banking system has been higher than the GDP growth rate of the country.
By the end of 1995, total outstanding loans amounted to 88 percent of the GDP that
year; and by the end of 2002, this amount had reached 138 percent of the GDP for that
year. This meant that the banking system was injecting more and more loans into industrial and commercial enterprises. With banks as intermediaries, China's high saving
rate is turned into a high investment rate, and this further turns into high GDP growth

---

[23] Shen Liantao and Xiao Geng, "The Financial Reform and Development, and Construction of Infrastructures with Firm Ownership (Zhongguo jinrong gaige yu fazhan jianli wengu de chanquan jichu sheshi)," *Mimeograph*, August 2003. See also Shan
Weijian, "Huge Paradox of China's Economic Growth (Zhongguo jingji zengzhang de juda beilun)," *Caijing Magazine (Caijing)*, 2003, No. 17.

Figure 10.2   Rapid Growth of Loans: Year-to-Year Growth %

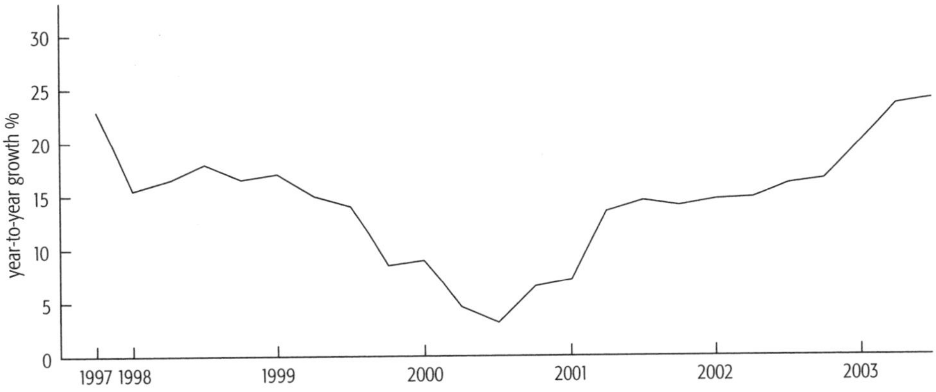

Source: Made by author with data from People's Bank of China.

rate. In this process, however, low efficiency in resource allocation leads to a huge waste of funds, and high-cost, low-efficiency growth leads to further accumulation of bad assets in the banking system.

The grounds for the conclusion of Paul Krugman, who in 1994 predicted the East Asian financial crisis, was that economic growth of East Asian countries was achieved almost entirely by heavy input of resources instead of enhancement of efficiency.[24] In his book, *The Return of Depression Economics* (1999), Krugman once again discussed this issue. He said that in 1994, he foresaw the East Asian financial crisis because Asia had fallen short in productivity growth, so that the area would eventually experience a period of diminishing returns. He pointed out that, as of 1997, Malaysia's investment amounted to 40 percent of its GDP, twice as much as that of the 1970s, whereas Singapore put 50 percent of its income into investment. However, even such high investment rates, which could not be higher, were still insufficient to sustain high-speed growth. For the whole region of Southeast Asia, this is demonstrated by the fact that the incremental capital-output ratio (ICOR), the indicator of the required investment growth rate needed to maintain a certain output growth rate, kept rising. The rising ICOR meant that the efficiency of investment kept falling, and the continuation of such conditions would definitely lead to the outbreak of a financial crisis.

It is alarming to note that since 1994, China's ICOR have continued to worsen (see Figure 10.3). Between 1998 and 2002, the required investment for every additional

---

[24] Paul Krugman, "The Myth of Asia's Miracle," *Foreign Affairs,* November/December 1994, pp. 62–78.

Figure 10.3   Increase in ICOR in China

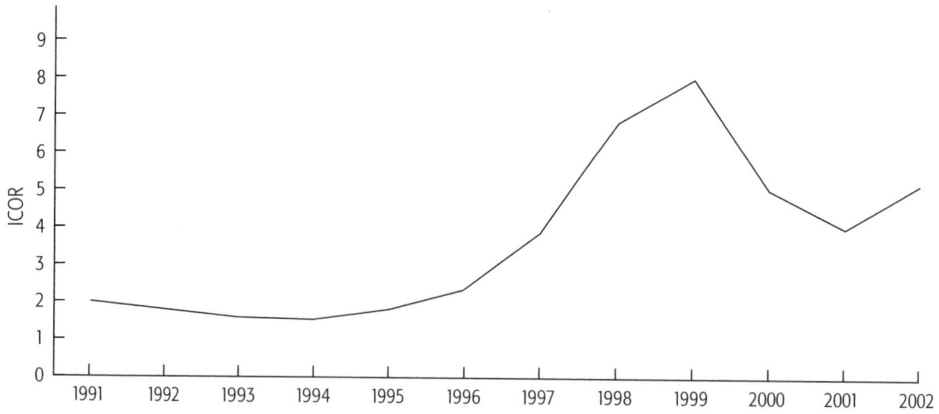

Source: Made by author with data from China International Capital Corporation Limited (CICC) and CEIC Data Company Limited (CEIC).

RMB in China's GDP jumped by 1.5 times the investment required for incremental GDP growth before 1994.

The evil consequence of this continuing high-cost growth is the huge increase of bad assets in the banking system. According to Chinese government figures, as of the end of 2002, China's four major state-owned commercial banks collectively had recorded a bad asset ratio of 25 percent. If the bad assets of RMB 1.4 trillion that had been turned over to four asset management corporations were included, bad assets would have been 45 percent of the four banks' total assets. This ratio came close to the Standard & Poor's Ratings Services 2003 estimate of the bad asset ratio of China's banking system,[25] and far exceeded that of Japan, which had been dragged down by its nonperforming financial system. The Standard & Poor's Ratings Services report further estimated that the Chinese government would have to spend as much as US$518 billion, equivalent to 40 percent of its current GDP, before it could completely eliminate all these nonperforming loans. Some scholars dubbed this kind of economic growth under this kind of financial process as "borrowed growth,"[26] that is, growth sustained by money borrowed from bank depositors.

---

[25] In June 2003, Standard & Poor's, in a report entitled *China Banking Outlook 2003–2004,* estimated that the proportion of nonperforming loans in China's banking system had reached 50 percent. With the substantial increase in the total outstanding loans of Chinese banks, Standard & Poor's in September 2003, revised its estimate to 44 to 45 percent.

[26] Shan Weijian, "Huge Paradox of China's Economic Growth (Zhongguo jingji zengzhang de juda beilun)," *Caijing Magazine (Caijing),* 2003, No. 17.

Of course, if certain conditions are met, "borrowed growth" can keep going on. Such conditions include (a) a high savings rate, (b) the monopoly status of state-owned banks, and (c) control of foreign exchange under the capital account.

What China has to attend to is that in the coming five to ten years, these conditions will definitely change. First, according to the commitment made when it joined the World Trade Organization, China will allow foreign banks to operate local currency (Renminbi) business free from any restrictions after 2007. It is predicted that in the future, many major customers may switch to foreign banks, and thus state-owned commercial banks, which currently carry the mountainous responsibility of supporting the growth of the economy, will lose their major sources of funds needed to keep their businesses going and to "dilute" their nonperforming loans. Second, a fully open China cannot everlastingly retain stringent control over foreign exchange under the capital account. If local businesses continue to operate with low efficiency and low profitability, and if the authorities relax exchange controls, Chinese citizens are very likely to invest their cash in better investment opportunities overseas. Third, as a result of China's one-child policy, the aging of the population will occur faster in China than in other countries. Around 2010, China will arrive at a turning point due to an aging population when saving deposits in banks will start to drop and withdrawals will rise. As accumulation of social security funds in China is disastrously falling short, and the phenomenon of empty individual accounts of social security is ubiquitous, the problem of bank asset quality will become even graver than it is currently.

Under such conditions, if necessary precautionary measures are not taken, a financial crisis like the one experienced by Japan and other East Asian countries will be hard to avoid.

10.4.2 Essential Measures Needed to Avoid a Crisis

Economists believe that to avoid a crisis, the Chinese authorities should take measures in two areas:

1. accelerate reform and strengthen the system to reduce the possibility of a crisis;

2. establish an anti-crisis mechanism so that the authorities will be able to limit the damage to a minimum if and when a financial crisis occurs.

In relation to the first recommendation, other than the measures made to stabilize banks (the core of the financial system) that were discussed in Chapter 6 of this book, what should be undertaken are the other reforms discussed in other chapters: (a) adjust the layout of the state sector and reform state-owned enterprises and enhance their governance; (b) establish a social security system for all citizens; (c) facilitate the development of nonstate enterprises; and moreover, include what is discussed in Chapter 11; and (d) build a basic framework for property rights and the rule of law.

In relation to the second recommendation, some finance scholars have proposed: (a) the formulation of professional standards for financial institutions based on international experience and the strict enforcement of regulations according to these standards; (b) clearly defined duties and responsibilities of different regulatory agencies, such as the China Securities Regulatory Commission, the China Insurance Regulatory Commission, and the China Banking Regulatory Commission, to reduce or eliminate overlapping functions and conflicts of interest; (c) improvement in the coordination among the central bank, financial regulatory agencies, and other government departments; (d) establishment and improvement of a crisis management mechanism; (e) improvement of the reporting system management and public disclosure of financial information; (f) strengthening of relevant departments of the central bank to enhance its ability to maintain financial stability; and (g) strengthening the study of financial stability problems by government departments and private institutions.[27]

---

[27] Huang Haizhou and Wang Shuilin, "A Few Suggestions for the Reinforcement of the Stability of Financial System (Jiaqiang Zhongguo jinrong xitong wendingxing de jidian jianyi);" Tang Min, "Build an Open-Style Anti-Financial-Crisis Mechanism (Jianli yige kaifangshi de fan jinrong weiji jizhi)," *Caijing Magazine (Caijing)*, 2003, No. 20.

CHAPTER 11

SOCIAL RELATIONS AND GOVERNMENT FUNCTIONS IN THE TRANSITIONAL PERIOD

China's transition from a planned economy to a market economy did not adopt the form of revolution, but rather of reform. In other words, the transition was not pushed forward by a new regime in leaps and bounds, but was led by the preexisting ruling party and government in a gradual, progressive way. From the point of view of maintaining social stability, reform had obvious advantages over revolution. Especially in the initial stage of reform, China adopted the strategy of economic reform preceding political reform so that economic reform could start in a stable political environment, successfully avoiding social unrest of epic proportions. Nevertheless, changes in the economic system always bring consequential changes in the social structure, which in turn demand corresponding changes in the superstructure of the society such as the political and cultural systems. As economic reform pushes forward, the superstructure of the society incompatible with the economic base will eventually become an obstacle to the proper functioning of the new economic system and the further advance of reform. Therefore, speeding up political reform, including the reform of the government, has turned out to be a pressing issue that warrants attention. However, political reform in a socialist country itself is a huge and complicated topic, and the study of it is beyond the scope of this book. This chapter gives only a brief discussion of social and political issues directly related to economic reform.

11.1 Social Contradictions in the Transitional Period

Many people used to believe that once reform started, it would be a smooth process of self-reinforcement: reform would improve productivity and the living standard of the people, and such improvement in turn would enlist more support from the public for further advance of reform. However, as reform in China deepened, we saw no sign of diminishing social contradictions; the preexisting contradictions and newly arisen contradictions showed signs of intensification from time to time. In this section, we will try to analyze the cause.

11.1.1 The Transitional Period Is a Period in Which Social Relations Are under Great Tension

The social transition driven by China's reform embraces a salient feature: the transition from a planned economy to a market economy is accompanied by the transition from a traditional agricultural society to a modern industrial society.

11.1.1.1 Social Contradictions in the Transition from a Traditional Society to a Modern Society

In their textbook titled *Economics of Development,* Gillis, Perkins, Roemer, and Snodgrass wrote, "once started, economic development does not necessarily proceed without interruption. Economic development itself, particularly in its early stages, can create enormous social and political tensions that can undermine the stability so necessary for growth." [1]

This situation occurs partially due to the nature of the modernization process. Samuel P. Huntington pointed out that "modernity breeds stability, but modernization breeds instability." [2] That is to say, society tends to be in a state of stability after modernization has been accomplished, but the process of modernization contains all sorts of elements that induce social unrest. In a society that has attained a high degree of modernity, because residents' income levels are generally high and individuals enjoy relatively great decision-making rights in economic affairs, the members of the society are satisfied with the existing social order and thus support a stable political order. The middle class plays a critical role in this process.[3] The expansion of the middle class, which does not have to worry about its livelihood and is accomplished politically and culturally, is an important symbol of modernity and a pivotal force in maintaining social stability. Therefore, the achievement of modernity will normally lead to social stability.

The process of modernization is defined as an increase in modernity or progress of society so as to enhance the stability of society. However, in a society in transformation, there are factors beneficial to stability as well as factors detrimental to stability. The massive transformation from a traditional society to a modern society has different impacts on different groups of people, which is likely to trigger social unrest. According to

---

[1] Malcolm Gillis, Dwight H. Perkins, Michael Roemer and Donald Snodgrass, *Economics of Development,* New York: W. W. Norton & Company, 1983, p. 37.

[2] Samuel P. Huntington, *Political Order in Changing Societies,* New Haven: Yale University Press, 1968, p. 41.

[3] In Western economics, level of income is generally used to demarcate class; in the initial stage of capitalist society, middle class is used as a synonym for bourgeoisie or capitalist. "In modern society this group is composed of professionals, white-collar workers, farmers, and the like, all far removed from the capitalist class of Marxist theory." Quoted from the "Middle Class" entry of *Microsoft Encarta,* 1994.

Samuel P. Huntington, the process of modernization is a shift from a traditional society where the flow of information is usually clogged to a society in transformation where information can flow freely. As a consequence, even those people in an impoverished, backward region may still be able to know how other people in this multifaceted world make and enjoy their living. In such a situation, people's expectation for improvement in living standards may substantially increase. When this expectation cannot be met, or is met to only a lesser degree, people become discontent. If there is not a powerful and flexible political system to restrain or control their actions, society will become vulnerable to outbreaks of turmoil. Any transformation will lead to a readjustment of interests and relations among all strata and all groups in the society. In the process of the readjustment of these interests, any stratum, group, or even individual, whether suffering from a real loss of interest or even a perceived loss, will become discontented, and this may lead to social unrest or turmoil. Increased expectation will be not only in terms of quantity but also of quality. Abraham H. Maslow's hierarchy of needs[4] theory tells us that when people's needs at the lower levels of the hierarchy are satisfied, they will pursue the satisfaction of needs at the next level. If their needs at this higher level are not satisfied, discontent may also grow, breeding social unrest.

Looking at history, countries like the United Kingdom and France, which have completed the process of modernization, all experienced a period of turbulence in their transformation from a traditional society to a modern society. Over a period of nearly two hundred years after the revolution in the seventeenth century, the United Kingdom suffered from social turbulence, gradually stabilizing in the mid- and late nineteenth century only after several civil wars and upheavals. With its tradition of championing revolution, France's entire eighteenth century was filled with firestorms of class antagonism and violent revolution. Many countries have paid a dear price for social unrest during their long process of modernization.

When a developing country tries to achieve in decades the level of modernization that developed countries have spent centuries to achieve, care must be taken to resolve social contradictions. Otherwise, efforts to expedite modernization, although economically successful, will eventually fail because of a lack of public support. (The experiences of countries like Iran and the Philippines can prove this point to some extent.) The enlarging income disparity among different social strata is the focal point of various social contradictions during the transition from a traditional society to a modern society.

---

[4] Abraham H. Maslow classified needs of human beings into five levels: (1) physiological needs; (2) safety needs; (3) belonging needs; (4) esteem needs; and (5) self-actualization needs. He pointed out that the lower the level of the need, the more easily it is satisfied; and human beings usually pursue the satisfaction of their needs in the above order, from lower levels to higher levels.

After World War II, the third- and fourth-echelon countries in the race for modernization, including those in Southeast Asia and Latin America, adopted measures to diminish the effect of the intensifying social contradictions caused by their strategy of rapid modernization. These measures achieved some success. Taking the problem of enlarging income disparity as an example, American economist Simon S. Kuznets proposed in 1955 that the relationship between gross national product (GNP) per capita and the level of inequality was represented by an "inverted U" curve. That is to say, in the initial stage of modernization, as GNP per capita increases, income inequality will enlarge; when income reaches a middle level, income inequality will reach its maximum; and when income reaches the level of industrialized countries, income inequality will then gradually shrink.[5] However, Simon Kuznets' point of view was based on historical data from affluent European and North American countries and on data from third-world countries during the early years after World War II.

To the contrary, the experience of rapid modernization of newly industrialized East Asian economies showed that it is indeed possible for developing countries to have both rapid economic growth and relatively low income inequality in the initial stage of their development and that a relatively equal distribution of income can promote social stability and rapid growth. The newly industrialized Asian economies such as Japan, South Korea, and Taiwan (China) solved this problem by formulating and implementing a series of policies and measures. For example, in the initial stage of modernization, farmers are always vulnerable to losses. Over a rather long period of time, Japan implemented a large subsidy for grain prices, ensuring farmers a rather high income. From the point of view of economics, the grain price subsidy was an unreasonable policy as it went against the optimal allocation of resources. However, given the fact that the interests of farmers were most vulnerable in the precipitant process of industrialization, this policy helped safeguard farmers' interests as well as social stability. In addition, over a rather long period of time after World War II, Japan also implemented a policy of holding back the expansion of large retail businesses. Although this policy did not follow theories of economics, it gave ample room for small retail businesses to survive, thereby making unemployment problems manageable. In the early stages of its development, Taiwan took great efforts to prevent the widening of income gaps. The World Bank's *World Development Report 1991: The Challenge of Development* suggested that in the so-

---

[5] In regard to Simon S. Kuznets' "Inverted U Hypothesis" for correlation between level of income and extent of inequality, for representative pros and cons, respectively, of Chinese scholars, see Chen Zongsheng, *Income Distribution in Economic Development (Jingji fazhan zhong de shouru fenpei)*, Shanghai: Shanghai Joint Publishing, 1991; and Zeng Zhaoning, *Fairness and Efficiency (Gongping yu xiaolü)*, Dongying, Shandong: China Petroleum University Press, 1994.

called "Jiang Jingguo[6] Era," both the level of income equality and the GDP growth rate stood relatively high in Taiwan.[7]

11.1.1.2 Social Contradictions in the Transition from a Planned Economy to a Market Economy

The effects on social contradictions of the transition toward a market economy are similar to those of modernization, and sometimes are even more violent. A scholar once said, "The large-scale institutional changes involved in transition are among the most complex economic and social processes one can imagine."[8] James Buchanan recognized that when changes in game rules occur during the transition, the lack of creditability of new rules can create social disorder.[9] Due to tremendous changes in the pattern of interests in the transitional period and due to the deconstructing effect of market mechanism on social relations based on personal dependence formed in the era of a planned economy, transition is often accompanied by intensified social contradictions and chaotic social relations.

For a country with a traditional planned economy to achieve such double transitions in decades, it must also solve in decades the social contradictions that developed countries faced in their transformations over centuries. As a result, the likelihood for social unrest is high, and if there is a bad policy, it will most likely induce social turbulence.

11.1.2 Evolution of the Social Structure and Social Contradictions during China's Transitional Period

In the two and half decades after China started the reform and opening up, its social structure underwent enormous changes: while some old social contradictions were alleviated, some new ones started to pop up, and some were aggravated. Analysis of the current situation and the development trends of those social contradictions to seek truth from facts is the foundation for understanding the contemporary Chinese society and formulating appropriate social policies.

Since the commencement of the reform and opening up, the Chinese social structure has undergone profound changes. According to *The Research Report on Social Strata*

---

[6] Jiang Jingguo (Chiang Ching-kuo, 1909–1988) was eldest son of Jiang Jieshi (Chiang Kai-shek) and, as his father, the top leader of the Chinese Nationalist Party (Kuomintang). After returning from his twelve-year stay in the Soviet Union in 1937, especially after the Nationalist retreat to Taiwan in 1949, he gradually rose to power and held the leadership between his father's death in 1978 and his death in 1988.

[7] World Bank, *World Development Report 1991: The Challenge of Development,* New York: Oxford University Press, 1991, Figure 7.2.

[8] Gérard Roland, *Transition and Economics: Politics, Markets and Firms,* Cambridge, Mass.: MIT Press, 2000, p. xviii.

[9] James M. Buchanan, *Explorations into Constitutional Economics,* College Station, Tex.: Texas A&M University Press, 1989.

in Contemporary China by the Chinese Academy of Social Sciences, by the turn of the century, the Chinese social structure had evolved from consisting of the working class, the peasant class, and the intelligentsia stratum in 1978, into a social structure consisting of ten major strata defined by their possession of organizational, economic, and cultural resources: (1) state and society administrators, (2) managerial personnel, (3) private enterprise owners, (4) professionals, (5) office workers, (6) self-employed in industry and commerce, (7) employees in commerce and service, (8) industrial workers, (9) agricultural laborers, and (10) urban and rural unemployed and semi-employed. These ten strata were respectively categorized into five classes: the upper class, the upper-middle class, the middle-middle class, the lower-middle class, and the lower class, resulting in a rudimentary form of a modernized structure of social strata. However, the report pointed out that according to requirements of a modern society, those strata that should have decreased had not, and those strata that should have enlarged had not; the middle class was still too small, while the stratum of agricultural laborers was still too large.[10] About 70 percent of the entire Chinese workforce was peasants, whereas in 1992 the share of agricultural employment in total employment was 2 percent in the United Kingdom, 3 percent in both Germany and the United States, 7 percent in Japan, and 17 percent in South Korea. The Chinese middle class accounts for only about 18 percent of the total workforce.[11] The histories of many countries of the world indicate that a lopsided structure of social strata was often the root cause for socioeconomic crisis.

In China, economic growth driven by reform simultaneously brought both positive and negative impacts on social relations. In the earlier stage of reform, positive influences took a dominant position, whereas in the later stage, negative influences became more and more prominent.

In the earlier stages, reform enhanced the degree of social stability. Not only did nonstate sectors experience rapid development, but the policy of power delegating and profit sharing adopted in the state sector succeeded in benefiting almost everyone as well, creating a sense of contentment within the whole society. As reform deepened, however, some social problems were not alleviated but aggravated. In recent years, the level of contentment has decreased. According to a research project in 2000 entitled *Social Stratification, Public Attitude, and Social Stability* by the Sociology Institute of the Chinese Academy of Social Sciences, people did not have an obvious sentiment of optimism, and 20 percent of those polled expressed a pessimistic attitude. When asked

---

[10]Lu Xueyi et al., *A Research Report on Social Strata in Contemporary China (Dangdai Zhongguo shehui jieceng yanjiu baogao)*, Beijing: Social Scientific Documentation Publishing House, 2002.

[11]Lu Xueyi, "Constructing a Well-Off Society; Social Indicators Are Harder to Be Attained than Economic Indicators (Jianshe xiaokang shehui, shehui zhibiao nanyu jingji zhibiao)," *Social Sciences Newspaper (Shehui kexue bao)*, November 28, 2002.

about the reform of the health care system, 36 percent believed that they would lose and 29 percent believed that they would either gain nothing or lose. When asked about the reform of the employment system, 14 percent believed that they would lose and 46 percent believed that they would either gain nothing or lose. In addition, according to other research conducted at the end of 2002, the number of urban residents who were discontented with their living standards reached one hundred to two hundred million, representing 22 to 45 percent of the total urban population; and the number of those who were very discontented reached thirty-two to thirty-six million, representing 7 to 8 percent. The discontented people were mainly those disadvantaged in the processes of economic transition and restructuring, including the laid-off and unemployed, peasants, low-income people, people with reduced income, and others. The conclusion of the research was that unfair distribution of social wealth was the ultimate root cause of social instability.[12]

Therefore, how to uphold social justice in the process of reform has become a key issue in determining whether reform can be carried out smoothly and successfully.

11.1.3 Increase in Corrupt Activities

Corrupt activities can be categorized into three major types by their economic sources: (1) taking advantage of the power of administrative intervention in market activities to make deals between power and money; (2) taking advantage of opportunities in the adjustment and change in property relations in the transitional period to misappropriate public property; and (3) taking advantage of the imperfections and anomalies in the market system to make exorbitant profits. These practices are all linked to power. Because mechanisms to check and balance power were not established early enough in the transitional period from a planned economy to a market economy, it was possible for some people to take advantage of this special situation by exploiting their unrestrained power to gain exorbitant wealth. These three practices are discussed next.

11.1.3.1 Taking Advantage of the Power of Administrative Intervention in Market Activities to Make Deals Between Power and Money

During the transitional period, there were two major resource allocation mechanisms: the market mechanism and the administrative mechanism. As discussed in Chapter 2, a prominent feature of China's "incremental reform," or the so-called "gradual transition," was that these two mechanisms coexisted and were intertwined over a long

---

[12] Wang Shaoguang, Hu Angang, and Ding Yuanzhu, "Social Instability behind Economic Prosperity (Jingji fanrong beihou de shehui bu wending)," *Strategy and Administration (zhanlue yu guanli),* 2002, No. 3.

period of time. Therefore, some people took advantage of the gaps and loopholes created by the coexistence of these two tracks by using their administrative power to intervene in economic activities to seek personal gain.

In the era of the planned economy, the state monopolized all industry and commerce, and the government was able to suppress the price of grain, cotton, and other raw materials produced by peasants as well as the price of products of upstream industry. In this way, the government was able to squeeze profits out of agriculture and upstream industry and transfer them to commerce, which had the highest degree of state monopoly (a situation that had been created during the socialist transformation of capitalist industry and commerce). Hence, the state was able to keep all the profits in the value-added process. After the inception of the reform and opening up when the party and government organs and nonprofit institutions started to be allowed to establish their affiliates in commerce, whoever got permission to establish a "labor service company" or a shop would be sure to rake in a huge sum of money, and thus the phenomenon of the industrial, agricultural, military, educational, and commercial circles all engaging in trade came into fashion in China. When enterprises were granted autonomy to a certain extent, they were allowed to sell the part of their products exceeding the planned quotas at the negotiated prices of the market rather than the allocation prices of the plan. Hence, for the same goods, market prices were much higher than planned prices. In 1985, this dual-track system of pricing was established as a formal system. Because of the huge gaps between market prices and planned prices, goods acquired at low prices and then resold at market prices would generate exorbitant profits. The secret of making a fortune by profiteering was power, and therefore people referred to those engaging in profiteering by buying and selling as "bureaucratic profiteers."

Two groups held opposing views about the phenomenon of bureaucratic profiteers. One group believed that corruption was an ugly phenomenon of the old society and it was the market-oriented reform that prompted people to pursue wealth; it was greed for money that caused the spread of corruption. They believed that to correct this incorrect orientation of reform, the discipline of plan rather than the role of money should be emphasized. Although the opposing group recognized that expansion of the roles of market and money would kindle human desires and consequently increase corruption, they emphasized that if China did not open the market or did not stress the role of money, the Chinese would never be able to improve their economic position and the whole country would stay in poverty. They argued that the spread of corruption should be tolerated as an unavoidable cost of economic development, and that people should not sacrifice the fundamental interests of economic development for the sake of moral purity. Some even believed that corruption served as a lubricant to reduce transaction costs, and that corruption should not only be tolerated, but used as a weapon to destroy the planned economic system.

Although these two groups were different in their positions, they shared the same assertion that corruption was linked to a market economy. However, this theory has little proof in history, which has shown that the rampant corruption in the remote mercantilist epoch of the primitive market economy during the sixteenth, seventeenth, and eighteenth centuries originated from the underdevelopment of markets and various interventions of administrative privileges.[13] Looking at countries that developed after World War II, not all of them suffered rampant corruption in the process of marketization. Contrary to the aforementioned assertion, the swifter and smoother the marketization of a country was, the less rampant corruption was.

Another group of economists held a third opinion. They recognized that the development of markets and emphasizing the role of money would intensify some people's desire to pursue wealth because the scope of wealth would no longer be limited to physical things. However, the problem did not center on how greedy these people were, but on whether there existed institutional conditions that allowed the realization of such greediness. To discover if these conditions existed in China, the economic theory of rent-seeking (as discussed in Chapter 2) was developed in the 1970s to analyze this phenomenon.

By the early 1990s, rent-seeking activities were still rampant, although almost all controls on commodity prices had been lifted and rent-seeking by reselling commodities was no longer profitable. Around that time, two new targets for rent-seeking emerged: bank loans and land. Hence, the bulk of bureaucratic profiteering activity shifted from commodity rent-seeking in the 1980s to production factor rent-seeking. Taking land as an example, in the era of a planned economy, all parcels of state-owned land were assigned through the plan to state-owned enterprises. In the early 1990s when China started large-scale land leasing, most local governments adopted the practice of leasing by private negotiation; thus, people who had personal connections were able to lease prime sites at low costs and make a great deal of profit once the leaseholds were sold. If speculation in real estate could generate bubbles, even the second-hand buyer, or the third-hand buyer, or the fourth-hand buyer would be able to earn a sizeable windfall, until the last buyer with bad luck was trapped. In those days, Beihai City of

---

[13] In the era of mercantilism in Western Europe in the seventeenth through nineteenth centuries, corruption proliferated: excessive intervention of administrative power in the economy created conditions for rent-seeking and the unhealthy growth of market mechanisms led to unfair competition. The sluggish reform of the public sector and the coexistence of the two mechanisms satisfy these two conditions: maintaining extensive administrative intervention of the government in an economy that emphasizes the role of money creates an immense opportunity for rent-seeking, resulting in surging corruption.

Guangxi Province was a hotspot in land leasing and speculation in real estate that attracted funds in the tens of billions from all over the country, breeding a crop of billionaires, corrupting a batch of cadres, and ruining countless public property after the eventual burst of bubbles.

In her 1974 paper *The Political Economics of the Rent-Seeking Society*,[14] Anne O. Krueger developed a model to calculate the ratio between total value of rents and gross national product in India and Turkey. This ratio immediately gained worldwide recognition as a standard measurement of a country's corruption. According to calculations by economist Hu Heli in 1987 and 1988, the total sum of rents in the Chinese economy reached the astounding proportions of 20 percent and 40 percent of GNP, respectively.[15] According to calculations by economist Wan Anpei, in 1992 when rent-seeking activities in the financial market and the real estate market were at their peak, rents in the whole country totaled RMB 624.37 billion, representing 32.3 percent[16] of the national income that year. Wang Shaoguang, Hu Angang, and Ding Yuanzhu classified corruption in the transitional period into four categories: (1) rent-seeking corruption, (2) underground economy corruption, (3) loss of taxation income corruption, and (4) public investment and public expenditure corruption. According to estimates, in the second half of the 1990s, these four types of corruption caused economic losses averaging between 13.3 to 16.9 percent of GDP; during 1999 to 2001, economic losses caused by corruption accounted for 14.5 to 14.9 percent of GDP.[17]

Such huge profits from rent-seeking nurtured a large and powerful group of vested interests. In the process of China's reform and opening up, they were not only hampering the marketization reform to maintain the institutional foundation for rent-seeking activities, but also aggressively engaged in rent-setting activities by increasing the intervention of administrative power in economic activities and expanding the scope of administrative approval in all sorts of good names to increase opportunities for rent-seeking. As a result, corruption became more and more rampant.

---

[14] Anne O. Krueger, "The Political Economy of the Rent-Seeking Society," *American Economic Review*, 1974, Vol. 64, No. 3, pp. 291–303. According to Krueger's calculation, India's total rent was 7.3 percent of its gross national product, whereas that of Turkey was above 15 percent. Since the costs of rent-seeking, such as bribes, are less than the total value of the rent, the total value of rent can be seen as the upper limit of costs of rent-seeking. If other conditions are ignored, the higher the ratio of total rent to gross national product, the higher the degree the corruption.

[15] Hu Heli, "Three Policies of Anti-Corruption (Lianzheng sance);" "Estimation of Rent of China in 1988 (1988 nian wo guo zujin de gusuan," in Editing Department of *Comparisons of Social Economic System (Jingji shehui tizhi bijiao)* (ed.), *Corruption: Making Deals between Power and Money (Fubai: quanli yu jinqian de jiaohuan),* 2nd edition, China Economic Publishing House, 1993, pp. 20–46.

[16] Wan Anpei, "Analyses of the Major Features and Composition of Rents in the Transitional Period of Chinese Economy (Zhongguo jingji zhuanxing shiqi de zujin goucheng ji zhuyao tedian fenxi) (1995)," in Wu Jinglian et al., *Building Up a Market Economy: Comprehensive Framework and Working Proposals (Jianshe shichang jingji de zongti gouxiang yu fang'an sheji),* Beijing: Central Compilation and Translation Press, 1996, pp. 331–364.

[17] Wang Shaoguang, Hu Angang, and Ding Yuanzhu, "Social Instability behind Economic Prosperity (Jingji fanrong beihou de shehui bu wending)," *Strategy and Administration (Zhanlüe yu guanli),* 2002, No. 3.

When people discovered that unrestricted power could make a person rich overnight, some sought that power by any means possible. One of these means was seeking and purchasing official positions. Therefore, starting in the mid-1990s, selling and buying official positions have quietly become a common practice in some parts of China.

11.1.3.2 Taking Advantage of the Adjustment of Property Relations to Seek Personal Gain

The transitional period was one of great change in ownership structure and great adjustment in interest relations. Because the original demarcation of property rights to public property was ambiguous and the re-demarcation of property rights was to be done under the government's leadership, if the exercise of power is not subject to strict monitoring and restriction, some people with power can make use of their unrestricted power to misappropriate public property. (Relevant issues have been raised in Chapter 5.) The following are some common situations.

First, in the reform of state-owned enterprises, the government as the real boss of the enterprise kept itself in the background and let the management handle the property of the enterprise.

For a long period of time, the main content of the reform of state-owned enterprises had been delegating power to and sharing profit with enterprise leaders (factory directors or managers), resulting in the problem of "self dealing" as it is called in management. In other words, as representatives of the owner vested with full authority, enterprise leaders were delegating power to and sharing profit with themselves.

One common practice was to transfer the profit from the public coffer of the state to the private coffer of the enterprise. After the commencement of the reform and opening up, state-owned enterprises were allowed to market the extra-plan part of their products themselves and to retain a certain percentage of the sales revenues of the extra-plan products to establish the "Three Funds," namely the employees' bonus fund, the employees' welfare fund, and the production development fund. Moreover, enterprises were allowed to make investments to set up their own labor service companies, tertiary businesses, etc. As a result, the assets of each state-owned enterprise were divided into two parts: state assets belonging to the state and self-owned assets belonging to the enterprise. Both types of assets were under the control of the enterprise leader. As a result, various means of transferring profit from the public coffer to the private coffer were invented. Some large state-owned enterprises, especially those in foreign trade, speculated in high-risk, high-return international futures markets; any loss would be a loss to the state while any gain would be a gain to the private coffer or even individuals' wallets.

Another practice was to misappropriate public property through subordinate enterprises. When the era of a centrally planned economy ended, state-owned enterprises as well as party and government organs were allowed to set up labor service companies or tertiary businesses, whose original purpose was to solve the employment problem of employees' children returning to cities from the countryside. Before too long, some people discovered the trick of appointing their trusted aides to establish subordinate enterprises and transferring profit to them. Since leaders of the parent organizations were representatives of the owner (the state) and vested with full authority, if they engaged in transferring profit, whether to the private coffers or to their own wallets, they would encounter little hindrance. Hence, it became a common practice for state-owned enterprises to invest money in organizing subordinate enterprises. Similarly, leaders of subordinate enterprises copycatted the same trick. Another rather popular way to misappropriate public property was, in the process of establishing the shareholding system, to sell tradable shares to investors at unreasonably high premiums to "grab money" and to give free or very low-cost initial shares to those within the enterprise.

Second, the concept of power delegating and profit sharing, which guided enterprise reform, provided large loopholes.

The root cause of the problem of state-owned enterprises was the ineffective enterprise system. However, for a very long period of time, the problems had not been addressed by the clarification of property rights and changes in the system. Instead, the enterprise reform had been limited to delegating power to and sharing profit with enterprises (mainly their leaders) in the hope of bringing their enthusiasm into play to improve the performance of enterprises. There were substantial drawbacks in such approaches as "enterprise contracting," "authorized management," and "authorized investment" adopted by the government during the process of power delegating and profit sharing. The practice of the owner of state-owned enterprises (the state) authorizing the management to exercise the property rights started when the enterprise contracting system was introduced into commercial and industrial enterprises. Modern economic theories consider the possession by the owner of residual control (ultimate control) and residual claim (claim to profit) as the basic requirement for the clarification of property rights. The basic principle of the enterprise contracting system is "fixing the base quota, guaranteeing the remittance, retaining what exceeds the quota, and making up what falls short of the quota." The substance of this practice was that, during the contract period, the owner (the party awarding the contract) relinquished complete control and claim to the portion of profit exceeding the base quota of the contract. This enabled the employed agent (the party awarded the contract) to become the real master of the property rights of the enterprise. Such an institutional arrangement of property rights made it possible for the party awarded the contract, by virtue of this control, to misappropriate public property by various means. This ambiguous institutional arrangement of property rights created a tremendous hotbed for managerial corruption.

The enterprise contracting system later evolved into a formal system of authorized management, written into the *Law on Industrial Enterprises of the Ownership by the Whole People*. This law interpreted the separation of ownership from management as the separation of the ownership of the state from the occupation, use, and disposition rights over the enterprises exercised by the factory directors or managers as the representatives of the state. The law provided the factory directors or managers as employees with some sort of legal basis to handle the enterprises' properties according to their own interests and desires.

Third, the enterprise system of transformed enterprises had inherent imperfection and the internal management system had huge loopholes.

A transformed enterprise (previously part of an existing state-owned enterprise) often adopted the form of a corporation, in which the owner of the state shares and the state-owned corporate shares was clearly defined; thus, appearing as if property rights were clearly established. Although the original state-owned enterprise (sometimes called a holding company, a group corporation, or an assets management company) acted as the investment institution authorized by the state to exercise the rights of the shareholder with a controlling interest, the authorized investment institution itself was an independent enterprise. Furthermore, the managers of the enterprise were at the same time representatives of the owner, vested with full authority. Therefore, the real owner was absent and it was impossible to develop checks and balances between the owner and the management, allowing insider control to continue to exist. When the managers of the authorized investment institution were not only representatives of the owner vested with full authority but also employed insiders, some of the leaders of the authorized investment institution could utilize their authority to seek gain for themselves or members of their cliques. One common practice was for the authorized investment institution as the parent to deliberately "hollow out" the listed company as the subsidiary by delaying payments for goods delivered or occupying the working capital.

In the absence of the owner, internal financial control of enterprises was lost. Once the last link was broken, the whole chain of principals and agents was broken. The problem was caused by the ambiguity about who was the owner in the last link. As a result, state-owned securities and futures companies sometimes engaged in "rat trading," where secret accounts were arranged so that any gain would go to the secret accounts, while any loss would come from the state's account. Although at the turn of the century, state-owned banks had written off RMB 1.4 trillion of nonperforming loans by establishing four asset management corporations, by 2002, RMB 1.8 trillion of nonperforming loans had shown up again in their books. A significant part of these astoundingly huge losses could be attributed to corruption in the state sector of the economy.

11.1.3.3 Taking Advantage of Market Imperfections and Anomalies to Make an Exorbitant Profit

In almost every market, information available to the two parties of a transaction is asymmetric, and the party with superior information can take advantage of the party with inferior information to gain profit. Thus, to put the market mechanism into action, it is necessary to regulate markets and transactions. The market economy in China is still in the process of being established, and we encounter not only problems caused by the inherent contradictions of a market economy but also problems caused by the nonexistence of market relations. Consequently, there are ugly deeds in a primitive market economy, such as bullying competitors and dominating the market, as well as ugly deeds in a market economy without the rule of law, such as deceiving and misleading consumers. In the securities market, illegal practices such as false statements, insider trading, and market price manipulating are rampant but punishment for these kinds of illicit market deeds is not very severe. As a result, some lawless persons have easily accumulated substantial wealth by taking advantage of the chaotic market environment; but few of them have been punished according to law.

Since the securities market is plagued with asymmetric information, normalization and regulation are essential. Relevant topics are covered in Chapter 6 of this book.

11.1.4 Enlarging Income Disparity among Social Strata

In its history, China has abounded with peasants, and the egalitarian ideology that "inequality rather than want is the cause of trouble" was a dominating social sentiment. In the environment of a planned economy, the income of the general public tended to be equalized except for a very few senior government officials who enjoyed the fringe benefits of their rank (such as housing and chauffeured limousines), but the income gap between factory workers and peasants was rather significant. After the inception of the reform and opening up, the citizens' income disparity gradually widened. In the era of incremental reform, the different policies adopted for different regions, for different industries, and for different sectors of the economy caused the enlargement of income inequality of people employed in various enterprises in various regions. In the early 1980s, Deng Xiaoping proposed a policy of "letting some people get rich first"[18] and the orig-

---

[18]"Some people in rural areas and cities should be allowed to get rich before other. It is only fair that people who work hard should prosper. To let some people and some regions become prosperous first is a new policy that is supported by everyone. It

inal intention of this policy was to let those who were working diligently or good at doing business get rich first and then to lead the great majority of people to gradually attain the goal of common prosperity. The widening income gap caused by this policy would have been a normal phenomenon. What was abnormal was that because of mistakes in implementing the policy, some corrupt officials with authority in resource allocation and others with connections for rent-seeking became nouveau riches, but the ordinary working people, including employees of state-owned enterprises and especially peasants, benefited little from the reform and their living standards were hardly improved or were even reduced because of the repeated emergence of inflation (as discussed in Chapter 10). In sharp contrast, neither soaring commodity prices nor surging securities prices caused any harm to those "wave riders" backed by power; instead, they got a chance to "fish in troubled waters," that is, gain advantage from other people's financial problems. Therefore, large fluctuations in macroeconomic conditions resulted in growing discontent of the masses and increasing social instability.

The laid-off employees of state-owned enterprises comprise one group of the lowest-income population. We discussed in Section 2.2 of Chapter 2 that the financial condition of state-owned enterprises had been deteriorating since the mid-1980s. The majority of ordinary employees of state-owned enterprises fail to see any great improvement in their income. In the initial stage of reform, state-owned enterprises facing financial difficulty were kept running mainly by subsidies from the government. In the mid-1980s, they switched to bank loans, and in the 1990s, when neither the treasury nor state-owned banks were able to "transfuse" enough "blood" to them, state-owned enterprises faced operation difficulties and even repayment crises. The deteriorating financial position of state-owned enterprises directly threatened the livelihood of their employees as well as the functioning of the social security system. Each year in the 1990s saw a great number of SOE employees get laid off. After the outburst of the East Asian financial crisis, China suffered from sluggish exports and decreasing demand, and the problem of laid-off SOE employees worsened. The registered urban unemployment rate was 3.6 percent in 2001, 4.0 percent in 2002, and 4.2 percent in the first half of 2003.[19]

Peasants without nonagricultural income comprise another group in the lowest income population (as discussed in Chapter 3). Since the beginning of the reform and

---

is better than the old one." See Deng Xiaoping, "Our Work in All Fields Should Contribute to the Building of Socialism with Chinese Characteristics (Ge xiang gongzuo dou yao youzhuyu jianshe you Zhongguo tese de shehuizhuyi) (January 12, 1983)," *Selected Works of Deng Xiaoping (Deng Xiaoping wenxuan),* Vol. 3, Beijing: People's Publishing House, 1993, p. 23.

[19] According to the speech made by Zhang Zuoji, Minister of Labor and Social Security, at the press conference on November 11, 2002 at the Press Center of the 16th National Congress of the CPC, as of September 2002, the registered urban unemployment rate in China was 3.9 percent, or 7.52 million. If the six million people laid off and still waiting for reemployment were included, it added up to fourteen million, representing an unemployment rate of 7 percent.

opening up, the poverty-stricken population in rural China has been substantially reduced (see Table 11.1). According to a report by the Rural Survey Team of the National Bureau of Statistics, the poverty-stricken population in rural China was reduced from 250 million in 1978 to 34 million in 1999.

However, in sharp contrast with the rapid increase in the income of urban residents, the increase in the income of rural residents has been very slow. At the inception of the reform, the implementation of the household contracted responsibility system with remuneration linked to output raised peasants' income considerably. Because a large number of rural laborers were absorbed by the development of township and village enterprises on the basis of leaving agricultural jobs but not rural areas, and a large number of peasant workers left both agricultural jobs and rural areas, income of the rural population increased quickly. However, after 1985, income disparity between the urban and rural populations started to widen.

Although income disparity between urban and rural residents narrowed in the first decade of reform, the gap widened rapidly again in the late 1980s. The disposable per capita income of urban residents exceeded the net per capita income of rural residents by RMB 209.8 in 1978, by RMB 286.3 in 1980, by RMB 341.5 in 1985, by RMB 823.9

Table 11.1   Standard of Poverty Line and Rural Poverty Reduction in China (1990–1998)

| Year | Chinese Official Standard | | | International Standard (US$1 per person per day) | |
	Poverty Line (RMB per Person per Year)	Rural Poverty-Stricken Population (Million)	Poverty-Stricken Population versus Rural Population (%)	Rural Poverty-Stricken Population (Million)	Poverty-Stricken Population versus Rural Population (%)
1990	300	85	9.5	280	31.3
1991	304	94	10.4	287	31.7
1992	317	80	8.8	274	30.1
1993	350	75	8.2	266	29.1
1994	440	70	7.6	237	25.9
1995	530	65	7.1	200	21.8
1996	580	58	6.3	138	15.0
1997	640	50	5.4	124	13.5
1998	635	42	4.6	106	11.5

Source: World Bank, China: Overcoming Rural Poverty (Joint Report of the Leading Group for Poverty Reduction, UNDP and the World Bank, Report No. 21105-CHA), Washington, D.C.: World Bank, 2000, p. xiii, Table 1.

in 1990, by RMB 2705.3 in 1995, and by RMB 3643.7 in 1999.[20] By 1993, the gap in the level of consumption between farming and nonfarming residents had widened to the same level as the record high in 1959.[21] After 1997, due to the inefficiency caused by the stagnant reform of urban industry and commerce, the low utilization of the capacity of urban enterprises, and the high incidence of layoffs, cities were unable to create enough new jobs to absorb rural surplus laborers coming to work in nonagricultural industries. Therefore the stock of rural surplus laborers was on the rise rather than on the decline, resulting in more and more rural laborers crowding into less and less farmland. According to a speech made by Vice Director Qiu Xiaohua of the National Bureau of Statistics in March 2003, the income gap between urban and rural residents in China might have reached a ratio of 6:1, while the same ratio in most countries in the world was 1.5:1.[22]

The combined effect of these factors was that income disparity of China's residents enlarged rapidly (see Figure 11.1). According to estimates by the World Bank, the Gini coefficient calculated for combined urban and rural areas rose from 0.3 in 1984 to 0.35 in 1989.[23] In those days, the extent of inequality still could be considered to be at a medium level. In the 1990s, it reached a high level, beyond 0.4. Two studies had come out with similar results. One was done by the Income Distribution Task Group of the Economics Research Institute of the Chinese Academy of Social Sciences, whose estimates showed that the national Gini coefficient had increased from 0.382 in 1988 to 0.452 in 1995, based on two random samplings of households.[24] The result of the other study was that the Gini coefficient had increased from 0.38 in 1988 to 0.45 in 1995.[25] Based on the information provided by the National Bureau of Statistics, the Economic Research Institute of Nankai University estimated that the Gini coefficient of residents' income had increased from 0.35 in 1988 to 0.40 in 1997; when tax evasion, official corruption, conversion of institutional consumption, and other sources of illicit income

---

[20] Xu Rui'e, "Summary of Views on Income Disparities among Residents in China (Wo guo jumin shouru chaju guandian zongshu)," November 14, 2002, http://www.drcnet.com.

[21] In 1993, the average consumption level of nonfarming residents reached 3.2 times that of the farming residents, equal to that of the historical high in 1959. (See The National Bureau of Statistics, *China Statistical Yearbook (Zhongguo tongji nianjian)*, Beijing: China Statistics Press, various years.)

[22] March 11, 2003, http://www.cei.gov.cn.

[23] United Nations Development Programme, *China Human Development Report: Human Development and Poverty Alleviation, 1997*, Beijing: UNDP China, 1997, p. 47.

[24] Keith Griffin and Zhao Renwei (eds.), *The Distribution of Income in China*, New York: St. Martin's, 1993. See also Zhao Renwei and Keith Griffin (eds.), *The Study of Distribution of Income of Chinese Residents (Zhongguo jumin shouru fenpei yanjiu)*, Beijing: China Social Science Publishing House, 1994; and Zhao Renwei, Li Shi, and Li Siqin (eds.), *The Restudy of Distribution of Income of Chinese Residents (Zhongguo jumin shouru fenpei zai yanjiu)*, Beijing: China Finance and Economics Publishing House, 1999.

[25] Azizur Khan, "Distribution of Income in China: Evolution of Inequality, 1988–1995 (Paper for Workshop on Income Distribution in China) (1997)," in United Nations Development Programme, *China Human Development Report: Human Development and Poverty Alleviation, 1997*, Beijing: UNDP China, 1997, p. 47.

Figure 11.1   Ratio of Per Capita Disposable Income of Urban Households to Per Capita Net Income of Rural Households in China

Source: The National Bureau of Statistics, *China Statistical Yearbook (Zhongguo tongji nianjian)*, Beijing: China Statistics Press, various years.

were included in the calculation, the actual Gini coefficient of residents' income had increased from 0.42 in 1988 to 0.49 in 1997.[26] Some scholars estimated that the actual Gini coefficient of residents' income in China exceeded 0.5, ranking China among countries of high income inequality in the world.[27] Judged by another indicator of the level of income inequality among all social groups, in China's neighbor, Japan, the total income of the richest 20 percent of all families was about four times as much as that of the poorest 20 percent, whereas, according to research done by Renmin University of China, in China the same indicator was 11.8, exceeding that of the United States, which has a high level of income inequality (around 11).[28] The continuously enlarging income gap definitely posed a threat to social stability.

In the 1980s, the intensifying problems of inflation, administrative corruption, and income inequality bred widespread discontent among the population, resulting in the political disturbance of 1989, in which many young students and ordinary citizens be-

---

[26] Cheng Zongsheng and Zhou Yunbo, "The Impact of Illicit Abnormal Income on Residents' Income Disparity and Its Economics Interpretation (Feifa feizhengchang shouru dui jumin shouru chabie de yingxiang jiqi jingjixue jieshi)," *Economic Research Journal (jingji yanjiu)*, 2001, No. 4, pp. 14–23.

[27] Wang Shaoguang, Hu Angang, and Ding Yuanzhu, "Social Instability behind Economic Prosperity (Jingji fanrong beihou de shehui bu wending)," *Strategy and Administration (zhanlüe yu guanli)*, 2002, No. 3.

[28] *China Market Economy Post (Zhongguo shichang jingji bao)*, July 26, 1995, p. 8.

came involved.[29] In the 1990s, the sluggish reform of state-owned enterprises caused deteriorating financial performance of enterprises, which not only led to instability and stagnation in wages of existing employees but also induced problems in social security payments to retired and laid-off employees, resulting in protests by SOE employees. Moreover, slow income growth and heavy burden of taxes and fees in rural areas as well as the sharp contrast in income between peasant workers and urban residents, caused considerable discontent among the population. The gap between the rich and the poor had enlarged to such a critical extent that it had undermined social stability and obstructed further reform and development of China.

11.2 Constructing a Good Market Economy

Accompanying the social problems in the transitional period, different interest groups emerged, forming social forces with different attitudes toward reform and development of the society; each had different expectations for the direction of China's social development.

11.2.1 Different Attitudes toward Reform

In the initial stage of reform, there were two different attitudes toward market-oriented reform in the Chinese society, one supporting it and the other opposing it.

Some opposing reform lacked full understanding of a market economy, while others opposing reform tried everything they could to maintain the dominant position of the planned economic system because they were concerned about their own power, status, and interests.

In marketization reform, the government had to reduce the scope of its own activities and return the power to allocate resources that it should not exercise to the market and enterprises, and it would inevitably face opposition from people with conservative ideas and vested interest in a planned economy. In these people's eyes, it was an unalterable principle of Marxism that a planned economy was equal to socialism while a market economy was equal to capitalism. They claimed that as the economic base for socialism, state ownership could only be reinforced, not undermined. Many of the drawbacks in the planned economies of the Soviet Union and China were not caused

---

[29] On May 31, 1989, in his talk to two leaders of the central government, Deng Xiaoping pointed out that, "One of the causes for the recent turmoil is the growth of corruption, which has made some people lose confidence in the Party and the government." ("We Must Form a Promising Collective Leadership That Will Carry out Reform (Zucheng yi ge shixing gaige de you xiwang de lingdao jiti)," *Selected Works of Deng Xiaoping (Deng Xiaoping wenxuan)*, Vol. 3, Beijing: People's Publishing House, 1993, p. 300.)

by the economic system itself, but rather by wrong forms or approaches. Therefore, a planned economy as an economic system should be reinforced and improved, not discarded. This opposition persists even now, with changes in its appearance but not in its substance. For example, given the common belief that implementing macroeconomic control is an important function of the government in a market economy, maintaining intervention in and control over microeconomic activities by administrative power in the name of macroeconomic control is the same old trick in a new disguise for administrative departments to keep their power.

The majority of the population supported the reform. At the beginning of the reform, most of the government officials and the masses were discontented with the extremely distorted economic and social conditions resulting from the ultra-left party line and policies, and they had a strong desire to change the status quo and motives for reform. They joined forces with statesmen who embraced political ambition and followed current trends, as well as with intelligentsia representing the social conscience to form the core of the reformist movement in the Chinese society. What they strived to build was a market economy based on the interest of the general public for the pursuit of social justice and the gradual realization of common prosperity.

As discussed earlier, the Chinese reform of "outside the system" preceding "inside the system" (i.e., incremental reform) in the mid-1980s gave rise to the coexistence of two systems. Although the market system did not take full hold, a breach was created in the existing system controlled by administrative power. The result was that the planned system and the market system not only confronted each other but also infiltrated each other. Under these circumstances, those with powerful connections could take advantage of the gaps and loopholes in the systems to make a fortune. These people were similar to mercantilists in the primitive market economy of Western Europe. Being rent seekers, they made their gains in the midst of the chaotic economic system of the transitional period by taking advantage of norms not yet established for a market economy where administrative power still played a prominent role; they had a vested interest in incremental reform. Unlike the old group of vested interests who were nostalgic for the "good old days" of the planned economy, this new group of vested interests did not want to revert to the system of a planned economy or to see the establishment of a normalized market with fair competition. Instead, they wanted to maintain or even intensify the existing disorder and administrative intervention in the marketplace so that they could continue rent-seeking and making a fortune by taking advantage of their privileged status. They tried their best to find fault with and create roadblocks to the real reform necessary to establish a normalized market.

Under such circumstances, further advance of reform encountered not only resistance from the first social force, people hoping to return to the planned system, but also from the third social force, people hoping to maintain their vested interest under the dual system.

Currently, the influence of the proposal for the planned system is declining and will not gain endorsement from the masses. Nevertheless, when blunders are made during the process of reform that give the third social force free rein to harm public interest, the first social force, advocating the planned system, may be able to capitalize on the discontent of the masses to boost their influence, leading to a resurgence of conservative ideas. In the most recent two and half decades of reform in China, resurgence of conservative ideas happened twice on a large scale. The first resurgence occurred between 1981 and 1983, after the initial experiments in the reform and opening up. At that time, the society was energized with an air of open-mindedness; people were reflecting on the old systems as well as the Great Cultural Revolution resulting from them, and people were longing for the new situation promised by reform. At that time, the political clout of conservative ideas appeared to be insignificant. However, because the urban reform in the period between 1979 and 1980 caused so many problems with economic chaos and inflation, reform met a setback and the conservative political force took the opportunity to launch an offensive. They promoted the view that the root cause of the chaos was the goal of reform to establish a commodity economy (then a politically correct name for a market economy). They argued that a socialist economy must be a planned economy.

The second resurgence happened between 1989 and 1991. The social contradictions and problems accumulated in the first decade of reform erupted as the hyperinflation of 1988 and the political disturbance of 1989. Reform suffered a heavy setback because of the eruption of crises and the conservative force seized the opportunity to claim that marketization was the root cause of social unrest as if they could succeed in turning back the trend of marketization reform at that point. It was not until 1992, when Deng Xiaoping made his South China speeches, that reform regained its momentum.

During the period of reform, one of the causes of these situations was that when blunders were made in either the execution of specific reform measures or the management of the overall economy, the interests of the general public were damaged. The public attributed their losses to reform and became nostalgic for the era of the planned economy, unintentionally becoming supporters of the conservative force. Because some of the conservatives' propositions gained sympathy from the general public, the conservative force became active and took the offensive against reform.

It should be noted that the conservative ideas gained momentum because of the existence of the third social force, which wanted to maintain a dual system. When the results of the initial stage of reform favored the interest of the third social force, they stayed in line with the overall direction of reform, hoping to break down the strict discipline of the state plan as soon as possible so that more room would be available for their profiteering. However, the further the marketization reform went, the more they sensed the danger of losing opportunities to make a fortune from the administrative interventions and economic chaos, and the more they felt they were becoming the targets of reform. Subsequently, the conservative side of their mindset began to surface. They took every excuse (including that of "protecting the fruits of reform") to block further advance of reform, even trying to pollute reform with their own agenda in order to create new opportunities for rent-seeking. For example, in the name of reform, they used land leasing to replicate the tragedy of the enclosure movement, they used their financial know-how to take advantage of numerous medium and small investors, and they used reform of property rights to take over public property. All these were praised as the panacea enabling the country to be prosperous and the people to be rich. Because these people had the credentials of being early participants of reform and they continued to wave the banner of reform even though they actually blocked or distorted reform, they could easily mislead the masses, making them believe the deceit to be truth. These actions were very damaging in two ways. First, they could take reform down the wrong path and hamper the construction of a sound market economy. Second, they led those who were ignorant of the truth to believe that the various despicable practices of the primitive market economy that run counter to social justice were the outcome of reform. These actions turned people against reform and encouraged the sentiment and even the actions to restore the old economy. These would adversely affect the smooth progress of reform and social stability during the transition period. Although it may seem that the first social force (in favor of a planned economy) and the third social force (striving to maintain the status quo of the existing system) were opposing each other, they were in fact supporting each other. Both sides have quoted the existence of the other side as proof of its own correctness, in order to gain public support. Frequently citing those who used reform as a front to embezzle public property—but were in fact damaging reform—the first social force denigrated the real reform to muster public support for their conservative propositions. The third social force, which waved the banner of reform to seek personal gain, used the existence of conservative force as a "scarecrow" to instill fear in the general public and to confuse the boundary between the two completely different criticisms of the existing system, which were based on two different sets of starting points and end results. Their goal was to oppose correct measures to further advance reform, to mislead the general public, and to make those dedicated to reform (but ignorant of the truth) believe that China would return to the old path of a planned economy if their propositions of false reform (which actually confounded right and wrong) were ignored. During this complicated transitional period, it was common for people to feel uncertain about their understanding of reform, resulting in vehement debates about the best direction to go and the right policies and measures to adopt.

It is inappropriate to attribute conflicts between different orientations of thoughts and policies completely to conflicts between interests of different social groups, and it is even more inappropriate to attribute each individual's attitude toward reform completely to his or her economic status. Ideological and cognitive factors also play important roles. However, even theoretical debates are caused to a great extent by differences in interests, in addition to ideological and cognitive differences. Examples of the topics of such theoretical debates would include (a) whether the scope of administrative approval should be reduced as much as possible, (b) whether interest rates should gradually be liberalized, (c) whether the two systems of pricing for foreign exchange should be merged, (d) whether control over commodity prices and factor prices should be rapidly and decidedly lifted when essential conditions are satisfied, (e) whether the reform of state-owned enterprises should be focused on power delegating and profit sharing or on institutional innovation, and (f) whether economic bubbles would do good or would cause great damage. In these debates, while some participants based their opinions on ideological and cognitive differences, others based their opinions completely on the motives of their personal interest.

All of these diverse phenomena and debates about theories and policies in contemporary Chinese society can be explained by conflicts between different orientations of reform.

11.2.2 Maintaining Social Justice Was a Critical Issue in the Transitional Period

As China has undergone two and half decades of the reform and opening up, the replacement of a planned economy with a market economy is inevitable. The question remains as to what sort of market economy China should build: one rife with power intervention, corruption, and distortion, or a normalized market economy that is fair and beneficial for all. Given the current domestic and international environments, the dream of the first social force (as described in section 11.2.1) to return to a planned economy is destined to fail. However, if the evil intention of the third social force is realized, China will fall into the trap of a bad market economy.

China was previously on such a ruinous track. In its developmental process from an agricultural society to an industrial society, Old China made a similar detour. In the 1920s and 1930s, the modernization of China first gained momentum. Unfortunately before long, especially after the outbreak of the Anti-Japanese War, the Kuomintang regime then in power moved full speed to adopt bureaucrat capitalism, that is, comprador, feudal, state-monopoly capitalism.[30] In view of this situation, Mao Zedong put forth the idea of overthrowing bureaucrat capitalism and constructing a New China. This united the overwhelming majority of Chinese people and it took only three years to topple the very powerful Kuomintang regime and to secure the success of the New-Democratic revolution.

According to the platform confirmed at the Seventh National Congress of the Communist Party of China of 1945, the historical goal in a rather long period of New China was to develop the New Democratic economy. As soon as the recovery period ended, Mao Zedong made a hasty switch to a centrally planned economy on the basis of nationalization and collectivization, believing that by using centralized planning to mobilize and allocate resources, he would enable China to achieve industrialization and to catch up with and overtake developed countries within a very short period of time. What he did not expect was that the centrally planned economy would not only cost China slow industrialization and stagnant living standards from 1957 to 1977 because of inefficiency in resource allocation, but also would gradually breed bureaucratic corruption rooted in bureaucratic privileges due to the suppression of the creativity and rights of the masses as the masters of the nation. When Mao Zedong launched the Great Cultural Revolution, he took the existence of a corrupted force inside the leading organs of the party and the government as a front to mobilize the masses and drum up support for his left-wing clique of leaders to seize power under slogans like "overthrow the capitalist roaders" and "impose universal proletarian dictatorship." The Great Cultural Revolution caused a mammoth catastrophe and drove the Chinese national economy to the verge of collapse, making the reform from a planned economy to a market economy inevitable.

The transition process from a planned economy to a market economy also can have detours. One wrong turn on the road to building a normalized market economy under the rule of law is to adopt crony capitalism. At the inception of reform, many people believed that *any* kind of market economy, regardless of its form, would ensure economic prosperity and happiness. The reality, however, is that a good market economy and a bad market economy are very different from each other. At present, although an absolute majority of countries in the world have adopted a market economy, only a few of them have built up a normalized market economy. Many countries are still struggling

---

[30] Mao Zedong, "The Present Situation and Our Tasks (Muqian xingshi he women de renwu) (December 1947)," *Selected Works of Mao Zedong (Mao Zedong xuanji) (The Four-in-One Edition)*, Beijing: People's Publishing House, 1966, pp. 1243–1262.

with a primitive market economy dominated by capital of power, or a bad market economy. If the job is not well done, a planned-economy country in the process of marketization reform may also fall into the trap of a bad market economy. The probability for this to occur is quite high because during the process of readjusting the pattern of interests in the transitional period, those possessing power to allocate resources are very likely to abuse their power to seek personal gains. If a country has built an effective democratic system and created an orderly environment under the rule of law, it may have enough force to counteract capital of power; unfortunately, a country in transition usually does not satisfy these conditions.

Lacking such an effective system, the former socialist countries of Central Europe, Eastern Europe, and the Commonwealth of the Independent States saw serious problems of social injustice surfaced. Some of these countries adopted the method of "voucher privatization" to equally distribute the existing public property among all individuals to first achieve equal original distribution of wealth, and then to allocate wealth to the hands of those most diligent and most talented in managing business through fair play in the market. But the actual outcome was not as expected. As in the case of Kornai's Strategy B (see Chapter 1 of this book), those with powerful connections received the better part of the wealth and then continued to prey on the public by virtue of their power and wealth.

China has chosen a different transitional path, but many forms of social injustice are so widespread that some scholars warn that crony capitalism or bureaucrat capitalism have become a real danger.[31] Since the beginning of the 1990s, scholars have been calling for fair reform and proposing the need to prevent those "in charge of the ladle" from dividing the "big-pot meal" or even taking over the "big pot" without authorization. After the mid-1990s, practices counter to social justice—such as those in power buying enterprises at rock-bottom prices while those not in power were "cleared away" from enterprises—emerged in the process of letting go of small and medium enterprises. Some scholars termed such practices as "custodian deals" made with the sellers in absentia.[32] The issue of social justice has become one of the most serious in the Chinese ideological circles since the late 1990s.

All in all, the type of market economy to be established has become an acute social issue in the transitional period. The core of the issue lies in whether to maintain social justice in such a great reform and, if so, how.

---

[31] See Wu Jinglian, "Tackling the Problem at Its Root and Distinguishing between Right and Wrong (Zhengben qingyuan, fenqing shifei) (2002)," *Reading Books (Dushu)*, 2001, No. 7. See also Wu Jinglian, *China in Transition (Zhuangui Zhongguo)*, Chengdu: Sichuan People's Publishing House, 2002, pp. 359–363.

[32] Qin Hui, "China's Transitional Path (Zhongguo zhuangui zhilu)," *Strategy and Administration (zhanlüe yu guanli)*, No. 1, 2003.

11.2.2.1 Pursuing Social Justice Is a Universal Value

Chapter 1 put forth that as a social ideal, the core of socialism is the pursuit of social justice and the demand for the realization of common prosperity.

Social justice is not only an ideal pursued by every genre of socialists but also a goal of many nonsocialist philosophers and statesmen in the contemporary world. John Rawls (1921–2002) of Harvard University stated his fundamental ideas at the very beginning of his book, *A Theory of Justice*,[33] saying, "Justice is of the very primary value of a social system." He proposed the theory of justice as fairness, which included two principles. The first was the equal basic liberties principle, which referred to the fundamental rights of citizens: every citizen should equally possess the most extensive fundamental freedoms, for example, freedom of thinking and belief; freedom of speech, assembly, and association; freedom of person; freedom to protect individual properties; and other freedoms and rights stipulated by the principle of the rule of law. The second principle combined the principle of equal opportunity and the difference principle, which referred to the issue of income distribution in a socioeconomic structure. Equal opportunity required the existence of fair opportunities to ensure its realization, for example, compulsory education for all citizens. To address unequal outcomes because of differences in natural endowment and social conditions, Rawls applied the difference principle to compensate disadvantaged groups of society by income redistribution. Another American professor of philosophy, Robert Nozick,[34] advanced the entitlement theory of justice in holdings, opposing Rawls's difference principle and his proposal of enlarging the function of the state to the realm of distribution. His so-called "justice in holdings" refers to holdings of properties coming from just sources, or a "fair starting point." Any holdings obtained by means of stealing, robbing, and swindling were considered to be illegal. According to Nozick, if the source or any chain in the source of holdings was unjust, the holdings were considered also to be unjust, and, therefore, it was necessary to run back over the past. However, insisting on an absolutely fair starting point on the retroactivity principle would be difficult, if not impossible, in real-life cases.

In summary, from the perspective of upholding a universal value like social justice, it is paramount in the transitional process to diligently maintain equality of opportunity and a fair starting point in order to prevent the emergence of crony capitalism.

---

[33]John Rawls, *A Theory of Justice,* Cambridge, Mass.: Harvard University Press, 1971.
[34]Robert Nozick, *Anarchy, State and Utopia,* New York: Basic Books, 1974.

11.2.2.2 Tirelessly Maintaining Social Justice in the Transitional Process

The foundation of a centrally planned economic system is unified state ownership. In the framework of a basic economic system like this, it is impossible for a market economy to survive. For the purpose of providing an institutional foundation for a market economy, an important mission of transition is to clearly establish all types of property rights. How to ensure a fair starting point in the process of establishing clear ownership is an important question. As mentioned, in the process of the reform of the state sector and the process of letting go of and invigorating small and medium enterprises, those in power or their cronies and connections gobbled up public property. To stop this practice, it is important to improve the rules and regulations for property-right transactions and a top-down supervision mechanism. It is even more important to make the transaction process transparent and to ensure that citizens can exercise their constitutional rights, such as the right to know, to effectively monitor the government.

Since 2003, the "original sin of the rich" and the "sin and penalty of the first bucket of gold" have been topics of heated debates.[35] The first opinion favored an unconditional amnesty to tax dodgers, to let bygones be bygones.[36] The second, opposite, opinion insisted on a thorough investigation of all illegal cases without any amnesty.[37] A third opinion suggested conditional amnesty; in other words, once properties are registered and overdue taxes are paid, these properties will be considered legal and their ownership will be protected by law.[38] Many people believed that the third opinion might be relatively reasonable and practical. Their reasoning was that during the transitional

---

[35] See "The Rich of China (Zhongguo furen)," *2003 Finance and Economics Observation,* http://finance.sina.com.cn. See also "On the Sin and Penalty of the First Bucket of Gold (Guanyu di yi tong jin de zui yu fa)," *New Economy (Xinjingji),* June 17, 2003, http://finance.sina.com.cn/roll/20030617/1521353589.shtml.

[36] Zhang Weiying believed that "A policy of amnesty for entrepreneurs' tax dodging should be executed; in other words, let bygones be bygones, because the past occurrences were due to historical conditions. If we wanted all enterprises to pay taxes according to a simple tax rate, few enterprises would be able to continue to survive. Therefore, would it be possible that from here on if anyone dares dodge tax, they will be subject to more serious penalties. In this way, entrepreneurs can cast off their mental burdens, so that from now on, they can make contributions to the country and to pay taxes." See Zhang Weiying, "A Policy of Amnesty for Tax Dodging Should Be Executed (Ying shixing shuishou teshe zhengce)," *New Economy (Xinjingji),* June 20, 2003, http://finance.sina.com.cn/roll/20030620/0851354932.shtml.

[37] Yang Deming believed that "If the accumulation of equity had come by any illegal means, it implied corruption and should not be tolerated. The law enforcement agencies have the duty to get to the bottom of it, and the government must persist in this principle. We absolutely should not concede on this critical principle. We must use anticorruption to get back these large amounts of public property, and we must try these lawbreaking suspects in court according to law, and we should not tolerate evil, or otherwise we are going to abet it, and commit evil against the state and the people." See "On the Sin and Penalty of the First Bucket of Gold (Guanyu di yi tong jin de zui yu fa)," *New Economy (Xinjingji),* June 17, 2003, http://finance.sina.com.cn/roll/20030617/1521353589.shtml.

[38] Larry H.P. Lang suggested that "Enterprises in the private sector could atone their sin by money; The specific methods can be building, operating, and transferring (BOT), and levying progressive legacy taxes. Of course, those cases proved to be intentionally committed fraud would be excluded, and those suspects should be brought to justice without any excuse. This is in line with the spirit of 'minor sin to be settled, major sin to be judged by law.'" See Larry H.P. Lang, "Dealing with the Original Sin of Enterprises in the Private Sector with a Mechanism (Zhiduhua chuli minqi yuanzui)," *Economic Observation Post (Jingji guancha bao),* June 16, 2003.

period, when the administration had great control over resource allocation, it was a common phenomenon for business owners to violate some regulations and laws in the process of acquiring wealth, yet there was a difference in principle between their infringements and the deeds of "giant crocodiles" who acquired their wealth mainly by manipulating administrative power. The conditional amnesty would lift the burden of a guilty conscience from the former while preventing the latter from escaping criminal punishment.

Another recent debate among scholars and officials has focused on how to manage the relationship between equality and efficiency. One viewpoint argues that equality in distribution is a basic requirement of socialism and therefore equality is of utmost importance, but efficiency is not important. The other viewpoint argues that China is still a poor country and consideration should be given to enhancement of efficiency, without simultaneously devoting attention to equality. According to the law proposed by the American economist, Arthur M. Okun (1928–1980), "there is a tradeoff between efficiency and equality" (negative correlation).[39] In fact, equality can be seen from the angle of equality of opportunity and also the angle of equality of outcome. The equality that Okun referred to is equality of outcome. As for equality of opportunity, it generally has a positive correlation with efficiency, rather than a negative correlation. Therefore, people may simultaneously have both equality of opportunity and efficiency. To address the issue of egalitarianism brought about by a planned economy, it should be emphasized that efficiency takes precedence; in addressing the issue of the current extreme disparity between the rich and the poor caused by inequality of opportunity, justice must be emphasized above everything else.

In China, the current phenomenon of rising income inequality among social strata is mainly caused by inequality of opportunity, not by inequality of outcome. To solve the problem of this extreme disparity between the rich and the poor, it is necessary to have market-oriented reform and to achieve equality of opportunity. In this sense, pursuing equality and boosting efficiency are consistent with each other.

Of course, inequality of opportunity also occurs even in a market economy. For example, in a knowledge economy, those with a higher level of knowledge and skill will have more and better employment opportunities and higher incomes. On the contrary, those without higher education or appropriate professional skills will face unprecedented difficulty in looking for employment and will have a lower income, a phenomenon known as "digital divide." This kind of inequality will have to be eradicated by public functions of the government, such as compulsory education.

---

[39] Arthur M. Okun, *Equality and Efficiency: The Big Tradeoff,* Washington, DC: The Brookings Institute, 1975.

Although inequality of outcome will be inevitable in a market economy, the government should be urged to alleviate the problem by adopting all necessary social policies, such as improved social welfare, and by levying estate tax and capital gain tax.

11.3 Government Functions in Economic Transition

Because the transitional period is rife with contradiction of interests and social conflicts, it is necessary for the government to play an important role in harmonizing different interests, overcoming contradictions, and pushing forward reform to create a smooth transition process. Given this, what functions should the government assume in the transition process? By what means should the government carry out these functions? What reforms should the government undertake to effectively carry out its functions? These questions will be discussed in this section.

Scholars specializing in studying transition gradually discover the nature of transition. Many believe that the sluggishness of reform is related to the lack of constitutional order. The government does not have constitutional constraint on its actions; therefore, many opportunities for reform are ruined by government officials who abuse their authority and engage in corrupt activities. Since the decision-making and administrative actions of the government are not subject to restriction by law, executive procedures lack transparency and vary from person to person and from case to case, breeding rampant corruption. Civil society is too weak to generate a significant enough pressure of checks and balances on government apparatuses to prevent most cases of power abuse. The process of decision making is not guided by universal legal norms. Therefore, the scholars propose that the core of reform should be a large-scale change in constitutional rules. The transition of the economy is only a part of the transition of the whole society.[40]

11.3.1 The Important Functions of the Government in the Transitional Process

There are two opposing opinions regarding the government functions in the transition from a planned economy to a market economy. One opinion claims that "a small government is a good government" and that if the government lifts its control over economic and social affairs and removes the suppression and constraint of administrative power on economic activities, a market economy will grow and prosper on its own. The

---

[40]Jeffrey Sachs, Wing Thye Woo, and Yang Xiaokai, "Economic Reforms and Constitutional Transition (Jingji gaige he xianzheng zhuangui)," *Opening Era (Kaifang shidai)*, 2000, No. 7.

other opinion proposes that a strong government is needed to promote marketization reform and enterprise restructuring, as well as to ensure that the allocation of resources is in the interest of the whole society. Apparently, both of these two extreme opinions have shortcomings.

The first opinion reflects the liberalistic views of both classical and modern times. However, living in the era of mercantilism in the late eighteenth century and emphasizing the need to reduce state intervention, Adam Smith also recognized that the government bore the responsibility of setting and enforcing the rules of property rights to build a platform to allow the functioning of the "invisible hand."

In the development process of market-economy countries thereafter, government intervention and market mechanism experienced a series of cycles of growth and decline. From the late eighteenth century to the late nineteenth century, government intervention in economic activities gradually shrank. However, in the late nineteenth century, government regulation of market activities began to increase. After the Great Depression of 1929, there was a surge in government function and many private businesses were nationalized or regulated by the government. Since the 1970s, the size of the public sector has been shrinking again; some government enterprises were sold to the private sector and the government deregulated many industries such as civil aviation and transportation.

At present, most people classify government functions in a market economy into three categories. The first function is to intervene in resource allocation where there is market failure; for example, to make all necessary adjustments to the production of goods with externalities (such as highly polluting products, products generating significant benefits to the society, and public goods) and to execute antitrust legislation to prevent unfair competition. The second function is to maintain macroeconomic stability in order to avoid extreme fluctuation in markets and economic activities. The third function is to redistribute income, to adjust income distribution determined by market forces in order to prevent polarization of income.

In a developing country, the government should play the leading role in supporting the growth of the market. This is demonstrated not only by the government's best efforts to establish a normalized market order and legal system and offer modern education, but also by the self-discipline of its own actions. The governments of newly industrialized East Asian economies have played this kind of role in the process of economic development. However, when promoting economic growth, the government of a developing country may make inappropriate interventions that will nurture problems like crony capitalism and sow seeds of trouble for the stable development of the economy in the long run.

For the transitional period, positive functions of the government should be strengthened, not be weakened. The positive functions of the government mainly include the following.

11.3.1.1 Eradicating Hindrances to and Opposition against Reform

As mentioned, reform is not a process that inevitably results from a spontaneous evolution of the economy; rather it is a rearrangement of the system. Hence, it implies a major readjustment of the structure of economic interests; this readjustment will definitely face opposition from those unwilling to give up their vested interest. Such opposition can be eradicated only if the government uses all its means of administrative, legal, educational, and economic policies. Of course, among all these measures, some are coercive, while the others are persuasive. For example, the reform of "outside the system" preceding "inside the system" was a persuasive arrangement to make the best use of the situation—and such arrangements would not have worked if they had not been introduced by the government.

11.3.1.2 Establishing Various Infrastructures of the New System

Establishing the necessary infrastructures of a market system is a prerequisite to the effective functioning of the market mechanism. The so-called infrastructures of the market system refer first to organizations such as industrial and commercial enterprises, intermediary organizations, and government apparatuses; and, second, to the full set of the rules of the game including laws and regulations. In the initial stage of China's reform and opening up, the government had problems with slow legislation and slack enforcement. As the reform and opening up has broadened and deepened, establishing the rules of the game has risen to the top of the government agenda; the state should devote more effort to making laws and regulations, and it should use its coercive power to ensure the enforcement of these laws and regulations.

11.3.1.3 Enhancing the Market and Remedying Its Failures

During the transitional period, because of the imperfections in the market system, the scope of deficiency in economic coordination is more extensive than that of market failure as defined in economics, and it is necessary for the government to play a bigger role. On the question of how a government could play its role in solving the problem of market failure, there exist three different viewpoints. The market-friendly view suggests that the role of the government should be restricted to maintaining macroeconomic stability and to remedying market failure as defined in neoclassical economics. The developmental-state view suggests that in this stage of development, the government should replace the functioning of the market with administrative intervention. The market-enhancing view proposes that the government should actively participate in development, but the major form of its participation should be supporting the development of the private sector, including business organizations, financial intermediaries, agricultural cooperatives, etc., and cooperating with them.[41] For a country still in its early stage of a market economy, this third view is the most suitable.

11.3.2 The Necessity of Change in Government Functions

A government keen on reform can play its role in remedying market failure in the process of an accelerated transition. However, a government is also an administrative organization and may also have failure. Government activities often result in government failure or nonmarket failure because: (a) government activities outside market institutions may cause low efficiency; (b) the internal operation of government organizations may deviate from common goals of the society; (c) government apparatuses will have to incur increased expenses; and (d) increased complexity, control of information, and government intervention may generate derived externalities and adverse distributional outcomes of unequal income and power.[42] The government should try to prevent failure by correctly designating areas for market functions and government functions and by determining an appropriate combination of market mechanism and administrative measures. It should be decided which problems should be solved by the market, which problems should be solved by government intervention, which problems should be solved by the market and the government in tandem, and how to coordinate the two.

The actions of statesmen and government officials to comply with the will of the people and to advance reform deserve support from people who are committed to social progress. However, since reform is executed under the leadership of the preexisting totalist government,[43] which has too much power but too little compatibility with a market economy, and the preexisting ruling party, which unavoidably has intertwined relations with the old system, there is the danger that the determination and drive for reform may be softened by the force of habit of the old system, antireform forces may be overaccommodated, and the advance of reform may be unnecessarily delayed. Worse still may be that some officials seek personal gain by abusing their power and become corrupt; to protect the institutional foundation of this fraudulence, the corrupt officials will go to great lengths to maintain the status quo, and thus they become an impedi-

---

[41] Masahiko Aoki, Hyung-Ki Kim, and Masahiro Okuno-Fujiwara (eds.), *The Role of Government in East Asian Economic Development: Comparative Institutional Analysis,* Oxford: Clarendon Press, 1997.
[42] Charles Wolf, *Markets or Governments: Choosing between Imperfect Alternatives,* Cambridge, Mass.: MIT Press, 1988.
[43] See the relevant content in Chapter 1 of this book.

ment to further reform. Therefore, avoiding the damage caused by government failure is more difficult for countries in the process of reform than for other countries.

In summary, the government in a transitional period must retain considerable power. However, as Lord Acton (1834–1902) said, "power tends to corrupt, and absolute power corrupts absolutely."[44] Hence, it is necessary to be vigilant against opposition to reform or attempts to use reform as a front for government officials to seek personal gain, and to mobilize all forces possible to stop them.

11.4 Active Promotion of Political Reform

11.4.1 The Necessity of Political Reform

The necessity of promoting political reform could be explained from two aspects: the values pursued by socialists, and the superstructure required by a market economic foundation. Looking from a values perspective, democracy and the rule of law are an ideal that progressive people have always yearned for, and the current political platform of socialists. Looking from the second aspect, a market economy rests on the foundation of free exchange among owners with equal rights and such an economic system can exist and develop only under a political system with democracy and the rule of law. However, in these two aspects, China's traditional political system in the era of a planned economy had numerous serious flaws that violated the principles of socialism and were detrimental to economic development and social stability. It should not be a surprise that such an abnormal phenomenon existed in China. As Deng Xiaoping once said, "This phenomenon is connected to the influence of feudal autocracy in China's own history and also to the tradition of a high degree of concentration of power in the hands of individual leaders of the Communist parties of various countries at the time of the Communist International."[45]

First, historically, China experienced autocratic rule for several millennia without any tradition of democracy or rule of law. Hence, autocracy had a far-reaching influence on all social strata. After the founding of the People's Republic of China, the importance of purging the influence of feudal autocracy was underestimated, and the hasty switch to socialist revolution left this task of vital importance half done.

Second, China's political system to a great extent had come under the influence of

---

[44] Lord Acton, "Letter to Mandell Creighton of April 5, 1887," *Essays on Freedom and Power,* in Gertrude Himmelfarb (ed.), New York: Penguin Books, 1972, p. 335.

[45] Deng Xiaoping, "On the Reform of the System of Party and State Leadership (Dang he guojia lingdao zhidu de gaige) (August 18, 1980)," *Selected Works of Deng Xiaoping (Deng Xiaoping wenxuan),* Vol. 2, Beijing: People's Publishing House, 1994, p. 329.

the Soviet Union. The political system of the Soviet Union, known as the "political mode of Lenin," corresponded with the economic mode of Lenin known as the "State Syndicate." Stalin established this political system amid bitter struggles within the Communist Party of the Soviet Union in the 1920s and 1930s. The political mode of Lenin, otherwise known as the proletarian dictatorship system, was further developed by Stalin. In many of his works, Stalin described the basic structure of this system in detail.[46] He said that the proletarian dictatorship system consisted of a "directing force" as well as various "transmission belts" and "levers" of the proletarian dictatorship, and that the proletarian dictatorship system was the totality of these components. Here, the "directing force" refers to the Communist Party as the vanguard of proletariat; the "transmission belts" and "levers" primarily refer to the government at various levels and to economic organizations such as factories and stores, as well as to social groups such as the trade union, the youth league, and the women's federation. Quoting Lenin's remarks, Stalin said, "the masses are divided into classes . . . classes are led by political parties; political parties, as a general rule, are run by more or less stable groups composed of the most authoritative, influential, and experienced members, who are elected to the most responsible positions, and are called leaders."[47] This mode of political system with highly centralized power had become a paradigm copied by all other socialist countries.

Under such a system, highly centralized power without constraint in China bred a large group of leaders of patriarchal dominance at various levels of the leadership structure. They suppressed democracy, marred the rule of law, drove the political life of the country into an abnormal state of dictatorial rule by a few individuals, and eventually led to national catastrophes such as the Great Cultural Revolution.

In view of this situation, at the very inception of the reform and opening up, Deng Xiaoping incisively pointed out that in the everyday political life of the party and the state, there were widespread phenomena of abusing power, suppressing democracy, acting arbitrarily, taking bribes, and perverting the law. "Such things have reached intolerable dimensions both in our domestic affairs and in our contacts with other countries."[48] Furthermore, Lenin's political system was interlinked with his economic system. Leaving aside the question of whether this system is reasonable or not, by relying on this system and on the foundation of the "State Syndicate," the party and the government

---

[46] Joseph Stalin, "Concerning Questions of Leninism (Lieningzhuyi de jige wenti) (1926)," *Selected Works of Stalin (Sidalin xuanji)*, Chinese edition, Vol. 1, Beijing: People's Publishing House, 1979, pp. 411–434.

[47] Vladimir I. Lenin, "Left Wing Communism, an Infantile Disorder (Gongchanzhuyi yundong zhong de 'zuopai' youzhibing) (1920)," *Selected Works of Lenin (Liening xuanji)*, Chinese edition, 2nd edition, Vol. 4, Beijing: People's Publishing House, 1972, pp. 197–198.

[48] Deng Xiaoping, "On the Reform of the System of Party and State Leadership (Dang he guojia lingdao zhidu de gaige) (August 18, 1980)," *Selected Works of Deng Xiaoping (Deng Xiaoping wenxuan)*, Vol. 2, Beijing: People's Publishing House, 1994, p. 320.

were able to enforce their orders and prohibitions and bring social and economic activities under control. However, this system was incompatible with a market economy characterized by diversified social and economic structures. Therefore, since the beginning of the reform and opening up, it has been more and more difficult for the preexisting political system to meet the needs of the ever-growing market economic system. As Deng Xiaoping said in 1986, "When we first raised the question of reform, we had in mind, among other things, reform of the political structure. Whenever we take a step forward in economic reform, we are made keenly aware of the need to change the political structure. If we fail to do that, we shall be unable to preserve the gains we have made in the economic reform and to build on them. . . . If we do not institute a reform of our political structure, it will be difficult to carry out reform of our economic structure." As the core of the second generation of leadership of China, Deng Xiaoping strongly expressed his feelings by saying, "We feel the need to reform our political structure is growing more and more urgent."[49]

Insight 11.1

Deng Xiaoping's View on the Reform of the System of Party and State Leadership

At the enlarged meeting of the Political Bureau of the Central Committee of the Communist Party of China on August 18, 1980, Deng Xiaoping voiced his view during the discussion on the issue of reforming the system of party and state leadership by pointing out:

> Due to the effect of long-term feudal despotism in China, also due to the long-standing belief that socialism must institute a highly centralized management system of economic, political, cultural, and social affairs, there are lots of defects in the present Party and State leadership system:
>
> 1. Bureaucracy. Its harmful manifestations include the following: standing high above the masses; abusing power; divorcing oneself from reality and the masses; being obsessed in putting up an impressive front; indulging in empty talk; sticking to a rigid way of thinking; being hidebound by convention; overstaffing

---

[49]Deng Xiaoping, "On Reform of the Political Structure (Guanyu zhengzhi tizhi gaige wenti) (September–November 1986)," *Selected Works of Deng Xiaoping (Deng Xiaoping wenxuan)*, Vol. 3, Beijing: People's Publishing House, 1993, pp. 176–180.

administrative organs; being dilatory, inefficient, and irresponsible; failing to keep one's word; circulating documents endlessly without solving problems; shifting responsibility onto others; and even assuming the airs of a mandarin, reprimanding other people at every turn, vindictively attacking others, suppressing democracy, deceiving superiors and subordinates, being arbitrary and despotic, practicing favoritism, offering bribes, participating in corrupt practices in violation of the law, and so on. Such things have reached intolerable dimensions both in our domestic affairs and in our contacts with other countries.

2. Phenomenon of overconcentration of power. It means inappropriate and indiscriminate concentration of all power in Party committees in the name of strengthening centralized Party leadership. Moreover, the power of the Party committees themselves is often in the hands of a few secretaries, especially the first secretaries. Now that ours has become the ruling party in the whole country, overconcentration of power is becoming more and more incompatible with the development of our socialist cause. The long-standing failure to understand this adequately was one important cause of the "Great Cultural Revolution," and we paid a heavy price for it.

3. Patriarchal ways. Besides leading to overconcentration of power in the hands of individuals, patriarchal ways within the revolutionary ranks place individuals above the organization, which then becomes a tool in their hands. After 1958, democratic life in the Party and the State gradually ceased to function normally. There was a constant growth of such patriarchal ways as letting only one person have the say and make important decisions, practicing the cult of personality and placing individuals above the organization. Many places and units have their patriarchal personages with unlimited power. Everyone else has to be absolutely obedient and even personally attached to them. Unless such ways are eliminated once for all, the practice of inner-Party democracy in particular and of socialist democracy in general is out of the question.

4. Political and economic privileges of all shades. All citizens are equal before the law and the existing rules and regulations, and all

Party members are equal before the Party Constitution and regulations on Party discipline. Everyone has equal rights and duties prescribed by law, and no one may gain advantages at others' expense or violate the law. The errors we made in the past were partly attributable to the way of thinking and style of work of some leaders. But they were even more attributable to the problems in our organizational and working systems. If these systems are sound, they can place restraints on the actions of bad people; if they are unsound, they may hamper the efforts of good people or indeed, in certain cases, may push them in the wrong direction.

According to Deng Xiaoping, the Central Committee of the Party was planning to gradually introduce the following major changes:

1. The Central Committee will submit proposals for revising the Constitution of the People's Republic of China, so as to really ensure the people's right to manage the state organs at all levels as well as the various enterprises and institutions, to guarantee to our people the full enjoyment of their rights as citizens.

2. A truly effective work system will be set up for the State Council and the various levels of local government. From now on, all matters within the competence of the government will be discussed and decided upon, and the relevant documents issued, by the State Council and the local governments. The Central Committee and local committees of the party will no longer issue directives or make decisions on such matters.

3. Step by step and in a planned manner we should reform the system under which the factory director or manager assumes responsibility under the leadership of the party committee. Then we institute a system under which factory directors and managers assume responsibility under the leadership and supervision of the factory management committee. We should also consider reforming the system under which university and college presidents and heads of research institutes assume responsibility under the leadership of the party committee.

4. Party committees at all levels are genuinely to apply the principle of combining collective leadership and division of labor with individual responsibility. Major issues must certainly be discussed and decided

upon by the collective. In the process of making decisions, it is essential to observe strictly the principle of majority rule and the principle of one man, one vote; the first secretary must not make decisions by himself.

This speech of Deng Xiaoping was discussed and endorsed by the Political Bureau on August 31, 1980.

(Compiled according to Deng Xiaoping, "On the Reform of the System of Party and State Leadership (August 1980)," *Selected Works of Deng Xiaoping*, Vol. 2, Beijing: People's Publishing House, 1994, pp. 320–343.)

The set goal of China's reform is to realize economic development and overall advance of the society and to construct a prosperous, strong, democratic, civilized, socialist country.[50] As Deng Xiaoping pointed out, to reach this goal, "Along with the expansion of our productive forces, we should also reform and improve our socialist economic and political structures, build a highly developed socialist democracy, and perfect the socialist legal system."[51] Deng Xiaoping repeatedly pointed out that China's political system originated from the Soviet model; this political system must be reformed and the reform cannot be delayed further, otherwise the reform of the economic system cannot be implemented and advanced further.[52] Deng Xiaoping not only made a general call to promote political reform but also put forth the two most important measures: separation of party leadership from government administration and separation of government administration from enterprise management. The third generation of leadership of China restarted political reform in the early 1990s. The 15th National Congress of the CPC in 1997 proposed a comprehensive goal for political reform "to expand socialist democracy, to perfect the socialist legal system, to run the country in accordance with the law, and to construct a socialist country with the rule of law."[53] In

---

[50] Jiang Zemin, *Hold High the Great Banner of Deng Xiaoping Theory for an All-Round Advance of the Cause of Building Socialism with Chinese Characteristics into the Twenty-First Century—the Report to the Fifteenth National Congress of the CPC (Gaoju Deng Xiaoping lilun weida qizhi, ba jianshe you Zhongguo tese shehuizhuyi shiye quanmian tuixiang 21 shiji—zai Zhongguo Gongchandang Di Shiwu Ci Quanguo Daibiao Dahui shang de baogao)* (September 1997), Beijing: People's Publishing House, 1997.

[51] Deng Xiaoping, "Speech Greeting the Fourth Congress of Chinese Writers and Artists (Zai Zhongguo Wenxue Yishu Gongzuozhe Di Si Ci Daibiao Dahui shang de zhuci) (October 30, 1979)," *Selected Works of Deng Xiaoping (Deng Xiaoping wenxuan)*, Vol. 2, Beijing: People's Publishing House, 1994, p. 208.

[52] Deng Xiaoping, "On Reform of the Political Structure (Guanyu zhengzhi tizhi gaige wenti) (September–November 1986)," *Selected Works of Deng Xiaoping (Deng Xiaoping wenxuan)*, Vol. 3, Beijing: People's Publishing House, 1993, pp. 176–180.

[53] Jiang Zemin, *Hold High the Great Banner of Deng Xiaoping Theory for an All-round Advance of the Cause of Building Socialism With Chinese Characteristics Into the Twenty-First Century—the Report to the Fifteenth National Congress of the CPC (Gaoju Deng Xiaoping*

2002, to promote political reform, the 16th National Congress of the CPC put forth goals to construct a country with the rule of law, to develop democratic politics, and to promote political civilization.

Although political reform has been included in the programmatic documents of leading organs of the party and the government, and much work has been done in elections at the grassroots level and in legislation for a market economy in the past twenty plus years, the advance of political reform has been far slower than originally anticipated and great efforts should be made in the future.

11.4.2 Major Contents of Political Reform

Political reform should make progress on the three aspects described: to construct a country with the rule of law, to develop democratic politics, and to promote political civilization. Here, the rule of law means that laws legislated according to the constitution shall prevail; the democracy we want is constitutional democracy, and constitutional government is exactly the essence of modern political civilization. Hence, the requirements of these three aspects focus on one issue—constitutional government.

Specifically, political reform should consist of the items discussed in the following sections.

11.4.2.1 Making Government Affairs Open and Protecting the People's Right to Know

Both *The Constitution of the People's Republic of China* and *The Universal Declaration of Human Rights* signed by the Chinese government outline provisions in principle on the fundamental rights of human beings. People's fundamental rights, including freedom of speech, freedom of the press, freedom of assembly, freedom of association, freedom of demonstration and protest, freedom of religion, rights of the person, and right to elect and right to be elected, must be protected, free from any infringement.

The monopoly of decision-making rights by government agencies and their officials often rely on their monopoly of public information. All information generated during the process of executing official duties is a public resource and is something the general public must have in order to understand public affairs and the government's working situation and to monitor government officials. Therefore, modern countries usually have legislation to ensure open information and a "sunshine government:" except for information related to national security and information exempted by law, all public information must be available to the public. Only when a system of transparent information

---

lilun weida qizhi, ba jianshe you Zhongguo tese shehuizhuyi shiye quanmian tuixiang 21 shiji—zai Zhongguo Gongchandang Di Shiwu Ci Quanguo Daibiao Dahui shang de baogao) (September 1997), Beijing: People's Publishing House, 1997.

is established can government agencies and their officials be monitored by the public. However, the totalist government of the past more often than not perceived the administration of public affairs and information that reflected this process as internal secrets of the party and the government. The operation of such a system over a long period of time has formed a whole set of established practices for handling crises: disregarding citizens' right to know, maintaining the approach of "being relaxed outside but tense inside," stringently keeping secrets and seeking resolution of the crises within the government without the public's knowledge. Hence, access to information has become a privilege and some corrupt government officials are able to turn what should be public information into their private information and to use it as a tool for rent-seeking. Taking advantage of this kind of nontransparent system, these officials can not only seek personal gain and deceive the public but also can blindfold higher authorities. In recent years, many corrupt officials were able to muzzle public opinion by abusing their power to hide the truth so that their wrongdoings of riding roughshod over the masses remained unexposed for years. In a modern society, mass media such as newspapers, magazines, television broadcasting, and the Internet are major means for society to exchange public information and for citizens to exercise their right to know and right to monitor granted by the constitution. If mass media cannot play the role it should play, society will be in a state of information blackout, resulting in serious negative economic, political, and social consequences.

The previous term of the Chinese government launched the reform to make government affairs open and promoted making information about government affairs open to the public by using modern information technology. Since this reform is essential to protecting people's right to know, continued effort should be made to fully implement it.

11.4.2.2 Separating Party Leadership from Government Administration and Separating Government Administration from Enterprise Management

Generally speaking, each country's party in power has three alternative ways to exercise its leadership in political life. The first is for the party in power to exercise its leadership by state power, that is, by drawing up the constitution, amending the constitution, and participating in other law-making activities of the representative institution of the country, and by implementing these laws by organs of state power. The second is for the party in power to circumvent state power and directly exercise the functions that should have been exercised by the representative institution and organs of state power. The third is for the party in power to control the government, making all decisions while the government implements the decisions. Nicos Poulantzas, a French scholar studying Marxism, once pointed out that "the political structure, in which the political parties and the administration of a country are entwined and integrated, does not have any connection at all with democracy or even with socialism."[54]

Because the Leftist party line in the past combined party leadership with government administration, government administration with enterprise management, and violated the principle of the rule of law of socialism, Deng Xiaoping reiterated in his works that the principle of separation of party leadership from government administration and separation of government administration from enterprise management must be carried out in China's political life. Given China's conditions, the achievement of separation of party leadership from government administration and separation of government administration from enterprise management will meet with difficulties and opposition. However, the realization of this important principle of Deng Xiaoping is the key in promoting the democratic politics of socialism; it must be achieved, with no effort spared.

11.4.2.3 Democratic Election System

The construction of democratic politics in China started from elections at the grassroots level. After the Third Plenary Session of the 11th CCCPC, the party clearly proposed to "realize step by step the people's direct democracy in the governments and the social life at the grassroots level." In the early 1980s, peasants in Guangxi Province and some other places established their autonomous organizations of villagers' committees after the implementation of the "all-round responsibility system" in agriculture. The new constitution adopted and implemented in 1982 defined this kind of autonomous system at the grassroots level. In 1987, the *Law on Organization of Villagers' Committees (Trial)* was enacted, stipulating that chairman, vice chairmen, and other members of a villagers' committee should be elected directly by the villagers. The Report of the 15th National Congress of the CPC in 1997 pointed out that "all grassroots organs of political power and grassroots autonomous organizations of the masses in urban and rural areas should institute a sound democratic election system." In 1998, the *Law on Organization of Villagers' Committee* was officially put into force, which further defined the autonomous nature of villagers' committees and instituted sound procedures of direct election. As of 2001, villagers' committees all over the countryside had generally completed four rounds of regular elections; the degree of democratization and normalization had increased with each round, and millions of village officials had been switched from a nomination system to a direct election system.[55] In the late 1990s, a few cases of competitive

---

[54] Wang Yan, "Promote Legalization of Political Life in China (Cujin guojia zhengzhi shenghuo de fazhihua)," *Methods (Fangfa)*, 1998, No. 4.

[55] Zhan Chengfu, "Several Issues Regarding Direct Election in Villages in China (Guanyu wo guo xiangcun zhijie xuanju de ji ge wenti)," *Research on Socialism (Shehuizhuyi yanjiu)*, 2001, No. 4.

election at the township/town level emerged in Sichuan and Guangdong. Then, in 2002, 40 percent of townships/towns (about two thousand) in Sichuan Province adopted competitive elections to elect township/town head and vice township/town head upon the completion of their office terms; some localities also adopted the competitive election of township/town party vice-secretaries. In cities, residents' committees of communities have ubiquitously been selected by direct election. However, due to the long-time absence of an election system and culture in China, the fundamental principles and significance of democratic election go beyond the understanding of many people; for example, some voters hold an indifferent attitude as to who is going to be elected, just swimming with the tide; some elections are manipulated; and various problems of bribery and fraud in election exist. Therefore, it is necessary to provide the masses with civic education, incorporating details of democratic election into the syllabus of high-school civil education courses.

11.4.2.4 Instituting the Rule of Law

The rule of law is a fundamental characteristic of a modern political system, and is a critical issue that every country must solve in the transition toward a market economy and democratic politics. China does not have a tradition of the rule of law. In the era of feudalism, the legal system was just a tool in the hands of the emperor. During a period after the founding of the People's Republic of China, some government leaders had been interested in starting the rule of law; but after 1957, the rule of law was condemned as the view of bourgeois Rightists. The press not only repeatedly propagandized the writings of Lenin that "proletarian dictatorship is a dictatorship that is bound by no law" but also advocated Mao Zedong's "supreme instruction" of defying all laws, human or divine.[56] Although leaders of the party and the government have been emphasizing administration according to law and institution of the rule of law in recent years, the ideological inertia is still a hurdle to be overcome. Furthermore, steps to institute the rule of law are necessary in the following aspects.

First, establishing the supremacy of the constitution. The *Constitution* is China's fundamental law; all other statutory laws, bylaws, or governmental orders of the administrative apparatuses must comply with the *Constitution*. The main content of the *Constitution* is the protection of citizens' fundamental rights. First of all, property rights, be they public or private, are under the protection of laws and free from any infringement. At the same time, the scope of the government authority must be defined to prevent the

---

[56] Xiong Xianghui, *My Intelligence and Diplomatic Life (Wo de qingbao yu waijiao shengya)*, Beijing: The Central Party History Press, 1999, p. 220.

government from abusing its authority and infringing upon citizens' fundamental rights. Corruption is in essence the abuse of entrusted public authority to infringe upon property rights and economic interests of citizens. One of the reasons for rent-seeking activities to become widespread is overly pervasive government control with too much discretionary power in the hands of government officials. A basic requirement for instituting a constitutional government is prevention of the existence of any entity with absolute, unconstrained power.

Second, instituting a transparent legal framework. Under the rule of law, the legal system must be transparent. There are three basic requirements of transparency. The first is that the public should extensively participate in the process of legislation and have a chance to take part in the drafting of laws. The second is that laws should be made known to the public. Right now, many government agencies treat laws and regulations as their private information, and outsiders are not allowed to know about the existence of relevant laws and regulations or their specific contents. This allows corrupt officials to control the situation officially or under the table so they can pervert laws and infringe upon the interests of citizens. According to the modern notion of the rule of law, a law not made known to the public is an ineffective law. The third requirement for transparency is that citizens should be able to predict the legal consequences of their actions. For example, according to the principle of the rule of law, a law can only be applied to actions carried out after the law has been issued; the law cannot be applied retroactively. Otherwise, citizens cannot control their own destinies and will be forced to seek backdoor connections and offer bribes to officials who have a lot of discretionary power to make an exception in their case.

Third, ensuring judicial impartiality and judicial independence. Independent trial by judges and law enforcement with justice are basic requirements for institution of the rule of law. At present, judicial corruption and administrative intervention are major obstacles to realizing these basic requirements. To remove these obstacles, in addition to improving the system, monitoring by the public and by party committees at various levels must be increased. The political leadership of the Communist Party of China in its capacity of the party in office and judicial independence required by the socialist rule of law are compatible with each other. First of all, the political programs and requirements of the party in office must be enacted into laws through legal procedures; every party member and every party organization can act only within the scope of the *Constitution* and law, and no one can be allowed to be above the law. Second, the monitoring of judicial practice by party committees at various levels should be exercised as monitoring of the justice of legal procedures, not as intervening in specific judicial processes or decisions. Nowadays, another important threat against judicial impartiality and judicial independence comes from so-called "judicial parochialization." The outcome of a cross-region case of economic dispute more often than not depends on which region possesses the judicial jurisdiction of the case. In view of this, several corrective measures have been proposed. For example, the power of local people's congresses in the nomination procedures of local judges should be restricted. Moreover, some scholars have recommended the People's Supreme Court to organize circuit courts to handle cross-region cases. This is a feasible method to curb local protectionism.

11.4.2.5 Correcting the Relationship Between the Government and the People

The major drawback of the political and social administration system in the era of a planned economy was that the system of a "big totalist government" reversed the original rightful relation of government as servant and the people as master. As early as 130 years ago, during discussion of the experience of the Paris Commune, the founder of Marxism repeatedly reiterated that the most important issue was the need to prevent the "transformation of the state and the organs of the state from servants of society into masters of society."[57] Under the system of a big totalist government, although some party and government organizations and their officials had slogans of "serving the people" or "acting as the servant of the people" on their office walls and on their lips, in reality they remained in the seat of "master of society" and "chief" of the masses and were able to impose their own will on society in the name of state objectives and to make decisions on behalf of "people of all family names" under their jurisdiction on all issues, including issues critical to citizens' vital interests. In a country like China with a long tradition of autocracy, this completely reversed relationship was able to gain acceptance by citizens. For example, such social aberrances as local officials being called "parent officials" of "people of all family names" and incorruptible officials being laurelled "parents of citizens" became the social norm. By virtue of their power and influence, some unlawful officials were unbearably arrogant toward people; they not only were free from the monitoring by voters and taxpayers but also considered people's petitions and visits to appeal to the higher authorities for help as illegal or rebellious actions, to be strictly forbidden.

It was the existence of these outmoded conventions and irrational practices that went against the grain of modern political civilization, that caused some government officials in charge to take very irresponsible actions—such as blocking the transfer of information, hiding the epidemic situation, and disseminating false information—on the vital issue of the SARS epidemic in 2003, while still believing what they had done was some-

---

[57] Friedrich Engels, "The 1891 Preface to Marx's 'The Civil War in France' (Makesi Falanxi Neizhan 1891 Nian Danxingben daoyan) (1891)," *Selected Works of Marx and Engels (Makesi Engesi xuanji),* Chinese edition, Vol. 3, Beijing: People's Publishing House, 1995, pp. 12–14.

thing right and proper and conforming to rules and procedures of the government. To rectify this reversed relation between master and servant, it is important to build a constitutional order that clearly defines fundamental human rights and establishes a set of explicit constraints on the government's authority, in accordance with the decision of the 16th National Congress of the CPC to promote political reform by promoting political civilization, developing democratic politics, and constructing a society with the rule of law. Officials of the party and the government who are vested with state power should be accountable for what they have done. The exercise of people's right to monitor and dismiss public servants should be ensured by legal procedures with operational feasibility.

Party Secretary-General Hu Jintao, in his speech at the Theoretical Seminar of Learning the Important Thought of Three Represents on July 1, 2003, decisively pointed out that "the essence of the important thought of Three Represents is to build the Party for public interest and to exercise power for the people. To realize the will of the people, to satisfy their needs, and to safeguard their interests are the fundamental starting point and underlying objective of the important thought of Three Represents. To build the Party for the public interest and to exercise power for the people is the most important measuring stick to determine whether one has really understood and practiced the important thought of Three Represents."[58] The *Decision* by the Third Plenary Session of the 16th CCCPC set further demands on the acceleration of the transformation of government functions from a management government to a service government and reform of the leadership and administration of methods appropriate for the new development of a socialist market economy.[59] These new demands and decisions made by leaders of the party and the government clearly showed the direction of the reform of the Chinese government in the future.

11.4.3 Nurturing a Civil Society and Improving the Self-Organizing Ability of the Society

A modern society has a multitude of interests and diverse activities. Public affairs should not purely rest on the shoulders of the party and the government organs and their officials and it is necessary for civil society to develop and for social groups to extensively exercise their autonomy. However, a significant trait of the conventional system

---

[58] Hu Jintao, "Speech at the Theoretical Seminar of Learning the Important Thought of 'Three Represents' (Zai Xuexi Guanche 'San Ge Daibiao' Zhongyao Sixiang Lilun Yantaohui shang de jianghua) (July 2003)," *Seeking Truth (Qiushi),* 2003, No. 13, pp. 3–11.

[59] "The Decision of the CCCPC on Issues Regarding the Improvement of the Socialist Market Economic System (Zhonggong Zhongyang guanyu wanshan shichang jingji tizhi ruogan wenti de jueding) (Passed by the Third Plenary Session of the Sixteenth Central Committee of the CPC)," *People's Daily (Renmin ribao),* October 21, 2003, p. 1.

of "big government and small society" was the full expansion of state power and the maximum control over activities of civil society. Therefore, after achieving the socialist transformation in 1956 and particularly after establishing people's communes that integrated government administration with commune management in 1958, other organizations of social groups completely vanished, except for the family, with its precarious independence. All walks of life in the whole society, no matter which trade they belonged to, were integrated into a unified and monotonous system of administrative hierarchy that was based solely on the standard of official positions. This was a fiber-like system without vitality and energy, also known as a "state without society." Once government leaders made a decision and issued an order, a system of organizations like this could wield state authority to mobilize every possible resource to achieve the specific goals of the state. Nonetheless, this system had a fatal weakness: its social groups had no self-organizing capability, any issue that cropped up had to be handled with government orders, and any project not based on official plans or any activity without official permission would be halted or would proceed with difficulty. In a country where its people are the ultimate master, it is necessary to enhance the self-organizing capability of civil society and to give organizations of social groups a free hand to deal with various public affairs. Only by doing so is it possible to have a colorful social life and a lively political situation, as well as all-round economic, political, and cultural prosperity.

PART 4

BRIEF CONCLUSION

CHAPTER 12

CONCLUDING REMARKS

China's reform has often been described as the "New Long March," where the word "Long March" indicates the great difficulties in the transition from administrative socialism to a socialist market economy. The foregoing eleven chapters, except Chapter 1 which runs back over the starting point of the transition, review this process from its different aspects to analyze the problems concerned in a framework of economic-social-political sciences. Chapter 12 will make a brief summary of the contents in the foregoing chapters.

12.1 Economic and Political Goals Becoming Increasingly Clear in the Process of Reform

China's reform started with economic reform, and economic reform started by "crossing the river by groping for the stones," an approach that lay emphasis on concrete results instead of arguments of theory and ideology. At the beginning, most people were keen on introducing some practices of developed market economies, only out of the belief that these practices effective in other countries would help China improve her economic performance. However, as reform advanced forward, people got to realize from the institutional contradictions and conflicts that unlike shopping in a supermarket when we arbitrarily choose consumer goods from the shelves and piece them into a "basket," reform could only be an overall transition toward a market economy. Moreover, a planned economy and a market economy are both huge systems, each consisting of many subsystems with "logical consistency" among them. In this respect, reform, as was often referred to in the 1980s, is a "project of systems engineering" requiring the coordinated implementation of every major subproject.

The practical needs of reform have accelerated the independent development of China's economic science on the basis of its integration into the world economic science; and this development in return provides theoretical guidance to the practice of reform. The interaction of theory and practice helps to make the goal of reform to establish a socialist market economy, set in the early 1990s, become clear and specific in the late 1990s.

The case of political reform is similar to that of economic reform. Almost at the same time when economic reform started, Deng Xiaoping, the chief architect of China's reform, put forward several pressing issues concerning political reform: "eliminating the surviving feudal influences," eliminating the "phenomenon of overconcentration of power"—"concentration of all power in Party committees . . . , the power of the Party committees themselves is often in the hands of a few secretaries, especially the first secretaries," realizing "separation of Party leadership from government administration" and "separation of government administration from enterprise management," and expanding the inner-party democracy and people's democracy.

China's political reform has undergone many twists and turns, which, however, enable those with insight in and outside the government to realize that the political superstructure compatible with the economic base of a market economy, or the "political shell" of a market economy, can be nothing else but a highly democratic political system that socialism ought to have.

The decisions made at previous national congresses of China's ruling party—the Communist Party of China (CPC)—are of significance to economic and political reforms. The 15th National Congress of the CPC in 1997 and the 16th National Congress of the CPC in 2002 are milestones for setting clear goals of economic reform and political reform respectively. The reports delivered by Jiang Zemin on behalf of the Central Committee of the CPC at these two national congresses and their decisions brought forward many thoughts of great significance on the goals of China's economic and political reforms, providing China's reform with correct guidelines.[1]

Thus, the goals of reform presented to people all over China by Chinese leaders become more and more clear, namely, to construct a prosperous, democratic, and civilized China.[2]

The biggest controversy over the concept of a socialist market economy is whether socialism can be combined with a market economy. The answer to this question, as is clear enough now, depends on the definition of socialism. If we stick to the definition in *Political Economy* of the Soviet Union and regard socialism as an economic system regulated by state planning on the basis of state ownership, then the answer can be nothing but negative. The "market socialism" proposed by some economists in the former socialist countries of Eastern Europe is confined to the Soviet-style prejudice and at-

---

[1] Jiang Zemin, *Hold High the Great Banner of Deng Xiaoping Theory for an All-Round Advance of the Cause of Building Socialism with Chinese Characteristics into the Twenty-First Century—the Report to the Fifteenth National Congress of the CPC (Gaoju Deng Xiaoping lilun weida qizhi, ba jianshe you Zhongguo tese shehuizhuyi shiye quanmian tuixiang 21 shiji—zai Zhongguo Gongchandang Di Shiwu Ci Quanguo Daibiao Dahui shang de baogao)* (September 1997), Beijing: People's Publishing House, 1997. See also Jiang Zemin, *Build a Well-off Society in an All-Round Way and Create a New Situation in Building Socialism with Chinese Characteristics—the Report to the Sixteenth National Congress of the CPC (Quanmian jianshe xiaokang shehui, kaichuang Zhongguo tese shehuizhuyi shiye xin jumian—zai Zhongguo Gongchandang Di Shiliu Ci Quanguo Daibiao Dahui shang de baogao)* (November 2002), Beijing: People's Publishing House, 2002.

[2] Jiang Zemin, *Speech at the Rally in Celebration of the 80th Anniversary of the Founding of the CPC (Zai qingzhu Zhongguo Gongchandang chengli bashi zhounian dahui shang de jianghua)* (July 1, 2001), Beijing: People's Publishing House, 2001.

tempts to base a new system on state ownership, and that is why it is criticized by most economists.[3] On the contrary, if we regard socialism as a cause of common prosperity and a social system to ensure the accomplishment of this cause as defined in Deng Xiaoping Theory, then the answer can be nothing but positive. It was based on this new understanding that the 15th National Congress of the CPC defined the ownership base for a socialist market economy by pointing out that: (a) state ownership plays a leading role only in important industries and key sectors concerning the lifelines of the national economy; (b) contrary to what was stated in *Political Economy* of the Soviet Union, public ownership can be realized in forms other than state ownership and collective ownership, it may and should be diversified, and all management methods and organizational forms that mirror the laws governing socialized production may be utilized boldly; (c) nonpublic sectors are important components of China's socialist market economy; and (d) the structure of ownership should be adjusted and improved according to the criterion of the three favorables (whether it is favorable to promoting the growth of the productive forces in a socialist society, increasing the overall strength of the socialist state, and raising the people's living standards). These thoughts free China from the fetters of *Political Economy* of the Soviet Union and prove scientifically the feasibility of a socialist market economy.

The case of the goal of political reform goes the same way. After Deng Xiaoping made his speech on August 18, 1980, China took some measures to fight bureaucracy, to overcome overconcentration of power and patriarchalism, to abolish life tenure in leading posts, and to realize the separation of party leadership from government administration and the separation of government administration from enterprise management, and achieved progress to a certain extent. Meanwhile, however, some unhealthy phenomena have not been eliminated; to the contrary, some social problems like corruption and the unrighteous work style of the party and government are deteriorating. Such a situation urges people to wonder whether there exists any problem in the Soviet political model that was introduced into China with the Soviet-planned economic system.

Just as the socialist planned economic system was originally intended to overcome the inherent defects of the capitalist system, the Soviet political system established by Lenin claimed in public to eliminate the chronic illnesses of the traditional state, a task raised by one of the founders of Marxism when he was summing up the experiences and lessons of the Paris Commune of 1871. Engels pointed out in his 1891 *Preface to Marx's "Civil War in France"* that "Society had created its own organs to look after its common

---

[3] As for the critiques and reflection on "market socialism," see Chapter 1 Section 4 of this book.

interests, originally through simple division of labor. But these organs, at whose head was the state power, had in the course of time, in pursuance of their own special interests, transformed themselves from the servants of society into the masters of society." In the view of Marx and Engels, after having seized the state power, the proletariat, just like the Paris Commune, should lop off at the earliest possible moment the worst sides of the state "until such time as a new generation, reared in new and free social conditions, will be able to throw the entire lumber of the state on the scrap-heap."[4] However, the practice later showed that the idea of Marx and Engels "to throw the entire lumber of the state on the scrap-heap" was overidealized. The fact was that after the founding of the Soviet regime, the state did not die out by itself, nor did the improvement measures made by the Paris Commune such as the election of officials on the basis of universal suffrage and the treatment of officials as equal to that of ordinary citizens. On the contrary, a political system was established under the leadership of Stalin in which power was highly centralized, a universal appointment system was applied, and the power of the leaders was subject to no constraint, resulting in a series of incidents gravely violating norms of inner-party behavior and the constitution and laws that the Soviet Union declared to the world. This historical fact cannot be denied even by Stalin's adorers.

As a result, China's political reform is not only to improve the work style of the Communist Party of China, and to enhance the moral qualities of the government officials for serving the people, but more importantly, to establish a political system that adheres to the principle of social justice and meets the requirement of a market economy. Deng Xiaoping said: "It is true that the errors we made in the past were partly attributable to the way of thinking and style of work of some leaders. But they were even more attributable to the problems in our organizational and working systems. If these systems are sound, they can place restraints on the actions of bad people; if they are unsound, they may hamper the efforts of good people or indeed, in certain cases, may push them in the wrong direction. Even so great a man as Comrade Mao Zedong was influenced to a serious degree by certain unsound systems and institutions, which resulted in grave misfortunes for the Party, the state and himself. . . . Stalin gravely damaged socialist legality, doing things which Comrade Mao Zedong once said would have been impossible in Western countries like Britain, France and the United States. Yet although Comrade Mao was aware of this, he did not in practice solve the problems in our sys-

---

[4]Friedrich Engels, "The 1891 Preface to Marx's 'The Civil War in France' (Makesi Falanxi neizhan 1891 nian danxingben daoyan) (1891)," *Selected Works of Marx and Engels (Makesi Engesi xuanji)*, Chinese edition, Vol. 3, Beijing: People's Publishing House, 1995, pp. 12–14. According to Engels, "the Commune made use of two infallible expedients. In this first place, it filled all posts—administrative, judicial and educational—by election on the basis of universal suffrage of all concerned, with the right of the same electors to recall their delegate at any time. And in the second place, all officials, high or low, were paid only the wages received by other workers."

tem of leadership. Together with other factors, this led to the decade of catastrophe known as the 'Cultural Revolution.'"[5]

Then, what kind of political system and leadership structure does China's reform aim to establish? The 15th National Congress of the CPC and especially the 16th National Congress of the CPC further clarified the answer to this question, that is, to promote political civilization, to develop democratic politics, and to build a country under the rule of law.[6] Constitutional government is the main content of modern political civilization. The new leadership of China has grasped the key link of democracy and the rule of law promoted by the 16th National Congress of the CPC, as they emphasized the role of the *Constitution* as soon as they took office.[7]

The reform of the traditional socialist system is an important part of the pursuit of a better society by mankind. For the whole twentieth century, mankind had been making explorations in many ways to eliminate existing social maladies. In addition to the effort made by various socialist countries under the leadership of communist parties as investigated in this book, there were also the New Deal of Franklin D. Roosevelt, experiments of social democracy, etc. These explorations had both successes and failures, which are worth learning from.

12.2 Promoting Reform and Comprehensively Improving Socialist Market Economic System

Having undergone over twenty years of economic reform in a steady and fundamental way, China has made a big step toward the goal it set: the outline of a market economy under the rule of law has appeared in front of the people. However, the situation faced by China in transition is one with multiple tasks of solving the remaining problems of the old system, resolving the contradictions brought about during the period when the new and old systems coexisted, and establishing a good environment for the new system. As discussed in previous chapters of this book, China is faced with a series of problems, including the "three rural problems" of stagnant rural economy, poor rural residents and backward rural society; incomplete restructuring of the state sector and

---

[5] Deng Xiaoping, "On the Reform of the System of Party and State Leadership (Dang he guojia lingdao zhidu de gaige) (August 1980)," *Selected Works of Deng Xiaoping (Deng Xiaoping wenxuan)*, Vol. 2, Beijing: People's Publishing House, 1994, p. 333.

[6] Jiang Zemin, *Build a Well-off Society in an All-Round Way and Create a New Situation in Building Socialism with Chinese Characteristics — the Report to the Sixteenth National Congress of the CPC (Quanmian jianshe xiaokang shehui, kaichuang Zhongguo tese shehuizhuyi shiye xin jumian — zai Zhongguo Gongchandang Di Shiliu Ci Quanguo Daibiao Dahui shang de baogao)* (November 2002), Beijing: People's Publishing House, 2002.

[7] Hu Jintao, "Speech at the Rally Held by All Circles in Beijing in Commemoration of the 20th Anniversary of the Promulgation and Implementation of the Constitution of the PRC (Zai shoudu gejie jinian Zhonghua Renmin Gongheguo Xianfa gongbu shishi ershi zhounian dahui shang de jianghua) (December 4, 2002)," *People's Daily*, December 5, 2002.

reform of state-owned enterprises; serious unemployment in cities; a fragile financial system; polarization between the rich and the poor; social disorders; and widespread corruption. Two possible futures lie in stark contrast in front of China. One road leads to a market economy under the rule of law with political civilization; the other leads to privatization of crony capitalism. It could be said that "it was the spring of hope, it was the winter of despair, . . . we were all going direct to Heaven, we were all going direct the other way."[8]

With the complicated contradictions and the possibility of economic and social crisis, the way out for China lies in furthering the economic, social, and political reforms and comprehensively establishing and improving the market economic system.

First, there is a long way to go to improve the structure of ownership, though nonstate sectors have made great progress. At present, enterprises of state ownership still have the control over the most important resources, especially capital resources. Therefore, besides making an effort to realize, as soon as possible, the adjustment of the layout of the state sector and carry out corporatization transformation of state-owned enterprises, we should enthusiastically explore, audaciously experiment, timely sum up new experience from practice, and blaze new trails of various forms for realizing public ownership that is compatible with socialized production. In the mean time, all the policies encouraging the development of the private sector that are beneficial to the national economy and people's livelihood must be earnestly implemented; all the rules and regulations prejudiced against nonstate enterprises must be abolished in order to help them develop. In this respect, attention must be paid to the fact that growing in an environment where administrative power still intervenes in market transactions in many ways, private business owners have often fallen into various bad habits of associating with government officials and rent-seeking by power, or have stepped into the wrong path of crony capitalism. That is what the government must take effective measures to prevent.

Second, apart from a small number of state-owned enterprises in special industries that, as special corporate bodies, need to adopt special rules and regulations by the government, ordinary companies controlled by the state or with noncontrolling state participation, as enterprises, do not have any privileges but participate in fair competition with other enterprises of all kinds of ownership in the same legal environment. Under the planned economy, those enterprises undertook many social functions that should not be undertaken by enterprises; meanwhile they got preferential treatment in many

---

[8]Excerpt from the opening remarks of *A Tale of Two Cities* by Charles Dickens. See Charles Dickens, *A Tale of Two Cities*, Chicago: F. Tennyson Neely, 1895.

aspects from the government. That made it difficult for the performance of the enterprises to be fairly and objectively measured. However, under the new market economy, all state-owned enterprises have to conduct businesses as incorporated companies in the market so as to realize the separation of party leadership from government administration and the separation of government administration from enterprise management and to enable enterprises to make decisions independently and assume sole responsibility for their profits or losses.

Third, it must be declared in the name of the constitution and law that the property gained legally is protected and all economic sectors receive national treatment without discrimination. Laws and regulations should be reviewed in an all-round way to eliminate the differences in treating different economic sectors and the discrimination against nonstate sectors in terms of pricing, taxation, financing, market-entry permission, and legal and social status. Great efforts should be made to create an environment for fair competition so that everyone is equal before the market rules and regulations and all sectors of the economy based on honest labor and lawful operation can perform their functions within the unified national legal framework.

Fourth, China officially entered into the World Trade Organization in December 2001. That means that after five to six years of transitional period, China will take overall participation in the global economic cooperation and competition according to the principle of free trade represented by the rules of the WTO. However, Chinese government apparatus, enterprises, and residents have not been accustomed to regulating their behavior by the norms of behavior and regulations generally used in world market and international contacts. In order to adapt herself to the new situation of overall opening up, China must abolish laws and regulations that are not in conformity with the rules of the WTO and establish rules and orders for fair competition. At the same time, according to China's commitments made upon the accession to the WTO, restrictions on foreign investors and foreign enterprises must be eliminated; special preferential treatment for part of foreign enterprises should be abolished so as to realize universal national treatment to all enterprises, with or without foreign investment, as soon as possible.

Fifth, the socialist principle of social justice and common prosperity must be adhered to. Currently, income gaps among residents and between urban and rural have enlarged to such a dangerous degree that it might cause social instability. The state should, by means of laws and policies, prevent public property from falling into the hands of a small number of people during the adjustment process of ownership structure and avoid polarization in the initial property possession. In the mean time, the government must, on the basis of general improvement in the living standard of the people, make full use of its policy tools, such as taxation for social welfare institutions, to assist widowers, widows, orphans, the childless, the aged, the crippled, and the ailing; to restrain over-concentration of personal wealth in a small number of people, to prevent polarization between the rich and the poor, and to ensure the gradual achievement of the socialist goal of common prosperity.

Sixth, the government must, in the first place, regulate the behavior of itself in order to regulate the behavior of various economic entities in the market and create a good market environment. So far, the reform of government functions has fallen behind the marketization progress. As the provider of public goods in a market economy, the government should only serve the society, not order ordinary enterprises and residents about; it should only play the role of referee, not that of coach or player. Governments at all levels should try their best to get their own business well done, namely, to provide the society with public goods at low costs, rather than meddle in the issues that should be coped with by enterprises, such as human, financial, and material resources as well as production, supply, and marketing.

Seventh, as a country with "a strong tradition of feudal autocracy and a weak tradition of democratic legality,"[9] China has a great and formidable task to put into effect the rule of law in constitutional democracy. However, time and tide wait for no man. That is a vital step for China to stand on her own feet among multitudes of nations in this era of constant progress. Therefore, in this new historical period of comprehensively improving the market economic system under the rule of law, promoting political civilization, establishing a democratic system, and building a society under the rule of law will be the main theme of reform.

---

[9] Deng Xiaoping, "On the Reform of the System of Party and State Leadership (Dang he guojia lingdao zhidu de gaige) (August 1980)," *Selected Works of Deng Xiaoping (Deng Xiaoping wenxuan),* Vol. 2, Beijing: People's Publishing House, 1994, p. 332.

BIBLIOGRAPHY

Aoki, Masahiko. *Towards a Comparative Institutional Analysis.* Cambridge, Mass.: MIT Press, 2001.

Aoki, Masahiko, and Qian Yingyi (eds.). *Corporate Governance Structure in Transitional Economies: Insider Control and the Role of Banks (Zhuangui jingji zhong de gongsi zhili jiegou: neiburen kongzhi he yinhang de zuoyong).* Beijing: China Economic Publishing House, 1995.

Atkinson, Anthony B., and Joseph E. Stiglitz. *Lectures on Public Economics.* London: McGraw-Hill Book Co., 1980.

Berle, Adolf A., and Gardiner C. Means. *Modern Corporation and Private Property.* New York: Commerce Clearing House, Loose Leaf Service Division of the Corporation Trust Company, 1932.

Brus, Wlodzimierz, and Kazimierz Laski. *From Marx to the Market: Socialism in Search of an Economic System.* Oxford: Clarendon Press, 1989.

Chen, Jiyuan, et al. *Agricultural Growth in the Most Populous Country (Renkou daguo de nongye zengzhang).* Shanghai: Shanghai Far East Publishers, 1996.

Chen, Qingtai, Wu Jinglian, and Xie Fuzhan (eds.). *Fifteen Critical Issues of the Reform of SOEs (Guoqi gaige gongjian shiwu ti).* Beijing: China Economic Publishing House, 1999.

Chen, Xiwen. *Rural Reform in China: Retrospect and Prospect (Zhongguo nongcun gaige: huigu yu zhanwang).* Tianjin: Tianjin People's Publishing House, 1993.

China Society of Economic Reform. *Macroeconomic Management and Reform—Selected Speeches of the International Conference on Macroeconomic Management (Hongguan jingji de guanli he gaige—hongguan jingji guanli guoji taolunhui yanlun xuanbian).* Beijing: Economic Daily Press, 1986.

Clark, Robert C. *Corporate Law.* Boston: Little, Brown and Company, 1986.

Eidem, Rolf, and Staffan Viotti. *Economic Systems.* New York: John Wiley & Sons, Inc., 1978.

Gregory, Paul R., and Robert C. Stuart. *Comparative Economic Systems,* 5th edition. Boston: Houghton Mifflin Co., 1995.

GTZ GmBH (ed.). *Analysis and Evaluation of SME Promotion Policy in Germany (Deguo zhong-xiao qiye cujin zhengce fenxi yu pinggu).* Beijing: China Economic Publishing House, 2002.

Gu, Junli, et al. (eds.). *An Analysis on Welfare State: A Comparative Study against the Background of Europe (Fuli guojia lunxi: yi Ouzhou wei beijing de bijiao yanjiu).* Beijing: Economic Management Press, 2002.

Hayek, Friedrich A. von. *Individualism and Economic Order.* Chicago: University of Chicago Press, 1948.

Hayek, Friedrich A. von. *The Road to Serfdom.* London: G. Routledge & Sons, 1944.

Heady, Christopher J., Wing Thye Woo, and Christine P. Wong. *Fiscal Management and Economic Reform in the People's Republic of China.* Hong Kong: Oxford University Press, 1995.

Huntington, Samuel P. *The Third Wave: Democratization in the Late Twentieth Century.* Norman: University of Oklahoma Press, 1991.

Institute of Economics of the Academy of Sciences of USSR. *Political Economy.* London: Lawrence & Wishart, 1957.

Jackson, Peter M. *Current Issues in Public Sector Economics.* New York: St. Martin's Press, 1992.

Jiang, Zemin. *Hold High the Great Banner of Deng Xiaoping Theory for an All-Round Advance of the Cause of Building Socialism with Chinese Characteristics into the Twenty-First Century—the Report to the Fifteenth National Congress of the CPC (Gaoju Deng Xiaoping lilun weida qizhi, ba jianshe you Zhongguo tese shehuizhuyi shiye quanmian tuixiang ershiyi shiji—zai Zhongguo Gongchandang di shiwu ci quanguo daibiao dahui shang de baogao)* (September 1997). Beijing: People's Publishing House, 1997.

Jin, Yan, and Qin Hui. *Economic Transition and Social Justice (Jingji zhuangui yu shehui gongzheng).* Zhengzhou: Henan People's Publishing House, 2002.

Kornai, János. *Reflections on Post-Socialism Transition (Hou shehuizhuyi zhuangui de sisuo),* Chinese edition. Changchun: Jilin People's Publishing House, 2003.

Kornai, János, and Karen Eggleston. *Welfare, Choice and Solidarity in Transition: Reforming the Health Sector in Eastern Europe.* Cambridge: Cambridge University Press, 2001.

Krugman, Paul R., and Maurice Obstfeld. *International Economics: Theory and Policy,* 3rd ed. New York: Harper Collins College Publishers, 1994.

Lardy, Nicholas R. *China's Unfinished Economic Revolution.* Washington, D.C.: Brookings Institution Press, 1998.

Lardy, Nicholas R. *Integrating China into the Global Economy.* Washington, D.C.: Brookings Institution Press, 2002.

Lau, Lawrence J. "A Proposed Pension System for the People's Republic of China (Guanyu Zhongguo shehui yanglao baozhang tixi de jiben gouxiang) (July 29th, 2000)." *Comparative Studies (Bijiao),* Vol. 6. Beijing: CITIC Publishing House, 2003, pp. 3–28.

Li, Jiange. "Reform of Enterprise and Development of Stock Market in China (Zhongguo qiye gaige he gupiao shichang fazhan)." *Reform (Gaige)* 6 (1996): 9–15.

Li, Shaoguang. "Analysis of the Point of Difficulty of the Basic Old-Age Insurance System and Its Policy Basis (Jiben yanglao baoxian zhidu de nandian he zhengce yiju fenxi)." *Comparative Studies (Bijiao),* Vol. 6. Beijing: CITIC Publishing House, 2003, pp. 29–42.

Li, Shaoguang. *The Pension System and the Capital Market (Yanglao zhidu yu ziben shichang).* Beijing: China Development Press, 1998.

Li, Yining. *Chinese Economy in Disequilibrium (Feijunheng de Zhongguo jingji).* Beijing: Economic Daily Press, 1990.

Li, Yining. "Giving Priority to Employment with Due Consideration to Price Stability (Jiuye youxian, jiangu jiage wending)." *Reform (Gaige)* 2 (1994): 10–13.

Li, Yining. "Several Theoretical Issues in Economic Reform in Urgent Need of Research (Guanyu jingji gaige zhong jidai yanjiu de jige lilun wenti)." *Economic Development and System Reform (Jingji fazhan yu tizhi gaige)* 5 (1986): 24–31.

Li, Yining. *The Theory of Transitional Development (Zhuanxing fazhan lilun).* Beijing: One Mind Press, 1996.

Lin, Justin Y. *Institution, Technology and Agricultural Development in China (Zhidu, jishu yu Zhongguo nongye fazhan).* Shanghai: Shanghai People's Publishing House and Shanghai Joint Publishing, 1994.

Lin, Justin Y., Cai Fang, and Li Zhou. *China's Miracle: Development Strategy and Economic Reform,* Revised edition. Hong Kong: The Chinese University Press, 2003.

Liu, Guoguang. *On Economic Reform and Economic Adjustment (Lun jingji gaige yu jingji tiaozheng).* Nanjing: Jiangsu People's Publishing House, 1983.

Liu, Guoguang, and Liu Shucheng. "On Soft Landing (Lun ruanzhaolu)." *People's Daily (Renmin ribao).* (January 7, 1997).

Long, Guoqiang. "Opportunities and Challenges for China in Opening-Up under Globalization (Quanqiuhua tiaojian xia Zhongguo duiwai kaifang de jiyu yu tiaozhan)." Wang Mengkui, et al. (eds.). *China's Economy in the New Stage (Xin jieduan de Zhongguo jingji).* Beijing: People's Publishing House, 2002, pp. 151–169.

Lou, Jiwei. *Reform in China: Advancing in Ups and Downs (Zhongguo gaige: bolangshi qianjin).* Beijing: China Development Press, 2001.

Lou, Jiwei, and Li Keping. "Establishing a Normalized and Effective New Fiscal System (Jianli yige guifan, youxiao de caizheng xintizhi)." Wu Jinglian, et al. (eds.). *Building up a Market Economy: Comprehensive Framework and Working Proposal (Jianshe shichang jingji de zongti gouxiang yu fang'an sheji).* Beijing: Central Compilation & Translation Press, 1996, pp. 59–70.

Ma, Xiaohe, et al. *A Study on Rural Tax and Fee Reform in China (Nongcun shuifei gaige yanjiu).* Beijing: China Planning Press, 2002.

Mao, Zedong. "On the Ten Major Relationships (Lun shida guanxi)." *Selected Works of Mao Zedong (Mao Zedong xuanji),* Vol. 5. Beijing: People's Publishing House, 1977.

Naughton, Barry. *Growing Out of the Plan: Chinese Economic Reform, 1978–1993.* New York: Cambridge University Press, 1995.

Office of Soft Science Committee of the Ministry of Agriculture (ed.). *The Issue of Grain Security (Liangshi anquan wenti).* Beijing: China Agriculture Press, 2001.

Party Literature Research Center of the CCCPC (ed.). *A Selection of Important Documents since the Third Plenary Session (Sanzhongquanhui yilai zhongyao wenxian xuanbian).* Beijing: People's Publishing House, 1982.

Party Literature Research Center of the CCCPC (ed.). *A Selection of Important Documents since the 12th National Congress of the CPC (Shierda yilai zhongyao wenxian xuanbian).* Beijing: People's Publishing House, 1986.

Party Literature Research Center of the CCCPC (ed.). *A Selection of Important Documents since the 14th National Congress of the CPC (Shisida yilai zhongyao wenxian xuanbian).* Beijing: People's Publishing House, 1996.

Qi, Guizhen (ed.). *Twenty Years of Ownership Reform in China (Zhongguo suoyouzhi gaige ershi nian).* Zhengzhou: Zhongzhou Ancient Book Publishing House, 1998.

Qian, Yingyi. "Government and the Rule of Law (Zhengfu yu fazhi)." *Modern Economics and China's Reform (Xiandai jingjixue yu Zhongguo jingji gaige).* Beijing: China Renmin University Press, 2003, pp. 41–54.

Qian, Yingyi. "Market and the Rule of Law (Shichang yu fazhi)." *Modern Economics and China's Reform (Xiandai jingjixue yu Zhongguo jingji gaige).* Beijing: China Renmin University Press, 2003, pp. 23–40.

Qian, Yingyi, and Huang Haizhou. "Financial Stability and Development in China after WTO Accession (Jiaru Shimao Zuzhi hou Zhongguo jinrong de wending yu fazhan) (2001)." Qian Yingyi. *Modern Economics and China's Reform (Xiandai jingjixue yu Zhongguo jingji gaige).* Beijing: China Renmin University Press, 2003.

Research Bureau of the People's Bank of China (ed.). *Modern Central Bank System of China: Major Reform of the Management System of People's Bank of China (Zhongguo xiandai zhongyang yinhang tizhi—Zhongguo Renmin Yinhang guanli tizhi de zhongda gaige).* Beijing: China Financial Publishing House, 1999.

Roland, Gérard. *Transition and Economics: Politics, Markets and Firms.* Cambridge, Mass.: MIT Press, 2000.

Rong, Jingben, and Liu Jirui. *Comparative Economics (Bijiao jingjixue).* Shenyang: Liaoning People's Publishing House, 1990.

Shi, Jinchuan, et al. *Institutional Change and Economic Development: Investigation on the Wenzhou Model (Zhidu bianqian yu jingji fazhan: Wenzhou moshi yanjiu).* Hangzhou: Zhejiang University Press, 2002.

Shleifer, Andrei, and Robert W. Vishny. "A Survey of Corporate Governance." *The Journal of Finance* 52, No. 2 (June 1997): 737–783.

Song, Hongyuan, et al. *Agriculture and Rural Economic Policies during the Ninth Five-Year Plan Period (Jiuwu shiqi de nongye he nongcun jingji zhengce).* Beijing: China Agriculture Press, 2002.

Song, Xiaowu, et al., *China's Social Security System Reform and Development Report (Zhongguo shehui baozhang tizhi gaige yu fazhan baogao).* Beijing: China Renmin University Press, 2001.

Stiglitz, Joseph E. *Whither Socialism?* Cambridge, Mass.: MIT Press, 1994.

Sun, Guofeng. "2000 Points in Year 2000: How Were the Bubbles Created (2000 nian 2000 dian, paomo shi zenyang xingcheng de)." *Caijing Magazine (Caijing)* 9 (2000): 54–56.

Sun, Guofeng. "Can China Avoid Bubble Economy (Zhongguo neng bikai paomo jingji ma)." *Caijing Magazine (Caijing)* 8 (2001): 60–63.

Sun, Guofeng. "Starting Up the Bond Market (Qidong zhaishi)." *Caijing Magazine (Caijing)* 3 (2002): 18–20.

Supachai, Panitchpakdi, and Mark L. Clifford. *China and the WTO: Changing China, Changing World Trade.* Singapore: John Wiley & Sons Ltd. (Asia), 2002.

Tong, Zhiguang, and Ding Jiatiao (eds.). *China and WTO: Discussions on Accession to WTO by Authoritative Experts (Zhongguo yu WTO: quanwei zhuanjia hua rushi).* Beijing: Xiyuan Press, 2000.

United Nations Conference on Trade and Development. *Trade and Development Report.* New York: United Nations, Relevant years.

Wang, Shuye, Dai Dingyi, and Wu Zhihui (eds.). *Facing WTO—Banking and Securities Industries and Basic Raw Materials Industries in China (Zhimian WTO: Zhongguo de jinrong zhengquanye ji jichu yuancailiao chanye).* Beijing: Economic Management Press, 2000.

Wolf, Charles. *Markets or Governments: Choosing between Imperfect Alternatives.* Cambridge, Mass.: MIT Press, 1988.

World Bank. *Averting the Old Age Crisis: Policies to Protect the Old and Promote Growth.* New York: Oxford University Press, 1994.

World Bank. *China 2020: Old Age Security: Pension Reform in China.* China 2020 series, Vol. 6. Washington, D.C.: World Bank, 1997.

World Bank. *World Development Report 1991: The Challenge of Development.* New York: Oxford University Press, 1991.

Wu, Jinglian. "An Analysis of the Trend of the Chinese Economy (Zhongguo jingji zoushi fenxi)." *Journal of Beijing Normal University (Beijing shifan daxue xuebao)* 2 (2003): 5–12.

Wu, Jinglian. "An Appraisal of Economic Situation and My Proposals (Dui jingji xingshi de guliang he duice yanjiu)." *Economics Information (Jingjixue dongtai)* 9 (1998): 4–7.

Wu, Jinglian, et al. *Building Up a Market Economy: Comprehensive Framework and Working Proposal (Jianshe shichang jingji de zongti gouxiang yu fang'an sheji).* Beijing: Central Compilation & Translation Press, 1996.

Wu, Jinglian. *China in Transition (Zhuangui Zhongguo).* Chengdu: Sichuan People's Publishing House, 2002.

Wu, Jinglian. "The Clean-up of Corruption in China (Zhongguo fubai de zhili)." *Strategy and Administration (Zhanlüe yu guanli)* 2 (2003): 1–8.

Wu, Jinglian. *Developing Chinese Hi-Tech Industries: Developing Institution before Developing Technology (Fazhan Zhongguo gaoxin jishu: zhidu zhongyu jishu).* Beijing: China Development Press, 2002.

Wu, Jinglian. "Economic Reflection on Corruption and Anti-Corruption (Fubai yu fanfubai de jingjixue sikao) (May 20th, 2002)." *China Supervision (Zhongguo jiancha),* 2002, August issue.

Wu, Jinglian. *Modern Corporation and Enterprise Reform (Xiandai gongsi yu qiye gaige).* Tianjin: Tianjin People's Publishing House, 1994.

Wu, Jinglian. "More on Maintaining a Good Economic Environment for Economic Reform (Zailun baochi jingji gaige de lianghao huanjing)." *Economic Research Journal (Jingji yanjiu)* 5 (1985): 3–12.

Wu, Jinglian. *Opinions on Stock Market during Its Ten Confused Years (Shinian fenyun hua gushi).* Shanghai: Shanghai Far East Publishers, 2001.

Wu, Jinglian, et al. *Overall Design of the Reform of China's Economic System (Zhongguo jingji gaige de zhengti sheji).* Beijing: China Outlook Press, 1988.

Wu, Jinglian. *Road to Market Economy (Tongxiang shichang jingji zhi lu).* Beijing: Beijing University of Technology Press, 1992.

Wu, Jinglian, et al. *The Strategic Restructuring of the State Sector (Guoyou jingji de zhanlüexing gaizu).* Beijing: China Development Press, 1998.

Wu, Jinglian. "The Transfer of Rural Surplus Laborers and the Three Rural Problems (Nongcun shengyu laodongli de zhuanyi yu "sannong wenti)." *Macroeconomics (Hongguan jingji yanjiu)* 6 (2002): 6–9.

Wu, Jinglian, and Justin Y. Lin. "Proposal on Transferring State-Owned Assets for Repayment of the Implicit Liabilities of Social Security Fund for Elder Employees (Guanyu huabo guoyou zichan guihuan guojia dui laozhigong shehui baozhang jijin qianzhang de jianyi)." *Comparative Studies (Bijiao),* Vol. 6. Beijing: CITIC Publishing House, 2003. pp. 1–2.

Wu, Jinglian, and Liu Jirui. *On Competitive Market System (Lun jingzhengxing shichang tizhi).* Beijing: China Financial and Economic Publishing House, 1991.

Wu, Xiaoling, et al. *China's Banking in the New Round of Reform (Xinyilun gaige zhong de Zhongguo jinrong).* Tianjin: Tianjin People's Publishing House, 1998.

Xie, Ping. "Theory and Debate on the Development of China's Monetary Market (Zhongguo huobi shichang fazhan de lilun yu zhenglun)." *PBC Staff Working Paper (Zhongguo Renmin Yinhang gongzuo renyuan lunwen)* 3 (2000).

Xu, Dianqing (ed.). *The Road of China's Financial Reform—200 Questions Concerning Private*

Banks (Jinrong gaige lu zai hefang: minying yinhang 200 wen). Beijing: Peking University Press, 2002.

Xu, Donggen. *An Explanation of the WTO Rules (WTO guize jiexi),* Chengdu: Southwestern University of Finance and Economics Press, 2002.

Xue, Muqiao. "Some Theoretical Issues Concerning Socialist Economy (Guanyu shehuizhuyi jingji de ruogan lilun wenti) (1991)." *Collected Works of Xue Muqiao in His Old Age (Xue Muqiao wannian wengao).* Beijing: Joint Publishing, 1999.

Xue, Wanxiang. *Model Selection and System Design of China's Monetary Regulation (Zhongguo huobi tiaokong moshi xuanze yu zhidu sheji).* Shanghai: Shanghai University of Finance & Economics Press, 1998.

Yang, Zhigang. *Public Finance: Theory and Practice (Gonggong caizheng: lilun yu shijian).* Shanghai: Shanghai People's Publishing House, 1999.

Zhang, Xiaoshan, et al. *Connecting the Farmer and the Market—An Exploratory Study on Farmers' Intermediaries in China (Lianjie nonghu yu shichang—Zhongguo nongmin zhongjie zuzhi tanjiu).* Beijing: China Social Sciences Press, 2002.

Zhou, Taihe, et al. *Economic System Reform in Contemporary China (Dangdai Zhongguo de jingji tizhi gaige).* Beijing: China Social Sciences Press, 1984.

Zhou, Xiaochuan, and Wang Lin. "Separation of Social Security Functions from Enterprises (Qiye shehui baozhang zhineng de dulihua) (1993)." Wu, Jinglian, et al. *Building Up a Market Economy: Comprehensive Framework and Working Proposals (Jianshe shichang jingji de zongti gouxiang yu fang'an sheji).* Beijing: Central Compilation & Translation Press, 1996, pp. 195–208.

Zhou, Xiaochuan, and Wang Lin. "Social Security: Economic Analysis and System Proposal (Shehui baozhang: jingji fenxi yu tizhi jianyi) (1994)." Wu Jinglian, et al. *Building up a Market Economy: Comprehensive Framework and Working Proposal (Jianshe shichang jingji de zongti gouxiang yu fang'an sheji).* Beijing: Central Compilation & Translation Press, 1996, pp. 211–258.

Zhou, Xiaochuan, and Yang Zhigang. "Taxation System Reform in China in 1994: Achievements and Problems (1994 nian Zhongguo shuizhi gaige: yi qude de chengji he dai jiejue de wenti)." Wu Jinglian, et al. (eds.). *Building up a Market Economy: Comprehensive Framework and Working Proposal (Jianshe shichang jingji de zongti gouxiang yu fang'an sheji).* Beijing: Central Compilation & Translation Press, 1996, pp. 365–388.

POSTSCRIPT BY THE TRANSLATOR

In 2003 mainland China acquired the rights to 12,516 books from overseas publishers and licensed the rights of 811 Chinese books to overseas publishers, with an inbound-outbound ratio of 15.4 : 1.[1] Because mainland China published 110,812 new books in 2003, this means that one out of every nine new books published in mainland China was introduced from overseas, whereas fewer than 1% of new books published in mainland China were available in any foreign language. While an overwhelming majority of acquired titles are in English, an overwhelming majority of Chinese titles are licensed to non-English-speaking regions, such as Hong Kong, Taiwan, Singapore, Malaysia, Japan, and South Korea. Therefore, for every 100 English books translated into Chinese, less than one Chinese book was translated into English. This imbalance is especially drastic between China and the United States, which has led Mr. Xin Guangwei of the General Administration of Press and Publication of the PRC to comment that "in sharp contrast to China's substantial rights acquisitions from the U.S., America's licensing from China is pathetically minimal."[2] Because most Chinese books introduced to foreign readers are in the fields of traditional Chinese medicine, arts, culture, and language, only a very limited number of Chinese books about contemporary China, especially about its economy and business, have been translated into English.

This huge imbalance can be partially attributed to the insufficient number of Chinese economic and business books published, especially high-quality ones. Only a few excellent books on China's reform have been published in Chinese up to this moment, with Professor Wu Jinglian's *Economic Reform in Contemporary China (Dangdai Zhongguo jingji gaige)* being the most prominent one. This huge imbalance can also be attributed to the language barrier, because thousands of Chinese terms about reform have been created in the past half century without counterparts in any other language. In the process of translating this book, about 3,000 special terms and phrases were identified, including more than 1,000 with a Chinese origin, many of which had never been translated into any other language. The language barrier is in turn partially caused by the ideological constraint. For example, because hiring workers by private business owners was considered committing the crime of exploitation by fundamentalists, when the Chinese government partially lifted the ban on private businesses in the early 1980s, it artificially divided private businesses into individual businesses (*geti qiye*), hiring seven or

---

[1] *China Publishing Yearbook (Zhongguo chuban nianjian),* Beijing: China Publishing Yearbook Press, 2004.
[2] Xin Guangwei, *Publishing in China: An Essential Guide,* Singapore: Thomson Learning, 2005, p. 238.

less workers each, and private enterprises (*siying qiye*), hiring eight or more workers each, and gave the green light only to the former.

The translation of this book was a Herculean task beyond the capacity of any single person, especially someone like me with an extremely tight teaching and administration schedule at the China Europe International Business School (CEIBS). Fortunately, many people lent helpful hands: Dr. Zhou Xuelin of CEIBS Translation and Publication Department, Dr. Liu Shengjun and Dr. Chen Junsong of CEIBS Case Development Center, and Ms. Ma Xiaoying and Ms. Yan Xiaoyun of Donghua University each reviewed a part of an early draft; Mr. Du Qian of CEIBS Translation and Publication Department, Ms. Xu Po of CEIBS Case Development Center, and Mr. Shen Baoshun and Ms. Hu Min of CEIBS Library helped check hundreds of quotes and references. The contribution of Dr. Zhang Chunlin of the World Bank Office Beijing deserves special acknowledgement because he reviewed all 12 chapters of the early draft. Special thanks also go to the editors of Thomson Learning for their professional expertise and advice on how to make this book more readable for an audience outside China. Of course, any remaining mistakes are my responsibility.

While some people in North America and Western Europe complain bitterly how imbalanced their trade with China is, they often ignore the fact that there is a huge imbalance between China and the West in terms of knowledge about each other. This imbalance causes difficulties and losses for both China and the West, more for the latter than the former, in my opinion. Therefore, efforts to deepen Western understanding of China benefit both sides. I believe that the publication of the English version of this book (under the title *Understanding and Interpreting Chinese Economic Reform*) by the most authoritative scholar on China's economic reform is a significant contribution to this undertaking.

In the twenty-first century, China is too important to be ignored or misunderstood.

Jianmao Wang
Professor of Economics
Academic Director of MBA Program
Director of Case Development Center
China Europe International Business School (CEIBS)

NAME INDEX

阿克顿勋爵 — Acton, Lord 417, 417n44

阿甘别疆 — Aganbegyan, Abel 23

青木昌彦 — Aoki, Masahiko 72, 72n52, 73, 161, 161n22, 416n41

巴伊特 — Bajt, Aleksander 26, 26n28

巴罗尼 — Barone, Enrico 10, 12n16, 13

伯格森 — Bergson, Abram 20, 20n23

伯恩施坦 — Bernstein, Edward M. 96

薄一波 — Bo, Yibo 32nn39,40, 33n44, 46n4, 49n9, 50nn10,13, 143n5

波伊索特 — Boisot, Max 267, 267n9

鲍恩斯坦 — Bornstein, Morris 56n28

布鲁斯 — Brus, Wlodzimierz 15, 16, 17n, 37

布坎南 — Buchanan, James M. 389, 389n9

布哈林 — Bukharin, Nikolai 6–9, 5n9, 10n13

蔡昉 — Cai, Fang 95n3

钱德勒 — Chandler, Alfred Dupont, Jr. 167n28, 168n30

陈伯达 — Chen, Boda 34, 100

陈吉元 — Chen, Jiyuan 118n41, 126n53, 136

陈锡文 — Chen, Xiwen 93, 127, 94n2, 104n20, 119n47, 127n54

陈云 — Chen, Yun 38, 38n59, 46, 46n4, 52, 97, 97n9, 98, 98n11,108, 361, 361n34

乔纳蒂 — Csanadi, Maria 140n

邓小平 — Deng, Xiaoping 5n9, 6n, 54, 63n39, 64, 68, 68n45, 75, 75n57, 76, 76n, 77n, 78, 82, 82n, 87, 88, 88n, 111, 112, 112n27, 181, 183, 183n17, 184n19, 234, 234n9, 235, 293, 294, 294nn4,5,6, 298, 363, 365, 366n11, 370, 371, 398, 399n18, 403n29, 405, 417–419, 417n45, 418n48, 419n49, 421, 422, 422nn51,52, 425, 433, 435, 436, 437n5, 440n9

邓子恢 — Deng, Zihui 34, 61–62, 96, 96n6, 97, 98, 108

董辅礽 — Dong, Fureng 58, 59, 59n35, 62, 248

杜润生 — Du, Runsheng 61, 62, 96n6

杜兰特 — Durant, William 167

恩格斯 — Engels, Friedrich 3, 5, 5nn6,7, 178–179, 178nn2,3,4,5, 179n7, 428n57, 435, 436, 436n4

费正清 — Fairbank, John King 52n18

方流芳 — Fang, Liufang 154n

费景汉 — Fei, John 119

费尔德曼 — Feldman, G A 9

费尔德斯坦 — Feldstein, Martin S. 342, 342n17, 343n18

弗里德曼 — Friedman, Milton 356

加尔布雷斯 — Galbraith, John K. 246n22

高西庆 — Gao, Xiqing 252n31

吉利斯 — Gillis, Malcolm 386, 386n1

哥穆尔卡 — Gomulka, Wladyslaw 27

戈尔巴乔夫 — Gorbachev, Mikhail S. 23, 24, 187

辜胜阻 — Gu, Shengzu 136n64

顾准 — Gu, Zhun 37, 38, 38n58

郭树清 — Guo, Shuqing 80, 81, 82n, 343, 343n19

哈耶克 — Hayek, Friedrich A. von 13, 14, 14n18, 18, 19n21

洪虎 — Hong, Hu 158n20

胡耀邦 — Hu, Yaobang 63n39, 182n16

华国锋 — Hua, Guofeng 112, 293, 293n2

黄海州 — Huang, Haizhou 379n22, 384n27

黄宗羲 — Huang, Zongxi 129, 129n58

亨廷顿 — Huntington, Samuel P. 386, 386n2, 387

贾康 — Jia, Kang 277nn15,16

蒋一苇 — Jiang, Yiwei 58, 59n34

江泽民 — Jiang, Zemin 86, 87, 88, 188n27, 189n29, 422nn50,53, 434, 434nn1,2, 437n6

卡达尔 — Kadar, Janos 26

卡德尔 — Kardelj, Edvard 24

考茨基 — Kautsky, Karl 96, 96n4

柯庆施 — Ke, Qingshi 50n13

凯恩斯 — Keynes, John Maynard 356

赫鲁晓夫 — Khrushchev, Nikita Sergeevich 21, 27, 45, 49n9

小宫隆太郎 — Komiya, Ryutaro 140n2, 367, 367n12

科尔奈 — Kornai, János 17n19, 28n30, 29, 30, 71, 73n54, 141, 142n4, 349, 349n24, 357, 357n1, 409

柯西金 — Kosygin, Aleksey Nikolayevich 21, 22, 24, 37n57, 60

克鲁格 — Krueger, Anne O. 394, 394n14

克鲁格曼 — Krugman, Paul 374n16, 381, 381n24

库兹涅茨 — Kuznets, Simon S. 388, 388n5

郎咸平 — Lang, Larry H.P. 411n38

兰格 — Lange, Oskar 13, 13n17, 14, 17

拉斯基 — Laski, Kazimierz 17n

刘遵义 — Lau, Lawrence J. 70, 70n49, 288n27, 341, 341n14, 342n17

列宁 — Lenin, Vladimir I. 3–5, 4n5, 5nn8,9, 7n10, 8n12, 7–10, 76, 86, 96, 96n5, 139, 179, 206, 217, 418, 418nn46,47, 426, 435

勒纳 — Lerner, Abba P. 13

李剑阁 — Li, Jiange 81, 363n5

李克强 — Li, Keqiang 136n63

李岚清 — Li, Lanqing 283n23

李先念 — Li, Xiannian 46n4, 59, 59n36, 148n13, 361

厉以宁 — Li, Yining 79, 81n, 82n, 246n29, 248, 364n6, 373n15

廖季立 — Liao, Jili 61

利别尔曼 — Liberman, Evsei Grigorevich 37, 37n57

林彪 — Lin, Biao 52

林毅夫 — Lin, Justin Yifu 95, 95n3, 99n13, 98n12, 103n15, 115, 115n31, 134n62

林子力 — Lin, Zili 182n13

刘国光 — Liu, Guoguang 62, 365, 365nn7,8, 368

刘吉瑞   Liu, Jirui 56n29, 80, 81, 82n, 266n8, 267n11, 283n24, 287n25

刘少奇   Liu, Shaoqi 32, 32n40, 33, 33n42, 39, 40, 44, 45n2, 52n19, 96, 99

楼继伟   Lou, Jiwei 26n29, 55n26, 78n61, 81, 82n

陆学艺   Lu, Xueyi 390nn10,11

马洪   Ma, Hong 58, 58n, 257n3, 377n18

马晓河   Ma, Xiaohe 129n36

麦基   Mackey, Charles 245n21

毛泽东   Mao, Zedong 3n1, 31–41, 31nn33,34,35, 32nn36, 37, 41, 33nn42, 43, 44, 45, 34nn46,48,50, 35n52, 39n60, 44, 44n1, 45, 46n4, 49, 49n9, 50n10, 50n12, 53, 53nn20, 22, 59, 60, 62, 62n, 96–100, 96n6, 97nn7, 8, 105, 107–108, 112nn26, 27, 143, 144, 144n8, 179n9, 180, 180n10, 186, 293, 408, 408n30, 426, 436

马克思   Marx, Karl 3, 4, 9, 12, 65n44, 62, 76, 95, 96, 178, 178n2, 179, 179n7, 182, 217, 217nn1,2, 436

马思洛   Maslow, Abraham H. 387, 387n4

米塞斯   Mises, Ludwig von 13, 14

墨菲   Murphy, Kevin 70, 70n48

诺顿   Naughton, Barry 74n56

诺斯   North, Douglass C. 56n30, 57

诺齐克   Nozick, Robert 410, 410n34

奥肯   Okun, Arthur M. 412, 412n39

欧文   Owen, Robert 217n1

帕累托   Pareto, Vilfredo 12

彭德怀   Peng, Dehuai 51

帕金斯   Perkins, Dwight H. 386, 386n1

彼得大帝   Peter I, the Great 9

费尔普斯   Phelps, Edmund S. 356

菲利普斯   Phillips, Alban W. H. 356

波特   Porter, Michael E. 214, 214n38, 215, 215nn39,40

普朗扎斯   Poulantzas, Nicos 424

普列奥布拉任斯基   Preobrazhenskii, Evgenii A. 5n9, 6, 7

钱颖一   Qian, Yingyi 57n31, 70, 70n49, 73n53, 161n22, 185, 186n21, 379n22

秦晖   Qin, Hui 129n58, 409n32

拉尼斯   Ranis, Gustav 119n46

罗尔斯   Rawls, John 410, 410n33

罗默   Roemer, Michael 386, 386n1

罗兰   Roland, Gérard 70, 70n49, 71n51, 389n8

萨克斯   Sachs, Jeffery 185, 185n20, 415n40

萨缪尔逊   Samuelson, Paul A. 356

熊彼特   Schumpeter, Joseph Alois 12n16, 119

希尔曼   Schurmann, Franz 55n28

石滋宜   Shi, Ziyi 215, 215n41

希勒   Shiller, Robert J. 246n25

施莱弗   Shleifer, Andrei 70, 70n48

锡克   Sik, Ota 28, 78, 78n60

斯隆   Sloan, Alfred, Jr. 167, 167n29

斯密   Smith, Adam 15, 414

斯诺德格拉斯   Snodgrass, Donald R. 386, 386n1

索洛   Solow, Robert M. 356

斯大林   Stalin, Joseph 8–10, 10nn13,14,15, 21, 24, 35, 45, 62, 140n1, 179, 418, 418n46, 436

斯蒂格里茨   Stiglitz, Joseph E. 17, 17n20, 282

孙冶方   Sun, Yefang 36, 36n55, 37, 37n56, 52n18, 54, 54n24, 58, 144, 144n10

泰勒   Taylor, Fred Manville 13

托宾   Tobin, James 365

托洛茨基   Trotsky, Leon 8

邹谠   Tsou, Tang 36n53

维什尼   Vishny, Robert W. 70, 70n48

万安培   Wan, Anpei 394, 394n16

王忍之   Wang, Renzhi 82n64

王则柯   Wang, Zeke 288n26

沃德   Ward, Benjamin 25, 25n27

威廉姆森   Williamson, Oliver E. 167n28, 168

沃尔夫   Wolf, Charles 416n42

胡永泰   Woo, Wing T. 185, 185n20, 268t, 413n40

吴家骏   Wu, Jiajun 140n2, 150n16

吴敬琏   Wu, Jinglian 20, 55nn26, 27, 56n29, 57n33, 63n39, 74n55, 78n61, 79, 79n63, 82n, 154n, 164n23, 165n25, 187n25, 188n26, 191n30, 243n15, 244n18, 247–250, 266n5, 267n11, 302n8, 337n6, 342nn15,17, 363n5, 368, 370n14, 373n15, 376n17, 394n15, 409n31

吴晓灵   Wu, Xiaoling 231n6

项怀诚   Xiang, Huaicheng 278n18

萧灼基   Xiao, Zhuoji 246n28, 248

谢平   Xie, Ping 231n6, 235n10

许成钢   Xu, Chenggang 57n31, 185, 186n21

许小年   Xu, Xiaonian 89t

薛暮桥   Xue, Muqiao 46n4, 58, 58n32, 61, 62n, 63, 63n38, 179n8, 181n12

杨之刚   Yang, Zhigang 276n13

于光远   Yu, Guangyuan 61, 62

袁宝华   Yuan, Baohua 144n11, 148n15

张维迎   Zhang, Weiying 162n22, 243n16, 411n36

张晓山   Zhang, Xiaoshan 131n59, 132n60, 133n61

张卓元   Zhang, Zhuoyuan 373n15

赵人伟   Zhao, Renwei 401n24

赵紫阳   Zhao, Ziyang 77, 77n58, 78, 78n59, 147

周恩来   Zhou, Enlai 46n4, 54, 208

周太和   Zhou, Taihe 47n6, 50n11, 53n21, 109n25, 143n6, 145n12, 144n9, 263n5

周小川   Zhou, Xiaochuan 55n26, 78n61, 81, 82n, 337nn6,7, 342n17

朱镕基   Zhu, Rongji 164n24, 277

朱绍文   Zhu, Shaowen 246n23

SUBJECT INDEX

巴山轮会议	ba shan lun hui yi	Bashanlun Conference 365
包产到户	bao chan dao hu	contracting output quota to each household 64, 64nn41,42,43, 65, 104–114
包干到户	bao gan dao hu	contracting responsibility to each household 64n42, 109–114
包工到组	bao gong dao zu	contracting job to each work group 109
保量放价	bao liang fang jia	assuring quantity while liberalizing price 123
包税制	bao shui zhi	tax farming 267
保险公司	bao xian gong si	insurance companies 217, 227, 228, 235, 236, 241, 242, 248, 249, 271, 272, 345
本益比	ben yi bi	P/E ratio 248, 249
闭关自守	bi guan zi shou	self-seclusion 291–293, 309
拨改贷	bo gai dai	substituting fiscal appropriations with bank loans 163, 238
布拉格之春	bu la ge zhi chun	Prague Spring 28
布雷顿森林体系	bu lei dun sen lin ti xi	Bretton Woods System 379, 379n19
不良贷款	bu liang dai kuan	non-performing loans (NPLs) 164–165, 231, 379, 382, 382n25. 383
布鲁斯的分权模式	bu lu si de fen quan mo shi	Brus' decentralized model 15–17, 37
部门承包	bu men cheng bao	department contracting 78n62
不完全合同理论	bu wan quan he tong li lun	incomplete contract theory 163
财政大包干	cai zheng da bao gan	all-round fiscal responsibility system 262
层级组织形式	ceng ji zu zhi xing shi	hierarchical organizational forms 167n28, 213
厂长（经理）负责制	chang zhang (jing li) fu ze zhi	factory director (manager) responsibility system 153
承包制	cheng bao zhi	contracting system 62, 64, 80, 93, 95, 101, 104n19, 108, 109n24, 113–121, 126, 142, 146–149, 153, 161, 182–183, 265, 328, 352, 396–397
出口导向	chu kou dao xiang	export orientation 293–294
传统的自然经济部门	chuan tong de zi ran jing ji bu men	traditional natural economy 119
存续企业	cun xu qi ye	remaining enterprises 160, 232
搭便车者	da bian che zhe	free-riders 174
大跃进运动	da yue jin yun dong	Great Leap Forward 44, 45n3, 46, 46n4, 49, 49n9, 50n10, 51–53, 52n18, 62, 100, 102, 107, 119, 143, 180, 255, 275, 292

代际转移支付	dai ji zhuan yi zhi fu	intergenerational transfer payment 329, 333
贷款五级分类	dai kuan wu ji fen lei	five-category loan classification 227, 227n5, 231
单一式组织形式	dan yi shi zu zhi xing shi	unitary structure (U-form) 57n31, 167, 167n28, 168
道布模式	dao bu mo shi	Dobb model 14
道德风险	dao de feng xian	moral hazard 346
第二次共产风	di er ci gong chan feng	second go-communism craze 51, 105
地方保护主义	di fang bao hu zhu yi	local protectionism 56, 57, 266, 274, 428
地区推进	di qu tui jin	regional advance 67
东亚金融危机	dong ya jin rong wei ji	East Asian financial crisis 200
独立董事	du li dong shi	independent directors 169, 170, 174–175
短缺经济	duan que jing ji	shortage economy 357
多级法人制	duo ji fa ren zhi	multi-tier legal person system 161–163, 167
恶税	e shui	vicious tax 373
恶意收购	e yi shou gou	hostile takeover 171
二板市场	er ban shi chang	second board market 210
二元经济	er yuan jing ji	dual economy 136, 198
法人	fa ren	legal person 153, 161–163, 167, 213, 227n4
法治	fa zhi	rule of law 88, 206, 249, 276, 285, 384, 398, 408, 410, 417, 418, 422, 423, 425–429
放权让利	fang quan rang li	power-delegating and profit-sharing/delegating power to and sharing profit with 395–396
放小	fang xiao	letting go of small enterprises 196, 202
非公有制经济	fei gong you zhi jing ji	nonpublic sectors 65, 66t, 86–88, 89t, 180, 187, 189, 199t, 205, 435
非关税壁垒	fei guan shui bi lei	nontariff barriers 295, 312, 313
非国有经济	fei guo you jing ji	nonstate sectors 43, 57, 59, 64, 65, 69, 70–73, 75, 134, 172, 177–205 (chapter 5), 219, 227, 232–233, 370, 390, 438, 439
非均衡	fei jun heng	disequilibrium 79–80, 355, 364
菲利普斯曲线	fei li pu si qu xian	Phillips curve 356, 373
非银行金融机构	fei yin hang jin rong ji gou	nonbank financial institutions 225, 230, 271, 272
分税制	fen shui zhi	tax-sharing system 78, 84, 261, 266, 269, 270, 274, 279, 280
分灶吃饭体制	fen zao chi fan ti zhi	revenue-sharing system 78, 255, 259, 261, 262, 265, 266, 268, 276
风险资本	feng xian zi ben	venture capital (VC) 210
高新技术	gao xin ji shu	high-technology (high-tech) 88n, 191, 204, 208–211, 286, 307
个人帐户	ge ren zhang hu	individual account 85, 310, 333, 334, 336–350, 383

个体经济   ge ti jing ji   individual business sector 65, 65n44, 86–88, 181–185, 377

公共财政   gong gong cai zheng   public finance 255, 256, 274, 279, 281, 283, 285

公共物品   gong gong wu pin   public goods 88n, 256, 276, 279, 281, 282, 285, 414, 440

公司财产   gong si cai chan   corporate property 161

《公司法》   gong si fa   Company Law 83, 85, 153–155, 158–161, 169, 173, 196, 244

公司制度   gong si zhi du   corporate system 147, 150, 155, 161, 165, 170, 172, 173, 213

公司治理   gong si zhi li   corporate governance 73n53, 152, 154–155, 158, 166, 168–176, 212, 232, 233, 240, 251, 253

工薪税   gong xin shui   payroll tax 336

公有制   gong you zhi   public ownership 3, 4, 4n4, 10, 11, 12, 35, 61, 80, 82, 86–87, 169, 178, 184–189, 198, 257, 435, 438

股份合作制   gu fen he zuo zhi   shareholding cooperative system 194, 197, 202

股份有限公司   gu fen you xian gong si   joint stock limited companies 160, 212

股份制   gu fen zhi   shareholding system 80, 147, 155, 161, 165, 194, 396

股票期权   gu piao qi quan   stock options 171

股权融资   gu quan rong zi   equity financing 163, 165, 166, 225, 237t, 238, 240

股市大辩论   gu shi da bian lun   big debate on the stock market 247–250

柜台交易市场   gui tai jiao yi shi chang   OTC market 210, 241, 242

国际会计准则   guo ji kuai ji zhun ze   International Accounting Standards (IAS) 175

国际市场   guo ji shi chang   international market 66, 67, 70, 126, 286, 291, 295, 297, 299, 301, 308, 312, 315–318, 324

国家能源交通重点建设基金   guo jia neng yuan jiao tong zhong dian jian she ji jin   state key energy and transportation projects fund 270, 275

国家所有制   guo jia suo you zhi   state ownership 5, 9–12, 14, 16, 29, 34, 35, 37, 59, 141, 162, 169, 177–181, 187–188, 257, 403, 411, 434–435, 438

国家推动发展论   guo jia tui dong fa zhan lun   developmental-state view 415

国家辛迪加   guo jia xin di jia   State Syndicate 4, 5, 9, 86, 139, 179, 255, 256, 258, 418

国家预算调节基金   guo jia yu suan tiao jie ji jin   state budget regulation fund 270, 276

国民待遇   guo min dai yu   national treatment 205, 287, 299, 305, 306, 439

国有经济   guo you jing ji   state sector 57, 64, 65, 68, 71–73, 75, 78, 81, 85, 86, 87, 132, 134, 135, 139, 169, 172, 177, 179, 180, 183–192, 196, 198, 203–205, 214, 218, 232, 239, 258, 267n9, 331, 370, 372, 374, 376, 377, 383, 390, 39–8, 411, 437–439

国有企业	guo you qi ye	state-owned enterprises (SOEs) 7, 13, 26, 29, 30, 44, 45, 50, 57–64, 69–88, 99, 132, 139–176 (chapter 4), 177, 181, 184, 185, 187, 190–197, 199, 201–203, 209, 219, 211–214, 232–233, 239, 242–253, 256–259, 263–270, 273, 276, 302, 308, 320, 327–333, 339–341, 349, 350, 370, 373, 374, 376, 380, 383, 393, 395, 396, 399, 403, 407, 438, 439
国有资产管理体制	guo you zi chan guan li ti zhi	state assets management system 158
国有资产经营公司	guo you zi chan jing ying gong si	state assets management companies 158, 160, 169
过渡时期总路线	guo du shi qi zong lu xian	General Line for the Transition Period 33–35, 180
合伙制企业	he huo zhi qi ye	partnerships 212
合作经济组织	he zuo jing ji zu zhi	cooperative economic organizations 131–133
合作制企业	he zuo zhi qi ye	cooperative enterprises 197, 212, 301
H型结构	H xing jie gou	H-form 167–168
宏观经济管理国际讨论会	hong guan jing ji guan li guo ji tao lun hui	International Conference on Macroeconomic Management 365, 365n10
宏观经济政策	hong guan jing ji zheng ce	macroeconomic policies 251, 355–384(chapter 10)
红帽子	hong mao zi	red cap 181
后发性优势	hou fa xing you shi	advantages of backwardness 66
黄宗羲定律	huang zong xi ding lü	Huang Zongxi Law 129, 129n58
汇率并轨	hui lü bing gui	merging the two exchange rates 85, 306
混合经济	hun he jing ji	mixed economy 31
混合所有制	hun he suo you zhi	mixed ownership 64, 88, 155, 186, 193n31
货币供应量	huo bi gong ying liang	money supply 223–226, 363, 364, 367, 369, 375
货币市场	huo bi shi chang	money market 217, 225, 234–237
基层选举	ji ceng xuan ju	elections at the grassroots level 423, 425
挤出效应	ji chu xiao ying	crowding-out effect 307
机构投资者	ji gou tou zi zhe	institutional investors 166, 232, 238, 241, 242, 248, 252, 322
计划经济体制	ji hua jing ji ti zhi	planned economic system 8, 9, 12, 18, 20, 22, 23, 27, 28, 31, 35, 36, 38, 49, 62, 101, 114, 121, 184, 219, 256, 258, 292, 295, 311, 348, 357, 393, 403, 411, 435
基金管理	ji jin guan li	fund management 247, 342n16
基金积累制	ji jin ji lei zhi	funded system 333, 337n8, 343, 345
激励成本	ji li cheng ben	incentive costs 18
激励机制	ji li ji zhi	incentive mechanism 13, 19, 81, 151, 153, 204, 211, 333

棘轮效应	ji lun xiao ying	ratchet effect 16, 258
基尼系数	ji ni xi shu	Gini coefficient 401−402
集群	ji qun	clusters 136n65, 201, 300
集体化	ji ti hua	collectivization 9, 27, 62n, 95, 230, 179, 408
集体企业	ji ti qi ye	collective enterprises 181, 185, 202n34, 273
集中解决法	ji zhong jie jue fa	centralized solution 13, 14
价格和工资改革闯关	jia ge he gong zi gai ge chuang guan	crashing through the pass of price reform and wage reform 368
价税财金贸配套改革	jia shui cai jin mao pei tao gai ge	coordinated reform in price, taxation, government finance, banking and foreign trade 261
家庭承包经营制	jia ting cheng bao jing ying zhi	household contracting system 62, 64, 93, 95, 101, 104n19, 108, 114, 118, 119, 121, 126, 146, 182, 183, 352
家庭经营	jia ting jing ying	household operation 63, 94−96, 104, 109
剪刀差	jian dao cha	price scissors 10n13, 117
渐进主义	jian jin zhu yi	gradualism 29
兼容性	jian rong xing	compatibility 162, 171, 416
交易成本	jiao yi cheng ben	transaction costs 12, 19, 94, 95, 163, 213, 300, 392
进口替代	jin kou ti dai	import substitution 293−294
金融市场	jin rong shi chang	financial market 63, 84, 217, 224, 225, 234, 245, 308, 322, 379, 394
金融压制	jin rong ya zhi	financial repression 27, 221, 233
金融中介	jin rong zhong jie	financial intermediaries 219, 416
经常项目	jing chang xiang mu	current account 85, 228, 314
经济过热	jing ji guo re	overheated economy 359, 359n2, 362, 364, 367, 370−372
经济合作与发展组织	jing ji he zuo yu fa zhan zu zhi	Organization for Economic Cooperation and Development (OECD) 175, 321
经济特区	jing ji te qu	special economic zones (SEZs) 66, 67, 184, 264, 287, 295−299
经济性分权	jing ji xing fen quan	economic decentralization 55, 56
竞争解决法	jing zheng jie jue fa	competitive solution 13
93基数	jiu san ji shu	1993 base number 279
居民消费价格指数	ju min xiao fei jia ge zhi shu	consumer price index 360t, 367, 378
凯恩斯主义	kai en si zhu yi	Keynesianism 365
柯西金改革	ke xi jin gai ge	Kosygin reform 22, 24, 37n57, 60
科学社会主义	ke xue she hui zhu yi	scientific socialism 187
控股公司形式	kong gu gong si xing shi	holding company structure (H-form) 167−168
宽松环境论	kuan song huan jing lun	argument for an easy-going environment 365
扩大企业自主权	kuo da qi ye zi zhu quan	expanding enterprise autonomy 45, 54, 57−60, 63−64, 142, 144−146, 259, 359n2

兰格模式	lan ge mo shi	Lange model 14
利改税	li gai shui	substituting tax payment for profit delivery 146, 147, 262, 264
利润留成	li run liu cheng	profit retention 49, 49n8, 60, 63n40, 145–146, 223, 257, 263, 264
利润中心	li run zhong xin	profit center 167–168
利益冲突	li yi chong tu	conflict of interest 94, 148, 162, 163, 169, 213, 384
利益相关者	li yi xiang guan zhe	stakeholders 176, 196
联产承包责任制	lian chan cheng bao ze ren zhi	contracted responsibility system with remuneration linked to output 110, 114, 146, 400
两个凡是	liang ge fan shi	Two Whatevers 112, 112n26
零和博弈	ling he bo yi	zero-sum game 245, 245n19
零售商业	ling shou shang ye	retail trade 190, 304t
零售价格指数	ling shou jia ge zhi shu	retail price index 222t, 360t, 361, 362t, 364t, 368, 369, 371
流动资金全额信贷	liu dong zi jin quan e xin dai	full loan financing for working capital 60, 238, 257
路径依赖	lu jing yi lai	path dependence 56, 56n30, 266
庐山会议	lu shan hui yi	Lushan Meeting 51
《论十大关系》	lun shi da guan xi	On the Ten Major Relationships 38, 39–41, 44, 59, 143
M型结构	M xing jie gou	M-form 57n31, 167, 167n28, 168, 186
贸易依存度	mao yi yi cun du	trade dependence ratio 66, 316, 316t, 316nn10,11
名义利率	ming yi li lü	nominal interest rate 222t
内部人控制	nei bu ren kong zhi	insider control 73, 152, 153, 161, 162n22, 168, 176, 193, 233, 253, 397
内涵增长方式	nei han zeng zhang fang shi	intensive growth 16, 22, 22t
逆向选择	ni xiang xuan ze	adverse selection 346
农产品购销体制	nong chan pin gou xiao ti zhi	purchase and marketing system of agricultural products 121
农村剩余劳动力	nong cun sheng yu lao dong li	rural surplus laborers 74, 119, 133–138, 199, 200, 201, 373, 401
帕累托效率	pa lei tuo xiao lü	Pareto efficiency 245
泡沫经济	pao mo jing ji	economic bubbles 244–247, 251, 407
破产清算	po chan qing suan	bankruptcy liquidation 164, 192
七国集团	qi guo ji tuan	Group of Seven (G7) 321, 322
期货市场	qi huo shi chang	futures market 193, 244n18, 246, 253, 395
七千人大会	qi qian ren da hui	Conference of Seven Thousand Cadres 52, 107

期权	qi quan	options 171, 376
企业部门	qi ye bu men	corporate sector 139
企业承包制	qi ye cheng bao zhi	enterprise contracting system 78n62, 142, 146–148, 265, 396, 397
《企业法》	qi ye fa	Enterprise Law 153–154, 161
企业改革主线论	qi ye gai ge zhu xian lun	argument for enterprise reform as the main theme 79–80
企业家	qi ye jia	entrepreneurs 71, 119, 181, 185, 205, 206, 210, 211, 215, 216, 411n36
企业家精神	qi ye jia jing shen	entrepreneurship 119
企业下放	qi ye xia fang	transferring enterprises to governments at lower levels 142, 143–144
企业自治	qi ye zi zhi	enterprise autonomy 21, 24, 44, 45, 54, 57–60, 62–64, 73, 142, 144–146, 259, 359n2
契约社会主义	qi yue she hui zhu yi	contractual socialism 25
全额利润留成	quan e li run liu cheng	full profit retention 49, 257
全球化	quan qiu hua	globalization 211, 295, 299, 320, 321
裙带资本主义	qun dai zi ben zhu yi	crony capitalism 216, 409, 410, 414, 438
人力资源	ren li zi yuan	human resources 18, 51, 209, 298, 310
人民公社	ren min gong she	people's communes 34, 49, 50, 51, 96, 99, 100–102, 103, 107, 114, 118, 119, 132n60, 180, 218, 260
人民公社化运动	ren min gong she hua yun dong	People's Communes Campaign 52n18, 100–102, 106, 107, 180
认可债券	ren ke zhai quan	recognition bonds 337, 337n7
软预算约束	ruan yu suan yue shu	soft budget constraint 73n54, 141, 152
三个有利于	san ge you li yu	criterion of the three favorables 435
三级所有、队为基础	san ji suo you, dui wei ji chu	three-level ownership with the production team as the basic accounting unit 101, 102, 107, 182
三就地原则	san jiu di yuan ze	three-locally principle 119, 135
三来一补	san lai yi bu	processing supplied materials, processing according to supplied samples, assembling supplied parts, and compensation trade 294, 311–312, 315
三年脱困	san nian tuo kun	getting out of the difficult position in three years 164
三农问题	san nong wen ti	three rural problems 120, 133, 134, 437
三提五统	san ti wu tong	three retention fees and five contribution fees 128, 128n55
商品经济	shang pin jing ji	commodity economy 37, 61, 62, 63, 75–77, 79, 81, 362, 365, 405
商品寻租	shang pin xun zu	commodity rent-seeking 393

上市公司	shang shi gong si	listed companies 159–160, 165, 174, 175, 238, 240, 243–244, 247, 249, 251, 252, 253
社队企业	she dui qi ye	commune and brigade enterprises 118–119, 183
社会保障体系	she hui bao zhang ti xi	social security system 83, 85, 195, 310, 325–353 (chapter 9), 374, 383, 399
社会大工厂	she hui da gong chang	immense social factory 4, 139, 255
社会公正	she hui gong zheng	social justice 172, 197, 332, 391, 404, 406, 407–411, 436, 439
社会主义	she hui zhu yi	socialism 3, 5–7, 9, 10–17, 19, 20, 24, 25, 30, 33, 35, 37, 38, 44n1, 45, 45n3, 53, 75, 76, 86, 87–88, 96, 97, 100, 139, 177–180, 187–189, 217, 403, 410, 412, 417, 419, 415, 431, 434, 435
社会主义论战	she hui zhu yi lun zhan	debate on socialism 13
社会主义者	she hui zhu yi zhe	socialists 188, 410, 417
审批制	shen pi zhi	approval system 48, 228, 242, 243, 244, 251, 252, 323
生产资料公有制	sheng chan zi liao gong you zhi	public ownership of the means of production 4, 10, 61, 184, 257
剩余控制权	sheng yu kong zhi quan	residual control 94, 147, 148, 150, 151, 153, 161n21, 168, 176, 396
剩余索取权	sheng yu suo qu quan	residual claim 94n2, 147, 148, 150, 396
市场亲和论	shi chang qin he lun	market-friendly view 415
市场取向改革	shi chang qu xiang gai ge	market-oriented reform 16, 38, 53, 56, 62, 63, 67, 68, 72, 82, 177, 187, 266, 357, 392, 403, 412
市场社会主义	shi chang she hui zhu yi	market socialism 12, 14, 15, 17, 24, 25, 434, 435n3
市场失灵	shi chang shi ling	market failure 349, 414–416
市场增进论	shi chang zeng jin lun	market-enhancing view 416
市场准入	shi chang zhun ru	market access 323
试错法	shi cuo fa	trial and error 13
实际利率	shi ji li lü	real interest rate 221, 222t, 223, 369
世界贸易组织	shi jie mao yi zu zhi	World Trade Organization (WTO) 56n29, 205, 229–230, 232, 234, 285, 286, 291, 294, 295, 299, 301, 302, 306, 313, 314, 318n13, 319–323, 383, 439
事业部制	shi ye bu zhi	multidivisional structure (M-form) 57n31, 167, 167n28, 168, 186
市盈率	shi ying lü	P/E 243, 244, 248, 249
首发	shou fa	initial public offerings (IPOs) 155, 157, 160, 166, 225, 232, 240, 243, 252n31
收购兼并	shou gou jian bing	mergers and acquisitions (M&A) 151, 163, 167, 192, 210, 230, 239
授权经营	shou quan jing ying	authorized management 161, 396, 397

受托责任	shou tuo ze ren	fiduciary duties 169–170
数码分化	shu ma fen hua	digital divide 412
双重汇率制	shuang chong hui lü zhi	dual exchange rate system 85, 294
双轨制	shuang gui zhi	dual-track system 68–71, 74, 80, 121, 228, 392
斯大林模式	si da lin mo shi	Stalin model 10, 24, 140n1
四分开一完善	si fen kai yi wan shan	four separations and one improvement 122
四沿战略	si yan zhan lue	four-along strategy 297
私营经济	si ying jing ji	private sector 29, 30, 65, 71, 86, 87, 88, 139, 177, 179, 182n15, 184–185, 255, 282, 411n38, 414, 416, 438
私有信息	si you xin xi	private information 130, 424, 427
松紧搭配政策	song jin da pei zheng ce	combination of a contractionary monetary policy and an expansionary fiscal policy 365
苏南模式	su nan mo shi	South Jiangsu model 201, 202
所有权	suo you quan	ownership 3–5, 9–12, 14, 16, 25, 29, 30, 34, 35, 37, 45, 54n, 59, 61, 62, 64, 64t, 65, 73, 76, 79, 80, 82n, 85–88, 89t, 94n, 96, 99, 101, 102, 104–107, 114, 118, 124, 126, 139–141, 149–153, 155, 158–166, 169, 171, 173, 176, 177–195, 198–205, 199t, 212, 230, 232, 233, 239, 257, 266, 273, 302, 312, 377, 178t, 395, 397, 403, 411, 434, 435, 438, 439
所有与控制的分离	suo you yu kong zhi de fen li	separation of ownership and control 76, 152, 153, 160, 161
所有者缺位	suo you zhe que wei	absence of the owner 169, 252–253, 397
体制外先行	ti zhi wai xian xing	"outside the system" preceding "inside the system" 43, 72, 404
田底权	tian di quan	field base right 105
田面权	tian mian quan	field surface right 105, 126, 128
调整、改革、整顿、提高	tiao zheng, gai ge, zheng dun, ti gao	readjusting, restructuring, straightening out and upgrading 361
统存统贷	tong cun tong dai	unified control over deposits and loans 220
通货紧缩	tong huo jin suo	deflation 318, 374
通货膨胀	tong huo peng zhang	inflation 25, 73, 74, 145, 222, 222t, 246, 356–373, 374, 379, 399, 402, 405
统收统支	tong shou tong zhi	unified control over revenues and expenditures 141, 228, 256, 259, 275
投资银行	tou zi yin hang	investment banks 322
土地租佃制度	tu di zu dian zhi du	land tenancy system 105
托拉斯	tuo la si	trusts 191
U型结构	U xing jie gou	U-form 57, 167, 168

外部性	wai bu xing	externalities 84, 191, 204, 207, 414, 416
外贸大包干	wai mao da bao gan	all-round foreign trade responsibility system 78n62
外商投资企业	wai shang tou zi qi ye	foreign-invested enterprises 66t, 183–184, 264, 272, 286, 287, 296, 300, 303, 304t, 305–312, 339
外商直接投资	wai shang zhi jie tou zi	foreign direct investment (FDI) 66, 67, 184, 200, 296, 300–309, 301f, 375
外延增长方式	wai yan zeng zhang fang shi	extensive growth 20, 22, 359
万言书	wan yan shu	ten-thousand-word article 187, 187n23
58 岁现象	wu shi ba sui xian xiang	phenomenon of age 58 171, 171n31
五保	wu bao	Five Guarantees 352
下岗	xia gang	layoff 401
现代公司制度	xian dai gong si zhi du	modern corporate system 147, 150, 165, 172, 173, 213
现代化	xian dai hua	modernization 36, 76, 188, 208, 386–389, 407
现代企业制度	xian dai qi ye zhi du	modern enterprise system 83, 85, 142, 154, 155, 161, 165, 308
现收现付制	xian shou xian fu zhi	pay-as-you-go system 328, 329, 332, 333, 337–345
先调后放	xian tiao hou fang	adjustment first and liberalization second 78
相对价格	xiang dui jia ge	relative prices 12, 19, 70, 79, 357
乡镇企业	xiang zhen qi ye	township and village enterprises (TVEs) 57, 64, 65, 68, 118, 119, 120t, 134–137, 183, 186, 193, 195, 201–203, 211, 202n34, 369, 374, 400
消费价格指数	xiao fei jia ge zhi shu	consumer price index 360t, 367, 378
消费者偏好	xiao fei zhe pian hao	consumer preferences 13
信贷额度切块包干	xin dai e du qie kuai bao gan	responsibility system of credit quota by region 78n62
新古典经济学	xin gu dian jing ji xue	neoclassical economics 12, 14, 17, 415
新经济政策	xin jing ji zheng ce	New Economic Policy 7, 8, 9
新奇士合作社	xin qi shi he zuo she	Sunkist Growers, Inc. 132
信息技术	xin xi ji shu	information technology (IT) 299–301, 317, 424
信息成本	xin xi cheng ben	information costs 18, 19, 20
行政社会主义	xing zheng she hui zhu yi	administrative socialism 9, 431
行政性分权	xing zheng xing fen quan	administrative decentralization 26, 39, 53–58, 144, 255, 257, 261, 266, 267, 284
休克疗法	xiu ke liao fa	Shock Therapy 29, 70n49, 185
寻租	xun zu	rent-seeking 70, 73, 74, 216, 266, 268, 393, 394, 399, 438
寻租活动	xun zu huo dong	rent-seeking activities 70, 73, 74, 216, 393, 394, 427

研究与开发　　　　　　　　yan jiu yu kai fa　　　　　　research and development (R&D) 22, 206, 209, 210, 300, 306

养老保险制度改革　　　　　yang lao bao xian zhi du gai ge　　reform of the pension insurance system 330, 338, 344

洋跃进　　　　　　　　　　yang yue jin　　　　　　　　Imported Leap Forward 46n4, 293, 359

要素寻租　　　　　　　　　yao su xun zu　　　　　　　factor rent-seeking 393

业主制企业　　　　　　　　ye zhu zhi qi ye　　　　　　proprietorships 182, 184, 202, 212

一大二公　　　　　　　　　yi da er gong　　　　　　　large in size and public in ownership 99, 180

一级市场　　　　　　　　　yi ji shi chang　　　　　　primary market 242, 244, 252

伊利里亚模式　　　　　　　yi li li ya mo shi　　　　　Illyrian model 25

隐性负债　　　　　　　　　yin xing fu zhai　　　　　　implicit debt 166, 289, 337, 341, 342

永佃制　　　　　　　　　　yong dian zhi　　　　　　　permanent tenancy system 105

用脚投票　　　　　　　　　yong jiao tou piao　　　　　voting with feet 171

有限合伙制企业　　　　　　you xian he huo zhi qi ye　　limited partnerships 210

有限责任公司　　　　　　　you xian ze ren gong si　　　limited liability companies 165, 194, 212

预算外收入　　　　　　　　yu suan wai shou ru　　　　extra-budgetary revenue 268, 273, 275–278

预算外资金　　　　　　　　yu suan wai zi jin　　　　　extra-budgetary funds 277n16, 283, 284

预算约束　　　　　　　　　yu suan yue shu　　　　　　budget constraint 29, 30, 73, 141, 152, 162n22, 173, 274, 346, 349, 358

增量改革　　　　　　　　　zeng liang gai ge　　　　　　Incremental Reform 43, 57, 58, 64, 68, 71, 72, 74, 75, 177, 185, 198, 391, 398, 404

增量资本产出率　　　　　　zeng liang zi ben chan chu lü　incremental capital-output ratio (ICOR) 381, 382f

增值税　　　　　　　　　　zeng zhi shui　　　　　　　value-added tax (VAT) 78, 207, 264, 270–274, 279, 285–286, 290n28, 306, 314

债权转股权　　　　　　　　zhai quan zhuan gu quan　　debt-equity conversion 163–165

债务重组　　　　　　　　　zhai wu chong zu　　　　　debt restructuring 192

战略A　　　　　　　　　　zhan lue A　　　　　　　　Strategy A 29, 30, 71, 232

战略B　　　　　　　　　　zhan lue B　　　　　　　　Strategy B 29, 30, 71, 232, 409

战时共产主义　　　　　　　zhan shi gong chan zhu yi　　wartime communism 5, 15

政府失灵　　　　　　　　　zheng fu shi ling　　　　　government failure 416, 417

政企分开　　　　　　　　　zheng qi fen kai　　　　　　separation of government administration from enterprise management 76, 122, 147, 422, 425, 434, 435, 439

证券交易所　　　　　　　　zheng quan jiao yi suo　　　securities exchange 197, 242, 244, 272n12

证券市场　　　　　　　　　zheng quan shi chang　　　　securities market 155, 171, 217, 219, 228, 237–240, 244–249, 251–253, 376, 398

证券私有化　　　　　　　　zheng quan si you hua　　　voucher privatization 409

整体推进战略　　　　　　　zheng ti tui jin zhan lue　　strategy of overall advance 85

整体协调改革论　　　　　　zheng ti xie tiao gai ge lun　argument for overall and coordinated reform 80

政治改革　　　　　　　　　zheng zhi gai ge　　　　　　political reform 88, 89, 385, 417, 422, 423, 429, 433–438

《政治经济学》教科书	zheng zhi jing ji xue jiao ke shu	textbook of Political Economy 10, 179, 188
知识产权	zhi shi chan quan	intellectual property rights 307, 318, 323
滞胀	zhi zhang	stagflation 373
中等阶级	zhong deng jie ji	middle class 386, 390
中共八大	zhong gong ba da	Eighth National Congress of the CPC 38, 39, 44
中共八届三中全会	zhong gong ba jie san zhong quan hui	Third Plenary Session of the Eighth CCCPC 46
中共十二届三中全会	zhong gong shi er jie san zhong quan hui	Third Plenary Session of the 12th CCCPC 75, 77, 79, 362
中共十六大	zhong gong shi liu da	16th National Congress of the CPC 88, 137, 171, 399n19, 423, 429, 434, 437
中共十四届三中全会	zhong gong shi si jie san zhong quan hui	Third Plenary Session of the 14th CCCPC 82, 83, 154, 155, 158, 161, 183, 186, 187, 193, 224, 225, 226, 255, 286, 269, 270, 327, 332–350, 372
中共十五大	zhong gong shi wu da	15th National Congress of the CPC 86, 87, 88, 135, 155, 172, 178, 186–189, 193, 198, 202, 205, 376, 422, 425, 434, 435, 437
中共十五届四中全会	zhong gong shi wu jie si zhong quan hui	Fourth Plenary Session of the 15th CCCPC 88n, 155, 158, 189
中共十一届三中全会	zhong gong shi yi jie san zhong quan hui	Third Plenary Session of the 11th CCCPC 57, 59, 64, 112, 183, 425
重商主义	zhong shang zhu yi	mercantilism 393n13, 414
抓大放小	zhua da fang xiao	grasping large enterprises and letting go of small enterprises 196, 202
专家治国主义者	zhuan jia zhi guo zhu yi zhe	technocrats 25
转型时期	zhuan xing shi qi	transitional period 313, 355–384 (chapter 10), 385–430 (chapter 11), 439
转移支付	zhuan yi zhi fu	transfer payment 129, 270, 274, 279–281, 344
准公共物品	zhun gong gong wu pin	quasi-public goods 276, 282
资本市场	zi ben shi chang	capital market 192, 197, 219, 225, 231, 235, 249, 308, 333
资产管理公司	zi chan guan li gong si	asset management corporations (AMCs) 164, 165, 231, 382
自治社会主义	zi zhi she hui zhu yi	self-management socialism 24, 25, 45
自然经济	zi ran jing ji	natural economy 37, 119
自我交易	zi wo jiao yi	self-dealing 395
自由人联合体	zi you ren lian he ti	association of free men 4, 178
资源配置	zi yuan pei zhi	resource allocation 12–14, 16, 18, 19, 38, 49, 50, 56, 65, 70, 81, 144, 168, 215, 216, 218, 265, 274, 346, 381, 391, 399, 408, 412, 414